The Modern Middle East

The Modern Middle East

A Sourcebook for History

Edited by
**Camron Michael Amin,
Benjamin C. Fortna,
and Elizabeth Frierson**

OXFORD
UNIVERSITY PRESS

OXFORD

UNIVERSITY PRESS

Great Clarendon Street, Oxford OX2 6DP

Oxford University Press is a department of the University of Oxford.
It furthers the University's objective of excellence in research, scholarship,
and education by publishing worldwide in

Oxford New York

Auckland Cape Town Dar es Salaam Hong Kong Karachi
Kuala Lumpur Madrid Melbourne Mexico City Nairobi
New Delhi Shanghai Taipei Toronto

With offices in

Argentina Austria Brazil Chile Czech Republic France Greece
Guatemala Hungary Italy Japan Poland Portugal Singapore
South Korea Switzerland Thailand Turkey Ukraine Vietnam

Oxford is a registered trade mark of Oxford University Press
in the UK and in certain other countries

Published in the United States
by Oxford University Press Inc., New York

British Library Cataloguing in Publication Data

Data available

Library of Congress Cataloging in Publication Data

Data available

Typeset by Newgen Imaging Systems (P) Ltd., Chennai, India
Printed in Great Britain
on acid-free paper by
Biddles Ltd., King's Lynn, Norfolk

ISBN 0–19–926209–8   978–0–19–926209–0

1 3 5 7 9 10 8 6 4 2

For all students of the Middle East and their teachers

Preface

The history of the modern Middle East has been written on the basis of a variety of sources: official and private archives, the periodical press, memoirs, Western journalists' and travelers' accounts, literature, and official reports (including statistical data). Middle East specialists, who have interpreted these sources and woven them into an ever longer and more detailed narrative, have done so with a variety of influences on their thinking. Since the late eighteenth century, European (and later American) researchers have investigated the Middle East against the backdrop of Euro-American hegemony in the region, with their work supported by and contributing to foreign policies that often furthered Western political and economic interests at the expense of Middle Eastern societies. Whether these scholars embraced the implications of Euro-American hegemony or reviled them, it colored their understanding of the Middle East. Indigenous Middle Eastern scholars were certainly no less affected by this state of affairs, with many embracing (and contributing to) methodologies and explanatory paradigms developed in Western academia even as they argued for different master narratives.

This volume does not seek to interrogate the historiography of the modern Middle East or to reconcile debates between 'Orientalists' and 'Revisionists' or to resolve other long-standing controversies. It does, however, seek to reflect the state of Middle East studies in the early twenty-first century, and therefore is a by-product both of the debates and the traditions of scholarship that characterize the field. Edward Said (d. 2003) was the most celebrated champion of the notion that the West had invented or created the construct of the 'East' in such a way as to suit its own interests and sense of self. In the realm of academic study this meant that all Western scholarship on the Middle East was affected by the fact that Western countries enjoyed considerable influence upon the politics and economics of the Middle East. Europe (Said's 1978 book *Orientalism* focused on British and French scholarship on the Middle East) and, later, American Middle East specialists were employed in the Western imperialist enterprise. Said argued that their characterizations of 'Oriental' societies as despotic and decadent ghosts of their idealized medieval selves, served the imperialist agendas of the nineteenth and twentieth centuries. If Westerners came to believe that Middle Eastern and Islamic countries were a mess, then they would consider it natural (even noble) for Europeans to take over those countries. Said was a literary scholar and his arguments largely rested on devastating critiques of the tone of

Orientalist scholarship, in which deep-seated biases were laid bare.[1] There were many responses to *Orientalism*, but the most pointed and durable have come from Bernard Lewis (whose works were part of the evidence marshalled by Said). Lewis was quick to point out the historical errors of Said's literary analysis, and took particular issue with the implication that Western Orientalists were incapable of providing meaningful and carefully researched analyses and critiques of the modern Middle East.[2]

The nuanced beginnings of this debate quickly gave way to more heated exchanges between 'Orientalist' scholars (Lewis's camp) and 'Revisionist' scholars (Said's camp), with the academic debate spilling over into policy disputes. Today's 'clash of civilizations' controversy (a phrase popularized by Samuel P. Huntington in 1996)—the notion that there is something irreconcilably different between West and East (or, more generally, 'the West and the Rest') and that conflict is unavoidable—is a legacy of the academic skirmishes between Orientalists and Revisionists and is at the heart of current policy deates over how best to wage a 'war on terror'.[3] That is why it is critical that students of the modern Middle East be able to reach past these debates and grapple with the kinds of sources that inform them. Developing a better-informed understanding of the modern Middle East is no longer merely an academic ideal (if it ever was); it is a civic responsibility as vital as voting.

Each document in this volume has been prefaced, translated, and annotated by a specialist in the particular history and culture from which it was drawn. Each specialist has endeavored to provide enough information so that the most novice student can appreciate the document's value and begin a further exploration either of its specific historical context or its relationship to broader themes in modern

---

[1] Incidentally, Said understood 'Orientalism' as a product of Western cultural history more than a result of the realities of the modern Middele East. His audience was Western. In the Middle East itself, the idea that Western 'Orientalism' was tainted by imperialism was an article of faith among the intelligentsia for at least two decades before the appearance of Said's *Orientalism*. Some in the Middle East, just as some in the rest of the world, have moved on from these debates. See, Mehrzad Boroujerdi, 'Iranian Islam and the Faustian Bargain of Western Modernity', *Journal of Peace Research*, 34/1 (Feb. 1997), 1–5.

[2] For the latest instalment of this argument, see Bernard Lewis, *The Middle East: What Went Wrong?: Western Impact and Middle Eastern Response* (New York: Oxford University Press, 2002). For a pointed critique, see Juan R. I. Cole, 'Review of Bernard Lewis's *What Went Wrong: Western Impact and Middle Eastern Response*', first published in *Global Dialogue*, 4/4 (Autumn 2002), and posted (with permission from *GD*) at <http://www.juancole.com/essays/rvlew.htm> on 27 Jan. 2003. Scholars such as Cole have been subjected to shrill personal invectives by admirers of Lewis such as Martin Kramer and Daniel Pipes.

[3] For an academic critique of Huntington, see Roy P. Mottaheddeh, 'The Clash of Civilizations: An Islamicist's Critique', *Harvard Middle Eastern and Islamic Review*, 2/2 (1995), 1–26. For a nuanced critique with an eye towards the policy implications of Huntington's work as it relates to the spread of democracy in the Middle East, see Fareed Zakaria, *The Future of Freedom: Illiberal Democracy at Home and Abroad* (New York: W. W. Norton & Co., 2003).

Middle Eastern history. For our colleagues in the field, we aimed to provide an array of primary sources to teach, discuss, and, perhaps, reconsider critical issues in modern Middle Eastern history. Some documents provide a window on the traditional order 'on the eve of modernity', to borrow a phrase from Abraham Marcus, but most deal with the process of modernizing change on a variety of fronts. The collection is expansive (from the Balkans to South Asia) but certainly not exhaustive. Nonetheless, for all the important differences in the region, it is striking how many issues—the expansion of state power, changing gender roles, religious revival, nationalist mobilization, increasing participation in a wider global culture and economy, and the redefinition of traditions and identities—are common and comparable across the greater Middle East.

Readers will note that words from various languages—the original documents assembled were written in Arabic, Armenian, English, French, Hebrew, Persian, and a number of Turkic languages—have been represented in a simplified form of conventional transliteration schemes. For precision, Middle East specialists resort to elaborate diacritical marks to indicate the original words they mean to represent in, or transliterate into, English (or other European language). For simplicity's sake, with the exception of the Arabic letters *ayn* (ᶜ) and *hamza* ('), these diacritical marks have been omitted. Furthermore, some words appear in several languages but are pronounced differently. We have taken that into account. For example, the word for 'book' in Arabic, Persian, and Turkish shares a common Arabic origin. When appearing in the script common to Arabic, Persian, and (until 1928) Turkish, the word looks the same but is transliterated differently. Our transliteration reflects that difference: in Arabic *kitab*, in Persian *ketab*, and in Turkish *kitap*. Turkish words are rendered in modern Turkish script, which is a Latin-based script. Sometimes, these different renderings reflect a question of historical interpretation. For example, the ruler of Egypt from 1805 to 1847 could be understood by some as an Ottoman officer (Mehmet Ali) or the man who initiated Egypt's emergence as an independent Arab country (Muhammad ᶜAli). At other times, the transliteration simply reflects the context in which a source was produced (e.g. a Persian-language newspaper, published in Tehran, Iran), and does not imply any particular historical debate. It is just one more way in which we wish to encourage readers to think carefully about the full context of each document in this collection, and the diversity of the greater Middle East.

This collection was developed as part of a larger (and continuing) project, funded by the National Endowment of the Humanities, to provide annotated translations of primary documents to scholars, students, and other people interested in the history and culture of the Middle East. Please go to our website, <www.umd.umich.edu/middleeastsourcebook> for more information about the project and to find additional documents.

Acknowledgements

The Modern Middle East Sourcebook Project (MMESP), under the auspices of which the content of this volume was developed, would not have been possible without the generous support of the National Endowment of the Humanities. We are especially grateful to the guidance provided by our program officers: Judith Jeffrey Howard and Bruce Robinson. Of course, any views, findings, conclusions or recommendations expressed in this volume do not necessarily represent those of the NEH. We also wish to acknowledge the support and patience of our advisory board: William Cleveland, Afsaneh Najmabadi, Hasan Kayalı, Laurie Zittrain Eisenberg, and Judith Tucker. We are also grateful for the help of our language consultants (John Perry, Marianne Kamp, and Şükrü Hanioğlu), whom we were fortunate enough not to have to pester too often, and our technical consultants, Diana Perpich, Michael Levine Hess, and Noah Levitt, whom we pestered a lot (especially poor Diana).

The very idea for this project began with our experiences in graduate school at the University of Chicago (Cam and Ben) and Princeton University (Elizabeth), and working at our current home institutions and at our first teaching jobs— North Central College (Cam), the University of New Hampshire (Elizabeth), and Washington University in St Louis (Ben). Through the years, our mentors and colleagues in all these places impressed upon us the value of such a project. We are also grateful for all the encouragement and advice from colleagues in Middle East Studies as we initiated the project and worked to see it through.

While we are grateful to all of our wonderful contributors, we must reserve a special acknowledgement to Herbert Bodman who made available to us the contents of the *Islamfiche* Project—a labor of scholarly love he developed with his colleagues Marilyn R. Waldman and William A. Graham. We offer special thanks also to Robert G. Landen who made documents from his 1970 collection, *The Emergence of the Modern Middle East: A Reader*, available to our collection. We are grateful for the permissions granted to us by *Iran*, *Iranian Studies*, *Ha'aretz*, *the Jerusalem Post*, *Turkish Studies*, *LeMan*, the British Broadcasting Corporation, and *iranian.com* to reproduce documents for this collection. Finally, we must express our great appreciation for our colleagues at Oxford University Press, especially Ruth Parr, for believing in this project, and Anne Gelling and Kay Rogers, and for our London-based editorial assistant, Claudia Pugh-Thomas, for her tireless efforts to get our damned manuscript into shape.

At the University of Michigan-Dearborn, Cam thanks his colleagues Mike Twomey and Ronald Stockton for their participation in the project. He could not have managed without his trusty student assistants Tricia King and Shelly Balogh, and the wonderful administrative staff at UM-D—Drew Buchanan (without whom he would never understand 'indirect costs' and 'cost sharing'), Kathy Hoskins, Martina Cucchiara, Betty Greco, Chalina Hillson, Paul Wong and Katic Anderson-Levitt—and, at UM-Ann Arbor's Department of Research and Development Administration, Julie Feldkamp and Addie Ryznar. On a personal note, Cam wishes his wife and sons (Amelia, Caelin, and Benjamin) to know that he is sorry for all the time this project stole from them and that he could not have done it without their patience and love.

Benjamin Fortna extends his thanks to Jacqui Arrol-Barker and Maureen Gaskin from the Research & Galleries Office for their help and professionalism in applying for and administering the NEH grant, and Professors Ian Brown and Gerald Hawting who as Heads of Department allowed him to make time for the MMESP among his teaching and administrative duties in the History Department. He is also grateful for the love and support of his wife and sons, Sarah, Will, Nick, and Benjy.

At the University of Cincinnati, Elizabeth offers special thanks also to Hope Earls, department administrator of the UC History Department, for taking on extra burdens of administration in managing the grant at the departmental level, and to Scott Roebuck, Ahoo Tabatabai, and Maribeth Mincey for their contributions. Thanks also must go to Liz Hamilton, who designed our project's first informational website and did a lot of work on our first demo of the electronic version of the MMESP. Elizabeth's husband and son, Philip and Tennant, were supportive throughout this effort—Tennant especially as the perfect traveling companion to MESA conferences! She also wishes to thank John Voll and Cathy Frierson, in particular, at the University of New Hampshire for their advice on grants, sourcebooks, and publishing.

Finally, we all owe a debt to our students, whose sacrifices for their own education and questions about the Middle East reminded us of the importance of this project.

Contents

List of illustrations

Notes on contributors

Camron Michael Amin, University of Michigan-Dearborn

Camron Michael Amin earned his Ph.D from the Department of Near Eastern Languages and Civilizations at the University of Chicago in 1996. He is an Associate Professor of History at the University of Michigan-Dearborn and the author of *The Making of the Modern Iranian Woman: Gender, State Policy and Popular Culture, 1865–1946* (2002).

Ali M. Ansari, University of St Andrews

Ali Ansari is Reader in Modern History at the University of St Andrews. His Publications include *Modern Iran since 1921* (2003) and *Iran, Islam and Democracy* (2000) as well as a number of articles in edited volumes and Scholarly journals.

Frederick Anscombe, University of London

Frederick Anscombe (Ph.D, Princeton University 1994) is Lecturer in Contemporary History at Birkbeck College, University of London. He is the author of *The Ottoman Gulf: The Creation of Kuwait, Saudi Arabia and Qatar* (1997) and editor of *The Ottoman Balkans, 1750–1830* (forthcoming).

Danny Ben-Moshe, Victoria University, Melbourne

Danny Ben-Moshe is an Associate Professor and director of the Social Diversity Key Research Area at Victoria University in Melbourne, Australia, and an Adjunct Professor teaching Zionism and Israeli studies at Gratz College in Philadelphia. He majored in Middle Eastern politics from the School of Oriental and African Studies at the University of London and completed his Ph.D in 2000 at Melbourne University. His book chapters and journal articles include 'The Impact of the Oslo Peace Process on Jewish and Zionist Identity in Israel' (*British Journal of Middle Eastern Studies*), and 'The True Meaning of The Rabin Assassination' (*Israel Affairs*).

Houri Berberian, California State University

Houri Berberian (Ph.D in 1997 at UCLA), is an Associate Professor in the History Department at California State University, Long Beach, and Director of the Middle Eastern Studies Program. Recent publications include: *Armenians and the Iranian Constitutional Revolution of 1905–1911: 'The Love for Freedom Has No Fatherland'* (2001); 'Armenian Women and Women in Armenian Religion', in the *Encyclopaedia of Women and Islamic Cultures* (forthcoming 2004); and

'Traversing Boundaries and Selves: Iranian Armenian Identity During the Iranian Constitutional Revolution', *Comparative Studies of South Asia, Africa, and Middle East* (forthcoming: Fall 2005).

Palmira Brummett, University of Tennessee

Palmira Brummett is Professor of History and Distinguished Professor in the Humanities at the University of Tennessee. She received her Ph.D in History from the University of Chicago in 1988. In 2003 she was awarded UT's College of Arts and Sciences Senior Research and Creative Achievement Award. She is currently engaged in a book project on 'Mapping the Ottomans: Early Modern Visions of the Ottoman Empire in Narrative and Image', for which she has been awarded an NEH Fellowship at the Folger Shakespeare Library in Washington DC. She is author of, among other works, *Ottoman Seapower and Levantine Diplomacy in the Age of Discovery* (1994) and *Image and Imperialism in the Ottoman Revolutionary Press* (2000). Her article, 'Imagining the Early Modern Ottoman Space from Piri Reis to World History', is forthcoming in Virginia Aksan and Daniel Goffman (eds.), *Exploring the Early Modern Ottoman World*.

Nazan Çiçek

NazanÇiçek received her BA and MA degree from Ankara University and is currently an advanced postgraduate student in the History Department at the School of Oriental & African Studies, University of London. She is completing her dissertation on the Young Ottoman opposition group and their relations with British Turophiles.

Juan R. I. Cole, The University of Michigan

Juan Cole earned his Ph.D in Islamic Studies from UCLA in 1984. He is the author of *Sacred Space and Holy War* (2002), *Modernity and the Millennium: The Genesis of the Baha'i Faith in the Nineteenth Century Middle East* (1998), *Colonialism and Revolution in the Middle East: Social and Cultural Origins of Egypt's 'Urabi Movement* (1993), and *Roots of North Indian Shi'ism in Iran and Iraq* (1989), in addition to many other articles and edited works. He has recently served as the director of UM's Center for Middle Eastern and North African Studies and editor for the *International Journal of Middle East Studies*. He also maintains the weblog Informed Comment <www.juancole. com>, which is devoted to current affairs in the Middle East and Islamic World.

Thomas Eich, Bochum University

Thomas Eich studied Islamic Studies, Medieval History, and Iranian Studies at the Universities of Bamberg, Damascus, and Freiburg, graduating from Bamberg University in 1999. He has been conducting a research project entitled 'Bioethical Questions in the Framework of Contemporary Islamic Law' at the Department of Oriental Studies at Bochum University since 2003. He received his Ph.D from the same university in 2002 for a study on Abu l-Huda as-Sayyadi (d. 1909), entitled *Abu l-Huda as-Sayyadi. Eine Studie zur Instrumentalisierung sufischer Netzwerke und geneal-*

ogischer Kontroversen im Spätosmanischen Reich (2003). This study was carried out in the junior research group 'Islamic Networks in Local and Trans-national Contexts (18th–20th centuries)', and funded by the Volkswagenfoundation, at the Department of Oriental Studies, Bochum.

Matthew Elliot, Unital Arab Emirates University, al-Ain

Matthew Elliot is currently Assistant Professor in the Department of History, United Arab Emirates University, Jerusalem. Previously he was Research Officer at the Kenyon Institute (incorporating the British School of Archaeology in Jerusalem) and a Research Fellow at the Ingiliz Arkeoloji Enstitüsü in Ankara. He gained a BA Hons. in Classics from Leeds University and an M.Phil. in Islamic Art and Architecture from St Antony's College, Oxford University. He received his Ph.D in History from the School of Oriental and African Studies, London University.

Halil İbrahim Erbay, Harran University in Urfa

Hail İbrahim Erbay completed his MA in Area Studies at SOAS, University of London, and is currently working towards his Ph.D degree at the same school. His doctoral research relates to education, religion, and state in the late Ottoman Empire. He is also a member of the teaching staff in the University of Harran, Turkey.

Ellen Fleischmann, University of Dayton

Ellen Fleischmann is currently Assistant Professor of History at the University of Dayton, having received a Ph.D in history from Georgetown University in 1996. Her specialties are the history of women and gender in the Middle East. Her book, *The Nation and Its 'New' Women: The Palestinian Women's Movement, 1920–1948*, was published in April 2003.

Bejamin C. Fortna, School of Oriental & African Studies, University of London

Benjamin C. Fortna is Senior Lecturer in the History of the Modern Middle East in the History Department of the School of Oriental & African Studies, University of London. He received his Ph.D from the University of Chicago in 1997. He has written a book, *Imperial Classroom: Islam, Education and the State in the Late Ottoman Empire* (2002), and a number of articles in journals and edited volumes. His current research focuses on learning to read and literacy in the transition from Ottoman Empire to Turkish Republic.

Ulrike Freitag, Centre for Modern Oriental Studies, Berlin

Ulrike Feitag received her Ph.D in 1991 from Albert Ludwig University in Freiburg, and, serves as the director for the Centre for Modern Oriental Studies in Berlin. In addition to a number of articles on the history of the Arab and the Islamic World, she is the author of *Indian Ocean Migrants and State Formation in Hadhramaut* (2003).

Nelida Fuccaro, School of Oriental and African Studies, University of London

Nelida Fuccaro received her Ph.D from Durham University. She is an expert on the Arab world, Kurds, and Yezidism. She is the author of *The Other Kurds: The Yazidis in Colonial Iraq* (1999).

Moshe Gershovich, University of Nebraska

Moshe Gershovich received his Ph.D from Harvard University in 1995. He is Associate Professor of Modern European History at the University of Nebraska at Omaha. His research focuses on French colonialism in Morocco. In addition to numerous articles, he has published *French Military Rule in Morocco: Colonialism and Its Consequences* (2000). Currently he is working on 'Serving the Tricolor: Oral History of Moroccan Soldiers in French Uniform', based on field research he conducted as a Fulbright Scholar in the Middle Atlas between 1998 and 2000.

Indira Falk Gesink, Baldwin-Wallace College

Indira Falk Gesink is Assistant Professor of Middle Eastern History at Baldwin-Wallace College in Berea, Ohio, where she has been teaching since receiving her doctorate from Washington University in St Louis in 2000. Her most recent publication was ' "Chaos on the Earth": Subjective Truths vs. Communal Unity in Islamic Law and the Rise of Militant Islam', *American Historical Review*, 108: 3 (June 2003).

Sarah Gualtieri, Loyola University, New Orleans

Sarah Gualtieri is Assistant Professor of Middle East History at Loyola University, New Orleans, where she teaches courses on Middle Eastern social, political, and gender history. She completed her undergraduate studies at McGill University in Montreal, Quebec, and holds an MA in Middle East Studies and a doctorate in History from the University of Chicago. Her field of specialization is the history of the modern Middle East, and her research focuses on migration, race, and national identity formation in Syria, Lebanon, Israel/Palestine, and in their respective diasporas. Her articles and reviews are published in *Encyclopedia of Chicago History*, *The Journal of American Ethnic History*, *The Journal of Religion*, *Radical History Review*, and *Comparative Studies in South Asia, African and the Middle East*. She is currently working on a book that traces changes in Arab racial identity in the United States from 1880 to 1924.

M. Şükrü Hanioğlu, Princeton University

M. Şükrü Hanioğlu is Professor of NearEastern Studies at Princeton University. He is a leading authority on the history of the late Ottoman Empire and the Young Turks period in particular. Among his many publications are *The Young Turks in Opposition* (1995) and *Preparation for a Revolution: The Young Turks, 1902–1908* (2001), both published by Oxford University Press.

Abigail Jacobson

Abigail Jacobson is a Ph.D candidate in History at the University of Chicago. She is researching the history of Jews in Palestine in the late Ottoman period.

Jahanshah Javid

Jahanshah Javid is the editor and publisher of web magazine *The Iranian* (www.iranian.com). As a journalist, he has worked for IRNA (Iran's news agency), the Associated Press, and the BBC. *The Iranian* has been published since 1995. His spirited exchange with *The Iranian* contributor Cyrus Kadivar appears in this volume.

Cyrys Kadivar

Author and regular contributor to *The Iranian*.

Karen M. Kern, City University of New York

Karen M. Kern received her Ph.D from the Department of Middle East and Asian Languages and Cultures at Columbia University in 1999. She specializes in the history of Turkey, the Ottoman Empire, and the Modern Middle East, focusing on law and legal institutions. Currently she is Assistant Professor in the History Department of Hunter College, City University of New York. She is the recipient of multiple grants, including the Fulbright Senior Scholar Fellowship (2000–1); American Research Institute in Turkey Post-Doctoral Fellowship (Summer 2000); and the Fulbright-Hays Fellowship (1994–5). Her honours include the J. Fulbright Foreign Scholarship Board and the US Department of State Certificate of Recognition (October 2002) and the City University of New York 'Salute to Scholars' Certificate of Recognition (December 2001). Her forthcoming publication is 'Women, Gender and Family Law: Modern Family Law, 1800–2000', *Encyclopaedia of Women and Islamic Cultures* (2004).

Adeeb Khalid, Carleton College, Minnesota

Adeeb Khalid is Associate Professor of History at Carleton College in Minnesota. His research focuses on the cultural history of Tsarist and Soviet Central Asia in the context of the broader Muslim world. He received his Ph.D in 1993. He is the author of *The Politics of Muslim Cultural Reform: Jadidism in Central Asia* (1998), and is currently working on a book on the multifaceted transformation of Central Asia in the early Soviet period.

Michael Laffan, Princeton University

Michael Laffan received his Ph.D in 2001 from the University of Sydney, Australia. He is the author of *Islamic Nationhood and Colonial Indonesia* (2003). He is currently Assistant Professor in the History Department at Princeton University.

Paul Losensky, Indiana University, Bloomington

Paul Losensky received his Ph.D from the University of Chicago in 1993. He currently serves as Associate Professor in the Departments of Central Eurasian Studies and Comparative Literature at Indiana University, Bloomington. His research concentrates primarily on Persian poetry of the sixteenth and seventeenth centuries, with a focus on intertextuality, literary biography and historiography, and the relations between poetry and material culture. His book *Welcoming Fighani: Imitation and Poetic Individuality in the Safavid-Mughal Ghazal* appeared in 1998, and he has recently completed a translation of Farid al-Din 'Attar's *Memorial of God's Friends*.

Shireen Mahdavi, University of Utah

Shireen Madhavi was born in Tehran, Iran, and educated at the London School of Economics and Political Science and the University of Utah. She holds a Ph.D from the University of London. Prior to the Iranian Revolution, she taught at the Institute of Social Research in Tehran and was involved in research in the field of social affairs and served as an advisor to the government. She has participated in numerous international and national conferences. Currently she is an independent scholar, affiliated with the Department of History, University of Utah. She has written extensively on various aspects of Iranian history, with special emphasis on the nineteenth century and the position of women. Her latest book is *For God, Mammon and Country: A Nineteenth Century Persian Merchant* (1999).

Weldon C. Matthews, Oakland University, Michigan

Weldon C. Matthews received his Ph.D from the Department of Near Eastern Languages and Civilizations at the University of Chicago in 1998. His primary research interests are the Palestinian national movement and the Arab–Israeli conflict. His publications include 'Pan-Islam or Arab Nationalism? The Meaning of the 1931 Jerusalem Islamic Congress Reconsidered', *International Journal of Middle East Studies*, and 'The Rise and Demise of the Left in West Bank Politics: The Case of the Palestine National Front', *Arab Studies Quarterly*. He is currently an Assistant Professor of History at Oakland University in Rochester, Michigan.

Flagg Miller, University of Wisconsin

Flagg Miller is an assistant professor of anthropology and religious studies at the University of Wisconsin at Madison (Ph.D, University of Michigan, 2001). He specializes in political discourse, media, and the Arab world. His articles include: 'Of Songs and Signs: Audiocassette Poetry, Moral Character, and the Culture of Circulation in Yemen 32: 1 (2005)', *American Ethnologist*. Also: 'Metaphors of commerce: Trans-valuing Tribalism in Yemeni Audiocassette Poetry', *International Journal of Middle East Studies*, 34: 1 (2002).

Gail Minault, University of Texas

Gail Minault (Ph.D, Pennsylvania, 1972) is Professor of History at the University of Texas in Austin, Texas. She is the author of *The Khilafat Movement* (1982) and *Secluded Scholars: Women's Education and Muslim Social Reform in Colonial India* (1998).

Eden Naby

Eden Naby received her Ph.D from Columbia University. She is an independent scholar devoted to Assyrian history, and Central Asian and Middle East Studies. Among her many projects is building Assyrian collections at American research institutions, notably Harvard University. She is the author of *The Modernization of Inner Asia* (1995) and *Afghanistan: Mullah, Marx and Mujahid* (1998, 2000, and 2002).

Mona Russell

Mona Russell completed her Ph.D at Georgetown University in 1998. Her manuscript, *Creating the New Woman: Consumerism, Education, and National Identity in Egypt, 1863–1922* is currently in production with Palgrave Press. She has held teaching positions at Framingham State College, University of Massachusetts—Amherst, and the Massachusetts Institute of Technology. Her current research project involves advertising, gender, and identity in Egypt from 1922 to 1952.

Barak Salmoni, Naval Postgraduate School's Department of National Security Affairs

Barak Salmoni earned his Ph.D in History and Middle Eastern Studies from Harvard University in 2002. He is the author of 'America's Iraq Strategy: Democratic Chimers, Regional Realities', *Current History* (Jan. 2004) and 'Ordered Liberty and Disciplined Freedom: Conceptualizing and Teaching Democracy in Mono-Party Turkish Education, 1923–1950', *Middle Eastern Studies*, 40: 2 (2004).

Cyrus Schayegh, Tehran Institute of Advanced Studies in Development, Planning, and Management

Cyrus Schayegh wrote his doctoral dissertation on science, medicine, and class in the formation of modern Iranian society at Columbia University (2003). Currently he is a postdoctoral fellow at the Tehran Institute of Advanced Studies in Development, Planning, and Management, working on a history of welfare paradigms in post-World War II Iran.

Paul Sedra, New York University

Paul Sedra is a MacCracken fellow in the Ph.D joint program in History and Middle Eastern Studies at New York University. His work has been published in the Middle East working paper series of Columbia and Yale Universities, as well as the journal *Islam and Christian–Muslim Relations*. Presently, he is teaching modern Middle Eastern history at Dalhousie University in Halifax, Nova Scotia.

Ryme Seferdjeli

Ryme Seferdjeli is currently completing her doctoral thesis on women during the Algerian war of national liberation at the London School of Economic and Political Science, University of London. She is also a Research Associate and part-time lecturer at the Simone de Beauvoir Institute, Concordia University. Prior to this she worked for a period of two years as a lecturer in gender and Middle Eastern history at the School of Oriental & African Studies, University of London.

A. Holly Shissler, University of Chicago

Holly Shissler is Assistant Professor of Modern Middle Eastern History in the Department of Near Eastern Languages and Civilizations at the University of Chicago. She received an AB from Vassar College and a Ph.D from UCLA. She is the author of *Between Two Empires: Ahmet Ağaoğlu and the New Turkey* (2003).

Mark L. Stein, Muhlenberg College

Mark L. Stein received his Ph.D from the University of Chicago in 2001, and is currently Assistant Professor of History at Muhlenberg College. His research focuses on the social, economic, and political dynamics of early-modern Ottoman frontiers.

Guido Steinberg

Guido Steinberg received a Ph.D in Islamic Studies at the Free University Berlin, 2000; his dissertation was on Religion and State in Saudi Arabia (*Religion und Staat in Saudi-Arabien: Die wahhabitischen Gelehrten (1902–1953)* (2002)). His research interests are Muslim religious scholars and reform movements, merchants and trade in the Persian Gulf region (nineteenth and twentieth centuries), and Islamism, Saudi Arabian history, and politics. He is currently working as an adviser in the German Federal Chancellery, Berlin.

Ronald Stockton, University of Michigan-Dearborn

Ronald Stockton is a Professor of Political Science at the University of Michigan-Dearborn. He is the author of two books and various academic articles. His 173-page curriculum unit on *The Israel–Palestinian Conflict* is in its second edition. He has been Chair of the Social Sciences Department, President of the Michigan Conference of Political Scientists, and Executive Director of the Michigan Committee on US–Arab Relations. He is a Principle Investigator on the Detroit Arab American Study, a benchmark study of 1,000 Arab Americans.

Steve Tamari, Southern Illinois University at Edwardsville

Steve Tamari earned his Ph.D from Georgetown University in 1998. He is the author of 'Ottoman Madrasas: The Multiple Lives of Educational Institutions in 18th-Century Syria', *Journal of Early Modern History* (2001) and 'Biography, Autobiography, and Identity in Early Modern Damascus', in Mary Anne Fay (ed.),

Auto/Biography and the Creation of Identity in the Middle East from the Early Modern to the Modern Period (2001).

Ernest Tucker, United States Naval Academy, Annapolis

Ernest Tucker is an Associate Professor in the History Department at the United States Naval Academy in Annapolis, Maryland, where he has taught since 1990. He has written numerous articles on the early modern history of Iran and is the co-author of *Russiam–Muslim Confrontation in the Caucasus* (2004).

Michael Twomey, University of Michigan-Dearborn

Michael Twomey received his Ph.D from Cornell University in 1974. Currently he is Professor of Economics at the University of Michigan-Dearborn. He has also taught in Peru, Colombia, and Mexico. He has worked for the UN Food and Agriculture Organization, and the International Potato Center. His most recent book is *A Century of Foreign Investment in the Third World* (2000).

Carole Woodall, New York University

Carole Woodall is a Ph.D candidate in the Departments of Middle East and Islamic Studies and History, New York University. Her research interests concern the interplay of the production of urban space and cultural practices on the formation of modern identities. Her dissertation is on cultural consumption and production in the late Ottoman and early Turkish republican periods, with specific emphasis on the construction of the Modern Woman.

Renée Worringer, University of Queensland

Renée Worringer received her Ph.D from the University of Chicago in 2001. From 2002 to 2003 she was Woodrow Wilson Fellow in the Department of History at the University of Minnesota. Currently she is a Lecturer in Islamic Studies and Middle East History at the School of History, Philosophy, Religion and Classics at the University of Queensland. She is the author of ' "Sick Man of Europe" or "Japan of the Near East"?: Constructing Ottoman Modernity in the Hamidian and Young Turk Eras', *IJMES* (May 2004).

David Yaghoubian, California State University

David Yaghoubian is Assistant Professor of History at California State University, San Bernardino. He received his Ph.D in Middle Eastern history from UC Berkeley in 2000, specializing in modern Iran and Iranian nationalism. He is currently co-editing the second edition of *Struggle and Survival in the Modern Middle East* (forthcoming) with Edmund Burke, III.

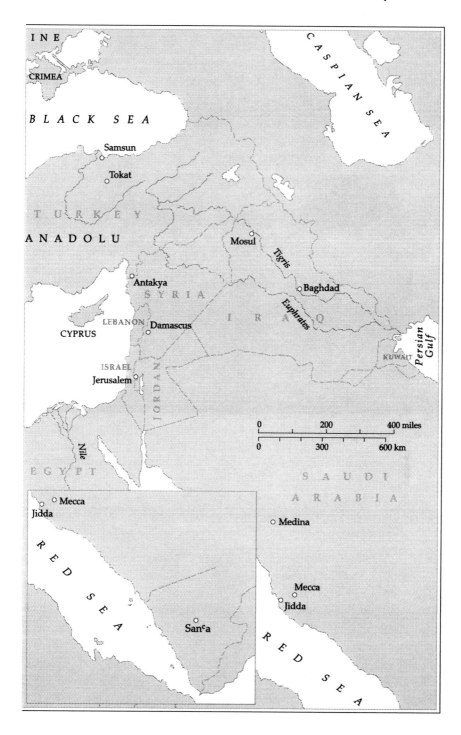

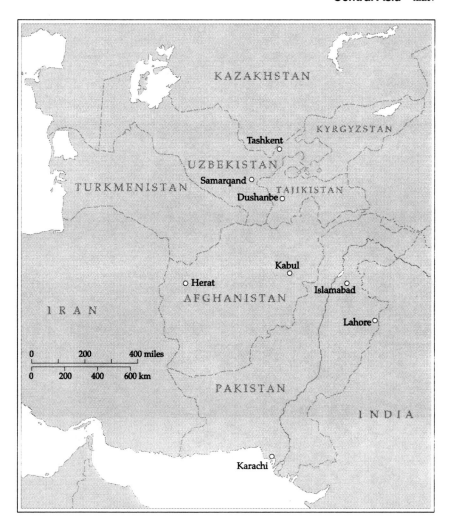

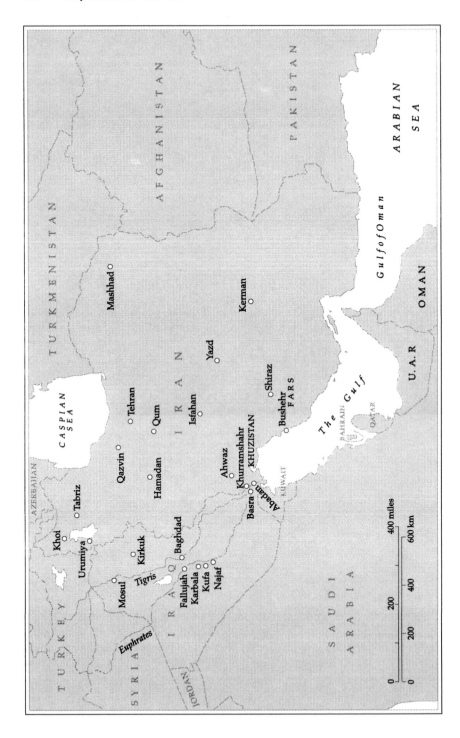

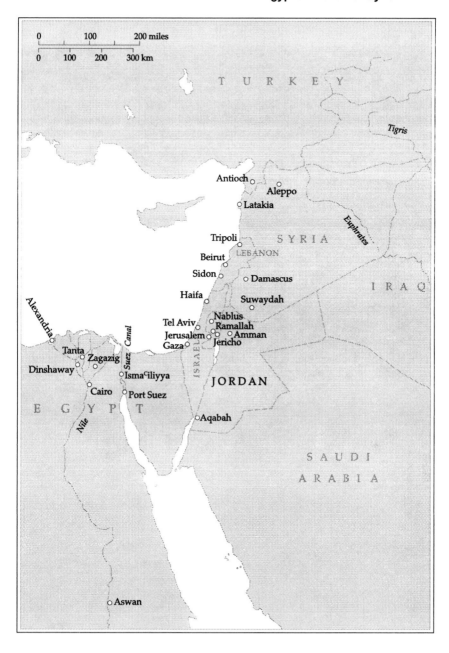

0   100   200 miles
0   100   200   300 km

TURKEY

Tigris

Antioch
Aleppo
Latakia

Tripoli
Beirut   SYRIA
LEBANON   Euphrates
Sidon   Damascus

Haifa   IRAQ
Suwaydah

Alexandria   Tel Aviv   Nablus
Ramallah
Jerusalem   Amman
Gaza   Jericho
Tanta   Zagazig
Dinshaway   ISRAEL
Ismaᶜiliyya   JORDAN
Cairo   Port Suez

EGYPT

Nile
Suez Canal

Aqabah

SAUDI
ARABIA

Aswan

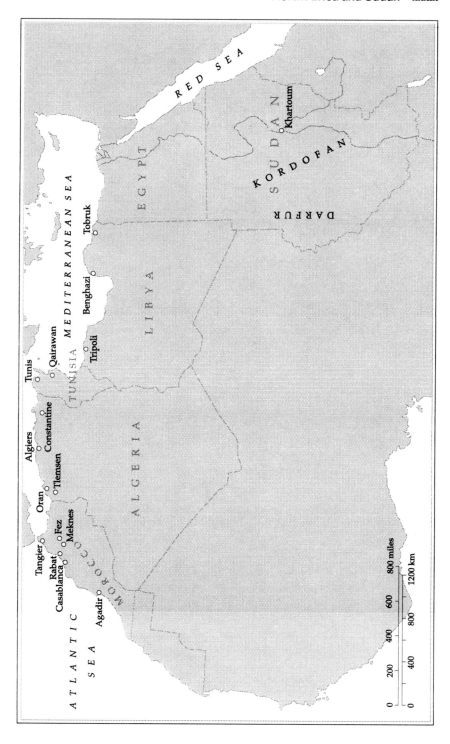

RED SEA

SOUDAN

Khartoum

KORDOFAN

DARFUR

EGYPT

MEDITERRANEAN SEA

Tobruk

LIBYA

Benghazi

Tripoli

TUNISIA

Qairawan

Tunis

Algiers

Constantine

Oran

Tlemsen

ALGERIA

Fez

Meknes

Tangier

Rabat

Casablanca

MOROCCO

Agadir

ATLANTIC
SEA

0   200   400   600   800 miles

0   400   800   1200 km

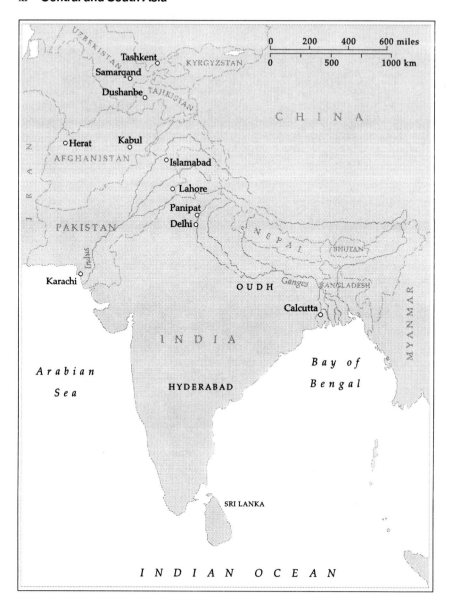

1

State and society

Introduction

Since the eighteenth century the Middle East, like the rest of the world, has witnessed dramatic change in the relationship between state and society. This series of changes took place in fits and starts, at times in response to a well-conceived plan, and at others appearing to lurch and sputter in response to a ruler's pressing circumstances and idiosyncrasies. One challenge for historians is that, while what constituted the 'state' and its purpose changed remarkably over these centuries, it is much easier for historians to approach, quantify, and analyze the state than to conceptualize, measure, and evaluate 'society', so that our sources lead us to top–down understandings which this section seeks to counterbalance with social history sources.

One feature of the modern state has been its concern, some might say obsession, with keeping records and producing paperwork. The combined weight of all of the orders, circulars, decrees, memoranda, drafts, financial records, and so on produced by modernizing governments has given historians an exceptionally rich reservoir of information. Most Middle Eastern states attempted to borrow models and techniques, including large bureaucracies producing reams of paper, that had recently been developed in Western Europe. To such reformers as Mehmed (Muhammad) ʿAli Paşa of Egypt (r. 1805–49) and Sultan Mahmud II (r. 1808–39) of the Ottoman Empire, the centralized model of the post-revolutionary French state in particular had a clear attraction in this regard.

Perhaps the best place to begin to understand the radical process of change in Middle Eastern state and society in the modern period is in the military sphere, as it encompasses both elites with their own reforming ideas versus the state, and the non-elites who were conscripted, sometimes with pay and sometimes not, into the armed forces for long periods. In the twentieth century the entry of people of non-elite backgrounds such as Jamal ʿAbd al-Nasir (Gamal Abd al-Nasser), into the officer ranks for the first time literally changed the face and shape of the Middle East. It is no exaggeration to say that the single most important development for the modern Middle Eastern state was the decision to adopt Western military methods—a reasonable response to the increasingly costly losses suffered at the hands of European armies in the early 1800s, but an extremely expensive strategy in practice.

From this simple decision flowed a number of crucial changes. The Western standing army relied upon conscription, training, education, drill, and uniformity. Developing this sort of regime required that ambitious governments of the Middle East develop the wherewithal to house, educate, feed, clothe, and pay the 'new style' troops upon whom the system depended. In the past, the states of the region had often been able to field troops without much money changing hands—exchanging the rights to collect taxes in certain regions for military service—or had come to rely on slave and mercenary troops who supported themselves in part by plunder, extortion, or intermarriage with artisanal and merchant classes.

The new standing armies required cash wages and were extremely expensive to equip and arm. This meant, in turn, that the state was forever seeking new ways of extracting more revenues from it subjects. This was usually done by sending out more men as surveyors, tax-collectors, and administrators, all of which inevitably swelled the government bureaucracy, and increased its profile in the provinces. In this they were largely successful.

The logic of the expanding government followed inexorably along its own course. States needed new clerks to staff and run this increasingly elaborate bureaucracy. Unhappy with the preparation children received from the religious schools that represented the vast majority of educational establishments, states began to involve themselves with providing education themselves.

Naturally enough, the increasing personal demands that the modernizing state was placing on its subjects produced a variety of results. While it is always difficult to determine how the 'silent majority' was affected, it is clear that the demands came at a price for the governments, who were increasingly confronted with elite and then popular demands for participation in the new arenas of social, economic, and political activity. With the rising costs of being an ordinary Ottoman or modern Syrian or Iraqi, many reasoned, should come a greater voice in what those costs should be, and how they should pay off in increasing standards of living.

The documents in this section have been selected to illustrate several aspects of the changing relationship between state and society in the modern Middle East. All of them shed light on the give-and-take relationship linking the burgeoning state—with its military, administrative, educational, and legal apparatus—with the much more inchoate, though no less important, subjects who were increasingly encouraged to think, act, and participate as citizens.

1.1 A provincial treasurer reports, *c.*1674
Mark L. Stein

Preface

During the seventeenth century the Ottoman and Habsburg empires faced one another across a military frontier that divided Hungary, each empire relying on a line of fortresses to defend its territory. Although there were few major campaigns during the seventeenth century, the frontier was the scene of constant raiding by both Ottoman and Habsburg forces. Border incursions by garrison troops to rustle livestock and capture prisoners for ransom were common, and a certain level of raiding was acceptable under the peace agreements between the two empires. Endemic raiding gave the soldiers opportunities to augment their salaries, and made life uncertain and dangerous for the local population.

This was also a period of increasing decentralization in the Ottoman state. Factionalism at the imperial center weakened the state's direct control over the provinces. Local officials gained new authority, as well as new opportunities to enrich themselves through corruption and exploitation of the peasants. Adding to the empire's difficulties was a continuing financial crisis. State revenues did not meet expenditure needs, and financial officials in both the central and provincial administrations were constantly scrambling to allocate limited resources properly.

The following document is the report of one such provincial official to his superiors employed in the central fiscal bureaucracy. The author, Mehmed, was a *defterdar*, or financial official, assigned to the important Ottoman frontier fortress at Uyvar, Hungary (modern Nove Zamky in Slovakia). This report appears in the back of Mehmed's record of revenues assigned to the garrison for the year 1084 AH/1673–4 CE. In it he asks the central administration to issue official orders to authorize—often retroactively—actions he has determined necessary for the effective functioning of the Uyvar treasury.

This report is seemingly unique. Such a list requesting official orders is not usually found appended to a financial ledger. From the layout of the register it is clear, however, that Mehmed finished his revenue calculations, then skipped a few pages and wrote out his list. In addition, the language of the list is simple and informal, even though the orders for which Mehmed is asking are nominally to come from the sultan himself. Formal requests for sultanic action were always filled with formulaic invocations and flowery language. This document is clearly more informal and thus provides a glimpse of the inner workings of the financial bureaucracy by illustrating one means by which provincial officials communicated with their superiors at the Imperial center.

Text

Başbakanlık Osmanlı Arşivi, Baş Muhasebe Kalemi, D.BŞM-UYH 17083, Defter of necessary imperial orders for the fortress of Uyvar

1. Absolutely nothing can be done without the necessary imperial edicts in response to the seven petitions. It is my sultan's to command.

2. 100,000 *akçe*[1] worth of robes of honor is spent at the fort of Uyvar from year to year. Because there are no people [worthy of it] it is a waste of the treasury. It is the sultan's to command.

3. When paşas come they cause the *defterdar*s[2] to expend furnishings worth 1,000 *guruş*.[3] As there is no customs house here, the treasury is incapable of finding [these funds]. It is the sultan's to command.

4. My sultan: forty or fifty thousand *akçe* are spent for the post station per year. Unless there is a really important matter to be reported to the Imperial Presence this is not necessary.

5. My sultan: The *cizye*[4] register of Uyvar has been sent and [*cizye* has been calculated as] two-thirds payment.[5] When you see this and know why it was done in this manner, an imperial edict must be sent accordingly. It is my sultan's to command.

6. There are also matters which we told orally to [my] brother slave. If it [the report] seems reasonable, *cizye* collection will be easy. Villages that are separated are made *mukataa*[6] and turned into *hass-ı hümayun*.[7] The rest [of the villages] will be given to the pashas and their *cizye* and *ispence*[8] and *öşr*[9] will be theirs. This is very reasonable and appropriate. It is my sultan's to command.

7. My sultan: Whenever paşas come to the fort of Uyvar [they order] unneeded, unnecessary repairs. There is no money for these repairs.

8. My sultan: the *kul*s[10] of Uyvar were to take possession of the allotted revenues from *mukataa* and *cizye* in accordance with our request. From now on the paşas should not take the *kalemiyye*[11] [from them]. If there is someone who wishes again to take the *kalemiyye*, the *kul*s will be upset and something unexpected may happen. Perhaps you could kindly give a handwritten imperial edict, for which you will receive good prayers until Judgement Day, saying that the paşas [must] never interfere with matters of imperial revenues. It is not a proper action. It is the sultan's to command. And the *defterdar*s need to have custody of keys to the government storehouses. It is the sultan's to command.

---

[1] Small silver coin.   [2] Bureaucrats from the financial ministry.   [3] Large silver coin.
[4] Poll tax on non-Muslims.
[5] Payment at two-thirds was a frequent bureaucratic gambit to make up for shortfalls in revenues.
[6] Tax farm.   [7] Imperial land.   [8] A type of personal tax.   [9] Tithe paid to the state.
[10] The military 'slaves of the sultan'.   [11] Scribal fee.

9. No action has been taken yet in collecting the '85 [1085 AH] *cizye*. The *cizye* collection will soon begin, however a kind imperial order should be ordered that in addition to [the *cizye*] one '*varabil*'[12] and one board will be given by each *cizye* payer. It is reasonable that [such] an order be addressed to the *alaybeyi*.[13]

10. My imperial sultan: You had ordered that the seed in the villages should be inventoried. However, around here all those [with *timar* income] have collected their share from the seed and they used it. There is no possibility of registration. Now, here is the solution: whatever can be found [should be registered]. There are many inhabitants in the villages and abandoned arable land, but not [registered] in households. A strong firman is necessary to register them as *hass-ı hümayun* for the imperial central treasury. It is possible for the *alaybeyi* to hide people away [from taxation]. The *defterdar*s should total up as *hass* whatever can be estimated [and put in the register], because the grandees do not show us what they have taken or given. It is my sultan's to command.

11. We intended to hold the Uyvar *mukataa* as soon as we arrived. [Before we arrived revenues were] collected with an order from the *beylerbeyi*[14] and the former *defterdar* Hasan gave a *berat*.[15] [They] accepted it in *guruş* and converted it to debased *akçe*. Now I, your slave, estimated and assigned it as 800,000 *akçe* to the *ocak*;[16] and such a firman should be sent such that Kel Ahmet [the tax farmer], who took it for the year '85, gives 800,000 *akçe* [if he does not] that man should be summoned to the imperial presence. Until he leaves Uyvar, Uyvar will not be safe. The merit shall be the sultan's and any sin be mine. In any case the people then will be safe from his hand. It is my sultan's to command.

12. My imperial sultan: there is little iron remaining in the armory of Uyvar. We had heard that iron at Varad is four *akçe* per *vukiyye*.[17] It is necessary to send 10,000 *vukiyye* of iron to Uyvar. A firman should be sent to the *beylerbeyi* [of Varad] ordering [this], and we have heard that transport via non-Muslim regions [here Transylvania] is easy. It is my sultan's to command.

13. My imperial sultan: We found nearly 400,000 *akçe* of the deceased *defterdar* Osman Efendi. This was allocated for the '84 salaries due for some people. If we should not do it that way 5,000,000 will not suffice. Further, we found 200 *guruş* in the Budin [treasury] and sent a *ruznamçe*[18] [for its delivery]. If they find a pretext not to pay, send an imperial edict with your brother *kul*. Also Osman Efendi had some properties and gardens so a strong imperial order should be sent so that no one can interfere. The *kadi*s[19] should work for the treasury's interests; this is the only way for this to be done.

---

[12] It is unclear what *varabil* means.   [13] Commander of all *timar* land-revenue holders in a district.
[14] Provincial military governor.   [15] Letter of patent.
[16] Janissary corps, here the garrison.   [17] A *vukiyye* was a weight of approximately 1.282 kg.
[18] Financial memorandum.   [19] Judges.

14. We heard that the former Budin *defterdar* Ömer Pasha is still in Bosnia. 500,000 *akçe* remain due from his tenure. However, saying, 'I have expenses from service', Ibrahim Pasha took it from the treasury and left a *temessük*.[20] Send a man to Ömer Pasha and take the *temessük* and take [the money] from Ibrahim Pasha. This is the truth of the matter; we received reliable information about this.

15. You should take the Gradişka *mukataa* for the year 6 [1086] and send 7,000 *guruş* as *irsaliye*[21] to your servant. The poor [garrison] can see some money in their hands and they will say kind prayers for the sultan. When I shall collect it for one year many benefits will come to [me as well as to] your slave [the revenue collector]. If it is [done] this way, it will be very reasonable. Also a *kadi* document concerning Gradişka is sent and there is a *temessük* for it. You may send a man to collect it. And as the deceased has no heir, only a wife, 3,000 *guruş* will go to the public treasury and 53,000 *guruş* will go to the Uyvar treasury for the debt left by Osman Efendi. It is my sultan's to command.

[Signed]
the slave, Mehmed, *defterdar* of Uyvar

---

[20] Bill of debt.   [21] Here, a financial disbursement.

1.2 An Armenian account of the Ottoman siege of Erevan, 1724[22]

George Bournoutian

Preface

In 1721 Afghans marched on the Iranian capital, taking advantage of the decline of the Safavid state. Isfahan fell in 1722 and the shah, Soltan Hosayn, abdicated. His son and heir, Tahmasp II, fled the region in order to regain strength and supporters, after which he intended to reclaim his empire. In 1723 the Ottomans invaded and captured a number of western Iranian cities, including Erevan, which was surrendered to the Ottomans in 1724.

Abraham, the author of the description of the siege of Erevan, which is included in a larger work entitled *History of the Wars (1721–1738)*, was a native of the city. The Ottoman invasion of Safavid domains, and the subsequent seventeen years of war and fighting, is probably what prompted him to write his history, which tends to favor post-Safavid Iranians and expresses disdain for the Ottomans and the Afghans. The *History of the Wars* begins with the 1721 invasion of Iran by the Afghans. A subtitle of the work is *Initiated by the Ottomans to Seize Armenian and Persian Towns Following the Campaign of Sultan Mahmud Afghan against the Persian King, Shah Soltan Hosayn*. This subtitle explains which wars in particular are considered in the work.

Much of Abraham of Erevan's information, received through second- or third-hand accounts, contains factual errors and omissions, yet his is the only source for many events that occurred in the region, particularly from March through September 1724. Furthermore, this history provides information on the societal roles of various groups, including elders, clergy, secular leaders, and gypsies, as well as descriptions of Erevan and its inhabitants. Abraham of Erevan further provides details on death tolls and those taken captive, adding to one's understanding of the lasting impact of the invasions on the inhabitants and victims.

The Armenians in western Iran, though outnumbered by the better-equipped Ottomans, still struggled to defend themselves. The following selection describes the eventual surrender of Erevan, after Ottoman troops succeeded in taking the town and the governor while other notables had sequestered themselves in the citadel. The surrender was effected by the intervention and negotiations made by an Armenian religious leader, the katʿoghikos Astuatsatur.

---

[22] Abraham of Erevan, *History of the Wars, 1721–1738*, ed. and intro. by George A. Bournoutian (Costa Mesa, Calif.: Mazda, 1999), 21–35.

Text

III

The Siege of Erevan and the Resistance of Its Populace. How the Armenians Bravely Fought Outside the Citadel and Routed the Ottomans

ᶜAbdullah Pasha moved from the plain of Eghvard and three days later reached Erevan. His army camped at a site called Sambeki Dalma, which was half an hour's distance from Erevan, and was named after a water canal (dalman) located in the vicinity. All those who lived in the villages and farms around Erevan fled and took refuge in the city.

After seven days of positioning his troops around Erevan, the Pasha decided to march on Ejmiatsin. A decree,[23] however, arrived from the Ottoman Sultan in which he ordered the Pasha not to attack Ejmiatsin. Instead, he ordered the Pasha to place some of his troops to guard it and not to allow anyone to damage it. No one was to loot it or to harm anyone residing in Ejmiatsin. The Katᶜoghikos of the Armenians, Astuatsatur, was not in Ejmiatsin at that time,[24] for he had gone to see Shah Tahmasp in Tabriz.

This occurred as a result of God's grace. For when the Ottoman army invaded Armenia, a pious Armenian notable called Seghbos, a most distinguished Armenian in Constantinople, who was an influential man and who held the rank of purveyor in the Sultan's court, interceded on behalf of Ejmiatsin. The Sultan cared for the Armenian people and, in the interest of the State, gave the order to the Pasha to protect Holy Ejmiatsin and to forbid his soldiers to invade that holy place. The Pasha, following the Sultan's decree, forbade his troops to attack Ejmiatsin and appointed a detachment of soldiers to guard it.[25]

When ᶜAbdullah Pasha marched forward with the intention of taking the fortress of Erevan, he sent delegates beforehand to discuss conditions for the peaceful surrender of the fortress. The governor of Erevan, who was called Mehr ᶜAli, replied, 'We shall submit your offer to our Shah and if he approves we shall surrender the fortress to you. If not, we cannot give it up on our own.' When the Pasha realized that the city would not surrender he prepared for war.

The Pasha brought his army forth and prepared the siege of Erevan. The next day he approached the fortress. He placed twelve cannons in the direction of the All Savior monastery, twenty-nine cannons near St Madr,[26] and seven cannons on

---

[23] MS a has the Arab-Persian term *farman*. Editorial note: Prof. Bournoutian is reconciling eight manuscripts of this text, he refers to them as MS a,b,c,e,f,g, via vz.

[24] MS a has the Armeno-Persian compound word, *en t'arighin* (from *tarik*, or 'on that date').

[25] MS a does not contain this paragraph.

[26] Persian for 'mother'; refers to the Monastery of St Anne (the Mother of Virgin Mary).

top of the three hills [across the river], thus surrounding and bombarding Erevan from four locations.[27]

Mehr ᶜAli then ordered the Muslims[28] to join the Armenians and give battle. They fought against the Ottomans for sixty days, killed many of the assailants, and did not allow them to enter the city. When ᶜAbdullah Pasha saw that his army was being slaughtered, he sent envoys to Bayazid and the Kurds[29] to ask assistance. Thirty-five thousand armed men arrived, but even with their help he could not conquer Erevan.

When the Pasha witnessed the firm resolve of the citizens of Erevan and his own casualties, he decided not to continue the battle. He sent a message to the Sultan stating, 'Erevan has too many defenders and I cannot take it.'[30] The Sultan then ordered the Pasha of Kutahya to proceed towards Erevan. The latter arrived with 10,000 armed men and camped near the city.

Three days later the two Pashas joined forces and, after conferring,[31] decided not to delay, but to move forward. At sunrise on a Thursday they prepared the army for an assault[32] on Erevan. A large river called Zangi[33] lies before the city, and when the Ottoman hordes began to cross it, the width of the river was covered with such a multitude that the water was not visible and it appeared as if the river had dried out. Although the Ottomans had crossed the river, they could not proceed much farther, for the defenders of Erevan attacked them. These were the Armenians, who fought them for half a day, for the Persians and the governor of the city had fled into the citadel and left the Armenians to do battle in town. Two thousand Christians fell to the sword on that day.[34]

There was a certain *vardapet*[35] in Erevan, called Grigor. He went to the St Sargis Church,[36] which was located in the neighborhood called Dzoragegh. He summoned and gathered a crowd of Armenians. At the first hour of the night the citizens sought the advice of the *vardapet* and asked, 'What are we to do? Tomorrow the Ottomans will kill all of us and will take our wives and children into captivity.' In Erevan, in the district called Kond, there lived some 100 households of Christian

---

[27] This sentence is absent from MS b.

[28] MS a has *Turks*, which in this case signifies Muslims.   [29] MS b has *Medes*.

[30] MS b has the following sentence in parentheses: '(What is Your Command? Send us reinforcements or let us withdraw).' On fo. 88a Karakashean explains the reason for the parentheses by stating that he wished to convey the meaning of Abraham's vernacular, which is *Yerevanay hzork'n shat ay, ch'em karum arnel.*   [31] MS a has the Perso-Arabic term *maslahat*.

[32] MS a frequently uses the word *erish*, which is the Persian term *yures* or the Turkish *yuruyus*.

[33] Present-day Hrazdan River.

[34] The Armenian commanders were the following: Hovhannes Hundibekean, Poghos K'ijibekean, Hovhannes Karjik, and Dawit' Mirzajanean. MS a has *Hohann Hundi Bekents'. K'ich'i Bekents' Poghos, Karchik Ovanes, Mirzayjaneants' T'avi.*

[35] Armenian celibate priests, who have graduated from a seminary; equal to archimandrites in the Orthodox Church.   [36] Also known as Hovhannavank.

Bosha.[37] They were wealthy, brave, and had armed men.[38] They and their men came to *Vardapet* Grigor. The Armenians, along with the *vardapet*, were in tears and begged the armed men to save them, their wives and their children from those who had besieged the town and were preparing to loot it.[39] Ghazaros said the following to Grigor: '*Vardapet!* I have 200 brave young men. They are armed and are capable of fighting with swords and guns. I shall gather them and shall fight with all my ability.' Hovhannes Hundibekean of Dzoragegh began to gather men as well. Other Armenian notables followed his lead and promised to resist with their followers.[40]

The Armenians gathered that night, conferred, and prepared their defenses against the Ottomans. At daybreak, God's mercy spared them, for it was Friday and the Ottomans did not attack. The Armenians gathered brave young men from the various villages around Erevan: from Parakar, Gok-Gumbed, Kanaker, Arinj, Avan, Gavan, Dzak, and Noragegh. 9,000 armed troops, that is, all the able-bodied men from the above villages, gathered outside Erevan to do battle. Young Armenians from the district called Old Erevan came, armed under the command of their chiefs.[41] On Saturday morning, Bosha Ghazaros, Bosha Klduz, and Bosha Dawit Bedik' came to Dzoragegh with 234 men. *Vardapet* Grigor ordered them to hold the road leading to the Forty Mills. The men from Dzoragegh, 3,000 strong, armed with swords or guns, were to defend Dzak. The men from Kond were to defend the road to the Tappakhana district. Nine hundred and fifty-five men from the Juhair neighborhood, with swords and guns, under the command of Ter-Movses, guarded the Darbinots' road. Four thousand men from Old Erevan were under the command of three men: Pahlavan Nikoghos, who was a horseshoe maker,[42] Andon, son of Maryam, and But'ik, son of Khatun. There were a total of 9,423 men[43] with guns and swords, who were capable of fighting. The rest, some 28,000, were not trained. They stayed to guard their homes.

All of them left their wives and children and those men who were unfit to fight, and gathered with their commanders in a suburb of Erevan that was called

---

[37] The Armenian gypsies were called *bosha*. Some 100 households lived in Erevan as late as the nineteenth century; see Bournoutian, *The Khanate of Erevan Under Qajar Rule*, 1795–1828 (Costa Mazda: Mesa, CA, 1992), 57.

[38] Their leaders at that time were Paron Ghazaros Baburean, Paron Klduz, Paron Dawit', Paron Beyram, and Paron Petros. (MS a has *Babur Oghli* and *Petik* instead of *Petros*.)

[39] MS a does not have this line.

[40] These were: Paron P'irigul, Paron Arzumbek, Paron T'adewos, Paron Mghun, Paron Mkrtich', Paron Malkhas', Paron Alexan, Paron Agham, Paron Galust, Paron Aghazade, Paron Nuri, Paron Zorahb, Paron Nikoghayos, Paron Awetis Srapionean, and Paron Eram. (MS a uses different spelling.)

[41] Nikoghos, Andon son of Maryam, But'ik son of Khatun, and the priest Ter-Movses.

[42] MS a has the term *nalband* from the Persian *na'lband*.

[43] MS b has 9,443 men. Although both manuscripts give exact numbers, the totals listed do not add up.

Dzoragegh. They were ready to do battle for their own sake and that of their wives and their children. They placed detachments in different parts of the city with instructions to block the entrances to Erevan. They waited in readiness to give battle should the enemy manage to enter the city and, if not, to hold their positions.[44]

The Ottomans surrounded the city on four sides. Dense gardens, orchards, and numerous ancient willow trees, which had been planted a long time ago for the defenses of the town, surrounded the city. Behind the tree-line flowed the big Zangi River. Because of this the Ottomans were afraid to move on Erevan, for they could not operate their guns because of the trees. They therefore set up their positions across the river and opened fire on the city. They sought a way to advance and occasionally they managed to move forward, but only in the direction of Dzoragegh, which had no gardens or trees and from there they attacked the town.

The governor of Erevan and all the notables were in the citadel and fought using their cannons. However, when the Ottomans came near the city, the cannons of the citadel were useless, for cannons fired from a height cannot hit the enemy if he is too near, but are effective only if he is located a certain distance away.[45] The governor of Erevan, Mehr ᶜAli Khan, had taken twelve Armenian families with him into the citadel.[46] The lesser nobles remained outside and prepared to fight. Harutᶜiwn, the son of Yesaman, was sent as envoy to the Pasha. When Harutᶜiwn, the Armenian, crossed the Zangi the Ottoman janissaries killed him.

The Armenians then prepared for renewed attacks. Meanwhile, 3,000 Egyptian[47] troops came to the aid of the Ottomans. They pitched camp near the villages defended by the Armenians. Being more courageous than the Turks, the Egyptians, ignoring discipline and without the permission of the commander-in-chief, ᶜAbdullah Pasha, attacked like wild beasts with the intention of breaking into Erevan from Dzoragegh. Many Turks followed their lead and moved *en masse* without formation. They thought that they alone would be able to achieve victory, gain glory, and at the same time be among the first to take booty and to accomplish their evil deeds. When the attack on the Dzoragegh district commenced, the defenders could not hold and retreated to the Forty Mills[48] district. News of this reached the Armenian gypsies, who were guarding other districts. They were afraid to move, but *Vardapet* Grigor shed tears and begged them to aid

---

[44] MS a does not contain this paragraph.   [45] MS a does not have these two sentences.

[46] The most important individuals were Melik Sahak, who was the son of Melik Aqamal, and his brother Aqa-Veli, Paron Karapet, Mikayel Barkhudarean, Babajan Motsakean, and other notables.

[47] MS a has *Mesra-ghul*, which translates as Egyptian slaves or *mamluks*.

[48] MS b has Aghoreats (Aghorik means mill in Armenian).

the defenders. Finally, 234 Armenian gypsy[49] warriors rushed to defend the road
leading to the Forty Mills. They attacked with swords and guns and with God's
help managed to defeat the enemy and kill six thousand. The rest fled across the
Zangi, for the Christians held the high ground and the enemy the low ground.
The Christians, however, also lost some 1,300 men that day. Witnessing the
disorganized behavior of the Egyptians, ʿAbdullah Pasha was extremely incensed
and ordered that no one attack without his express order.

<h1 style="text-align:center">IV</h1>

*The Weakening of the Armenian Defenders. Sending Envoys for
Peace to the Ottomans. The Capture of Erevan and the Slaughter and
Enslavement of its Armenian Defendants*

The Sultan then ordered Saru Mustafa Pasha and Rajab Pasha to march on
Erevan and to join ʿAbdullah Pasha. The latter received news that Saru Mustafa
and Rajab Pasha would soon arrive. Prior to their arrival, however, ʿAbdullah
Pasha made another assault by deploying his janissaries against the district known
as Kond. The Armenian units were immediately sent to that location. The
Armenian gypsies gave battle, defeated them, and forced the enemy to flee.
Four hundred Armenians and forty Armenian gypsies were wounded in this
engagement. They did not die, but were confined to bed. After that the Ottoman
army did not advance until the arrival of the two pashas, who came fifteen
days later with an army totaling 38,000 men. After conferring with the new
commanders, ʿAbdullah Pasha gave orders to attack from four directions, to
continue fighting without interruption, and not to retreat.

   When the Christians saw that two Pashas had arrived and had substantially
increased the Ottoman army, they realized that they were surrounded from all
sides and the enemy would swallow them like the sea. They were filled with
horror. It became clear that no matter how many of the enemy they killed, new
soldiers would appear and take their place. The Christians, however, could not
follow suit, for they were locked in the city and were blocked from all sides, like
fish in nets. They could not expect any aid from anywhere.[50] The Armenians
gathered around *Vardapet* Grigor and said, 'What can we do? The enemy is
increasing its strength daily, while we decrease in numbers day after day.' The
Vardapet replied, 'We shall send them envoys to discuss terms of submission and
ask for peace.' They asked: 'Whom shall we send?' Everyone was afraid to take on
this mission. Prior to this, an envoy by the name of Harutʿiwn had not been able
to reach the Pasha—the janissaries had seized and killed him because they wanted
to take and loot the town and did not wish a peaceful end to the conflict.[51]

---

[49] MS b has 300 gypsies.   [50] MS a does not contain the last five sentences.
[51] This sentence is absent from MS a.

An Armenian by the name of Mirza, son of Akhijan, who was willing to sacrifice his life for his fellow citizens, came forward and said, 'For the sake[52] of our Lord, Jesus Christ, I shall take it upon myself to be a messenger. If I die, I will accept death gladly, and if not, I shall go to the Pasha and shall relate whatever message you entrust to me.' They provided him with gifts and he left, accompanied by his servant. He crossed the Zangi River and when he reached the Ottoman camp the janissaries seized him, took him to Khan Bag[53] and cut his throat. When his servant, who was called Sargis, and who was from Ejmiatsin, saw what happened to his master, he fled and when the soldiers pursued him he threw himself from a cliff into the Zangi. Thanks to God he did not faint or die, but survived, reached the defenders of Erevan, and related what had occurred to his master. He added, 'Woe be to us Christian brothers, there is no hope. Our sins have been great and have made us unworthy of God's benevolence.'

Then the people raised their voice and, groaning loudly and mourning the dead, began to call on God to redeem them and not to deprive the Christians of his mercy. *Vardapet* Grigor then gathered the people in the church and said Mass. Having confessed their sins they were ready to receive communion, the life-giving body and blood of Christ. Then each man stood in readiness in his assigned place.

The next morning, on Friday, the Ottoman forces, led by five pashas and divided into four advance detachments, attacked the city from all directions. The battle continued from morning until evening. Here and there Armenian and Ottoman groups continued to kill each other until the twenty-fourth hour. There was so much bloodshed that the Zangi and the earth adjoining it turned red. The smell of blood and the corpses of the dead in the town reached even the outlying districts. The city was taken on the seventh day of the month of June, in the year 1173 of the Armenian calendar (1724). The citadel, however, remained in Persian hands. The Armenian fighters thus fell to the sword. All died or were taken captive. Many drowned in the Zangi. The Ottomans took their wives with them and defiled them with evil acts.

Why did this occur if God did not wish them to fall into the hands of the enemy? Why did God hand them over, they whom He had redeemed and cleansed through the blood of His Only Son and had adopted as His own? He did not give them up willingly, but because their sins and waywardness brought upon them His just retribution. For their sins and unlawful acts cried out to heaven. What were the causes of their sins? Mainly it was because the clergy and churchmen generally neglected the commands of God and other teachings of Christian doctrine, preferring to take care of only the physical aspect of life.

---

[52] MS a frequently uses the Persian term *kater*.

[53] This was a large orchard outside the citadel; see Bournoutian, *Khanate*, 41.

Although the churches conducted daily Masses and services, they were performed in ignorance, without comprehending the mystery and without honoring God. I shall simply state that in their soul they lacked the Holy Christian spirit and kept their Christian faith in name only and through outward acts. They lacked the required knowledge and the inner meaning of the Holy Trinity, His words of Incarnation, His Salvation and Passion. They were not only unconcerned about acquiring it, but did not strive to at least understand or learn it. Therefore, it is not surprising that God permitted the unbelievers to defile such Christians with evil deeds and to turn them away from their faith. For those who do not know God and who do not observe the commands of Christ and are careless in learning them, even if they do not experience such hardships, are not of the true faith and should be severed from the Christian faith and viewed the same as heathens.[54]

V

On How the Governor of Erevan, Through the Mediation of Kat'oghikos Astuatsatur, Received Assurances of Safety from the Ottoman Pasha and Surrendered the Citadel

The governor of Erevan, together with the Persian and Armenian notables who had taken refuge in the citadel, and who had observed what had occurred, fell into despair and confusion, lost hope of holding out in the fortress, and sought ways to save their lives.[55] During the time when the Ottomans had besieged Erevan, Shah Tahmasp, who was in Tabriz, marched to Karosan with an army of 6,000 men, for he did not plan to go to the defense of Erevan with such a small number of troops.[56] On his departure, he permitted Kat'oghikos Astuatsatur, whom, as noted, he had kept by his side, to return to Ejmiatsin.

When the Kat'oghikos arrived in Ejmiatsin, ʿAbdullah Pasha learned of this and sent 300 men to summon the Kat'oghikos to his presence. The troops went to Garni[57] and told the Kat'oghikos, 'The Pasha wants you.' The Kat'oghikos replied, 'I am obedient to the Pasha.' When the Kat'oghikos arrived, the Pasha received him with honor and ordered that he be given splendid garments. He seated the Kat'oghikos beside him and spoke with him with great courtesy. He kept the Kat'oghikos in his camp for three days and continued to honor him. After that he spoke to him about the war and said, 'How are we to behave if after taking the town, those in the citadel still hold out and refuse to surrender? How

---

[54] The last paragraph is absent from MS a. Father Karakashean's criticism of the Armenian clergy echoes that of Abbot Mekhit'ar, whose dissatisfaction led him to become a Catholic and to establish the Mekhitarist order of priests.   [55] This sentence is absent from MS a.

[56] This sentence is absent from MS a.

[57] This should be Karbi; that is, Karbi-basar, a district in the Khanate of Erevan where Ejmiatsin was located, see Bournoutian, *Khanate*, 36.

can we achieve peace?' The Kat'oghikos replied, 'Be patient for a little while, tomorrow I shall go and talk with them and point out the necessity of submitting, and they will surrender the fort.'

The next day the Kat'oghikos left the camp and approached the fortress. The governor was informed that the Kat'oghikos had arrived and was standing outside the gates. He ordered one of his subordinates, Mohammad Qasem Beg, not to open the gate but to inquire from the inside the reason for the Kat'oghikos' presence and what news he had of Shah Tahmasp. The messenger came, stood in a place where he could be heard, and asked, 'Why have you come and what news do you have of our Shah?' The Kat'oghikos answered, 'There is no hope of aid from the Shah. You must think[58] and decide what is best for your own interests.' When the governor heard this he was filled with grief and shed tears. He then exclaimed, 'Woe unto us. Our king has deserted us.' He dispatched three Armenian notables who were in the fortress with him, Paron Karapet, Melik Sahak, and Paron Andon, and told them, 'Go and find out the implications of your Patriarch's statement.' When they came, the Kat'oghikos, standing outside the gate, explained the situation once again. He told them about Shah Tahmasp, and presented the peace proposal of the Pasha, stating, 'He promises to let all of you go in peace if you surrender the citadel.' They returned and related these words to the governor. The Kat'oghikos went back to the Pasha to relate what had taken place. He begged that the Pasha wait for several days for the defenders to make up their minds and then he left for Ejmiatsin.[59]

The governor summoned his notables[60] and asked their opinion. One of them, who was called Mejlum Beg, said, 'I think that we should surrender the citadel in exchange for our lives. If we resist we will lose the fortress and our lives in a few days' time.' The *jarci basi* said the following: 'If you surrender the fortress to the Ottomans, then know for certain that our homes will be looted and our families will be taken into captivity, for although they now promise us freedom, after we give up the fortress they shall go back on their word.' Mohammad Qasem Beg said, 'I also have an opinion.' The Khan ordered, 'Speak your mind.' Mohammad Qasem replied: 'May the Khan prosper.[61] Let us ask the messenger of peace, the Armenian Kat'oghikos, to come again so that we can assess the situation.' Mehr °Ali accepted his advice and summoned the Armenian chiefs, Melik Sahak and

---

[58] MS a has the Persian term *fekr*.   [59] This sentence is absent from MS a.

[60] Among them [were] Mohammad Qasem Beg, Salakan Beg, the stable-master (text has the Persian term *mirakor*), Shiekh °Ali Beg Rehanlu, the chief herald (text has the Perso-Turkish term *jarci basi*), °Abbas Ali Beg Bayat, Hajji Elias, Abbas Khan Beg, Gazar Ramazan Beg, and Naqd °Ali Beg of the Demir Bulag district.

[61] The Armenian word is *voghj* (to be alive and healthy); the Persian term is *salamat* (secure from danger, good health). The Armenian term is used here.

Melik Karapet, and said, 'This is what my advisors and I think. What is your opinion?' They responded, 'Your will be done.' Mehr ʿAli said, 'We shall send someone to bring the Katʿoghikos here.'

But they decided not to send a Persian, for they were certain that the Ottomans, upon seeing a Persian, would immediately cut his throat. They therefore decided to dispatch an Armenian to bear an official communication to the Pasha, requesting that the Armenian Katʿoghikos come once more to the fortress so that the terms of peace could be negotiated through his office. Paron Andon was asked to act as an envoy. They lowered him down from the wall by a rope, for they did not wish to open the gates of the citadel, even though they had already hoisted a white flag of peace on the citadel tower. When Andon approached the Ottoman camp, a number of soldiers surrounded him and took him to the Pasha, who asked him, 'Where are you from and why were you sent?' Andon answered, 'I was sent from the fortress with a letter for Your Excellency.' He then took out the note and handed it to the Pasha. After reading it the Pasha immediately sent one of his officers with fifty men to Ejmiatsin to bring the Katʿoghikos to him. The officer came to the Holy See and said, 'The Pasha wants you.' The Katʿoghikos replied, 'I obey.' When the Katʿoghikos arrived he saw Paron Andon standing next to the Pasha. The Pasha asked the Katʿoghikos to sit down and said, 'Mehr ʿAli Khan has asked for you. Go and find out what he has to say.' The Katʿoghikos replied, 'Your wish is my command.' The Katʿoghikos then went to the fortress for the second time. They let him into the fort and took him to the audience room of the governor. All the Persian and Armenian notables had gathered there and waited patiently to hear what he had to say so that they could follow his advice and save their lives. The Katʿoghikos spent a long time in discussion. After going back and forth carrying messages between the governor and the Pasha, he told the latter that Mehr ʿAli Khan wanted assurances that he would not be killed. He wished to leave Erevan and join the Shah. The Katʿoghikos thus persuaded the Persians to trust the word of the Pasha and to surrender the fortress.

Having their word that they would surrender the fort, he went back to the Pasha. He delivered their message and begged the Pasha to accept the agreement and to permit them to leave freely. The Pasha agreed and presented the Katʿoghikos with a kalʿat. He then ordered some 3,000 janissaries to go with the Katʿoghikos, who carried the official document of peace.

The Katʿoghikos and the janissaries approached the fortress and presented the writ. The Persians took it, examined what was in it, and opened the gates. The Katʿoghikos entered the fortress first and the 3,000 Ottoman troops followed. The first group of soldiers immediately took charge of the 300 cannons of the fort. The Katʿoghikos sat in the square until all the Ottoman troops had entered the fort in an orderly fashion. After that the Katʿoghikos escorted the Pasha into the fortress. The Pasha came to Mohammad Qasem Beg's house and alighted. The Kat'oghikos went to bring the Khan of Erevan. The Khan said, 'Caliph,[62] I am scared!' Astuatsatur replied, 'Do not be afraid!'[63]

After that, Mehr ᶜAli Khan and the Kat'oghikos, together with all the notables and military chiefs, went to the Pasha to offer their respects. Mehr ᶜAli Khan was received by the Pasha, who gave him the kiss of peace. The Kat'oghikos told the Pasha that the Khan wished to leave. The Pasha permitted the Khan and 200 of his close subordinates to depart. Escorted by the Kat'oghikos, they left and after six days of travel the Kat'oghikos returned to Erevan.[64]

The Pasha hereby ordered that all the Muslims[65] had to come out of the citadel and they did. The Pasha announced that he had to send Qasem Beg, Shaykh ᶜAli Beg, and ʿAbbas ᶜAli Beg to Istanbul, for Sultan Ahmet had asked for them. The Pasha then took the three men, ordered that they be taken out of town, wrapped in sacks,[66] and thrown into the Zangi River. He thus killed them.[67] Mehr ᶜAli and all the others were set free to go anywhere they pleased. When all was done and the Ottoman army had settled down, the Kat'oghikos returned to Ejmiatsin.

The Ottomans took Erevan on 20[68] August 1173 (1724). The Ottoman army rested there until November.

---

[62] The Muslims considered the supreme patriarch of the Armenian Church as the caliph (*kalifa*) of the Armenian nation.   [63] These three sentences do not appear in MS b.

[64] These two sentences do not appear in MS b.

[65] MS a has *Turks*, the term used by Abraham when referring to Muslims. MS b has *Persians*. Abraham also uses the tern *Tajik* to refer to Turks or Muslims.

[66] MS a has the term *jval* from the Persian *joval*.   [67] The reason for this action is unknown.

[68] MS b has *21 August*. If one adds eleven days (for the Julian calendar), the surrender of Erevan falls in the beginning of September. Von Hammer's date of 28 September, however, is cited by most historians, see *Histoire de l'Empire Ottoman*, 4 (Persian translation, Tehran, 1988), 3112.

1.3 Concord and harmony among Ottoman provincial governors: a grand vizier's advice and warning: Abdullah Paşa, 1749
From the Islamfiche *project*

Preface

Boynuiğri Seyyid Abdullah Paşa became grand vizier of the Ottoman Empire in 1160AH/1747CE after many years of service as a provincial governor, a rank to which he reverted after his dismissal from office in 1163/1750. Of particular interest with regard to his background were both his ethnic origin (some historians believe that he was an Arab from Kirkuk, now in northern Iraq) and his title of honor, *seyyid* (from the Arabic, *sayyid*), which denoted descent from the Prophet Muhammad. The text of the personal letter that he wrote to the governor of Sidon, a certain Sarı Mehmed Paşa, first of all illustrates the values and thinking of the Ottoman ruling elite; and second, it demonstrates the importance of the annual Damascene pilgrimage caravan to the structure of Ottoman rule in the region and the prestige of the Ottoman state as a whole.

From a stylistic point of view, the letter displays the high-flown language, love of euphemism, and knotty syntax that were typical of this genre and period; the content, on the other hand, is far more significant. The reader should bear this point in mind while wading through the prose, which was part of what the Ottomans called *edeb-i Osmani*, roughly translatable as 'the Ottoman way', the values, etiquette, language, and conduct of those selected to serve *din ü devlet*, the faith and the state. Appearances to the contrary, the letter contains three distinct sections. The first speaks in general terms of the practical goals of Ottoman rule in the provinces, namely, the protection of the *reaya* (literally, flock), the non-privileged majority, and the advancement of state interests. The second section describes a very intricate and dangerous situation in the province of Sidon and the nearby province of Damascus. During the twelfth/eighteenth century the Ottoman state moved to subordinate its fiscal and military politics in greater Syria to enhance the administration of the annual Muslim pilgrimage caravan, which departed from Damascus to Arabia. The pilgrimage, as a sacred obligation for Muslims, had to be conducted every year and thus the sultan's prestige was at stake every year. The costs of this enormous operation were borne principally by the province of Damascus (at least from the early twelfth/eighteenth century onward) and its neighbors, including Sidon, where the semi-autonomous Druze notables played an intricate political game, serving as feudal tax farmers and keeping their distance from the imperial government and its agents.

The Druze, a religious-political community that was originally an offshoot of Shi'i Islam, thus had both religious and political differences with the Sunni Ottomans. In practical terms, this meant that the governors of Sidon would have to exercise great caution in maintaining their suzerainty while continuing to collect taxes that had to be remitted to the governor of Damascus for financing the pilgrimage caravan. Sarı Mehmed's failure to do so was thus the occasion of Abdullah Paşa's letter. That failure, however, cannot be explained convincingly, given the evidence that is at hand: was it Druze resistance to paying ever-increasing amounts, or was it the presence in the province of exiled enemies of the famed governor of Damascus, Esat (in Arabic, As'ad) Paşa al-'Azm? The result, nonetheless, was bad blood between two colleagues, a situation that the grand vizier blamed squarely on Sarı Mehmed. The last section of the letter contains not-so-veiled threats of reprisal and an insistence that the two governors observe the etiquette of the Ottoman way and continue to serve the faith and the state.

Text

My honorable, felicitous colleague, Excellency:

Because offices in the Exalted Everlasting State were originally arranged according to good and wise principles arising out of acceptance of good order, in the well-protected imperial dominions, to protect, comfort, and arrange the affairs of the poor *reaya*[69] who are in the safekeeping of God; and to regulate and advance, according to a desirable method, the interests of the Exalted State in the provinces; and in order to achieve good and beneficial causes, to each of the great provinces in the well-protected imperial dominions, by appointing and assigning a governor from among the great viziers (those holding the highest rank), their concord and unity are needed for continuously advancing [state] interests and obtaining the comfort of the people, which is the fundamental purpose cited [above].

And in particular, collecting the *miri* revenues[70] which are entrusted to the obligation of the governors of Sidon, and supervising and advancing the other interests of the Exalted State, are dependent on the conformity and mutual support of the governors of Damascus. And likewise, governors of Damascus are appointed to the duty of administering, as required, the matter of the caravan of the commander of the Muslim pilgrims. Because it is known to their excellencies that they are dependent on the establishment of the necessities of love and friendship with the great viziers who are appointed to and aided with the affairs

[69] Literally 'flock', the non-privileged sector of Ottoman society, by far the vast majority of the population; it included both Muslims and non-Muslims and consisted chiefly of peasants and the lower urban orders.　　[70] Government taxes on land held under various forms of tenure.

of the *cerde*,[71] according to the requirement that their excellencies demonstrate rectitude and watchful attention, the honorable governors of the provinces near those environs [i.e. near Damascus] are ordered nonetheless to esteem the exalted path of amity and friendship.

At this time, however, because of the allegations of some hypocrites and because of the annulment of the means of concord by contentious persons, some coolness has resulted between you and the current governor of Damascus, the honorable vizier, Esat Paşa. Because the occurrence of this state of affairs is discerned and understood, the matter with which you are charged—collecting the *miri* revenues—entails agitation and difficulty. If it were necessary to listen to the Druze *şeyhs*,[72] payment of the *miri* revenues charged to them would be accomplished carelessly, and supervising the matters of the Noble Pilgrimage, collecting the money to be transferred for [purchasing] provisions for the imperial fortresses [lying on the route of Damascus to Arabia], and assigning the duty of dispatching the *cerde* at the proper time would become impeded by delay. In this way, it is evident that both you and the said vizier's affairs would necessarily suffer disorder.

In this manner, the change in the hearts of the two parties, and the disorder in the affairs of the land and people which are thus occasioned, and which are circulating in the mouths of men, upon reaching the Sovereign Earshot, will cause a change in the favorable inclinations of the Elixir of the Imperial Signs with respect to you, and will result in a reprimand to you. Because the degree of [your] relapse is evidently the cause of the Royal Disposition, and because it is Our Benevolent Necessity, in accordance with our relationship of the heart with you in the past, to reclaim the relationship and purify the hearts of the two parties, by explaining the said particulars, for the purpose of unrolling the carpet of love and amity with respect to you, along with our special message [*kayime*], by recommendation [to] the said vizier [i.e. Esat Paşa], a message to you characterized by affection has also been written and sent by messenger of the Council of the Abode of Glory.[73] God Almighty willing, on its arrival [you should] esteem the said vizier as holding the rank of your virtual son and be assiduous in the protection of his influence. And also, the latter should adopt and continue to be in the position of a virtual father to you.[74]

[71] Pronounced 'Jerdeh' in Turkish, from the Arabic *jardah*, this was the military relief force that met the returning pilgrimage caravan roughly at the midpoint between Damascus and Mecca. Normally, during the twelfth/eighteenth century, the governor of Tripoli was charged with this duty, hence the frequent references in the text to governors of neighboring provinces, particularly because the financing of the *cerde* depended on revenues from Sidon and other nearby provinces.

[72] The hereditary tax-farming aristocracy of the region corresponding roughly to modern Lebanon. The Druze are a sect which split from mainstream Islam in the fourth/tenth century. The rugged domain of their region and their legacy of political independence made Ottoman rule in Lebanon quite tenuous.   [73] The Imperial Council in the Ottoman capital, Istanbul.

[74] The implication here is that the two paşas are basically equal in rank and therefore worthy of mutual respect, so that each one might be a 'virtual son' or a 'virtual father' to the other.

By prudence and meaningful friendship, by showing respect to the established practices of your dignity, you should also reflect on these points. Because of some hypocrites' allegations and the debt problems that necessarily ensue, with deliberation on the consequences of the matter to be guarded against and which was previously spoken of at length, take pains and care to remove and obliterate totally the annoyance that exists between you and the said vizier [i.e. Esat Paşa] and to fulfil and practise the essence of the necessities of concord and unity and the established usages of love and friendship that are the means of regulating affairs. As written before, [let] the above-mentioned situation—which influences the quality of the summit of the Sovereign Earshot and which is our sincere idea regarding you—be simple talk. According to the important, single-tracked order which you are charged to aid and support fully, [you will] doubtless show and offer your constancy to the Bountiful, Abundantly Brilliant Royal Presence, and obtain an increase in Sovereign Good Will toward you. In order to demonstrate the decisive argument, it is expected that you will deign to exert yourself to confirm mutual confidence with [writing] official letters of sincere signs containing continuation of [your] patron's daily-increasing happiness and success and containing your complete amity.

[Seal of]
Esseyid Abdullah ibn Hasan
15 Cemaziyelahir 1162
[3 June 1749]

1.4 Negotiating the power of the sultan: the Ottoman Sened-i İttifak (Deed of Agreement), 1808

Ali Akyıldız and M. Şükrü Hanioğlu

Preface

In the 1550s central authority in the Ottoman Empire began to weaken due to world economic changes and internal disruptions, as the state slowly changed from a perennially expanding military-conquest state to a sedentary empire, struggling to maintain its boundaries and the socio-political order within those boundaries. Beginning in the late 1300s, the Ottomans had built their state structures around a vast array of local cultures from the Balkans around the Mediterranean to North Africa, imposing systems of taxation and justice that often allowed local populations to maintain traditional practices. As long as these systems were followed, and as long as local populations provided support to Ottoman imperial troops passing through on their annual campaigns, hybrid cultures of Ottoman imperial rule and local custom could develop with minimal disruption. As the dynasty retreated increasingly into the palace, however, and left annual military campaigns either poorly waged or not waged at all, local notables (*ayan*) in distant cities and provinces started to gain political and economic power that endured from one generation to another. Ottoman military officers, including those in the elite Janissary (or slave-recruit) corps, and administrators in the provinces found themselves struggling to survive on their tax-shares and salaries, and often actively abetted the rise of strong local dynasties, simply by becoming part of them through intermarriage, bribery, and military alliances between imperial forces and local militias to maintain order. By the late 1600s influential family dynasties appeared in Anatolia and Rumelia, often with their own military forces, control of economic resources in their area, and increasing social authority, and the Ottoman government was forced by its own weakness to accept the power of these families. Subsequently, the shifting struggles and alliances between the state and the notables, and among the notables themselves, changed the local balances of power throughout the empire, and created new hybrid classes of ruling families whose roots lay both in the slave military and administrative recruitment of the empire in its strongest days, and in local cultures, speaking both the imperial language—Ottoman Turkish—and local languages such as Czech and Arabic.

Several sultans from the late 1700s onwards sought to recapture their power, most signally by establishing a new standing army loyal only to the sultan, not to barracks officers or local military heroes. The first

Westernizing sultan, Selim III (r. 1789–1807), lost his throne to an uprising of the palace Janissaries whose livelihood and status were threatened by Selim III's 'New Army' with their European-style uniforms and European-style training. In July 1808 a Balkan governor, Alemdar Mustafa Pasha, marched at the head of a mixed force of Bosnians, Albanians, and provincial janissary troops in an effort to return Selim III to the throne. The appearance of this force at the gates of Istanbul led to the execution of Selim, but Alemdar Mustafa Pasha's military success gave him the power to enthrone a new, reform-minded sultan, Mahmud II (r. 1808–39), and to install himself as the grand vizier. With this incident the *ayan*s rose to the rank of grand vizierate for the first time in Ottoman history.

Aware of the need to bring state authorities and the *ayan*s together, the new grand vizier Alemdar invited the *ayan*s to Istanbul. In October 1808 a document of agreement called the *Sened-i İttifak* (Deed of Agreement) was signed between the sultan, state officials, and the *ayan*s in attendance. This document marked a startling change in Ottoman political and social order at the centre and in the provinces. Some scholars compare the *Sened-i İttifak* to England's Magna Carta of 1215, while others are of the opinion that the constitutional movement in Turkey started with this document. They even argue that the *Sened-i İttifak* was a kind of basic constitutional draft and the first step towards democracy.

Though exaggerated, these views indicate that the *Sened-i İttifak* marked a turning-point in Ottoman history. For one, the sultan himself signed an agreement binding his state authority to work in co-operation with local notables. Another important aspect is the use of four Qur'anic verses (two in the text, two in the *Hatt-i Humayun*). The first verse is stated at the beginning of the *Sened*. The verse, 'take warning, then, o ye with eyes (to see)' (Q. 59: 2), points out that lessons should be learned from the problems that the Ottoman Empire had been facing and a consensus should be reached. The verse, 'if anyone changes it [the bequest] after hearing it, the guilt shall be on those who make the change. For God hears and knows (all things)' (Q. 2: 181), aims to urge the parties to keep their promises. The verses in the *Hatt-i Humayun* are: 'not if thou hadst spent all that is in the earth, couldst thou have produced that affection between their hearts, but God hath done it' (Q. 8: 63), and 'to fulfil the contracts you have made' (Q. 2: 177). These two verses stress the importance of the document and remind the parties of their responsibilities.

The full text presented below is translated not from the original, but from a copy approved by Mehmed İzzet, director of office of the Imperial Divan (*Beylikçi*) and author of the original document.

Text

In the Name of God, the Most Merciful, the Most Compassionate.

A Copy of the Imperial Decree[75]

I seek refuge in God. 'Not if thou hadst spent all that is in the earth, couldst thou have produced that affection between their hearts, but God hath done it.' According to the tenor of this illustrious verse of the Qur'an, it is manifest that the reinvigoration of the religion, the Sublime State, and the whole Muslim community depends upon the sincere unity of and concord among the high officials and ministers, and it is evident that the accomplishment of this goal, with the help of God, is contingent upon the continuous implementation of these auspicious promises and compacts. Therefore, with the grace of God, I, myself, in my imperial capacity, undertake the execution and implementation to the letter of the promises and recognized conditions written in this deed of agreement, and thus let my grand vizier, my *şeyhülislâm*,[76] the viziers, the ulema, the ministers of my state, and the notable houses of my Imperial Dominions, too—I seek refuge in God—exert their power and resources for the execution and implementation of the aforementioned promises to the letter for love of God, in compliance with the sacred order 'to fulfil the contracts you have made,' and by applying them as a guiding principle in the capital and provinces. If anyone commits the smallest infraction, or, God forbid, dares to avoid the contract, let him be the object of God's curse and suffer serious consequences and punishment in this world and the next.

Praise be to God, who strengthened Islam by means of men who acted with one accord and in harmony. Peace be upon our Master Muhammad, who removed hypocrisy and strife from his community, and his family and companions, who struggled in concord for his cause. Now to our subject. The reason for writing this auspicious document is that the Sublime Ottoman State, which is the benefactor of all, is an Islamic sultanate, and it is a self-evident fact that the conquests, victories, glory, and might that it enjoyed from its early foundation to this very day have been accomplished through union, unity, and the removal of selfishness and strife; however, for some time, the passage of time has caused the elements of order to deteriorate beyond recovery, and the power of the Imperial Sultanate to disintegrate, and its domestic and foreign influence to be disturbed in connection with situations of selfishness and strife among the ministers of the state and the provincial notable houses, and this situation brings about weakness and disorder in the entire Muslim community, that is to say, rich and poor, high and low alike. Young and old acknowledge that this situation has taken on a horrendous form, and because of these aforementioned unjust and shameful acts it has reached a point at which the very foundation of the sultanate is in utter ruins. In the name

---

[75] This translation is based on the transliterated text of the 'Deed of Agreement' in Ali Akyıldız, 'Sened-i İttifakın İlk Tam Metni', *İslâm Araştırmaları Dergisi*, 2 (Istanbul, 1998), 209–22.

[76] This is the chief mufti (an official who provides legal opinions) in the Ottoman Empire.

of God, the most merciful, the most compassionate, all of us comprehend and understand that for the sake of the blessed intention of turning this disorderliness into unity and exerting efforts toward securing and manifesting the Sublime State's full power, a warning must be taken from previous affairs, the pillars of the order of state and religion must be maintained, and the highest word of God be exalted in compliance with the illustrious verse of the Qur'an 'take warning, then, o ye with eyes'. This is incumbent upon piety and an obligation of loyalty. Hence numerous meetings were held, and we exerted efforts for the reinvigoration of the religion and the state, as a single body and in union and concord. We discussed strengthening personal power and other administrative issues, and consulted on agreeable rules and recorded the articles of this unity in the contract below.

First Article

Since our glorious, generous, majestic, and powerful sultan, who is our and the entire world's benefactor, is the most eminent person in the Eternal State, all of us undertake and guarantee both the [protection of] his sovereign imperial person and the strengthening of the structure of his imperial sultanate by depending upon God the Almighty's grace and benevolence and by drawing near to the spiritual influence of the Prophet Muhammad. If at some time either ministers, ulema, high officials, notable houses, or any Janissary corps commit a betrayal or actions against orders by word or deed, secretly or overtly, let us all, in the capital and provinces, unite to strive and exert efforts to have the individual who dared to commit such an act punished and used as a warning to others after an investigation. In this matter, let serious efforts also be made in union to punish anyone who manifests tolerance [of such actions] and to make him an example to others. And if someone does not join this mutual alliance, let all of us take action against him and force him to obey [this] article of the agreement by words and deeds. In short, let all of us personally and with our resources undertake and guarantee to maintain both his imperial personality and the state and power of the Imperial Sultanate, and ensure [the implementation of] his orders and wishes, and safeguard these against betrayal and conspiracy. As long as we live let us guarantee this, and afterward let our sons and noble families do so. In this way the good will of His Majesty the Sultan toward all of us becomes apparent, and consequently let us give necessary thanks and continuously serve and increase our merit.

Second Article

Since the maintenance of the Sublime State and the increase of its power and glory result in the maintenance of our personalities and noble families, all of us agreed upon discussion that the soldiers and privates to be drafted from the Imperial Domains for the strengthening of the power of the sultanate should be drafted and recruited as state's soldiers in accordance with the order decided at the councils that met for discussion, and this policy should be maintained, and all of us should strive and exert efforts toward this [goal]. Let all high officials, officials, and notable houses in the capital and provinces work seriously toward the orderliness and orderly arrangement of [the draft]. Since this decision on the issue of [drafting] soldiers was taken unanimously for the sake of bringing the religion and state to the right point, if anyone permits its modification by stirring up conspirators by claiming that this [rule] has been voided because of the changing times or something else, or if the Janissary corps disapprove or oppose this, then let all of us take action in concord and consider anyone even uttering such ideas, let alone those who dare to censure or terminate or alter it, to be a traitor, and strive and exert efforts toward his punishment, rejection, and removal; let not a single person among us differ on this issue. And since exerting efforts toward the prevention and repression of any enemy act regardless of its origin, and reaching against the enemy in the swiftest way, are principal rules, let no action against this tenet be taken at any time.

Third Article

The strength and brightness of the sultanate is our primary aim, and we undertake to work on this matter in concord. Thus, just as we work toward increasing the number of troops in order to increase the power [of the state], so also we undertake the maintenance of the Imperial Treasury and increase the revenues of the Sublime State. We will, in concord, undertake the punishment of anyone who opposes the collection and payment of them in their locations, their protection from damage and hampering, or the execution and implementation of the orders and decrees of the sultan, as of anyone who disobeys them. Let this rule be obeyed perpetually.

Fourth Article

Heretofore the order and the rule of the Sublime State has been that the orders and prohibitions of the sultan issue to all high-ranking statesmen and ministers, whether in the capital or in the provinces, through the Grand Vizier. Thus, henceforth let everyone know his superior and not set himself to interfere with affairs other than his duties. And let such orders and prohibitions be considered orders and prohibitions of the sultan, and let nobody dare to disobey them. And we will act together against anyone who interferes with affairs which are not his own or which fall under the authority of others, and we all undertake to dismiss such an individual affirming that, despite the universal ban on interference, he had interfered in an affair that fell under the authority of someone else. All affairs must be submitted to the Grand Vizier and authorization be asked from him, and everyone must [act] in accordance with the orders and judgements [issued]. In addition, let all of us act against unlawful subornation and corruption violating mutual agreement, and work toward preventing other disagreeable actions that may be initiated by the illustrious offices of the Grand Vizier and may immediately harm the provinces and the Sublime State's internal situation. And we unanimously promise that if a Grand Vizier falsely calumniates anyone or holds a personal grudge on the grounds of his telling him to prevent [such actions], we will prevent the former and protect the latter, thus let these [rules] be perpetually respected.

Fifth Article

As we all guarantee and undertake to protect the sultan's imperial person, the sultanate's power, and the state's order, let all the local notable houses, notables, ministers, high officials, and dignitaries who participated in this agreement, alike guarantee and undertake each other's personal safety and that of their families, because it is a clear fact that the local notable houses and chief men in the provinces must have confidence in the Sublime State, that the trust between the high officials and dignitaries of the state in the capital is of utmost importance, and that security and tranquility of mind may only be acquired through the union and mutual agreement of all and through their joint guarantee and pledge for each other. In this manner, if an assault or act of treachery or a conspiracy is perpetrated by the Sublime State or viziers in the provinces against one of the local notable houses, when it has not committed any act violating the conditions of the agreement, or if such acts are carried out by notable houses against each other, then let all of us in concord work toward punishment and preventing it, regardless of distance. And since all ministers will guarantee and undertake the continuance and maintenance of the leaders of the notable houses as long as they are alive, and afterward of their families, those local notable houses should likewise provide pledges and guarantees for those notables and chief men under their administration. And let nobody be permitted to plot against the lives of those local notables or chief men out of greed or anything else. If the guilt or treachery of one of them in violating his guarantees and agreement becomes apparent, then let the local notable house in charge work toward his dismissal, punishment, and replacement with somebody else, after carrying out an investigation and submitting information to the Grand Vizier. And let nobody force his way or transgress into any area that is even a span outside the region entrusted to him. Let all take action, regardless of distance, if somebody carries out such an assault, and prevent him. And if he does not take warning, let us work unanimously toward prevention and punishment of the person who is responsible for the strife. And let all chief men, local notable houses, and local notable leaders unanimously strengthen their work toward suppressing revolts and strife. And let us also unanimously work toward punishment and correction of anyone who mistreats and oppresses the poor or opposes the implementation of the sacred *şeriat*. And since all the local notable houses and chief men in the provinces guarantee and undertake to work toward preventing any treachery or plot arising out of provocation or conspiracy, against ministers, ulema, high officials, and state officials at any time, and to prevent any punishment unless somebody's guilt has become apparent in the eyes of all, just as in the case of the guarantee given to all local notable houses and notables, let nobody act against this. And if because of human nature somebody's guilt becomes apparent, upon manifestation of this guilt to all, let the person be punished by the Grand Vizier's Office according to the degree of his offence.

Sixth Article

If any rebellion or conspiracy led by the Janissary corps in Istanbul or elsewhere should occur, all local notable houses will hasten to reach Istanbul and those persons and Janissary corps who dared [to act in this way] will be removed or abolished. That is to say, those persons or military groups who caused such rebellion and conspiracy should be investigated, and in the case of a military group, they should be subdued and punished, and their revenues and muster rolls should be annulled, as in the case of the soldiers of the Bosphorus Castle [palace corps] who engaged in conspiracies; in the case of individuals, they should be executed upon investigation regardless of their class. All local notable houses and chief men in the provinces undertake this, and they all guarantee Istanbul's security and orderliness. Thus let us unanimously and continuously work and exert efforts toward acquiring the means necessary to establish such a strong bond.

Seventh Article

Since it is essential to protect and support the poor and taxpaying subjects, it is necessary that the local notable houses and chief men in the provinces pay attention to public order in the districts under their administration, and that they be moderate in levying taxes on the poor and taxpaying subjects. Thus, let everyone give serious attention to establishing and continuously implementing any decision to be taken by ministers and local notable houses after discussion in regard to preventing oppression and adjusting taxes, and let everyone give serious attention to preventing oppression and transgression from taking place in contravention of these decisions. And let local notable houses scrutinize each other and inform the Sublime State if one such house commits oppression and transgression in violation of orders and the sacred *şeriat*, and let all local notable houses unanimously work toward preventing such actions.

Since the said seven articles have been decided upon through discussion, and an oath in the name of God and Prophet has been taken not to act against it, the present legal document is written and copied for the sake of preserving these solemn promises. 'If anyone changes it [the bequest] after hearing it, the guilt shall be on those who make the change. For God hears and knows.' Written in the middle ten days [*evasıt*] of the honored month of *Şaban* in the one thousand two hundred and twenty-second year of the noble and glorious *hicret* (*hijra*) [October 1808].

Appendix

The articles included in this legal document are fundamental principles in strengthening and reinvigorating the religion and the Sublime State with the help of God. Thus its perpetual implementation as a guiding principle is a duty. In order to prevent it from being altered because of changing times and new appointments, those persons who henceforth honor the posts of the Grand Vizirate and the *Meşihat* [office of the *şeyhülislam*] by their presence will read and sign this document, and work toward its execution to the letter upon their initial appointment in their offices. And in the event of replacement, in order to avoid any delay in the reading of this deed, the Director of the Imperial Divan should immediately take the original deed from the office upon a new appointment to the Grand Vizierate and *Meşihat*, inform the steward of the Grand Vizier and the Minister of Foreign Affairs, and bring it to the persons who sit on the posts of the Grand Vizierate and *Meşihat*. Let this practice be recorded in the office of the Imperial Divan, and regarded as a guiding principle. And since copies of this deed will be given to the necessary people, let a copy of it be kept by His Majesty the sultan, and let our Imperial Majesty personally supervise its continued and perpetual implementation.

Guarantor of its contents, Mustafa, Grand Vizier (seal)[77]

Guarantor of the execution of its contents, Mehmed Salihzâde Ahmed Esᶜad, may they be forgiven (seal)

Guarantor of the execution of its contents, Esseyyid Abdullah Râmiz, Grand Admiral (seal)

Guarantor of its contents, Abdurahman, Vizier, Governor of Anatolia (seal)

Guarantor of what is written in it, Mehmed Derviş Chief Military Judge of Rumelia (seal)

Guarantor of the execution of its contents, Dürrizâde Esseyyid Abdullah, Representative of the Sharif of Mecca in Istanbul (seal)

I have looked at the contents and found them to be correct, and I guarantee its contents. Written by Emin Paşazâde Mehmed Emin, the servant who prays for the Sublime State. Holder of the rank of Military Judge of Rumelia (seal)

Guarantor of what is written in it, Hâfız Ahmed Kâmilî, Military Judge of Anatolia (seal)

Guarantor of what is written in it, Mehmed Tahir, Qadi of Istanbul (seal)

And one of the guarantors, Mustafa Refik, Steward of the Grand Vizier (seal)

And one of the guarantors, Mustafa Ağa, Agha [Commander] of the Janissaries at the Sultan's Court (seal)

And one of the guarantors, Mehmed Emin Behic, Minister of Finance (seal)

[77] 'Cây-ı Mühr': Literally place of the seal, i.e. his seal appeared here in the original document, of which this is a copy.

And one of the guarantors, Esseyyid Mehmed Sa^cid Galib, Minister of Foreign Affairs (seal)

And one of the guarantors, Mustafa Reşid, Former Steward of one of the Sultan's Equerries (seal)

And one of the guarantors, Esseyyid Ali, Minister of the Navy (seal)

And one of the guarantors, Mehmed Emin, Senior Officer in charge of daybook of receipts and expenditures (seal)

And one of the guarantors, Süleyman Cabbarzâde (seal)

And one of the guarantors, İsmail Serezî (seal)

And one of the guarantors, Elhac Ömer Karaosmanzâde (seal)

And one of the guarantors, Ahmed, who is the senior accountant (seal)

And one of the guarantors, Mehmed, Agha [Commander] of the Cavalry Troops at the Sultan's Court (seal)

And one of the guarantors, Mehmed İzzet, Director of the Imperial Divan, the writer of this (seal)

And one of the guarantors, Hüseyin Hüsni, Director of the office in charge of correspondence between the Imperial Palace and the Grand Vizier's Office (seal)

And one of the guarantors, Mustafa, Governor of Çirmen (seal)

1.5 Creating new institutions: Clot Bey's organization of Egypt's first modern medical establishment, 1827–1837[78]

Robert G. Landen

Preface

In order to support and staff the modernized military and administrative apparatus that he constructed in Egypt, the ambitious Ottoman governor Muhammad (Mehmet, in Ottoman/Modern Turkish) ʿAli had to recruit a large group of men educated in a broad spectrum of subjects. Relying heavily upon foreign experts, the pasha undertook a program of introducing his subjects to a modern education. Many students were sent to Europe; others were trained in a hastily improvised educational enterprise which tried to convert religious schools into elementary schools, which could in turn feed students into a new state system of modernized secondary and higher education.

Muhammad ʿAli's ambitions for Egypt, and his long reign there, from 1805 to 1848, saw the rise of this critical province to nearly independent status—largely through his ability to use ancient despotism to force through reforms meant to catch up with the West (or at least with Istanbul), and his ability to play off the interests of Western powers in the strategic location of Egypt at the head of the Red Sea, the site of a possible canal that would cut transit time to British and French colonial possessions in Asia and Africa. Both the British and French were willing to provide foreign experts in fields such as military science, medicine, and the training and health of factory-workers, in exchange for a better diplomatic position in Egypt. Ironically, much of what was touted as 'modern' and 'new' Western science in Egypt was still quite controversial in the West, especially in the dramatic changes taking place in the practice of medicine, the understanding of contagion theory, and the new professional status accorded doctors, working to discredit traditional healers, such as midwives, in their own societies, such as the United States of America, where the American Medical Association was first formed in 1847. Egypt became one of the primary fields of experimentation in rapid industrialization, the transition from mixed subsistence and market crops to cash crops, and management of contagious disease. Developments there were followed with great interest by 'new

[78] Clot Bey, 'Historico-Statistical Account of the Present State of Medicine in Egypt', in John Bowering, 'Report on Egypt and Candia, A Report addressed to the Right Hon. Lord Viscount Palmerston and presented to both Houses of Parliament', House of Lords, Sessional Papers, 35 (1840), 139–42. This report appears in House of Commons, Sessional Papers, 21.

men' of science and social reform throughout Europe, many of whom looked on a stint as an adviser in Egypt as an opportunity for funded research.

The first schools established were military academies designed to provide the armed forces with officers conversant with modern military science. A government press and a bureau charged with translating European works into local languages was established to facilitate the spread of those kinds of Western knowledge considered useful by the government. For example, the press published numerous works on recent developments in science and technology, but few in Western philosophy or the humanities in general. In some cases, education had to be provided in subjects entirely foreign to Egyptians, such as the nascent system of modern Western medicine. Beginning in the second quarter of the nineteenth century, European and North American physicians began to systematize the practice of medicine, regulating subjects taught in medical schools, instituting standardized examinations for the certification of new doctors, and supporting experimentation in such fields as quarantine, contagion theory, and inoculation. These developments in Western medicine occurred in tandem with Muhammad ᶜAli's efforts to reduce infant and maternal mortality, and to build a healthier population better able to staff his growing military, his new factories, and his new cash-crop plantations, such as those where cotton was grown for export. Testament to his interest in using modern medicine to build a modern population was Muhammad ᶜAli's early introduction of training in midwifery as part of state-funded schooling, and his assigning of newly certified midwives married off to newly certified doctors to rural provinces and newly industrialized districts. Throughout the world during the nineteenth century, wherever imperial powers or reformist anti-imperial rulers needed to increase military strength to achieve their objectives, there one could also find experimental programs in field medicine, including not only the treatment of combat casualties but also new anti-contagion protocols to reduce cholera, dysentery and smallpox among troops barracked in large numbers in tight quarters.

The report below provides a first-hand account of this sort of pragmatic encounter between the new West and the new East. It was written by a European expert, Clot Bey, hired by Muhammad ᶜAli to create a modern medical corps to support his modern army. The audience for the report was the British government, which was concerned with resolving a conflict between Muhammad ᶜAli and his nominal sovereign, the Ottoman sultan, in such a way as to preserve British strategic and commercial interests vis-à-vis other European competitors for influence. This mix of 'outsider' and 'insider' interest in developments in Egypt reflects the mix of influences—native and foreign, state and private—that went into the process of modernization throughout the Middle East.

Text

Organization of the Service

In Egypt, as in other parts of the East, all the sciences were buried under the ruins of the empire of the caliphs; hardly have some disfigured and badly understood manuscripts transmitted to us a dim reflection of that era of glory and intelligence.

Medicine was given up to the achievements of empiricism; surgery passed into the hands of the barbers; pharmacy to the traffic of the merchant. But when more friendly political relations between Christian Europe and Turkey rendered communication more easy and more frequent, the East was over-run with physicians, who easily established their superiority over ignorant pretenders. Since that time the Orientals have attributed to Europeans a general medical reputation; and even in our day, the public credulity is but too often practiced upon by men whose foreign extraction is the only scientific title they possess.

In commencing the great work of reformations that he determined upon, Mahomet Ali [Muhammad ʿAli]made offers to European officers of every rank and department; a general military organization was introduced, and then, as a matter of course, a medical service was created for the preservation of the Egyptian forces.

Clot Bey, engaged as physician and surgeon-in-chief to the new army, arrived in Egypt, followed by a number of medical officers, who were immediately appointed to the different regiments and hospitals then in progress of establishment. Thus began a regular service.

The surgeon, the physician, and the apothecary constituted the general council of health, placed under the immediate authority of the minister of war, and having under its authority secondary councils for the land and sea forces established upon all the possessions of his highness.

The medical service is almost exclusively organized according to the spirit of the French regulations.

The foreign physicians and apothecaries employed among the troops and in military hospitals belong to the different nations of Europe, and appear on the medical list in the following proportions:

Italians	105
French	32
English	6
Germans	5
Poles	4
Spaniards	2
	154

The title of 'doctor of medicine' from one of the faculties of Europe is required to obtain the rank of major.

The general council of health, at present, is composed as follows:

M. M. Clot Bey, inspector-general—president.
Gaetani Bey, private physician to his highness—honorary member.
Delsignore, inspector physician—incumbent member.
Destouches, inspector apothecary—incumbent member.

The salary given to the different ranks was fixed as follows:

	Francs.
Inspector-general of the land forces and the marine; president of the general council of health	30,000
Inspectors and members of the council general of health	10,000
Inspectors of the army	8,500
Principals	5,000
Majors	3,400
Assistant-majors	2,200
Under-assistants	1,500

Formation of the Hospital and Medical School at Abouzabel

The opening of the hospital at Abouzabel dates from the year 1825. The camp of instruction, situated in the vicinity of this establishment, and composed of the infantry of the army, the staff, and artillery schools (in all 25,000 men) provide it on an average with about 1,500 or 2,000 sick.

The death of native physicians and the existence of materials proper for the formation of a school suggested to Clot Bey the idea of establishing within the hospital itself a medical class, destined to furnish surgeons and apothecaries for the service of the army. His views were approved of; and in 1827, young men, chosen from the schools of the mosques, were the first initiated in the science of the Avicennas and the Albucazars.[79]

The program of the studies comprised the following subjects:

1. Anatomy and physiology.
2. Pathology and external clinique.
3. Pathology and internal clinique.
4. *Materia medica* and therapeutics.
5. Hygiene and forensic medicine.

[79] This is a reference to Islamic medical practice, informed by Hellenistic medicine but advanced a good deal by Muslim physicians in the Middle Periods. Avicenna, or Ibn Sina (981–1037), for example, was an Iranian philosopher and physician whose contribution to medical knowledge was collected in his work *Al-Qanun fi al-Tibb* ('The Canon of Medicine'), which influenced medical thinking in the Western world on its translation into Latin.

6. Physics and chemistry.
7. Botany.

Clot Bey was appointed director of the school and professor of pathology and of external clinique. This school has produced, in the ten years since its formation, 420 medical officers, incorporated in the army and navy, with the rank of under-assistants, assistants, and majors.

Twelve young Arabians were brought in 1833 to Paris, by Clot Bey, for the completion of their medical studies; and six of them have been employed since their return to Egypt as assistant professors in the national school of Abouzabel, where they had received, as pupils, instructions in the art they practice. The six others, still in Paris, will be forthwith restored to their country, where they will turn to good account, like their predecessors, the knowledge they have acquired.

Creation of the Secondary Schools at Alexandria and Aleppo
In 1837, two secondary medical schools were created, one at Alexandria and the other at Aleppo, for the improvement of the practical instruction of the pupils who leave the school at Abouzabel. They were instructed in descriptive anatomy, pathology, internal and external clinique, and practical pharmacy. The instruction devolved upon the physicians, surgeons, apothecaries (en chef) of the army and navy.

Removal of the Hospital and Medical School from Abouzabel to Cairo
In consequence of the suppression of the camp, which had given rise to the creation of the hospital and the school of Abouzabel, the sick-ward received none but individuals laboring under chronic affections. From that time the usefulness and the success of the two establishments ceased; and their removal to a more convenient place for the sick, and for instruction, became an absolute necessity. The vast edifice of Kasr-el-Ein, occupied by a preparatory school, was destined to receive the sick, and the pupils from Abouzabel, and vice versa. It was an exchange profitable both to science and humanity.

The edifice of Kasr el-Ein is situated on the eastern bank of the Nile, and about a quarter of a league from Cairo, and upon the site of the summer farm of Ibrahim Bey, where the French, at the time of their conquest, established their military hospitals.

It is formed by four ranges of buildings, in a square; sixty-four spacious apartments, of forty beds each, composed of two storeys; a separate building for the pharmacy, the chemical laboratory, the museum of physics and natural history, for the amphitheatre, baths, kitchens, &c.

Since the creation of the medical school, works on the following subjects have been translated into Arabic:

1. Anatomy.
2. Surgical pathology.

   3. Physiology.
   4. Physics.
   5. Chemistry.
   6. Botany.
   7. *Materia medica*.
   8. Toxicology.
   9. Hygiene.
 10. Midwifery and diseases of women and children.
 11. Treatise on general anatomy.
 12. Treatment of asphyxia.
 13. Guide to military surgery.
 14. Treatise on bandages.
 15. Diseases of the skin.
 16. Rules of military hospitals.

The duration of medical studies is five years.

The renewal of the students takes place by fifths every year. The pupils wear a uniform, and are subject to military rule; fed, dressed, lodged at the expense of the government; and receive, besides, pay, which varies according to the class to which they belong. Thus, the pupils of the first year receive forty piastres a-month (ten francs), those of the second year fifty piastres, and thus progressing to the fifth year.

The lectureships are given by caencaems, or in some cases to those whose services have sufficiently deserved the reward.

The salary of the professors is 5,000 francs a-year; that of the directors of the school, 7,000 francs.

The following is a list of the professors and the courses of study:

> M. M. Duvigneau, director—pathology and internal clinique.
> Scisson—pathology and external clinique.
> Fischer—anatomy and physiology.
> Perron—medicine and chemistry.
> Figari—botany and materia medica.
> Pacthod—pharmacy.
> Pruner, chief physician to the military hospital—ophthalmology.

Each European professor is assisted by an Arabian professor, who understands French.

Formation of a Lying-in Establishment
The importance of a maternity was sensibly felt in Egypt, where lying-in women were entrusted to the care of the most ignorant and superstitious midwives.

In 1832 Clot Bey proposed and obtained the establishment of a school for midwives; twenty negresses and Abyssinians were collected in a place for this purpose, under the direction of a midwife of the maternity at Paris, an Arabian physician, who had graduated in France, and an ulema,[80] to instruct in religion and literature. The pupils read and write Arabic and learn the theory and practice of midwifery. This school of obstetricity [*sic*] daily acquires importance; the number of pupils now amounts to fifty, and their instruction is confided to the five most skilful among them, under the direction and surveillance of the principal midwife physician and ulema.

Formation of the Hospital

The removal of the hospital from Abouzabel to Kasr-el-Ein caused the suppression of that of Cairo, situated in the great Esbekieh-square, which has just been converted into a civil hospital, divided into five departments—a hospital for men, a hospital for women, a maternity, a lying-in hospital, and a lunatic establishment: it is capable of accommodating 500 sick.

The Civil Hospital at Cairo was the first erected in the Ottoman Empire since the Caliphs, and although they had in the height of their power erected some, they never were so complete as the Asylum of Piety, which Mahomet Ali has opened for human sufferings.

Thus in the regeneration of Egypt, medicine has been, as it ought to be, one of the most powerful instruments.

The ascendancy which its ministers exercise throughout the whole of society by their mission of philanthropy, has rendered the union of the people of two religions essentially different, more intimate, exacted gratitude on the one side, created devotedness on the other, and has broken down the barrier which had been erected between the worshippers of Christ and those of the prophet by a superstitious but popular hatred.

The devotedness of the European physicians, their heroic struggles against the most fatal disorders, their praiseworthy and entire disregard of their own lives, have produced invaluable and incalculable results; but it was especially the formation of the school at Abouzabel which gave a new era to medicine in Egypt—a glorious epoch for a humane and imperishable sovereign.

Initiated in the different sciences which belong to the art of medicine, and which constitute the well-informed man, the medical pupils are become so many apostles destined to spread the light of knowledge in the midst of a people still enslaved by prejudice and ignorance.

Henceforward to apply the dissecting knife to a dead body is not a sacrilege worthy of damnation. The wonders of medicine and chemistry are no longer supposed to be brought forth by magic, or by the devil.

The ulema himself has progressed—has applauded the acquirements of the young girls, knowing the Arabic language equally with those who study in the

[80] Properly, the text should have read 'an *'alim*' for which *'ulama* is the plural form in Arabic.

mosques. They are able to give an account of the structure of the organs, to explain the phenomena of conception, the principal functions of life, the sublime discovery of Harvey, the chemical decomposition of air, the geometrical proportions of the pelvis, parturition, both natural and unnatural, and have quoted, by turns, the names of Smellie and Baudeloque.[81]

Mother of all the schools established in Egypt—their model by its regular organization, its order and discipline, by the professorships given at the annual public examinations, or in recompense of distinguished merit, worthy of the patronage which presides over its destinies and of the gratitude of the country, by the numerous scientific treatises which are, in some degree, naturalized by translation—the school of medicine has given the first impulse to the regenerative movement, and has not stopped one single instant, continuing, with success, the humane and intellectual task it has thus auspiciously undertaken.

December 27, 1837.

---

[81] These are references to physicians and obstetricians William Harvey (1578–1657), William Smellie (1697–1763), and Jean-Louis Baudeloque (1746–1810).

1.6 Observing Muhammad ᶜAli Paşa and his administration at work, 1843–1846
Paul Sedra

Preface

There are few figures in the history of the modern Middle East who generate as much controversy as Muhammad ᶜAli Paşa. Indeed, that controversy extends as far as his name, with one set of scholars insisting upon the Ottoman Turkish rendering, Mehmed 'Ali Paşa, and a different set endorsing the prevalent Arabic rendering, Muhammad ᶜAli Paşa. As this particular question of naming suggests, the general controversy hinges upon differing conceptions of the Paşa's relationship with Egypt, and with the Ottoman Empire, respectively. Partisans of the Arabic rendering tend to identify Muhammad ᶜAli as the 'founder of modern Egypt', a visionary to whom they attribute the genesis of an independent Egyptian state and nation. In stark contrast, partisans of the Ottoman Turkish rendering caution against such a sanguine view of the man, insisting upon viewing Mehmed ᶜAli within an Ottoman imperial context, and rejecting the notion that an independent Egypt figured in Paşa's aims as *vali* or viceroy of the province.

Whatever one's position in this controversy, there can exist little doubt that Muhammad ᶜAli was a savvy, often ruthless leader who aimed to secure control of the wealthy Ottoman province for himself, and his family after him. He employed a variety of methods to secure this control, including the development of schools, a monopoly-based agricultural policy, and, above all, a well-structured and disciplined army.

Joseph Hekekyan was among the technicians Muhammad ᶜAli entrusted with such projects. (For complete biographical details, please refer to 'The Journals of an Ottoman Student in England, July 1829 to January 1830', Sec. 6.3 in this volume.) In 1830, after detailed studies of weaving and spinning technology and hydraulic-engineering works in Britain, undertaken at Muhammad ᶜAli's expense, Hekekyan was recalled to Egypt and subsequently dispatched to examine and enhance the pasha's cotton factories. Muhammad ᶜAli soon entrusted him with a leadership role in expanding the nascent education system, with particular reference to engineering education.

The extracts from Hekekyan's journals drawn together below give an impression of the scope of Muhammad ᶜAli's ambitions, the lengths to which he ultimately went to achieve them, and the consequences of his projects for the inhabitants of the Nile Valley, as well as his leadership style and idiosyncrasies. They were written in the final years of Muhammad ᶜAli's rule, at a time when his debts had reached unprecedented levels, and the shortcomings of his various projects were becoming plain.

Text

Selections from the Journals

[Hekekyan on the Translation Committee of the Department of Schools, January 1843]
During the discussions I perceived three distinct parties—the first party was composed of such persons as had already given in translations and whose translations had been printed. Their argument was that they had already given out works of which hundreds of copies were printed, and no body read them, and that they were in heaps in the Central Magazine of Books near the Mehkeme—that they had recommended their publication—that Government had incurred a great expense—and they were liable to be called to account on some future day—and consequently they opposed the publication of such works as were not absolutely of an immediate necessity in the schools, and even of these the numbers were warmly disputed. The arguments of the second party were—that the more books we had the better chance there would be of people reading them, that we should not look merely to the present—but more particularly to the future—that there was a great demand in Constantinople, the Hedjaz [*sic*] and other parts—and by proper measures some might be disposed of in India and Persia. The third party insisted on the publication of such elementary works as were especially wanted in their respective establishments. The most complete work we shall have will be that of the programme of the Polytechnic School, the entire course of studies of which is based on that adopted in the French School. The themes and exercises are first translated by the Professors and taught for the first year—the second year the same are lithographed in the school—the third year the same are improved and revised with a view of ulterior printing: by which means we shall possess a complete course of the Theoretical Branches of Mathematics and Natural Philosophy, Chemistry and Astronomy &c.[82]

[Hekekyan on Government in the Countryside, April 1843]
Many cultivators or fellahs[83] ruined by the exactions of the government had taken refuge in the towns, and in particular Cairo, when acting as servants or artisans they gained a pittance for their families and for themselves.[84] The Government, latterly making great efforts to restore cultivation adopted the arbitrary measure of seizing and conveying to the provinces all individuals of the above description their agents could lay their hands on. But many of them contrived to elude vigilance, and to secrete themselves in their masters' houses; several, in fact,

---

[82] British Library, Hekekyan Papers, Additional Manuscript 37,449, Vol. 2, Journals 1841–1844, pp. 89–90.   [83] Peasants.

[84] Muhammad ʿAli imposed a range of taxes upon peasants, most significant among them a land tax, which rose by 5% in 1839, and 12½% in 1844. For a detailed account of government exactions in the countryside, refer to Kenneth M. Cuno, *The Pasha's Peasants: Land, Society, and Economy in Lower Egypt, 1740–1858* (Cambridge: Cambridge University Press, 1992).

emigrated to Syria, and many of them putting on the bedoween [i.e. bedouin] garb entered the service of the independent sons of the deserts.[85] Hence the edict of the government to the purport that whoever should be found to connive or abet in the secretion of a fellah should be decapitated, and all fellahs found away from their villages after a certain time fixed, I believe forty days, should be immediately executed. It is the property of a weak and barbarous government to proclaim laws which it cannot put into execution, though acquiring all the odium which it would acquire, could it put such sanguinary and murderous edicts into execution. But if the government actually sent back to their own villages the unhappy individuals who fell into its hands, in order to assist their fellow villagers to pay the land tax, which is fixed and not diminished on account of drafts into the army, epidemics, emigration and some part of the odium would be palliated; instead of which all men who are caught are chained by the neck, put into boats and sent to the Pasha's farms.

When a boat full is collected, an endless chain is passed around their necks, so that they have to march in a body and no individual can separate or run away: two or three men are sufficient to manage two hundred so shackled. They are crammed into a boat, and as they descend the Nile, their wives and children follow them along the banks. The fellah wife never abandons her husband.[86]

[Hekekyan on the Paşa's Factories, June 1843]

Latiff Bey long since proposed to substitute fellahs instead of oxen to turn the Pasha's cotton machinery—the cost of maintaining an ox being equal to that of four or five men, and because there were a great number of infirm, weak, sick and blind and who would not be of any use in the army or navy or any other employment. The Pasha did not listen to the proposal, but when the murrain deprived us of cattle, men were pressed at a time when any body able to work can get from three to five piastres in the country, there being a great demand for men in agriculture. They get a piastre a day—but it is managed in the following manner—half of it is given to them in bread—the remainder is kept back on account of deficiency in their daily work which is arbitrarily fixed. In Mabieda alone they prefer to put an end to their miserable existence by throwing themselves out of the windows, and attempting to hang themselves. Formerly two men were allotted to each machine—now only one. The Pasha has ordered criminals to the Mills—so that we stand a chance of seeing some of them burnt down to the ground.[87]

[Muhammad ʿAli on the Urgency of the Census, 1846]

Hekekyan! We have no men—we have no men—every body hides his money. They will not believe they are safe—their children will. Egypt is small: but is

---

[85] Nomadic tribesmen.   [86] Vol. 2, p.120.   [87] Vol. 2, p. 148.

there a finer country? How rich it might be made. What think you, that we have five millions of inhabitants? The highest number allowed was three millions, and it was generally supported to be only two millions and a half. I told the Shaikhs at Mansourah that they must assist me in the census. They understand what it means—but as they wish to escape the just burden of service in men and money they are induced to give indirect opposition. I have determined to effect the entire establishment of the European system. I told the Shaikhs that I would surround some of their villages, and if I found they had deceived me that I would put them to death. I think the true number must be more than five millions—but the census must be repeated—and by and by we shall have a correct one.[88]

[The Paşa Discusses the Census with Cairo Shaykhs, 1846]

PASHA: I hope authority has been found to sanction it.

LEADING SHAIKH: We trust much in the wisdom of the Prophet and of our Lord.

PASHA: I wish to do nothing against common reason. I am working for your advantage and that of all Musselmans. We must introduce order in our house. I am old and before I depart I must sow the seed, for you, for yours and those who will come hereafter. I declare before God and the Prophet it is not for myself I am giving myself so much trouble. But I will have no opposition.

SHAIKH: We all know our Lord's good wishes and intentions, and we pray daily of God to give us the means of pleasing him—but our Lord certainly knows that such great things cannot be done at once. It is well known that the revelations were made not in one day or one year—they took twenty-three years to come down.

PASHA: Surely in the mass of divine revelation which took twenty-three years to come down there must be not one but several passages authorizing the census, as some have been found for the Nizam Gedeed,[89] for the European costume, for quarantines &c. Go and see—go and see.[90]

---

[88]   British Library, Hekekyan Papers, Additional Manuscript 37,450, Vol. 3, Journals 1844–1850, p. 134.

[89]   Hekekyan's transliteration of *nizam al-jadid*. Literally, 'new order.' A reference to the reform of the Ottoman army in terms of structure and discipline.   [90]   Vol. 3, pp. 135–6.

1.7 A manifesto for educational reform in Qajar Iran, 1859

Monica Ringer

Preface

Modernization in Iran began with a series of defensive military reforms prompted by the losses of Crown Prince ᶜAbbas Mirza's forces to Russian military might in the first quarter of the nineteenth century.[91] Even before such reforms were under way in the Qajar Empire, Iranians had traveled to Europe and the Ottoman Empire as students, diplomats, and merchants. Some were convinced of the necessity of implementing modernizing reforms in Iran in order to strengthen the country in the face of increasingly strong, commercially invasive, and colonizing European powers.[92]

Preliminary military reform measures centered around standing forces and a revision of taxation and supporting administrative structures. Reformers believed that training a new cadre of leaders astute in the new internationally competitive diplomatic and economic world was essential to maintaining Iran's political autonomy and territorial integrity. In 1851 the first European-style secondary school, the Dar al-Fonun, was established in Tehran under the initiative of Naser al-Din Shah's reform-minded prime minister, Mirza Taqi Khan 'Amir Kabir'. Staffed initially by European teachers, this school taught a plethora of European subjects, mostly,

---

[91] Crown Prince ᶜAbbas Mirza was a son of Fath ᶜAli Shah and had been named governor of the key province of Azerbaijan—an appointment that began the tradition of the crown prince assuming governorship of that province for the rest of the Qajar period. Together with his prime minister, Mirza Bozorg Farahani Qaem Maqam, ᶜAbbas Mirza instituted a defensive military reform program along the lines of that instituted by Sultan Selim III (r. 1789–1807) in the Ottoman Empire. Called the *nezam-e jadid* or 'New Order', after Selim's program (the *nizam-i cedid*), this program consisted of the introduction of European military technology and modern methods of training troops. It also served as a catalyst for the introduction of a number of other measures, such as the translation of European books, the establishment of a printing-press, the publication of a newspaper, as well as attempts to regularize the tax system, that were all believed to be necessary prerequisites to substantive military reform. The *nezam-e jadid* began following the loss of two 'wars' to an expansionist Russia: the First Russo-Persian War of 1803–13 (ended by the Treaty of Golestan), and the Second Russo-Persian War of 1826–8 (ended by the Treaty of Turkomanchai). Both defeats resulted in losses of territory to Russia, large indemnities owed to Russia, and a concomitant expansion of Russian influence in Iranian affairs.

[92] Crown Prince ᶜAbbas Mirza was the first in Iran to instruct diplomats to investigate the 'secret of European strength' while in Europe. Travelers' accounts not only of superior military might, but also of the political, economic, and social systems that generated it, convinced ᶜAbbas Mirza to dispatch the first group of Iranian students to Europe in 1811 to complete their studies. This group of two was followed by a second student mission in 1815 of five persons, and subsequent dispatches of individual artisans, largely to Russia. Accounts of travelers abroad in this period have not been translated into English.

although not entirely, with military applications. The school represented the use of Europe as a model, albeit modified, for modernization, and as such served as a lightning-rod that polarized opposition to and support for such changes.

Despite the fall (and subsequent assassination) of Amir Kabir prior to the school's official opening, the Dar al-Fonun was permitted to function, albeit under court control.[93] Many of the graduates hailed from elite families and obtained coveted positions in the ministerial and diplomatic bureaucracies. As such, the school confirmed the existing social and political status of its students. Over the course of the nineteenth century the educational goals of the reformers broadened to include calls for compulsory, universal primary education for all Iranians as a building-block for a modern citizenry. The Dar al-Fonun expanded its curriculum, and was joined by some two dozen primary and secondary 'New Schools' that sought to embody these new expanded roles for education as a motor of social and political change.[94]

In 1860 the minister of sciences and education, ⁽Ali Qoli Mirza E⁽tezad al-Saltaneh,[95] used the forum of the government-sponsored newspaper, *Vaqaye⁽-e Ettefaqiyeh*, to promulgate his visions for education as a tool of reform, and his reform of the function, curriculum, and program of the Dar al-Fonun. It provides a window on the many expectations placed upon Iran's emerging state education system.

Text

Translation of declaration of educational intentions of the Dar al-Fonun schools in Tehran and Tabriz

(Published in the *Ruznameh-e Vaqaye⁽-e Ettefaqiyeh* #456, 19 Jomadi I 1276/14 December 1859)

Proposals concerning the training and progress of the people of the state have always, from the outset, come from His Majesty, Power of Powers, the Emperor,

[93] Mirza Taqi Khan Amir Kabir was removed as prime minister and assassinated on the orders of Naser al-Din Shah. He is generally considered to be the 'founding father' of modernizing reform in Iran, alongside Crown Prince ⁽Abbas Mirza. He was determined to curb many of the prerogatives of the court and religious establishment. For this reason, many court figures who sought to preserve the status quo agitated against him, finally winning the shah's support for the man who ousted him.

[94] These 'New Schools' were usually primary schools, and employed different teaching methods, discipline and organization than 'traditional' *madraseh* schools did. Their express purpose was the provision of functional literacy, and the teaching of a curriculum that represented a synthesis of European and Iranian subjects.

[95] ⁽Ali Qoli Mirza E⁽tezad al-Saltaneh was named superintendent of the Dar al-Fonun from 1857 until his death in 1880. In 1858, he was named minister of sciences, two years prior to the formal establishment of the Ministry of Sciences. E⁽tezad al-Saltaneh was a Qajar prince, a son of second Qajar ruler Fath ⁽Ali Shah, and he enjoyed the support of the powerful Queen Mother—*Mahd ⁽Oliya*.

may God perpetuate his kingdom and his reign. The means of progress of every state have always been primarily the spreading of useful sciences and new arts. It was thus desired [by the shah] that the customary sciences and arts of European countries (most of which, in truth, in previous times were specialties of Iran, [yet] due to lack of attention and effort on the part of kings and sultans gradually became obsolete and disappeared), [would] again be established and propagated in their location of origin and rightful place. It was decided to bring in from Europe knowledgeable instructors and qualified teachers in all of the sciences and industries, and build the blessed school Dar al-Fonun in the royal citadel [in Tehran] in order to teach and instruct all the sciences and mining arts.

In the beginning, the people of this kingdom still were not familiar with the foreign sciences and unfamiliar technologies. To the contrary, they had not heard of even a few of these sciences and technologies, and considered their study and mastery to be mere fantasy. For this reason [the shah] determined to send children to the school. Another factor was that in the field of arithmetic, except for Shaykh Baha'i's *Kholasat al-Hesab*, no other books were available. [Furthermore], [scholars] considered some of the [mathematical] problems in this very book to be so ancient and precious that they did not wish to teach them to others and even attempted to hide them. Now the students in the second and third levels of the exalted school can write to such an extent better and more completely than the *Kholasat* and were able to challenge some of this book's [solutions to] problems. The same goes for geometry, [where] except for Euclid's *Tahrir*, there was nothing, and although several articles from the *Tahrir* had been learned it was just this science which had no practical application. Now in the exalted school, engineers have been fully trained both theoretically and practically. In addition they are masters of the problems and difficulties of that book. The same is true concerning [the science of] engineering [where] there are only a few [good] examples like balances and weighing instruments and oil-pressing equipment from Isfahan and now in this field, books and treatises have been written and complete skill is demonstrated and machinery and instruments of this art are able to be constructed. The same goes for surgery where, without viewing and [performing] surgery, it cannot be fully undertaken. Except for the vocabulary and terms from the old books, they did not know anything. Now they have seen various [kinds of] European surgery and have become masters in hands-on practice. Each one of the medical students has written a treatise in the art of medicine and surgery. The same is true in the rest of the sciences, like physics, the telegraph, handicrafts, infantry, cavalry, artillery, cartography, and the building of telescopes. [These fields] were not practiced at all in this country before. In each of these sciences, fully experienced and tested students have been trained.

Because some of the students, owing to their youth, had no facility and fluency in Persian and Arabic, and, because observing national culture is of the highest importance, out of respect for the true Law, Aqa Shaykh Mohammad Saleh, who is a man of knowledge and known for his devotion and piety, has been given an office in one of the rooms of the school to teach the children Persian, Arabic and issues and traditions of prayer and fasting. He is to lead them in prayer and together the students are to perform their group prayer with him.[96]

Since some of the people of Iran are not convinced of European medical practice, in order to inform medical students of the prevailing Persian medical practice, Mirza Ahmad Hakimbashi Kashani, who, both in terms of practice and knowledge is the best of the Iranian doctors, was assigned to teach Persian medicine in the blessed school.

The people of Iran now know, due to the favor of His Imperial Majesty towards them regarding the training of children, what a foundation of progress for children as well as many benefits for this steadfast government the Dar al-Fonun has provided, and that each of its students, in a thousand ways and means, has been advanced and has attained a position as official deputy or royal [deputy] in the victorious troops or a postal clerk in the rest of the government service. Owing to their studies in the blessed school and progress in knowledge, each [student] according to the extent of his competence [in a particular field] has attained the high post of colonel in the victorious troops, head of the country's doctors, positions outside the military, translator in the Ministry of Foreign Affairs and [positions in] domestic affairs. It is incumbent on all Iranians from [amongst] the royalty, ministers, holders of government office in the administration and military, large merchants and tradesmen not to leave their sons uneducated, [but rather] to occupy them with [one of] these sciences.

But since these students that are now at the blessed school of the Dar al-Fonun and the Dar al-Saltaneh school of Tabriz, those that graduated and are [now] occupied in service outside [the school], and the many students who (along with Hasan ʿAli [Garrusi], Minister Plenipotentiary of Iran) are residing in the capital of Paris (under the supervision of Colonel ʿAbd al-Rasul Khan) and are now completing their studies in every [branch of] science and industry, [all] have been committed to government service. New stipends will not be granted to new students unless they are children of the highest notables who have a hereditary stipend already established—these will continue. But the other children of the highest notables will not be granted the hereditary positions or stipends they seek unless they have attended and graduated from the Dar al-Fonun.[97]

---

[96] The attempt here may have been to create a 'student community' using a traditional communal religious practice while simultaneously familiarizing the students with an important aspect of national culture.

[97] The first class graduated from the Dar al-Fonun in 1858. In the same year, a similar school of the same name was established in Tabriz, the capital of Azerbaijan province and seat of the crown prince.

To favor (*makhz-e enayat*) in truth the people of Iran—for every Iranian who desires to place his sons to study these sciences, clothing and lunch will be provided, and after the students graduate and receive confirmation from the Minister of Sciences E^ctezad al-Saltaneh, suitable employment in accordance with their studies will be granted. Details of their study and the favor of His Majesty, the Refuge of the World, are as follows: if students are residing in Tehran they go before the Minister of Sciences E^ctezad al-Saltaneh, who, with permission from the government deputy Reza Qoli Khan, director of the *Dar al-Fonun* and first deputy of the Ministry of Sciences, will approve each field of study that is [determined to be] appropriate. If the student resides in the capital of Tabriz, he should go before Army Commander ^cAziz Khan. He then will entrust the student to Muhammad Sadeq Khan, director of the Tabriz school and second deputy of the Ministry of Sciences, so that he becomes occupied with [his] studies. If [the student] resides in other locales, he should go before the governor of that province. After the number [of students] from that locale has reached ten, the governor of that province shall submit a report to the Ministry of Sciences and he shall send [the report along] to the land of His Highness, then, in accordance with royal decree, a teacher shall be sent to them, and clothing and lunch will be provided. In each place that the governor of the province deems it advisable, [students] shall become occupied with studies.

Each year in the middle of the month of Esfand [February/March] in the capital and the rest of the regions of Iran the teachers and the expert instructors will give exams. For the first level of progress a copper medal will be awarded, and, for the second level a medal of silver will be awarded along with an appropriate bonus to each student. For the third level of progress a gold medal with a partial stipend shall be awarded. After completing the fourth level, which is [synonymous] with graduation, the student will be given a letter from the Ministry of Sciences along with the certification of his instructor. [Furthermore,] in accordance with his studies a position outside or inside [the military] and occupations and the commensurate salary, [along] with a gold medal shall be bestowed [on him].

It must not be imagined that in all of the fields of study students require five or more years to graduate, but rather this process depends on [the students'] intelligence and understanding, and on how hard the student studies. Sometimes it is possible to graduate in one or two years, and sometimes it requires a particularly lengthy period [of study]. All the governors must pay attention to the details of this newspaper—the high and the low—so that they receive the recent favor of His Imperial Majesty Power of Powers regarding the people of Iran. In addition to the praise they gave him before they should continuously be busy praying more for the long life and prosperity of His Majesty.

1.8 Discipline in a late Ottoman provincial secondary school, 1903
Benjamin C. Fortna

Preface

During the reign of Sultan Abdülhamid II (1876–1909), the Ottoman state carried out an ambitious school-building campaign. In spite of a bankrupt treasury and a host of problems at home and abroad, the Hamidian government found the time and money necessary to complete an empire-wide school network that had been only partially implemented during the preceding Tanzimat period (1839–76). Partly in imitation of Western architectural models, partly because a considerable portion of their curriculum was devoted to subjects associated with Western Europe, and partly because the new schools appeared to be radically different from the religiously affiliated education that had previously prevailed in the empire, the Ottoman schools of the late nineteenth and early twentieth centuries have been labeled 'Western' and 'secular'. In fact, much of their curriculum was devoted to such 'traditional' subjects as Arabic, the Qur'an, and classical Ottoman history, to name only a few. Moreover, the schools had their own mosques and employed members of the ulema in a variety of functions. Even their architecture, although originally based on plans borrowed from France, was modified to include such characteristically Ottoman orna-mentation as the crescent moon and the calligraphic seal of the reigning sultan (*tuğra*). Furthermore, life in the late Ottoman state schools followed the major events of the Muslim calendar. The case presented here, for example, turns on the question of student observance of Ramadan, the Muslim month of fasting.

The state schools attempted to inculcate an Ottoman and Islamic sense of identity in their students. Young men were expected to emerge from these institutions as well-trained subjects; many of whom would fill the burgeoning ranks of a government bureaucracy that had swelled from approximately 2,000 scribes in the 1790s to approximately 35,000 roughly a century later.[98] Regardless of their career path, the state sought to produce students who would be loyal to the sultan and his empire and remain true to Ottoman and Islamic customs. In their fledgling attempt at state-sponsored identity formation, the Ottoman schools were responding to the rapidly growing presence of missionary schools on Ottoman territory.

The following documents from the Ottoman archives in Istanbul offer one of the very few recorded instances in which the students of an Ottoman

---

[98] This estimate is given by Carter V. Findley, *Ottoman Civil Officialdom: A Social History* (Princeton: Princeton University Press, 1989), 22–3.

state school speak in their own words. In this case, the students of the *idadî*, or preparatory school, in Manastır (today's Bitola in Macedonia) delivered a petition to the inspector-general of Rumelia (Ottoman Europe) in November of 1903, complaining about their treatment at the hands of the school's officials. That such a case is preserved at all is due perhaps to the existence of the office of the inspector-general, a post created by Abdülhamid II under pressure from the Western powers for 'reform' in Macedonia. In fact, this petition was submitted thirteen days after the Ottoman government accepted the terms of the Mürzteg Program (9 November 1903), which stressed the right of Ottoman subjects to complain.[99] It is interesting to note that the signatures on the petition include both Muslim (e.g. Ali Rıza) and non-Muslim (e.g. Lazaraki, Eftim) names.

The first document presented here is the students' signed petition, drafted by a professional petition writer, which explains their grievances. The second source contains the depositions taken from two of the students involved.

Texts

1. To the Illustrious Office of the Inspector-General of Rumelia

The petition of your humble servant:

We cannot know how long this inauspicious practice will last: when even a correct accusation is brought against an official, his superior protects and defends him instead of punishing him. For instance, as a result of his inefficacy and, what's more, his obliviousness, Şevki Efendi, one of our assistant directors and teachers, far from effecting progress among the children of the fatherland, has rather engendered incidents and so forth that make one recall the training of the era of the Janissaries[100] with affection. It is probable that someone must have submitted [the information about] the aforementioned [i.e. Şevki Efendi] to your Excellency and that is why the director and teachers who are his companions are eagerly hatching several plans on his behalf. Actually, it is clear that being of the sort that attempts to cover the light of the sun with a finger, their plans to keep everything secret will not produce a beneficial result. [Their] plotting to take revenge against the students as a result of their suspicion that it was the students that denounced him, combined with the director and others turning a blind eye, their going so far as stooping to be instruments [in this plot], reveals an unscrupulousness that cannot be imagined.

---

[99] This agreement between the Russian tsar and the Austro-Hungarian emperor marked an attempt to impose Great Power controls on Ottoman Macedonia, by appointing, for example, foreign advisers and a foreign-controlled gendarmerie.

[100] The elite units of the Ottoman infantry, abolished by Sultan Mahmud II in 1826 in an event that is known as the 'Auspicious Incident'.

If the director had at least considered his legally stipulated duties once a year, let alone implemented them, then no such incidents involving the students would have occurred, and the food given as alms during the present month of Ramadan (which is a sign of pride) would not fall far from what is just. As if that were not enough, he summoned us by number[101] at 4:30 in the evening,[102] and insisted that it was necessary for us to go to bed, no matter what. But when the students requested that, as in previous years, they be allowed to stay up in the school until as late as 8:00, and then eat the pre-dawn Ramadan meal (*sahur*),[103] he flew into a rage and threw as many as ten of our companions into the street at 4:30 before they had the chance to get properly dressed, saying, 'I am now expelling you by order of the [provincial] Education Director'. Can such unscrupulousness be imagined? After wandering around in the rain and mud for an hour and a half, and since every one of us was from the countryside we had no places in which to take refuge, and although we were prepared to submit our secret thoughts to you by troubling your lofty vizierial personage, we followed your commands and returned to school, but again the threatening continued. These actions of theirs stem from their aim of both exacting revenge and securing their personal repose in the evenings, so that they can be free to go to the theatre and frequent the coffeehouses. Just as the horizon-extending kindnesses of our greatest benefactor [i.e. Sultan Abdülhamid II] will by no means accept this, therefore your khedivial, intelligent personage will likewise not show it the face of approval. It is requested of your just and mark-hitting judgement that we should be rescued, that such impropriety should not be allowed in the future, and that the proper measures are taken with respect to them [i.e. the officials]. In that respect, and in any case, the command belongs unto Him to whom all commanding belongs.

8 Teşrin-i sânî 1319 (1 Ramadan 1321/21 November 1903)
Your servants, the boarding students of the civil *idadî* school in Manastır
[25 signatures]

2. The deposition of the eighth grader, Şevki Efendi from Manastır

Whom did you have write this petition?

We had one of the petition-writers (*arzuhalci*) write it. His shop is in the market, next to the Municipality. A boy came out of his shop. We related the contents of

---

[101] Each student had an identification number.

[102] Using the traditional method of marking time, namely counting the hours from sunrise and, as in this case, sunset (i.e. the time would have been around 10.30 p.m.).

[103] During the holy month of Ramadan Muslims are enjoined to fast from sunrise to sunset. Consequently, the meals both prior to, and immediately after, the fast take on a special significance.

the petition. We waited in the street. He wrote it and brought it out. Everybody took something out [from his pocket] and paid. I don't know what they paid.

[Signed]

This is not what your friends say. You, almost fifteen people, entered the shop. You related the contents of the petition to a mustachioed petition-writer. He wrote it.

We, fifteen people, did not enter the shop. That's a lie. [Saying the shop] is in Drahor is a lie. It is next to the Municipality. I didn't relate the contents [by myself]. We all did.

Everyone related his ideas separately. I spoke first.

The idea of having a petition-writer occurred to everybody. They said, 'Let's go to the petition-writer.' We got up and went. We signed it in Ali Ağa's coffeehouse.

I don't know who took the petition. I gave the first statement but I wasn't the first to take the petition. Whoever says so is a liar.

How many hours were you out in the streets?

For an hour and a half. The servant Hüseyin Ağa threw me out. Zokman Ağa was by his side. Whether or not he got involved, I don't know.

When the director said, 'Go to bed' did you go to bed or not?

No, I didn't.

Why did you not [go to bed]?

We didn't go to bed because we were not going to wake up for *sahur*. I followed my friends [in this].

[signed] Şevki
8 Teşrin-i sânî, 5[:00] in the evening.

3. The deposition of the eighth grader, Ali Rıza Efendi from Hanya[104]

Whom did you have write this petition?

I had a petition-writer write it, but I don't know him. His shop is in [the vicinity of] the Municipality. If a gendarme is allowed to accompany me, I'll show [him]. We went after five o'clock. We were a few in number, [i.e. between five and ten]. We entered the shop one by one. We sat down in the shop. Şevki Efendi related the contents of the matter. He explained it all precisely. I didn't say anything to the petition-writer. My friends spoke. I know Lazaraki Efendi [did] but I couldn't recall the others. I gave five para (piasters). We went to the coffeehouse near

---

[104] City on the island of Crete (Gk. Khania).

the school, the one designated by the school. We signed it there. Şevki Efendi signed it first and then I did.

What is your complaint?

Our food is meagre. It doesn't suffice. We don't get filled up. We requested to stay up until *sahur*. Because [our request] was not accepted, they threw us out in the street. Şevki[105] and Artin Efendis told us to go to bed. I said, 'I won't go to bed. If my friends do, then I will also. But I just won't go to the dormitory. Perhaps I'm ill.'

What is your illness?

I don't have one.

Who is your companion in class? With whom do you study?

They are all my companions. At exam time I study with Abdurrahman Efendi and Receb Efendi.

[signed] Ali Rıza

---

[105] This is the school official named Şevki, mentioned in the petition, and who is not to be confused with the student who has the same name.

1.9 An Armenian-Iranian promoted to Amir Tuman of the Persian Cossack Brigade: firman of Mohammad ᶜAli Shah Qajar, 1908

David Yaghoubian

Preface

On 4 August 1906, following more than six months of strikes and protests centered in Iran's capital Tehran, Mozzafar al-Din Shah Qajar (r. 1896–1907) conceded to popular pressure and proclaimed his acceptance of the concept of constitutional monarchy and the formation of a representative assembly (majles). The First Majles, composed primarily of members of the ᶜolama (clerics), merchants, and guild members who had participated in the movement to constrain or qualify the power of the Qajar shahs,[106] convened for the first time in October with the immediate goal of drafting a national constitution. The Fundamental Law (as the Belgian-modeled constitution was termed) was signed by Mozaffar al-Din Shah on 30 December 1906, less than one week before his death.[107] It was also signed grudgingly by Mozaffar al-Din's successor, his anti-constitutionalist son Mohammad ᶜAli. In addition to the drafting of the constitution, between October 1906 and June 1908, the First Majles worked to achieve several goals, which included limiting the powers of the shah, subordinating government ministers to the Majles, balancing the budget, restructuring taxes, implementing land reform, and initiating judicial reforms.[108]

Throughout the initial stages of the Iranian Constitutional Revolution and twenty-month tenure of the First Majles, tensions between the Qajar monarchy and the constitutionalists remained high, and in June 1908 Mohammad ᶜAli Shah launched a successful *coup d'état*. After issuing a series of ultimatums to the Majles to regain his autocratic powers, the shah

---

[106] Homa Katouzian explains that the word used in the movement for a constitution, *mashruteh*, means constrained, conditioned, or qualified. The central demand of the 'revolution' was for a constrained or qualified monarchy; a limitation of the arbitrary power of the shah, who was taking out large foreign loans and was perceived widely to be selling out to the interests of foreigners. Radical political, social, or economic change was not on the agenda for the majority of revolutionaries as they rallied in support for the movement. Homa Katouzian, *The Political Economy of Modern Iran: Despotism and Pseudo-Modernism, 1926–1979* (New York: New York University Press, 1981), 156. See also id., 'Nationalist Trends in Iran, 1921–1926', *International Journal of Middle East Studies*, 10/4 (1979), 533–51.

[107] Janet Afary, *The Iranian Constitutional Revolution, 1906–1911: Grassroots Democracy, Social Democracy, and the Origins of Feminism* (New York: Columbia University Press, 1996), 57–66; Nikki Keddie, *Qajar Iran and the Rise of Reza Khan, 1796–1925* (Costa Mesa, Calif.: Mazda Publishers, 1999), 56; and Edward Granville Browne, *The Persian Revolution of 1905–1909* (London: Frank Cass, 1966 [1910]), 131–2.   [108] Afary, *The Iranian Constitutional Revolution*, 63–4.

ordered his military forces, including the Persian Cossack Brigade under the command of Russian Colonel Vladimir Platonovich Liakhoff, to close the Baharestan (house of parliament) and arrest several leading constitutionalists. On 23 June over 1,000 troops surrounded the Baharestan and opened fire with artillery, leaving the building in ruins, and dozens of dead and wounded constitutionalist fighters (*feda'i*).[109] Following the surrender of the constitutional forces, Majles members were arrested and put in chains, or summarily executed. Majles records were destroyed, houses of constitutionalists and their sympathizers were sacked and looted, and Tehran was placed under martial law under Colonel Liakhoff and the Cossack Brigade.

One month after the bombardment of the Majles, Eskandar Khan Setkhanian (1865–1953), an Armenian-Iranian officer of the Persian Cossack Brigade who had participated in the engagement, was promoted from the rank of Mir Panj (Brigadier-General) to Amir Tuman (Major-General), which was the highest-ranking position within the Brigade below its Russian commander, Liakhoff.[110] Descended from a line of Setkhanians who had served the Qajar government and military since the reign of Fath ᶜAli Shah (r. 1797–1834), Eskandar Khan was educated in Russian military school and had been a loyal member of the Cossack Brigade since 1894. As a staunch supporter of the Qajar monarchy, Eskandar Khan's political views and military efforts contrasted with those of the Armenian political parties and the Armenian-Iranian *feda'i*, who supported the constitutional movement, and who would rally with military forces from around the nation to march on Tehran, oppose Mohammad ᶜAli and the Cossacks, and restore the constitution and Majles in July 1909.[111] Eskandar Khan, who was 43 years old at the time of his promotion in 1908, survived the subsequent battles with the constitutionalists, and would remain Amir Tuman of the Cossack Brigade for eight years. During this period he served as commander of all Cossack regiments, including that of a young officer named Reza Khan, who would crown himself Reza Shah Pahlavi in 1926.[112]

---

[109] Browne *The Persian Revolution*, 205–9. See also Jangahir Qa'immaqami, *Tarikh-e tahavvolat-e siyasi-e nezam-e Iran* ('History of the political transformation of Iran's military') (Tehran: ᶜAli Akhbar, 1326/1947), ch. 9.   [110] Amir Tuman translates literally as 'Commander of Ten Thousand'.

[111] On the role of the different corporate groups that participated in the Constitutional Revolution see Afary, *The Iranian Constitutional Revolution*. Cosroe Chaqueri (ed.), *The Armenians of Iran* (Cambridge, Mass.: Harvard Center for Middle East Studies, 1998), focuses on the contributions and role of Armenians in the Constitutional Revolution and Armenian political parties active in Iran at the turn of the century. Houri Berberian provides insight into the activities and motivations of the Armenian Dashnak, Hunchak, and Social Democrat parties that contributed to the struggle for the constitution and parliament in '*The Love for Freedom Has No Fatherland*': *Armenians and the Iranian Constitutional Revolution of 1905–1911* (Boulder, Col.: Westview Press, 2001).

[112] For a detailed social biographical portrait of the life and military career of Eskandar Khan Setkhanian, see David Yaghoubian, 'Ethnicity, Identity, and the Development of Nationalism in Iran', Ph.D thesis, University of California, Berkeley (2000).

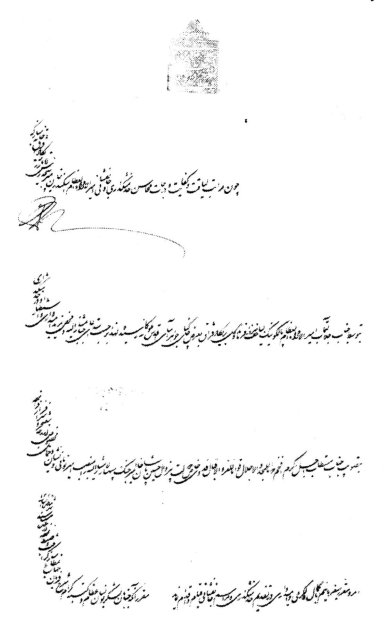

1. *Farman* of Mohammad ᶜAli Shah dated 20 Jumada II (20 July 1908)

Eskandar Khan's promotion to Amir Tuman was decreed and recorded in a *farman* (royal edict) of Mohammad ᶜAli Shah dated 20 Jumada II (20 July 1908), utilizing the ornate language and honorific epithets characteristic of Persian imperial edicts dating back to the sixteenth century.[113] The *farman* was issued on a 55 cm. by 42 cm. piece of parchment and written using the highly stylized *shekasteh* (literally 'broken hand') script—another centuries-old feature of Persian farmans that continued throughout the late Qajar era. The document bears the official seals of Mohammad ᶜAli Shah and Minister of War Hosayn Pasha Khan, who led the combined attack of Cossack and Persian Army forces on the Majles. It is signed in blue ink with an illegible flourish.

Text

Seal of Mohammad ᶜAli Shah

Because the account of the capability and virtues of service and sacrifice of His Honor Eskandar Khan Mir Panj, head of the glorious house of Cossacks by means of his glorious excellency, the commander of all the great commanders, Palkovnik Sardar Liakhoff, Commander-in-Chief of the Cossack Brigade, has been brought to the attention at the feet of the adorned and sacred King [Mohammad ᶜAli Shah], it is therefore by that request determined that the said person, with hope of excelling in his service to the approval of his most glorious, noble and elevated excellency never to be eclipsed, Hosayn Pasha Khan, Minister of War and Field Marshal, be promoted to the rank of Amir Tuman and that all of the medals and sashes pertaining to that rank be given to honour him and make him stand proud.

By way of perpetuating his glory and splendor, we ordain and establish this to be law with warm hearts and with hope he will apply himself to his offering of service and sacrifice. Be it that the secretary of the army describes, records, and notarizes this glorious farman, month of Jumada II, 1326.

[Seals on back of document]
Moshir al-Saltaneh   Amir Jang Sepahsalar
Entered in the private register of the monarchy
Dated 20th month of Jumada II
Number: 1833

---

[113] I am indebted to Ali Sadrpour for his essential work in deciphering and transcribing the *shekasteh* script of the Setkhanian firmans. Special thanks go to Dr Hamid Algar for his assistance in the translation of several complex passages.

1.10 Wahhabi *ʿulama* and the state in Saudi Arabia, 1927[114]

Guido Steinberg

Preface

The Saudi state, which re-emerged on the Arabian scene in 1902, was based on an alliance between the rulers of the Saʿud family and the Wahhabi religious scholars, the *culama* (sing. *ʿalim*).[115] Some years after the new ruler ʿAbd al-ʿAziz Ibn Saʿud (r. 1902–53) had conquered Riyadh in 1902, he embarked upon a campaign to settle the Bedouin. These had hitherto threatened every effort to establish central rule in the Arabian Peninsula. Because of their military prowess, the rulers of the settled communities feared them as enemies. But even as allies they proved to be notoriously unreliable, changing sides whenever the general situation promised greater rewards on the opposite side.

As part of his effort to build a modern state in the Arabian Peninsula, Ibn Saʿud had to eliminate the Bedouin as a military threat. By a combination of persuasion, economic and military pressure, and religious indoctrination, Bedouin began to settle in small agricultural colonies from about 1911/12 and called themselves *Ikhwan* (brethren). Wahhabi scholars and their students were sent to the tribes and their settlements in order to teach them the principles of the Wahhabi interpretation of Islam and administer justice. Central to their teachings was an aggressive interpretation of *jihad* (in the meaning of holy war) against non-Wahhabi Muslims. As a result, the *Ikhwan* transformed themselves into fanatical warriors of the faith and played important roles in the military campaigns that led in 1934 to the unification of the Saudi state in its present form.

From 1915/16, and especially after 1918/19, problems emerged. Although the *Ikhwan* had settled and lived according to Wahhabi precepts, they were far from giving up their tribal way of life. Arguing that they were spreading the faith and fighting the unbelievers, they attacked neighboring tribes who had not settled and Muslims in neighboring countries like Jordan, Iraq, and Kuwait.

---

[114] The translation is a revised version of the text in Sheikh Hafiz Wahba, *Arabian Days* (London: Arthur Barker 1964), on the basis of the original text in Hafiz Wahba, *Khamsuna ʿamman fi jazirat al-ʿarab* (Al-Qahira: Al-Halabi 1380/1960).

[115] The Wahhabiya is an Islamic reform movement that strove to rebuild Najdi (i.e. Central Arabian) society along the lines of an idealized vision of the community of the early Muslims in Mecca and Medina, the so-called pious forefathers (*Al-salaf al-salih*). Founded in the eighteenth century, it has since been a prominent force in Saudi history. The Wahhabis enforced a puritan code of conduct, prohibiting smoking, music, and laughter, obliging Muslims to attend the communal prayers five times a day. More importantly for their neighbours, they—under the leadership of the Saʿud family—led a *jihad* against Muslims not following the Wahhabi interpretation of the faith.

In 1924/5 the *Ikhwan* took part in the military campaign which led to the establishment of Saudi rule in the Hijaz.[116] After the military campaign had ended, however, their role had been played and they increasingly became a political liability. Ibn Saʿud had to consolidate his realm and centralize power. Consequently, he recalled the unruly *Ikhwan* from the Hijaz and sent them back to Najd. In the following months the *Ikhwan* attacked especially Iraqi territory in their raids against non-Wahhabi tribes, and threatened to bring the Saudi state into conflict with the British government of Iraq. Ibn Saʿud ordered the *Ikhwan* leaders to come to Riyadh, where they presented their demands. The Wahhabi ʿulama were now asked to decide whether these were justified. In a famous religious ruling of February 1927, they showed a marked ambivalence. On the one hand, they sympathized with the *Ikhwan*'s demands for a more ideologically based policy with regard to the conversion and control of non-Wahhabis within the Saudi state and a more aggressive approach towards non-Wahhabi neighbours. For them, the *Ikhwan* were a force pressuring for the ideal puritanical state that they would have liked to establish. On the other hand, they had experienced that their own influence depended on the existence of a strong Saudi–Wahhabi state. The outcome of these deliberations was the fatwa of 11 February 1927. It is one of the most important documents concerning the relation of religion and state in Saudi Arabia.

The fatwa repeats the *Ikhwan*'s main demands; Ibn Saʿud had introduced telegraphs after the conquest of the Hijaz. The *Ikhwan* rejected this innovation, ostensibly on religious grounds, but also because by employing modern communication methods Ibn Saʿud enhanced his abilities to control his realm. Secondly, the *Ikhwan* had demanded a more radical religious policy in the Hijaz, *inter alia* forcing the more liberal and open-minded Hijazis to adopt Wahhabi Islam. Most importantly, they wanted to enforce the Wahhabi prohibition of the veneration of saints and graves by destroying all the tombs of prominent Muslims in the Hejaz. Thirdly, they demanded the application of Islamic law as interpreted by the Wahhabis in the Hijaz, where the Ottomans and Hashemites had introduced positive law in some fields. Fourthly, they rejected the tradition of the Egyptian *mahmal*. This was a splendidly adorned camel litter, accompanied by an Egyptian armed escort and traditionally leading the Egyptian pilgrimage caravan to Mecca. In 1926 the *Ikhwan* attacked it. Over the following months the *Ikhwan* repeatedly reproached Ibn Saʿud for having protected the *mahmal* from further damage. Fifthly, the *Ikhwan*, again sharing the views of the Wahhabi ʿulama, demanded a forceful conversion of all Shiʿites in the country. Shiʿites formed a strong minority in Eastern Arabia and were considered to be the unbelievers par excellence in Wahhabi lore. The *Ikhwan* furthermore demanded the right to attack Bedouin entering Najd from

[116] The Hijaz is a region in Western Arabia ruled by the Ottoman Empire until 1919. Between 1919 and 1924/5 Sharif Husayn ruled it. Its most important cities are Mecca, Medina, and Jiddah.

their pastures in Iraq and, most importantly, continuing the jihad against all non-Wahhabi territories, aiming at the British mandates in Iraq and Jordan, but also the smaller emirates of the Persian Gulf.

In this fatwa, the *ʿulama* showed a marked pragmatism in navigating between the *Ikhwan*'s demands and the needs of the Saudi state.

The *Ikhwan* did not end their raids into Iraq and, after several months of low-intensity conflict between the two sides, they rebelled. Ibn Saʿud had their uprising crushed in 1929/30. A large majority of the *ʿulama* sided with him and gave up their former allies, although the *Ikhwan*, more than anyone else in Arabia, embodied original Wahhabi ideals.

Text

The Wahhabi *ʿUlama*'s *Fatwa* Concerning the Demands of the *Ikhwan*, 11 February 1927

From Mohammad b. ʿAbd al-Latif Al al-Shaykh, Saʿd b. ʿAtiq, Sulayman b. Suhman, ʿAbd Allah b. Abd al-ʿAziz al-ʿAtiqi [ʿAtiq?], ʿAbd Allah al-ʿAnqari, ʿUmar b. Salim, Salih b. ʿAbd Allah al-ʿAziz Al al-Shaykh, ʿAbd Allah b. Hasan Al al-Shaykh, ʿAbd Allah b. ʿAbd al-Latif, ʿUmar b. ʿAbd al-Latif, Mohammad b. Ibrahim Al al-Shaykh, Mohammad b. ʿAbd Allah b. ʿAbd Abd al-Latif, ʿAbdallah b. Zahim, Mohammad b. ʿUthman al-Shawi, ʿAbd al-ʿAziz al-Shithri[117]—to all who may see it of our Muslim brothers—may God guide us and them to the right path! Peace be upon you! We have received from the Imam ʿAbd al-ʿAziz,[118] may God preserve him, a question addressed to him by some of the *Ikhwan* relating to certain problems. We have answered as follows:

With regard to the wireless telegraph, this is a recent invention which has not been in use long enough for us to know its true nature. We can find nothing about it in the works of the great religious scholars (*ahl al-ʿilm*), and consequently cannot pronounce any opinion on it, and as we cannot speak in the name of God and His Prophet without knowledge, we cannot say whether or not it is permissible until we know its exact nature.

With regard to the Mosque of Hamza and Abu Rashid, we have told the Imam that according to our legal reasoning it should be destroyed at once.[119]

With regard to un-Islamic laws (*qawanin*), if any such exist in the Hijaz, they should be abolished at once. Nothing should be applied other than pure Islamic law (*al-sharʿ al-mutahhar*).

---

[117] The list of names varies in the different versions of the fatwa. This is a slightly modified list on the basis of all available sources, mainly drawing from Wahba's text in Arabic.

[118] Until the twentieth century the Wahhabis called their ruler 'Imam'.

[119] Hamza b. ʿAbd al-Mutallib had been an uncle and prominent companion of the Prophet Muhammad. He was buried in a small but beautifully adorned mosque close to Medina.

As regards the entrance of Egyptian Pilgrims into the sacred city of God [i.e. Mecca] escorted by an armed force, we have advised the Imam not to allow such a show of strength and to forbid other polytheist and forbidden phenomena.

Nor should they be allowed to bring the *mahmal* into the sacred Mosque; no one should be permitted to touch or kiss it, nor to perform any of the other sinful or forbidden actions to which the people of the *mahmal* are accustomed. If it should be possible to forbid the entrance of the *mahmal* into Mecca entirely, without any ill effects (*mafsada*), this is obligatory; if not, in accordance with the legal principle, the lesser evil must be permitted in order to prevent the greater.

As to the Shi꜀ites (*al-rafida*),[120] we have told the Imam that our religious ruling is that they must be obliged to become true Muslims, and should not be allowed to perform the rites of their misguided religion publicly. It is incumbent on the Imam to order his governor in Hasa[121] to summon the Shi꜀ites to Shaykh Ibn Bishr [i.e. the Wahhabi judge of the oasis], before whom they should swear to follow the religion of God and His Prophet, to cease all prayer to the saintly members of the Prophet's house or others, to cease their heretical innovations (*bid꜀a*, pl. *bida꜀*) such as the commemoration rites performed on the anniversaries of the deaths of members of the House of the Prophet and all other such rites of their misguided creed, and that they should cease to visit their so-called sacred cities Karbala and Najaf.[122] They must also be forced to attend the five prayers in the Mosques, along with the rest of the congregation. Sunni Imams, muezzins and religious policemen (*nuwwab*) should be appointed to instruct them. They must also force them to study Ibn Abd al-Wahhab's *Three Principles*.[123]

Any places specially erected for the practice of their rites must be destroyed, and these practices forbidden in mosques and anywhere else.

Any Shi꜀ites who refuse to keep to these rules must be exiled from Muslim territory. With regard to the Shi꜀ites of Qatif,[124] the Imam should compel Shaykh Ibn Bishr to go and see personally that all the above-mentioned requirements are carried out. We have advised the Imam to send missionaries and teachers to certain districts and villages which have only recently come under the rule of the Muslims, and to order his governors and other officials to bring these people back to Islam and forbid sinful behaviour.

[120] The Wahhabis use the disrespectful term *al-rafida* (lit. renegades) to designate the Shi꜀ites, indicating that they do not consider them to be Muslims.

[121] Hasa (or Al-Ahsa) is the name of an oasis in Eastern Arabia, where most Saudi Shi꜀ites live. The term has frequently been used for the whole Eastern province, including Qatif, the second-largest oasis.

[122] These are important Shi꜀i pilgrimage cities and centers of learning in Southern Iraq. Many Shi꜀ites from the Eastern province studied there.

[123] Muhammad b. ꜀Abd al-Wahhab's *Al-Usul al-thalatha* was and is one of the textbooks every young student had to learn by heart. It contained the most important principles of Wahhabi thought.

[124] Qatif, on the Persian Gulf coast, was populated nearly exclusively by Shi꜀ites.

As to the Shi'ites of Iraq who have infiltrated and become mingled with the desert people under Muslim rule, we have advised the Imam to forbid them entry into Muslim pastures or other territory.

Worldly taxes (*mukus*), we have ruled, are completely illegal and it is the King's duty to remit them, but if he refuses to do so we do not feel it permissible to break up Muslim unity and revolt against him solely on this account.

As to the *jihad*, we leave this to the Imam, whose duty it is according to our religious teaching (*shari'a*), to see what is best for Islam and for the Muslims. We ask God, on our and his behalf and that of all Muslims, to give us His guidance and His help. Written on the 8th day of Sha'ban 1345 (11 February 1927 A.D.). Signatures follow.

1.11 Crime and society in Iran: press and court transcripts, 1934

Cyrus Schayegh

Preface

ᶜAli Asghar Borujerdi 'Asghar Qatel' (the Murderer) was arrested by the Tehran police in March 1934, charged with the sexual abuse and murder of thirty-three children—twenty-five in Baghdad and eight in Tehran—in a trial which seems not to have deviated from the then standard judicial procedure. He was publicly executed a year later. His name still reverberates in the Iranian national memory today, in part because of similar murder cases receiving press attention in the 1930s.[125] The press coverage of this case cited below comes from Iran's main daily newspaper, *Ettelaᶜat* ('Information'). Summary reports of criminal proceedings and transcripts from parliamentary proceedings were printed in the press routinely. However, the publication of criminal-court transcripts was rare and highlights the importance of this case. The coverage of the trial of Asghar the Murderer allows us to focus on some important aspects of the attitudes of the modernizing class during the period of Reza Shah Pahlavi (1921–41).

As the modernizing class—journalists, lawyers, judges, and magistrates—confronted the reality of Asghar the Murderer, questions were raised about the ability of such figures to educate, elevate, and reform not only exceptional criminals, but society at large: the same state that was charged with protecting society from crime had committed itself to a variety of legal, administrative, and social reforms under the stern and authoritarian rule of the Pahlavi Dynasty. In a process that mirrored experiences in Europe in the late nineteenth century[126] and colonial India in the nineteenth and early twentieth[127] centuries, perceptions of increasing instances of criminality and immorality were considered alongside anxieties about the pace and nature of change in Iranian society.

[125] See D.M. Rejali, *Torture and Modernity: Self, State and Society in Modern Iran* (Boulder, Col.: Westview Press, 1994), 86; and the specific case of Seyyed Mohammad ᶜAli 'Sayf Al-Qalam Qatel' as reported in "Seyyed Mohammad ᶜAli ya Sayf al-Qalam qatel-e dah nafar" ('Seyyed Mohammad ᶜAli, or Seyf al-Qalam the murderer of ten people'), *Ettelaᶜat* (22 Esfand 1313/12 March 1935).

[126] e.g. see J. Walkowitz, *City of Dreadful Delight: Narratives of Sexual Danger in Late-Victorian London* (Chicago: University of Chicago Press, 1992).

[127] G. Prakash, *Another Reason: Science and the Imagination of Modern India* (Princeton: Princeton University Press, 1999).

Texts

1. Pre-trial press commentary, 12 March 1934[128]

Each time that his name is pronounced, the common people—i.e. the very same huge mass in the midst of which this predacious creature has openly lived— deprive him by their curses, determine ways of punishment for him, and sentence him in their own courts to suffer the hardest punishments one can imagine. [. . .] They spoke with very serious faces about all these ways and methods of punishment which they had in mind for him, but never discussed or studied their own thoughts and statements from a rational standpoint. For instance, they did not think about how it is possible to cut him into thirty-three pieces, what legal grounds the performing court officials have in order to cut him into pieces, and for what absurd motives they would like to cut him into thirty-three pieces. [. . .] However, under no circumstances—even not once for this miserable and impure creature—can the concessions of a democratic government's justice be rescinded. In clearer words: our judicial regulations, which are congruent with the laws of the most civilized countries in the world, do not discriminate in the punishment of criminals.

2. Published court transcripts, 4 June 1934[129]

HEAD JUDGE: ᶜAli Asghar, there is one thing which I have not really understood: You said that you killed them because they had bad morals and were causing corruption, and that their existence was harmful for the country. But you have said something else to your interrogators, there you said that you liked killing them and that you enjoyed it. Now I want to know whether you also liked and enjoyed killing a *Seyyed* or a respectable/reasonable person.

ᶜALI ASGHAR: I killed the ones I did (kill) because their morals were bad, and I liked killing them.

HEAD JUDGE: When he was a reasonable person, did you kill him?

ᶜALI ASGHAR: No—why should I have killed him?

HEAD JUDGE: If you killed (them) because their morals were bad, why then did you sell their clothes?

ᶜALI ASGHAR: Those which were good I sold, and those which were torn and not worth the pain, I threw away. [. . .]

---

[128] *Pishnehad-e mojazat-e ᶜAli Asghar Qatel* ('Propositions for punishing ᶜAli Asghar the murderer'), *Ettelaᶜat* (21 Esfand 1312/12 March 1934). Although the absence of a signature makes it impossible to identify the author of this article with complete certainty, the fact that it is an editorial suggests that the editor of the newspaper and influential intellectual of the period, ᶜAbbas Masᶜudi, probably wrote it.

[129] Process protocol reprinted in *Mohakemeh-ye ᶜAli Asghar dar mahkameh-ye jenaʾi* ('ᶜAli Asghar's Trial in Criminal Court'), *Ettelaᶜat* (15 Khordad 1313 H. S./4 June 1934) and Process protocol reprinted in *Defaᶜ-e Aqa-ye Shariᶜatzadeh* ('Mr Shariᶜatzadeh's defence'), *Ettelaᶜat* (17 Khordad 1313, 6 June 1934).

[PROSECUTOR, SIYASI]: [N]ever in my life have I seen a person [i.e. ᶜAli Asghar Borujerdi] who perpetrated such homicides and carnage, and it is clear that such crimes have a bad influence on the thoughts and minds of the common people. Basically, if his deeds remain unpunished, it is possible that everybody will perpetrate murders out of personal whim, and will be sure that they will not be punished. [. . .]

[DEFENSE COUNSEL, SHARIᶜATZADEH]: Honored judges! First, I have, in your presence, proven that ᶜAli Asghar Borujerdi is a degenerate individual, i.e. that he is not like a normal human being with regard to his state of mind, physiognomy, and anatomy. Secondly, I have demonstrated that, from the point of view of criminology, this man is a natural-born criminal (*jani-ye fetri*). [. . .] Although the acceptance of scientific thought and principles concerning natural-born criminals is not explicitly mentioned in our laws, in my opinion paragraph 40 of the General Penal Code contains the acceptance of these principles and standards, and is implicitly ruled by the spirit of this same scientific theory. [. . .] Paragraph 40 (states that) 'a person who was insane (*majnun*) at the moment of committing a crime, or who suffers from a cerebral disorder, is not considered guilty, and will not be punished, but needs to be transferred to a mental hospital if his insanity persists'.

3. Post-trial press commentary, 6 June 1934[130]

All the endeavors which the great spokesmen and reformers, and the leaders of the nation and the state's ruling group undertake for the improvement of the condition and situation of our life, all the schools that are being established, all the articles and the literary and social texts that are being published in newspapers and journals, all the advice, guidance, and counsel that the elderly are giving to us, are made so that we will educate our own children and offspring well, will assign them to teaching and send them to school in time, will ensure that they do not associate with malicious persons, and will not let them acquire vile habits. [. . .] We must be warned, accept our own good and bad actions as the result of our own beings, and educate our own children in such a good way that they will be useful and beneficial beings for the country, the nation, and themselves.

[130] *Tamasha-ye Asghar Borujerdi dar mahkameh* ('Watching Asghar Borujerdi in Court'), *Ettelaᶜat* (17 Khordad 1313/6 June 1934). Again, this article was unsigned.

1.12 A protest of the Jewish women workers of Palestine against the new municipal ordinance which deprives the women of Palestine of their civic rights, 1934[131]

Ellen L. Fleischmann

Preface

Even before the British Mandate in Palestine was official, Jewish Zionist women had begun to organize themselves. Unlike Palestinian Arab women, however, the Jewish women had numerous women's organizations that reflected sometimes specifically focused, differentiated goals. This reflected the highly organized and institutionalized Zionist movement overall, which essentially was able to organize almost a state within a state under the terms of the Balfour Declaration, which promised that the British government would 'facilitate the achievement' of a 'Jewish National Home'. As early as 1914, women associated with the Labor Zionist informally organized movement in pre-Mandate Palestine for fuller representation and rights within the Labor Zionism movement, particularly on work-related issues, such as rights to work in the same jobs as men in agriculture and the construction trades. A few years later (1918–19) the Palestine Jewish Women's Equal Rights Association (ERA) was formed with the purpose of winning women's suffrage in the Jewish national constituent assembly, Vad Leumi. The ERA also worked for women's full participation in other elected bodies in the Yishuv (the Jewish community in pre-1948 Palestine), for replacing the religious laws that regulated personal status with civil law, and for a woman's right to practice law. When the Jewish Federation of Labor (the Histadrut) was formed in 1920, a Women's Worker Council was established under its organizational umbrella the following year. The ERA participated in the international women's suffrage movement, attending conferences of the International Woman Suffrage Alliance and succeeding in becoming the 'Palestinian' delegation. Palestinian Arab women were thus excluded from this international arena, as the ERA was explicitly for Jewish women.

In 1920 Jewish women obtained the right to vote in, and stand for, election in the National Assembly, although there were numerous attempts by more conservative, religious male elements to restrict this right. On the local level, however, the situation was more complex. Women gained the

---

[131] The original document is undated, but a letter accompanying it in the archives is dated 21 May 1934.

right to vote in some local Jewish councils depending on the particular council. As of 1947, however, women did not have the right to vote in municipal elections, with two exceptions: Tel Aviv and Petah Tikva. The document below, sent by the General Council of Women Workers under the Histadrut, protests an ordinance denying women the right to vote in municipal elections. The document is interesting for what it reveals about the women's attitudes about suffrage rights, women's work, and the Palestinian Arabs.

Text

A protest of the Jewish women workers of Palestine against the new municipal ordinance, which deprives the women of Palestine of their civic rights [1934]

(FO 317/1/17883 E3421 and 2, Israel State Archives)

On behalf of the twenty thousand Jewish working-women, members of the General Federation of Jewish Labor, this Council voices its Protest against the provisions of the new Municipal Ordinance, which deny the female population in the towns of Palestine (excepting only the city of Tel Aviv) the suffrage in municipal elections.

We cannot ascribe this distrimination [sic] to the consideration that there is in the towns of Palestine a great number of ignorant and illiterate Arab women; because there are a great number of illiterates amongst the Arab men as well, and still the law grants them all the civic rights. It is, therefore, evident that the law places a limitation upon the women solely because they are women.

This limitation is indefensible, even if the reason behind it is the low cultural level of some women in Palestine. The cultural level of a country cannot be raised by means of denying the people elementary civic rights, but on the contrary—the exercise of civic duties prompts and stimulates education among the people. In this connection we cannot but emphasize that the educational activities of the Government have always been exceedingly limited, especially so among the women. And now, instead of contributing to the uplifting of the Arab women from their pitiful medieval status by giving them civic rights, the Government, by means of the new Municipal Ordinance, reduces the position of the Jewish women, who always have been enjoying full equality in the Jewish community.

What has proven the experience of the civic equality of women in the city of Tel Aviv for the twenty-five years since the city has been founded? Not only have any negative results from the franchise of women never been pointed out, but, on the contrary, women have repeatedly been elected to high municipal offices and have always discharged their duties to their full credit—facts which are sufficiently known to the Government.

The social maturity of the Jewish working woman is further proven by the following facts: women constitute fifty per cent of the membership of the Jewish Federation of Labor; the Jewish woman is particularly active in the professions and in political parties, in the fields of social, municipal and national activities.

For years, we see our women in Palestine working side by side with the men in all fields of activity: in the colonization of waste localities and in their transformation into flourishing agricultural settlements; in building, manufacture and industry as well as in the sphere of education and literature. In fact, there is not a responsible enterprise in which the woman has not shared.

By means of persistent efforts and at the cost of great sacrifice did the Jewish Working woman prove the fine attainments she is capable of achieving when no artificial barriers are put in her way.

The Women Workers' Movement of Palestine, which has been fighting for the cause of the social and professional advancement of female workers for tens of years, cannot but see in this inequality placed upon the woman by the new Municipal Ordinance an unjustified attempt to retard the emancipation of women in Palestine.

We call upon the women of the country, and especially the Jewish women, as well as all fair-minded citizens, to join us in our protest against this Ordinance, which on the one hand is humiliating the women of this country, and on the other hand deprives the municipalities of the women's valuable cooperation.

The General Council of Women Workers in Palestine, by [hand-signed; illegible].

1.13 The rise of mass doctrinal parties: the program of Hasan al-Banna and the Muslim Brotherhood, 1936

Robert G. Landen

Preface

This pamphlet, addressed to King Faruq, Prime Minister Nahhas, and the other notables of the Arab world, summarizes the aims of Shaykh Hasan al-Banna (1906–49), Supreme Guide of the Muslim Brotherhood. The Muslim Brotherhood was and remains a many-faceted organization. In some respects it was a modernized Sufi (Muslim fraternity) organization offering a blueprint for social and economic reorganization according to commonly understood Muslim principles, and a vehicle for resistance to foreign control. Much of its early success can be attributed to the imaginative leadership and attractive Islamic teachings, and its active role in the Egyptian struggle against imperialism. By the time of Al-Banna's assassination in 1949, the Brotherhood numbered some 2 million members, many of them from the lower middle class, in Egypt, Sudan, Syria, and most other Arab countries. When it rose in the 1930s, it offered an attractive alternative to the vaguely liberal parliamentary regimes then governing much of the Arab East. The Brotherhood was instrumental in pioneering the ideology and technique of mass political organization employed by the revolutionary regimes that arose in the Arab world in the 1950s.

It is significant that members of Jamal ᶜAbd al-Nasir (Nasser)'s Free Officers movement were at one time or another closely connected with the Brotherhood and borrowed heavily from its secret, cellular structure before the 1952 revolution and from its techniques for appealing to the masses after the uprising. Indeed, ᶜAbd al-Nasir (d. 1970) and other similar leaders stole the Brotherhood's thunder not only organizationally, but also in their concern for pan-Arab unity and social justice for the masses. The violent suppression of the Muslim Brotherhood in Egypt in the 1950s and 1960s spawned a more uncompromising branch of the movement that followed the teachings of Sayyid Qutb (d. 1966) and disavowed Arab nationalism and socialism completely. Indeed, this document was written before the Muslim Brotherhood had turned to militant opposition to the monarchy that resulted, ultimately, in the government's assassination of Al-Banna in 1949. This document addresses the practical expressions of the Sunni Islamic revivalist world-view before the rise of Arab Socialist political ideologies. It should be noted that moderate branches of the Muslim Brotherhood have also survived the suppression and radicalization of the movement, and many of the steps suggested here would be more in line with their perspective than with such radical Muslim Brotherhood offshoots as Islamic Jihad or *Takfir w'al-Hijrah*.

Text

Toward An Effective Reform[132]

After having studied the ideals which ought to inspire a renascent nation on the spiritual level, we wish to offer, in conclusion, some practical suggestions. We will list here only the chapter headings because we know very well that each suggestion will require profound study as well as the special attention of experts; we know also that the needs of the nation are enormous; we do not believe that the fulfilling of the needs and the aspirations of the country will be an easy thing; what is more, we do not think that these goals can be reached in one journey or two. We realize the obstacles which these problems must overcome. The task will require a great deal of patience, a great deal of ability, and a willing tenacity.

But one thing is certain: resolve will lead to success. A dedicated nation, working to accomplish the right, will certainly reach, with God's help, the goals toward which it strives.

The following are the chapter headings for a reform based upon the true spirit of Islam:

I. In the political, judicial, and administrative fields:
1st To prohibit political parties and to direct the forces of the nation toward the formation of a united front;

2nd To reform the law in such a way that it will be entirely in accordance with Islamic legal practice;

3rd To build up the army, to increase the number of youth groups; to instill in youth the spirit of holy struggle, faith, and self-sacrifice;

4th To strengthen the ties among Islamic countries and more particularly among Arab counties which is a necessary step toward serious examination of the question of the defunct 'Caliphate';

5th To propagate an Islamic spirit within the civil administration so that all officials will understand the need for applying the teachings of Islam;

6th To supervise the personal conduct of officials because the private life and the administrative life of these officials forms an indivisible whole;

7th To advance the hours of work in summer and in winter so that the accomplishment of religious obligations will be eased and to prevent all useless staying up late at night;

---

[132] Translated from *Nahw al-Nur* ('Towards the Light') (Cairo: Jamʿiyat al-Ikhwan al-Muslimin, 1936), 38–48.

8th To condemn corruption and influence peddling; to reward only competence and merit;

9th Government will act in conformity to the law and to Islamic principles; the carrying out of ceremonies, receptions, and official meetings, as well as the administration of prisons and hospitals should not be contrary to Islamic teachings. The scheduling of government services ought to take account of the hours set aside for prayer.

10th To train and to use the 'Azharis', that is to say, the graduates of Al-Azhar University [a Cairo institution specializing in Islamic learning], for military and civil roles;

II. In the fields of social and everyday practical life:

1st The people should respect public mores: this ought to be the object of special attention—to strongly condemn attacks upon public mores and morality;

2nd To find a solution for the problems of women, a solution that will allow her to progress and which will protect her while conforming to Islamic principles. This very important social question should not be ignored because it has become the subject of polemics and of more or less unsupported and exaggerated opinion;

3rd To root out clandestine or public prostitution and to consider fornication as a reprehensible crime the authors of which should be punished;

4th To prohibit all games of chance (gaming, lotteries, races, golf);

5th To stop the use of alcohol and intoxicants—these obliterate the painful consequences of people's evil deeds;

6th To stop attacks on modesty, to educate women, to provide quality education for female teachers, school pupils, students, and doctors;

7th To prepare instructional programs for girls; to develop an educational program for girls different than the one for boys;

8th Male students should not be mixed with female students—any relationship between unmarried men and women is considered to be wrong until it is approved;

9th To encourage marriage and procreation—to develop legislation to safeguard the family and to solve marriage problems;

10th To close dance halls; to forbid dancing;

11th To censor theatre productions and films; to be severe in approving films;

12th To supervise and approve music;

13th To approve programs, songs, and subjects before they are released, to use radio to encourage national education;

14th To confiscate malicious articles and books as well as magazines displaying a grotesque character or spreading frivolity;

15th To carefully organize vacation centers;

16th To change the hours when public cafes are opened or closed, to watch the activities of those who habituate them—to direct these people towards wholesome pursuits, to prevent people from spending too much time in these cafes;

17th To use the cafes as centers to teach reading and writing to illiterates, to seek help in this task from primary school teachers and students;

18th To combat the bad practices which are prejudicial to the economy and to the morale of the nation, to direct the people toward good customs and praiseworthy projects such as marriage, orphanages, births, and festivals; the government should provide the example for this;

19th To bring to trial those who break the laws of Islam, who do not fast, who do not pray, and who insult religion;

20th To transfer village primary schools to the mosque and to carry on all beneficial activities there (selecting officers, matters of health, interested support for young children learning their religious duties, introducing the old to science);

21st Religious teaching should constitute the essential subject matter to be taught in all educational establishments and faculties;

22nd To memorize the Qur'an in state schools—this condition will be essential in order to obtain diplomas with a religious or philosophical specialty—in every school students should learn part of the Qur'an;

23rd To develop a policy designed to raise the level of teaching, to unify the different teaching specialties, to bring together the different branches of culture—emphasis should be put upon teaching morality and physics;

24th Interested support for teaching the Arabic language in all grades—absolute priority to be given to Arabic over foreign languages (primary teaching);

25th To study the history of Islam, the nation, and Muslim civilization;

26th To study the best way to allow people to dress progressively and in an identical manner;

27th To combat foreign customs (in the realm of vocabulary, customs, dress, nursing) and to Egyptianize all of these (one finds these customs among the well-to-do members of society);

28th To orient journalism toward wholesome things, to encourage writers and authors who should study specifically Muslim and Oriental subjects;

29th To safeguard public health through every kind of publicity—increasing the number of hospitals, doctors, and out-patient clinics;

30th To call particular attention to the problems of village life (administration, hygiene, water supply, education, recreation, morality).

III. The economic field:

1st Organization of the 'zakat tax'[133] according to Islamic precepts, using zakat proceeds for welfare projects such as aiding the indigent, the poor, orphans; the zakat should also be used to strengthen the army;

---

[133] A tax upon one-fortieth of the total possessions of individuals of means. This is one of the few taxes that flow directly from Islamic law. Historically, most taxes collected in the Islamic world were in accordance with 'customs' that did not violate Islamic law.

2nd To prevent the practice of usury, to direct banks to implement this policy; the government should provide an example by giving up the 'interest' fixed by banks for servicing a personal loan or an industrial loan, etc.;

3rd To facilitate and to increase the number of economic enterprises and to employ the jobless there, to employ for the nation's benefit the skills possessed by the foreigners in these enterprises;

4th To protect workers against monopoly companies, to require these companies to obey the law, the public should share in all profits;

5th Aid for low-ranking employees and enlargement of their pay, lowering the income of high-ranking employees;

6th Reducing the number of posts for employees, to be satisfied with a job necessary for the country, payment of employees should be apportioned on a fair basis;

7th To encourage agricultural and industrial works, to improve the situation of the peasants and industrial workers;

8th To give special attention to the technical and social needs of the workers, to raise their level of life and aid their class;

9th Exploitation of certain natural resources (unworked land, neglected mines; etc.);

10th To give priority to projects whose accomplishment is vital to the country. [. . .]

1.14 Jamal ᶜAbd al-Nasir (Gamal Abd al-Nasser) from *Egypt's Liberation*, 1953[134]
From the Islamfiche *project*

Preface

Jamal ᶜAbd al-Nasir's *Egypt's Liberation: The Philosophy of the Revolution* is still an important text for radical nationalists in much of the Middle East. Although al Nasir had been involved in the revolutionary government of Egypt for only a year when he put his philosophy onto paper in 1953, *The Philosophy of Revolution* contains the basic points of the program he promoted for the rest of his life.

Nasir was born into a middle-class family in Alexandria in 1918 and received primary and secondary education in Cairo, Helwan, and Alexandria. As a teenager he was involved in student nationalist protests against the British domination of Egypt. In 1936 he received his first lesson in the corruption of Egyptian politicians, when the leading nationalist party, the *Wafd* (delegation), agreed to continued British presence in Egypt in return for the formation of a Wafdist government. After attending the Military Academy, Nasir became a commissioned officer in 1937 and soon joined an informal group of young nationalist officers who were discontented with the state of their country. Five years later these officers became outraged when the British forced a Wafdist government upon the king, as Egypt was nominally independent at the time. A further jolt was delivered by the 1948 defeat of the Arab armies in Palestine, where the young Major Nasir served as commanding officer at the important battle for the town of Faluja. Defective arms, a lack of supplies, and virtually non-existent co-ordination of planning shocked Nasir and his comrades, who became increasingly determined to fight for Egypt's salvation. The right time finally came for the Society of Free Officers in July 1952, when their military coup put in place General Muhammad Neguib [Najib] as the figurehead ruler of Egypt. Nasir took control of the revolutionary government within two years; he was elected president in 1956 and remained in office until his death in 1970.

The following selection presents Nasir's basic ideas about the nature of Egyptian society, the role of the army in politics, and the reasons for the revolution. His political legacy is complex. His efforts to unify the Arab world led to such political experiments as the United Arab Republic, a union of Syria and Egypt, from 1958 to 1961. His commitment to 'Arab Socialism' contributed to an 'Arab Cold War' in which Egypt competed both with rival revolutionary regimes in Syria and Iraq and conservative

[134] Gamel Abdel Nasser, *Egypt's Liberation: The Philosophy of the Revolution* (Washington, DC: Public Affairs Press, 1955).

monarchies, such as Saudi Arabia and Jordan. Saudi Arabia and Egypt fought a proxy war in the 1960s by supporting opposite sides in a civil war in Yemen. Nasir's efforts to modernize the Egyptian economy led to achievements both grand (the Aswan High Dam) and costly (the nationalization of the Suez Canal), as well as a state-led economic system that his successors began dismantling, with mixed results, soon after his death. His efforts to lead the Arab confrontation with Israel proved disastrous in 1967. His political charisma and mastery of mass politics allowed him to survive and thrive in his leadership of Egypt, but his crackdowns on domestic opposition helped to create an oppressive political climate in Egypt that persists to this day. It is worth noting that Nasir's political legacy is truly a global one. He was the moving force behind the Asian African Conference of Non-Aligned Nations, which first met at Bandung, Indonesia, in 1955.

Text

First, I should like to dwell for a moment on the word 'philosophy'. It is a big word. As I contemplate it, I feel that I stand before a boundless world, a bottomless sea—and a trepidation restrains me from plunging into it since, from my point of vantage, I see no other shore to head for.

The truth is, I want to avoid the word 'philosophy' in what I am about to say. Besides, it is difficult to discuss the philosophy of the Egyptian revolution—difficult for two reasons. In the first place, an exposition of the philosophy of the revolution of 1952 would require the thorough investigation by scholars into its roots, which strike so deeply into the history of our people. The story of national struggle contains no gaps filled with nothingness; neither does it feature any surprises that leap into existence without introduction. The struggle of any people, generation after generation, is a structure rising stone upon stone. And just as each stone finds firm support beneath it so, too, do the episodes in the struggles of a people support each other. Each new event stems from the one preceding, and each becomes in turn the basis for a new one to follow.

Elementary School Student

I do not want to claim for myself the role of a history professor; nothing could be further from my mind. But were any elementary school student to attempt a study of the struggles of our people, he would discover that the revolution of 23 July marks the realization of the hope held by the people of Egypt since they began, in modern times, to think of self-government and complete sovereignty.

There was an unsuccessful attempt to realize this hope when Sayyid ʿUmar Makram led the movement to install Mohammad ʿAli as ruler of Egypt in the name of its people. Another attempt failed when ʿUrabi tried to secure a constitution. Many other attempts that also ended in grief were made during the period of intellectual ferment between the ʿUrabi revolution and the 1919 revolution.

This 1919 revolution, led by Saᶜad Zaghul, was no more successful than the others in fulfilling the hopes of the people.

The Ultimate Roots

It is not true that the successful revolution of 1952 stemmed from what happened in the Palestinian War; nor is it true that it was due to the defective weapons that caused the death of our men and officers. Still further from the truth are statements that the cause lay in the electoral crisis in the Army Officers Club in 1951.

In my view, the real cause must be sought further and is more profound. Had the Army officers attempted the revolt on their own account because they were inveigled into the Palestine War, or because they had been shocked by the defective weapons scandal, or because of the attack on their honor in the club elections, it could not have been called a revolution—mutiny would have been a more appropriate name.

These were only incidental causes. Perhaps their greatest influence was to give us added impetus to going ahead with our plans for the revolution, although we had already embarked on this course for other reasons.

Whence the Revolution?

Let me now try, after all that has happened and after the long years that have gone by since the idea of revolt began to take root, to go back in my memory to the first day I discovered within myself the seeds of this idea.

The seeds were planted long before those days of November 1951, when the crisis in the Army Officers Club began. For by that time the Free Officers' organization was in existence and active. In fact, it is no exaggeration to say that the election crisis in the club was due chiefly to the activity of the Free Officers, for we intended at that time to enter the battle to test our strength of solidarity and organization.

The day we conceived that idea was also long before the scandal of defective weapons broke upon us. The Free Officers were already in existence, and it was their pamphlets, in fact, which first sounded the alarm. Their activity inspired the uproar that followed the scandal.

Egypt was the Center of Our Dreams

No, the idea started long before that. It was further back even than 16 May 1948, the day that marked the beginning of my involvement in the Palestine War.[135]

When I now try to recall the details of our experience in Palestine, I find a curious thing: we were fighting in Palestine, but our dreams were centered in Egypt. Our bullets were aimed at the enemy in his trenches before us, but our hearts hovered over our distant country, which we had left to the care of the wolves.

[135] For a fuller account of Nasir's participation in the war, see 'Gamal Abdul Nasser', trans. Walid Khalidi, *Journal of Palestine Studies*, 2/2 (Winter, 1973), 3–32.

In Palestine, Free Officer cells found opportunities to study and investigate and to meet in the trenches and command posts. Salah Salem and Zakaria Muhyi al-Din[136] came to me in Palestine after breaking through the siege lines into Faluja. We sat there in our besieged positions, not knowing what the outcome would be, but our conversation dwelt only upon our country, which it was our soldiers' duty to defend.

One day, Kamal al-Din Husayn[137] was sitting near me in Palestine, looking distracted, with nervous, darting eyes. 'Do you know what Ahmad ʿAbd al-ʿAziz said to me before he was killed?' he said.

'What did he say?' I asked.

He replied with a sob in his voice and a deep look in his eyes, 'He said to me, "Listen, Kamal, the biggest battlefield is in Egypt." '

A Greater Faluja

Not only did I meet in Palestine the friends who collaborated with me in the work for the sake of Egypt, but I encountered there also the ideas which illuminated the path ahead of me. I recall a time when I was sitting in the trenches thinking of our problems. Faluja was surrounded, and the enemy was subjecting it to a terrific air and artillery bombardment. I used often to say to myself: Here we are in these foxholes, surrounded, and thrust treacherously into a battle for which we were not ready, our lives the playthings of greed, conspiracy and lust, which have left us here weapon-less under fire.

And when I would come to this point in my thinking, I used to find my thoughts suddenly leaping across the field and over the borders into Egypt, and I would say to myself: Over there is our country, another Faluja on a larger scale. What is happening to us here is a picture in miniature of what is happening to Egypt. Egypt too is besieged by difficulties and enemies; *she* has been deceived and forced into a battle for which *she* was not ready, *her* fate the toy of greed, conspiracy and lust, which left *her* without weapons under fire.

Even the Enemy

In addition to the companions who discussed with me in Palestine the future of our country, and the experience which hammered out our ideas as to the possibilities of its fate, the enemy, too, played a role in reminding us of our country and

[136] He was later a member of the Revolutionary Command Council who served as prime minister, 1964–5, before retiring from political life.

[137] A member of the Revolutionary Command Council who retired from political life in 1964. During the 1948 war he served with an advance force of Egyptian army volunteers under Col. Ahmad ʿAbd al-ʿAziz. The Egyptian volunteer force met up with a force of civilian volunteers who were members of the Muslim Brotherhood. The combined forces had entered Palestine on 6 May, before the expiration of the British Mandate and Israeli declaration of independence but during the ongoing hostilities between the Jewish settlers and Palestinians.

its problems. A few months ago, I read some articles written about me by an Israeli officer named Yeruhan Cohen, which appeared in the *Jewish Observer*. In these articles the Jewish officer relates how he met me during the armistice negotiations.

'The subject which Jamal ʿAbd al Nasir always talked about with me,' he wrote, 'was the struggle of Israel against the English, and how we organized the underground resistance movement against them in Palestine, and how we were able to muster world public opinion behind us in our struggle against them.'

Before February 4[138]

The seeds of the revolution were present within me long before the episode of 4 February 1942, a day after which I wrote to a friend, saying, 'What is to be done now that the die was cast and we accepted what happened on our knees in surrender? As a matter of fact, I believe the Imperialist was playing with only one card in his hand, with the object of threatening us. But once the Imperialist realizes that some Egyptians are ready to shed their own blood and meet force with force, he will beat a hasty retreat, like any harlot rebuffed.'

Such, of course, is the usual practice of Imperialism. As for us, as for the Army, the episode had a new electrifying effect on our spirit and sensibilities. Heretofore, officers who had talked only of selfish amusement now began to talk of self-sacrifice and their readiness to die in defense of their honor. They all voiced their regret for not having intervened, despite their obvious weakness, to restore to their country its honor and cleanse it with their own blood.

But for him who waits, tomorrow is close.

Some indeed tried to do something afterwards by way of retaliation, but the opportunity was irretrievably lost, leaving our hearts full of bitter anger and sorrow. Actually this action (on the part of the Imperialist), or rather this stab, revived the spirit of some of us and brought home to us the fact that when our honor was involved we might be prepared to defend it. It was a lesson, but it was a hard lesson.

And Before 1935

The day of my awakening was even earlier than that explosive period when, as a student, I marched in 1935 with the demonstrators, who clamored for the restoration of the 1923 Constitution (which was actually restored), and when I was going around with delegations of Egyptian leaders in an attempt to get them to unite on behalf of Egypt. The National Front was formed in 1936 as a result of those efforts.

[138] On this date, British troops forced a change of government by surrounding King Faruq's palace. The British wanted to ensure a compliant Egyptian government as they confronted Axis forces in North Africa during World War II.

I recall that during that period of ferment, I wrote a letter to one of my friends. It was dated 2 September 1935.

'Dear Brother,

'I talked to your father on the telephone on the thirtieth, asking after you. He told me that you were at school. So I decided to put down in writing what I intended to communicate to you on the telephone. Allah said: "Oppose them with whatever forces you can muster." But where are these forces we are supposed to have in readiness for them? The situation today is precarious, and Egypt's situation is even worse. We are on the verge of collapse and death, for truly the temple of despair has mighty columns. But, who is to pull it down?' I continued my letter in this vein.

When was the day on which I discovered the seeds of revolution within me? The truth is that these seeds were not only hidden in me; I found them also in the hearts of a great many others, who in turn could not pinpoint the exact beginnings of their existence. Is it not clear then that these seeds were implanted in us when we were born, and that they were a hope concealed in our subconscious, put there by the generation before us?

Truth . . . and Vacuum

I have made this long digression in order to describe the primary reason for the difficulty confronting me in speaking of the philosophy of the revolution because such a discussion requires the deep research of scholars into the historical origins of our people.

The second reason is that I myself was inside the maelstrom of the revolution, and from those who find themselves in a maelstrom, some of its more distant details are hidden. I was heart and soul involved in everything that happened and the way it happened: how, then, can I deal with it objectively, or with the hidden significance behind it?

I am one of those who believe that nothing can exist in a vacuum; even truth cannot so exist. Truth is that which we feel and know in our hearts to be right, or to be more exact, that which our souls embrace. Our souls are the vessels in which everything we are is contained; and everything we are, everything placed in these vessels, must take their shape, even truth. I try as much as humanly possible to prevent my soul from altering the shape of truth very much, but how far can I succeed? That is the question.

Beyond this, I want to be fair to myself and fair to the philosophy of the revolution. So I leave it to history to draw up its outlines as I see them, as others see them, and as they are demonstrated by events—and then to distil from all the full truth.

Aspirants and Measures

What, then, can I say? I am qualified to talk of two things. The first is embraced in the term 'aspirations', which began in the form of a vague hope, then developed into a defined idea, and finally into a practical program at midnight on 23 July.

The second is the measures we have taken to put these aspirations, with all their vague hopes, their defined ideas and their practical programs, into practical execution since midnight on 23 July up to now.

It is about these aspirations and measures that I wish to speak.

For a long time I have been asking myself: Was it necessary for us, the Army, to do what we did on 23 July 1952?

I have already observed that the revolution marked the realization of a great hope felt by the people of Egypt since they began, in modern times, to think in terms of self-government and to demand that they have the final word in determining their own future. But if that is so, and if what happened on 23 July was neither a military mutiny nor a popular uprising, why then was it entrusted to the Army, and not to other forces, to bring it about?

I have always been a confirmed believer in the ideal of military service. It imposes one duty on the Army: that it should die on the frontiers of the mother-land. Why did our Army find itself obliged to act in the capital of the motherland instead of on the frontiers?

Again, let me draw your attention to the fact that the rout in Palestine, and the defective arms, and the crisis in the Officers' Club were not the real sources from which the torrent poured out: all these were only contributory factors to the speed of the flow; but, as I said before, they never were the real origin.

But why the Army? I have long asked myself this question; I asked it during the stages of hope, thinking and planning prior to 23 July, and I have continued to ask it during the many stages of action since then.

There were various justifications before 23 July that made it clear to us why it was necessary for us to do what we did. We used to say, 'If the Army does not do this job, who will?' We also used to say, 'We have been used by the Despot as a bogey to give the people nightmares; now it is high time that the bogey be turned against the Despot to shatter his own dreams.' We said many other things, but we felt to the depth of our beings this was our soldiers' duty and that if we failed to discharge it, we would be failing in the sacred trust placed in us.

I confess, however, that the full picture did not become clear in my mind until after a long period of trial after 23 July. It was the details of this experience which filled in the details of the picture.

The Role of the Vanguard

I can testify that there were certain critical occasions since 23 July when I accused myself, my comrades and the rest of the Army, of stupidity and madness for doing what we had done on that day.

Before 23 July, I had imagined that the whole nation was ready and prepared, waiting for nothing but a vanguard to lead the charge against the battlements, whereupon it would fall in behind in serried ranks, ready for the sacred advance towards the great objective. And I had imagined that our role was to be this commando vanguard. I thought that this role would never take more than a few hours. Then immediately behind us would come the sacred advance of the serried ranks and the thunder of marching feet as the ordered advance proceeded towards the great objective. I heard all this in my imagination, but by sheer faith it seemed real and not the figment of imagination.

Then suddenly came reality after 23 July. The vanguard performed its task and charged the battlements of tyranny. It threw out Faruq and then paused, waiting for the serried ranks to come up in their sacred advance toward the great objective.

Symbol of Revolution

For a long time it waited. Crowds did eventually come, and they came in endless droves—but how different is the reality from the dream! The masses that came were disunited, divided groups of stragglers. The sacred advance toward the great objective was stalled, and the picture that emerged on that day looked dark and ominous; it boded danger. At this moment I felt with sorrow and bitterness that the task of the vanguard, far from being completed, had only begun.

We needed order, but we found nothing behind us but chaos. We needed unity, but we found nothing behind us but dissension. We needed work, but we found behind us only indolence and sloth. It was from these facts, and no others, that the revolution coined its slogan.

Weapon in the Hand of Hate

We were not yet ready. So we set about seeking the views of leaders of opinion and the experience of those who were experienced. Unfortunately we were not able to obtain very much.

Every man we questioned had nothing to recommend except to kill someone else. Every idea we listened to was nothing but an attack on some other idea. If we had gone along with everything we heard, we would have killed off all the people and torn down every idea, and there would have been nothing left for us to do but to sit down among the corpses and ruins, bewailing our evil fortune and cursing our wretched fate.

We were deluged with petitions and complaints by the thousands and hundreds of thousands, and had these complaints and petitions dealt with cases demanding justice or grievances calling for redress, this motive would have been understandable and logical. But most of the cases referred to us were no more or less than demands for revenge, as though the revolution had taken place in order to become a weapon in the hand of hatred and vindictiveness.

The Evils of Egotism

If anyone had asked me in those days what I wanted most, I would have answered promptly: To hear an Egyptian speak fairly about another Egyptian. To sense that an Egyptian has opened his heart to pardon, forgiveness and love for his Egyptian brethren. To find an Egyptian who does not devote his time to tearing down his views of another Egyptian.

In addition to all this, there was a confirmed individual egotism. The word 'I' was on every tongue. It was the solution to every difficulty, the cure for every ill. I had many times met eminent men—or so they were called by the press—of every political tendency and color, but when I would ask any of them about a problem in the hope he could supply a solution, I would never hear anything but 'I'.

Economic problems? He alone could understand them; as for the others, their knowledge on the subject was that of a crawling infant. Political issues? He alone was expert. No one else had got beyond the a-b-c's of politics. After meeting one of these people, I would go back in sorrow to my comrades and say, 'It is no use. If I had asked this fellow about the fishing problems in the Hawaiian Islands, his only answer would be "I".'

Duties and Responsibilities

I remember visiting once one of our universities where I called the professors together and sat with them in order to benefit from their scholastic experience. Many of them spoke before me and at great length. It was unfortunate that none of them advanced any ideas; instead, each confined himself to advancing himself to me, pointing out his unique aptitude for making miracles. Each of them kept glancing at me with the look of one who preferred me to all the treasures of earth and heaven.

I recall that I could not restrain myself, so I stood up and said, 'Every one of us is able in his own way to perform a miracle. His primary duty is to bend every effort to his work. And if you, as university professors, were to think of the welfare of your students, and to consider them as you should, to be your basic work, you would be in a position to provide us with the fundamental strength to build up our motherland.

'Everyone must remain at his post, to which he should dedicate all his efforts. Do not look at us—we have been forced by circumstances to leave our posts in order to perform a sacred duty. If the motherland had no need for us other than to stay in the ranks of the Army as professional soldiers, we would have remained there.'

What I did not do at that time was to give them the example of the members of the Revolution Council. I did not want to tell the professors that, before they were called to a greater duty, these men had been devoting all their energies to their jobs. I did not point out to them that most members of the Revolution Council were professors at the General Staff College, and that this constituted a proof as to their distinction in their field as professional soldiers.

Likewise, I refrained from pointing out that three of the Revolution Council, ᶜAbd al-Hakim Amir,[139] Salah Salem and Kemal al-Din Husayn, were given exceptional promotions on the field of battle in Palestine. I did not want to mention all this, because I do not want to boast about members of the Revolution Council, they being my brothers and comrades.

The Complete Picture

I confess that this whole situation produced in me a psychological crisis; but the events that followed, and my reflections thereon, together with the real meaning I could adduce from them, tended to ease my distress and set me to seek a justification for this situation, which I found when the whole picture of the motherland's plight rose somewhat clearly before my eyes. This clarification, moreover, brought me the answer to the question that had long bothered me, namely: Was it necessary for us, the Army, to do what we did on 23 July?

The answer is yes, beyond any subterfuge or equivocation. I can say now that we did not ourselves define the role given us to play; it was the history of our country that cast us in that role.

I can now state that we are going through two revolutions, not one revolution. Every people on earth goes through two revolutions: a political revolution by which it wrests the right to govern itself from the hand of tyranny, or from the army stationed upon its soil against its will; and a social revolution, involving the conflict of classes, which settles down when justice is secured for the citizens of the united nation.

Peoples preceding us on the path of human progress have passed through two revolutions, but they have not had to face both simultaneously; their revolutions, in fact, were centuries apart in time. For us, the terrible experience through which our people are going is that we are having both revolutions at the same time.

Between the Millstones

This terrible experience stems from the fact that both revolutions have attendant factors that clash and contradict violently. To be successful, the political revolution must unite all elements of the nation, build them solidly together and instill in them the spirit of self-sacrifice for the sake of the whole country. But one of the primary features of social revolution is that it shakes values and loosens

---

[139] He became head of the Egyptian military after the revolution of 1952, rising to the office of first vice-president in 1964. After the June war of 1967 he was removed from office and subsequently committed suicide.

principles, and sets the citizenry, as individuals and classes, to fighting each other. It gives free rein to corruption, doubt, hatred and egoism.

We are caught between the millstones of the two revolutions we are fated now to experience. One revolution makes it obligatory that we unite and love one another, fighting side by side to achieve our ends; the other brings dissension upon us against our desires, causing us to hate each other and think only of ourselves.

Between these two millstones, for example, the 1919 revolution was lost; it was unable to make secure the results it should have achieved. The ranks which formed in 1919 and faced up to tyranny were soon scattered by the outbreak of strife and conflict between individuals and classes. The result was dismal failure. Tyranny tightened its grip afterwards, overtly by means of occupation troops, and covertly through its masked stooges led by Sultan Fuad and King Faruq after him. The people harvested nothing but self-doubt, evil, hatred and rancour between individuals and classes.

Only the Army

The hope reposed in the 1919 revolution was thus dimmed. I say dimmed, but not extinguished, because the natural forces of resistance called into being by the great aspirations of our people did not cease to be active and to prepare for a new attempt.

This was the state of affairs which existed after the 1919 revolution, and which singled out the Army as the force to do the job. The situation demanded the existence of a force set in one cohesive framework, far removed from the conflict between individuals and classes, and drawn from the heart of the people: a force composed of men able to trust each other; a force with enough material strength at its disposal to guarantee a swift and decisive action.

Only the Army could meet these conditions.

In this way, as I have already remarked, it was not the Army that defined its role in the events that took place; the opposite is closer to the truth. The events and their ramifications defined the role of the Army in the great struggle to free the nation.

I have been aware since the beginning that our unity is dependent upon our full realization of the nature of the circumstances in which we found ourselves, the historical circumstances of our country. For we could not alter the circumstances by the mere stroke of a pen, nor could we turn back the hands of the clock, or advance them—we could not control time. It was not within our power to stand on the road of history like a traffic policeman and hold up the passage of one revolution until the other had passed by in order to prevent a collision. The only thing possible was to act as best we could and try to avoid being ground between the millstones.

It was inevitable that we go through the two revolutions at the same time. When we moved along the path of the political revolution and dethroned Faruq, we took a similar step on the path of the social revolution by deciding to limit land ownership.

I continue to believe that the 23 July revolution must maintain its initiative and ability to move swiftly in order to perform the miracle of travelling through two revolutions at the same time, however contradictory our resulting actions might at times appear.

When one of my comrades came to me saying, 'You want unity to face the English, but at the same time you allow the treason courts to continue their work,' I listened to him with our great crisis in mind, the crisis of the millstones— a revolution on the one hand which obliges us to unite in one phalanx and to forget the past, and on the other hand, another revolution which demands that we restore lost dignity to our moral values by not forgetting the past. I might have replied that our only salvation lies, as I said before, in maintaining our speed of movement and our initiative, and our ability to travel through two revolutions simultaneously.

This situation does not exist because I wished it, or because all those who participated in the revolution have wished it. It is brought about by the act of fate, the history of our people, and the stage it is passing through at the present time.

1.15 The Program of the *Baʿth* (Arab Socialist Resurrection) Party, 1963[140]

Robert G. Landen

Preface

The Baʿth Party was founded in Syria in the early 1940s by Michel Aflaq and Salah Bitar. Syria had barely achieved some measure of democratic rule in 1943 and independence from France in 1946 when it was rocked by a series of factional coups ultimately resulting in a shaky unity government in 1956 in which Baʿthist participation was essential. In 1958 the Baʿthi Party helped to engineer a union with Jamal ʿAbd al-Nasir[Nasser]'s Egypt but left the United Arab Republic in 1961. Since that time, Syria and Egypt have remained rivals for 'revolutionary' leadership of the Arab World, even as Egypt began to abandon Arab Socialism after the death of Nasir in 1970. The Baʿthist dominance of Syrian politics did not end internal strife until 1970, when Hafez al-Asad seized control of the party and the state. A Baʿthist takeover of Iraq in 1963 created another radical rival for Syria, with Al-Asad and Iraq's Saddam Husayn [Hussein] becoming implacable foes. Syria supported Iran during the Iran–Iraq War of 1980–8 and joined America and its allies during the First Gulf War of 1990–1. Hafez Al-Asad died in 2001, and Syria seems to have taken a more conciliatory stance towards Iraq under Hafez's son, Bashar, and opposed the American overthrow of Saddam Husayn in the Second Gulf War of 2003. The future of Baʿthism rests again with Syria and will depend on how well Bashar negotiates external pressures to reform, Syria's role in the peace process with Israel and Palestine, its relations with Lebanon, and its ability to withstand internal challenges from Islamists and liberal opponents.

The Baʿth Party's chief theoretician was Aflaq, a French-educated Syrian Christian who abandoned an early allegiance to communism. Theoretically, the Baʿthist attraction has been its strong advocacy of pan-Arab nationalism, and its socialist-statist development policy, which has gained the support of intellectuals, if not the masses. A major point of disagreement between 'Nasserites' and Baʿthists had been the latter's insistence on collective, regionally decentralized leadership. The party's main preoccupation from the beginning has been with revolutionizing the social and economic order on the basis of nationalization of the economy, redistribution of wealth, and worker participation in management.

---

[140] 'Text of the Published Deliberations of the Sixth National Congress of the Baʿth', trans. Center for Near Eastern and North African Studies in Ann Arbor, Michigan. Original Arabic Text in *Al-Nahar* (Beirut: 29 Oct. 1963).

The platform cited below, published eight months after the Baʿthist coup of February 1963, provides a window on the ideology and aspirations of the party. Before it became a somewhat discredited vehicle of authoritarian rule in Syria and Iraq, it is important to understand Baʿthism's initial appeal.

Text

Party Matters and the Party's Relationship with the Masses and the Authority of the state

Principle of Collective leadership

1. The Congress studied the question of Party organization in general, and emphasized the importance of maintaining the principle of collective leadership in the Party, since collective leadership represents Party democracy 'at the summit.' The Congress agreed also that the experience of the Party has confirmed the wisdom of the principle 'of democratic centralization' as applied by the Party. The Congress considers that only the establishment of a balance between centralization on the one hand and democracy on the other will permit the Party and the masses to exercise an effective responsibility; it considers also that this balance guarantees the unity of the Party and its momentum on the one hand, and the realization of its democracy and flexibility on the other.

Socialist Structure of the Party

In making a deep study of the Party's situation in Syria and Iraq, the Party gave special attention to the circumstances of the socialist revolution put forth by the popular masses. The Congress emphasized that the Party's socialist composition will leave its imprint on the revolution itself. Therefore, the Party decided that the socialist goals of the Party must be put into operation right away, because a thorough socialist revolution must use the workers and peasants as the basis for the Revolution and the Party simultaneously.

Right of the Popular Masses to Criticize the Party

Under the prevailing conditions, where the Party is in power in each of the Syrian and Iraqi Regions, the Congress cautioned against the infiltration of opportunist elements into the Party. It also cautioned against the possibility that some elements of the Party might succumb to the temptations of power, and the danger of turning the heads of these elements, making them feel superior to the non-party masses. The Congress emphasized that membership in the Party means no more than an awareness of the wide and great responsibility assumed by members toward the Party. The Congress reminded the Party members of their duty to concern to themselves solely with their responsibilities. As to the rights of Party members, they are the same rights enjoyed by any citizen, without any addition or privilege. The Congress emphasized the right of the non-party popular masses to criticize the Party and to watch over its members. The Congress considers criticism, besides being a natural right of the masses, a guarantee of the operation of the process of rectification and interaction between the masses on the one hand and the Party and that State machinery on the other. The Congress also considers this watch as a curb on the temptations of power and on the excess manifestation of authority by the Party's members, and as a means to prevent the occurrence of bourgeois manifestations by them. The Congress also stressed the necessity of paying careful attention to the quality and moral character of members of the Party, and emphasized the need for strict standards in agreeing to their affiliation and the need to prolong the period of party experimentation so as to be able to ascertain during this period the moral fitness and general aptitude of the candidates.

Party's Relationship with the State Machinery

With respect to the relation between the Party and the state machinery, the Congress decided upon the need for making a complete distinction between the Party and the state machinery. It warned against the danger of the state machinery swallowing up the Party, and against the possibility of the Party becoming submerged in the detailed and every-day affairs of the work of the state machinery. The Congress considers the Party as the leader of the state machinery and as the director of general policy and basic administration questions. The Congress emphasized the need for the majority of the Party leaders to give their full time to Party affairs. [. . .]

Socialist Transformation Within a Democratic Context

6. The Congress discussed the questions of socialist transformation in the Syrian and Iraqi Regions, and decided to proceed with the task of a socialist transformation of society on a democratic basis with the participation of the popular masses. After a scientific analysis of the social, political and class conditions in the Syrian and Iraqi Regions, the Congress emphasized that the Party's dedication to the cause of the masses is preparing for the establishment of a democratic, rational, and revolutionary experience, which will be reflected not only in the two Regions but in the entire Arab country. This will be because it is preparing a realistic and objective experience which will be able to interact with the other experiences in the Arab country.

Forces of the Socialist Revolution

In accordance with a scientific analysis of the political and economic circumstances in the two Regions, the Congress has reached basic conclusions as to the bourgeois middle class, which has become incapable of playing a constructive role on the economic level. Its opportunism renders it qualified only to play the role of an ally of the new imperialism. The Congress considers the workers, the peasants, the revolutionary intelligentsia, and the petty bourgeoisie to be the forces whose alliance will support the socialist revolution in its first stage.

Workers' Democratic Management

8. In an attempt to indicate the possible horizons of the socialist evolution in the two Regions, and in the light of other revolutionary socialist experiences in the world, the Congress emphasized the need to bring about a democratic system of administration of the means of production by the workers. The Congress considers that this type of administration may enable the development of socialism in the two Regions to bypass the stage of state capitalism experienced by most socialist experiments. The Congress emphasized the need for being alert to the dangers of bureaucracy and the continual need to curb it and control it.

State Machinery and its Relationship with the Party and the People

9. The Congress gave special attention to the subject of developing the state machinery and the relationship between it and the Party in particular, and between it and the popular masses in general. The Congress adopted a detailed policy to promote the revolutionary and democratic evolution of this machinery, to enable it to participate effectively in the socialist transformation. The Congress emphasized that its task is to promote evolution, not amputation. Evolution is the basis and the jumping-off point. Amputation is an exceptional course. The Congress adopted this policy both from human considerations and from its belief in the conscience of the citizen on the other hand.

10. With respect to the question of the land, the Congress adopted resolutions which countered the problem of land in a revolutionary and social manner. It agreed on the necessity of regarding the problem of land from a revolutionary and social manner. It agreed on the necessity of regarding the problem of land from a revolutionary outlook. It considers the agricultural revolution to be an essential step towards speedy development in the industrial sector. It considers a policy of collective farms, independently run by the peasants on land covered by Agrarian Reform, to be the sound socialist course toward developing social progress in the rural areas. It considers the establishment of these farms as a revolutionary goal towards which the Party strives. It considers the participation of peasants in the execution of the agricultural revolution to be a basic condition for the success of this revolution.

Socialist Planning

11. In its resolution, the Congress emphasized the necessity for socialist planning on regional and Arab levels, because this is the only effective means to utilize all the national, natural, and human resources in a scientific and realistic

manner. It emphasized the importance of industrialization and economic development in the most important sectors to guarantee the real development of the national economy and to avoid external achievements which do not contribute to the development of production.

Socialist Policy in the Field of Services
12. The Congress adopted in its resolutions a socialist policy in the field of services. It drew attention to the open contradiction between the aspects of extravagance and waste in the state machinery and the standard of living of the popular masses. It emphasized that austerity is the duty of the well-to-do classes and of the state machinery in particular. The congress dealt with education questions, and emphasized the need to make compulsory education a real fact. It also stressed the necessity of overcoming illiteracy, and of giving education a national and scientific aspect so as to give the coming generation a deep, complete, and coordinated understanding of human knowledge. The Congress also agreed on the need to coordinate education so as to give the requirements of development and specialization a high priority. The Congress decided to expand scientific faculties in universities, and to raise the standards of teaching in the universities. The Congress decided to expand services in the rural areas and in the remote and poor provinces. The Congress also considered that providing free medical treatment to citizens is a fundamental element of socialism, and it laid down the guidelines for executing this policy, starting with the expansion of the teaching of medicine and with the expansion of medical services given by the state, in order to liquidate the private sector in the field of medicine.

The National Guard and its Revolutionary Tasks
13. The Congress studied the experience of the National Guards, and it considers this experience, despite its drawbacks and some mistakes that accompanied it, a bulwark for the protection of the revolution, to be developed and expanded so as to be able to perform revolutionary tasks in the field of socialist construction and in awakening the Arab popular masses. The Congress emphasized the necessity of taking a firm stand towards any errors into which the National Guard members may fall.

The Congress decided that labor, student, professional, and feminine popular organizations should have full freedom within a socialist and national framework. It emphasized the need for them to be independent of the state authority, so long as that authority is marching towards the socialist transformation and so long as the current situation has not yet been transformed into a socialist reality. The Congress considers the independence of these organizations to be a necessity dictated by the interests of those groups and classes. The Congress agreed to the right of the working class to go on strike.

Ideological Education in the Army

14. The Congress gave special attention to the ideological and doctrinal education of the Army. It emphasized the right of the military elements to exercise their full political rights. The Congress considers that an organic merger of the military and civilian revolutionary vanguards will bring about an ideological interaction between them, permitting unity of thought, permitting a direct and realistic joint approach to the problems of creating a socialist structure, and permitting a merger of the Army and the people into a joint revolutionary venture. The Congress concluded that the introduction of doctrinal education in the Army will create a new revolutionary understanding of discipline between the superior and his subordinate. The Congress emphasized also the importance of compulsory military service in an under-developed country, so that such service may become a training-ground for the peasant enlisted men, contributing to the overcoming of illiteracy and mental under-development in the rural areas. [. . .]

Position Toward ʿAbd al-Nasir (Nasser)'s System

20. The Congress studied ʿAbd al-Nasir's system in its positive and negative aspects. It emphasized the necessity of the presence of the UAR, with its overall and specific gravity, in any unity. The Congress considers that the positive aspects in al-Nasir's system drive the Party to accept al-Nasir's system as a partner in the unity but not as its foundation. The Congress considered that only such a form would give an opportunity to the operation of rectification and interaction between the Arab experiences. The Congress emphasized that it was al-Nasir himself who imposed on the Party a struggle which is only justified by the nature of the dictatorial and autocratic system of government which he himself exercises. The Congress drew attention in its resolutions to the fact that the present circumstances of Arab struggle require that this struggle be stopped, and that points of meeting and understanding be created between the liberative Arab movements on the level of the entire Arab country. [. . .]

Selected bibliography

ABDUL MALEK, ANOUAR, *Egypt: Military Society* (New York: Random House, 1968).

AFARY, JANET, The Iranian Constitutional Revolution, 1906–1911: Grassroots Democracy, Social Democracy, and the Origins of Feminism (New York: Columbia University Press, 1996).

ABRAMS, RUTH, 'Pioneering Representatives of the Hebrew People: Campaigns of the Palestinian Jewish Women's Equal Rights Association, 1918–1948', in Ian Fletcher, Philippa Levine, and Laura Mayhall (eds.), *Women's Suffrage in the British Empire: Citizen, Race and Nation* (New York: Routledge, 2000).

AHMED, LEILA, 'Early Feminist Movements in the Middle East: Turkey and Egypt', in Freda Hussain (ed.), *Muslim Women* (New York: St Martin's Press, 1984).

AL-RASHEED, MADAWI, *A History of Saudi Arabia* (Cambridge: Cambridge University Press, 2002).

AMANAT, ᶜABBAS, *Pivot of the Universe: Nasir al-Din Shah Qajar and the Iranian Monarchy, 1831–1896* (Berkeley: University of California Press, 1997).

ANTONIUS, SORAYA, 'Fighting on Two Fronts: Conversations With Palestinian Women', *Journal of Palestine Studies*, 8 (1979), 36–45.

ARJOMAND, KAMRAN, 'The Emergence of Scientific Modernity in Iran: Controversies Surrounding Astrology and Modern Astronomy in the Mid-Nineteenth Century', *Iranian Studies*, 30/1–2 (Winter/Spring 1997), 5–24.

ATAI, MUHAMMAD FARHAD, 'The Sending of Iranian Students to Europe, 1811–1906', Ph.D thesis, University of California, Berkeley (1992).

AVERY, PETER, GAVIN HAMBLY, AND CHARLES MELVILLE (eds.), *The Cambridge History of Iran: Volume 7: From Nadir Shah to the Islamic Republic* (Cambridge: Cambridge University Press, 1991).

BADRAN, MARGOT, *Feminists, Islam and Nation: Gender and the Making of Modern Egypt* (Princeton: Princeton University Press, 1994).

BAKHASH, SHAUL, *Iran: Monarchy, Bureaucracy and Reform Under the Qajars, 1858–1896* (London: Ithaca Press, for the Middle East Centre, St Antony's College, 1978).

BARBIR, KARL K., *Ottoman Rule in Damascus, 1708–1758* (Princeton: Princeton University Press, 1980), 108–77.

BARKEY, KAREN, *Bandits and Bureaucrats: The Ottoman Route to State Centralization* (Ithaca, NY: Cornell University Press, 1994).

BARON, BETH, 'Mothers, Morality and Nationalism in Pre-1919 Egypt', in Rashid Khalidi et al. (eds.), *The Origins of Arab Nationalism* (New York: Columbia University Press, 1991).

BAYERLE, GUSTAV, *Ottoman Diplomacy in Hungary* (Bloomington: Indiana University Press, 1972).

—— *The Hungarian Letters of Ali Pasha of Buda 1604–1616* (Budapest: Akadémiai Kiadó, 1991).

BEATTIE, KIRK J., *Egypt During the Nasser Years: Ideology, Politics and Civil Society* (Boulder, Col.: Westview Press, 1994).

BERBERIAN, HOURI, *Armenians and the Iranian Constitutional Revolution of 1905–1911: 'The Love for Freedom Has No Fatherland'* (Boulder, Col.: Westview Press, 2001).

BERNSTEIN, DEBORAH, *The Struggle for Equality: Urban Women Workers in Pre-State Israel* (New York: Praeger Press, 1987).

—— 'In Search of a New Female Identity: Pioneering Women in Pre-state Israeli Society', *Shofar: An Interdisciplinary Journal of Jewish Studies*, 9/4 (Summer 1991), 78–91.

—— (ed), *Pioneers and Homemakers: Jewish Women in Pre-State Israel* (Albany: State University of New York Press, 1992).

BOURNOUTIAN, GEORGE A., *A History of the Armenian People* (Costa Mesa, Calif.: Mazda Publishers, 1993).

BROWNE, EDWARD GRANVILLE, *The Persian Revolution of 1905–1909* (London: Frank Cass, 1966 [1910]).

CHAQUERI, COSROE, *The Armenians of Iran: The Paradoxical Role of a Minority in a Dominant Culture* (Cambridge, Mass.: Harvard University Press, 1998).

CUNO, KENNETH M., *The Pasha's Peasants: Land, Society, and Economy in Lower Egypt, 1740–1858* (Cambridge: Cambridge University Press, 1992).

—— and MICHAEL J. REIMER, 'The Census Registers of Nineteenth-Century Egypt: A New Source for Social Historians', *British Journal of Middle Eastern Studies*, 24/2 (1997), 193–216.

DARLING, LINDA T., 'The Finance Scribes and Ottoman Politics', in Caesar E. Farah (ed.), *Decision Making and Change in the Ottoman Empire* (Kirksville, Miss.: Thomas Jefferson University Press at Northeast Missouri State University, 1993), 89–100.

DAVISON, RODERIC J., *Essays in Ottoman and Turkish History, 1774–1923: The Impact of the West* (Austin: University of Texas, 1990).

DICKIN, PAUL, GEORGE COURTICE, *et al.*, *Nasser: A Personal View* (Film) (Cairo: AVE, 1988, 1986).

EHLERS, E. AND W. FLOOR, 'Urban Change in Iran, 1920–1941', *Iranian Studies*, 26/3–4 (1993), 251–75.

EKHTIAR, MARYAM, 'The *Dar al-Fonun*: Educational Reform and Cultural Development in Qajar Iran', Ph.D thesis, New York University (1994).

FAHMY, KHALID, *All the Pasha's Men: Mehmed Ali, His Army and the Making of Modern Egypt* (Cambridge: Cambridge University Press, 1997).

—— 'Women, Medicine and Power in Nineteenth-Century Egypt', in *Remaking Women: Feminism and Modernity in the Middle East* (Princeton: Princeton University Press, 1998), 35–72.

FLEISCHMANN, ELLEN, 'Young Women in the City: Mandate Memories', *Jerusalem Quarterly File*, 2 (Autumn 1998), 31–9.

—— 'Selective Memory, Gender and Nationalism: Palestinian Women Leaders in the British Mandate Period', *History Workshop Journal*, 47 (Spring 1999), 141–58.

—— 'The Other "Awakening": The Emergence of Women's Movements in the Middle East, c. 1900–1940', in Margaret Lee Meriwether and Judith Tucker (eds.), *A Social History of Women and Gender in the Modern Middle East* (Boulder, Col.: Westview Press, 1999).

—— 'The Emergence of the Palestinian Women's Movement, 1929–1939', *Journal of Palestine Studies*, 29/2 (Spring 2000), 16–32.

—— 'Nation, Tradition, and Rights: The Indigenous Feminism of the Palestinian Women's Movement (1920–1948)', in Ian Fletcher, Philippa Levine, and Laura

Mayhall (eds.), *Women's Suffrage in the British Empire: Citizen, Race and Nation* (New York: Routledge, 2000).

FLOOR, WILLEM, *The Traditional Crafts of Qajar Iran* (Costa Mesa, Calif.: Mazda Publishers, 2003).

FOGIEL-BIJAOUI, SYLVIA, 'On the Way to Equality? The Struggle for Women's Suffrage in the Jewish Yishuv, 1917–1926', in *Pioneers and Homemakers: Jewish Women in Pre-State Israel* (Albany: State University of New York Press, 1992).

FORTNA, BENJAMIN C., *Imperial Classroom: Islam, the State and Education in the Late Ottoman Empire* (Oxford: Oxford University Press, 2002).

GIACAMAN, RITA AND MUNA ODEH, 'Palestinian Women's Movement in the Israeli-Occupied West Bank and Gaza Strip', in Nahid Toubia (ed.), *Women of the Arab World* (London: Zed Press, 1988).

GORDON, JOEL, 'The False Hopes of 1950: The Wafd's Last Hurrah and the Demise of Egypt's Old Order', *International Journal of Middle East Studies*, 21/2 (May 1989), 193–214.

GURNEY, JOHN, AND NEGIN NABAVI, 'Dar al-Fonun', in *Encyclopedia Iranica*, 6 (Costa Mesa, Calif.: Mazda Publishers, 1993), 662–8.

HABIB, JOHN S., *Ibn Sa'uds Warriors of Islam: The Ikhwan of Najd and Their Role in the Creation of the Sa'udi Kingdom, 1910–1930* (Leiden: Brill, 1978).

HANAWAY, WILLIAM L., and BRIAN SPOONER, *Reading Nasta'liq: Persian and Urdu Hands from 1500 to the Present* (Costa Mesa, Calif.: Mazda Publishers, 1995).

HARRIS, CHRISTINA PHELPS, *Nationalism and Revolution in Egypt: The Role of the Muslim Brotherhood* (The Hague and Stanford, Calif.: The Hoover Institution, 1964).

HARRIS, R., *Murders and Madness: Medicine, Law and Society in the Fin de Siècle* (Oxford: Clarendon Press, 1989).

HEGYI, KLÁRA, 'The Ottoman Military Force in Hungary', in Géza Dávid and Pál Fodor (eds.), *Hungarian–Ottoman Military and Diplomatic Relations in the Age of Süleyman the Magnificent* (Budapest: Hungarian Academy of Sciences, 1994), 131–48.

HEYWORTH-DUNNE, J., *An Introduction to the History of Education in Modern Egypt* (London: Luzac & Co., 1939).

HOPWOOD, DEREK, *Syria: 1945–1986, Politics and Society* (London: Unwin, 1988).

HOVANNISIAN, RICHARD G. (ed.), *The Armenian People from Ancient to Modern Times* (New York: St Martin's Press, 1997).

HUNTER, F. ROBERT, *Egypt Under the Khedives, 1805–1879: From Household Government to Modern Bureaucracy* (Berkeley: University of California Press, 1984).

INALCIK, HALIL, and DONALD QUATAERT (eds.), *An Economic and Social History of the Ottoman Empire, 1300–1914*, 2 vols. (Cambridge: Cambridge University Press, 1994).

IZRAELI, DAFNA, 'The Zionist Women's Movement in Palestine, 1911–1927: A Sociological Analysis', *Signs*, 7 (1981), 87–114.

—— 'The Women Workers Movement: First Wave Feminism in Pre-State Israel', in *Pioneers and Homemakers: Jewish Women in Pre-State Israel* (Albany: State University of New York Press, 1992).

JAD, ISLAH, 'From Salons to Popular Committees: Palestinian Women, 1919–1989', in Jamal R. Nassar and Roger Heacock (eds.), *Intifada: Palestine at the Crossroads* (Birzeit and New York: Birzeit University and Praeger Press, 1991).

KANDIYOTI, DENIZ, 'Identity and its Discontents: Women and the Nation', *Millennium*, 20/3 (1991), 429–43.

KEDDIE, NIKKI, *Qajar Iran and the Rise of Reza Khan, 1796–1925* (Costa Mesa, Calif.: Mazda Publishers, 1999).

KHOURY, PHILIP, *Syria and the French Mandate: The Politics of Arab Nationalism, 1920–1945* (Princeton: Princeton University Press, 1987).

KIENLE, EBERHARD, *Baʿth vs. Baʿth: The Conflict Between Syria and Iraq, 1968–1989* (London: I.B. Tauris, 1990).

KOSTINER, JOSEPH, 'On Instruments and their Designers: The Ikhwan of Najd and the Emergence of the Saudi State', *Middle Eastern Studies* 21/3 (1985), 298–323.

—— *The Making of Saudi Arabia: From Chieftaincy to Monarchical State 1916–1936* (New York: Oxford University Press, 1993).

KUHNKE, LAVERNE, *Lives at Risk: Public Health in Nineteenth-Century Egypt* (Berkeley: University of California Press, 1990).

LAWSON, FRED H., *The Social Origins of Egyptian Expansionism During the Muhammad ʿAli Period* (Boulder Colo.:Westview Press, 1992).

LAYISH, AHARON, 'Ulema and Politics in Saudi Arabia', in Metin Heper and Raphael Israeli (eds.), *Islam and Politics in the Middle East* (London and Sydney: Croom Helm, 1984).

LEPS, M.-C., *Apprehending the Criminal: The Production of Deviance in Nineteenth Century* (Discourse: Duke University Press, 1992).

LITTLE, DOUGLAS, 'The New Frontier on the Nile: JFK, Nasser, and Arab Nationalism', *Journal of American History*, 75/2 (Sept. 1988), 501–27.

LIPPMAN, THOMAS W., *Egypt After Nasser: Sadat, Peace, and the Mirage of Prosperity* (New York: Paragon House, 1989).

MARSOT, AFAF LUTFI AL-SAYYID, *Egypt in the Reign of Muhammad Ali* (Berkeley: University of California Press, 1984).

MENASHRI, DAVID, *Education and the Making of Modern Iran* (New York: Cornell University Press, 1992).

MOGHANNAM, MATIEL, *The Arab Woman and the Palestine Problem* (London: Herbert Joseph, 1937).

MURPHEY, RHOADS, *Ottoman Warfare 1500–1700* (New Brunswick: Rutgers University Press, 1999).

MUSTAFA, AHMED ABDEL-RAHIM, 'The Hekekyan Papers', in P. M. Holt (ed.), *Political and Social Change in Modern Egypt* (London: Oxford University Press, 1968).

NAJJAR, ORAYB, AND KITTY WARNOCK, *Portraits of Palestinian Women* (Salt Lake City: University of Utah Press, 1992).

NYE, R. A., *Crime, Madness and Politics in Modern France: The Medical Concept of National Decline* (Princeton: Princeton University Press, 1984).

PASQUINO, P., 'Criminology: The Birth of a Special Knowledge', in G. Burchell *et al.*, (eds.), *The Foucault Effect: Studies in Governmentality* (Chicago: University of Chicago Press, 1991), 235–50.

PETEET, JULIE, *Gender in Crisis: Women and the Palestinian Resistance Movement* (New York: Columbia University Press, 1991).

POLK, WILLIAM, AND RICHARD CHAMBERS (eds.), *Beginnings of Modernization in the Middle East: The Nineteenth Century* (Chicago: University of Chicago Press, 1966).

RAFEQ, ABDUL KARIM, *The Province of Damascus, 1723–1783* (Beirut: Khayats, 1966), 189–92.

RAHNAMA, ALI (ed.), *Pioneers of Islamic Revival* (London: Zed Books, 1994).

RAʿIN, ISMAʿIL, *Iraniyan-i Armani* [Iranian-Armenians] (Tehran, 1349/1970).

REJALI, D. M., *Torture and Modernity: Self, State and Society in Modern Iran* (Boulder, Col.: Westview Press, 1994).

RINGER, MONICA, *Education, Religion, and the Discourse of Cultural Reform in Qajar Iran* (Costa Mesa, Calif.: Mazda Publishers, 2001).

RIVLIN, HELEN A. B., *The Agricultural Policy of Muhammad Ali in Egypt* (Cambridge, Mass.: Harvard University Press, 1961).

SANEY, P., 'Iran', in E. H. Johnson (ed.), *International Developments in Criminology, II* (Westport, Col.: Greenwood Press, 1983), 357–69.

—— 'Criminology', in E. Yarshater (ed.), *Encyclopaedia Iranica*, 6 (Costa Mesa, Calif.: Mazda Publishers, 1993).

SEALE, PATRICK, *Asad: The Struggle for the Middle East* (Berkeley: University of California Press, 1988).

SHAW, STANFORD J., *Between the Old and New: The Ottoman Empire Under Sultan Selim III, 1789–1807* (Cambridge, Mass.: Harvard University Press, 1971).

SIVAN, EMMANUEL, *Radical Islam: Medieval Theology and Modern Politics* (New Haven: Yale University Press, 1990).

SMITH, MARGARET, 'The Women's Movement in the Near and Middle East', *Asiatic Review* (Apr. 1928), 188–203.

SONBOL, AMIRA EL-AZHARY, *The Creation of a Medical Profession in Egypt, 1800–1922* (Syracuse, NY: Syracuse University Press, 1991).

STEIN, MARK L., 'Ottoman Bureaucratic Communication: An Example From Uyvar, 1673', *Turkish Studies Association Bulletin*, 20/1 (1996), 1–15.

STEPHENS, ROBERT, *Nasser: A Political Biography* (New York: Simon & Schuster, 1971).

SWEDENBURG, TED, *Memories of Revolt: The 1936–1939 Rebellion and the Palestinian National Past* (Minneapolis: University of Minnesota Press, 1995).

TATAR, M. LUSTMORD, *Sexual Murder in Weimar Germany* (Princeton: Princeton University Press, 1995).

TOLEDANO, EHUD, 'Mehmet Ali Paşa or Muhammad Ali Basha? An Historiographical Appraisal in the Wake of a Recent Book', *Middle Eastern Studies*, 21 (1985), 141–59.

VASSILIEV, ALEKSEI, *The History of Saudi Arabia* (London: Saqi, 1998).

WAHBA, SHAYKH HAFIZ, *Arabian Days* (London: Arthur Barker, 1964).

WALKOWITZ, J., *City of Dreadful Delight: Narratives of Sexual Danger in Late-Victorian London* (Chicago: University of Chicago Press, 1992).

WEDEEN, LISA, *Ambiguities of Domination: Politics, Rhetoric and Symbols in Contemporary Syria* (Chicago: University of Chicago Press, 1999).

WOODSMALL, RUTH, *Moslem Women Enter a New World* (New York: Round Table Press, 1936).

WRIGHT, DENIS, *The Persians Amongst the English* (London: I. B. Tauris, 1985).

ZAID, ABDULLAH S., 'The Ikhwan Movement of Najd, Saudi Arabia 1908–1930', Ph.D thesis, University of Chicago (1989).

2

Press, media, and society

Introduction

In the Middle East in the nineteenth century, the press developed into the main vehicle for mass communication. Initially fostered by modernizing states like the Ottoman Empire, Khedival Egypt, and Qajar Iran in the 1820s and 1830s, the press quickly diversified into numerous official, semi-official, and private publications surviving (or not) on an income derived from a combination of subvention, subscriptions, and advertisements. In addition to the importation and adaptation of printing technology from Europe, the periodical press in the Middle East became a forum for translated technical and cultural literature. The urge to educate the masses was a theme echoed by all participants in the press right through the middle of the twentieth century, when the commercial potential of the press seemed both more viable and less stigmatized. The twentieth century also witnessed the emergence of a professional class of journalists and editors who supplanted the idealistic amateurs, and of graphic artists who illustrated the newspapers to aid newly literate or illiterate readers' comprehension of ideas being discussed.

The press thrived alongside other communication technologies. Initially, it was the main means of distributing information from the telegraphic wire services. Starting in the 1920s, journalists commented on radio and cinema entertainment and, as the century progressed, print journalists teamed together with those media plus television to support co-ordinated commercial and political propaganda campaigns. Indeed, the state's reaction to the rise of the periodical press created the tension that persists today between freedom of expression and state censorship of the media. The contest between state censors and media participants has continued with the rise of the Internet in the twenty-first century. It is important to remember that the state's reaction to potentially subversive ideas transmitted over the Internet has its roots in the anxiety over subversive ideas transmitted through the press in the nineteenth century. The gradual diffusion of education and the rise in literacy in the Middle East in the twentieth century, coupled with the commercial viability and increasing diversity of the press and other media in the region, has ensured that new ideas about culture, religion, society, and the media itself have circulated despite state efforts to stem the tide.

The media is a critical source for the study of the modern Middle East, and many documents featured in other sections of this sourcebook are from the press and other media. The documents in this section have been selected to illustrate both attitudes toward the press itself and ways in which different participants used the press to reach a mass audience. Nonetheless, any press excerpt will offer a window on other issues and opinions that have shaped modern Middle Eastern societies.

2.1 'The Statement of Purpose' of an early official gazette in Qajar Iran, 1851

Camron Michael Amin

Preface

The Qajar Dynasty ruled Iran from 1797 to 1925, and Naser al-Din Shah (r. 1848–96) was its longest-reigning monarch. From 1848 to 1852 the young Naser al-Din's government was dominated by the personality of his prime minister, Mirza Taqi Khan Amir Kabir (d. 1852). Amir Kabir's brief time at the pinnacle of the Qajar bureaucracy reflected his ambition to modernize and centralize government. It was during his tenure as prime minister that a technical school modeled on Ottoman examples of education reform was established in Tehran, and with it, a government printing-house. The school, called the Dar al-Fonun, was intended to train modern officials for the bureaucracy and officers for a new military (see Sec. 1.7): eventually it became one of a number of government colleges consolidated as the University of Tehran in 1935. The Dar al-Fonun's printing-house produced textbooks, translations of European books, and, from 1851, government newspapers, magazines, and announcements, starting with *Vaqaye͑-e Ettefaqiyeh* ('Chronicle of Events').

In fact, *Vaqaye͑-e Ettefaqiyeh* was not the first Iranian government newspaper. The first was *Kaghaz-e Akhbar* ('Newspaper'), published for the government by Mirza Saleh Shirazi in 1837. Shirazi had been sent to England as a student in 1815, where he had acquired his interest in publishing and printing-presses. *Kaghaz-e Akhbar* was something of a latecomer to the world of government journalism in the Middle East. In Egypt, the independent-minded Ottoman governor Muhammad (Mehmed) ͑Ali had established *al-Waqayi͑ al-Misriya* ('The Egyptian Chronicle') in 1828. In 1831, under the direction of the Ottoman sultan, Memhed II, *Takvim-i Vekayi* ('Calendar of Events') was produced in the Ottoman capital, Istanbul. Although *Kaghaz-e Akhbar* was abandoned after a few years, Amir Kabir revived the idea of an official gazette. Like the Dar al-Fonun, *Vaqaye͑-e Ettefaqiyeh* survived its creator by many years. It was supported by a staff of government translators, writers, and editors under the auspices of the Office of Publications, which was established to supervise the production of all government publications and, eventually, to censor all publications produced in or imported into the Qajar Empire.

Text

The Newspaper of Tehran, the Capital[1]

Because His Most Sacred Imperial Majesty expends effort towards the education of the people of Iran, and towards informing them of internal affairs and foreign happenings, it was established that, from week to week, royal commands, internal news of the country and such things, which are called '*gazet*' in other realms, should be printed in the government printing-house and distributed to all the cities of Iran. Each week, the people of the Iranian Empire will also obtain information of celebrated commands from the capital and such things from [this newspaper]. One of the advantages of this *gazet* is that it is the cause of knowledge and clear-sightedness of the people of this sublime state. Another [advantage] is that the lying news of false rumors, which occasionally before this ([and] contrary to the commands of the *divan*[2] and the truth of the situation) was the cause of the error of the public mind in this empire, [and] in some of the cities and frontiers of Iran, henceforth shall be stopped by means of this newspaper. For this reason, it is necessary that all the trusted ones of the state of Iran and the governors of the provinces and the reliable functionaries and the honest subjects of this state have this newspaper, and in accordance with the above arrangement on Friday, 5 Rabi[c] II of the Year of the Dog, 1267 [7 February 1851], this work began. The supervisor will deliver these newspapers from week to week to whosoever seeks them.[3]

---

[1] The term *dar al-khilafa* (seat of the caliphate) is used, but this translation seems more appropriate.

[2] The *divan* is the council of the king's ministers and advisors.

[3] *Vaqayeʿ-e Ettefaqiye*, 5 Rabi[c] II, 1267 (7 Feb. 1851), 1.

2.2 Nationalist imagery in Egypt's tabloid presses: a drawing from the *Egyptian Papagallo*, 1904
Indira Falk Gesink

Preface

One of the most prominent features of life in early twentieth-century Egypt was the development of a nationalist movement directed specifically against British imperialism that had as its objective the independence of Egypt, which had been under direct British rule since 1882. Traditional accounts of the Egyptian nationalist movement detail the activities of Mustafa Kamil, the French-educated lawyer, journalist, and Nationalist Party leader, who demanded the unconditional and immediate withdrawal of British troops. When the British argued that their occupation had brought prosperity to the country, Mustafa Kamil retorted that: 'the chains of slavery are still chains, whether they be forged of iron or gold.'

During this period Egypt's public was becoming increasingly literate, and the last decade of the nineteenth century witnessed an explosion in the number of presses operating in its cities. Mustafa Kamil's political newspaper *Al-Liwa'* ('The Standard'), was one of the most popular papers of the early twentieth century. Between 1900 and 1904 one could find a copy in every café where men gathered together in the evenings to share a *shisha* (waterpipe) with their neighbors and catch up on the day's news.

As *Al-Liwa'* was one of few newspapers that could boast a large number of regular subscribers, Mustafa Kamil could afford both to have it machine-printed on durable paper and to maintain a staff of trained editors who ensured the quality of its classical literary Arabic. Most press owners, however, could not afford such quality. Much of the reading material available to Egyptian café patrons was not as neatly printed and was less eloquent and much less profitable than *Al-Liwa'*, to say the least. Yet, although some of these less profitable newspapers lasted only a few months, nonetheless they might acquire a certain degree of notoriety during that brief period. Especially popular were the 'tabloid presses', characterized by their ribald humour and ripe political sarcasm. Some tabloids were written in the colloquial dialects of Egypt, using an idiom more familiar to working people and peasants than *Al-Liwa's* classical Arabic. Moreover, as many of their readers could not actually *read*, these tabloids often employed drawings to convey their political messages.

The sample below is from a handwritten tabloid called the *Egyptian Papagallo*, printed by one ʿAbd al-Majid Kamil. This tabloid was printed only a few times before the government shut it down, but it achieved a small degree of lasting fame by libeling Egypt's chief jurisconsult, the Grand Mufti Muhammad ʿAbduh. The first issue, shown below, depicted a monkey in topcoat and hat, holding the leashes of trained dogs wearing Ottoman-style fezzes. In the background, a helmeted European is shown reading, while another grinning dog provides him with a seat. To Cairo's café audiences, the monkey clearly represented Great Britain and the dogs Egypt's Europeanized elite. Cows wearing turbans, which symbolized Egypt's religious scholars, lay somnolent in the foreground. Their complacent appearance conveyed the impression, popular at that time, that

2. A drawing from the *Egyptian Papagallo*, 1904

religious scholars had either accepted British rule, or were simply too involved in their own scholastic interests to rouse themselves on behalf of the nationalist effort.

Although the *Egyptian Papagallo*'s paper was of such poor quality that it barely survived the century, and although the ink showing through from the opposite side renders it almost illegible, this paper and others like it were staples of early twentieth-century Egyptian popular culture. They were imbued with the nationalist principles of Mustafa Kamil's *Al-Liwa'*, and played a significant role in the spread of nationalist ideas to the less literate audiences of urban workers and rural peasants.

2.3 'The world of journalism, or the reasons for the establishment of the newspaper *To'jjor*', 1907[4]
Adeeb Khalid

Preface

This editorial to the first issue of the Tashkent newspaper *To'jjor* ('Merchants') provides an excellent example both of the high hopes invested in the press by modernist reformers in Central Asia, and the difficult political situation that often set strict limits to their activity. The tone of earnest didacticism is also typical of the early twentieth century.

Intellectuals in the Muslim world shared the view of the newspaper as a source of enlightenment and a tool for the expression of political demands during this period. The political constraints were peculiar to Turkestan.[5] The October Manifesto, granted by Nicholas II as a result of the First Russian Revolution of 1905, promised freedoms of press, assembly, association, and speech, but the government treated these promises very much as temporary concessions, which it attempted to retract as soon as revolutionary activity eased. In Turkestan, a distant possession of the Russian Empire, the government's patience with opposition was even shorter. The first two non-official newspapers published in Turkestan were quickly banned.

The weakness of the market also set stringent limits on the utility of the newspaper. Despite the wealth of its founder, *To'jjor* lasted only three months before folding for economic reasons. The editorial is also interesting for the exploration of the idea of the nation (*millat*), which is defined in terms of a combination of language, territory, and faith, with explicit and implicit boundaries defining the community.

Despite the use of the first person by its author, the editorial is not signed. The editor of *To'jjor* was Said Karim Azimboyev, scion of the wealthiest Muslim family in Tashkent. He was active in public life and philanthropic causes. His father, Said Azimboy, was a leading merchant with extensive

---

[4] *To'jjor* (Tashkent), 21 Aug. 1907. *To'jjor* is the proper Uzbek transliteration for the word *tujjar* (Arabic) or *Tojjar* (Persian). It means 'merchants'.

[5] In contrast, other Central Asian states, such as Bukhara and Khiva, became Russian protectorates. While its administration had local peculiarities, Turkestan was a part of the Russian empire, ruled by a governor-general. In addition, there were other areas (the Tatar lands, Azerbaijan, Kazakhstan), also inhabited by Turkic-speaking Muslims, that had been conquered earlier (dating back to 1552), but where social and political developments were very different. The problem arises when people (including many academics) use 'Central Asia' to mean all Muslim areas ruled by Russia. Bukhara and Khiva remained separate until 1924, when they, together with Turkestan, were abolished and the whole of Central Asia delimited according to the national principle of the Soviet Union.

trading interests in Russia even before the Russian conquest of Tashkent in 1865. With the conquest, the new Russian authorities lionized him. Said Azimboyev received many decorations and became an important notable on whom Russian administrators depended for dealing with the native population. The wealth and the status remained in the family, and were inherited by Said Karim Azimboyev. Said Karim's interest in publishing *To'jjor* was part of his interest in public life. In 1909 he was one of the founders of the *Imdodiya* ('Aid') benevolent society, the first attempt at organized philanthropy among the Muslim population of Turkestan.

Text

O Co-religionists,

Our age is the age of the highest development of journalism. In the present age, the flame of journalism lights the heart of every nation, and the eyes of each nation are decorated with the mirror of the press. The press comprises newspapers and magazines published in each nation's own language. With these means, people become aware of the affairs of the world as well as those of their own situation. Thus it can be said the press is a mirror that shows the world. The press is a just ruler, before whom kings and paupers, rich and poor, friend and stranger all appear equal [. . .] the names of those who do good are made famous throughout the world and they are decorated with the medal of praise; and those who do evil are rendered notorious [. . .] and thrown into the prison of disgrace. The press is like an itinerant preacher who goes from city to city, street to street, encouraging people on the path of civilization and education, giving them sincere advice on the difference between good and bad, sin and virtue, and who thus becomes the source of the reform of the national and economic affairs of the people.[. . .]

O Brothers, don't you see that in our time there is not a single nation that doesn't have tens or hundreds of newspapers and magazines in its own language, for time itself deems any nation living in the twentieth century without a press in its own language to be savage and uncivilized. And indeed, this verdict is just, because today a nation living without a press is like a person living in a dark house without windows, unaware of the progress of ideas and deprived of the sun of civilization.

O Compatriots, don't you think that for a long time, we have lived with various kinds of superstition (e.g. our surroundings stand on the horn of a great bull . . . etc., etc.). By virtue of the Manifesto granted by our Emperor on 17 October 1905, we too acquired ten or fifteen newspapers and magazines and thus became aware of the world, and [able to] differentiate that which benefits us from that which harms us, and our friends from our enemies. But because these newspapers and magazines were in Turkish or Tatar, and not in the pure language of Turkestan, it was generally not possible for the Muslims of Turkestan to benefit from them. Instead, they were limited only to those among us who knew Turkish and Tatar, while the rest of us continued to exist without a press, unaware of the affairs of the world. Now it is obvious to any intelligent person that the solution to this is, of course, to publish a newspaper in the language of Turkestan, i.e. in Chaghatay.[6]

With this is mind, last year Ismail Abidov[7] and Munavvar Qori[8] published the newspapers *Taraqqiy* ('Progress') and *Xurshid* ('The Sun'),[9] but they were both shut down for being against our present government, and the Muslims of Turkestan were again left without a press, as if without a tongue and without ears.

For a long time, I have had the desire to provide a sincere service to my beloved nation, but was debating the best way to do so. Now I know that the Muslims of Turkestan require nothing more than a newspaper in their own language, because no matter what needs and rights we have, they cannot be acquired without a newspaper, for our age is the age of the press. This is an age in which needs, religious or worldly, national or economic, can only be demanded through the press (newspapers). Thinking of this, with the most honorable intentions, I acquired permission to publish *To'jjor*. While presenting this humble newspaper of mine to the exalted judgement of the readers, I also have a sincere request. In publishing this newspaper, my purpose is not personal gain, but rather to serve the nation to the best of my ability, for it is well known that those publishing newspapers suffer great losses. I nevertheless took on my own neck as heavy

[6] Chaghatay was the name of the Eastern Turkic literary standard (as opposed to Osmanli' (Ottoman), the Western predecessor of modern Turkish used in the Republic of Turkey). It was called many different things at the same time: Turki, Turkcha, Eastern Turkic, Chaghatay. By the turn of the twentieth century Chaghatay was being used synonymously with Uzbek. The Soviets called it 'Old Uzbek'. Until the 1920s it was written exclusively in the Arabic script. Then it became known officially as Uzbek, and has been written in about six different orthographies in three scripts.

[7] Ismail Abidi (Abidov) (b. 1880), a Tatar born in Kulja in Chinese (Eastern) Turkestan, and educated in Kazan and Moscow. He became interested in radical politics and joined the Social Revolutionary Party. He arrived in Tashkent not long before the revolution of 1905, and the following year began publishing *Taraqqiy* ('Progress'), one of the first non-official Uzbek-language newspapers.

[8] Munavvar Qori Abdurashidxon o'g'li, (also known as Munavvar xon Aburashidxonov), (1878–1931), was the leading reformist figure in Tashkent, the capital of Russian Turkestan. Born to a family of Islamic scholars, Munavvar Qori received a seminary education in Tashkent and Bukhara. He opened Tashkent's first new-method school in 1901, which soon became the largest and best-organized in the city. Munavvar Qori also wrote many textbooks for such schools, and ran a publishing house specializing in modernist works. He was also editor and publisher of *Xurshid*. He continued to work in the field of education in the early Soviet period, but fell foul of the regime by the late 1920s and was arrested and sent to prison camp in 1931.

[9] *Tarraqiy* was started in June 1906, and published nineteen issues before it was shut down in August 1906 by the courts for publishing an editorial containing unacceptable material. *Xurshid* began publishing in Tashkent in September 1906 under the editorship of Qori, but was closed down in November 1906 after only ten issues for 'its extremely harmful direction'.

and delicate a burden as publishing a newspaper. Now, I hope that my dear co-religionists will not leave me alone under this heavy burden, and will not spare me any material and moral support, because *To'jjor* is not just for me, but is the eyes, ears, and tongue of all of us, i.e. a great advocate for demanding our national and economic rights. There is also no fear that it will be shut down by the government, like *Taraqqiy* and *Xurshid*, for unlike them, the political and social position of *To'jjor* is not against the government, but rather it is to be the friend and supporter of the Russian State as long as our religion is not harmed. In addition, it will inform Turkestan Muslims of all sorts of useful articles and examples published in Russian and Muslim newspapers, and it will give the honorable readers news of the very latest happenings everywhere and of events in the police stations and other government offices. Since the name of our newspaper is *To'jjor*, we will also publish useful articles about commerce and serve merchants by providing information about prices of various commodities in each province. We will also keep the Muslims of Turkestan informed by printing letters to the editor containing various ideas and news, and telegrams from our reporters in every city containing all sorts of information.

2.4 The aftermath of revolution in the Ottoman cartoon space, 1909–1910

Palmira Brummett

Preface

Cartoons bridge the gap between what is imagined and real. The cartoonist plays upon the concerns of his or her audience, presenting images suggestive of how society is, or how it might be perceived. Those images may be designed to amuse, to criticize, or to spur the audience to action.

In 1908, prompted by the second Ottoman constitutional (or Young Turk) revolution, there was an explosion of publishing in Istanbul.[10] The pens of writers and cartoonists, long constrained by the vigorous censorship of the sultan, Abdülhamid II (r. 1876–1909), were suddenly active once again, producing over 200 new gazettes in the first year after the revolution. While some of the gazettes contained exclusively satirical articles, many others included cartoons. Ultimately, censorship was reimposed, but during the first years after July 1908 a dazzling and diverse array of publications, both primitive and sophisticated, emerged. Editors and cartoonists vigorously critiqued both the old regime and the new. They created and reflected the anxieties of a public long accustomed to monarchy and ambivalent as to whether a parliamentary regime could protect the empire. Their cartoons touched a raw nerve: they revealed the hopes, the fears, and the ironies circulating in the capital of an empire that had endured for over 500 years, but which was now faced with possible extinction.

Istanbul cartoons in the years immediately following the revolution were concerned with two primary themes: the threat of European political, economic, and cultural imperialism; and the general Ottoman condition. Cartoonists portrayed the Ottomans as being trapped between the old and the new, freedom and despotism. They suggested that the constitutional revolution might be a glorious event (similar to a distant and romanticized French Revolution), or one that was potentially disastrous (as in nearby Iran, which was plagued by a bloody civil war). Nor were they persuaded that European 'modernity', represented by constitutional government, women in French fashions, Western-style theatre, or a new calendar, would enhance the lives of the average Ottoman citizen.

---

[10] See Palmira Brummett, *Image and Imperialism in the Ottoman Revolutionary Press, 1908–1911* (Albany: State University of New York Press, 2000). On the Young Turks and their revolution, see Feroz Ahmad, *The Young Turks: The Committee of Union and Progress in Turkish Politics, 1908–1914* (Oxford: Oxford University Press, 1969); M. Şükrü Hanioğlu, *The Young Turks in Opposition* (New York: Oxford University Press, 1995) and *Preparation for a Revolution: The Young Turks, 1902–1908* (New York: Oxford University Press, 2001); and Erik Zürcher, *The Unionist Factor: The Role of the Committee of Union and Progress in the Turkish National Movement 1905–1926* (Leiden: E. J. Brill, 1984).

The two cartoons reproduced here reveal the fears and the realities of territorial loss suffered by the Ottomans in the aftermath of revolution. The empire had already lost Egypt and Cyprus to Britain during Abdülhamid's reign. Subsequently, only a few short months after the 1908 revolution, Austria-Hungary annexed Bosnia and Herzegovina in the Balkans. The Ottomans protested, but had little recourse except to launch a boycott of Austrian goods—an act that helped rally Ottoman support for the parliamentary elections and the new constitutional regime. Meanwhile, Russia was moving its troops into Iranian territory at the borders of the empire.

The Ottoman revolution occurred soon after a constitutional revolution in neighboring Iran. The Iranian revolution of 1905–6 resulted in intervention by imperialist European states and a protracted civil war from 1908 to 1909. Britain and Russia signed an agreement in 1907 to divide Iran into spheres of influence; and an autocratic new ruler, Mohammad ᶜAli Shah (r. 1907–9), fought the Iranian constitutionalists with the help of Russian Cossack brigades (see Sec. 1.9). The Ottoman constitutionalists did not ignore the problems that beset Iran during the aftermath of its revolution. They too feared reactionary monarchy and imperialist intervention, as evidenced by an Ottoman cartoon published in 1910 (Ill. 3).[11] The cartoon depicts Iran as a naked bather, immersed in the 'constitutional waters'. As he bathes, Britain and Russia run off with his clothes, which represent the two territories of Bouchire and Azerbaijan (in the south-west and north-west of Iran respectively). The bather cries out to an Ottoman soldier sitting on the bank of the river: 'Help, Help . . . While I was bathing in the constitutional waters, which for me are like the Water of Life, they stole my clothes!'

This cartoon, like many others published in the Ottoman press at the time, suggested the degree to which the Ottomans felt vulnerable in the aftermath of the Young Turk revolution. The empire had a long and glorious history under the rule of kings, whereas a parliamentary regime was untested. Ottoman editors and cartoonists feared that their own constitutional revolution might subject the empire to the same woes suffered by Iran. The 'constitutional waters' were life-giving, but 'bathing' in them left a state exposed and unprotected. The press suggested that Ottoman rivals, like a pack of hungry wolves, were drawn to the upheaval caused by revolution. Monarchical rule was problematic but familiar. Although modern readers may assume that constitutional government is a necessary good, for the Ottomans constitutional rule implied a new system, one that would take time to establish. In the meantime the empire might end up at the mercy of its enemies, as had occurred in Iran where Russia and Britain had intervened.

[11] *Kalem*, 104/7, 2 Kanun-ı evvel 1326/15 Dec. 1910. For Iranian press satire on the greed of Britain and Russia, see Hasan Javadi, *Satire in Persian Literature* (Rutherford: Farleigh Dickinson Press, 1988); and Janet Afary, *The Iranian Constitutional Revolution, 1906–1911: Grassroots Democracy, Social Democracy, and the Origins of Feminism* (New York: Columbia University Press, 1996), 131–44.

Le Persan. — Pendant que je me plongeais dans la jouvence Constitutionnelle, on m'a volé mes effets... Au secours! Au secours!

3. Cartoon published in the Ottoman gazette *Kalem* depicting Iran as a naked bather, immersed in the 'constitutional waters'

In this first cartoon, the 'stolen' territories of Iran are represented as essential parts of a man's clothing. Iran is 'naked' without them. Britain, Russia, and Iran are all embodied as male. In other cartoons, however, the state or its parts were embodied as female, revealing another, gendered dimension of satire and the contest for territory. For example, a cartoon published in the gazette *Kalem* shows how dress and gender figured in cartoonists' depictions of the Ottoman revolutionary struggle (Ill. 4).[12] The cartoon shows Bosnia and Herzegovina as two young women wearing exaggerated 'traditional' dress (harem pants, fezzes, sashes, and pointed shoes), being lured into the clutches of dirty-old-man Austria.[13] While they stand tentatively at an open gate, Austria, in the form of the aged emperor Franz Josef, in military uniform, beckons to them. 'Please Mesdemoiselles,' he says, 'Come. I've been waiting for you too long!'

[12] *Kalem*, 10/7, 23 Teşrin-i sani 1324/6 Nov. 1908. A similar cartoon in *Kalem*, 22/4, 15 Kanun-ı sani 1324/28 Jan. 1909, compares Bosnia and Herzegovina to Alsace and Lorraine (between France and Germany), all as female bodies representing contested territory.

[13] For broader treatments of the gendering of Ottoman cartoons, see Palmira Brummett, 'New Women and Old Nags: Images of Women in the Ottoman Cartoon Space', *Princeton Papers* (Spring/Summer 1997), 13–57; and 'Dressing for Revolution: Mother, Nation, Citizen, and Subversive in the Ottoman Satirical Press', in Zehra Arat (ed.), *Deconstructing Images of the Turkish Woman* (New York: St Martin's Press, 1998), 37–64.

L'Autriche racolle.

4. Cartoon published in the Ottoman gazette *Kalem* depicting Bosnia and Herzegovina as two young women wearing exaggerated 'traditional' dress (harem pants, fezzes, sashes, and pointed shoes) being lured into the clutches of dirty-old-man Austria

Although Austria had annexed Bosnia and Herzegovina outright on 5 October 1908 (a month before this cartoon was published), it had, in fact, occupied those territories since the Congress of Berlin in 1878. Nonetheless, in the Ottoman cartoon imagination Bosnia and Herzegovina were still parts of the empire, symbols of its integrity, its 'national' honor, and the rapacious nature of European aggressors. In the cartoon space, the struggle for territory was often cast in sexual terms, a battle of contending males for possession of the female. The cartoonist drew imperialist enemies such as Britain, France, Russia, and Austria as males, often in military dress. They, and other forces, attempted to snatch or seduce the empire or its parts, drawn as female, in 'traditional' or 'ethnic' dress. The female (a figure of the mother or the beloved) was depicted as being at risk and in need of protection. But in this cartoon there appear to be no Ottoman males to defend the young and attractive Bosnia and Herzegovina. Just like Iran bathing in the 'constitutional waters', they too are vulnerable. In both cartoons the 'nation' is shamed by the loss of its territories.[14] In the second cartoon, however, because that land is embodied in the female form, the 'nation' is doubly shamed. European aggressors would seem to have compromised not only the empire's territorial integrity, but its sexual honor as well.

[14] It is not, of course, entirely accurate to characterize either Iran or the Ottoman Empire at this time as 'nations': they were empires in transition. But the rhetoric of national identity was already in place in both states at this time and was intimately connected to the rhetoric of constitutional revolutions.

2.5 *Seruan Azhar*: a paper published by Southeast Asian students in Cairo, 1925
Michael Laffan

Preface

Although parts of Southeast Asia were formally Islamized by the late thirteenth century, Southeast Asians are first noted as being active participants in scholarly networks beyond the region in the late sixteenth century. By this time there was a small community of expatriate scholars studying in Arabia who were joined each year by fellow countrymen participating in the hajj. Over the following centuries, this expatriate community was instrumental in the further Islamization of their homelands.

By the late nineteenth century there was also an intensification of colonial control throughout the Muslim world, and new modes of thinking, pioneered in Cairo by the modernist Muhammad ᶜAbduh (1849–1905), proved very attractive to many Malay students abroad. A smaller community therefore developed around the student lodgings at the Al-Azhar mosque, where these students were personally connected with ᶜAbduh's follower Rashid Rida (1865–1936), who promulgated his ideas of religious reform, and the material advancement of Muslims through modern education and the press.

Like Rida, many Malay reformers were also interested in publishing their ideas. Some had already launched periodicals in Southeast Asia modelled on Rida's *Al-Manar*. Meanwhile, the first Malay periodical to appear in the Middle East was *Al-Ittihad*, which served briefly as the mouthpiece of some twenty students enrolled at Al-Azhar at the end of 1912. The advent of World War I meant that such activities had to be put on hold. After the war the community rebuilt quickly, with students numbering around 150 by the mid-1920s. This time these students were drawn from a wider range of Southeast Asian communities, including Javanese and some Patani Malays from Southern Thailand. The increase in student numbers merited the publication of another periodical, and in October 1925 a second Malay paper was released in Cairo.

The following extract was written by one of the key movers of that paper, Mahmud Yunus (1899–1982). This Sumatran had moved to Cairo in 1925, where he remained for five years. He would become the first Indonesian to graduate from Cairo's modern Dar al-ᶜUlum, and his later career was devoted to Islamic education, culminating in the establishment in present-day Jakarta of the Syarif Hidayatullah Institute, now the Universitas Islam Negeri. He is well known as the author of many Indonesian textbooks and histories, including *The History of Islamic Education in Indonesia*, and a Malay–Arabic dictionary.

Text[15]

Praise be to Almighty God who sent the messenger to call to all people, great and small. Peace and blessings to our Prophet Muhammad possessed of faith and truth, and upon his family and clever companions.

Thus said, this journal (periodical)[16] called *Seruan Azhar* is put out by the students[17] living in the city of Cairo at the Azhar Mosque. This journal emerges[18] from the East like [the sun at] dawn, giving light and illumination to their homeland, bringing knowledge of this life and that to come, and many lessons besides. It calls their homeland to the broad and expansive field of progress, calling for the study of the sciences of religion and the world that bring benefit. It calls so that all of us awaken and become aware, because the foreign peoples have already raced to the field of progress and have laboured [hard there]. It is appropriate that we should emulate [them] and draw a lesson [from this].

Seruan Azhar calls upon all mothers and fathers whoever they are. We call on our children to study religion and to enact it whilst going to primary school. And if, thereafter, the child likes the study of religion, then encourage him to study it as deeply as possible. Or should he[19] be attracted to medicine, agriculture[20] or the advanced sciences, then let him continue his schooling. And should he be attracted to some other form of expertise not forbidden by religion, then urge him to complete its study and not quit halfway through lest our fees be wasted.

Seruan Azhar calls upon the kings or heads of state to be ready to dispatch students to other countries, whether to Europe or Egypt, in order to study at advanced schools. This is because fathers and mothers alone cannot afford the fees. Therefore we should all bear them together because the benefit is for the people (*isi negeri*), and for the future, which the kings and heads of state will administer together.

[15] Extract from *Seruan Azhar: Surat kabar bulanan menyeru menuntut pengetahuan, kemajuan dan persatuan. Diterbitkan oleh pemuda-pemuda bangsa kita di Mesir* ('The Call of Al-Azhar: A monthly periodical advocating the search for knowledge, progress and unity, published by the youth of our people in Egypt'), 1/1 (Rabiᶜ al-akhir 1344/Oct. 1925), 3–5.

[16] The article often features alternative glosses in round brackets. In this case the word for journal (*majalah*) is followed in brackets by the word for newspaper (*surat khabar*). Material in square brackets is my addition or interpolation.

[17] The Malay word *penuntut* is a direct translation of the Arabic word *talib*. Both mean 'a seeker' of knowledge.

[18] The word for 'published', *diterbitkan*, is also a pun on its alternative meaning as 'the rising' of the sun.

[19] The Malay third-person is not gendered; however, as all the students concerned here were male, I have maintained the masculine form.

[20] Here the first word used is the Dutch *landbouw*, which would have been familiar to readers from the Netherlands Indies, and is followed by the Malay gloss: *bercu'cu' tanam*, for those readers in the Malay Peninsula.

Seruan Azhar calls to its people who are wealthy and with possessions that it is fitting to disperse a small portion of this wealth for the support[21] of students, to found schools or for whatever general good is of benefit. This is because Almighty God has given His grace to them and it is obligatory to show gratitude to God by spending this [wealth] to advance one's people and homeland.

Seruan Azhar calls to its people who have rank or position that it is fitting to carry out your work rightly and appropriately. Do not exceed your authority, which has been fixed in order to advance the people and homeland, [rather] be willing to sacrifice it because 'to love the homeland is a part of belief'.[22]

Seruan Azhar calls to its people who till the soil, who trade or who labour as coolies: none of your work is scorned by religion, but rather it urges that you carry it out diligently and with a genuine intention to obtain wealth to advance the people. Recall the saying of our Prophet [Muhammad], God's peace and blessings be upon Him, the meaning of which is approximately: 'There will come a time when you still seek dirhams (silver coins) and dinars (gold coins) to support your world and your religion.' Isn't this the time in which we now find ourselves? Isn't money now useful to establish religion and to advance the land? Why not indeed? It takes money to establish schools, it takes money to go to school, it takes money to buy books—yes—everything needs money these days.

Seruan Azhar calls to the youth and students of like age—whether in Europe or in our homeland—to race together, with diligence and effort, in search of knowledge of science, and of this world and that to come, so that we might advance our homeland and people. Certainly such knowledge should not be like what the old people say:

> Hunt in the plain
> And catch the deer with banded legs,
> But to seek the most distant teacher
> Is like having a bloom that never opens.[23]

For instance, brothers who study religious science, astronomy, natural science, mechanics,[24] medicine, agriculture, chemistry, history, literature, education, engineering, geography, and all the other sciences; let it be with absolute

---

[21] Here the Sanskrit-derived *derma* is followed by the Arabic *sadaqa*.

[22] This is a Malay version of the popular Arabic tradition that 'love of the homeland is a part of belief' (*hubb al-watan min al-iman*). Some reform-minded intellectuals, attracted to the notion of cultivating nationalism and patriotism in the Middle East in the nineteenth century, circulated this tradition as though it were a Hadith (report about the life and sayings of the Prophet Muhammad). It is not.

[23] *Berburu ke padang datar dapat rusa belang kaki, berguru ke paling akhir seperti bunga kembang ta'jadi.* The format of this poem conforms to a traditional Malay quatrain known as a *pantun*. In this case it implies that the search for distant knowledge is a pointless quest, whilst to hunt in nearby fields will reap the prized result.   [24] Again this has a Dutch (*mekanika*) and English (*meshin*) gloss.

diligence in order to obtain a diploma. So it should be too with those brothers who study foreign languages, such as Arabic, French, English, Dutch, and other such languages. There is no point to the lassitude of indolence having not obtained perfection.

Seruan Azhar calls to its people in general, be they in Java or Sumatra, or even in Borneo and the Malay Peninsula: Let all of you be as one heart and mind [on the path] to the field of progress, seeking the general good and averting that which is evil.[25] Let us not break up into factions. Remember what our Prophet said [in Arabic]: *al-jamaʿa rahma wa al-firqa naqma.* This means that to join together (in agreement) brings mercy whilst to break into factions brings misery and suffering.

Seruan Azhar calls and prays to God: Oh God, strengthen our unity and grant long life to this [journal] *Seruan Azhar,* and may it be received warmly by its people who will send in subscriptions. Amen, O Lord of the Worlds.

Mahmud al-Yunusi [of] Batu Singkar,
A graduate of Al-Azhar

[25] This pairing of enjoining good and prohibiting evil is found repeatedly in the Qur'an. See e.g. Q. 3: 104, 'Let there arise from you a community, inviting to all that is good, enjoining what is right and forbidding evil.'

2.6 Journalism in Egypt in the 1920s and 1930s: from *The Education of Salama Musa*, 1947[26]
From the Islamfiche *project*

Preface

When *The Education of Salama Musa* was first published in 1947, the author was 60 years old and could look back on a prolific career as one of Egypt's most iconoclastic writers. Despite his rejection of traditional society and culture, Musa himself came from a conservative, wealthy, Coptic (Christian) family in Egypt. He was the sixth and youngest child of a provincial landlord and local official and was raised and educated in the Delta town of Zagaziq. Growing up Christian in a Muslim society greatly influenced Musa, doubtless contributing to the development of his critical attitudes toward the customs of his homeland.

In addition, like other liberal intellectuals of his generation, Musa witnessed an age of conflicting values and loyalties for middle-class Egyptians and especially the intelligentsia. On the one hand, they admired European society for its relative openness in politics and social relations; on the other hand, their country was occupied and controlled by the same Europeans. The tensions inherent in such a situation were more difficult for some writers than others. Salama Musa apparently resolved the conflict for himself by advocating a Westernization program that was more thorough and radical than that proposed by other Egyptian intellectuals of his time.

This generation was in agreement in feeling a strong obligation to use its education for the enlightenment of the Egyptian public. A popular press developed and expanded significantly during the first quarter of the twentieth century; it was frequently owned and written by liberal Christian Arabs, often of Syrian and Lebanese background. Musa gained his reputation as a provocative writer through his work for such journals, where he especially liked to expound on the superiority of modern science over traditional religious belief. He was also one of the first of his time to identify himself as a socialist, although his socialism was of the liberal, parliamentary variety.

In this selection, Musa provides a window on the vitality of intellectual life in Cairo in the 1920s and 1930s, especially in the field of journalism. His career spanned a period in which a private Arab press emerged, thrived in British-occupied Cairo (the 'capital of Arab journalism', in the words of historian Ami Ayalon), and became a cultural

---

[26] Salama Musa, *The Education of Salama Musa*, trans. L. O. Schuman (Leiden: E. J. Brill, 1961), 123–33. Original Arabic Source: *Tarbiyat Salama Musa* (Cairo, 1947).

institution (albeit an embattled one) with the rise of quasi-independent Arab nation-states.

Text

Culture is either stagnant, or struggle and movement. It is stagnant when it is concerned with subject matters that do not give rise to discussion. Such a situation may be due to the state of society itself being stable, when it is embedded in an unchanging milieu, an agricultural milieu for instance; or it may be due to a society having lost its right of self-destination, when it is governed as a colony or part of an empire. We were in that condition for about forty years, from 1882 till 1922. During that period, our society was robbed, and divorced from its own governmental management, until at last we had our rights established in the Constitution.

The British caretakers of course had no use for newspaper discussions on such subjects as education, health conditions, or economics. I remember that the late ʿIwad Wasif,[27] writing in the first issue of his magazine *Al-Muhit* in 1903 that political and governmental affairs would be regularly dealt with in it, was promptly brought down to earth by *Al-Muqtataf* which argued it would be completely useless to do so, as those who were managing our affairs, the British, could not read Arabic.

Yet there was, in those days, a certain measure of discussion in our society. There was a religious debate going on about the reforms advocated by Muhammad ʿAbduh,[28] and there was a social debate going on in which Qasim Amin played the leading part; and those debates were very lively indeed. But on the whole our position in those years must have resembled that of Czarist Russia, where the intellectuals were prevented from criticizing political affairs, and therefore turned to literature. In Egypt, we were likewise prohibited any form of criticism on politics and government; and we turned to social questions.

When I was first becoming intellectually and culturally conscious, I found myself greatly stimulated by the magazines *Al-Muqtataf* ('Selections'),[29] *Al-Hilal* ('The Crescent'),[30] and *Al-Jamiʿa* ('The Community').[31] I must say that I

---

[27] ʿIwad Wasif was a journalist and minor author, who published a book on King Alexander and Queen Draga of Serbia (murdered in 1903), and a book on Japan in 1906.

[28] The most important and influential of the early twentieth-century Islamic modernists.

[29] This was a scientific and literary magazine founded in Beirut in 1875 by Faris Nimr (1857–1951) and Yaʿqub Sarruf (1852–1927), two instructors at the Syrian Protestant College (later the American University of Beirut). It moved to Cairo in 1884 and continued for seventy-five years. Ami Ayalon, *The Press in the Arab Middle East: A History* (New York: Oxford University Press, 1995), 50–69.

[30] This magazine was founded by Jurji Zaydan (1861–1914) in 1892, and was still being published 100 years later. Zaydan, a Christian, was originally from Beirut and moved to Cairo in 1886.

[31] Farah Antun (1874–1922) was a Christian Lebanese journalist who immigrated to Cairo in 1897 and, along with *Al-Jamiʿa*, began a long intellectual rivalry with the Islamic revivalist Rashid Rida (d. 1935), publisher of *Al-Manar* ('The Minaret'). While Rida saw himself as the bearer of the

was rather contented with their cultural approach, and I think that, but for the Dinshaway[32] incident, I would not have turned to politics; at any rate, that event shocked me so much that I set myself to study its origins and to trace in much detail the political developments in Egypt during the first decade of the present century.

On the other hand, the theory of evolution as I had understood it from *Al-Muqtataf* was the germ from which sprouted my whole personal culture. It stimulated me to acquire both knowledge and method, and it also provided me with a criterion by which I classed all authors and thinkers as either friends or opponents. At the same time it made the habit of struggle take firm root in my heart, for the idea of evolution was contrary to all our accepted convictions and traditions, so it had to be defended. Once adopted, and after it had been focused for the sake of defending the idea of evolution, my attitude of struggle also came to cover other subjects, and I think this explains why I never withdrew to hide in an ivory tower. The leading idea of evolution, applied to social and scientific thought, made me continually doubtful and strongly inquisitive. All my standards changed and were replaced by new values; in a rather immature form, these may be found in *The Advent of Superman*, which I wrote when I was only nineteen years old. In that essay I discussed how, in my opinion, socialism, eugenics, evolution, and new political and social conditions would together produce Superman, a higher species of man, who would be advanced over us as much as we are advanced over the chimpanzee. But my thought was at that time still very close to what might be designated as 'scientific occultism,' in which scientific elements were still blended with former religious concepts. In that year, 1909, I also contributed an article to *Al-Muqtataf* under the title *Nietzsche and the Son of Man*, while for *Al-Hilal* I wrote an article on socialism; I called it *al-ijtima'iya*, as I found this word was closer to the European concept of socialism than the word *al-ishtirakiya*, which we now commonly use for it. I also wrote another essay on these subjects, which I sent to *Al-Muqtataf* to be printed. They returned the manuscript to me, while I was still in London, with only eight pages of it printed, apologizing for not printing the rest of it because of the prevailing Egyptian laws under which it was a punishable offence to divulge such opinions. I had to pay the printing expenses of those eight pages.

Herbert Spencer used to say that he was able to assess anybody's intellectual level after having talked with him for a few moments. By this, he meant of course that we have certain words or expressions that have some central function in our

authentic legacy of the Islamic modernist Muhammad Abduh, Antun was influenced by the secularism of Ernest Renan. Ayalon, *The Press*, and Albert Hourani, *Arabic Thought in the Liberal Age, 1798–1939*, 2nd edn. (Cambridge: Cambridge University Press, 1983), 253–9.

[32] The site of a 1906 incident where British officers murdered an Egyptian peasant. This was a very radicalizing event for the Egyptian intelligentsia.

mind and which we use so often that they are a sure indication of our interests, and therefore of our personal culture, materially as well as ethically. When I look at myself in order to ascertain what expressions I have used most often in my writings, I find that I am always using the words evolution, international, freedom for women, the sciences, industrial civilization, reactionary, the future—all words, therefore, that call for change from us. In fact, I find that my ideas about politics and culture have always been leftist, and on the whole prospective and progressive. It is remarkable that all authors in Egypt have started their literary careers as adherents of some progressive, pioneering doctrine, and that so many of them have ended by turning again to the traditions that bind us to the past, instead of continuing to prospect the future. Similarly, I find I have shown a democratic *parti-pris* in all my writings, which made me relentlessly struggle against the tyrannies that still live in the Arab East, keeping the people down economically and socially as well as in matters of conscience. My standpoint was never changed, whether as a leftist writer I was struggling against the reactionaries who found their only wisdom in the past, or against the feudalists who opposed the advent of democracy among the Arab peoples. To a certain extent of course my leftist attitude was due to cultural influences that came with my economic and social position, namely, my belonging to a Christian minority. The Jews, as a European minority, always were and still are the bearers of the standard of leftist culture there, in matters of politics and society generally as well as in economy.

My journalistic life in Egypt was indeed cultural to the highest degree. As early as 1914, I produced the magazine *Al-Mustaqbal*, which I wanted to make an instrument for the struggle of mind. I did not discuss political issues in it—but of course I could only issue sixteen numbers. Shibli Shumayyil[33] was one of its editors and supporters. After that, I worked on *Al-Hilal*, and next on *Al-Balagh*.[34] While working on that last paper I became in fact enmeshed in politics, but my first concern and my main interest remained in the literary page. Then, there were three books: *The Theory of Evolution and the Origin of Man, Egypt and the Origin of Civilization*, and *Renewal in Modern English Literature*, all of which I had published in installments in *Al-Balagh* before they appeared in book form. In that time I always received much encouragement from ᶜAbd al-Qadir Hamza.[35]

I was editor of *Al-Hilal* from 1923 till 1929. It was part of the conditions of my work there that I should write a new book every year, which was to fill the gap of the vacations when the magazine was discontinued for two months. Some of

---

[33] The first 'official' socialist in the Arab world; a Syrian Christian popularizer of science.

[34] This paper served as an unofficial organ of the Wafd Party in Egypt. It was first published by ᶜAbd al-Qadir Hamza in January 1923.

[35] ᶜAbd al-Qadir Hamza is considered a minor author; in 1923 he published *On the Victims of the Passion for Gambling*.

these books were for entertainment only, such as *The Most Famous Love Stories in History*, which I composed in the routine of my daily work, without spending much effort on it. But others required much study and research, so that I did my writing and learning at the same time. Such was the case of *Freedom of Thought and the Story of its Pioneers*, and *The Subconscious*. As a matter of fact, this book-writing while I was editing *Al-Hilal* was rather like going to school again, and I must say that this period taught me much that was very useful for future work. In the meantime, some articles that I had published in *Al-Hilal* and *Al-Balagh* caught the attention of other publishers. They were reprinted in collections entitled *Selections from Salamah Musa, Today and Yesterday*, and *Life and Literature*.

I was quite happy on account of my literary output. Though it brought me little material gain, I was gratified because I was continuing my own education and at the same time contributing to the overall change in mentality and public opinion, which was then gradually taking place. These changes certainly amounted to an evolution among the reading public, and sometimes even to a revolution. In those years between 1923 and 1929, a good deal of dust was raised in Cairo as everybody, each according to his temperament and his personal outlook, took part in very lively discussions on all sorts of questions connected with renovation in matters of culture. I think the various modernizing tendencies that were advocated with so much energy could now be summarized as follows:

1. We ought to have a modern Egyptian literature, which must not be based upon the classical Arabic literature.

2. We ought to have a modern mode of expression, an idiom that must not laboriously cultivate its relationship with Al-Jahiz[36] and the like, but to the contrary enter into a vitalizing flirtation with the colloquial language—provided that this flirtation be conducted chastely.

3. We must take to European standards and values in literary criticism, without bothering about the example of ancient critics and their values, like Al-Jurjani[37] or Ibn al-Athir[38] or Ibn Rashiq.[39]

4. We must connect literature with the life of society, and treat social subjects as subjects of literature, integrating ourselves with its problems.

5. We should introduce to the Egyptian public the novel and the theatre.

---

[36] The reference means: we don't have to use elegant but incomprehensible language. Al-Jahiz was a writer of the classical Islamic period.

[37] Al-Jurjani: probably Abu Bakr ʿAbd al-Qahir al-Jurjani, a philologist, author of *Asrar al-Balagha*, d. 1078 CE.

[38] Ibn al-Athir was the name of three princely brothers, all of whom lived about 1200 in Syria. One of them achieved lasting fame as the author of important historical works.

[39] Ibn al-Rashiq was a historian and philologist who lived in North Africa about 1025.

6. We have to make literature serve the common interest of humanity, and make it respond to the problems of the world at large.

The author, in comparison with the journalist, is considered to live the secluded life of a monk. He withdraws in his room, to study and do research, whereas the journalist goes out in order to mix with people, and to report on society. Though most of my work as a journalist was of a cultural character, as it consisted of scientific and literary studies, I also came in touch with politics. Occasionally the dust whirled so high about me that the inference of such a violent storm shocked me, but on second thoughts I was confronted by the idea that what was blowing at me was also blowing throughout the nation, and that by my journalistic struggle I helped in the struggle for democracy, of which the tyrants tried to deprive us.

My very first experience in journalism has been in connection with *Al-Liwa'* ('The Banner') in 1909. As I have already stated, I worked on it some four months, together with Farah Antun. Our chief, 'Uthman Sabri, a brother-in-law to Mustafa Kamil,[40] was a cultured and enlightened man. He had taken charge of the paper after the late Shaykh 'Abd al-'Aziz Jawish—the one who angered the Copts by the use of improper words. We supported the demand for evacuation, writing that there should be no negotiations until after the evacuation. At that time, some Egyptian leaders repudiated this formula, but nowadays nobody would repudiate it. The Indians acted upon this principle when, throughout World War II, they insisted on their demand with the watchword: 'Leave India!'

Farah, as long as I worked with him on *Al-Liwa'*, believed that I was a Muslim, because my name admits both Muslim and Coptic connotation, whereas in the things I wrote there was never any sign of a special group allegiance. 'Uthman Sabri knew that I was a Copt. He often spoke to me of the articles of Shaykh 'Abd al-'Aziz despisingly, and carefully avoided publishing any articles that might have prejudiced the fraternization between Muslims and Copts. I acquired at *Al-Liwa'* a good training in journalism, writing reports and articles on domestic and foreign affairs. There was not really much scope for a reporter in those days, as the newspapers were editorial rather than informative. The struggle for independence absorbed nearly all our energy, and most of our writing staff consisted of editors.

In the first decade of this century, *Al-Liwa'*, which was the Nationalist Party's mouthpiece, set the tone for our new journalism. It was quite successful. Its methods were essentially didactic, as Mustafa Kamil had formed the correct opinion that a newspaper's main task was to serve the cause of nationalism by stirring the people's enthusiasm and stimulating their national consciousness.

---

[40] The founder of the modern Egyptian nationalist movement, who became the leader of the National Party after Dinshaway. He founded *Al-Liwa'* in 1900. Ayalon, *The Press*, 50–60.

Therefore, not much care was given to covering the foreign news; all international news reports were summarized in half a column or a quarter of a column of telegrams. As most other papers also criticized the English occupation or tried to stir up the public mind in some other way, a journalist's first duty was to write clearly and with much fierceness. This situation prevailed until about 1930, when the papers began to give 'news' instead of 'editorials'. But even at present, we still find journalists of the old stamp who care for cultivated language more than for improved knowledge of international, scientific, or social problems, and as a matter of fact among the public there are still those who have a predilection for reading that old-fashioned sort of writing.

In those days, the newspapers were still 'personal', in so far as we used to read them not because of the news or pictures they contained, but because of the particular authors who were on their staff. Discussions also had a personal character. *Al-Mu'ayyad* ('Empowered')[41] for instance was vituperative with Mustafa Kamil, because the Khedive had slapped him, and *Al-Liwa'* was constantly attacking Shaykh ʿAli Yusuf, the owner of *Al-Mu'ayyad*, for his not being a suitable match for the Princess Safiya. Even *Al-Muqattam*[42] entered into this quarrel to add its share in the discussion of ʿAli Yusuf's marriage.

The first comic paper had made its appearance about 1900.[43] It contained many derisive comments about Muhammad ʿAbduh, the Great Imam. Rumor had it that the Khedive ʿAbbas Pasha was encouraging this attitude, because he hated the modern spirit of thought advocated by the imam in Al-Azhar.

I think I was the first to produce a weekly magazine. When I had left *Al-Liwa'* and returned to Europe, I could not take my mind off the idea to try my hand at publishing. When I came back to Egypt, my plans quickly matured, and in 1914 I managed to publish the weekly paper *Al-Mustaqbal*. However, when the Great War started, and the price of newsprint went up to ten times higher than what it used to be, I had to discontinue the work after only sixteen issues. There was another reason compelling me to stop, for just when I was going to close down on account of the soaring paper prices, I was summoned by the Directorate of Press Affairs. Though there were many rumors about newspapers and magazines going to be suppressed, I went there without suspicion. There I sat, opposite one of the Syrian officials, who just began a friendly chat and ordered coffee. While he was asking me about the magazine, and enquiring whether it was going well or

---

[41] This daily paper was founded in 1889 by ʿAli Yusuf (1863–1913) with the support of the khedival family. It had an anti-British tone and took care to cultivate an Islamic perspective on the news. Ayalon, *The Press*, 56–60.

[42] The name of the paper is a reference to hills east of Cairo: it was founded by the publishers of *Al-Ahram* with support from the British government in 1889 (indeed, *Al-Mu'ayyad* was a response to it). Ayalon, *The Press*.

[43] See examples of cartoons and satire in the press in the present chapter, especially the document by Indira Falk Gesink (Sec. 2.2).

whether I was losing on it, he sent to ask an Englishman in. The latter sat down in front of me without saying a word. The Syrian official then proceeded to explain how difficult the situation was, and that it would be necessary to suspend (to *suppress* was of course what he meant) publication of certain papers. Though I did not mind anymore to discontinue publication of my magazine, I was tempted to seek more elucidation for psychological reasons, especially in front of that Englishman. So I stated that I was quite capable to continue publishing *Al-Mustaqbal* regardless of any financial difficulties. I must say that I rather enjoyed seeing them look at each other when I boldly went on to say that I wanted to keep on publishing the paper until the end of the war, and that I intended to use it for the promotion of socialism. When the Syrian official again tried to placate me, addressing me very politely as *ustadh*[44] and explaining that I, as an intellectual . . . etc., I stubbornly repeated my intentions. Finally he became so angry that he forgot his suave demeanor. He shouted that the Directorate of Press Affairs had the competence to enforce suppression of any paper whose influence was considered undesirable, and that anybody opposing the law under the present exceptional conditions exposed himself to arrest or exile. That was what I wanted to hear, so I got up, told them that I would stop publication of the magazine, and left them without another word.

I am not myself in possession of a complete set of *Al-Mustaqbal*, but some readers have kept those sixteen issues bound in one volume. Its articles furnish an indication as to how and what I thought at that time. Some were on Nietzsche, and one, entitled 'Allah,' contained an unrestrained exhibition of my unbelief. Besides that, there were poems and articles by Shibli Shumayyil advocating the theory of evolution and materialistic doctrine. In short, *Al-Mustaqbal* stood for extreme modernism,[45] and even futurism. We usually sold about 600 copies per week, not counting the subscriptions of enthusiastic socialists, and I believe that we might have succeeded to carry out the mission of demolition and reconstruction we were so much in need of, but for the circumstances of the war of 1914. After *Al-Mustaqbal*, no other magazine was edited on similar lines. When I prepared to produce *Al-Majalla al-Jadida* in 1929, I had already been influenced by the persistent tradition in our journalism, as well as tamed miserably by Egyptian conditions at large. The fire was extinguished, my enthusiasm frustrated: moderation had taken the place of exaggeration.

After the suppression of *Al-Mustaqbal*, I received a letter from Mayy in which she asked me to become editor of *Al-Mahrusa*, a daily paper of limited

---

[44] A word of Persian origin used with the meanings of 'master in an art or profession', 'doctor', 'professor'.

[45] Here: a mode of analysis using modern scientific method, as opposed to older religious forms of thought.

circulation published by her father.[46] I accepted and worked with them for several months; but soon I was fed up with having to write under the excessively sharp censorship of the Directorate of Press Affairs. My hardship was only mitigated by Mayy's friendliness when she visited us from time to time—her sweetness was mixed with so much charm and *finesse*!

For the rest of the first Great War, I remained unemployed. As I have already related, I spent most of those years in the countryside, on our estate near Zagaziq. This was like a period of incubation. I devoted much time to readings in literature and science, and profited a good deal of my enforced leisure. I also took up teaching for a while.

When the revolution of 1919 broke out, I returned to Cairo in order to be in touch with the events and to find a new opening in journalism. After teaching for a short time in Tawfiqiya College, I joined the staff of *Al-Hilal* and next that of *Al-Balagh*.

I have already referred to the fact that I entered into politics, together with the late ᶜAbd al-Qadir Hamza, with whom I used to visit Saᶜd. ᶜAbd al-Qadir was one of those rare authors who whenever they tackle a subject, never cease their inner debate with it until they have reached the bottom of its problems and emerge victoriously. He was very fair in his judgment, even on developments that were contrary to his own opinions. After he had left the Wafd in 1931, he continued his former friendship with many of its members.

In 1929, I produced *Al-Majalla al-Jadida*, and in the next year, *Al-Misri*. The former was a monthly magazine, the latter a weekly.[47] Both of them advocated freedom of culture and political opinion. But in 1939, we had a political hurricane. The Prime Minister, Ismaᶜil Sidqi Pasha, abolished the constitution and replaced it with another one that was far from democratic. My magazines were suppressed, and the new Press Law required a deposit of £150 [Egyptian] from anybody who applied to have a license for publishing a newspaper or a magazine. I paid the amount in cash, but it was refused. Only three years later, when ᶜAbd al-Fattah Yahya Pasha became prime minister, I was allowed to resume publication of *Al-Majalla al-Jadida*—but on condition that as a guarantee I should employ in our printing works a worker appointed by the government. Such is our situation in Egypt: under one government, cash payment of a guarantee deposit is refused, and under another, the guarantee of a worker is accepted who possesses nothing.

---

[46] This paper was founded by Syrian Christian Selim Naqqash in 1880, but by the time Musa joined the paper it was being run by Iliyas Ziyadah. Ayalon, *The Press*, 44, 76, and 238. The name of the paper means 'the protected', as in the traditional way to refer to a kingdom, *mamalik al-mahrusa/mamalek-e mahruseh* or 'well protected domains'.

[47] This weekly paper *Al-Misri* ('The Egyptian') is not to be confused with the daily paper of the same name belonging to the Wafd political party, which was taken over by the republican government after the dissolution of political parties in 1953.

At the beginning of the second Great War, the Ministry for Social Affairs was established, and I was asked to edit its magazine. This I accepted, for I thought it would give me a good opportunity to spread modernism and advocate a socialistic orientation. For about two years I wrote for this magazine, signing some of my articles with my name and contributing others anonymously. But when it pleased my supervisors they made them appear under somebody else's name, even though the person in question had not the slightest connection with the ministry. This procedure sometimes caused a lot of fun, but on other occasions it was certainly regrettable.

I took a salary of £20 [Egyptian] per month for my work as editor, without being bound to contribute a fixed amount of work or to attend office at regular hours. Sometimes a month would pass without my going to the ministry, and I wrote what suited me. But the ministry begrudged me my freedom, even though the salary was so small; it changed the conditions, fixing my pay at 40 piasters a day. At the end of that month, I found that I had only earned £2 [Egyptian], so I quit the job.

While I had been working for the ministry, I had continued publishing *Al-Majalla al-Jadida*. I kept it up until 1942, when I transferred it to some friends who were to take care of its publication while I was going to specialize in political editing. But the unbridled democratic tendency they displayed soon irritated the imperialists so much that the magazine was repressed by order of the military authorities that same year.

The following year I bought a license for a daily paper, that is to say, the Directorate of Press Affairs, against the payment of £30 [Egyptian], accepted to change my old license for one that bore the mention 'daily paper'. But when I had thus overcome all official obstacles, and prepared everything for the publication of a daily newspaper, the Wafd cabinet went out of office. On the day following its resignation, in October 1944, the Directorate of Press Affairs informed me that after all I was not licensed to publish a daily paper, and that I could have a monthly only.

When I now compare the journalism of the former generation (from 1900 to 1920) with that of the present, I find that we have certainly made progress in several respects, but that in others the reverse is true. In the art of printing and layout, we have made very great progress indeed. Our newspapers show a technical perfection that compares well with the highest journalistic standards of Europe. But we are certainly a good deal behind in editing. At present, we have not a single editor who might be compared to Mustafa Kamil, ʿAli Yusuf, or Lutfi al-Sayyid; with the death of ʿAbd al-Qadir Hamza, the last of that generation disappeared.

Nevertheless, there is one good symptom in our modern editing, namely, the great concern given to foreign news. The idea that world news should be fully covered was greatly stimulated by two world wars, and I think it is a good thing that readers are informed in such a way that they acquire an international outlook, and are taught to look at our own political situation in the wider scope of the world situation.

On the other hand, the fact that the papers run after advertisements has done much to restrict their freedom and responsibility. They pay, for instance, much attention to the cinema business, which brings them a fine crop of advertisements. But very little attention is given to agriculture, which in Egypt is the daily concern of millions of people, but from which the papers do not benefit through advertisements.

What I have experienced in political and non-political writing has taught me that a few articles on politics may sometimes bring just as much financial gain as is yielded by a complete book that has perhaps required years of special studies. For this reason, it is clear that writing books in Egypt implies a great sacrifice, which only those who are fully and blindly devoted to cultural ideals will be prepared to make. This is also the reason why so many literary persons who started to be authors have changed their mind and become journalists.

On the evening of 12 July 1932, I was trying to get some sleep on the asphalt floor of a dark room in the Ezbekiya prison, where I was confined with some forty other people who were accused of theft, fighting, fornication, murder, possession of narcotics, and similar crimes. I was accused of writing on socialism and communism. The rough surface of the asphalt caused me a pain that kept me awake, so in that long night I reviewed, like a film, my past life. I recalled the freedom that I had enjoyed when I was writing articles for *Al-Mustaqbal*—articles which, if they were to have been written in 1932 instead of 1914, would certainly have lead to imprisonment much more quickly. I recalled all the hardships that I had met with in my studies and my writing, and I went through the list of nearly twenty books which I wrote for my compatriots—books that were the best products of my intellect, sincere efforts to enlighten and reform, to lead the young people out of the darkness of our past by showing to them the examples set by the great men of the twentieth century. In my painful position on the hard asphalt floor of prison, I was for the first time sharply conscious of what it meant for me, not having collected the wealth nor reached the status of distinction that might be considered as the just rewards for one who works and spends his best forces in order to serve. Beside me was just half a loaf of bread, all the Egyptian government allotted to me as my supper and as a reward for a life spent in the service of Egypt. Thinking of all this, and repeating the same thoughts over and over again, I tortured my mind till morning, when a man entered with a basket of bread. He gave me a loaf for my breakfast, which I put on top of the other half that had been given to me the previous night. That was how the combined forces of imperialism and tyranny dealt with us!

2.7 Cartoon from the satirical Turkish weekly comic *LeMan* [48] entitled 'Sözde Mini Öykü . . .' ('A So-Called Short Story'), 27 January 2001 [49]

Matthew Elliot

Preface

This humorous cartoon touches, albeit in an indirect manner, on one of the most sensitive political subjects in Turkey: the Armenian deportations and massacres that occurred during World War I. While most Turks concede that massacres did occur, they argue that atrocities were committed by both sides and that Armenian revolutionary violence, together with Turkish fears of Armenian collaboration with Russia, led to the catastrophic decision to effect large-scale deportations. Further, they fiercely oppose the definition of these deportations and the massacres that followed as a deliberate genocide perpetrated by Turks against Armenians. [50]

For the majority of Turks, France's Armenian genocide law and the proposal in Congress (not adopted subsequently) to commemorate those events as genocide constituted a straightforward attack on their national reputation. The psychological importance of Western, and particularly European, acceptance, of a Turkey still guided by Kemalist ideals of Westernization, combined with the sense of rejection implied by such a bill to produce a passionate anti-French reaction in the Turkish press and in public life. Similarly furious (and also relatively short-lived) public reactions were seen in Turkey after an earlier rejection of its application to join the European union and after a row with Italy over the latter's reception of Abdullah Öcalan, leader of the Kurdish PKK (a terrorist

---

[48] From the issue dated 27 January 2001. *LeMan*'s website may be found at <http://www.leman.com.tr/>. The first Turkish satirical comic of this modern type was named *Gırgır*, appeared in 1972, and achieved a circulation of over 600,000 in the 1980s (Devrim Çakır, '70'li yılların karikatür dili: Gırgır', in *Popüler Tarih*, (Temmüz-Agustos 2001, Sayı 14), 90–5. On the earlier history of Turkish political cartoons, see Palmira Brummett, 'New Woman and Old Nag: Images of Women in the Ottoman Cartoon Space', and Ayhan Akman, 'From Cultural Schizophrenia to Modernist Binarism: Cartoons and Identities in Turkey (1930–1975)', in Fatma Müge Göçek (ed.), *Political Cartoons in the Middle East* (Princeton: Markus Wiener, 1998), 13–57, 83–131.

[49] A pun on the phrase *Sözde Ermeni Soykırımı* (the 'so-called Armenian genocide'). References to the *Ermeni soykırımı* (Armenian genocide) in the Turkish press are normally preceded by the word *sözde* ('so-called').

[50] A short but intelligent examination of the Armenian genocide from a Turkish perspective has been published by the academic Taner Timur: *1915 ve sonrası Türkler ve Ermeniler* (Ankara: İmge, 2000).

organization with nationalist objectives). Although in January 2001 the Turkish government withdrew its ambassador from France in protest at the adoption of the Armenian law and threatened to cancel important contracts with French firms, the Franco-Turkish relationship reverted to normality within a few months.

The cartoon strip recorded below, like the wider Turkish furor over the Armenian genocide law, demonstrates far more concern for the Franco-Turkish relationship and Turkish national pride than for the historical fate of the Armenians. It presents a variation on an old tradition in Turkish comics of contrasting a traditional, patriotic Turk with a more modern, Western-oriented one. Here, both men are Westernized, but one more thoroughly so than the other. The difference can be seen in their physical appearance, clothes, choice of European objects, and attitude towards the anti-French boycott. The clean-shaven man's interest in French literature reflects the long-standing admiration of French culture by Turkish intellectuals, and it is clear that he comprehends the Armenian genocide law more philosophically than the moustachioed man (whose attempt to impose a personal boycott is presented as futile and inconsistent). Their argument, in essence, is one over Turkey's proper relationship with, and behaviour towards, Europe, while the contrast between the two men may be understood as a comment on the state of modernization in urban Turkey. The irony of the situation, as evidenced by the cartoon, is that two such Westernised Turks could become so bitterly divided over whether or not to boycott France without even addressing the issue of the Armenian genocide itself.

Text

First Row, Box 1:

MOUSTACHIOED MAN:[51] 'May I have a light?' ('Ateş alabilir miyim?')
CLEAN-SHAVEN MAN: 'Pardon?'

Box 2:

MOUSTACHIOED MAN: 'Ahem, "Pardon" is a French word, sir, so please don't use it again . . .' ('Fakat, "pardon" fransızca bir sözcük, bir daha kullanmayın beyefendi! . . .')

CLEAN-SHAVEN MAN: 'Pardon me—you're talking nonsense! ' ('Pardon ama söylediğiniz çok saçma! . . .')

---

[51] During the conversation that follows, the moustachioed man adopts a nationalistic, anti-French stance whereas the clean-shaven man refuses to do so. Both men are Westernized, though the clean-shaven man more thoroughly so: he dresses casually and demonstrates a cultural sympathy with Europe, while the moustachioed man wears business clothes and has a more limited, material relationship with Europe.

5. Cartoon strip from the satirical Turkish weekly comic *LeMan* entitled 'Sözde Mini Öykü. . . ' ('A So-Called Short Story')

Box 3:

MOUSTACHIOED MAN: 'Where's the nonsense? But, but . . . I can't believe it . . . are you actually smoking a French cigarette . . .' ('Neresi saçma? . . . Fa . . . fa . . . fakat olamaz bu içtiğiniz sözde fransız cigarası? . . .') 'I'm not lighting my cigarette with a French cigarette!' ('. . . Ben bir fransız cigarasıyla cigaramı yakmam!')

CLEAN-SHAVEN MAN: 'Yes, I smoke Gitanes . . . what of it?' ('Evet, "citanes" içiyorum . . . ne var bunda?')

Box 4:

MOUSTACHIOED MAN: 'But my dear friend,[52] as you know, the French have passed their so-called Armenian bill[53]. . . consequently we must boycott French goods!' ('Ama arkadaşım, Fransızlar bildiğin gibi "sözde Ermeni yasa tasarısı"nı kabul ettiler!. . . Bu durumda yapmamız gereken Fransız mallarını boykot etmek! . . .')

CLEAN-SHAVEN MAN: 'Fine, but surely you've noticed that there's no smoke without fire?'[54] ('İyi de farkındaysan ateş olmayan yerden duman çıkmıyo [r] . . .')

Second Row, Box 1:

MOUSTACHIOED MAN: 'Oh my God! You're . . . you're even reading Victor Hugo's *Les Miserables*! You've a French novel in your hand!' ('Aman allahım siz . . . siz . . . üstelik Victor Hugo'nun "sefiller" ini okuyorsunuz, elinizdeki bir Fransız romanı . . .')

CLEAN-SHAVEN MAN: (beginning to seethe)

Box 2:

CLEAN-SHAVEN MAN: 'Well then, mate,[55] so should we abandon the Galatasaray–Paris St. Germain[56] match in the Champions League?'[57] ('İyi be, oldu olucak bari Şampiyonlar Liginde Gaassaray-Paris St Germain maçını da iptal edelim?!')

---

[52] The more intimate, but nevertheless polite, form of address indicates growing tension.

[53] The Armenian genocide law (passed on 18 Jan. 2001) made public denial of the Armenian genocide a punishable offence on the same lines as the existing 1990 law governing denial of the Jewish Holocaust.

[54] This remark appears to be a straightforward joke about the moustachioed man's obstinate refusal to light his own cigarette with a French one rather than a veiled comment on the Armenian issue.

[55] *Be* is a discourteous form of address (unlike *bey* (sir), which is polite).

[56] Paris St-Germain and Galatasaray are both top soccer clubs, the latter being Turkish and based in Istanbul.

[57] Turkey's participation in European football championships is regarded in Turkey as an important sign of its acceptance by Europe; withdrawing from the competition might therefore be more damaging to Turkey itself than to France.

MOUSTACHIOED MAN: 'Of course we should! Why not? And what's more Nouma should go back to France!' ('Tabi niye olmasın, ayrıca Nouma[58] da Fransa'ya geri dönsün! . . .')

Box 3:

MOUSTACHIOED MAN: 'You, you're a typical traitor . . . I feel ashamed to sit beside you!' ('Siz, siz tipik bir vatan hainisiniz, sizinle yanyana oturmaktan utanç duyuyorum! . . .')

CLEAN-SHAVEN MAN: 'Oh well but I see that your suit is of French manufacture . . .' ('İyi ama görüyorum ki takım elbiseniz Fransız malı! . . .')

MOUSTACHIOED MAN: 'So what? Am I supposed to wander around stark naked like an orphan?' ('Ne yani çırçıplak yetim gibi mi dolaşsaydım?!')

Box 4:

MOUSTACHIOED MAN (driving away in his Renault car): 'You ungrateful traitor, bugger you with the Eiffel Tower!' ('Nankör hainler, topunuza Eyfel Kulesi girsin! . . .')

CLEAN-SHAVEN MAN: 'And up yours with the Statue of Liberty,[59] you prick!' ('Sana da Özgürlük Heykeli, hadi çaav!')

---

[58] Pascal Nouma, a black French striker then playing for the Turkish club Beşiktaş. It had been briefly suggested that Nouma be repatriated as one of several measures of retaliation against France's adoption of the Armenian genocide bill.

[59] The Statue of Liberty was first designed and built by Bartholdi in France.

2.8 From the Internet magazine, *The Iranian*, 25 January 2002: a debate on the legacy of the Persepolis celebrations of 1971
Cyrus Kadivar and Jahanshah Javid

Preface

Since its establishment in 1995 by editor/publisher Jahanshah Javid, *The Iranian* has become an important electronic forum for the Iranian Diaspora; just as the composition of this Diaspora is diverse, so too are the opinions expressed in *The Iranian*. The exchange below is between Pahlavi loyalist, and regular contributor to *The Iranian*, Cyrus Kadivar and Javid. Kadivar and Javid represent two of the many streams within the Iranian Diaspora in the West: Kadivar left Iran as a result of the revolution and Javid actually returned from studies in the West to serve the Islamic Republic as a journalist until 1984.[60] As Javid describes himself on *The Iranian*'s FAQ page, 'I used to love the Shah when I was a kid. Then I became a supporter of the revolution in my late teens. I became religious, grew a beard and changed my name to Muhammad. I snapped out of that too and settled permanently in the U.S. in 1990.'[61] Typical or not, Javid became one of 226,123 Iranian immigrants to the United States recorded in the 1990 US Census (up from 128,240 in 1980).[62]

Kadivar's article revisited a controversial event in Iran's past, the Persepolis Celebrations of 1971. The Persepolis Celebrations were reviled by opponents of the Pahlavi regime as the very essence of the regime's arrogance, authoritarianism, and poor judgement. These two articles reveal both an insider's view and one strong reaction it provoked in the Iranian expatriate community. More generally, they give some indication of the political culture of Iranians before and after the revolution of 1977–9, the culture of the Iranian Diaspora and its relationship with Western host cultures, and the impact of globalization on the Middle East. *The Iranian*, and sites like it, provide a unique opportunity for Iranians to express diverse points of view. Although the government in Iran attempts to monitor Internet access, just as with press censors in the nineteenth and twentieth centuries, expatriate publications (electronic in this case) are available to Iranians. It is worth noting, however, that *The Iranian*, which publishes both Persian and English contributions, cannot protect its

[60] For Jahanshah Javid's education and professional career in journalism, see his resumé at <http://www.iranian.com/Writers/jjavid.html>.

[61] <http://www.iranian.com/JahanshahJavid/Publish/index.html#9>.

[62] Mehdi Bozorgmehr, 'From Iranian Studies to the Study of Iranians in the United States', *Iranian Studies*, 31/1 (Winter 1998), 9.

contributors from the consequences of what they write, be it personal or political. Javid warns his contributors: 'If you write about how you hate the Islamic Republic and then decide to go to Iran for a vacation, too bad. I will not remove your article. If you write how great your boyfriend is and then he turns out to be a jerk, tough!'[63]

Text

1. We Are Awake: 2,500 Year Celebration Revisited[64]

The sky was dark on that Christmas Day in Paris. As I walked down the quiet Avenue du President Wilson the leaves lay sodden in the streets and the howling wind drove the rain against my face. Turning into the deserted Trocadero I rushed inside a smart café where I had agreed earlier to rendezvous with a former high-ranking official of the late Shah's *ancien régime* [. . .] I was going to meet a man who had played a key role in organizing the lavish ceremonies staged at Persepolis in 1971 to commemorate 2,500 years of monarchy in Iran [. . .]

Abdolreza Ansari had been part of the Pahlavi elite. Born in 1925, he had been educated in the United States. He had degrees in economics and agriculture. He had started his career working as a Special Assistant to Bill Warne, the Country Director of Iran under Truman's Point 4 Technical Assistance Program. Under the Shah he had served in various posts: Governor of Khuzestan, Deputy Finance Minister, Treasurer, Minister of Labour. In 1968, after a disagreement with Prime Minister Hoveyda he had resigned as Minister of Interior to join Princess Ashraf's inner circle where he assisted her in the numerous activities, including the sixty-eight charities and welfare organizations under her royal patronage. He was regarded as a capable and energetic technocrat with suave manners [. . .]

We sat down near the window facing each other at the table. After exchanging polite preliminaries, Mr Ansari glanced at me with alert eyes and said, 'What is it that you want to know?'

'Tell me about the party at Persepolis,' I said. 'Whose idea was it and what was your role in it all?'

Surrendering to a current of memories, Mr Ansari remained silent for a while as he contemplated my question. I knew that he had thought about the questions and the answers he wished to provide. But I also sensed a burden lifting. 'It's a long story,' he sighed. 'My memory is a bit rusty but I will try to give you a picture, as accurately and detailed as possible, even though it was so many years ago . . .'

---

[63] Ibid.

[64] This is an abridged version of Cyrus Kadivar, 'We Are Awake: 2,500 Celebrations Revisited', *The Iranian* (Iranian.com), 25 January 2002 <http://www.iranian.com/CyrusKadivar/2002/January/2500/index.html>.

'The idea of holding a ceremony which would highlight Iran's glorious past in the world was nothing new,' Mr Ansari said calmly [. . .]

In 1960, Shojaeddin Shafa, an Iranian scholar had sent a proposal to the Shah of Iran suggesting that he hold a colorful pageant thirty miles outside Shiraz in the ruins of *Takht-e Jamshid*, or Persepolis, the 'City of Persians', built by King Darius and burned to the ground by Alexander the Great in 331 BCE.

The Shah had given his tacit approval and a small committee headed by Amir Homayoun, a venerable senator, had been formed to consider a festival to mark the 2,500th anniversary of the original [Achemenid] Persian Empire founded by Cyrus the Great in the sixth century BCE.

'A small budget was allocated to the project,' Mr Ansari continued. 'But for ten years nothing happened, partly because the country was in the full throes of development and the government could not afford to allocate time or funds to such a celebration.'

In 1969, Michael Stewart, the British Foreign Secretary visited Iran and after meeting the Shah he was taken on a private tour of the famous ruins by Court Minister Alam, Prime Minister Hoveyda and Deputy Foreign Minister Abbas Ali Khalatbari. Later, during an evening reception thrown by Amir Khosrow Afshar, in Stewart's honor, the British Foreign Secretary had described how deeply impressed he had been by the fabulous Persepolis.

'Your Empire was founded by Cyrus. Xerxes extended it and Darius preserved it,' Michael Stewart told his hosts. 'Your present ruler seems to me to possess something of the qualities of all three of these mighty kings.' When Assadollah Alam had reported this to HIM [His Imperial Majesty], the Shah revived his interest in holding some sort of celebration and the Court Minister was asked to look into the details [. . .] In early September 1970, thirteen months before the festivities, Mr Ansari, then aged forty-six, received a phone call. It was Princess Ashraf. She wanted to see him at once.

'Arriving at Saʿadabad Palace,' Mr Ansari continued, 'I was taken to see HRH, Princess Ashraf. She greeted me in her reception room and informed me that HIM, her twin-brother, had finally decided to push ahead with organizing an international gathering at Persepolis. Court Minister Alam had set up a High Council and I was to report to him without further delay.'

The High Council responsible for the celebrations which reported directly to Empress Farah comprised of nine people: Court Minister Assadollah Alam; Hormoz Qarib (Chief of Protocol); Mehrdad Pahlbod (Minister of Culture); General Nematollah Nassiri (Head of Security and SAVAK); Amir Motaqi (Deputy Court Minister); Dr Mehdi Bushehri (Princess Ashraf's husband and the Director of the Maison d'Iran in Paris); Reza Qotbi (Head of the National Iranian Radio and Television), Shojaeddin Shafa (Assistant Court Minister for Cultural Affairs), and Abdolreza Ansari.

'We would meet once a week at the Ministry of Court under Mr Alam's chairmanship,' Mr Ansari recalled. 'HM, Shahbanou Farah, took a direct interest in the details and the High Council would meet with her every two weeks at Niavaran Palace. I set up my headquarters in a rented office on Elizabeth Boulevard [Now Keshavarz Blvd.] with a staff of twenty. The conference room was used to hold meetings and we often set up organizational and progress charts to keep track of what had to be done.'

That autumn, Court Minister Alam went to Paris where by chance he met Monsieur Pierre Delbée, the Honorary President of Jansen, an interior decoration firm in Paris's fashionable Rue Saint-Sabin a few blocks from La Bastille. Alam spoke about the planned festivities and Delbée suggested that perhaps Jansen could help.

'When Mr Alam returned from his European trip he mentioned his meeting with Monsieur Delbée,' Mr Ansari recalled. 'A few weeks later Monsieur Deshaies, the Managing Director of Jansen flew to Tehran to meet with the Shah.'

Monsieur Deshaies discussed the project with the Ministry of Court and suggested that a tent city inspired somewhat by François I's sumptuous royal camp in Picardie erected in 1520 to entertain Henry VIII of England be modified and installed in the Iranian desert. A few months later Jansen presented a model of the proposed site, which delighted the Shah and Shahbanou [Queen]. A contract was signed and Jansen began preparations for the royal tents.

'At first we thought we would only invite thirty heads of state,' Mr Ansari said after swallowing a glass of mineral water. 'But as our intentions leaked out to the foreign embassies we were flooded with requests and soon our list had grown by another thirty-four, bringing the total number of world leaders expected to attend to sixty-four. We also made provisions for the entourage of the leaders whom we expected would bring a maximum of five people with them. All these people would be housed in blue and yellow tents that were actually prefabricated apartments with a plastic cover thrown over them to protect them from the elements. Our team worked very hard as our country's prestige was at stake.'

Invitations were sent to a galaxy of monarchs, queens, crown princes, presidents, sheikhs, sultans, vice presidents, a pride of prime ministers, ambassadors, legates, business figures and stars of the jet-stream too numerous to mention.

'From the start we realized that we were facing a colossal challenge,' Mr Ansari confessed. 'There was so much to be done and so little time. So we divided the tasks between ourselves. For instance, Mr Shafa spent a month in Europe and America meeting with famous scholars who were invited to present papers at Pahlavi University in Shiraz. I was responsible for coordinating the activities between the various organs dealing with the celebrations, and providing necessary support and removing bottlenecks. I spent a lot of time on the phone, calling this person or that. I reported directly to Court Minister Alam. Mr Pahlbod busied himself with cultural programs to be held in Iran while Mr Hormoz Qarib, a former ambassador traveled to England, Belgium, Holland, Scandinavia and France to discuss protocol details.'

In an interview with Habib Ladjevardi, the head of the Iranian Oral History Project at Harvard University, Sir Peter Ramsbotham (Britain's ambassador to Iran) described a conversation he had at the time with Hormoz Qarib, a close and personal friend of his. In some ways it reveals the pressures that the organizers faced. 'You know, the English, we acknowledge, are better than anybody in the world at protocol and arranging these things,' Hormoz Qarib told the British ambassador. 'We are new to this Western style; we could do it, of course, our own way, but we are having everybody here. We would like you to advise on this.'

During the weeks that followed, every Iranian embassy in the world was instructed to hold cultural seminars and publish literature extolling Iran's great past and contribution to human civilization. Moscow's Hermitage, Paris's Louvre and the British Museum in London were invited to promote the planned celebrations by sending a team of archaeologists and Iranologists to Shiraz.

'We were very happy when the British Museum agreed to lend us the original cylinder of Cyrus the Great,' Mr Ansari told me. 'We later created a logo with a picture of this famous object acting as a center-piece and small copies were made in clay as special gifts for the guests. Mr Pahlbod, the Minister of Arts and Culture, invited several of Iran's best artisans to workshops in Isfahan, famous for its wool. These people worked day and night to produce small, immaculate, silk carpets bearing the portraits of the important leaders who were to descend on Persepolis. It was a wonderful idea as it revived a practically extinct art.'

This was the easy part. The organizers were now faced with turning a dream into reality. Given the remoteness of Persepolis, which is located in the desert, there were many things to consider. Where would the guests stay? How would the security of so many heads of state be guaranteed? What kind of food should be served?

'You must understand that we Persians are hospitable people,' Mr Ansari said thoughtfully. 'Our Ministry of Court was very capable of hosting small state dinners. But to do this in the middle of the desert with all those distinguished heads of state required an expertise that we did not have. We contacted the head of the Pahlavi Foundation's hotel services and were told that they lacked the proper staff. Besides, we had little experience in catering. So we turned to the French who are experts.'

Court Minister Alam and his deputy Mr Amir Motaqi contacted Maxim's of Paris who agreed to help, while Dr Mehdi Bushehri's office at La Maison d'Iran on the Champs–Elysées dealt with other essentials.

As it turned out, it was this aspect of the celebrations, among other things, that was to gain press attention, overshadowing the main reason for the celebration.

The French press gloated over the details. It was said at the time that Master Hôtelier Max Blouet had come out of retirement to supervise a staff of 159 chefs, bakers, and waiters, all of whom were to be flown in from Paris ten days in advance of the banquet that was to be attended by 500 guests.

When the menu, a closely guarded secret, was leaked to the press it almost caused a scandal. Headlines spoke of roast peacock stuffed with *foie gras*, crayfish mousse, roast lamb with truffles, and quail eggs stuffed with Iranian caviar. For dessert, the master chef suggested a glazed fig and raspberry special.

For almost six months the Imperial Iranian Air Force made repeated sorties between Shiraz and Paris flying goods that were then trucked carefully in army lorries to Persepolis. Each month supplies were driven down the desert highway to deliver building materials for the Jansen-designed air-conditioned tents: Italian drapes and curtains, Baccarat crystal, Limoges china with the Pahlavi coat of arms, Porthault linens, an exclusive Robert Havilland cup-and-saucer service and 5,000 bottles of wine (including a 1945 Chateau Lafitte-Rothschild).

'Persian designers, not French ones as often claimed, came up with the idea of producing ancient uniforms of our illustrious ancestors,' Mr Ansari explained. 'Military workshops in Tehran came up with various costumes, and replicas of ancient trumpets were reconstructed to produce sounds not heard for 2,500 years.'

The responsibility for the great parade at Persepolis was given to General Minbashian, the Commander of the Imperial Army: his brother, Mr Pahlbod, the Minister of Arts and Culture, oversaw the details. Hundreds of Iran's finest horses, camels and 1,724 soldiers were mobilized for the great parade day. Costumes, fake beards and wigs, flamboyant uniforms, chariots, weapons, and regalia were made, based on detailed research by teams of military historians. There was even a replica of three ancient ships dating back to the glorious days of Xerxes for the occasion.

Meanwhile, Carita and Alexandre, two of Paris's top hairdressers were invited to provide a service to the foreign guests and their companions.

At one point the Ministry of Court realized that the Shah's adjutants needed smart new uniforms. 'There was an old court tailor by the name of Zardooz,' Mr Ansari recalled nostalgically. 'He had an atelier in Sepah Avenue near the Army HQ building in Tehran. I had my ceremonial uniform, usually worn during the royal audiences, sewn by him. When we asked him to prepare thirty new uniforms for the celebrations, Mr Zardooz complained that he did not have the people or necessary tools, so Mr Alam turned to Lanvin and asked them to duplicate the extra uniforms.'

An Iranian publisher arranged to take stills of a 700-year-old *Shahnameh*[65] under the supervision of Mrs Attabai and 2,000 copies were superbly reproduced and later became a collectors' item. William MacQuitty, a famous photographer came to Iran and snapped photos for a marvelous book called: *Persia: The Immortal Kingdom*. Ramesh Sanghvi, the Bombay-born author of a biography on HIM, produced it. This rare book was translated into a dozen languages and many experts like Ghirshman and Minorsky wrote the text.

'MacQuitty and I became good friends,' Mr Ansari recalled fondly. 'He was an extraordinary man who had been the producer of *A Night To Remember*, the 1958 film about the sinking of the Titanic. He was a rather tall man and had salt and pepper hair and was in his sixties when we met. He was absolutely fascinated by Iran.'

Shahrokh Gholestan, a prominent filmmaker, was commissioned to gather a crew to make a film of the events. Hollywood director-actor, Orson Welles came to Iran to discuss the project. It was called, 'Sholehayeh Pars', or, 'Flames of Persia'.

Mr Ansari stressed to me that many people outside the High Council for the festivities provided crucial services. For instance, Amir Aslan Afshar, Iran's ambassador in Washington D.C., hosted interesting seminars on Persian history and modern Iran. Mr Parviz Khonsari, Assistant Foreign Minister, dealt directly with the various diplomatic missions hosting numerous receptions at Tehran's brand new Hilton Hotel. General Khademi, the Director of Iran Air, took control of the skies, and Mr Mansour Rouhani, the Minister of Water & Power, took charge of the electrification of the vast area in and around Persepolis, Naqsh-e Rostam and Pasargad.

We stopped talking and ordered a coffee. Once again I found myself remembering a trip with my parents and my brother Darius sometime before the ceremonies. Mr Ansari listened to me politely as I described how General Boghrat Jaffarian, a marvelous officer later killed during the revolution, had given us a tour of the encampment. Driving us around in an army jeep, Jaffarian seemed proud of his men. He pointed at the soldiers, most of them naked to the waist and

---

[65] The *Shahnameh*, or 'Book of Kings', is an epic poem completed by Abul-Qasem Ferdowsi Tusi (940–1020 CE) in the eleventh century. It contains much pre-Islamic Iranian folklore and became a source of legitimizing rhetoric for dynasties that emerged in the wake of the weakening of Abbasid caliphal power in the tenth century. Due to its role in preserving Iranian folklore and reviving Persian as a post-Islamic literary language, the *Shahnameh* also became a source of inspiration for Iranian nationalism in the nineteenth century, when themes of national revival in the face of foreign domination were quite salient. It was of particular value to the Pahlavi Dynasty in the twentieth century, which sought to firmly link national revival to the idea of monarchy. Reza Shah Pahlavi (r. 1925–41) sponsored celebrations of the 1,000th anniversary of the poet in 1934 with elaborate ceremonies that anticipated the 1967 Coronation Ceremony of Mohammad Reza Shah and the 1971 Persepolis celebrations discussed here.

sporting long beards under the boiling sun. These were the men, he said, who would later march in the greatest parade of history representing the armies of the successive dynasties that had ruled Iran. Later, General Jaffarian, dressed in olive green fatigues had given us a preview of the royal blue tents and the private chambers of the king and queen.

Each tent was decorated differently in classical and modern style. The walls of the banqueting rooms were made of velvet sewn in France covered by a gigantic blue-pink canopy made, I later found out, of synthetic plastic of reliable and durable quality.

'How many tents were there?' I asked.

'There were two enormous tents, one being a reception area and the other a banqueting hall,' Mr Ansari explained. He pulled out a fine looking pen and began to draw a number of circles on a white napkin. 'The largest of these tents was the Tent of Honor, about 34 meters in diameter,' he said. 'The Banqueting Hall was 68 by 24 meters in length and width. There were fifty smaller tents painted in yellow and blue that branched out in five avenues in a star-shaped pattern. There was also an enormous fountain which was flood-lit at night.'

While the workers sweated to complete the camp at Persepolis, the Hessarak Institute had to launch a campaign against the thousands of poisonous snakes that populated the desert and whose sting could have killed the distinguished guests. An area of 30 kilometers was cleared and disinfected. 'I will never forget the sight of all those jars of exotic creatures, snakes, scorpions, and lizards,' Mr Ansari recalled creepily. 'On one of my inspection trips there a team of zoologists had collected hundreds of unknown species in special jars kept in a big van. In some ways we had unwittingly helped research.'

In addition to collecting crawling creatures the Agricultural department planted acres of small pine trees along the newly asphalted road leading to the stone ruins. In order to light up the dark road that ran thirty miles from Shiraz to Persepolis, the National Iranian Oil Company (NIOC) placed torches fueled by oil barrels set 100 meters apart from each other. Hundreds of thousands of commemorative posters, stamps and coins were made to mark the auspicious occasion.

Teams of bulldozers demolished a few old village houses in the area known as Pasargad where the opening ceremony would later be held in the shadow of Cyrus's empty tomb. The town of Shiraz, famous for her poets and beautiful gardens, was cleaned and the façades of shops and houses repainted. The Ministry of Tourism ordered the construction in Shiraz and Persepolis of two brand new hotels, named Koroush and Daryoush, each with a 150-room capacity.

The dormitories at Pahlavi University were repainted and the cafeteria refurbished to accommodate the various scholars and journalists. In April 1971, a delegation headed by the Court Minister arrived in Shiraz to inspect the project work at Persepolis.

'When we arrived in Shiraz,' Mr Ansari recounted, 'we were met with great pomp and circumstance by Mr Sadri, the Governor of Fars, and General Zarghami. We traveled in a government car with a heavy escort to see the works so far.' The delegation met with workers who expressed great pride in their achievements, as they were keen to demonstrate to the visiting foreigners the best aspect of Iran. In his slightly old-fashioned, feudal way, Alam who had a feel for the common man had thanked them all warmly for their patriotic efforts before moving swiftly to inspect the building works at the nearby Daryoush Hotel.

'When we got there,' Mr Ansari said laughing, 'Mr Alam's face went completely white. Instead of a modern hotel the only thing visible was a metal structure stuck in the ground.' The Court Minister could not believe his eyes. Six months to the big event and no hotel. 'Mr Alam was fuming all the way to the Governor's Palace in Shiraz,' Mr Ansari remembered. 'Once the delegation members had settled down in their seats, Mr Alam exploded. He shouted that the Persepolis events were of national importance. Pointing his finger like a pistol at the faces around the table he warned them that if they failed in their duties he would personally shoot everyone present in the room before killing himself. I believe he meant every word of it.'

Throughout the hot summer months the feverish pace of work continued unabated. Every day in Tehran, millions of residents in the capital drove past the monumental white Shahyad tower as the finishing touches were made under the supervision of Mohsen Foroughi, one of Iran's most revered architects. Almost every other city, town and village in Iran underwent a facelift and newspapers reported how four hectares of earth were being delivered to the Tent City in Persepolis so that George Truffault, the Versailles florist, could create a perfumed garden with a variety of roses and tall cypresses.

By early October, a dark cloud had descended over the celebrations. The liberal press was very critical. Anti-Shah activists began to spread rumors that the 'dictator' Shah was planning to hold a fabulous party at the expense of the 'starving Iranian people'. In Pahlavi University several students were caught by the secret police for writing slogans in the campus toilets denouncing the planned festivities. The most scathing attack came from the exiled Khomeini who from his Iraqi base in Najaf condemned the 'evil celebrations'. 'I say these things because an even darker future, God forbid, lies ahead of you,' the Ayatollah warned the Shah.

There were a number of security problems just beforehand because Iraq had been training assassins in Iraqi territory to start a wave of terror to disrupt events, so that they could demonstrate that the Shah could not maintain security in his own realm. It was hoped that consequently a lot of people would cancel their trip or that the whole atmosphere would be spoiled.

'SAVAK[66] was particularly active during that time,' Mr Ansari conceded. 'There were many serious acts of terrorism during this time. The American ambassador was almost kidnapped one night in Tehran. Then there was the Siahkal incident in Gilan. Terrorists attacked a number of banks, assassinated police officials and blew up cinemas. Security became tough especially after the Mujahidin and Fedayeen guerrillas threatened to drown the Persepolis events in a bath of blood.'[67]

'How many were arrested?' I asked.

'I once asked General Nassiri[68] the same question,' Mr Ansari said. 'This was after the ceremonies were over. He smiled and said that in addition to the extraordinary security measures he had instructed SAVAK to detain 1,500 suspects.'

'What happened to them later,' I asked, having read that they had disappeared.

'Nassiri, who was later executed after the revolution told me that they were released after a few days,' Mr Ansari said. 'Let's face it. We were not as sophisticated as the West. Sometimes the methods were crude and some innocent people may have been arrested. But imagine if a terrorist had succeeded in getting through.'

The Shah's enemies did not succeed in boycotting the celebrations, but a few important guests had a change of heart, among them the Queen of England, President Pompidou of France (he sent his prime minister, Jean Chaban Delmas) and Richard Nixon (represented by US Vice-President Spiro Agnew). According to documents released in October 2001 to the Public Records Office in London, Queen Elizabeth was urged by the Foreign Office not to go on the grounds that the celebrations were likely to be 'undignified and insecure'. Prince Charles turned down the opportunity to stand in for his mother because the trip would clash with his naval training commitments. This decision threatened to cause a rift between Iran and Britain as diplomats warned that the Shah would take this as a personal rebuff, 'with possible unfortunate consequences.' Ultimately, the Duke of Edinburgh and Princess Anne volunteered to attend, and by all accounts had a good time.

---

[66] SAVAK is the acronym for (*Sazman-e Amniyat va Ettela'at-e Keshvar*, or 'The National Security and Intelligence Agency'), the shah's dreaded secret police, established with CIA help in the late 1950s.

[67] These are references to the two major 'Islamic-Marxist' organizations that challenged the Pahlavi state in the 1970s and the Islamic Republic after the revolution of 1978–9: *Mojahedin-e Khalq* ('People's Holy Warriors') and the *Cherikha-ye Feda'i-e Khalq-e Iran* ('The Iranian People's Guerillas'). It was the Feda'i group that was responsible for the assault on a police station on 8 February 1971 in Siahkal.

[68] He was the head of SAVAK from 1964–1978. He was replaced by the Shah during the revolution and was one of the first to be executed by the Islamic Republic in 1979.

Muhammad Reza Shah was a proud man and although he may have felt snubbed by some of the key defections he did not show it. As he told the French prime minister later, 'The great desert wind and the blue sky of Persepolis have banished the alleged dark clouds between our country and that of France.'

By the time the last roses of Truffault had been laid and the fountains switched on, the Shah had a list of important VIPs which included: Emperor Haile Selassie of Ethiopia, King Hussein of Jordan, Prince Juan Carlos of Spain, the King and Queen of Belgium, the Kings and Queens of Sweden, Norway, Denmark, and Holland, President Tito of Yugoslavia, President Podgorny of the Soviet Union, Prince Rainier and Princess Grace of Monaco, President von Hassel, president of the German Bundestag, the Grand Duchess of Luxembourg, Abdul Rahman of Malaysia, Cardinal de Furstenberg, the Pope's special envoy, ex-King Constantine of Greece, President Ceaucescu of Romania and his wife, President Svoboda of Czechoslovakia, the President of Lebanon, and President Marcos and his wife Imelda.

The show that everyone had waited for could now begin. [. . .]

'We had established a Control Room in the Darius Hotel,' Mr Ansari said, filling my head with more details. 'Here, the team had everything worked out, closely monitoring events, ticking off names and checking organizational charts. The telephones never stopped ringing. Too much was happening. For all the arrivals, protocol had to be kept and observed. The late Mr Hormoz Qarib, a small and intense man, who passed away last year in Lausanne, almost had a nervous breakdown . . .'

The Shah and Empress Farah were in constant attendance on the arriving guests, their hands stretching a hundred times in welcome. The various leaders who came to Persepolis had a unique opportunity for relaxed conversation, visiting each other in their respective tents. Prince Philip piloted his own plane down, racing Prince Bernhard because they were great friends. When they arrived, they hobnobbed, visiting different tents. Prince Philip's great friend was the King of Jordan. They were all about the same age. King Constantine of Greece and Baudouin of Belgium. And they had fun. They would go to each other's tents and have drinks in the evening. They loved it. It was all a great success. And Princess Anne enjoyed herself too . . .

The Celebrations began with a simple and moving ceremony at the tomb of Cyrus the Great at Pasargad shortly before noon on 12 October 1971, 2,510 years after the Persian conquest of Babylon in 539 BCE. Accompanied by the Empress Farah and Crown Prince Reza, the Shah, dressed in his emperor's uniform, delivered an emotion-packed eulogy to his illustrious predecessor and vowed that Iranians would continue to prove worthy heirs of their glorious past. In his prayers to the founder of the Persian Empire, his unforgettable words were beamed live on television worldwide:

'O Cyrus [Koroush], great King, King of Kings, Achaemenian King, King of the land of Iran. I, the Shahanshah of Iran, offer thee salutations from myself and from my nation. Rest in peace, for we are awake, and we will always stay awake.'

Mr Ansari who witnessed the event had, like his monarch, been visibly moved by the solemn occasion, but he could not recall the moment, shortly after the Shah had finished his speech, when a desert wind had swept over the onlookers.

Later that night, the Shah and the Empress Farah received their guests in the red damask reception room of the state-banqueting tent that dominated the canvas city. The roll call of impressive titles, the aides-de-camp hovering in attendance, the chandeliers hanging high above the tables, the music playing from a minstrel's gallery, the gold plated cutlery used by the heads of state all seemed to hark back to a European court of a century or more ago.

The Shah, with the Queen of Denmark beside him, led the procession into the banqueting hall, which was draped in pink and blue: the Empress and Emperor Haile Selassie of Ethiopia followed him. The principal guests were ranged on one side of a long zigzag table designed to accommodate the maximum number of people, as well as blur questions of protocol. The other guests, who included ambassadors and members of the suites of heads of state among their number, sat in groups of twelve at smaller tables. All in all, over 600 guests feasted on a menu never to be repeated or forgotten. The peacocks were mainly for decoration, as the peacock was an emblem associated with the Persian crown. Journalists were quick to notice that the Shah did not like caviar and ordered artichoke hearts instead. It was indeed a night to remember.

The next day, on 13 October, a magnificent parade was staged at Persepolis.

'The setting sun gilded the columns of the palace of Persepolis,' wrote Fereydoun Hoveyda, the Shah's UN ambassador and brother of the ill-fated prime minister, Amir Abbas. 'Guards dressed as Achaemenid warriors with their curled hair and beards were lining the great double stairway, their lances flashing . . .'

Mr Ansari recalled that several days before the parade a shipment of umbrellas had been ordered to shade the guests. 'To my horror they were not black but dozens of colors. At the end, this mistake turned out to be a great photo opportunity when the distinguished guests opened them creating a rainbow effect.'

'After sundown,' Mr Ansari continued, 'the guests followed their hosts into the starlit Persian night for a marvelous *son et lumière* performance among the great stones. Given the chill in the air, I had taken the precaution of supplying the guests with electric blankets. I still remember watching the Emperor of Ethiopia who was sitting next to Her Majesty, the Shahbanou. He was a very old man and grateful to be wrapped tightly in a blanket.'

From the tomb in the mountainside overlooking the ruined palaces where he ruled 500 years before Christ, the voice of Darius the Great spoke in the dark, but in French. Andre Castelot, France's eminent historian, recounted the glories of Xerxes and the last days of the Persian Empire. The columns of Persepolis were bathed in white light that gradually turned red and the sound of fire mingled with the drunken orgy of Greek soldiers. It was the sacking of Persepolis by Alexander all over again. The guests were thrilled and applauded.

Until now everything had gone well. The *son et lumière* lasted for about thirty minutes. It had been planned that after this the lights would come on and a few minutes later the night sky would have been lit up by a stunning fireworks display.

'But even the best of plans can go wrong,' Mr Ansari said. 'When the *son et lumière* show ended, the lights went out and we were plunged into darkness for about three or four minutes. Then suddenly, there was an explosion. A fantastic display of fireworks lit the sky sending shivers down a few people who thought it was a terrorist attack. Well, this went on for a few minutes and still the lights did not come on.'

'At this point everybody became worried,' Mr Ansari recalled, 'I ran quickly to the control room while the fireworks exploded above me. The man responsible for the lights was an ordinary worker. He was standing outside his room so overwhelmed by the show that he had forgotten to switch the lights back on. Well, I got that fixed.'

The lights came back and everyone gave a sigh of relief. The Shahbanou turned to Alam and whispered angrily, 'Whose silly idea was it to have fireworks?'

The Court Minister bowed politely and in a calm voice addressed Empress Farah. 'Your Majesty,' he said in his candid manner, 'it was my idea and I think it was a rather nice display.'

The Shah, on the other hand was amused. He had enjoyed himself. He stood up, proud as a peacock, and walked back to the tents. 'It was an emotional moment to see the high and mighty following behind HIM,' Mr Ansari said. 'During the Conference of Tehran in 1943, the representatives of Russia, Britain and America had paid scant attention to HIM, who had to swallow many insults to his pride. Now, in 1971, it was the other way around. The world was paying respect to his achievements and position as a world-class leader. I recall how some of the other international delegates had fought with our chief of protocol to get a room in a tent instead of lodging at a hotel. . .'

'How did you feel when it was all over?' I asked.

Mr Ansari finished his espresso. 'Frankly,' he said, 'I was so tired and exhausted that I crept into my bed and slept for two whole days. It had been quite nerve-wracking. Like my colleagues I had worked sixteen hours a day for thirteen straight months. Throughout this period, I had lived and breathed nothing but Persepolis. I dreamt about it and had my shares of nightmares worrying that it would all go wrong. Fortunately, the whole event was something that made us all proud . . .'

Shortly after the ceremonies had ended, almost every major newspaper in Europe and America began to criticize the lavish display which, only a few days before, had been praised as the 'greatest gathering of the century'. Speculating on the cost, *Time*, a magazine usually sympathetic to the Shah, put the figure at a shocking $100 million, while the French press doubled the numbers. Under heavy criticism for the expenditures, Minister of Court Alam called a press conference on 24 October to announce the celebration expenses at $16.8 million.

The Shah, finding himself somewhat on the defensive, described critics who alleged the celebration had cost $2 billion as 'not sound of mind'. In any case, he told one journalist, Iran 'couldn't care less'. As far as he was concerned, the whole thing had been a success. Besides, what were people complaining about? Did they expect the Imperial Court of Iran to offer their guests 'bread and radishes'?

Strangely enough, thirty years after the event, the British press resurrected a story about how the Foreign Office had advised the Queen, who wanted to go, to not attend the Shah's party, and referred to the Persepolis event as 'one of the worst excesses of the Pahlavi regime'. Once again, they alleged that the ceremonies had cost $50–$500 million. Where did these figures come from, I wondered?

'So how much did it cost, Mr Ansari?' I asked, praying that he would not feel insulted.

Once again the fine-looking pen came out as Mr Ansari totted up the numbers in Persian.

'One hundred and sixty million *tomans*,' he said. 'That's about $22 million dollars in those days.'

'Is that all?' I gasped. 'So, what about all these astronomic figures we read in the press?'

'Not true,' he said. 'One third of the money was raised by Iranian industrialists to pay for all the festivities. Another third was from the budget of the Ministry of Court and went to pay for the Tent City. The rest of the money came from the original budget under Senator Amir Homayoun, which he had invested in 1960, and was spent on the building of the Shahyad tower. The remaining funds amounting to $1.6 million were, by order of HIM, allocated towards the ongoing construction of a mosque in Qom which, on completion, was to be named after the late Ayatollah Boroujerdi, the most prominent Shiah leader in the world.'

When I asked Mr Ansari what had been his proudest moment in the celebrations his answer was unexpected. 'Before the Persepolis event,' he said, 'I had suggested to the High Council that we should build 2,500 schools in the poorest rural areas. People were invited to sponsor a school for $4,000 that would bear their name. HIM liked and approved the idea and I later submitted a lengthy proposal to the Education Minister, Mrs Farrokhro Parsa. She agreed to supply the teachers drawn from the Literacy Corps. On the first day of the events, 3,200 schools had been opened and when the bells were rung, 110,000 children went to their classrooms. That, I believe, was my biggest joy.'

'Sadly,' I said, 'the foreign media seemed to have been more interested in Haile Selassie's little dog Chu Chu and her diamond collar than what you just mentioned.'

'True,' Mr Ansari replied. Then he added, 'Did you know the French government spent $200 million dollars on the 200th anniversary of the fall of the Bastille? And what about the hundreds of millions of dollars spent on the late Ayatollah Khomeini's tomb?'

Since the revolution, an estimated forty per cent of the Iranian population lives under the poverty line, and yet the hardliners in the ruling Islamic regime continue to spend millions on sponsoring terrorism and anti-American street demonstrations.

Even in the West, many projects have cost more than Persepolis ever did. In the summer of 2002, the Queen's Golden Jubilee was held across Britain to promote the monarchy and thank Her Majesty's subjects for half-a-century of loyalty and service. That night, while talking to Mr Ansari, I wondered about the millions that would be spent. I cited the costly Millennium Dome project and the £53 million fund raising campaign for renovating the fifty-year old Royal Festival Hall in London. And this was being done in a city with hundreds of unemployed and homeless persons sleeping rough on the bridges and street corners.

Was the West guilty of hypocrisy . . . ?

2. Shah bee Shah [With or Without the Shah]: When you think 'monarchy', 'freedom' is not the first thing that comes to mind[69]

'Good God . . . here we go again . . .' was my reaction when I saw Cyrus Kadivar's email. He had said he would write an article about something (it didn't matter what; he always shamelessly glorifies the Pahlavis) and I had told him, fine; send it. A bit later I'll tell you why I publish things that are totally alien to my taste or beliefs. But anyhow . . . I figured I have to DEAL with Cyrus's article sooner or later, and I'd much rather do it sooner than later.

So I thought I would run his article with all the pictures on Friday (today) and let it be there for the weekend. This way it would get more exposure since I don't publish anything else until Monday. BUT I wouldn't put the teaser on top of the Today page. That would make the *shahis* a bit too happy for my comfort; they might *fekr konan khabareeye!* (think, 'Something is going on').

The thought of using the article as a cover story didn't even cross my mind. Well, it did, but it was so disturbing that I immediately dismissed it with an 'eeew!'

---

[69] <http://www.iranian.com/JahanshahJavid/2002/January/Shah/index.html>.

Earlier this morning and afternoon I published a couple of okay features. One was an excerpt from an award-winning novel ('A Winner'),[70] and the other was again one of those vintage weird iranian.com features; the ones that have a catchy title and teaser, and you think, hmmm . . . interesting, but then you go to the actual piece and you soon notice that it really sucks ('Visiting Shushtar'),[71] although in an interesting way:—)

Then I thought, okay. Let's get this over with. I opened Cyrus's first email and . . . I couldn't believe it. How LONG is this thing? I keep scrolling down and scrolling down . . . *nakheyr, tamoomi nadaareh*! (There's no end to it!) And I thought: you're kidding me . . . I have to read and edit all of this? . . . hmmm. I don't think so.

I copied the entire text, pasted it on the web page and fixed all the line breaks. As I was doing all that I noticed a few words here and there, and shook my head . . . Unbelievable! He's in TOTAL denial! Sigh! I decided not to read it. I had no time or patience. I only edited one or two words in the entire piece.

Then I started working on the pictures. TWENTY-THREE of them, in giant sizes; some of them were literally twice the size of my 19-inch monitor! *Cheh khabareh*! *Baba*, we know you think the Pahlavis were the best things that ever happened to Iran, but come on *deegeh* . . .[72]

Meanwhile I get an email from Mersedeh. She's been fired from her job. Good. I need a break. I call her to console myself. She goes on and on about something, and I'm staring at my monitor, looking at this humongous photograph of the Shah and Farah arriving for the 2,500-year anniversary thing.

'Wow . . .'

'Huh? Wow what? Are you even listening to me?'

'This would be such a cooool cover photo . . .'

It was right there in front of me: the Shah's and Farah's head in the bottom of the frame, with a double meaning: that very little is left of the monarchy (only symbols) and yet monarchists are on the rise (or just getting louder?). Thanks to our brilliant imagination Reza Pahlavi, the former Crown Prince and now Reza Shah II is suddenly the talk of the town.

As you move your eyes above the royal heads, you see a group of young guards or officers and a man carrying the imperial flag moving about. They represent today's monarchists, proud and determined. But notice the eyes; they're in the

---

[70] <http://www.iranian.com/Books/2002/January/Lailee/index.html>.

[71] <http://www.iranian.com/Arts/2002/January/Shushtar/index.html>.

[72] *Cheh khabareh* means 'What is going on here?' (literally, 'What is the news?'), and the next line might be rendered in American English (as opposed to 'Persianglish') as: 'Man, we know you think the Pahlavis were the best things that ever happened to Iran, but come on already . . .' *Baba* literally means 'father'.

dark. Blind faith? The helicopter on top gives the sense of urgency, as if we're going to witness an operation, a military operation of some sort. A coup? And finally, those two scary guys standing in the back. SAVAKIS?:-)))[73]

I know what you're thinking: I'm nuts. How could I come up with such total nonsense and actually believe in what I'm saying? I dunno . . .

Then I got another idea. I was sooo excited.

'Oh my God! . . . I'm going to start a storm.'

'Huh? What are you talking about? What's the point of talking on the phone when I'm talking and you're working?'

'I'm going to run this as the cover story, but then write an editorial against it.'

'An editorial against what?'

'The monarchy. I'll say why the 2,500-year anniversary thing was so wrong.'

'Yeah. Be sure to write in there that they brought all the food from Paris on a Concorde.'

'You're sure about that?'

'Yes I'm sure. So and so said so.'

So I published Cyrus's piece, 'We are Awake,' as the cover story and started thinking about this editorial. One of the first things that came to my mind was the title, '*Shah bee Shah*' (Shah no Shah). It was catchy and to the point.

We don't need a Shah. We can take care of ourselves.

If there's anything to be learned from 2,500 years of monarchy and twenty-three years of the Islamic Republic, it's that all our problems stem from this *aqaa baalaa sar*—the absolute ruler squatting on our head.

Oh, I hear your protests, dear monarchists. You say you want a secular, democratic monarchy, not like the undemocratic ones of the previous 2,500 years? I see. We laugh at 'Islamic democracy' but admit it, 'democratic monarchy' is pretty funny too, considering the history of monarchy. Was there a democratic dynasty that we've missed? Was there a period when the individual's inalienable right to freedom and self-determination was respected?

Oh I forgot! The 2,500-year-old Cyrus Cylinder! The 'First Declaration of Human Rights':

'My great army entered Babylon peacefully and I did not allow any harm to come to the land of Babylonia and its people,' Cyrus' edict reads. 'Babylonians' respectful manner and their places of worship touched me deeply and I ordered that all should be free to worship their god without harm . . . I ordered all closed places of worship, from Babylonia to Assyria, Susa, Akkad and the lands beyond the Tigris, which were built in ancient times, to be reopened . . .'

There you have it! The pillars of our democratic monarchy. Satisfied? I'm not.

---

[73] A *sâvâki* would be a member of SAVAK (see n. 66).

Monarchists say Iran should have a modern, democratic, constitutional monarchy, and then they tell us how great the Pahlavi era was. Well which is it? That tells me you want a king more than democracy. You're willing to sacrifice democracy, as long as we enjoy His Majesty's grace.

What's wrong with keeping 'secular' and 'democracy' and dropping 'monarchy'? Just for the sake of efficiency. We could have a secular, democratic state without the pomp and ceremony of the monarchy. Are you saying we NEED the pomp and ceremony of the monarchy? Why?

What's so special about monarchy? Honestly, what qualities—reasonable qualities—can you ascribe to monarchy as a system of government? Whatever those qualities are, they do not include freedom. I mean, when you think 'monarchy', 'freedom' is not the first thing that comes to mind. Instead it's things like 'pride', 'glory', 'motherland', 'empire'. It's *naamoose vatan*,[74] whatever that is.

At best, monarchy is about the monarch graciously serving his subjects. It's not about the monarch being held accountable by the people and their representatives. It's never been that way. Not in our country it hasn't.

You insist that *bekhodaa*[75] Reza Pahlavi is not thinking about monarchy RIGHT NOW. Right now he's calling for a referendum. 'What's wrong with a referendum?' You ask. There's nothing wrong with asking the people what kind of government they want.

In fact I hope to God there is a free and fair referendum. Maybe then you'll realize that Iranians today have their own ideas about how the country should change, and that doesn't include crowning Reza Pahlavi. Maybe then he will be freed from the shackles of history, and distance himself from all the imperial symbols that are preventing him from potentially becoming a viable opposition leader.

But, no. Right now it looks highly unlikely that we'll see a referendum, much less one with the monarchy being a choice on the ballot. Therefore this myth about the popularity (nostalgia is NOT popularity) of the monarchy will live on. And chances are Reza Pahlavi will never be able to be what he CAN be, instead he has to be what his family and fans WANT him to be.

No one wants Khamenei[76] or any of his cruel clowns to run our country. They have managed to make most of us and the rest of humanity sick and ashamed

---

[74] *Namus-e vatan* means the 'the honor of the homeland'. The term *namus* is also used to refer to a man's honor in 'protecting' the women of his family. See Asfaneh Najmabadi, 'The Erotic Vatan [Homeland] as Beloved and Mother: To Love, to Possess, and To Protect', *Comparative Studies in Society and History*, 39/3 (July 1997), 442–67.

[75] *Beh khodâ* means 'to God'. So this English translation of the Persianglish phrase is: 'You swear to God that . . .'

[76] Ayatollah ʿAli Khameneʾi is the current Supreme Leader of the Islamic Republic. This office was previously held by Ayatollah Ruhollah Khomeini (d. 1989), the leader of the Islamic Revolution of 1977–9 that ended the Pahlavi Dynasty's rule in Iran.

of Islam, let alone the Islamic Republic. They must go. They have no choice
but to go. They will be forced out of power or they will dissolve in the reform
movement. We know they're history; they know they're history. But the question
is, when, and who will replace them?

We don't know. All we know is that *velayte faqih*[77] does not enjoy an ounce of
legitimacy. Its leaders and staunchest supporters have abandoned reason, thrown
away conscience, turned against the people who brought them to power, and then
disobey the words of the very god they claim to worship. VF has been tried,
tested, discredited, and now utterly hated. That's why we look at Iran today and
we think, '*Sad rahmat beh oon khodaa beyaamorz.*' (The Shah was a hundred times
better.)[78]

That's the dilemma. If the monarchy was so bad, why do some of us want it
back? Not just some people, but it seems like a growing number. Is it because
Afghanistan's deposed monarch has been rehabilitated?[79] Could it be that we
don't have any 'real' opposition forces other than monarchists and the
Mujahidin?[80] Could it be that the Western media finds Reza to be a breath of
fresh air compared to the angry *mollas*?[81] Or has it gotten to a point where
ANYTHING is better than the IRI [ie. Islamic Republic Iran]?

It's a combination of all that and more. But whatever it is, monarchy has
become a hot topic among Iranians abroad. It's not all hype. What's amazing is
that republicans—as in supporters of a republic—are so overwhelmed that they
have gotten defensive. They used to be dismissive, but now they feel obligated

[77] The concept of *velayat-e faqih* or 'deputyship of the jurist' is the Twelver Shiᶜite Muslim idea
that in the absence of the Hidden Imam (who will return one day to restore justice to the world), a
qualified religious scholar can serve as the Hidden Imam's 'deputy' so that the faithful will not be
without guidance. This concept was given a decidedly political interpretation by Ayatollah, and is the
fundamental organizing principle of government in the Islamic Republic, giving the Supreme Leader
tremendous authority in Iran's constitution.

[78] In more formal Persian, *Sad rahmat beh ân khodâ bi-âmorz*, with a more literal translation of 'May
God forgive him a hundred times'.

[79] This is reference to the reinstallation of Zahir Shah as symbolic leader of Afghanistan in the wake
of the US-led removal of the Taliban regime in the Fall of 2001. The Taliban had allied itself with
the terrorist organization *Al-Qaᶜida*, which was behind the destruction of the World Trade Center in
New York on 11 September 2001. Zahir Shah had been ousted from power in 1973 and was living
in exile in Italy prior to his rehabilitation. The leadership of the Islamic Republic of Iran, which
continued a longstanding Iranian interest in Afghanistan as part of a 'sphere of influence', was not
pleased by this result.

[80] The *Mojahedin-e Khalq* (or 'People's Holy Warriors') are a Islamic-Marxist organization that
carried out armed struggle against the Pahlavi Dynasty in the 1970s but found itself at war with the
leadership of the Islamic Republic soon after the revolution of 1979. Effectively expelled from Iran in
1984, the organization enjoyed continuing support from the regime of Saddam Hussein [Husayn] in
Iraq (which, at the time of the Mujahedin's retreat from Iran, was itself in the middle of an eight-year-
long war with Iran) and still mounts terrorist and guerilla incursions into Iran from Iraq.

[81] *Molla* is the Persian word for a Muslim cleric.

to counter this surge in monarchist activity. I get dozens of emails from these *shabollahis*[82] every day. *Dahanemoono service kardan.*[83] Suddenly there's a creeping suspicion that maybe *jeddan khabariye* (something IS going on).

Is monarchy also gaining popularity in Iran? Is it more than nostalgia? That's the real question, that's where it matters. The prospect of monarchists gaining power does not look good at all. But who would predict the Shah's downfall and Khomeini's rise to power in the span of a year. You never know, *yeho deedee een Reza kaar dastemoon daad!* (Reza might actually get somewhere).

So be it. I don't care that much about Iran, and especially its politics, as I care about publishing. I care about the thrill of watching Cyrus Kadivar, his opponents, and everyone in between, voicing opinions and expressing feelings about whatever they please, no matter how bad, dumb or distasteful some of them might seem, to me, or anyone.

Cyrus *jaan!*[84] Send me more!

---

[82] This pejorative epithet for exiled Iranian royalists is a pun on the word *Hezbollahi* ('member of the Party of God'), which is the name given to supporters of the regime in Iran as well. The Iranian government, with the complicity of the Syrian government, also sponsors the main political and military organization of the Twelve Shiʿites based mainly in southern Lebanon, known (in Arabic) as the Hizbullah.

[83] In more formal Persian, *dahan-e mâ râ servis kardand*, 'they have serviced our mouths'. Servicing how? The meaning here is 'they are trying to sell us on this idea', or 'they have fed us a line', or, more plainly, 'fed us all this bullshit'. To 'eat shit' in Persian slang (*goh khordan*) is to be gullible.

[84] *Jan* literally means 'life' or 'soul', but the context here is more like the Arabic (and Persian) ʿ*aziz* or 'dear', or, still more freely, 'dude'—as in: 'Dude, send me more.'

Selected bibliography

ABRAHAMIAN, ERVAND, *Iran: Between Two Revolutions* (Princeton: Princeton University Press, 1982).

AMIN, CAMRON, 'Selling and Saving "Mother Iran": Gender and the Iranian Press in the 1940's', *International Journal of Middle East Studies*, 33/3 (Aug. 2001), 335–61.

AVERY, PETER, *Printing, the Press and Literature in Modern Iran: The Cambridge History of Iran*, 7 (Cambridge: Cambridge University Press, 1991), 815–69.

AYALON, AMI, *The Press in the Arab Middle East: A History* (New York and Oxford: Oxford University Press, 1995).

AZIMI, FAKHREDDIN, *Iran: The Crisis of Democracy* (New York: St Martin's Press, 1989).

AZRA, AZYUMARDI, 'The Transmission of Islamic Reformism to Indonesia: Networks of Middle Eastern and Malay-Indonesian Ulema in the Seventeenth and Eighteenth Centuries', Ph.D thesis, Columbia University (1992).

BARON, BETH, *The Women's Awakening in Egypt: Culture, Society, and the Press* (New Haven: Yale University Press, 1994).

BROWNE, E. G., *The Press and Poetry of Modern Persia* (Los Angeles: Kalimat Press, 1983 [1914]).

DOUGLAS, ALLAN, and FEDWA MALTI-DOUGLAS, *Arab Comic Strips: Politics of an Emerging Mass Culture* (Bloomington: Indiana University Press, 1994).

ELWELL-SUTTON, L. P., 'The Iranian Press, 1941–1947', *Iran*, 6 (1968), 65–104.

GENDZIER, IRENE, *Practical Visions of Ya'qub Sanu* (Cambridge, Mass.: Harvard University Press, 1966).

GESINK, INDIRA FALK, 'Abduh *ad hominem*', in 'Beyond Modernisms: Opposition and Negotiation in the Azhar Reform Movement, 1870–1911', Ph.D thesis, Washington University in St Louis (2000).

HOURANI, ALBERT, *Arabic Thought in the Liberal Age, 1798–1939*, 2nd edn. (Cambridge: Cambridge University Press, 1983).

KHALID, ADEEB, *The Politics of Muslim Cultural Reform: Jadidism in Central Asia* (Berkeley: University of California Press, 1998).

KISHTAINY, KHALID, *Arab Political Humour* (London: Quartet, 1985).

LAFFAN, M. F., *Islamic Nationhood and Colonial Indonesia: The* Umma *below the Winds* (London and New York: Routledge Curzon, 2003).

MacKENZIE, DAVID, 'Turkestan's Significance to Russia (1850–1917)', *Russian Review*, 33/2 (Apr. 1974), 167–88.

MAHDI, ALI AKBAR, 'Ethnic Identity Among Second Generation Iranians in the United States', *Iranian Studies*, 31/1 (Winter 1998), 77–95.

ROFF, WILLIAM R., 'Indonesian and Malay Students in Cairo in the 1920s', *Indonesia*, 9 (1970), 73–87.

Rugh, William A. *The Arab Press: News, Media and the Political Process in the Arab World* (Syracuse, NY: Syracuse University Press, 1979).

Snouck Hurgronje, C., *Mekka in the Latter Part of the 19th Century: Daily Life, Customs and Learning of the Moslems of the East-Indian-Archipelago*, trans. J. H. Monahan (Leiden: Brill, 1931).

Soucek, Svatopluk, *A History of Inner Asia* (Cambridge: Cambridge University Press, 2000).

3

Gender and society

Introduction

Perhaps nothing has reflected the anxieties and aspirations of the modern Middle East more than the redefinition of gender roles. While discussions of gender have been most recognizable in public debates about 'the woman question', redefining the roles of women has necessarily had an impact on men. Indeed, the first framers of 'the woman question' were men—nineteenth-century men who had ambitions to liberate both themselves (not yet women) from authoritarian governments and their societies from traditions that, they argued, restrained creativity and productivity. Men argued that if women could be made valued partners in a household—providing for the early education and hygiene of their children—society as a whole would be stronger, with healthier, smarter adults resulting from early childhood intervention. Before the end of the nineteenth century, however, women had begun to enter into 'woman question' debates and to organize around certain key issues: women's education, women's rights within the family, and women's employment. In all cases, the push was for more and higher levels of education, qualifying women for jobs previously reserved for men and justifying more state attention to protecting their legal rights. Beginning in the nineteenth century, but with increasing rigor and ideological commitment, states in the Middle East began to co-opt issues raised by 'the woman question'. They did this both to make better use of their population resources, and to gain status by the stated standards of Western civilization.

State feminism projects were key to opening doors in employment and education for women, and legal reforms benefiting women often dovetailed satisfactorily with state efforts to expand its effective dominion over individuals and institutions and efforts to bolster national sovereignty with respect to international (European) standards of legal and judicial practice. As states changed from sacral kingships to constitutional monarchies or republican forms of government, the question of women's political enfranchisement became more salient and urgent. Yet the quest for women's suffrage also signalled a change in the nature of 'the woman question' in the middle of the twentieth century. Granting women the same political rights as men meant recognizing the principle of 'equal rights'. Until the 1920s and 1930s, most Middle Eastern feminists argued for an improvement in the conditions of women based on some understanding of 'complementary rights', in which women and men were not complete equals but, rather, were members of a partnership in which both had a defined role to play. Men went from being fathers, brothers, husbands, and sons to being supervisors, teachers, classmates, and co-workers of women—but the essential dominance of men was retained with these changes. 'Equal rights' feminism in the Middle East, then, is no different from elsewhere in the world, in that it questions remaining male privileges and the limitations placed on the aspirations of women.

But that is not the end of the story. In the Middle East, feminism must also contend with the politics of religious and national identity—made sharper by the accusation that feminism is just another import from the West and a tool of Euro-American hegemony. The documents in this chapter highlight the highly visible 'woman question' debates, the identity politics that are interwoven into discussions of gender and, in some cases, give testimony to the agency of women in times and places where it has been assumed, mistakenly, to be absent.

3.1 A view of Indian Muslim womanhood from Hali's *Majalis un-Nissa*, 1874
Gail Minault

Preface

Majalis un-Nissa (Assemblies of Women) is a fine example of male feminist advocacy, written carefully to simulate a 'woman's voice'. It earned its author, Khwaja Altaf Husain 'Hali' (his pen-name, meaning 'modern' or 'up to date'), a 400-rupee prize from the Director of Public Education in the Punjab and was adopted as a textbook for girls' schools. Hali was born in Panipat, fifty miles north of Delhi in 1837. He joined government service for the British in India at a time before knowledge of English was required. His education included a thorough grounding in the Qur'an and a subsequent reading, with a succession of teachers, of the standard classical works regarded as preparatory for government service: Arabic grammar, Persian literature and composition. At the age of 17 he entered a religious school in Delhi, where he became involved in literary life, mentored by the greatest Indian Muslim poet of the age, Mirza Asadullah Khan Ghalib (1797–1869). His relatives were not impressed by the news of his participation in poetic gatherings (*mushaʿirah*), and his brother dragged him back to Panipat, where he took a job as a clerk and settled back down with a wife he had married a year-and-a-half before. The character of his wife, Islam un-Nissa, apparently impressed him and influenced his later writing of *Majalis un-Nissa*. He returned to Delhi with her and was employed by a powerful landlord (and friend of Ghalib's), remaining in this comfortable position until 1869, when his employer died. From 1870 to 1874 he worked for the Punjab Government Book Depot in Lahore, where his duties involved revising the style of textbooks that had been translated from English to Urdu for the Education Department. It was only at this point in his life that Hali became familiar with Western ideas, albeit in translation. He had just published *Majalis un-Nissa* when he came to the attention of the Muslim reformer Sir Sayyid Ahmad Khan (1817–98), the founder of Aligarh University and the man who encouraged him to write his most famous poem, *Mussadas: Madd o Jazr-i Islam* ('The Ebb and Flow of Islam'), in 1879. The patronage of the ruler of Hyderabad allowed Hali to retire from teaching in 1887. He died in his ancestral home of Panipat in 1914, after having helped establish schools for girls and a public library.

In contrast to some of his contemporaries (including Sir Sayyid Ahmad Khan, who felt the state of Muslim women's education at the time was 'enough for domestic happiness'),[1] Hali's suggestion that a girl in *purdah*

---

[1] Report of the Indian Education Commission, Appendix Vol., *Report From the Northwestern Provinces and Oudh with Testimony* (Calcutta: Government of India, 1884), 300.

(the Urdu term for veiling) in 1874 should benefit from a thorough vernacular education, including learning to write, was very advanced. *Majalis un-Nissa* is divided into two parts and nine chapters, or *majalis* (gatherings, sittings). The first part tells the story of Zubaida Khatun, a young girl who was educated by her parents and thus prepared for all vicissitudes of life. At the end of Part 1, Zubaida Khatun is married to a young man from a good family, and Part 2 tells the story of Sayyid ᶜAbbas, the son of that marriage, raised by his mother to be a resourceful and forward-looking individual, the very model of a modern *sharif*[2] gentleman. In these two parts, we can see much of the late nineteenth-century rationale for women's education in the greater Middle East and the priorities of early Islamic feminism. The transgendered aspect of these selections—men writing as women (and vice versa)—is another persistent feature of 'the woman question'. *Majalis un-Nissa* draws upon two traditional literary forms: the Sufi *majalis*, which detail the religious advice given by venerated mystics to their disciples, and practical advice literature, or 'mirrors for princes'. It is interesting to note that *Majalis un-Nissa* also contained lavish praise for Queen Victoria as India's sovereign and as a model of ideal womanhood.

Text

From Part 1, Third *Majlis*

'In addition, if you ask me, we are like blind people when compared to the truly learned. We do not recognize our strengths nor understand our weaknesses. We are not skilled in discussion nor clever in understanding. In many homes the husband and wife do not get along, and the women sit around conversing with each other, blaming the men for this situation. If someone asked me to explain this, what would be my answer? I'll tell you. Alas! It is the dreadful times we live in! There is no justice! Oh stupid ones (women)! How can there be any understanding between you and men? God granted men greater skill and intelligence in the first place, and secondly, they alone get an education. Even the most worthless of men possess some talent. If nothing else, a man can hear learned people conversing and can pick up lots of information that way. After all, he is a man. He can meet all kinds of people. He can go to other people's houses and converse with all sorts. He can sit with *maulvis* [South Asia equivalent of *mollah*] and learn about religion. He can learn the pros and cons of many questions. He can meet doctors and learn something about medicine. He can go to the court house and learn about new laws and regulations. Sitting with his elders, he can learn about the

---

[2] In kinship terms, the *ashraf* (singular, *sharif*) are the descendants of foreign-born Muslim settlers in India, or perhaps descendants of high-caste converts to Islam who successfully established a claim to a foreign connection. In cultural terms, being *sharif* is a somewhat more complex concept. It implies inward nobility as well as outward status, a sense of honor, knowledge of what is correct, discrimination in behavior and taste, and a tradition of learning.

past and take heed for the future. In other words, no matter what he does, he becomes civilized. But tell me, where and how can you become civilized? The knowledge that you can pick up around the house is not worth mentioning. If the thought entered your head, you could not hear any learned discussion around here. From your point of view, just as moving about, going abroad, and earning a living are the men's responsibilities, so too is getting an education.

'All that leaves for you is the possibility of learning from conversation. But God bless me! The jabber around here would drive anyone to distraction! In your natal home, you can talk to grandmothers, mother, sisters, nieces and aunts, and in your future in-laws' home, your mother-in-law, sisters-in-law, brothers' wives, aunts-in-law, etc. In sum, in the entire clan, from young to old, there is no one with whom you could spend time and become cultivated. No matter whom you meet, when several of them get together, they sit around and start complaining. Some complain about their mothers-in-law; others weep about their sisters-in-law. Some pour vitriol on their daughters-in-law; others retail their grievances against their husbands. Some find fault with x's marriage or joke about the amount of y's dowry or cast aspersions on z's ancestry. If anyone disagrees with anything another says, they quarrel. If anyone is the least bit impetuous, she picks fights with the slightest provocation. Such women abuse and wound each other. They say tasteless things to their husbands. They curse their children for no reason. They grumble and argue with the servants, right or wrong. As for those with any delicacy of temperament, they are so lazy that they can't get up to get a drink of water. Whatever the cook cooks, they eat it. Whatever the seamstress produces, they wear it. If there is too much salt in the food, too bad. If the clothes don't fit, they think nothing of it. If the water vessels are standing uncovered, no one notices. If the cooking pots need retinning, no one cares. Sitting with such people, how can one pick up any civilized manners? Indeed, you might learn a new religion which is unique in all the world, a strange sort of faith which you won't find mentioned in the Qur'an or the *hadith*.[3]

I said: 'What, Mummy? God forbid, have all these women changed their religion?'

She answered: 'Daughter! Haven't you heard the old saws that they repeat?—But true, how could you have heard them? If I, your mother, had taught you those things from the beginning, and instead of teaching you about prayers and fasting had rather heeded their advice, then you too would believe the fatuities contained in those women's heads.'

I said: 'Mummy dear! What are some of the things they say? Can't you give me just a few examples?'

[3] Traditions of the Prophet Muhammad; together with the Qur'an, the main sources of Islamic belief and practice.

She said: 'Daughter! If there were only a few things, I could tell you, but they have strung together thousands of useless superstitions: If two pieces of metal strike together it is inauspicious, so when cutting with scissors or using tongs, don't strike the two sides together. Nor should you rest your hand on the vessel while drinking water; that too is unlucky. If you drink water with a bare head, cover your head with your hand. Don't touch a door frame while you are standing up, but if by chance you should do so, then kiss both your hands. Don't pass between two people carrying fire, or they may quarrel. Don't put a sifter (for culling grain) on your head or you will become bald. Don't weigh anything while standing up, or the *barakat*[4] will disappear from the commodity you have weighed. Don't yawn immediately after eating, or else everything you have eaten will end up in a dog's stomach. If a broom touches your body, you will become thin as a broomstick. If a ladle touches your body, you will become greedy for food. Don't drink water from a vessel that has been stepped over. Don't lift the sides of a bed in which a child is sleeping, but if you do, then you should clasp your hands together and kiss them. A water vessel that has passed through three hands should either be touched by a fourth person, or else the water thrown out. When you sit down, don't jiggle your feet, or your means of livelihood will be endangered. If you put out a lamp by blowing on it, you will get bad breath. Whenever you give the children milk, curd, or rice (white things) to eat, give them a slight taste of ashes as well, or else the evil eye will affect them. From stitching clothes while wearing them comes ruination. From keeping a porcupine quill in the house, quarrels arise. If the veil of a woman whose child has died touches someone, her child will become sick, unless she cuts off a corner of the veil and burns it. If you go to someone's house for a visit, don't return on the third day. Don't go visiting on Wednesday. When you are making a bride's costume, get seven married women to touch it.

'If you hear a crow calling first thing in the morning, you can be sure that some relative is returning from abroad. Therefore, you should mention the names of all your relatives who are away, and the name at which the crow flies away is the one who will return. When you get up in the morning and want to mention the *hakim*,[5] use the term 'the one who wears a turban', and if you want to mention the washerwoman, you should call her 'the one with clean clothes'. You should call the moon 'the one upstairs' and a snake 'a rope'. Cholera should never be mentioned by name and bronchitis should be called 'the nameless one'. At night, when a dog barks, you can be sure that he has caught a glimpse of the devil. When you take the griddle off the fire, and something is burning on its underside, the griddle is 'smiling' and you can be sure that something pleasant

[4] Abundance, prosperity, blessing; good fortune, auspiciousness; inherent prosperity which produces success or abundance. The word is commonly used in weighing grain, etc. in place of the number 'one.'   [5] Practitioner of the traditional Islamic *yunani* medicine; a doctor.

will happen. If someone sneezes when you stand up, sit back down. If you stand a cot up against the wall with its legs facing out, it will bring bad luck. If you are cutting out clothes, touch the floor for good luck. Don't look at your face reflected in water. When you take medicine, put the cup down upside down. Putting one foot on top of the other is bad luck. If a shoe falls on top of another shoe, then you are going to take a trip. When serving someone food, don't pass the vessel over his head, or that food will have to be given to the poor as alms. Don't step over anyone or you will get a headache. If your nose itches, then get the shoe of someone who has come from outside and touch it seven times, or else you will fall ill. Don't strike a metal vessel, that too is bad luck. If a woman has remarried, don't let her take part in the ritual of the *sahnak* of Fatima.[6] The third, thirteenth, and twenty-third and the eighth, eighteenth, and twenty-eighth are unlucky, so don't take up new tasks on those dates. Don't take a trip on Wednesdays. On Thursdays, don't go to the *hakim*, or take a purge, or have someone bled. Don't tighten the bed strings at night. If a lizard falls on your clothes, dip a gold ornament in water and sprinkle that water on your body. If you get the hiccoughs, then someone misses you. If a fly gets into your mouth, you are going to eat something sweet. If a child gets pink-eye, use the straws from a broom to cast a spell to get rid of it. If a child comes down with smallpox, don't cook seasoned meat nor go visiting wearing white clothes or having just bathed. Don't sweep the bed with a broom; it brings bad luck. When you fill a new earthen vessel with water, you should offer the water first to a man. If you touch someone's nose, then you should put his hand on your own nose, otherwise he will fall ill. And so forth and so on.

'In short, there are hundreds of these superstitions that I could tell you about, my daughter! Since women in this city have started to get some education, they have dropped some of these silly beliefs, but women in small towns still believe them. A gentleman came from outside and settled into our neighborhood, and we got to meet his womenfolk. They were always mouthing hundreds of such stupid things.'

From Part 1, Fourth *Majlis*

'Now run and see if there are any servants loitering about and listening. No? Good. Now I am going to tell you how to get things from the bazaar day by day, so that those wretched people don't pilfer things. They think it is their birthright to keep aside four *annas*[7] out of every rupee. As long as I was able to move about

[6] A small earthen dish or plate used for making offerings or oblations to the Prophet's daughter, Fatima: a women's ritual usually connected with marriage observances. Remarried women were excluded from this ritual, a tradition presumably dating from the time of Nur Jahan's remarriage to Jahangir, as discussed in Sayyid Ahmad Dehlavi, *Rasum-e-Dehli* (repr. Rampur: Kitabkar, 1965), 109–12.

[7] 1/16 of a rupee; hence 4 annas equals a quarter-rupee, 8 annas, a half-rupee.

and my heart was still strong, I was able to foil their plans, but now for a year I have been an invalid. I can't get about as I used to and my memory is failing. I want to say something, and something else comes out. Furthermore, I hate arguments. So they can get away with anything. If they want to take eight *annas* out of every *rupee*, there is no one to check up on them because no one is keeping proper accounts. My daughter! You must take over all these arrangements. You should ask all those who come to the house from outside (the water-carrier, the sweeper-woman, the vegetable-seller, the miller-woman, the bangle-seller) what the current market prices are. Ask them periodically, and when you detect a discrepancy between the reported price and what you have spent, then chastize the person who did the shopping. Get into the habit of buying those commodities for which there is no fear of spoilage, like oil, *ghi*, spices, *gur*, sugar, cardamoms, tobacco, and lime for *pan*, either when they are in season and cheap, or else buy them from month to month. The remaining things, like fresh vegetables, meat, yoghurt, milk, have to be bought on a daily basis. For those, it is not good always to send the same person. Fortunately, there are a number of maidservants in the house, and at the outer doorway there are two menservants. Vary the person whom you send to do the shopping. That will keep the servants on their toes. That leaves the grain, for which you do not need to concern yourself, since we get supplies of wheat, *dal*, barley, corn, etc. for the whole year from our lands. In addition, every day, morning and evening, you should go to the storeroom and have all the flour, *dal*, *ghi*, rice, etc. for that day's use weighed out before you. You should have a good idea of how much is used in the house on a daily basis. You should mete out enough for that day's needs. On those days when something new is being cooked, or when you are sending some food to another house, or when guests are expected, you should increase the day's portion. From time to time, you should go to the kitchen and taste the salt, or peel vegetables, or fry the spice or something. This too keeps the servants on their toes, so they will not get careless in their work, and they will cook better. You too will get in the habit of keeping track of things.

'You should also have ten kilos of grain husked every day and put into containers so it is ready when the miller-woman comes. Weigh the grain you give her and also the flour which you get back from her and do the accounts and pay her on a daily basis. You should also have the daily rations for the horses and bullocks weighed out in your presence and sent out to them. When the food is prepared and ready to serve, and your father comes in from the men's quarters, go to the kitchen and have the food dished out in front of you. First of all, you should send special food outside to any male guests, and then you should lay the cloth for your father and place the food before him with your own hands. Then help him to wash his hands with the ewer and basin. When he has started to eat, leave the maidservant there to serve him water to drink and return to the kitchen. If there are some purdah-observing women guests in the house, take food to them and to your *ustani* [female ustad/governess] in the *zanana* [women's quarters] and sit and eat with them. When there are no guests, then just eat with Ustani-ji. You should also send ordinary food out to the menservants and feed the maidservants inside. You should always cook enough bread so that after everyone has been served, there is enough left over for one extra person. Sometimes, guests will bring children with them, and heaven only knows when they will get hungry and want something to eat! You should also keep a little bit of partially prepared meat on hand, since a guest might arrive at any time, and then you will only have to worry about making bread.

'When everyone has finished eating, open the *pan dan* and make *pans* for everyone. For those eating outside in the men's quarters, put some in a *khas dan* and send out to them; for those inside, serve them yourself.[8] On special occasions, you should send food out to other houses. Make sure it is properly wrapped and that the cloth is perfectly clean. When sending *pans* out, make them plain, with less lime than usual, and put a little tobacco in a separate container.

'After all this, make sure that the servant cleans all the utensils thoroughly and puts them back in the storeroom, and be sure to get the utensils retinned at least every two weeks, if not every week. Every second or third day you should have the bottoms of the pans recoated with mud, and the *chulhas*[9] replastered every ten days to two weeks. Every four months or so the spice grinding stone should be rechiselled. You need to pay special attention to the arrangements for water. The mouths of the water vessels must be covered, and the ladles always kept next to them. Drinking water should always be kept in a shady place. The vessels for stale water should be kept separate from those for fresh water, and care must be taken that fresh and stale water not be mixed. There are scores of illnesses which arise from the mixing of water. Estimate the amount of oil needed for the lamps in the passageways and the reception room and make sure you know when, and for how long, they burn, and that lamps never burn unnecessarily. Once you have learned this, you should measure out the oil each evening and give the job of filling the lamps to a trustworthy servant.

'When you give the clothes to the washerwoman you should count them, and when you get them back, count them again, and if you can't remember such things write it all down. When giving the clothes, you should tie the men's and women's clothes in separate bundles. You should also examine each item before

---

[8] *A pan dan* is a box, usually of metal, in which the *pan* leaves, betal nut, lime, tobacco, and flavorings are kept for making *pan*, the digestive chew which is so much a part of convivial occasions. Large, elaborate *pan dans* with separate compartments for each condiment are an important item in a woman's dowry. *Khas dans* are small containers for carrying prepared *pan*, more portable than large *pan dans*. For a discussion of *pan*, see Abdul Halim Sharar, *Lucknow: The Last Phase of an Oriental Culture*, trans. E. S. Harcourt and Fakhir Hussain (London: Elek, 1975), 218–23.   [9] Cooking stove.

the washerwoman takes it so that if she brings it back torn, she can't claim that it was already torn when she got it. Every year you should take all the clothes out into the sun several times and pay special attention to clothes that are made of wool or silk. Before winter comes, get out the winter clothes and see which ones are worn out and which ones are still wearable. Quilts which need to be undone and new stuffing put in them, or new covers made for them, should also be inspected and put right before the cold weather. Any clothes that are all right, let them be, but any that are old and torn should be set aside and given to the servants. Make a list of the new cloth that needs to be ordered so that you don't have to send out to the bazaar for it several times. The cotton stuffing from the old quilts should be used to make thin quilts, or have it exchanged for new, and then buy more new cotton stuffing as you need it.

'In preparation for winter, order four or five *angithis*[10] from the potter. During the year, be sure to remind the maidservant to save the coals from the kitchen fire every day and put them aside in the storage area. If you do this regularly, then you will never have to order charcoal for your *angithis* from the bazaar in the winter. Similarly, when warm weather comes, you should get the house whitewashed, get the *punkas*[11] hung from the ceilings, attend to the garden, change the water vessels, look after the clothes for the warm weather, and get the house repaired before the monsoon. Get mud plastered on the thatched roofs and get the cracks filled in the masonry roofs. Get the gutters and downspouts cleaned out and repaired. All these things need to be kept in mind.'

From Part 2, Sixth *Majlis*

Atuji, Miriam Zamani, and Bari Begam's conversation

ATUJI: There my dears, you have heard Zubaida Khatun's story! You see how her mother educated her and made her a worthy person. Aren't we also human beings? If we wish, we can turn our children into even better persons. If we don't, how will they ever learn to be worthy?

MIRIAM ZAMANI: Honored one! If you don't mind my asking, how did you conclude from all this that mothers can also teach their sons? We were talking about my son, Ahmad Mirza, and you brought up the story of Zubaida Khatun. The latter has to do with the education—education of girls and the former has to do with the education of boys. They are as different as heaven and earth!

ATUJI: Bari Begam! Do you hear what Miriam Zamani is saying? Do you also feel that a mother cannot educate her son?

BARI BEGAM: Atuji! To tell you the truth, the discussion was about one thing, and you diverted it to another! I too realize that if a mother can read and write,

---

[10] Charcoal burner; brazier.
[11] Fan, a large awning-like cloth hung from the ceiling and pulled by a rope to create a slight breeze.

she can educate her daughter and teach her good judgement. But the education of boys is not a mother's job.

ATUJI: Thank heavens, at least, that you have agreed on one thing! Now the time has come to take up the second question. That is, if we listen to the will which Sayyid ʿAbbas's father wrote during his last days, you will have the answer to your question.

From Part 2, Seventh *Majlis*

Sayyid ʿAbbas recounts the story of his upbringing

Until I was 8 or 9, my mother did not send me to a *maktab*, but rather educated me herself at home, for three hours in the morning and for two hours in the afternoon. These five hours were devoted to my education, but otherwise, from early morning until late at night, my time was entirely spent in other tasks. After the morning prayers, I took a man with me and went out for a walk in the forest. I returned when the sun came up, bathed in hot water, put on clean clothes, and ate whatever was prepared for breakfast. At that point it was usually 7:00 and time for my lessons. Mother sat with me until 10:00 and taught me to read. After that, until 11:00, I played in the stables with my nursemaid's elder son, Ghulam Imam, who was about a year older than me. Boys from the surrounding neighborhood used to come and join us there to play. Coming back at 11:00, I had my meal, and then looked at the newspaper until noon. After that, I went to a calligrapher who lived in our neighborhood and practised *nastaʿliq* with him for an hour. At 1:00 I returned, said my afternoon prayers, and then studied with Mother again until 3:00. From 3:00 until 5:00 I practised my shooting. Islam Beg, who had been a servant in the household since my father's boyhood, was a very good shot. He took me to the stables and put up a target and taught me to shoot. Thereafter, I said my late afternoon prayers. At 5:30 during the hot weather, I took another bath, otherwise I went for an outing on horseback outside the city walls. On my return in the evening, I said my sunset prayers and then ate my dinner. After dinner, I played around in the courtyard for a while, and then it was time for the evening prayers. I performed my ablutions, said my prayers, and then read for an hour or so. After that, I sat with Mother and listened to what she had to say until 10:00. During that time, she sometimes quizzed me on what I had learned that day, or sometimes she told me a story, or sometimes she gave me good advice. Then at 10:00 I went to bed.

Now I should tell you a few more details of my childhood. Mother always had sturdy clothes made for me. She gave as reasons for this first, that fine clothes need a lot of care, and secondly, that the body is not properly covered, and finally, that in light clothes, one doesn't sweat adequately. She felt it was better for the health if the pores were kept open. That way, people avoided all sorts of illnesses. She also admonished me always to wear clean clothes, and she belittled people who went around in filthy clothes, so that I would become averse to wearing them and always wear clean ones. I cannot remember if I ever wore and embroidered cap or shirts with decorated collars or borders on the hems. But I do remember that if anyone came visiting with a boy in fancy clothes, Mother would say to her visitor in my presence: 'My dear! You dress your boy in such fancy clothes, one might mistake him for a *hijra*[12] or a woman!'

In hot weather, cold weather, the rains—whatever the weather—she made me wear an undergarment under an *angarkha*,[13] and said that under no circumstances should I ever expose my breast. She also placed tremendous emphasis on bathing. Except for days when I was ill, I don't believe I ever missed a bath. She explained that the sweat would clog my pores if it weren't washed off, and that one should bathe daily so that dirt did not collect on the body.

When eating, I was under orders to eat less bread, since eating too much grain causes the body to become fat and the heart and mind also become thick. But I could eat all the meat or milk I wanted. She also ordered me not to eat my fill at any one time. 'If you want, you may eat four times a day, but each time you finish eating, you should remain a little bit hungry. Eating your fill impedes digestion and makes you sluggish. Your hands and feet will also become sluggish and your mind dull, and all kinds of illnesses will ensue. Also chew each mouthful well before swallowing.'

She also prohibited my drinking too much water as sternly as she forbade me doing bad deeds, as she said that any man who could not control his thirst was no better than an animal. A thirst may be false, and to drink water at such times is harmful. After eating, one should refrain from drinking water for at least an hour. Nor is it a good idea to drink water right after waking up, at the end of a walk, or after working hard.

As for my recreation, it so happened that there was a large unpaved enclosure not very far from our house in which cattle and fodder and straw to feed them were kept. There, we made a wrestling pit where we played and wrestled. The men who supervised us were under strict orders from Mother not to let us play games other than with bat and ball, *kabaddi*,[14] running races, or wrestling. Islam Beg, who taught me how to shoot, was a very experienced rifleman who knew many tricks, but Mother said that he should not teach me anything fancy, only how to fire straight at a target. Similarly, the horseman who taught me how to ride was

[12] Eunuch; female impersonator; transvestite entertainer.
[13] A loose over-shirt with a front yoke and side opening which sometimes exposes one breast.
[14] A traditional Indian game, described in Shurreef, *Qanoon-e-Islam*, as follows: 'a game among boys who divide themselves into two parties, one of which takes its station on one side of a line . . . made on the ground, and the other on the other. One boy, shouting "kabaddi, kabaddi", passes this line and endeavours to touch one of those on the opposite side. If he is able to do this and return to his own party, the boy that was so touched is supposed to be slain . . .', and so on, alternatively, until all on one side are 'slain', the other side winning.

a great master of his art and also had a great deal of experience. But he was under orders to teach me only the necessary skills: to squeeze the horse firmly with my thighs, to understand the use of the reins, to have a proper seat, not to remain weak in any of the gaits: walk, trot, canter, or gallop. In riding at a gallop, I should not lose my grip on the horse's flanks. I should be acquainted with all the horse's dispositions and moods. I should be able to bridle him, saddle him, tie the girth properly, curb him, attach a cropper, and know how to use a curry comb, so I would not be deficient in any tasks of harnessing and grooming. I should also know the cures for the common maladies of horses. In the same way, the man who taught me handwriting was a master of the calligraphic arts. He knew *naskh*, *gulshan*, *ghubar*, *tughra*, and many other styles besides. But Mother told him to teach me only *nasta ʿliq*.[15] I should know how to write well enough so that anyone seeing my hand would not be contemptuous, and would be able to read it easily. More calligraphy than that was superfluous.

The room that my mother gave me to live in was located on one side of the courtyard. All the other rooms in the house were built in the old style, but my father had built this room for himself in a new way. It had good ventilation from all directions, East–West and North–South, and all around it was a veranda about a meter and a half wide plus three meters of open ground for flowerbeds. I was told to live in this room day and night and also to keep my books and other possessions there. All the other rooms in the house were equally solidly built, but she wouldn't let me live anywhere else.

She said: 'All those rooms are filled with air that doesn't circulate. The properties of air are much like those of water. When water stands for a few days without circulating, it goes bad. So too when the air in a house does not circulate, illness results. For the air to circulate, fresh air must come from outside. For this reason, doctors have said that there should be free space on all sides of a house. Son! In olden times, people were very straightforward, and they built their houses in the old style because that was the only way they knew. Your father, however, had studied all the latest methods of construction and had great knowledge of these questions. Several times he declared his intention to tear down the old house and build himself one in the new style. But the old place was a symbol of his past and an inheritance from his elders, so I strongly counselled against doing such a thing. Instead, he had this room built.'

Until I started going to school, Mother spent a lot of time raising me properly. Actually, it is not very difficult to improve a child's behavior, but she supervised my upbringing to such an extent that whatever I am today is largely the result of her attentions. She was able to do this, not only because her own habits and

---

[15] Different styles of calligraphy; *naskh*, the standard Arabic script; *gulshan*, a florid, ornamental script; *ghubar*, a delicate, miniature script; *tughra*, 'imperial' script used for signatures and headings; *nasta ʿliq*, the standard script for Urdu and Persian.

qualities served as examples to anyone who observed them, but also because she trained both the outdoor and household servants with such care that, whether men or women, they all became slaves to her will. From the moment she decided that there was no more important a task for a mother than to bring up her son properly, Mother exercised as much restraint over me as the servants did. Whether I stayed in the house or went out, admonishing voices reached me from all sides, saying: 'Look here, what are you doing? That is not good! That is very naughty! This is what you should do, not that!' And so on.

Then too, Mother treated me in such a way that I always wanted to do what she said. I cannot recall if Mother ever so much as slapped me, nor if she spoke harshly to me more than once or twice. Nevertheless, I was so afraid of her that I was very subdued in her presence. The truth of the matter is that I never even laughed out loud in front of her, and playing before her was out of the question. It was not her custom to kiss me, embrace me, or show undue affection. Not only that, but the servants terrorized me with threats of her displeasure. And I, who had never felt so much as a blow, so lived in fear of a beating that I did as I was told. Finally, it was her habit, if I committed some offense, to ignore my existence and treat me as a complete stranger. And if I committed the same offense three or four times, she took me aside and quietly explained: 'Look here, son! I have ignored this offense of yours this time, but if you ever do it again, I will disgrace you in front of everyone. If you have any self-respect, then don't ever do such a thing again!'

Up until I was seven or eight years old, she always advised me to eat and wear the kinds of things I found at home: 'He who picks up the bad habits of wearing fine clothes and eating rich foods, when fallen on hard times, will end up a beggar, a gambler, or a thief. Don't grab a second morsel before you've finished the first. While eating, don't let your clothes be soiled by the food. Don't start to eat before your elders. Don't get into habits that disgust others: shaking your fingers, chewing loudly, letting things drop from your mouth onto the cloth, belching, taking food out of your mouth and putting it back onto the plate. Such execrable manners are to be avoided. Similarly, you should not spit in others' direction, nor blow your nose in front of them, nor sit with your back turned toward them. If anyone offers you something, don't take it without the proper formalities.' She also kept me from other bad habits: begging, interrupting and interfering in other peoples' conversations, chattering foolishly, cursing, swearing oaths, lying, sleeping in the afternoons or not getting up early in the mornings, bending down in the dark without first groping (to check for obstructions), sitting in the sun, basking before a fire, not paying attention while out walking, walking too quickly or too slowly, not keeping my feet together, and going about with a bare torso.

Most of all, however, she emphasized conversational mistakes which should be avoided. First, she taught me the rules of what to say to older people, and then what to say to younger people. She advised me: 'Never use the *tu* form, even with the poorest sweeper, rather use *tum*. With elders, or with people your own age whom you do not know very well, use *ap* or *hazrat* (honored one), and with a person who is your equal in age or status and with whom you are on familiar terms, you may use *ap* or *tum*.[16] To describe the arrival of an elder, say *tashrif lana* ("to bring your greatness in", to come in), and their departure, *tashrif le jana* ("to take your greatness away", to take leave). When they summon someone, use *yad karna* (to remember), and their health should be termed *mizaj mubarak* (your blessed condition) or *mizaj-e-'ali* (your great/high condition). In greeting them, say *taslim* (obeisance), or *adab* (respects), or *kornish* (salutations), or *bandagi* (at your service). Call their home a *daulat khana* (a wealthy house), and what they say *farmana* (to decree), or else *irshad karna* (to instruct or command). Their children are *sahibzada* or *sahibzadi* (son/daughter of a gentleman), and their name is *ism-e-mubarak* (blessed name), or *ism-e-sami* (exalted name), or *ism-e-sharif* (noble name). Their native place should be called *watan-e-ma'luf* (familiar/ beloved country).[17] In a like manner, you should refer to your own arrival as *hazir hona* (to be present), and to what you say as *arz karna* (to submit). Refer to your own house as a *gharib khana* (a poor house), and to your children as *bandazada* or *bandazadi* (son/daughter of your slave).[18] You should refer to yourself as "we", but to use the titles Sayyid, Shaikh, or Mirza with your name is foolish and bad form.'

In addition to this, whenever I pronounced something wrong, she would immediately correct me. One day I happened to say *phul walon ki sail*.[19] Mother overheard me, smiled and said: 'Son! Most of the fine points of the culture of our city have disappeared, and now you are also butchering our poor language— the only thing left—with your pronunciation! Do you want to destroy that too? Listen! From this day forth, whenever you hear someone say an unfamiliar word, come and ask me whether it is correct or not. There are a number of errors of pronunciation that ignorant or street people make which should not be repeated. For example, *sail* for *sair* (trip), *majaz* for *mizaj* (health/condition), *nukhsa* for *nuskha* (copy/model), *qabutar* for *kabutar* (pigeon), *phattar* for *patthar* (stone), *darwazza* for *darwaza* (door/gateway), *buzaar* for *baazaar* (market), "underprivileged" for deprived, "disinformation" for untruth, and so on; there

[16] *Tu, tum,* and *apare*: forms of the second-person pronoun 'you', in ascending order of formality.

[17] All of these are polite or formal forms of expression used with one's elders or superiors. Some have fallen into disuse; others are still heard in polite society.

[18] All of these are forms of self-deprecation, again used to honor one's superiors.

[19] The proper pronunciation should be *phul walon ki sair*, referring to the annual flower festival in Mehrauli, near Delhi.

are hundreds of examples![20] Talking in such a low-class manner is unforgivable. There are even some errors that one hears from the educated as well as the uneducated, such as: *tabe'dar* (dependent), *badshahat* (kingdom), *khairad* (charity, alms), *chaku* (knife), *bakrid* (a festival), *murraghan* (fatty food), *shaabaash* and *shaabashi* (bravo congratulations), *lachar* (helpless), and so on.[21] There is no such great harm in such (relatively educated) mistakes.

'In addition, there are a number of unique words that women use, but which men should never use. For example: *nauj, dur par, chhain phuin, ab se dur* (all inter-jections meaning God forbid; heaven forfend), *chal dur* (get out of here, begone), *sidharna* (to go away), *muva* (dead), *picchalpai* (demoness, witch), *bodli* (transvestite, whore), *vari, acchi, bua* (terms of endearment), *bhayya, bhaina* (brother, younger sister, also terms of endearment used with other women), *ujra* (ruined, a family in decline), *marne joga, janihar* (worthy of death, deadly curses), *pinda* (body), *nikhattu* (worthless, useless), *nigora* (unfortunate, without support), *bakhtavari* (lucky), *rasna basna* (fortunate, one who stays at home), *jhulsa* (fiery, quarrelsome), *ag lago, bhar men jae, chulhe men jae* (burn up, go into the fire/stove—curses, the equivalent of "go to hell"), *dar gor* (into the grave—another curse), and so on.[22] Never use these words in front of anyone! They won't say anything to you but they will certainly say to themselves that this boy has started talking like a woman from hanging around his mother too much. Men must make especially sure that they know their own language well and speak it correctly before they think

---

[20] These examples are somewhat like saying 'nucular' for 'nuclear' in English, common but uncouth. I have defined the correct terms (the mispronunciations are usually meaningless), but the meanings are irrelevant to Zubaida Khatun's point. The last two examples are somewhat harder to translate; I have tried to capture the sense with examples of bureaucratic 'newspeak', also a common but uncouth affliction of today's language.

[21] Some of these examples are slight mistakes of usage, others are mispronunciations, and some have become common usage today. *Tabedar* is an Arabic word with a Persian suffix, thus an improper compound, but it is commonly used. *Badshahi* is preferable to *badshahat*. *Khairad* (which actually means lathe) is a mispronunciation of *khairat*. *Chaqu* is preferable to *chaku*. *Bakrid* is a mispronunciation of *Baqr 'id* (*Bakr 'id* is now the most usual pronunciation). *Murraghan* is an improper derivative of *roghan* (fat, butter). *Shaabaash* is now common, but *shaabaashi* is more usual than *shaabashi*. *Lachar* is another improper but common compound of an Arabic prefix and a Persian word.

[22] All these expressions come from *begamati zuban*, the women's dialect of Urdu, and are used only by women, or in this case, by a man (Hali) writing in a woman's voice for a largely female readership. The idioms of *begamati zuban* have to do with the world of the household, the women's world, and tend to be earthy and colloquial. There are few Persian and Arabic loanwords in it, but rather expressions from *khari boli*, the local vernacular. Hence the educated (both men and women) regard *begamati zuban* as low-status. From the examples given, one sees that *begamati zuban* is especially rich in interjections, in terms of endearment or abuse, and in forebodings of disaster. See the above description of supersti-tions in the Third *Majlis* for the consciousness of bad luck, the evil eye, and inauspiciousness in secluded women's lives. For a further discussion of *begamati zuban*, see Gail Minault, 'Begamati Zuban: Women's Language and Culture in Nineteenth-Century Delhi', *India International Centre Quarterly*, 11/2 (June 1984), 155–70; and Muhiyuddin Hasan, *Dilli ki Begamati Zudan* (New Delhi: Nai Avaz, 1976).

about learning other languages. If they don't, this proverb illustrates what will happen:

> The crow, wishing the goose to imitate
> Forgot how to walk in his own gait.

'Let me reiterate my point that whenever you hear someone say a new word, you should ascertain whether that person is speaking authoritatively or not. If he is an illiterate bazaar vendor, then don't imitate his expressions until you hear them spoken by a more highly educated person. You should also keep in mind that you don't learn proper speech from reading and writing, but rather from paying attention. He who only reads a language does not have any idea about its pronunciation and will always make mistakes. Whereas he who pays attention, whether illiterate or from abroad, will be able to learn the language quickly.'

Besides all this, she taught me a variety of other subjects from time to time: the meaning of Arabic and Persian words in Urdu; the names of the months in Arabic, English, Persian, and Hindi; the explanation of the Hijri, Christian, Fasli, and Vikram calendars, and how to calculate the date from one to the other;[23] the forms of address in letters; how to set a clock, how to tell time; how to read a thermometer and a compass, how to use a microscope and a telescope, and how to read maps. Thus, she taught me verbally how to use all sorts of instruments and other similarly useful information.

Finally, it so happened that a woman from Baghdad, who knew how to speak not only Arabic but also Persian very well, had come to Delhi for a visit. Since she was very old and far from home, and it seemed that she didn't have a penny to her name, she decided that her days were numbered and that she might as well spend them here. She therefore indicated interest in becoming a household companion in return for her upkeep. When she arrived in Delhi, she was staying at the home of Nawab Zil-Qadir ud-Daulah. My mother heard good things about her and invited her over one day. From this meeting, my mother saw that she really did know both languages very well, so she employed her, undertook to meet her expenses, gave her a place to live, and looked after her so well that she never had reason to go elsewhere. From time to time when I was free from other work, I sat and talked to her. Although I had not studied much Arabic and Persian, I learned to speak them both quite fluently from our conversations. My pronunciation was good, and I never felt shy about speaking them.

Well, so much for my oral or informal instruction. Now I should tell you about my reading and other formal studies. When I was in my seventh year and had learned one full section plus five Suras[24] of the Qur'an, Mother started teaching

[23] The Hijri calendar is the Muslim lunar calendar, beginning from the hegira in 622 CE; the Fasli calendar is the Persian solar calendar, approximately 590 years behind the CE date; and the Vikram calendar is the Hindu dating system, also solar. [24] Chapters in the Qur'an.

me Urdu and arithmetic. To recount all the details of the education she gave me through my ninth year would take too long, but a few of the things I remember from those years were: First, from the day I began to read my first book, Mother kept nothing in my room except my school materials. The room contained my books, tablets, slate, pens, ink, paper, blotter, pencils, erasers, all those things, and had maps of various countries hanging on the walls. Aside from my writing desk, my bed and bedding, a candlestick, floor coverings, and a clock, there was nothing else in the room to distract me from my studies, as if the sole purpose of the room was my education.

When Mother began to teach me to read, I wasn't as enthusiastic about it as she thought I should be, even after the first ten days to two weeks. As long as she sat and taught me, I studied dutifully for fear of her, but as soon as she got up to do something else, I started playing around. So, in order to increase my enthusiasm, she invited Ghulam Imam, my nursemaid's elder son, to join in the lessons. He was older than I was and also had a much better memory, so I began to worry that he would humiliate me. Once or twice Mother congratulated him on his reading and didn't say anything to me, so I was hurt by that. In addition, she started giving us examinations, so whether I wanted to or not, I had to work very hard.

Mother's habit was that she would ask us more questions than she would teach us (so we had to learn on our own). The first thing she did when we sat down for a lesson was to ask us a few questions about the last lesson. And in the evenings, when it was our habit to sit together, she also asked me some questions about the day's lessons. Thursdays were regularly set aside for examinations. Then she would ask such easy questions that it did not take me long to answer them, since on exam days, I was always nervous and thus even slower-witted than usual. When she asked a more complex question which obliged me to give a longer recitation, she would also correct my pronunciation and style of speaking. While correcting my speech patterns, she would also ask about the meaning of the book from time to time. When I couldn't explain its meaning clearly, she would go no further. In this way, my understanding or lack of understanding of the text became clear.

I learned Urdu style largely from reading the newspaper.[25] A weekly newspaper from Agra was delivered to our house. First Mother read it and then she gave it to me to read. Whatever I read during the day, I had to tell Mother about it that evening, so partly out of fear and partly out of a growing interest in the news, I read the newspaper with avidity. On the seventh day, when the newspaper delivery was expected, I waited for the mailman with such anticipation that I would run in and out of the house watching for him.

---

[25] Learning Urdu style from the newspaper implies that Sayyid ᶜAbbas was learning a simplified, straightforward style, rather than flowery, Persianized Urdu. This fitted in with the down-to-earth nature of the education his mother was giving him, and with Hali's own stylistic predilections.

My mother was particularly concerned about teaching me good reading style. First, she had me go through the lesson pronouncing each word. Then, she had me read the whole lesson phrase by phrase. If I read it badly, or ran one phrase into another, or dropped an *izafat*,[26] she would repeat the correct way to me several times. Then, if I still didn't read it properly, she would mimic me and make me feel ashamed. I was also in the habit of reading very softly. She would sit far from me and call out: 'Son! Read so that I can hear!' So whether I liked it or not, I had to read it louder, but if I began to shout too much while reading, she would say: 'Son! You should read the book as if you were talking to someone. You should consider the book as a friend sitting beside you, with whom you are conversing.'

---

[26] In Persian (and Urdu) grammar, an *izafat* is the connection of a noun with its modifier or possessor by the use of -e-; or, as in this case, the -e- sound itself, which is often not indicated in the text, and hence easily dropped by neophytes (example: *ism-e-sharif*).

3.2 'Should a woman demand all the rights of a man?' From the Cairo periodical, *Al-Hilal*, 1894
Sarah Gualtieri

Preface

In 1894, the Cairo-based literary and scientific periodical *Al-Hilal* ('The Crescent') published a series of letters in its correspondence section, all of which addressed the question: 'Should a woman demand all the rights of a man?' The debate continued over several months and was part of a broader discussion around 'the woman question', that is, questions about the place of women in a modernizing Middle Eastern society. Egypt was especially suited to this debate. It had a more open press that circumvented the strict Ottoman censorship laws (an environment that attracted many Syrian émigrés, including Jurji Zaydan (1861–1914), the publisher of *Al-Hilal*), and it was a society undergoing social and political transformation in the wake of the British occupation in 1882. Egyptian intellectuals were at the forefront of an emerging anti-colonial discourse in which a central concern was how best to reform old institutions and customs in order to build a modern nation, independent from the British. Many (and we may count the anonymous author of this letter among them) argued that women had an essential, albeit circumscribed, role to play in building a modern Egypt. As Beth Baron and other scholars have demonstrated, the press became a key forum for disseminating ideas about the 'new woman' and for staking claims to modernity.

In her defense of women's rights, the author of this letter incorporates several familiar motifs of the 'woman question'. Writing in a flowery and rhyming style, she argues, for example, that modern civilization is distinguished from a traditional one by the status of its women. Like many participants in the debate on the woman question, she contends also that women have a special role in shaping modern society. 'It is well known', she writes, 'that the basis of modern civilization is good upbringing and refinement of morals', and it is in this area that women make a specific imprint, distinct from that of men. It is important to note that the author does not so much define the rights of woman, as delimit her *ideal* responsibilities. The modern woman is to be the guardian of virtue, the consummate educator and nurturer, and mistress of the house. In this capacity, her contributions are as important as those of men in the realm of politics and science. We see here an early example of what would become (especially in Egypt) the main argument for implementing primary education for girls, namely, that this would make them more efficient homemakers, and ultimately, better mothers of the nation. In the discourse around the woman question, it is as mistress of an increasingly rationalized domestic space that women acquire a modern subjectivity. Implicit in this argument is the idea that the modern homemaker produces the modern man, 'for he who is not happy in his home will not be effective in his work or capable of invention or discovery'. This document thus shows how the woman question was not only about women, but about defining notions of ideal modern manhood as well.

Finally, the author's mention of the Syrian doctor Shibli Shumayyil (1850–1917) and his initially disparaging opinion of women's rights, foreshadows what would become a central problem for Arab feminists: the lack of a genuine commitment of male elites, nationalists and socialists alike, to female emancipation.

Text

'Should a woman demand all the rights of a man?'[27]

To the esteemed publisher of *Al-Hilal*:

I was apprised of what was discussed between the esteemed doctor, Amin Efendi al-Khuri, and those among the defenders of the woman in (the articles) 'Should a woman demand all the rights of a man?', and I have seen in the discussion of both sides varying evidence in the face of the question. And I saw support for what they set forth traced to words of learned men and leaders of both sides. However, I do not see in all of this anything satisfactory because the declarations on this issue are irreconcilable, and they are for the most part based on premises that are not suitable to the purposes of this study now. Therefore, the inclination towards them is to participate in defence and postponement to no avail, because the rights about which we are presently concerned do not grant to either of the sides civil power or political authority or [determine] the weight of the brain, or its ability. The main issue in all of this is the impact of men or women on the condition of civilization and, strictly speaking, on the condition of modern civilization; because what was true of ancient civilization does not apply to our present concerns in a variety of cases, political, literary, and subjective.

Therefore it is clear that a woman, at present, has the right to demand all the rights of a man. The purpose of this is not that she has exactly the same rights as a man, but that she has rights that are no less important than his with regard to modern civilization.

As I already said, modern civilization has moved beyond the condition of the past because the woman had less of an impact [on society] than now because of

[27] *Al-Hilal*, 2/16 (April 1894).

her delicateness, tenderness of her character, and gentleness of her face. Those times [were characterized by] roughness and the reliance on physical power where victory and triumph went to he who was the most forceful and the strongest at enduring the hardships of long journeys, he who perpetrated the most atrocities and killing of people, he who was far from the woman's gentle nature and compassionate heart. Women did not participate in the regime of Napoleon Bonaparte in killing four thousand men from the garrison of Jaffa, struck down by bullets, their only sin being their surrender of [their positions] out of a desire to preserve their lives, and she was not involved in the tricks of the Mamluks,[28] and their killing in the Citadel of Cairo, nor in the massacres of the Circassians,[29] for these types of massacre are far from the character of women and it is impossible for one of them to have been an advisor or one who permitted their perpetration.

Though the [typical] woman in those days did not participate in those types of deliberations and did not aspire to have practical views before her emergence from violence to action, she was the one who reared those men and planted in their hearts courage and boldness. Rarely do historians mention her [while] the defenders paid no attention to her, wanting from her years of childhood and youth in which she is relied upon for her influence in upbringing. And this is the meaning of the saying: 'She who rocks the cradle with her right hand, shakes the earth with her left.'

All this concerns past times, and [as] I have said the woman rarely exerted an influence in them. In truth, the crucial topic of our study is modern civilization, based on peace, the safeguarding of the variety of humanity, and the raising of feelings towards delicateness and compassion and good works. The writer Jirjis Efendi Elias al-Khuri said it excellently when he said: 'The man will lessen his position in relation to the woman the day the reason takes the place of harshness, and wisdom becomes noble feelings.' This is the time he is pointing to ... for the woman is purer emotionally and more subtle in feeling than the man, therefore she has a greater influence on the condition of modern civilization.

It is well known that the basis of modern civilization is good upbringing and refinement of morals and the development of literary and religious rites [that are] the source of love and courtesy, and compassion for the oppressed and succor of the unfortunate, and the enduring of calamities and the correction of catastrophes [which the woman is better at]. We do not think that the esteemed doctor denies

[28] This is a reference to the Turkish and Circassian military Mamluks (literally, slaves) whose factions ruled Egypt and Syria from 1250 to 1517, and continued to dominate the local politics of those areas under Ottoman rule into the nineteenth century.

[29] In 1811 the Ottoman governor of Egypt, Muhammad ᶜAli (d. 1849), massacred a large number of Mamluk commanders and troops and set the stage for his own dominance of the local political scene, the modernization of Egypt's administration, military, and economy, and the establishment of Egypt's autonomy within the Ottoman system.

our weak sex its specialization in these qualities...There is no reason for [him to make] selfish claims for his sex. He exalts the active sex distinguished by rough muscles and a wide skull, and a long right hand and the likes of which do not grant him the right of preference over woman with regard to modern civilization.

I will not deny the esteemed doctor's [opinion] on the effect of man's roughness and power, or the hardness of his heart on the exigencies of civilization but [these qualities] were of no less influence than the weakness of woman and do not suggest superiority.

Our sex does not ask to compete with men in war or in politics, and not in science and industry as some of our defenders seek, especially after we have been forced into seclusion [away] from these types of pursuits and separated in the house from the beginning of time. Indeed those activities [war, politics] have now become his specialty and area of expertise and it is therefore not surprising that he should excel in them. But I do not agree with [the doctor] that civilization is based on these activities alone and that inventions and discoveries are the source of the happiness of humanity. As for true happiness it is [to be found] in the life of the inner family that does not extend beyond the walls of the home, but is the origin of civilization of this universe, for he who was not happy in his house, is not capable in work and he cannot invent or discover. The woman is the axis of this happiness. She alone is the carrier of life's burdens for her man, and she is his comforter in his sadness and his troubles, and she is the subduer of his anger, the one who makes gentle his morals, the tutor of his feelings, the restrainer of his recalcitrance, the one who softens the cruelty of his heart. This the esteemed doctor admits to in some of what he said.

This is thanks to the natural accomplishments that the woman possesses in greater measure than the man and, [therefore] she takes these hardships on for her [own] sake, and [though] the heart of man trembles [to her dismay] from his [own] cruelty and hardness, I think he would acknowledge her abilities to bear what a man cannot.

In summary, woman does indeed have an influence on modern civilization equivalent, if not exceeding, that of the man and she therefore has the right, at the very least, to request the same rights that he has.

The doctor [should] return to what is right as his colleague doctor Shibli Shumayyil did before him after he was full of rancor towards women and emphasized his disapproval of them.[...]

3.3 Two Ottoman officials on gender and class in early twentieth-century Nablus, 1916
Weldon C. Matthews [30]

Preface

The following selection is from *Wilayat Beirut* ('The Province of Beirut'),[31] a two-volume work commissioned by the governor of the Ottoman province of Beirut as a guide for government officials. Published in Arabic and in Turkish in 1916, it surveys the geography, economy, society, and administration of the province, as it also includes ethnographic studies of the province's populace. The translated passages are taken from the section describing the city of Nablus, located in what is now the West Bank region of the Palestinian National Authority.

The work was written by two Arab Ottoman schoolteachers and administrators, Muhammad Rafiq al-Tamimi and Muhammad Bahjet. Al-Tamimi, 30 years old when the work was published, was a native of Nablus and a son of one of the city's notable families. He was educated in the empire's secular school system in the city of his birth as well as in Istanbul, where he studied at the Ottoman school of civil service, the Mülkiye Mektebi. In 1911 he was selected to study in Paris on a scholarship from the Ottoman Ministry of Education. There he specialized in history and gained a command of the French language. After his return three years later, he taught at several imperial secondary schools and served as director of the Damascus branch of the ruling party, the Committee of Union and Progress.[32] Perhaps even more significantly, he was an early member of the secret Arab nationalist association, the Young Arab Society (Jami'at al-Fatat al-'Arabiya).[33] By the time of the publication of *Wilayat Beirut*, at least eleven Arabs had been hanged in Beirut for their suspected wartime involvement in clandestine Arab nationalist societies on orders of the Ottoman governor.[34]

Muhammad Bahjet was born in Aleppo in 1889 to an Arab father who made a career in the empire's secular law courts. Bahjet's mother was a Turk

[30] I am grateful to professors Rashid Khalidi, Farouq Mustafa, and Robert Dankoff for their advice on translating the document, and also to Ms Erin Gettling for her editorial aid.

[31] Muhammad Rafiq al-Tamimi and Muhammad Bahjet, *Wilayat Beirut* (Arabic), (Beirut: Iqbal Press, 1916; Beirut: Dar Lahd Khatir for Publishing, Printing, and Distribution, 1987; *Beirut Vilayeti* (Turkish) Beirut: The Provincial Government Press, 1916). The translation and references are all from the Arabic version.

[32] Al-Tamimi and Bahjet, *Wilayat Beirut*, 2; Ya'qub 'Awdat, *Min 'Alam al-Fikr wa al-Adab fi Filastin* ('From the Leaders of Thought and Literature in Palestine') (Jerusalem: Dar al-Isra', 1992), 79–81.

[33] 'Awdat, *Min 'Alam al-Fikr wa al-Adab*, 80.

[34] Hasan Kayalı, *Arabs and Young Turks: Ottomanism, Arabism and Islamism in the Ottoman Empire, 1908–1918* (Berkeley: University of California Press, 1997), 192–200.

from Istanbul, a fact implying that he grew up in a bilingual home. He received his education in the imperial primary and secondary schools, graduating from the school of law in Istanbul where he was witness to the constitutional revolution of 1908. Nineteen years old at the time, he supported the revolution, and the atmosphere that followed allowed him to publish his poetry and to join the editorial boards of two Turkish newspapers. In addition to his career as a teacher, he served in the statistical office of the Ministry of Justice and edited its journal. While teaching at the imperial lycée in Beirut (Sultani Beirut), he studied European literature and Turkish linguistics at the Jesuit Université St Joseph.[35]

Although *Wilayat Beirut* is a description of the province and its people, it is also no less a reflection of the world-view and ideology that were prevalent among the elite of the Ottoman official class in the final years of the empire. As members of this bureaucratic elite, Al-Tamimi and Bahjet were products of institutions generated by three-quarters of a century of reforms modeled on the practices of Western Europe.

Texts

Classes of the people and the way of life

It is possible to divide the people of Nablus on the basis of religion into the three groups: Muslims, Christians, and Samaritans.[36] Each of these groups has its well-known customs. But the paucity of Christians and the Samaritans, who are not more than a thousand, does not allow them a disproportionate influence on public life. Thus, we should look at Nablus generally as an Islamic city.

However, there are classes among the Muslims that are revealed by their respective, well-known characteristics. It is possible to place them into three groups: the elite, the common people, and the Jabalis.

When one speaks of the elite in Nablus, money and wealth come to mind before anything. So it is more fitting to call this class 'the wealthy'. Calling them nobles implies the 'Khanadanat'.[37] The ancestors of this elite class governed Nablus with their influence for hundreds of years. They divided among themselves the adjacent lands even to the point of dividing the city into eastern and western

---

[35] Al-Tamimi and Bahjet, *Wilayat Beirut*, 3.

[36] The Samaritans regard themselves as descendants of the inhabitants of the Kingdom of Israel, which had its capital at Shechem, near modern Nablus, until the kingdom's destruction by the Assyrian Empire in 722 BCE. Although Arabic has become the Samaritans' first language, they continue to use Hebrew as a liturgical language and preserve the Torah in Hebrew. Their beliefs and practices diverge from Judaism on key points. At present, the Samaritans number a few hundred. The original text contains a footnote at this point stating: 'We will explain what our research revealed about the Samaritans, so there is no need to repeat it here.'

[37] *Khanadanat* is the Arabized plural of the Turkish word *hanedan* meaning 'dynasty' or 'household', and here indicates the status of the established families of Nablus.

sections. Disputes and fights have frequently occurred between them because of this. These are the ones whose descendants are called today by the title 'Khanadanat'. Nevertheless, one [also] finds in Nablus families that had a limited degree of influence in comparison to these people. But [these less influential people] settled in Nablus and made reputations for themselves. This group is the more conservative.

In spite of the fact that the elite families are alike in the drive to maintain influence and increase wealth, they are divided into two main groups, as will become apparent in what follows.

However, this division is superficial because [the elite families] are bound by mutual interests. In any case, believing that the positions of the families do not change over time is simplistic and naive. We can say with certainty that some of the families are allied to one of two sides to preserve their positions from encroachment or usurpation.

The varying clothing of the leaders of these families reflects their diversity. Some of them wear clerical clothes. The other group—especially the young—generally wears pants and jackets.

The elite depend on agriculture, industry, and trade for their livelihoods. The farmers cultivate the lands that they own through the medium of the peasants. [The elite] frequently engage in the business of tax farming. In truth, they take all that [the peasants] harvest from the land, whether they harvest a little or a lot. As for those who occupy themselves with trade, most of them are in the grain trade and the sale of manufactured garments. The richest classes in Nablus are merchants who engage in soap manufacture and sales. Most likely, they engage in a mixture of trade, manufacturing, and agriculture. Those engaged in agriculture sometimes make soap for themselves. Many times, they also engage in moneylending. Debt in Nablus is a very grave problem. Most of the complaints of the villagers are in reference to these usurers. In any condition, those [usurers] own thousands of lira in property, land, and wealth. Thus, those who have annual incomes of thousands of lira are few in Nablus, and they are entirely of the elite.

Since the elite become comfortably rich in their livelihoods, everything in their houses is in abundance. They do not deprive themselves of anything. However, those engaging in farming become wealthier than those engaging in trade. Because they have little with which to occupy themselves, those who preserve the old way of life of Nablus—namely the *diwan*[38] life—belong to the elite. You see their homes open night and day to receive visitors.[. . .]

As for the women of this class, they live in a way that saddens the heart. It is forbidden for them to go out of the houses into the alleys. They spend all their time in those damp houses preserving their natural beauty; they are constantly

[38] *Diwan* is used here to mean the area of a home used to entertain guests. More strictly, it refers to the hall of a royal council or to the council itself.

concerned with beautifying themselves. One can say that expenditures for powder and cosmetics are very large. The young and old women still dye their hands with henna, yet are inclined to adorn their hair in the European style. There is no doubt that the devotion of the women to 'fashion' is epitomized by the tastes of a number of seamstresses in Nablus.

As for the second Islamic class, it is the common people. The livelihood of these people is from laboring, cutting stones, selling vegetables, and other such small jobs. The houses they live in and the shops they work in are just huts. These people generally wear the kinds of clothes called '*ghunbaz*', which are made of the local cloth. The sides are in the form of a triangle, open in the front, and one part is wrapped around the other. They wrap over it a sash, fifteen centimeters in width. Over that, they wear a robe or cloak (jacket). Usually, their legs are bare. Wearing leggings is not a custom among them. They wear a kind of local shoe called a '*madas*'. Sometimes they cover their heads with a fez, and at other times with a turban.

Their life is hard. They are of no importance at all among the elite. The elite feel that it is their right and privilege to use the services of the common people in any job. Every individual of the common people feels that belonging to the elite is an unmatched blessing.

As for the third class, they are the Jabalis. They dwell in the neighborhood of Qaysariyah. They are from the neighborhood of Jabaliyah in Ghaza. One does not find a lower class of people in Nablus than these people. Their women go unveiled. Because of their tattered clothes and their miserable jobs, such as begging and the like, the Nabulsis call them 'tramps'. [The Nabulsis] feel that beating them and abusing them is permissible. It is said that their number does not exceed three hundred. Because of a peculiarity of their speech, they are distinguishable from the class of common people.

As for the Christians dwelling in Nablus, most of them engage in iron-working and dyeing. Because of their poverty, you can find only a semblance of order or cleanliness. Neither can one find among the youths a great resurgence of learning. It is strange that the women of these Christians veil themselves when passing through the markets. The people of Nablus do not permit the women of these faiths to go unveiled unless they are foreigners.

As for the Samaritans, we must consider them as the wretched of God's creation in Nablus. The contempt, disdain, and scorn with which they are viewed by the people of Nablus—even by the young—has ingrained in them a sense of inferiority that is hard to describe. The Samaritan women do not go about the alleys unveiled, as is consistent with their doctrines.

Customs and social conditions: the matter of marriage

The Muslim classes are distinctly divided in the matter of marriage. In that matter, they each have special conditions. It had been the custom in Nablus that noble families married only within their own circle. One could not marry a noble daughter unless he was of this group of families. Even if he were rich, he did not have the right to take the daughter of one of these families, unless he was himself of noble descent by two hundred years. They honored this tradition completely. They sometimes went to such extremes that some [extended] families restricted the marriage of their daughters to their male members. They clung to their traditions intensely. However, the attribute of wealth took the place of nobility in recent times. The wealthy gained the right of taking the daughter of any of the noble families. One of the odd manifestations of wealth in Nablus is that some of the rich families prohibit the marriage of their daughters to anyone who is not of a family that can marry its [own] daughter to a suitable man. This is from fear of the wealth leaving the family. It has happened frequently that the daughters are married to married men more suitable to them out of fear of [the family] falling victim to a pretext for the [family's] wealth going to a family unsuitable for sharing in that wealth.

However, the obvious custom followed is that the members of each class marry within their own class. The people of Nablus honor this custom completely. If a family of the common people becomes rich, it immediately becomes a part of the elite because of its wealth.

The common people display no difficulty with the matter of marriage. Not one of them considers his ability to feed his wife and children when he rushes into marriage. It is frequently witnessed that a man who does not earn more than 100 piastres a month in salary marries and divorces three out of four times, while he also has a family he must provide for. Sometimes they marry a young girl to a man over 60 out of greed for his wealth. They ruin the life of the girl and deprive her of her youth.[. . .]

The people of Nablus are greatly inclined towards having children. However, they prefer boys to girls. They marry several times hoping to attain this goal. In Nablus, they conduct circumcisions without much fanfare before the [male] child is twenty days old.

Family life

I am doing my best here to explain the disease that afflicts our societal life here in the East and that has become apparent to us in the investigations we conducted recently in Nablus. There is no doubt that my data here is of an important scientific nature. Family life here appears very sad. We can say that women here have no influence at all, as is the case in other parts of the land. [The men] did not want these daughters to come out of the stomachs of their mothers into this world, and they want to dispossess these creatures of everything. Education of the daughters is necessarily lacking. Nor is there any need of education for the women. If we assume that [the men of Nablus] were good to [their daughters] and sent them to school, they would erect barriers in the way of [the daughters'] education after they completed the glorious Qur'an. They would remove them from school before they learned the addition of simple numbers. The daughter remains in the house until 5 or 6 years of age. She is not important. Because she is female, they look on her with disgust and disrespect, especially if she was the reason for bringing another wife into the mother's house. Then the life of the daughter is subject to increasing disrespect against her. She is beaten and slapped. She can flee the house only with great difficulty. You see these girls fleeing their homes by going out into the alley and playing with their companions in the clay and dirt. When evening comes, they gather in the marketplaces and begin dancing and singing songs. In the nights of Ramadan, they tour all the sections [of town], one by one, with lanterns in their hands. If [a girl] goes out of the house, she is not free of the contempt of the smallest male child. She is forced to tolerate this. She suffers all kinds of pranks. When she reaches 6 years of age, leaving the house is forbidden. She is sentenced to breathing the damp, dark, musty air of her house. If she manages to leave the house once in a year, it is in the company of her mother. It is a rule that she bows her head to the ground and looks to neither side. After five or six years, they send this poor girl, knowing nothing of the world but the stones of the alley, to a house in which she is a total stranger. There, she becomes an instrument for bearing children, a servant to the man, and a slave girl to the mother-in-law and to her female cousin. This little woman, who is thrown into the hands of strangers, cannot raise her voice to complain of her condition, her new home, or her husband. She can only consent to her life as it is. However, even if we suppose that she bears all these hardships and she was aware of no indolence or defect [on her part], it may not be long before she sees another wife sharing her life. Then her patience is broken and she begins complaining about her life. Confusion results among the mother-in-law, the female cousin, the first wife, the second wife, the man, the sons, and the sons of the various wives. Then that house becomes a house of torment. The life of the woman withers away and she becomes a victim. It is unusual to consider a woman's illness important. It is even unusual to get a doctor or buy medicine for a woman who is sick. If the illness gets worse, they send for a doctor once or twice, but by then, it is too late to save her. The poor woman leaves behind her children in a lamentable condition, since they clung to her since they were babies. The woman dies and the man pays no attention to her death. The next day, he marries another woman. It is not customary to put the name of the woman on her grave. In Nablus, it is difficult to find the name of a Muslim woman written on her grave. The Nabulsis believe it is shameful to mention the name of the deceased woman.

3.4 Excerpts from Antun al-Gamayyil's textbook, *Al-Fatat wa'l-Bayt* ('The Young Woman and the Home'), 1916
Mona Russell

Preface

Although Islam as a religion encourages learning from all adherents, historically education for women in Egypt was a luxury reserved for the upper and upper-middle classes. Even within those classes, education for girls was not necessarily a given. Prior to the nineteenth century, this education, like that of boys, was primarily a religious one. The reforms of Muhammad ᶜAli (r. 1805–48), which included bureaucratic centralization, the creation of a new army, the intensification of agriculture, and industrialization, all necessitated a new educational system (see Sec. 1.6). Although a number of his advisers believed in the importance of female education for the progress of society, aside from a school for midwives, little was done to advance its cause. On a personal level, the viceroy set an example by bringing European women into his own harem to educate his wives, consorts, slaves, and their children.

The practice of hiring European governesses for girls (and young boys) spread among the upper classes in the 1840s and 1850s, despite the fact that Muhammad ᶜAli's successors, ᶜAbbas (r. 1848–54) and Saᶜid (r. 1854–63), did little to promote education generally. In contrast, Ismaᶜil (r. 1863–79) made education a priority, placing special emphasis on it both in his home and throughout the country as a whole. It is during his reign that the first primary school for girls opened in 1873. Nevertheless, Ismaᶜil is also famous for his grandiose schemes for development, and plunging Egypt into debt. This sequence of events helped to bring about both his deposition in 1879 and the British occupation in 1882.

While the British paid lip-service to the necessity of girls' education, they were more concerned with the country's fiscal solvency. Thus, while the demand for education was increasing, the British did little to meet that demand, and in fact, obstructed it by adding fees where none had previously existed. The desire for girls' education overlapped with the desire of missionaries from Europe and the United States to bring Christianity to Egypt. Although the missionaries converted few individuals, their influence in girls' education was considerable. The existence of missionaries helped to spur various communities within Egypt to open their own schools for girls: Coptic, Jewish, Muslim, Catholic, Greek, and Armenian.

By the turn of the century, among those contributing to the press there was general agreement on the necessity of girls' education and the need for the government to expand its efforts. What differed among contributors to this discourse was the question of definition. Should education for girls be the same as that for boys? What subjects should it encompass? While there was a general agreement that home economics should be at the core of any curriculum, there was great debate over what 'home economics' meant. For upper-class women, it was a theoretical and philosophical topic, while most men argued that it needed to have a practical component. In other words, many men believed that even if a woman had a household staff to take care of the cooking, cleaning, and laundry, she should still know how to carry out all of these tasks herself.

Textbooks ran the gamut, from the extremely pragmatic to those offering little or no practical advice. Initially, many textbooks were translated from European languages to meet the needs of schools. Nevertheless, for the same reasons that many Egyptians found missionary education unaccept-able, so too did they object to foreign textbooks. Furthermore, as the British presence in Egypt persisted, Egyptians focused on reform from within to combat the occupation. Reform of the individual, the home, and the family was uniquely tied to reform of the nation and the Egyptians' capability for self-government.

The selection which follows represents the Introduction of the first chapter of a text book *The Young Woman and the Home* edited by Antun al-Gamayyil (d. 1948). The author was a journalist who also served in various government posts. He later was the editor of the semi-official newspaper *Al-Ahram*.

Text[39]

In the name of God, the Beneficent, the Merciful.

The esteemed rector, his Excellency Isma°il Sabri Pasha,[40] graciously sent me the following, after having examined this book:

My dear friend Antun Effendi al-Gamayyil,

I read your book, *The Young Woman and the Home*, and I am writing to you because I am overwhelmed with delight. How could I not be delighted having

[39] Antun Al-Gamayyil, *Al-Fatat wal-Bayt*, 'Introduction and Chapter One', 2nd edn. (Cairo: Matba°at al-Ma°arif, 1916).

[40] Like Saad Zaghlul, Isma°il Sabri Pasha was not born into Egypt's elite. Nevertheless, his merchant family was well enough off to send him to school, where he excelled in a number of subjects including calligraphy. Around 1870 he was 'discovered' by °Ali Mubarak and changed career paths from calligra-phy instructor to law. After studying in France, he was an attorney for the courts of Cairo, Mansura, and Alexandria consecutively, not simultaneously. He was appointed Chief Justice in Benha and later (1886) in Alexandria. In 1895 he became the first Egyptian Attorney-General. The following year he was appointed the governor of Alexandria, a post held until 1899. He then returned to law as the Deputy Minister of Justice until his retirement in 1907—a response to the events of Dinshawal. He was also a poet, influenced by both traditional Arabic poetry and his studies of French literature.

witnessed your style of writing and grace of composition? Before you, writers have been unsuccessful translating subjects, which are related to our cultural life and tied to our intellectual renaissance, from a foreign language into Arabic. [...]

We are in dire need of education for our sons and our daughters. Indeed, our need to educate our daughters is even more extreme, because the girl of today is the mother of tomorrow. The wise man knows that the mother's bosom is the first school in which the baby finds nourishment for his body and his mind. Women are half of the community and it is unquestionable that their half is crippled. If the infirmity of this half is not remedied—which includes our mothers, our sisters, and our daughters—and if they are not properly raised in the presence of knowledge and sound morals, then their uplift will be in vain.

The book *The Young Woman and the Home* addresses this need and fills the void that we have witnessed in our textbooks. Thus, I extend to you dear friend, the greatest expression of congratulations, and ones like them to the virtuous woman who knew how to simplify the duties of the young woman and the mistress of the household by the most beautiful means and in the most comprehensive style. [...] Peace be upon you and upon all who follow your example in writing and translation.

Isma'il Sabri

[*There follows an open letter praising the book and the author from Mustafa Lutfi al-Manfaluti that was published in* Al-Ahram.][41]

Introduction

Many books on girls' upbringing have been written from all of the nations which have attempted to raise their ethical and material fortunes. Writers and intellectuals have given this subject great significance, connecting it to national life and discussing its influence in the creation of morals. Nevertheless, in writing my book, I did not broach the subject like this or take it up from any single point of view, which for me did not fulfill this need.

I have attempted to fill this void, at least partially. I did not believe that I should translate one of the many Western books on the topic, because they are not suited to our Eastern life and our national customs. Nor did I feel qualified to take the subject up directly, since it is the specialty of women and full comprehension of its subject matter in all of its detail is impossible. Thus, I referred to the wisdom and experience of a woman. This was offered to me by Dr G. S. Dubuk, who is among the virtuous women who have studied a great deal and have achieved expansive expertise in implementing this knowledge.

[41] Two Lebanese Greek Catholic immigrants, Salim (1849–92) and Bishara (1853–1902) Taqla established *Al-Ahram* ('The Pyramids') in Alexandria in 1876. With its emphasis on reporting the news over partisan polemics it survived censorship and many changes of government to become Egypt's main daily newspaper. See Ami Ayalon, *The Press in the Arab Middle East* (New York: Oxford University Press, 1995), 42–3, 55–6, and 148–51 (for circulation estimates through 1948).

Regardless, the book *The Young Woman and the Home*, which I offer today for the Arab woman, is distinguished by its conformity with our life and our customs, as well as by its combining both the rules of moral upbringing and the prerequisites for household organization. [. . .] Our household happiness and our national renaissance both depend upon the upbringing of our women and I would like this book to provide assistance for young women and housewives to help them understand their lofty mission and to undertake their duties with precision.

Chapter 1: Moral and household education: girls' upbringing—The mission of the young woman—The science of home economics—How to benefit from this knowledge

The need for girls' education

One of the great kings once said to a woman, who had long been in charge of administering a woman's institute, 'What is missing in our young women that is needed to complete their upbringing?' She responded, 'Mothers.' This is a profoundly complete, yet condensed response. We must understand its meaning and give its aim careful consideration. If the man who has the greatest influence in the future of his countrymen's sons is nothing more than what the hands of his mother have created and the fruit of her upbringing, then why are our young women not admired? If the matter of your education was made contingent upon such great significance, then you could become complete mothers, able to raise men of the future.

[. . .]Women, like men, have an intellect that must be nurtured, organized, and strengthened[. . .]How can a woman possibly undertake her duties without sound knowledge?[. . .]Thus, if we want the young woman to be prepared to take on her obligations, then we must cast open the door of learning for her because the developed mind is more capable of completing those duties and more.

Young women, I am not providing you with information to obstruct you from other matters: take from the sciences correctly, drill what is important, study and teach, but there are two matters of which you must never fail to take note: first, your studies should not interfere with your duties as a daughter, wife, or mother, because your home is more significant than any other locale. Second, do not use your knowledge to curry favor or to boast, instead use your influence in ways that are worthy of praise.

The importance of the housewife in our age is not limited to what it was in the past: it necessitates that she organize her home, regulate its finances, and carry out its support from within. She must know how to use her mind and her time. Her position in societal life is to extract maximum benefit, or at least benefit from, wherever she may be.

The man must not concern himself with his wife's loyalty; rather he needs to have faith in her wisdom and intellect. He does not summon her, drawing him away from his work; nor should he seek her opinion for everything, because her errands require more devotion than others and her opinion is more relevant. By the same token, after the hearts are united, so too must the minds of the couple be joined. They should create a beautiful agreement from which neither can deviate. This total agreement is based solely upon mutual respect and trust between the two parties. [. . .] Each realizes what is incumbent upon him/her and strives to do it.

The young woman's mission in the family with respect to morals
The young woman, whose upbringing is carried out as we describe, brings happiness to her family and herself. She is the flower beautifying the garden and scenting her environs [. . .] She rejects selfishness and seeks the happiness of others. [. . .]

Is there no greater outlook than that of a mother and a daughter who live one life, who feel with one heart? [. . .] You, young woman, from a young age accustom yourself to opening your heart to your mother and letting her enter. This mutual trust eases mothers in their mission to raise their daughters, and young women should guard against obstructions along this path.

The relationship between the daughter and her father is no less affectionate or less worthy of mention than that with her mother. The father, who spends most of his day outside the home, returns to it and he is gladdened if he finds the love and devotion of his daughter. If the work day tires him and his duties weigh heavily on his mind, then the virtuous wife and the devoted daughter are the most capable of alleviating his anxiety, returning ease to his heart, and a smile to his mouth, thus increasing his energy level and ability to return to his duties anew.

The properly raised, happy, good daughter is not content to just think of herself, she sees the responsibility of her mother in the house without her [mother] saying anything. She takes an interest in both household affairs and the individuals of the family. If her mother were sick and unable to do her work, the young woman would take her place in the administration of the household. [. . .] These duties are required of you [. . .] and they are the most beautiful adornment for you when you are wealthy and the most beneficial assistance to you in poverty.

The science of home economics: its content and its utility
You are probably surprised to see these words and are asking yourself, 'Is home economics really a science among ones that one must study, or whether it is something easy to attain?' Yes, there is a special science for the home which you must learn [. . .] The science of home economics teaches the woman how she can undertake this administration in a wise and effective manner; how she can administer the affairs of her small kingdom; how to elevate its order, cleanliness, and ease of body and mind; how to arrange its finances from within and from outside [. . .]

An understanding of all of these matters necessitates diverse areas of knowledge, such that making girls' education household education, in both its moral and material aspects, could not possibly be rejected by anyone. God created woman to be man's partner, taking care of his needs, raising his children, caring for him in sickness, and assisting him in health. She was granted with a nature capable of undertaking this lofty mission. [. . .]

It is well known that the happiness of the family rests upon the ability of the mistress of the household, just as its misery and ruination are a necessary result of her efforts.

So for the happiness of the family and the future of the community, and in the noble name of marriage and the majesty of motherhood, the young woman's education is among the most important and significant matters.

How to take on the science of home economics
The mission of each spouse in a family is defined. The man undertakes outside work, exerting himself and taking his work seriously in order to provide sustenance for his children; the woman is concerned with internal matters, and she judiciously uses the money provided for her, which is returned to the family with ease, harmony, and comfort. [. . .]

There is no doubt that the young woman should take on this work gradually from an appropriate age. The principles of home economics—order and efficiency, love of work, and the principles of economy—these concepts should be easy for her to attain from a young age. Knowledge in the child is like engraving a stone [. . .] If a girl has her own room, then she should begin by caring for it—she would learn to put everything in its place and keep it clean. When she is a bit older she can be given a budget for her clothing. In this very useful way, she will learn the value of money and how to spend it wisely. [. . .]

So prepare your mind young woman to comprehend all of the household chores and train yourself to observe carefully such that you guard the knowledge pertaining to your gender in the present and in the future. If you truly want to become a proper housewife one day, then the matter is in your own hands, apparent in your deeds and desire.

The concerns of a housewife are numerous and diverse, so do not slack off in doing them. Do not make light of anything that depends upon you, for there is no doubt that the housewife is concerned with all matters in her home [. . .] He who brings her respect and honor knows her duties and how well she carries them out, just as her ignorance in these duties or neglect is an indication of a deficiency in education and/or morals.

The young woman does not know what the future will bring or for what place life is preparing her. [. . .] If peoples' expectations and desires are only in this life, then wealth will create huge disparities among them and in their ability to achieve them. Thus, it is incumbent that the woman uses her knowledge and expertise in meeting these needs, real or imagined, by creating a household budget, achieving an accommodation between income and expenditures through the guidance of her mind and her heart, devising all possible means to bring harmony, happiness, and clarity to them.

Before researching the things which a woman must know to run her home, we must say something about the characteristics of a housewife because the happiness of most families depends upon them. Organization, thrift, and energy are the pillars upon which flourishing homes rest, just as we will see in the coming chapter.

If we want to prepare the young woman to undertake her duties, then we must cast open the door of knowledge.

The happiness of the family is contingent upon the housewife's excellence in organization.

3.5 The Turkish 'Modern Woman': two press articles, 1924 and 1926[42]

Carole Woodall

Preface

> The new way of life made its strongest appearance in Istanbul. The old families run in a patriarchal way are falling off one by one. Young girls are dropping into the streets, the bars, and the dance halls . . . and ruining their futures in the process.[43]
>
> (*Illustrated Thursday*, 1926)

In the early twentieth century Ottoman state and society experienced profound changes marked by the defeat of the empire in the aftermath of World War I (1918). This event coincided with the decisive dismantling of the imperial domains in the Arab lands and the Balkans. Demographically, Istanbul had swelled in size due to an influx of Muslim refugees after the Balkan Wars (1912–13) and later of Russian refugees following the Russian Revolution (1917). The Allied Entente—French, Italian, and British forces (1918–22)—occupied Istanbul. With the founding of the Turkish Republic in 1923, Mustafa Kemal, later to take the name Atatürk, and his entourage composed of military officials, bureaucrats, and journalists instituted a series of secularist reforms. These reforms transformed the cultural and political appearance of society, including the abolishment of the caliphate and changes to dress, the calendar, and the alphabet occurring between 1924 and 1928.[44] The appearance of the modern-dressed Turkish woman participating in public activities became a banner for the republican ethos.

In the early republican years the status, position, education, employment, rights, and visibility of women were discussed amongst feminists, bureaucrats, and writers, continuing a debate that had been current since the nineteenth century. Ottoman elite women had become active in the public arena during the late Ottoman period, becoming involved in charity and social organizations as well as a thriving women's press. In addition,

[42] I would like to thank Professor Sibel Erol for her time and assistance in the preparation of this document.

[43] 'What sort of women do men look for when they decide to set up a new life for themselves?', *Resimli Perşembe* ('Illustrated Thursday'), 2/71 (Sept. 1926), 2. Translation taken from Alan Duben and Cem Behar, *Istanbul Households: Marriage, Family and Fertility, 1880–1940* (Cambridge: Cambridge University Press, 1991), 198.

[44] In 1926 the adoption of the Swiss Civil Code secularized family law. Women gained the right to vote in municipal elections in 1930 and in national ones in 1934.

educational reforms had occurred providing opportunities and training for women.[45] However, in the mid-1920s the image of the 'feminine' Kemalist woman was added.[46] A Turkish woman dressed in Western fashions and attending a republican ball with chaperone was appropriate. The image of the feminine 'modern woman' dancing unaccompanied, drinking, and attending the cinema became the subject of a heated debate in the popular press.[47] Not only was she meant to be active in the public domain, but she also had to present an appropriate visible image becoming her role as mother and/or daughter of the family and citizen of the nation.

During a period characterized by war, occupation, and political consolidation (1918–28), urban centers, such as Istanbul, experienced changing patterns of consumption, sexuality, morality, and behavior, which reconfigured the public and private. New modes of communication and technology increased individual access to various forms of entertainment. In the early twentieth century the gramophone and phonograph—albeit elite luxury items—were available in retail stores in both the more traditional Muslim districts of Istanbul and the more Europeanized district of Pera. In addition, the radio, and advances in cinematic production, increased accessibility to dancing and cinema-going. By the mid-1920s the popularizing of jazz, dances such as the Charleston, Black Bottom, and Shimmy, the films of Charlie Chaplin and Mary Pickford, and performances by Josephine Baker (1929, 1934) as well as by Hungarian and Russian dancing girls were just part of a developing cultural scene whereby Turkish women were participants as spectators and cultural consumers. In the various illustrated magazines, women's press, and periodicals, intellectuals, writers, feminists, and reformers debated not just the moral appropriateness of these activities, but the suitability for Turkish Muslim women. The modern Turkish woman, although representative of the republic, became linked to popular debates about the Turkish family, society, and the nation.

The increased presence of Turkish women in public continued a 'family crisis' debate, which was linked to a larger dialogue on the social, economic, political, and cultural transformations occurring in various urban and rural centers during the interwar period. The idea of the 'modern woman' as a

---

[45] e.g. in 1842 a midwifery program was introduced at the medical school, and in 1870 the Dar ül-Muallimât, or Teacher's Training College for Women, was founded.

[46] Ayşe Durakbaşa, 'Kemalism as Identity Politics in Turkey', in Arat (ed.), *Destructing Images of the 'Turkish Woman'* (New York: Palgrave, 2000), 147, states that the image of the 'feminine woman entertaining men at balls and parties' was a new addition to the roles that women assumed in public and private spaces.

[47] In the late-nineteenth century Güllü Agop, a successful Armenian theater-owner in Istanbul, expanded his troupe's repertory by including works by Turkish writers in order to appeal to an increase of elite Turkish women as spectators. His theaters also provided latticed boxes to maintain the discretion of Muslim women. However, the appearance of a Muslim woman on stage was not deemed as appropriate. In 1920 a protest ensued when Afife Jale (1902–41), the first Turkish Muslim female stage actor, made an historic stage appearance.

threat to the moral fabric of the family and the role of women as mothers and citizens was not new to the republican period. Ziya Gökalp (1876–1924), sociologist, poet, and intellectual figure, advocated the importance of the family unit as being essential to the strength of Turkish culture and the attitude that Turks should have regarding Western civilization.[48] But it was not until the mid-1920s, in a period of rapid social change and the destabilization of cultural norms, that the conflict over changing patterns of lifestyle, consumption, and sexuality went so far as to question the role of the family and the identity of the 'modern Turkish woman'.

The two readings presented here, both selections from the early Turkish Republican press, reveal two different ways in which debates over women and the family were approached. The essay drawing a contrast between the 'family oriented' woman and the materialistic woman takes on the subject from a societal perspective, preaching a clear, moralizing message which emphasizes the connection between the correct role for women and the welfare of the nation. The article on dancing is both a much more personal reflection and a considerably more ambiguous view of the direction in which society was moving under the new republic.

Texts

A Turkish woman: 'How I began to dance for the first time and how I felt'

(*Resimli Ay*,[49]s.3, Nisan 1340/April 1924, *translated by Carole Woodall*)

In Istanbul dancing reached the level of a contagious disease that worked its way as near as the *na-mahrem*[50] of all families both rich and poor. We don't know how and from where this storm came; however, today dancing has become the most interesting topic of conversation for everyone, both men and women, in all social settings. Because of the instantaneous and infectious manner [in which it came], this trend that is dragging off our youth and making them drunk with excitement is also removing the loving affection and familial connection, the sincerity and purity of our young girls. In this new life it seems to be a remarkable thing to learn

---

[48] His ideas became the backbone of republican nationalist thought.

[49] In 1924 the husband and wife left-wing journalistic team of M. Zekeriya (1890–1980) and Sabiha Sertel (1895–1968) began the monthly publication of *Resimli Ay* ('The Illustrated Month'). In her memoir *Roman Gibi* ('Like a Novel') (Istanbul: Belge Yayınları, 1987; first pub. 1969), 79, Sabiha Sertel states that the main intention of the magazine was to address the needs and interests of the readers. Topics of interest ranged from critical commentaries on the social and economic conditions of Turkish society as well as serial stories and articles on fashion styles, beauty, and the latest trends. During the cultural purges of 1925 the magazine was closed down, resuming publication under the title of *Sevimli Ay* ('The Lovable Month'), and continuing subsequently under the original title in 1927. Publication continued until 1930.

[50] According to Islamic law, *na-mahrem* refers to an individual who is distantly related to another by blood, meaning that marriage with her/him is permissible.

about the excitements and feelings of a Turkish woman who until yesterday was
not used to sitting next to men. We requested a writing of sentiments from a
woman addicted to dancing. She promised to communicate her genuine feelings
on the condition that she not reveal her name. The article that you will read
below is a statement of those sentiments:

I laughed when I analyzed my emotions. However, I hesitated from saying
my exact feelings when asked what I felt at the first dance. After I had got the
go-ahead to write anonymously, I was able to convey my sentiments entirely.

At a time when dance came through all polite circles like a storm, I became
opposed to it in my little house in the village of Meçri.[51] My friends, whom
I accepted, belonged to the polite society of Şişli[52] and Kadiköy[53] and had joined
life. The more I listened to them the more my hair simply stood on end. I saw
dancing in a man's arms as buffoonery, when earlier we were not used to sitting
next to them.

Why did I see dancing like that? According to me, in that day I had some rights;
however, today I see that my [attitude about] dancing was because I didn't have
rights. At first new things create opposition psychologically, then later one warms
up to them. Dancing had this effect on me. After setting aside my conservatism, I
accepted this [new] feeling.

The first time that I accepted dancing, the social environment had an effect on
my embrace [of it]. Those who were dancing accused me of thick-headedness and
stupidity. Making oneself fit a trend is a woman's first duty. For me, while my
friends were accepting the clothing of modern life, conservatism was going to
leave its stamp on me. Given that this was the fashion, given that one had to
accept these [trends] to be modern, it was necessary to embrace these [things]
before being labeled. I accepted this fashion with my heart before my mind.

I danced for the first time at my friend's house in Erenköy.[54] At this social
[gathering] there were also foreigners. To tell you the truth everyone there was a

[51] I have been unable to identify the location of this village based on the spelling provided by the
writer. However, in C. Mostras's *Dictionnaire Géographique de l'Empire Ottoman* (St Petersbourg, 1873;
repr. Pera Turizm ve Ticaret Ltd.: Şirketi, 1995), there is a listing for the village of Mégri, or Makri,
located in the Edirne province near Gallipoli. There was no listing of the village in *Son Teşkilat Mülkiye'de
Köylerimizin Adları* ('The names of our villages in the last Civil Service Organization') (Istanbul: Hilal
Matbaası, 1927). In 1927 the first official census of the Turkish Republic was taken. A result of this project
was the listing of villages by province, provincial subdivisions, and provincial districts.

[52] By the early part of the twentieth century increasing urban development and tramway lines
expanded the residential boundaries of the city. Located in the European quadrant of Istanbul, Şişli
became a residential area for Muslim and non-Muslim upper-middle-class families and individuals
who resided in European-style, luxury apartment buildings.

[53] Kadıköy, ancient Chalcedon, located on the Asian side of the city, developed into an upper-middle-
class residential area by the turn of the century.

[54] Erenköy, located on the Asian side, was an exclusive residential Muslim district, hosting
luxurious kiosks.

complete stranger to me. I had no friends apart from my friend's husband. When bashfully entering my first boy–girl gathering I mumbled to the men presented to me. My wildness continued for a considerable time. Today mixed male–female society is an extremely normal thing. But to dance in the same hall is an event.

In order to be able to dance at my friend's social gathering I took lessons night and day for three months. There were even nights that I didn't eat or only slept for three hours. I was taking lessons from a Greek lady, [and] [my dancing partners] were my female friends. This also was not an extraordinary thing.

But, the dance at my friend's house was extraordinary.

First of all, my husband annoyed me the most. His glances, which couldn't bear to see me 'naked'[55] among strange men, passed harshly over my arms, breast, and eyes sometimes irritatedly sometimes lustfully. When my eyes made contact with his eyes, it was like taking a cold water bath.[56] I had persuaded him to come. Now, regretting this, he would have pulled me out from the midst of these naked women, these men who were stiff like mannequins, if this was possible. For a moment I was afraid that he was going to act out his Easternness.

In an excited manner, my eyes sometimes timidly gazed upon women, who were adorned like flowers of different colors (red, white, pink, and purple), and sometimes on my husband and men who filled the night.

My husband almost acted disrespectfully at the gathering. He danced with no one. He was pleasantly hanging out with fine and pretty girls. As his eyes alighted on mine, he almost acted wildly. I hesitatingly looked at the men around me. None of them was the object of his nervousness or his excitement. The only target of his anger was me.

In response to his egotism I almost became angry. Come what may I decided not to pay attention. The women around me were only acquaintances of the night. Standing up with big peacock-feathered fans and with crowns on their heads, each was as majestic as a queen. Next to them I was incredibly incapable and ungraceful. My crown was the irritable glances of my husband and my fan was my heart.

At this moment a blond youth approached.

'Would you be so kind,' he said . . .

We mixed in with a wild group of people who were entangled dancing to a wild tune. I did not know that young man. Even my friend had not introduced him. However, it would be shameful to refuse [an invitation], whoever it may be. If it were necessary to refuse on the grounds that I didn't know the person, then it would be necessary to dance with no one.

Certainly, in my expensive evening gown and in all my excitement, I had come here in order to dance. And how I danced with this young fellow. In order to narrate this entirely, I need to be aware of my senses. However, I was drunk with

---

[55] Literally, *décolleté*, French for a low neckline.   [56] Or, 'I was left feeling cold or frigid'.

joy. I don't know if the thing that made me drunk was the embarrassment of dancing in the arms of a young man, or his touch on my body, the intoxicating music, or the warmth of his breath. Amongst these couples who ran hither and thither in merriment from the exuberance of the music, I don't know how I was dancing or whether my steps fitted the music.

The touch that turned me, the hot breaths that descended to my soul made me sweat and made me faint to the point that I lost all my senses. This was the modesty of the first dance. I could not control how my feet [moved]. [Instead] I supposed that everyone was looking at my feet. I was dancing with the help of my cavalier, [because] I was so weak that I was not able to do what I knew. For a moment my eyes sought out my husband. He was not in his place. Later I saw him dancing with a woman who had been the subject of gossip between us for a long time. [At that moment] my husband took the night's revenge on me. However, I intended to take revenge myself.

That night I danced until morning. I paid no attention to the clumsiness of my feet or to my shyness. I was trying to punish my husband for his rude behavior. This feeling allowed me to quickly become used to the dancing festivities.

That night when we returned, while there was no reason, my husband and I were not talking to each other. What for! Why? After entering this world, these things were very natural. Why didn't we accept this? If I had been frightened by my husband's dancing with that woman, would it not be the same for me that my husband would be frightened by my dancing with another? Because it was I who persuaded him to come to the dance, it would have been a little chancy to ask him to [accept this situation]. [After all] I had tricked him to come to the first dance, and I had brought him. I wonder if [my] actions didn't give him some justification to be angry. Finally I decided not to say anything in order not to be accused.

My husband gradually began to attend dance school early every night. At this school, it is apparently reported that we weren't able to learn dancing together, [and] the families weren't able to go. While my husband was going there in order to learn how to dance, we [myself and friends] were dancing in our salons. At this festivity, we were accompanied by the brothers and husbands of my friends. I wasn't able to persuade my husband to come [to these gatherings].

The excitement of the first dance completely disappeared. Now, I could dance with whomever and wherever. However, I sometimes think that this new life ruined the old one and that one day we will face the danger of missing [the old life]. Nevertheless, I feel that the necessity of accepting all the requirements of modern life is pushing me toward this sacrifice.

Enver Behnan [Şapolyo],[57] 'Family Oriented Woman, Woman of Luxury'

(*Türk Kadın Yolu*,[58] published September 1926, written on 15 June 1926)

In today's society, two types of women catch the eye. The first one is married and bound to her children; the other is preoccupied with flighty things like dancing and fashion. A close examination of these two types may give us a more solid idea [about and the reasons for their differences]. The family oriented woman is a member of society, and the woman of luxury is [interested in] material things. That is to say that one is a social woman who conforms to [the dictates of] society, [whereas] the other one is materialistic.

It is appropriate to investigate carefully the sociology of the family oriented woman and also the physiology of the woman of luxury. Firstly, let's take the woman of luxury. There is no function in society for these kinds of women. They are a group living on society like parasites, [and are thus] harmful creatures to that society. They do not like marriage, [and] are not pleased with [the idea] of raising children. For them, becoming a mother is the biggest torment. [Instead,] they are slaves to material pleasures. Social rules do not dictate [their actions]. There are certain physiological reasons. These women have a weakness of their skin. Skin is active and often sensitive. In all creatures there is an importance [placed on] the sense of touch. However with these women, their skin is so sensitive that it is about to explode. Mirrors do not fall from their hands, as they always want to see their beauty. At the time when some of them [notice] a weight loss, they are pessimistic. It is as if life is extinguished. They own all beauty materials: powders, perfumes, ribbons, and colorful clothes.

The inside of a house is an annoyance for the women of luxury. They want to go out and [when they do so] they want each guy to turn his head [when he passes by]. When one does not [turn his head], they have a nervous breakdown. They are envious, cross-tempered, and addicted to hysteria. They betray men, commit

---

[57] Enver Behnan, [Şapolyo] (1900 Istanbul—1972 Ankara), history teacher, writer, and journalist for several newspapers and magazines including *Yeni Gün* ('New Day') (1922), *Hakimiyet-i Milliye* ('National Sovereignty') and *Öyğüt* ('Advice') (1923), *Tanin* ('The Echo'), *Son Telegraf* ('Latest Despatch'), and *Cümhüriyet* ('Republic'). He was also a member of the Court of Honor of the Ankara Newspaperman's Association and the Turkish Hearth Organization (*Türk Ocağı*). For a more detailed yet brief biographical entry refer to Osman Nebioğlu's *Türkiye'de Kim Kimdir* ('Who's Who in Turkey') (Istanbul: Nebioğlu Yayınevi, 1961–2), 576. Nebioğlu numbers his written works at 86. In addition, he is credited with being Atatürk's biographer, and also fought in the nationalist forces.

[58] *Türk Kadın Yolu*, or *Kadın Yolu*, the original title of the illustrated weekly magazine for the first four issues, covered topics of interest for modern Turkish women. Owned by Turkish feminist intellectual, Nezihe Muhittin (1889–1958), the publication began in 1925, ending in 1927 after thirty issues. It is considered to be the last women's periodical published in the Ottoman script before the language reform of 1928.

suicide, and lead their lives to prostitution. They are the sick and unhappy members of society. They do not have a single happy minute. Everyday they want to acquire a new ornament, exchange letters and be together with a new young man. However, if they realize these goals, they quickly change their mind and give him up. Many of them contract tuberculosis, or they go mad. They harm the society, and they destroy the comfort of its young girls. [Thus,] it is necessary to protect these [girls] from them, to marry them off quickly, or to cure them.

These kinds of women exist everywhere in the world. In Europe these women fill dance salons, brothels, and bars. In Istanbul, there are a lot of dance salons. Go there and examine them [yourself]. You will not encounter one woman with a clean face or a beautiful color.[59] [However] you will come in contact with [female] curiosities composed of sensitive skin, flesh, and bones . . . Amongst them, you will not come across a young girl who will be tomorrow's mother. This is how it is in Europe. When I was in Germany, I saw them in the dance halls. While there, apart from women with unpleasant grins, bare naked arms and painted lips, I was not able to see a family oriented woman. I did not see a woman who was better than a painted one with bare arms. There is dancing in Germany. It's part of their social life, because dancing is an entertainment that is done in the family with relatives and friends. Without getting permission from her family a young girl should never surrender her purity to men who aren't known for their moral character, who have blood shot eyes, and whose breath reeks of *rakı*.[60] Of course a young girl who goes there without permission has a tragic end. Youth is a time of strong sensations. An artificial glance [from a young man] may steal her heart, and may drag [it] into a dangerous abyss.[61] A family who is aware that this [is happening] can't give up its daughters to Beyoğlu's[62] cosmopolitan society, saying it's a necessity of civilization. If this is the case, that man becomes an enemy of the family and of the country.[63]

The family and the country want an honorable mother, an up-standing citizen, and an ethical individual. A girl who is up to no good and [indulges in] sensual pleasures can never raise children for the country. In the country, before everything else [or other responsibilities], there's the responsibility to motherhood.

[59] Clean face (*temiz siması*) more appropriately refers to a good character, whereas beautiful color (*güzel rengi*) aptly describes the woman as having a pale skin color due to her remaining primarily indoors.

[60] *Rakı* is a traditional Turkish alcoholic drink distilled from grapes and flavored with aniseed.

[61] In other words, 'her heart may be crushed'.

[62] Beyoğlu, or Pera as it was once called, was a predominantly non-Muslim district. In the nineteenth century vast changes took place to the urban structure, including the construction of European embassies, department stores, etc. The growth of leisure and entertainment facilities in Beyoğlu reflected changing notions of styles, fashion, and entertainment.

[63] The term translated here as 'country' can also mean hometown, neighborhood, or the place one hails from.

Marriage is the perpetuity of society. With this explanation I am not against those who dance. But I am against the manner and situation in which dancing occurs. There is no offense in a family dancing with each other or a member of society, or a society or an official club giving a social ball. The honor and background of the people who enter into this society is evident. It is necessary to trust them, because they are friends of mankind. Those who are loved and [can be] trusted are no harm to anyone.

It's like this; physiological problems push people toward sick aspects of social life. Women of luxury are [examples] of this type. They are sick and hysterical. Hence, there is a need to control the moral and ethical character of those who are inclined in this direction.

In that case, how is the family oriented woman? She is the woman of society, and she has a function. At home, she raises children for the country and she breathes happiness from the clean air of the family.[64] Families should simply be cultured.

To be cultured has the [same] meaning as to be national. The family association fits into this group. If families don't adapt themselves to the culture of that nation and if families become imitators of other countries' [culture], tragedy will again rear its head. Again, this family is not the true family. In a country, [this family] is a foreign element. The family should be national. In other words the family should conform to the culture of the Turkish nation. These are the cultural components of the nation.

Morality, good manners, language, religion and economics are wonderful things. A family that does not abide by these regulations is considered a cosmopolitan family and is thus harmful to that society. For this reason the family oriented woman is the representation of the nationality to which she belongs. The nationally minded woman is the family oriented woman. These women offer a living gift to the motherland: a soldier, a teacher, a writer, and clerk. That is to say that they produce good citizens. It is as if the family that is not cultured leaves to the country children that are ruined and corrupted, who fear military service, who are afraid of official duty, and anyone who is flippant and snobbish. At home, a European group, or 'monşerler',[65] speaks a language that does not love the streets of his country, and does not appreciate holidays and pleasures. Nevertheless, neither Europe accepts this type, nor is this type a child of the country. Cosmopolitans are wretches. Each family and woman of the country is cultured and is national. European civilization is a rose. However, when we

[64] She, the family oriented woman, gains a sense of security from the family.

[65] 'Monşerler', or *mon chermes chers*, was an expression heard in Turkey in the 1920s. It refers to members of late Ottoman/early Turkish elite Turkish society who adopted European styles, mannerisms, and language. Monşerler were also popularly referred to as *alafranga* as opposed to *alaturka*.

examine various European countries, French, German, English families, et cetera, catch the eye. They have accepted aspects of one civilization; however, culture is separate for each country. They never accepted that culture is shared.

We, the Turks also, accept European civilization. However, in no way can we accept their culture. Let's not even try European culture. A nation takes its existence from ideals, national passions, and national feelings. That this exists is possible by the power of its culture. The cultural strength of the Turkish nation is that it has shown its own existence against the ways of the civilizations of the world. For years [the nation] has been living freely and its independence is an example to the world. Presently, after the Turkish republic accepted its [political] position, it got rid of all the foreign cultural elements, and while prevailing over the Turkish country, it declared its governance. A national state was established. This [nation] and also the family organization will not resemble European nations, and will exist as a clear Turkish family. This family will raise good citizens with national sentiments for the Turkish nation. Thus there are differences between a woman of luxury and a family oriented woman. A woman of luxury is detrimental to all societies. The family oriented woman is useful. However, being national is a condition for the family.

3.6 Gender, morality, and state policy in modern Iran: a Ministry of Education memorandum, 1935

Camron Michael Amin

Preface

On 7 January 1936 the regime of Reza Shah Pahlavi in Iran embarked on a bold and brutal social experiment called the 'Women's Awakening' (*Nahzat-e Banovan*). Iranian women were compelled to remove their Islamic veils in public as part of an attempt to modernize Iranian society's attitudes toward women. In addition to this forced unveiling, some professional and educational opportunities were made available for women and their increasing presence in the fields of medicine, education, and government was encouraged. The coercive aspects of this social experiment were ignored and its beneficent and modernizing aspects lauded: an intense propaganda campaign involving the press, the arts, and radio, and public education speeches by prominent citizens and humble employees of the Ministry of Culture was launched. The propaganda effort continued from 1936 until the Allied occupation of Iran in 1941. Its ostensible aim was to emancipate women by ending their traditional social seclusion, and by creating 'new' men and women who could address the moral implications confronting the two sexes in working and socializing together in public. Neither the goals nor the tactics of the Women's Awakening project appeared overnight, but had been anticipated by decades of discussion of 'the woman question' in treatises, in the Iranian press, and in parliamentary debate.

The following document is a Ministry of Education memorandum written on the eve of the Women's Awakening and derives from a collection of published documents relating to this initiative.[66] For approximately a year before the Women's Awakening was prompted by the appearance of Reza Shah with his unveiled wife and daughters at a graduation ceremony in Tehran, the Iranian government had begun experimenting with unveiling in schools and organizing the Women's Society (*Kanun-e Banovan*), which replaced all independent women's organizations. These quiet efforts had not gone unnoticed, however, and in the summer of 1935 Iranian troops violently suppressed an uprising in the Gawhar Shad Shrine at Mashhad, in which demonstrators had protested against Westernized government dress codes, particularly the unveiling of women. That the Women's Awak-

---

[66] *Mottahed al-Mal-e Vezarat-e Ma'aref beh Shahrestanha*, 25 Azar 1314 (No. 3 Ministry of Education Memorandum to the Counties, 25 Azar 1314), in *Khoshunat va Farhang: Asnad-e Mahramaneh-e Kashf-e Hejab* (1313–1322) ('Violence and Culture: Confidential Documents of the Removal of the Veil (1934/5–1943/4)') (Tehran: *Entesharat-e Sazman-e Asnad-e Melli-ye Iran*, 1371/1992/3), 2–4.

ening was undertaken at all testifies to the high expectations Iranian leaders had in the power of the state to change society.

This document suggests that the high expectations were accompanied by anxiety about gender, violence, religious sentiment, national honor, and social morality.

Text

Ministry of Education, Pious Endowments and the Fine Arts Provincial [Departments of] Education. Memorandum No. 51561/17224. 25/9/14 [16 December 1935]. Confidential

Director of Education and Pious Endowments,

It is clear and observable that for many years women—who are half the population of this country—have strayed from the royal road of science and knowledge due to ignorance and have been the captives of superstitions and groundless imaginings, and for this very reason have been judged as the palsied limb of the social body which could in no way be beneficial and useful for practical and moral affairs. Now that a new movement has consolidated the country's social issues and affairs under the shadow of royal attention, and now that everyone's vices are being reformed, it is necessary that this great shame and deficiency also be eliminated. Women, who are the mothers of the great men of tomorrow, should benefit from the blessings of science, knowledge, civilization, and education, just like the women of other civilized countries. [It is also important] that they become able to form healthy and useful families and to educate brave patriotic children for the country. In order to execute this auspicious intent, the Ministry of Education is pursuing an orderly and fixed program that is being precisely and confidentially forwarded to you so that [Ministry of] Education operations in your jurisdiction will conform to this program, and so that you will refrain from useless delay and hesitation, or inappropriate zeal and extremism.

First of all, in regard to very young children, it has been decided that, from this year on, mixed beginning schools called 'kindergartens' will be formed throughout the country so that the boys and girls of the country's new generation will be educated there following a single course of instruction. This way, brothers and sisters will profit from the benefits of science without discrimination. In this regard, detailed and necessary instructions have been provided already, and you must try to proceed with those same arrangements so that gradually all the elementary schools will be mixed and under the instruction of female teachers.

Secondly, the children of the primary and secondary schools must be made accustomed to plain clothing, and you should ban the decoration and ornamentation, which is the cause of great social harm. You must immediately see to it that the girls of the primary and secondary schools regularly wear the uniforms that have been ordered. This is so that wealthy girls have no opportunity to be proud and boastful, and so that everyone will be accustomed to simplicity, cleanliness, and purity. They should wear the clothing that has been selected out of the utmost modesty and taste at school, at home, in the street, and everywhere. They should know that the ideal morality of women must be firm and strong and that its firm veil (*pardeh-e mohkam*) is self-possession and morality. The great father and crowned monarch of Iran has always preferred that the girls of Iran all wear simple clothing and be adorned with the ornaments of chastity, honor, and modesty, and that they keep far from their faces any sort of adornment which is of foreign manufacture or the cause of extravagance and waste. Education officials, teachers, and principals must have this clearly in mind when they nurture the girls who, with pure hearts and untroubled minds, are prepared to receive an education in the virtues of chastity, economy, purity, and simplicity.

Thirdly, regarding other women, two procedures must be implemented. Firstly, for the education of women in the jurisdiction of your primary and secondary school you must form a special conference for women at which female teachers will be present, and to which other genuine ladies will be invited and will attend with their husbands to partake of the scientific, moral, or social papers and lectures. To such conferences, you should invite persons possessing virtue, experience, and those who are known for [their] good record, friendliness, knowledge, or information, or who are [notable] people of the town, or who are distinguished government people, scholars, and academics who happen to be passing through, so that they may discuss personal hygiene, family issues, protection against infectious diseases, economics, thrift, and other such useful and scientific issues. The secondary school [students] should likewise give speeches or recite moral poetry. They must especially educate [the women in attendance] in the etiquette of sitting, rising, dressing, and such social graces as are typical among the chaste and genteel families of the civilized countries of the world. The [local] government and the police have been instructed to fully co-operate and render you complete aid in this matter so that these sorts of conferences for women will be administered in a useful and respectable way. You must especially endeavour to spread the word that the clothes that all the women of the world wear today are the same clothes that were typical in ancient days in Iran, were common for up to two centuries after the spread of Islam, and are in the same form that has been ordered by the sacred *shari'a* of Islam during worship—such as prayer, or on the pilgrimage—which is that [a woman's] face and shoulder are to be uncovered (*baz va goshudeh*). Today, the fact that good ancient practice has been revived is not out of imitation of other countries, but rather is due to the natural and social uses and advantages that this form of clothing possesses. You must especially endeavour that no corrupt women or women of bad reputation find their way into the gatherings of respectable ladies, and that they not dress in their clothing, but rather that they should be kept far from these sorts of conferences and denied entry into parties, receptions, and such things. Secondly, the honorable government, chief of police, and the honored and influential people, of the city, who are of good intentions and enlightened thought, must act in concert as soon as possible to form gatherings in which they all socialize with their families in an approved way and with the utmost composure. [This is] because family socializing is very useful for moral education. In the company of women, men, perforce, become accustomed to modesty and politeness, and [the company of women] reduces the violence and rudeness that is requisite of their nature. In the presence of virtuous and moral men, women obtain virtue, and the shyness and bashfulness, which usually is their only disagreeable weakness, is diminished. Instead, [the women] gain knowledge and information from their discussions and conversations with knowledgeable and informed men.

For this assignment you must show the utmost caution that you not allow unmarried or rash men [into the gatherings] and that this sort of social intercourse is placed upon a strong foundation of learned morality, or else harm, rather than benefit, will result. This has been a summary of the details of the program which has already commenced in the capital according to orders, and must now be appropriately executed everywhere in the provinces [in accordance] with the exigencies of the moment and the environment, and in accordance with the specifications and clarifications of the officials in [the Ministry of] Education, who are in charge of educating public morality. Of course, you must conduct yourself and operate with the utmost intelligence, composure, and organization in co-operation with government officials and officials within your jurisdiction.

Minister of Pious Endowments.

Related note: It should be especially emphasized that in this important matter all sorts of harshness, posturing (*tazahor*), and rudeness is to be avoided and that matters should not depart from planning and composure.

The enclosed points will be sent to Eastern Azarbayjan, Western Azarbayjan, Fars, Kerman, Gilan, Mashhad, Mazandaran, Esfahan, Kermanshah, Khuzestan, Hamadan, Yazd, Borujerd, Kordestan, Eraq, Qazvin.

(Series J—51018–10A ±)

3.7 Interview of a deputation of the Arab Women's Committee in Jerusalem at Government House on Thursday, 24 March 1938[67]

Ellen L. Fleischmann

Preface

Beginning in the late nineteenth century, middle- and upper-class, educated women in the Middle East, like their counterparts in other parts of the world, began to form women's organizations. Globally, the issues that prompted the establishment of these associations varied widely: from women's suffrage to the abolition of slavery to educational and legal reform, amongst others. In the Middle East, although many of these groups initially tended to be constituted within the context of religion—such as the (Christian) Orthodox Aid Societies in Greater Syria—and focused on reform and social welfare concerns, issues of nationalism and feminism increasingly came to the forefront of their agendas. The groups, founded as individual societies, frequently with disparate aims and organizational methods, began to consolidate as women's movements in the 1920s and 1930s. The women's movement in Egypt, which had been established early, with its renowned, celebrated feminist leader Huda Sha'rawi, provided inspiration and a model for other women's movements in the region. Each movement had its own character, goals, personalities, issues, and distinct history, yet a sense of regional solidarity and common efforts also developed. Regional women's conferences were held in the 1930s and 1940s in Beirut, Damascus, Tehran, Baghdad, and Cairo.

In Palestine, Arab women's organizations followed simultaneously a parallel and distinct trajectory as they evolved. The earliest women's societies were the Orthodox Aid societies established in towns and cities, such as Acre (whose Orthodox Aid Society was founded in 1903), which had significant Christian populations. Their goals were to assist poor girls by educating them—in some instances founding schools—and helping to provide dowries for marriage. In the course of the early twentieth century more groups followed, though not many. In the 1920s, however, different kinds of women's organizations appeared, due to growing tensions over the political situation.

Until World War I, Palestine had been part of the Ottoman Empire. In the war settlements, Great Britain and France extended their control in the

[67] Sources: Khayr al-Din Zirikil, *Al A'lam*, 7, 4th edn. (Beirut, 1949), 174, kindly provided by Arnoud Vrolijk, curator, Middle East Collection, Leiden University; and Kayalı, *Arabs and Young Turks*, 20, 57, 74.

Middle East through securing League of Nations' Mandates over Greater Syrian territories. France's Mandate covered present-day Lebanon and Syria, while Great Britain had two: Iraq, and what is now Palestine/Israel. But the Palestine Mandate was significantly different from the others; included in its text was the Balfour Declaration, which promised the Jews a 'National Home'. The Zionist movement, founded in Europe in the nineteenth century, had been successful in gaining sympathy among some of the British political establishment during the war. One result of this was the ambiguous promise contained in the Balfour Declaration, which also guaranteed that 'nothing [would] be done which [would] prejudice the civil and religious rights of existing non-Jewish communities in Palestine'. However, the Palestinian Arab population rejected the Balfour Declaration from its inception. In the 1920s a Palestinian nationalist movement formed which resisted the Mandate and the imposition of the Jewish home, and agitated for an independent, parliamentary government for the people of Palestine. At the same time, the Zionist movement began to make its presence felt through the acquisition of land and immigration of Jews from Europe. Periodic outbreaks of violence occurred between the Arabs and Jews in Palestine, one of the worst in 1929 in Jerusalem and Hebron, where 133 Jews and 116 Arabs died. Such incidents stimulated the founding of the Palestinian women's movement.

In October 1929 Palestinian Arab women convened a national congress in Jerusalem and founded their own women's movement, which united local women's associations within a national framework. From this point on, the movement: established local women's associations; demonstrated on the streets; protested via a barrage of memoranda and telegrams to the British government and others; accosted government officials in private meetings and interviews; delivered speeches in public and published articles and protests on the Palestinian cause in the press; provided financial, material, and emotional support to prisoners and their families; participated in regional, Middle Eastern, and international women's conferences; and raised funds for and financed arms purchases during the 1936–9 Revolt.

The document below was produced during the revolt, which broke out against the British in 1936. Palestine during the 1930s witnessed increased tension over the issues of Jewish immigration and land acquisition. Underground militant groups had begun to form amongst both the Jewish and Arab populations. In 1936 the death of ʿIzz al-Din al-Qassam (one of the popular leaders of an underground group) in a skirmish with British police provoked a general strike, which lasted for six months before escalating into a full-scale armed rebellion against the British in Palestine, which continued sporadically for three years. The British response was severe: the government drafted large numbers of troops and threw all the weaponry and military might a major European power could wield against largely peasant forces. The government also used arrests, detention, and collective punishment against the Palestinian population to put down the Revolt. The women's movement energetically protested to the government, held frequent and large demonstrations, and assisted the families of men killed or imprisoned. In another response to the rebellion, a royal commission, the Peel Commission, was sent to Palestine in 1937 and recommended partition of the country into Jewish and Arab states. The Arab population rejected this proposal, and the Revolt continued until the eve of World War II.

The document below is an interview between many of the key leaders of the Palestinian women's movement's main Jerusalem organization and the British high commissioner of Palestine. In it, they not only protest against the measures used by the government to repress the Revolt, but also present their own political positions on a variety of topics. The document is also interesting for what it reveals about the character, tactics, and strategies of the movement's leadership.

Text

Interview of a deputation of the Arab Women's Committee in Jerusalem at Government House on Thursday 24 March 1938

The following were present:

His Excellency the High Commissioner [Sir Harold MacMichael];[68] Madame Labibeh Budeiri,[69] Mrs M. S. Moghannam,[70] Miss Shahinda Duzdar,[71] Miss Zahia

---

[68] Sir Harold MacMichael replaced Sir Arthur Wauchope as High Commissioner on 3 March 1938.

[69] Not much is known about Labibeh Budeiri, other than that she came from a prominent Jerusalem family.

[70] Matiel Moghannam: Mrs Moghannam, a Lebanese Christian by birth but brought up in the USA, was a prominent leader of the Palestinian women's movement in the 1930s. She was the wife of Moghamman Moghannam, a lawyer originally from Jerusalem, who was associated with the Nashashibi faction, which opposed the dominant Husayni faction in the Palestinian national movement during the Mandate period. Mrs Moghannam was the English-language secretary of the Arab Women's Executive Committee (founded 1929), which dominated the leadership of the women's movement in its early years. She wrote a book, *The Arab Woman and the Palestine Problem* (1937), and contributed numerous articles to the Palestinian press. Her name is on many of the letters and memoranda of protest sent to the British government during the 1930s. Her husband's family was middle class, and not particularly prominent in Palestinian society. He attended law school in the USA, where he met and married his wife, and subsequently they returned to Palestine.

[71] Shahinda Duzdar. Born (1906) and died (1946) in Jerusalem, Shahinda Duzdar lived her entire life in her native city. Her family was not a particularly prominent one. Little is known about her social background. A founding member and treasurer of the Arab Women's Executive Committee, she was the president of the Arab Women's Association (exactly when this began is not entirely clear, but her tenure continued throughout the 1940s up until her death), from which the Arab Women's Union split (effectively fragmenting the women's movement) c.1937–8. She was very active in the movement from the 1930s until her early death, attending numerous meetings with British government officials. She never married.

Nashashibi,[72] Miss Zuleikha Shihabi,[73] Miss Badra Canaan,[74] Private Secretary; Chief Arabic Translator in attendance.

Mrs Moghannam said that the Arab Women's Committee was anxious to take this early opportunity of meeting His Excellency to welcome him to this country and to wish him a successful term of office. At the same time, the Committee wished to convey to His Excellency an expression of the Arabs' deepest concern at the deplorable condition to which Palestine has been drawn.

She thought it was hardly necessary for them to state the grievances of the Arabs, for they felt sure that His Excellency must have acquainted himself by now with all the details of the Palestine case.

Mrs Moghannam added that as women, they were compelled to express their alarm and great anxiety at the future of their children. Hundreds of Arabs are now under arrest or in concentration camps, while many people deserted their homes and families, and a good number meet their death daily through military operations or execution, and the heavy burden of all that falls on women.

In the opinion of the Arabs, the policy of His Majesty's Government in Palestine will result in the subordination of the Arabs in their own country, while at the same time, that policy was contrary to the natural rights and prerogatives of the Arabs and has been the cause of all troubles and will continue to be so until it is fundamentally changed. The more the British Government persists in the present policy, the more tension will increase, and people are impelled, most reluctantly, to do things which they know well would bring them disaster and sorrow.

---

[72] Zahia Nashashibi came from a (still) prominent Jerusalem family. The Nashashibi clan competed with the Husayni family for leadership of the Palestinian national movement in the Mandate period, although not all individual members held the same political views. This competition was reflected to a certain extent in the women's movement. There is little personal information about Nashashibi: she was a graduate of the Sisters of Zion school in Jerusalem; a member of the AWE; and a founding member of the Arab Women's Association in 1929. She was president of the AWA after the death of Shahinda Duzdar in 1946 until her own death in 1977. She never married.

[73] Zuleikha Shihabi (1903–92) came from a middle-class family in Jerusalem. She was a member of the AWE and one of the founders of the Arab Women's Association (AWA) in 1929. In 1937 she was elected to the Arab Women's Union (AWU), which split from the AWA as a result of personal rivalry among the women and some fallout from the Husayni–Nashashibi competition. Shihabi was aligned with the Husaynis. She held this position until her death, and was very active in the women's movement throughout her life. Those who remember her, consider Shihabi to be '*the* founder' of the Palestinian women's movement, (which is not entirely accurate). She owned property in Jerusalem, which she donated for the use of the AWU. She never married.

[74] Little is known about Badra Canaan. She was probably related to Tawfiq Canaan, a prominent Palestinian physician and amateur anthropologist of his own people. She was Christian, and according to Moghannam, an active member in one of the earliest Arab women's associations, *c.*1919, in Jerusalem. Reports of her activities surface in the press. In 1938 she is reported to be the treasurer of the Arab Women's Association. She was one of the Palestinian delegates who attended the 1938 Eastern Women's Conference in Cairo.

Mrs Moghannam assured His Excellency that the Arabs were not enemies to the British and added that the traditional friendship between the two nations has been maintained for generations in Palestine, as well as in other territories. The Arabs of Palestine were driven to a state of despondency and despair; for them the issue is one of life or death. They cannot keep silent, nor will anyone else on the subject of what, she considered, is a continual trespass of their rights. If some of the Arabs, under pressure of circumstances beyond their control, carried arms to defend their country in their own way, it was because they were convinced that many forces were working against their interests. In her opinion, the majority of members of Parliament and most of the British Press were amongst such forces.

Arab women, Mrs Moghannam asserted, abhor the destruction of life in whatever form. They harbor no hatred toward any people or race, and dislike to see Palestine, from which the message of peace was first given to the world, to be converted into a warlike state. It was unfortunate, she added, that His Majesty's Government, who is upholding the cause of peace at this moment of international anxiety, should fail in its sacred duty in this country. Something greater than punitive measures was necessary to restore peace and to remove the causes of anxiety. Unless the Arab people were assured of their natural rights, there could be no reason to believe that their anxiety would be removed or even diminished.

Commenting on the quotation made by His Excellency in his broadcast address that 'man does not live on bread alone', Mrs Moghannam said that it was immaterial to the Arabs whether they were now living under better conditions than those obtained under the Turks, or whether some of them are now richer and their standard of living higher, so long as they see that they are being supplanted from the land, outnumbered by immigration and subordinated politically, economically, and socially.

Referring to the partition scheme proposed by the Royal Commission, Mrs Moghannam wished to reiterate what has been said by every Arab spokesman in Palestine and elsewhere, that partition was not a solution to the Palestine Problem and cannot and will not be accepted by any Arab.

Mrs Moghannam expressed the hope that, through His Excellency's wise judgment, a new era of peace and prosperity would be established in Palestine and the memory of the deplorable events that marred the recent history of this country would be wiped out. She implored His Excellency to be instrumental in restoring to the Arabs their rights and to the Holy Land its peace. His Excellency enquired whether any other lady would like to speak.

Miss Shahinda Duzdar said that the position of the Arabs has been reduced to one who finds himself facing an extreme danger and endeavors to defend himself. The Jews were the aggressors. They invaded the country with their men and wealth and the Arabs find themselves facing a sweeping invasion. It was the intention of the Jews to supplant the Arabs and to take their places in the country in all walks of life. If Europe has been stirred to oust the Jews from countries in which they lived for centuries, why should the Arabs of Palestine be made the victims?

Referring to the position of the Arabs of Palestine under the Turks, Miss Duzdar added that the Arabs were restive under the Ottoman rule and had made every endeavor to rid themselves of that rule. It was with this object in view that the Arabs had joined the side of the British Government and fought against the Turks, their co-religionists. For taking that attitude, they were subjected to many calamities and difficulties: many of their leading men were executed by the Turkish tyrant, Jamal Pasha, and a great number lost their lives in war. The Arabs were motivated to take that thorny course in order to attain their freedom and independence, and they will never agree that a Jewish state or even a Jewish National Home should be set up on the land that is so dear to them.

Discussing the consequences of His Majesty's policy, Miss Duzdar added that the present situation in the country might be cited as the best example of the failure of that policy. The heaviest burden fell on the *fellahin*. Many of them are being killed daily, while others have deserted their homes and left their wives and children helpless. Every day a number of them are brought to trial before the Military Courts that, in most cases, end with their conviction. Miss Duzdar inquired whether these Courts were primarily intended for the Arabs.

The Arabs are aware, Miss Duzdar added, that Great Britain was powerful. They realize that she has an innumerable number of airplanes, guns and men, but they also realize that in the annals of history, such strength will have no recognition and only acts of justice will be acknowledged, for it has been truly said 'Justice is the foundation of rule.'

Reverting to the Ottoman rule, Miss Duzdar said that the Turks had governed this country for over 500 years, but they failed to erase its Arab character. The Arabs enjoyed full constitutional rights and were the actual rulers. The Jews enjoyed their rights as citizens, but their language was not officially recognized and there were no Jewish Municipalities or Jewish mayors. Now the Jews control almost all the resources of the country and are rapidly lending the country a Jewish character.

Referring to Syria, Miss Duzdar said that France has acknowledged the rights of the Arabs in that country and restored to them all that is their due, while the Arabs of Palestine are still living under Zionist pressure.

Miss Duzdar hoped that His Excellency will appreciate their point of view and will see to it that this state of tension and unrest be removed by granting to the Arabs their legitimate rights.

Miss Shihabi wished to make special mention of the deportees and detainees. The government thought, she said, that by deporting some of the leaders, the situation would be improved, but experience has shown that the contrary was the case. The deportees were the spokesmen of the people and were claiming their legitimate rights, and there was no reason why they should have been deported.

Supplementing Miss Duzdar's statement with regard to the rights and pre-rogatives the Arabs enjoyed under the Turks, Miss Shihabi said that Arabs were even appointed by the Sultan as Prime Minister and cited Mahmud Shawkat Pasha[75] as an example. They had full representation in the Ottoman Parliament, but under British rule they were deprived of all such prerogatives and the only Muslim institution in the country has now fallen into foreign hands.

Discussing the case of the detainees, Miss Shihabi said that they realized that the detainees are now living under better conditions than before, but their condition is still far from satisfactory. Fifty men are grouped in one room and the sanitary conditions leave much to be desired. Families of these detainees are living in a state of distress and misery.

Miss Shihabi appealed to His Excellency to consider the case of the deportees and detainees with a view to their release.

Miss Shihabi criticized the manner in which Arabs are detained or arrested. She assured His Excellency that, in certain cases, a man is kept for months under investigation while his parents are hardly allowed to know of his whereabouts or to see him. She cited the case of Diab Fahoum as one of such cases.

Miss Canaan wished to speak on the particular question of immigration. Immigration, she said, was the cause of all trouble. The British Government promised the Jews a national home in Palestine, but not to convert all Palestine into a Jewish National Home. Lord Samuel once said in 1921 that the term 'national home' means that the Jews should be allowed to establish for themselves a national home in Palestine to the extent required by the interests of the Jewish people settling there. At the beginning of the British Administration the number of Jews in the country did not exceed 60,000. Now they have reached the figure of 420,000. This immigration has adversely affected the interests of Arab

[75] Mahmud Shawkat, a leading member of the Young Turk movement, was born in 1858 in Baghdad, an Iraqi of Circassian (Georgian) descent. After graduating from the military academy in Istanbul, he had a distinguished army career. He was a prominent member of the CUP, taking part in the Young Turk Revolution in 1908 and the ensuing deposition of Sultan Abdülhamid II. Commander of the Third Army, which crushed the counter-revolution against the CUP in 1909, he was subse-quently appointed minister of war in 1910, and then became grand vizier in 1913. As an Arab, he opposed the Turkification policy of the Young Turk regime. He was assassinated in June 1913.

merchants and cultivators. Even Arab laborers were displaced. The Jews took control of almost all the economic resources of the country. When they reached this number, they asked not only for equal rights with the Arabs, but also that the country should be divided into two parts and they be given one part thereof. The Arabs will not accept partition. The British Government has given sufficient assistance to the Jews and enabled them to reach this position. That should be enough. If the Jews were sincere, they would not insist on further immigration and would live peacefully with the Arabs, as continual immigration would increase the anxiety of the Arabs as to their future and the future of their children. The Jews state that this country was once their own, and that they are entitled to return to the land of their ancestors: this statement cannot be accepted by any men of reason.

Miss Canaan asserted that Jewish immigration to Palestine would not solve the international Jewish problem. At the most, Palestine will not absorb more than two to three millions, and the number of Jews in the world exceeds 18 million. If it is argued that the Jews were promised this land, it may be stated that no promise that would affect the rights of other people who are living in the land should be upheld. Many promises and pledges made as a consequence of the Great War have disappeared, and it is in the interest of peace that the Balfour Declaration, which has caused so much trouble, should also be wiped out.

His Excellency, after thanking the members of the deputation for their expression of welcome, said that he could not be expected to reply seriatim to the points they had raised, for they had in fact put forward the Arab case in the same form in which it had been presented and considered by the Royal Commission. But he wished to make a few general remarks, although he did not expect that the deputation would agree with them all, just as the deputation would not expect him to agree with all they had said.

The first remark His Excellency had to make was in regard to Mrs Moghannam's statement that the Arabs harbored no hatred. It appeared to His Excellency that this was far from the case, and he was very sorry for it.

His Excellency's second remark was in reply to the statement made by Miss Canaan that, though the British Government had promised to give the Jews a national home, it had not offered to them the whole of Palestine. That, His Excellency said, was true and it explained why His Majesty's Government favored partition.

Thirdly, His Excellency noted that the deputation had made many points, but had omitted one very important one: that was that it was the duty of every Government to govern. One would have thought from the tenor of the deputation's remarks that Palestine has been an independent Arab state from the beginning of time. That was not so and it seemed to have been forgotten that

British troops conquered Palestine and that the British people are entrusted with the task of governing it. The Arabs must realize that there is a Government in the country to which respect must be paid and His Excellency's advice to the deputation was to advise their friends to co-operate with that Government.

When Mrs Moghannam replied to this that it was in accordance with the spirit of co-operation that His Excellency advocated that the deputation had asked for the interview then being accorded, His Excellency referred Mrs Moghannam to certain statements which she had already made in her address to him:

1. 'The policy of His Majesty's Government has been the cause of all the trouble and will continue to be so until it is fundamentally changed.'
2. 'Partition cannot and will not be accepted.'

After the meeting, the deputation put in a memorandum for His Excellency's consideration.

3.8 Two views of women fighters during the Algerian War of National Liberation, 1957
Ryme Seferdjeli

Preface

Algeria achieved independence from France in 1962 after 132 years of French colonization and eight years of a brutal war.

Unlike other French colonies, Algeria had been integrated into the French territory as early as the nineteenth century and was administrated by the French Ministry of the Interior. The attachment of France to Algeria was reinforced by the presence of nearly 1 million European *colons* or settlers, the majority of who, in 1954, were born in Algeria, with roots in France or the Mediterranean, and were commonly known as *pieds noirs*.[76] Consequently, at the beginning of the 1950s the independence of Algeria, an integral part of France, was almost unthinkable. Moreover, during the course of the war oil was discovered and a decision taken to use the Sahara for the first nuclear and space experiments.

Several attempts to fight colonialism through legal means by the main Algerian nationalist party, the *Mouvement pour le triomphe des libertés démocratiques* (MTLD), failed. In March 1954 a faction within the party called for immediate action, leading to the creation of the *Front de libération nationale* (FLN), with an armed branch, the *Armée de libération nationale* (ALN). On 1 November 1954 the FLN staged an armed insurrection in Algeria with the sole aim of achieving total independence from France.

The insurrection marked the beginning of a long and brutal war in Algeria between the FLN/ALN and France. Political repercussions in France included the fall of six prime ministers and the collapse of the Fourth Republic. Ultimately, the war led to the total independence of Algeria after more than a century of French colonization.

One of the most remarkable features of the war was the involvement of a large number of young Muslim women in the revolutionary movement. Although the participation of women in such movements is common, the presence of young Muslim women in the Algerian war as nurses, liaison agents, but also as political and propaganda agents, was largely exceptional. Prior to 1954, Muslim women were largely confined to the home. Few were educated, few worked beyond the domestic sphere. Their daily lives were regulated by *shariʿa*, and by traditional rules and

---

[76] The *pieds noirs* (literally 'black feet') represented approximately 10% of the population in Algeria on the eve of the 1954 insurrection, with 984,000 in 1954, 79% of whom were born in the country.

customs that antedated Islam which categorized them—socially, judicially, and politically—as second-class citizens. This situation was further exacerbated by the strict segregation enforced between the Muslim and European communities in Algeria.

Consequently, the participation of women in the revolutionary movement had a novelty value. The French, perceiving Muslim women to be uneducated, backward, and oppressed in a patriarchal society, did not anticipate the role they would undertake as fighters. The FLN, too, did not appear to anticipate the large-scale participation of women.

The Algerian war was not a conventional one, but a guerrilla war, in which the population was the best weapon the FLN could employ against the French. The population was the FLN's main target for recruits, and its support was crucial in a war where France had clear military superiority. With the support of the Algerian people as a whole, the FLN sought to sign up new combatants, establish a politico-administrative organization in order to extend its influence, collect money for the revolution, and ultimately, legitimize its action within the international community.

The FLN needed the participation of women, and encouraged them to join the cause from the very beginning of the war. However, it endeavored to confine their roles to what could be described as 'female tasks'. Although not discussed in the FLN document below (Document 2), women went well beyond what the FLN expected them to do (as can be seen from the accompanying photographs). Women acted as nurses and social and political commissioners, and were vital in the effort to shelter and provision combatants. Beyond these support roles, they also served as liaison agents, carrying weapons and, in exceptional cases, planting bombs. However, the FLN made sure to severely regulate them and to confine their role to specific assignments. Close supervision was also considered a necessity, especially as the tasks assigned to women gradually grew beyond the limits imposed by their gender identity. The heavy media coverage of the participation of women during the famous 'Battle of Algiers', in which they played a significant part by planting bombs in European quarters of Algiers, and their significant participation during demonstrations further reinforced this view. It also supported the view amongst the FLN that women should be employed as political instruments.

For the French, the involvement of women was probably the most surprising element in the organization of the FLN. Until the war started, the French had never paid attention to Muslim women. However, by the time the French note was issued in November 1957 (Document 1, below), the French had already become aware of their activities in the war, and it was widely known some had joined the ranks of the ALN.

Within months of the outbreak of the insurrection in 1955, names of the young Muslim women arrested had been already reported in the local press[77] and, in July 1956, pictures of young Muslim women dressed in military uniforms were published. For the first time, the press reported the presence of women in the battlefield. The Battle of Algiers further confirmed their active contribution.

The French note reveals French awareness in 1957 of the growing involvement of women in what the French defined as 'rebel activities', and its view of female Muslim fighters. From 1957 onwards, France's attention towards women increased. As a response to female involvement in the war, the French authorities, while intensifying their contact and control of the population, kept a separate agenda for women, mainly through social and medical assistance. Moreover, attempts to emancipate Muslim women through assimilation to France were offered as an incentive to keep them from joining the fight. Specifically, the French authorities granted Muslim women suffrage, reformed the marriage law in their favor, and encouraged them to unveil.

Although many historians have studied the Battle of Algiers, there is very little mention in most of the literature covering the war of the participation of women. These documents illustrate not only their contribution to the war effort, but more importantly, the psychological effect their participation had during the course of the war on both the Algerians and the French. Through the course of the war, it came to symbolize for French and international public opinion the depth of Algerian commitment to the cause of independence from French rule.

Texts

1. Information note from the Xe military region, Army Corps of Constantine. Command of the North of Constantine and of the 14th infantry division, headquarters, second bureau[78]

7 November 1957
Object: Note No. 9 from the *Wilaya*[79] No. 2
Were dispatched the enclosed translation of two notes of the Wilaya 2 found on the body of Harane Saïd, political [officer] responsible for the Nahia de JEMMAPES (Nahia 2—Mintaka 2), shot down on 4 October 1957.
[referring to] Note No. 9 dated 2 May 1957
This note [No. 9 dated 2 May 1957] refers to the organization of the body of women fighters (*'Moudjahidat'*).

---

[77] *Dépêche quotidienne d'Alger*, 28 June 1955, 7 Sept. 1955, 13 Dec. 1955.
[78] File 1H2582/D1, Service Historique de l'Armée de Terre (SHAT), Vincennes.
[79] Province in Arabic; the FLN organized its struggle by dividing Algeria into six *wilayas*.

Independently from their role as nurses, 'in hospitals and outside hospitals' assigned to '*Moudjahidat*', the rebel higher command intends as well to use the latter as official representatives to the Algerian woman on a social and political level. The note indicates that women fighters are required to become more than just nurses but also real political agents of the FLN. The note No. 9 materializes their role by subordinating them to political responsible of Kasma, when it comes to dealing with their political and social activities.

The presence of women within the rebels' ranks has been reported several times in the territory of the *Wilaya* 2.

Moreover, recent information, although unconfirmed, collected in Z.O.E.M, reports arrangements made by BOUALI Messaoud, chief P.M. of the Mintaka No 1, in view of proceeding with the insertion of some fifty women within the ranks of the HLL.[80]

This set of facts indicates the growing part taken by women in rebel activities. We are witnessing, in that sphere, an evolution that needs to be followed very closely. The O. R.[81] will pay careful attention on that point, and all evidence collected regarding female political activities will be subject for review to be performed under the present stamp.

Signed: General Desfontaines, Commander of the 14th infantry division and the North of Constantine.

2. Note No. 9. Wilaya of the North Constantine[82]

2 May 1957

Object: Role of 'women fighters' (*Moudjahidat*)
In accordance with a decision taken by the Committee of *Wilaya*, the body of 'women fighters' will be organized as follows:

1. Specialization
Women fighters are intended to serve in hospitals (or nurseries); they must first complete an internship which indudes medical instruction; the director of the health service of the *Wilaya* is entrusted with providing medical instruction.

Women fighters are subject to the same laws and regulations as men, except for accommodation and discipline, which were subject to earlier instructions.

2. Role of women fighters
Medical role.
Political and social role.

---

[80] HLL, in French *Hors La Loi*, i.e. outlawed.
[81] O.R., in French *Officiers Regionaux*, i.e regional officers.
[82] File 1H2582/D1, Service Historique de l'Armée de Terre (SHAT), Vincennes.

Duty of women fighters at the medical level:

—in hospitals as nurses.

—Outside hospitals where they treat civilian women.

Within her medical role, the woman fighter is put under the authority of the nurse-in-chief (male).

Duty of women fighters at the political and social level:

Within the framework of the organization of the sector in which she is employed, the woman fighter has towards her sisters a social and a political role.

Social role

The woman fighter must be a real social assistant at the service of the Algerian woman. She must give useful advice to the Algerian woman in order to help her to look after her house, to bring up her children, to observe rules of hygiene, etc [. . .] Her role should be confined to that.

Political role

The woman fighter must 'instruct' the Algerian woman by familiarizing her with the current situation. With this aim, she must do her best to explain to the Algerian woman:

—what the ALN is.

—what the FLN is.

—what the goals of the Algerian revolution are and what we are expecting from it.

She must be in a position to answer all questions that will be asked by her sisters, to whom she should indicate their duty and what is expected from them by the ALN and the FLN.

In her politico-social role, the woman fighter fulfils her activities under the responsibility of the political adviser of Kasma.

The committees of Mintaka, of Nahia, and of Kasma, as well as medical doctors are in charge of the enforcement of the present note.

Seal of the FLN

6. Zohra Drif following her arrest in September 1957. Drif, the daughter of a qadi and one of the few Muslim students at the University of Algiers, became a member of the FLN in 1956 after clashes with Ultra Students at the university revealed discrimination against Muslims, on whom a curfew was imposed. She joined Yacef Saadi's network in Algiers. Saadi was responsible for organizing the guerrilla cells in Algiers and relied heavily upon women during the Battle of Algiers. Drif became Saadi's assistant and is believed to have participated actively in the direction of the Battle with Saadi. She, together with Saadi, was arrested in September 1957 and sentenced the following year to twenty years of forced labor for having planted bombs in public places in the European quarters of Algiers. She survived the war and married Rabah Bitat, one of the leaders and founders of the FLN. Source: Museum of Moud-jahidine, Algiers

7a–c. Moudjahidate (women fighters) in the maquis. The Moudjahidate, members of the ALN, represent the most remarkable group of women participants. The idea of the Moudjahidate emphatically shat-
ters the traditional image of Algerian women as backward, veiled, and oppressed Muslims. The
Moudjahidate left their homes for the mountains and countryside from where the revolutionary underground army would hide and operate. They were armed and dressed in military uniforms. Many of the
Moudjahidate remained in the maquis for years. The role of Moudjahidate varied according to circumstances; they mainly carried out auxiliary services such as nursing, communication, engineering and
food preparation. Some, in exceptional conditions, took part in combat. One of their tasks was to give
female civilians a political and social education, by gathering women in meetings and explaining to them
the significance of the revolution. Source: Museum of Moudjahidine, Algiers. Year: approximately
between 1956 and 1959

Selected bibliography

ABRAMS, RUTH, 'Pioneering Representatives of the Hebrew People: Campaigns of the Palestinian Jewish Women's Equal Rights Association, 1918–1948', in Ian Fletcher, Philippa Levine, and Laura Mayhall (eds.), *Women's Suffrage in the British Empire: Citizen, Race and Nation* (New York: Routledge, 2000).

ABU-LUGHOD, LILA (ed.), *Re-making Women: Feminism and Modernity in the Middle East* (Princeton: Princeton University Press, 1998).

—— 'Feminist Longings and Postcolonial Conditions', in Lila Abu-Lughod (ed.), *Remaking Women: Feminism and Modernity in the Middle East* (Princeton: Princeton University Press, 1998), 3–32.

AHMAD, NAZIR, *The Bride's Mirror: Mirat ul-ʿArus: A Tale of Life in Delhi a Hundred Years Ago*, trans. G. E. Ward, with an afterword by Frances W. Pritchett (New Delhi: Permanent Black, 2001). Originally published in 1903, this is a translation of a novel first published in 1869.

AHMED, LEILA, 'Early Feminist Movements in the Middle East: Turkey and Egypt', in Freda Hussain (ed.), *Muslim Women* (New York: St Martin's Press, 1984).

—— *Women and Gender in Islam* (New Haven: Yale University Press, 1992).

AMIN, CAMRON MICHAEL. *The Making of the Modern Iranian Woman: Gender, State Policy, and Popular Culture, 1865–1946.* (Gainesville, Fla.: University Press of Florida, 2002)

AMIN, SONIA NISHAT, *The World of Muslim Women in Colonial Bengal, 1876–1939* (Leiden: Brill, 1996).

AMRANE, DJAMILA, *Les Femmes algériennes dans la guerre* (Paris: Plon, 1991).

ANTONIUS, SORAYA, 'Fighting on Two Fronts: Conversations With Palestinian Women', *Journal of Palestine Studies*, 8 (1979).

ARAT, ZEHRA F., 'Introduction: Politics of Representation and Identity', in Zehra F. Arat (ed.), *Deconstructing Images of 'The Turkish Woman'* (New York: Palgrave, 2000), 1–36.

BADRAN, MARGOT, *Feminists, Islam and Nation: Gender and the Making of Modern Egypt* (Princeton: Princeton University Press, 1994).

—— and MIRIAM COOKE (eds.), *Opening the Gates: A Century of Arab Feminist Writing* (Bloomington: Indiana University Press, 1990).

BARON, BETH, 'Mothers, Morality and Nationalism in Pre-1919 Egypt', in Rashid Khalidi *et al.* (eds.), *The Origins of Arab Nationalism* (New York: Columbia University Press, 1991).

—— *The Women's Awakening in Egypt: Culture, Society and the Press* (New Haven: Yale University Press, 1994).

BEAUVOIR, SIMONE DE, and GISÈLE HALIMI, *Djamila Boupacha: The Story of the Torture of a Young Algerian Girl Which Shocked Liberal French Opinion* (London: Andre Deutsch/Weidenfeld & Nicholson, 1962).

BERNSTEIN, DEBORAH, *The Struggle for Equality: Urban Women Workers in Pre-State Israel* (New York: Praeger Press, 1987).

—— 'In Search of a New Female Identity: Pioneering Women in Pre-state Israeli Society', *Shofar: An Interdisciplinary Journal of Jewish Studies*, 9/4 (Summer 1991), 78–91.

—— (ed), *Pioneers and Homemakers: Jewish Women in Pre-State Israel* (Albany: State University of New York Press, 1992).

DAVIDOFF, LEONORE, 'Regarding Some "Old Husbands' Tales": Public and Private in Feminist History' in *Worlds Between: Historical Perspectives on Gender and Class* (New York: Routledge, 1995).

DOUMANI, BESHARA, *Rediscovering Palestine: Merchants and Peasants in Jabal Nablus, 1700–1900* (Berkeley: University of California Press, 1995).

DUBEN, ALAN, AND CEM BEHAR, *Istanbul Households: Marriage, Family and Fertility, 1880–1940* (Cambridge: Cambridge University Press, 1991).

DURAKBAŞA, AYŞE, 'Kemalism as Identity Politics in Turkey', in Zehra F. Arat (ed.), *Deconstructing Images of 'The Turkish Woman'* (New York: Palgrave, 2000).

ELIAS, NORBERT, *The Civilizing Process: The History of Manners and State Formation and Civilization*, trans. Edmund Jephcott (Cambridge: Blackwell, 1994; originally pub. 1939), 1–9.

FANON, FRANTZ, *Studies in a Dying Colonialism* (London: Earthscan Publications, 1989).

FERAOUN, MOULOUD, *Journal 1955–1962: Reflections on the French–Algerian War* (Lincoln, Nebr.: University of Nebraska Press, 2000).

FLEISCHMANN, ELLEN, 'Young Women in the City: Mandate Memories', *Jerusalem Quarterly File*, 2 (Autumn 1998), 31–9.

—— 'Selective Memory, Gender and Nationalism: Palestinian Women Leaders in the British Mandate Period', *History Workshop Journal*, 47 (Spring 1999), 141–58.

—— 'The Other "Awakening": The Emergence of Women's Movements in the Middle East, c. 1900–1940', in Margaret Lee Meriwether and Judith Tucker (eds.), *A Social History of Women and Gender in the Modern Middle East* (Boulder, Col.: Westview Press, 1999).

—— 'The Emergence of the Palestinian Women's Movement, 1929–1939', *Journal of Palestine Studies*, 29/2 (Spring 2000), 16–32.

—— 'Nation, Tradition, and Rights: The Indigenous Feminism of the Palestinian Women's Movement (1920–1948)', in Ian Fletcher, Philippa Levine, and Laura Mayhall (eds.), *Women's Suffrage in the British Empire: Citizen, Race and Nation* (New York: Routledge, 2000).

FOGIEL-BIJAOUI, SYLVIA, 'On the Way to Equality? The Struggle for Women's Suffrage in the Jewish Yishuv, 1917–1926', in *Pioneers and Homemakers: Jewish Women in Pre-State Israel* (Albany: State University of New York Press, 1992).

FRIERSON, ELIZABETH B., 'Unimagined Communities: Women and Education in the Late-Ottoman Empire, 1876–1909', *Critical Matrix*, 9/2 (1995), 55–90.

GIACAMAN, RITA, and MUNA ODEH, 'Palestinian Women's Movement in the Israeli-Occupied West Bank and Gaza Strip', in Nahid Toubia (ed.), *Women of the Arab World* (London: Zed Press, 1988).

GÖKALP, ZIYA, 'What is Turkism—A Recapitulation', 'Culture and Refinement', 'Culture and Civilization', and 'Modern Family and National Culture', trans. Niyazi Berkes, *Turkish Nationalism and Western Civilization* (London: George Allen & Unwin, 1959).

GORDON, DAVID C., *Women of Algeria: An Essay on Change* (Cambridge, Mass.: Harvard University Press, 1968).

GRAHAM-BROWN, SARAH, 'The Political Economy of Jabal Nablus, 1920–1948', in Roger Owen (ed.), *Studies in the Economic and Social History of Palestine in the Nineteenth and Twentieth Centuries* (Urbana, Ill.: Southern Illinois University Press, 1982).

GROSSMAN, ATINA, 'The New Woman and the Rationalization of Sexuality in Weimar Germany', in Ann Snitow, Christine Stansell, and Sharon Thompson (eds.), *Powers of Desire: The Politics of Sexuality* (New York: Monthly Review Press, 1983).

HELIE-LUCAS, ARIE-AIMEE, 'The Role of Women During the Algerian Liberation Struggle and After', in Eva Isaksson (ed.), *Women and the Military System* (Brighton: Harvester-Wheatsheaf, 1988), 171–89.

HORNE, ALISTAIR, *A Savage War of Peace: Algeria 1954–1962* (Basingstoke and Oxford: Pan Books, 2002).

HOURANI, ALBERT, *Arabic Thought in the Liberal Age, 1798–1939*, 2nd edn. (Cambridge: Cambridge University Press, 1983).

IZRAELI, DAFNA, 'The Zionist Women's Movement in Palestine, 1911–1927: A Sociological Analysis', *Signs*, 7 (1981), 87–114.

—— 'The Women Workers Movement: First Wave Feminism in Pre-State Israel', in *Pioneers and Homemakers: Jewish Women in Pre-State Israel* (Albany: State University of New York Press, 1992).

JAD, ISLAH, 'From Salons to Popular Committees: Palestinian Women, 1919–1989', in Jamal R. Nassar and Roger Heacock (eds.), *Intifada: Palestine at the Crossroads* (Birzeit and New York: Birzeit University and Praeger Press, 1991).

KANDIYOTI, DENIZ, Emancipated but Unliberated? Reflections on the Turkish Case', *Feminist Studies*, 13 (Summer 1987), 317–38.

—— 'Identity and its Discontents: Women and the Nation', *Millennium*, 20/3 (1991), 429–43.

KHALIDI, WALID, *Before Their Diaspora: A Photographic History of the Palestinians, 1876–1948* (Washington DC: Institute for Palestine Studies, 1991).

LAZREG, MARNIA, *The Eloquence of Silence: Algerian Women in Question* (New York: Routledge, 1994).

MARDIN, ŞERIF, 'Super Westernization in Urban Life in the Ottoman Empire in the Last Quarter of the Nineteenth Century', in Peter Benedict, Erol Tümertekin, and Fatma Mansur (eds.), *Turkey: Geographic and Social Perspectives* (Leiden: E. J. Brill, 1974).

METCALF, BARBARA (trans.), *Perfecting Women: Maulana Ashraf 'Ali Thanawi's Bihishti Zewar* (Berkeley: University of California Press, 1990).

MINAULT, GAIL (trans.), *Voices of Silence: English Translation of Hali's Majalis un-Nissa and Chup ki Dad* (Delhi: Chanakya, 1986).

—— *Secluded Scholars: Women's Education and Muslim Social Reform in Colonial India* (Delhi: Oxford University Press, 1998).

MOGHANNAM, MATIEL, *The Arab Woman and the Palestine Problem* (London: Herbert Joseph, 1937).

NAJJAR, ORAYB, and KITTY WARNOCK, *Portraits of Palestinian Women* (Salt Lake City: University of Utah Press, 1992).

PETEET, JULIE, *Gender in Crisis: Women and the Palestinian Resistance Movement* (New York: Columbia University Press, 1991).

SCOTT, JOAN W., 'Gender: A Useful Category of Historical Analysis', in *Gender and the Politics of History* (New York: Columbia University Press, 1988).

SHAKRY, OMNIA, 'Schooled Mothers and Structured Play: Child Rearing in Turn-of-the-Century Egypt', in *Remaking Women: Feminism and Modernity in the Middle East* (Princeton: Princeton University Press, 1998).

SMITH, MARGARET, 'The Women's Movement in the Near and Middle East', *Asiatic Review* (Apr. 1928), 188–203.

SWEDENBURG, TED, *Memories of Revolt: The 1936–1939 Rebellion and the Palestinian National Past* (Minneapolis: University of Minnesota Press, 1995).

TOPRAK, ZAFER, 'The Family, Feminism, and the State During the Young Turk Period, 1908–1918' in *Première rencontre internationale sur l'empire Ottoman et la Turquie moderne* (Istanbul: Editions ISIS, 1991).

TUCKER, JUDITH, *In the House of Law: Gender and Islamic Law in Ottoman Syria and Palestine* (Berkeley: University of California Press, 1998).

WOODSMALL, RUTH, *Moslem Women Enter a New World* (New York: Round Table Press, 1936).

ZÜRCHER, ERIK J., *Turkey: A Modern History* (London: I. B. Tauris, 1998).

4

Religion and society

Introduction

As the Middle East is the celebrated cradle of monotheism, it is perhaps no surprise that religious questions figure in its modern history as well. Indeed, from the break-up of the Ottoman Empire in the nineteenth century to the rise of Israel and the Islamic Republic of Iran, the story of the modern Middle East might be characterized as merely an updating of religious strife that has characterized regional politics and the relation of 'East and West' for centuries. But religion does not transcend other historical processes—it is part of them. The rise of ethnic nationalism and liberal ideals has triggered religious responses that have contributed sometimes to discord and sometimes to a new sense of unity. Furthermore, seeing religion as the root cause of conflicts ignores the diversity that exists within religious traditions in the Middle East and the ways in which that diversity can affect local debates about the nature of society.

Undoubtedly, however, radicalized forms of religion have played a major role in Middle Eastern history as a response to Western imperialism and authoritarian political environments in the twentieth and twenty-first centuries. The distinction between 'religious reform' (with its implication of embracing the modern world and liberalism) and 'religious revival' (with its connotation of wild-eyed fundamentalism and social conservatism) is in some ways a false one. All those who seek to incorporate religion into the routines and institutions of the modern Middle East are at once mindful of contemporary developments and the fundamental sources of religious tradition. The general tendency is to focus on these debates among Muslims in the Middle East, but they are played out in Jewish and Christian contexts as well.

The documents of this section were selected to highlight the way religious sensibilities are deployed in public discourse to mobilize opinion and to create (or challenge) a sense of community in the modern Middle East.

4.1 An intellectual biography of a religious scholar in Ottoman Damascus: from Isma'il al-Ajluni's 'The Finest and Most Perfect of Men who are Connected by Chains of Transmission to all other Fine Men,' 1739

Steve Tamari

Preface

The following is an excerpt from the *thabat* of Isma'il al-Ajluni, a Muslim scholar of eighteenth-century Damascus. A *thabat* is a kind of intellectual biography in which the author details his educational and scholarly achievements by compiling the teaching certificates, or *ijazas*, he has acquired over his career. *Ijazas* are among the most ubiquitous documents in the scholarly Islamic corpus and constitute the primary source for Islam's rich biographical tradition. Their use dates back to the first Islamic centuries, though compilations, like Al-Ajluni's *thabat*, are a more recent phenomenon. There are four main parts to Al-Ajluni's *thabat*: (1.) an introduction in which he describes the years in which he grew up and pronounces on the importance of Hadith studies and the significance of verifiable and trustworthy lines of transmission; (2.) verbatim copies of three of his most valued *ijazas* or teaching certificates; (3.) excerpts and copies of other *ijazas* arranged according to the cities in which he received them; (4.) a list of 164 books he read (and whom he read them with) arranged alphabetically; and (5.) a final section containing five Hadith reports and their lines of transmission. The document printed below is an excerpt from the introduction.

Isma'il al-Ajluni was first and foremost a Hadith scholar. Hadith are reports of the words and deeds of the Prophet Muhammad (d. 632) and are key to the elaboration of Islamic law. Since there was so much potential for fabricating Hadith, Muslim scholars developed an elaborate system for verifying the authenticity of these reports. The heart of this system was documentation of the circumstances of the transmission of Hadith from individual to individual, referring back to the companions of the Prophet and the Prophet himself. Each link in these chains of transmission is called an *isnad*. The Islamic educational system developed in tandem with the collection of Hadith and the elaboration of Islamic law. Consequently, during Al-Ajluni's time and, in some circles, to this day, Muslim scholars put a premium on documenting the personal connection between teacher and student, not only for the transmission of Hadith, but in terms of the transmission of all knowledge.

As a specialist in the collection of Hadith, Al-Ajluni was a member of the ʿulama, a body of Muslim scholars who provided spiritual, legal, and educational guidance to Muslims across the world. Throughout the course of Islamic history, military and other political elites depended on the ʿulama to legitimize their power.

Damascus had been under Ottoman rule for more than 200 years when Al-Ajluni composed his *thabat* around 1737. The city of Damascus was the capital of the province of Damascus, which encompassed most of what is known as Greater Syria, including the modern-day states of Syria, Lebanon, Israel/Palestine, and Jordan. Historians agree that the eighteenth century witnessed a significant decentralization of power throughout the empire that allowed local leaders to exercise unprecedented levels of power. For Damascenes, the most dramatic illustration of this phenomenon was the rise to prominence of the ʿAzm family, several of whom were appointed as governors for uncommonly long terms from the 1720s to the 1780s.

Damascus had been a center for Islamic education since the first Islamic century. Many of the Prophet's earliest companions settled there, and Damascus was the first capital of an Islamic empire under the Umayyad dynasty. Throughout Islamic history, the Umayyad Mosque in the center of the walled city remained a focal point of Muslim scholars and pilgrims from around the Islamic world.

Al-Ajluni was born in 1676 in Ajlun, today a city in Jordan. As described in the excerpt below, he made his way to Damascus, where he studied with the most prominent teachers in the city. He reached the pinnacle of his scholarly career when he was appointed the city's chief Hadith scholar with a stipend and post at the Umayyad Mosque in 1708. He died in 1749.

Text[1]

In the name of God the merciful and the compassionate and in whom we trust, praise be to God who elevated the scholars of Hadith and prayers and peace be upon our Prophet Muhammad, lord of creation and humanity, and upon his family and his companions who followed him in all matters, and upon the followers and the conscientious imams, and all believers upon whom the light of the sun and the moon shine.[2]

Now on to our topic: Ismaʿil al-Ajluni b. Muhammad Jarrah, the unfortunate—may his Lord forgive him—declares: some of my esteemed brothers have asked me to gather a *thabat* that verifies the *isnads* I have acquired from the exalted teachers with whom I studied and who certified me in their glorious writings.[3]

---

[1] This translation is based on a manuscript held in Berlin (Staatsbibliothek zu Berlin: Preussischer Kulturbesitz Orientabteilung. We (II), fos. 1b–7a).

[2] In this context, 'imam' and 'shaykh' are simply terms of respect for scholars.

[3] The 'b.' between names stands for 'ibn' which translates as 'son of'.

I was also asked to reproduce the certificates they wrote for me in their hand and sealed with their exalted seals. I do this so the certificates (and what I have transmitted on the basis of those certificates) may be preserved from loss and that we may emulate our predecessors among the Hadith scholars. I answered this request hoping I have fulfilled the expectations made of me and called it The Finest and Most Perfect of Men who are Connected by Chains of Transmission to all other Fine Men.

I know it is in the tradition of scholars of Hadith in the past and today to mention their *isnads* and their connections to the imams and the shaykhs because these chains of transmission are the expression of their lineage to the imams and the shaykhs and from them and the means by which scholars of Hadith listen to them and are supported by them. Thus, the imam al-Shafi'i, may God be pleased with him, said that he who seeks knowledge of Hadith without an *isnad* is like the wood gatherer who gathers firewood at night and is unaware of a snake in its midst.[4] And the imam Ahmad, as transmitted from him by Al-Bukhari, said that the measure of a person rests in the weightiness of his shaykh and that if the shaykhs depart, with whom would one thrive?[5] And the imam 'Abd Allah ibn al-Mubarak says *isnad* is part of religion and he also said that he who seeks knowledge without *isnad* is like one who tries to ascend a roof without a ladder. [...][6] Al-Hafiz Ibn al-Hajar says that he heard some esteemed scholars call *isnad* the lineage of books.[7] And the imam Sufiyan al-Thawri said it is a weapon of the faithful and that if one doesn't have a weapon, what is one supposed to fight with?[8] And Hafiz al-Gharb Yusuf b. 'Abd al-Birr said an *ijaza* in knowledge is to the scholar what capital is to the merchant.[9] And some of our reliable shaykhs have said the *isnad* to the shaykhs is the lineage of the working 'ulama and they are the fathers of religion. The *isnad* is part of the essence of Muhammad's *umma* so it is incumbent to travel to gather them even if it means going to the farthest Indian provinces.[10] This knowledge carries with it perfection, as when Al-Hafiz al-Suyuti says that an *ijaza* from a shaykh is not just permission to transmit Hadith but is a prime condition of becoming part of the family of transmission

[4] Muhammad b. Idris al-Shafi'i (d. 830) was the founder of the Shafi'i school of law, one of four major schools of law among Sunni Muslims. Al-Ajluni identifies himself as an adherent of the Shafi'i school of law.

[5] Muhammad b. Isma'il al-Bukhari (d. 870) was the most important collector and compiler of Hadith. (It is not clear from the text who the imam Ahmad is.)

[6] 'Abd Allah b. al-Mubarak was a scholar of the ninth century CE.

[7] Ahmad b. al-Hajar al-Asqalani was a scholar of the fifteenth century CE. 'Al-Hafiz' is an honorific for those renowned for their knowledge.

[8] Sufyan al-Thawri was a Hadith and legal scholar of the eighth century CE.

[9] Yusuf b. 'Abd al-Birr, who was from Islamic Spain, was a Hadith scholar of the eleventh century CE. He was known as the 'Hafiz of the West' (al-gharb).

[10] 'Umma' refers to the worldwide community of Muslims.

and knowledge. [...][11] The most important thing is that one's intentions be pure. [...]

Following the examples set by my predecessors, like Al-Suyuti and others like him among the most renowned ʿulama, I start my autobiography from the beginning. The purpose of mentioning this is to avoid ambiguity, asking God to make this book useful to me and to others.

I, humble before God the almighty, am Ismaʿil b. Muhammad Jarrah b. ʿAbd al-Hadi b. ʿAbd al-Ghani b. Jarrah al-Jarrahi, an ascription that refers to Al-Jarrah who is said to be buried in Jerusalem in a shrine which pilgrims visit and which I had the good fortune to visit. I am from the town of Ajlun, a citizen of Damascus, and adhere to the Shafiʿi legal rite. It has become a commonplace in our town of Ajlun that our family traces its roots back to Abu ʿUbayda Amir b. ʿAbd Allah b. al-Jarrah, one of the companions of the Prophet, one of the 10 who were told they would go to heaven, and one of the guardians of the faith, may God be pleased by him. Al-Tabari says that Abu ʿUbayda had two sons who died during his lifetime without issue.[12] But it is possible that he had another son after these two. I heard from reputable sources that they had seen evidence that Abu ʿUbayda married a Bedouin woman near the end of his life and died while she was pregnant. This story is supported by the fact that there is a group of Bedouins in the Hawran who claim to be descended from Abu ʿUbayda and are known as Al-Jarrah.[13] They sent letters to my father, God protect him, asking him to visit them because of their kinship ties. I noticed that Al-Jalal al-Suyuti mentioned that Yazid b. al-Jarrah, may God be pleased with him, Abu ʿUbayda's brother and also a companion, was married in Egypt when, in fact, he was married in Yemen.[14] Perhaps the ascription and the kinship ties derive from him. My colleague Shaykh Salih says he met with a man in Egypt who said his Abu ʿUbayda ascription also derived from Abu ʿUbayda ibn al-Jarrah. My friend Shaykh ʿAbd al-Rahman al-Kafarsusi says he has relatives in the Biqa who have the same ascription.[15] If these claims are certain, then it is probable that our lineage derives from this noble companion of the Prophet. [...]

Abu ʿUbayda died of the plague in Imwas and was buried in Ghur Bisan and his domed tomb there is well known. I visited it and wrote a few lines of verse in praise of Abu ʿUbayda. [...]

I was born around 1087 (AH; 1676 CE) and my parents and others informed me later that I was named Muhammad for about a year when my name was changed to Mustafa for about six months before they settled on Ismaʿil, the son of Abraham,

[11] ʿAbd al-Rahman al-Suyuti was an Egyptian scholar of the fifteenth century CE.
[12] Ahmad al-Tabari (d. 1295 CE) was a historian from Mecca. He is not to be confused with the historian of the early Islamic period, Muhammad al-Tabari (d. 923 CE).
[13] The Hawran is a mountainous area to the south of Damascus.
[14] 'Al-Jalal', like 'Al-Hafiz', is an honorific.   [15] The Biqa is a valley to the west of Damascus.

God grant them prayers and peace.[16] Our friend Al-Sayyid Mustafa al-Bakri alluded to this in a few lines of poetry when he wrote in my book, *Revealing the Hidden Meaning and Clearing the Confusion of the Most Widely Repeated Hadiths.*

Once I reached puberty, I started studying the Qur'an until I had memorized it by heart. In mid-Shawwal of the year 1100, when I was thirteen, I headed for Damascus, may God bless it and the other countries of Islam, to study the religious sciences.[17] I studied, law, Hadith, Qur'anic commentary, Arabic, and other subjects with a number of shaykhs and imams (who will be mentioned later) until I distinguished myself from among my student colleagues. Among the reasons that I sought knowledge was a dream I had when I was a child. In the dream, I was at school and a man dressed me in a grass-green cloak lined with white fur from head to foot. When I told my father, he was very happy and told me he hoped I would become one of the ʿulama. In fact, I ended up pursuing the life of a scholar and had the good fortune to write a number of books.

I studied with many shaykhs and imams including Syrians, Meccans and Medinans, Egyptians, and Rumis.[18] I studied a variety of subjects with them including theology, Qur'anic commentary, Hadith, law, Qur'anic recitation, arithmetic, Arabic and related topics, logic, mysticism and other fields of learning that benefit the faithful. Let me mention the names of my teachers who taught me or certified me orally or in writing. I do this in order to amplify the blessings that come from mentioning the righteous ones, *al-salihun.* Al-Jalal al-Suyuti said that when God says 'the martyrs and the righteous ones', He means the Hadith scholars. Others have said that the *salihun* are those who have no doubts about their faith, who work without compromising their faith, and who are dutiful to God and the community of the faithful. In all cases, the *salihun* encompass scholars of Hadith, who are the masters of piety and the foremost ascetics. Shaykh Muhi al-Din Ibn ʿArabi says that it is recorded in some sources that mercy comes with mentioning the *salihun* because when they are mentioned God and the Prophet are also mentioned. [...][19] Mentioning the *salihun* makes one recognize one's own fragility for they separate one from God and, at the same time, connect one to God. [...] Now, on to the brief biographies of my teachers I promised together with written mention of the subjects they certified me in, thus preserving this information from loss. [...].

---

[16] 'AH' stands for 'Anno Hegirae', and refers to the lunar Muslim calendar that begins with the migration of Muhammad (the *hijra*) and his earliest followers to Medina from Mecca in 622 CE. Thus, Al-Ajluni was born in the eleventh century AH, which corresponds roughly to the seventeenth century CE.

[17] Shawwal is the sixth month of the Muslim calendar.

[18] 'Rum' is the Arabic term for the area around Constantinople, 'the second Rome' or more generally for Anatolia which had been part of the Byzantine, or Eastern Roman Empire. In Ottoman times 'Rumi' generally referred to Turks, who ruled the Ottoman Empire from this area.

[19] Muhi al-Din Ibn ʿArabi (d. 1240 CE) was the most important mystical thinker of Islam.

4.2 Three letters from Imam Shamil to his followers, 1834–1858

Ernest Tucker

Preface

The following three documents are letters from Imam Shamil to his followers in the Caucasus at critical points during his long struggle with the Russians in the mid-nineteenth century (1834–59). Shamil, a follower of the Khalidiya branch of the Naqshbandi Sufi order, became the third leader of Muslim resistance (called an 'imam') against Russian encroachment in Daghestan, a key part of the north-east Caucasus. The first imam, Ghazi Muhammad, had begun the struggle against the Russians in 1829, but was killed in battle in October 1832. The second, Hamza Bek, was assassinated in September 1834. Shamil continued to fight the Russians intermittently until his surrender in September 1859. After spending time under a relaxed form of 'house arrest' in Kaluga and subsequently Kiev for several years, he was permitted to make the hajj pilgrimage and died on the journey to Medina in 1871.

Daghestan, immediately south of Chechnya, had been a center of Muslim struggle against the Russian move south for many decades before the 1830s. This mountainous region proved advantageous to members of the Muslim resistance who could always retreat into the wilderness. When Shamil assumed command of the movement in 1834, he began to build a government, and by the 1850s he had a functioning state structure. In essence, this structure depended upon local *naibs* (deputies) whom he nominated to rule over certain areas. This system, although very loosely administered, succeeded in keeping a certain amount of unity among the disparate mountain peoples of this region, who spoke a myriad of dialects and languages. Although mostly Muslim, they were affiliated with different Sufi and other groups.

An archive of Arabic letters sent by Shamil to his Muslim followers in Daghestan has been published recently by the Daghestani Center of the Russian Academy of Sciences in Makhachkala. The three letters included in this selection were all sent during important and distinct phases of Shamil's imamate. The first, written between October 1834 and April 1836, was addressed to the scholar Ghalbatz and the notables of the village of Andi when Shamil had gone into scholarly seclusion for a period of time. The Russian commander Klugenau was attempting to secure a peace agreement with Shamil that he could only accept if the Russians would make sure that Islamic holy law (*sharī'a*) would be enforced diligently among Caucasian Muslims. The second was written just before Shamil's major showdown with the Russians at Akhulgoh in 1839. The third was written on 16 February 1858, at the beginning of what would be Shamil's final campaign, which resulted in his capture and surrender at Ghunib on 6 September 1859.

Texts

Letter 1

(Kh. A. Omarova (ed. and trans.), *100 Pisem Shamilya* (Makhachkala: 1997), 188)

From the humble Shamil[20] to the heroic and distinguished scholar Ghalbatz and to the notables and all of the population of the area of Andal, upon you be peace and may excellence continue for you! So, go swiftly on horse and on foot and do not hesitate after this letter reaches you. God willing, we will achieve our desire and reach our goal. Do not give in to pleasure and weaken. 'You will be exalted' in the two abodes [this world and the next].[21]

[On the margin:] O adept scholar Ghalbatz, do not give way to the lies of the hypocrites, go quickly even if alone, and urge your people to be quick.

Letter 2

(Ibid. 190)

From the scribe Shamil to his brothers, the judge [*kadi*], the notables, the disciples [*murids*], and believers of Karata: peace, mercy, and blessing be upon you!

So, assist our reliable brother Qurban Muhammad in examining the case presented by [the people of] Akhkhal that some Botlikh men and youths killed one of their uncles who lived among them [in Botlikh]. Actually, they killed him by my order because he corrupted religion and harmed the disciples. If you are Muslims, then have them refer their case to us, since we will resolve it according to the Holy Law [*shari'a*].

Letter 3

(Ibid. 154)

In the name of God, the Merciful, the Compassionate.

From the Commander of the Faithful Shamil to his brothers, the deputies [*naibs*] Talkhik [a Chechen], Abakardibir, Kadi, Dibir [an Avar], peace and mercy be upon you! So, a reliable source has informed me that the cursed ones [the Russians] are now planning to attack Tawzen, Makhkita, and Aghishta. Do not be heedless but prepare yourselves well for them. Do not doubt it. Yet God, may He be exalted, said, 'The ruse of the infidels is only in error'.[22] Be careful not to neglect this [warning] by tarrying. Peace. Rajab 2, 1274 [16 February 1858].

Ali Kayayev [scribe].

---

[20] In all three letters Shamil is referred to as Shumayil, a diminutive form of his name. However, for continuity with all other sources about him, I have chosen to render his name as Shamil.

[21] Qur'an 3: 139.

[22] Qur'an 40: 25. This passage is from the middle of a sura describing the struggle of Moses with Pharaoh.

4.3 Kemal Atatürk on the abolition of the Ottoman caliphate, 3 March 1924[23]
Robert G. Landen

Preface

In October 1923 Mustafa Kemal gained the final, reluctant assent of the Grand National Assembly to the abolition of the office of the sultan and their subsequent approval of the proclamation of a republic with himself as president. Moreover, the capital was shifted from Istanbul, filled as it was with ghosts and physical reminders of an imperial, Islamic heritage, to Ankara, deep in the Turkish heartland, a symbol of the new Turkey that was to be built. Nevertheless, although the office of sultan was dead, the office of caliph, supposedly a religious but not a political dignity, had been retained, occupied by the scholarly Ottoman prince, Abdulmejid (Abdülmecid, 1923–4). Increasingly, Mustafa Kemal viewed the caliphate as a focus around which traditionalists and others opposed to his goals were rallying. Indeed, many Turks did view Abdulmejid rather than Kemal as the legitimate head of state as well as the head of Islam. Finally, in March 1924, the Kemalists acted, receiving the Assembly's assent to the suppression of the caliphate and the banishment of the Ottoman royal house. Abdulmejid was placed aboard the Orient Express for the ride westward. The abolition of the caliphate had repercussions throughout the Islamic world and served to emphasize that the old era was indeed gone and irrecoverable; it strengthened the thrust of those who were building modern nation-states throughout the Middle East.

Text

During my stay [in Izmir] I believed that the moment for the abolition of the Caliphate had arrived. I will try to follow the course of this affair as it actually happened.

On the 22nd January, 1924, I received from Ismet Paşa, President of the Council of Ministers, a telegram in cipher which I will read to you in full:

Telegram in cipher.

To His Excellency the President of the Turkish Republic.

The First Secretary of the Caliph sends me the following: For some time there have been articles in the newspapers concerning the situation of the Caliphate

[23] Kemal Ataturk, *Nutuk*, 2 (Ankara: Ministry of Education, 1950), 846–51; translated into English as *A Speech Delivered by Ghazi Mustapha Kemal, President of the Turkish Republic, October 1927* (Leipzig: K. F. Koehler, 1929), 681–6.

and the person of the Caliph, which gave rise to misunderstandings. The Caliph is very much afflicted about the articles which seem to lower his authority without reason, and particularly the fact that the leaders of the Government coming from time to time to Stanbul, as well as the official corporations, avoid him. The Caliph had thought of making his feelings and wishes on this question known either by sending a Chamberlain to Angora [Ankara] or by requesting that a trustworthy person should be sent to him, but he declares that he has abandoned this idea, because he was afraid that this step might be misinterpreted.

The General Secretary writes at length about the question of allocations, and asks that the question should be examined and the necessary steps be taken in this matter according to the communications of the Government of the 15th April, 1923, which state that the Ministry of Finance would help if the expenses were beyond the means of the Treasury of the Caliphate or outside the obligations of the Caliphate. The question will be discussed in the Council of Ministers. I shall have the honour of informing Your Excellency of the result of the discussion.

(Signed) Ismet.

In reply to this telegram, being myself by the side of the instrument, I sent the following reply to Ismet Paşa:

At the instrument.
    Smyrna.
    To His Excellency Ismet Paşa, President of the Council of Ministers, Angora.
    Reply to the telegram in cipher of 22nd January, 1924.
    It is to the attitude and manner of acting of the Caliph himself that the origin of the misunderstandings and the unfavourable interpretations regarding the Caliphate and the person of the Caliph must be attributed. In his private life and especially in his public appearances the Caliph seems to follow the system of the Sultans, his ancestors. As a proof: the Friday ceremonies, the relations of the Caliph to foreign representatives to whom he sends officials; his drivings out in great pomp; his private life in the Palace where he goes even so far as to receive dismissed officers to whose complaints he is listening, mixing his own tears with theirs. When the Caliph considers the situation, placing himself face to face with the Turkish Republic and the Turkish people, he must adopt as a measure of comparison the situation of the Caliphate and the Caliph towards the British Kingdom and the Muslim population of India, of the Government of Afghanistan and the people of Afghanistan. The Caliph himself and the whole world must know in a categoric manner that the Caliph and the office of the Caliph as they are now maintained and exist, have in reality neither a material nor a political meaning or any right of existence. The Turkish Republic cannot allow itself to be influenced by fallacies and cannot expose its independence and existence to danger.

To complete the analysis, the dignity of the Caliphate can have no other importance for us than that of an historical memory. The demand of the Caliph that the dignitaries of the Turkish Republic and the official corporations should enter into connection with him constitutes a flagrant violation of the independence of the Republic. The fact that he wants to send his First Chamberlain to Angora or his demand to inform the Government of his feelings and his wishes through a trustworthy person sent to him, shows likewise that he is taking up a position antagonistic to the Government of the Republic. He has no competency for doing this. It is also suggested that he should commission his First Secretary to act as mediator in the correspondence between him and the Government of the Republic. The First Secretary must be told that he must abstain from such impudence. Allocations inferior to those of the President of the Turkish Republic must suffice to secure the means of subsistence of the Caliph. Luxury and pomp are out of place. The question is only to secure a decent living for the Caliph. I do not understand what is meant by the 'treasure of the Caliphate.' The Caliphate has no treasure, and ought not to have any. If this should be an inheritance of his ancestors, I request you to make inquiries and to give me official and clear information about this question. What are the obligations which the Caliph cannot fulfill with the allocations he receives, and what promises and declarations have been made to him through the communication of the Government dated the 15th April? I ask you to inform me of this. A duty which the Government ought to have fulfilled hitherto is to specify and fix the place of residence of the Caliph. There are a great number of palaces in Constantinople which have been built with the money raised from the bread of the people, and the furniture and valuable objects they contain; in short, all is given over to destruction, because the Government has not exactly defined the situation. Rumours are spread to the effect that persons who are attached to the Caliph are selling here and there at Pera the most precious objects of the palaces. The Government must take the treasures which still remain under its guard. If there is a reason for selling anything it is for the Government to do so. It is necessary to submit the administrative functions of the Caliphate to a serious examination and reorganisation, for the fact that there are 'First Chamberlains' and 'First Secretaries' always sustains the dream of power in the mind of the Caliph.

If the French to-day, a hundred years after the Revolution, are still of the opinion that it would be dangerous for their independence and sovereignty to allow members of the royal family and their confidants to come to France, we, on our part, in the attitude which we have to adopt in view of a dynasty and its confidants who are eager to see on the horizon the sun of absolute power rise again, cannot sacrifice the Republic for considerations of courtesy and sophism. The Caliph must be told exactly who he is and what his office represents and must content himself with this situation. I ask you to proceed in such a manner that the Government takes fundamental and serious steps and to inform me of this.

(Signed) Ghazi Mustafa Kemal,
President of the Turkish Republic.

After this exchange of correspondence Ismet Paşa and Kiasim Paşa, Minister of War, arrived at Smyrna for the 'Kriegspiel.' Fewsi Paşa, Chief of the General Staff, was already there. We agreed about the necessity of suppressing the Caliphate. We had decided at the same time to suppress also the Ministry for Religious Affairs and the 'Evkaf'[24] and to unify public instruction.

On the 1st March, 1924, I had to open the Assembly.

We had returned to Angora on the 23rd February. I informed the competent authorities of my resolutions.

The Assembly began to discuss the budget. This afforded us an opportunity of occupying ourselves for a short time with the question of the allocations to the members of the dynasty and the budget of the Ministry for Religious Affairs and the *Evkaf*. My comrades began to make remarks and criticisms aiming at attaining the proposed aid. The debate was intentionally prolonged. In the speech which I delivered on the 1st March, the fifth anniversary of the opening of the Assembly, I especially emphasized the three following points:

The nation demands that now, in the future, forever and unconditionally the Republic shall be protected from every attack.

The wish of the nation can be expressed through the fact that the Republic will be founded a moment earlier and completely on the whole of the positive principles which have been put to the test.

We declare that it is necessary without loss of time to apply the principle of unity of instruction and education which has been decided by the vote of the nation.

We also recognize that it is indispensable in order to secure the revival of the Islamic Faith, to disengage it from the condition of being a political instrument, which it has been for centuries through habit.

---

[24] *Evkaf* is the plural of *vakif* (Arabic *waqf*). A *waqf* is a pious endowment set up in perpetuity from private property. It could serve any worthy purpose but was often used to support mosques, shrines, and religious schools. The administration of a *waqf* could be lucrative in that it often included a stipend and the right to control the wealth generated by the endowment. The Ottoman Empire had moved to establish more direct state control over these endowments in the nineteenth century. The step proposed here would allow the state to seize and reallocate the wealth contained in these endowments. Though there was an ideological edge to this twentieth-century effort by the Turkish Republic—the removal of financial support from religious institutions—*waqfs* had been historically vulnerable to seizure in the event of a state financial crisis or a major change in the political order, such as the collapse of a ruling dynasty and installation of another.

The group of the Party was invited to a sitting on the 2nd March. The three points I have just mentioned were brought forward and discussed. We were united in principle. Amongst other matters received, the following motions were read on the 3rd March during the first sitting of the Assembly:

Draft of the law of Shaykh Safvet Effendi and fifty of his colleagues concerning the abolition of the Caliphate and the expulsion of the Ottoman Dynasty from Turkish territory.

Draft of the law of Halil Hilki Effendi, deputy for Seerd [Siirt], and fifty of his colleagues concerning the suppression of the Ministry of Religious Affairs, of the Evkaf and the Ministry of the General Staff.

Motion of Vassif Bey, deputy for Saruchan, and fifty of his colleagues concerning the unification of instruction.

Fethi Bey, who presided, announced: 'Gentlemen, there are proposals with numerous signatures, demanding immediate discussion of these questions of law. I put this demand to the vote.'

Without referring it to commission, Fethi Bey immediately put the motions to the vote, and they were accepted.

The first objection was raised by Halid Bey, deputy for Kastamuni. One or two joined him in the course of the discussion. Numerous important speakers ascended the platform and gave long explanations in favour of the propositions. Besides the signatories of the motions the late Sejid Bey and Ismet Paşa made convincing speeches which were of a highly scientific nature and which will always be worthy of being studied and borne in mind. The discussion lasted for nearly five hours. When the discussion closed at 6:45 p.m. the Grand National Assembly had promulgated the Laws No. 429, 430 and 431.

In virtue of these laws the 'Grand National Assembly of Turkey and the Government formed by it is authorised to give legal form to the stipulations which are in force in the Turkish republic with reference to public affairs and to carry through their application. The Ministry for Religious Affairs and the *Evkaf* have been suppressed.'

All scientific and educational institutions in Turkish territory [...] all ecclesiastical schools, are transferred to the Ministry of Public Instruction.

The Caliph is declared deposed and the dignity abolished. All members of the deposed Ottoman dynasty are forever forbidden to reside within the frontiers of the territory of the Turkish Republic.

Certain persons who wrongly believed that it was necessary, for religious and political reasons to maintain the Caliphate, proposed at the last moment when the decisions were to be taken, that I should assume the office of the Caliphate.

I immediately gave a negative reply to those men.

Let me emphasise another point which arose: When the Grand National Assembly had abolished the Caliphate, Rassih Effendi, an ecclesiastic and deputy for Adalia, was president of the deputation of the Red Crescent, which was in India. He came back to Angora via Egypt. After soliciting an interview with me, he made statements to the effect that 'the Muslims in the countries through which he had been travelling demanded that I should become Caliph, and that the competent Muslim bodies had commissioned him to inform me of this desire.'

In the reply which I gave to Rassih Effendi, I expressed my thanks for the benevolence and affection which the Muslims had shown me and said: 'You are a Doctor of Religious Right. You know that Caliph signifies Chief of the State. How can I accept the proposals and desires of people who are governed by kings and emperors? If I should declare myself ready to accept this office, would the sovereigns of those people consent to it? The orders of the Caliph must be obeyed and his interdictions submitted to. Are those who want to make me Caliph in a position to execute my orders? Consequently, would it not be ridiculous to rig me up with an illusionary role which has neither sense nor right of existence?'

Gentlemen, I must frankly and categorically declare that those who continue to occupy themselves with the chimera of the Caliphate and thereby mislead the Muslim world, are nothing but enemies of the Muslim world, and especially of Turkey. They are only ignorant or blind men who could attach hopes to such jugglery.

Is it from love of our faith that such people as Rauf Bey,[25] Tsherkess Edhem and Reshid, all the 'Hundred and Fifty,' all members of the deposed dynasty of the Sultanate and the Caliphate with their adherents, all enemies of Turkey, are working with so much bitterness? Is the aim of those who are working so energetically against us, sheltering themselves under the words 'holy revolution,' but who use means such as murderous attempts, and gangs of brigands, and who maintain organization centres at our frontiers, who have always made the destruction of Turkey their aim—is this aim actually a holy one? Indeed, to believe this would mean that we were possessed of unmitigated ignorance and boundless blindness.

From now onwards it will not be so easy to suppose that the Muslim peoples and the Turkish nation would have fallen to such a low level as to continue in the abuse of the purity of the conscience and the tenderness of the sentiments of the Muslim world to criminal aims. Impudence has its limits.

[25] Hüseyin Rauf [Orbay], a Circassian naval officer who led the opposition against Mustafa Kemal in the People's Party. Accused of organizing the 'Izmir conspiracy' of 1926, he lived in exile until 1936.

4.4 An appeal from the Iraq Minorities (non-Muslim) Rescue Committee, 1931
Nelida Fuccaro

Preface

The Iraq Minorities (non-Muslim) Rescue Committee was a charitable organization established in Great Britain on the eve of the termination of the British Mandate (1920–32). The activities of this organization are representative of trends of political mobilization that affected the Iraqi minorities after the stipulation of the 1930 Anglo-Iraqi Treaty. This treaty paved the way to Iraq's independence while raising widespread concerns about the welfare of minority groups after the departure of Great Britain as mandatory power. Between 1930 and 1932 representatives of local communities addressed increasing numbers of petitions to the League of Nations to voice their fears and express their grievances against the Iraqi government. As a result, the League, which supervised the Iraqi Mandate through the Permanent Mandate Commission, came to play an active role between minority groups and the Iraqi administration, while British influence was on the wane. The main goal of the Rescue Committee was to provide humanitarian assistance to non-Muslim communities living in northern Iraq, particularly to groups of Assyrian Christians who had arrived in the region as refugees during and after World War I. In October 1930, three months after its establishment, this organization pledged to gather evidence on abuses that were being perpetrated by the Iraqi administration against non-Muslim groups living in the Mosul province. It also put forward proposals for the creation of an autonomous Christian region within the Kingdom of Iraq under the direct supervision of the League.

This document is a fund-raising appeal that was circulated to attract donations from Great Britain, Europe, and the United States. It details the political agenda of the Rescue Committee by highlighting its quest for international assistance. The activities of this Committee added a controversial dimension to the reputation of the Iraqi Christians, particularly to that of the Assyrians who were perceived by many Iraqis to be the main supporters of British colonialism in the region. The appeal presents the Christians as a nation with historical rights of self-determination and thus offers an interesting example of the impact that discourses of race and independent political development had on Iraqi society under mandatory rule. As the numerous references to the Semitic race suggest, ethnicity (rather than religion) defines the boundaries of the new political community. Moreover, the Christian nation was considered possibly to be capable of providing the framework for the political action of non-Christian groups, particularly of Yazidi Kurds and Jews. This document illustrates the extent to which the Rescue Committee was prepared to manipulate notions of race to suit its political agenda, a phenomenon that is very common in the nascent stages of modern nationalism in the region. Chaldeans and Assyrians, the two main Christian denominations represented in Iraq, belong to the Semitic race, as they are the descendants of the ancient Assyrians, who ruled Mesopotamia in the first millennium BCE. The Yazidis, a Kurdish heterodox community, are generically described as 'of traditional Semite origin', although they did not speak a Semitic language. The passing reference to the Jews (in the nineteenth century the Semites par excellence) can be explained by their scarce numbers in the Mosul hinterland whose populations the Committee claimed to represent.

Text

An Appeal from the Iraq Minorities (non-Muslim) Rescue Committee

Formation

This Committee was formed in London on 11 July 1930, under the Chairmanship of Captain Hormuzd Rassam, as a consequence of the consternation felt by these Peoples when the proposal to terminate the Mandate in 1932 was made known. This fear was especially prevalent in northern Iraq among the inhabitants of the Mosul Vilayet [province], which had only been assigned four years previously by decree of the League of Nations to the Arab Kingdom of Iraq, on the understanding that the Mandate would remain in force for at least twenty-five years.[26] The Peoples concerned comprised Chaldeans, Assyrians, and Jews (all Semites), Yezidis (of traditional Semite origin) and others.[27] These, together with the Kurds, are in a vast majority over the Arabs in this Territory, although a minority of the whole Kingdom of Iraq. Their apprehensions were confirmed when, on the publication of the Anglo-Iraqi Treaty dated 30 June 1930, it was found that no provisions of any kind for their welfare after the lifting of the Mandate had been made in the Treaty.

Captain Hormuzd Rassam is the legally constituted Accredited Representative of these Peoples (so-called Minorities), with power to negotiate on their behalf

[26] This is a reference to the dispute with Turkey over the Mosul province that was awarded to Iraq by the League of Nations in 1926.

[27] Chaldeans and Assyrians were Eastern Christians who belonged to Churches of Syriac language and tradition. While the Chaldeans were the largest Christian group living in the Mosul province, the Assyrians (also known as Nestorians) were originally from the Hakkari region, which after 1926 was included in Turkey. During the Mandate they were temporarily settled in northern Iraq. The Yazidi Kurds were the second largest non-Muslim community of the Mosul province. Under Ottoman rule they had suffered from religious persecutions as a result of their heterodox beliefs.

with the League of Nations and all Governments concerned. His acknowledged pre-eminence as a Chaldean (through his father), his British birth and Army Service, and his distinguished Irish descent (through his mother), constitute an unequalled status as their Representative.

Preparation and Presentation of Petitions

Having ascertained that this omission in the Treaty was deliberate, as the Mandatory Power considered that the guarantees for the welfare of these Minorities was a question to be decided directly between the League of Nations and the Arab Government of Iraq, two Petitions were drawn up by the non-Muslim inhabitants—one by the Chaldeans and Assyrians, the other by the Yezidis—and forwarded to the Committee for presentation to the League of Nations, through the Mandatory Power, in accordance with the procedure laid down. This was done—and a separate Petition from Captain Rassam himself, a non-resident in the Territory, was also sent in. These three Petitions were considered in June last by the Permanent Mandates Commission.

This completes the first chapter of the Committee's work.

Preliminary Investigation

In order to ascertain at first hand the true conditions existing among these Peoples, Captain Rassam, with his family, went out to Mosul and lived among them from January to June 1930. This was very necessary to ensure, when petitioning the League of Nations, that all statements made were as free as possible from Oriental exaggeration. He was joined there, in February 1930, by Mr Matthew Cope and his family, and the latter remained in Mosul at the unanimous request of these Peoples, until June this year, when they returned to England. It was due to Mr Cope's presence that these Peoples dared to risk their lives to make out and send in their petitions, although such action is an undoubted right.

The Preliminary Expenses, prior to the formation of the Committee, amounted to (approximately) £1,800, and were met by Captain Rassam and friends.

The Expenses of the Committee in London and Mosul between 11 July 1930 and 31 July 1931 amounted to £1,200, which sum has been raised by private subscriptions, including £150 from the Archbishop of Canterbury's Assyrian [Fund], £200 from the Assyrian Relief Committee of the U.S.A., and £73 (the final balance) from the Sir Henry Lunn Fund.

The League of Nations

As a result of the sittings of the Permanent Mandates Commission between 9 and 27 June last, and of the Council [of the League of Nations] on 4 September last, it was decided that Captain Rassam should be informed that his petition had been considered, and that the League will continue to see that the rights of the minorities are respected. It was also decided that *effective* [emphasis in text] guarantees for the protection of Racial Linguistic and Religious Minorities should be obtained from Iraq before the mandate is lifted; and, that when considering their Report to be presented to the Council [of the League of Nations] in January 1932, the Mandates Commission should pay particular regard to any special circumstances that obtain in Iraq, as distinct from other territories under the mandatory system.[28]

These decisions represent all that it was possible for this Commission to obtain from the League up to the present time, and are a very gratifying proof of the success of its efforts.

The Final Petition

On 23 September last, there was forwarded to the Chairman of the Permanent Mandates Commission, for consideration at their next meeting commencing on the 26th instant:—

'The Petition of Captain Anthony Homuzd Rassam for and on behalf of the Chaldee-Assyrian Nation to be preserved as a National Entity and for the protection of the Jews, Yezidis and other Racial and Religious Minorities.'

In this Petition are clearly and logically put forward the reasons why, in the opinion of this Committee, the special circumstances in regard to the minorities in Iraq can only be met by the formation within and as an integral part of that Kingdom, of an ENCLAVE in which these non-Muslim Races *can preserve* their national Entities, Faiths, Languages, Schools, Laws and Customs.

THE PRESERVATION OF THE NATIONAL ENTITY OF THE SURVIVING MEMBERS OF THE ONCE MIGHTY ASSYRIAN EMPIRE—known now as Chaldeans and Assyrians according to the religious community to which they adhere—is a matter that concerns the whole World. The fame of this Race for centuries prior to and after the Christian era is emblazoned in the annals of History, scriptural, archaeological and secular. At the centre of that Empire, in the land watered by the Tigris, and in sight of the ruins of ancient Nineveh, their Capital City, there still dwell some 120,000 people, lowlanders for the most part, but now reinforced by the return of their highlanders (Assyrians).[29] During the 2,500 years since the downfall of their Empire, despite the vicissitudes of war and changing governments and the oppression of alien rulers, here have these People endured and remained, recognised even under the late Turkish dominance as a small

---

[28] When this appeal was circulated Great Britain was preparing a report for the League of Nations that included evidence on the progress of Iraq during the Mandate. In order to release the country from mandatory rule, the League was to provide recommendations to the Iraqi government based on this report.

[29] The Assyrian refugees are called highlanders with reference to their original settlement in the Hakkari Mountains. The Chaldeans are lowlanders as they lived in the plain around the city of Mosul.

Nation (*millet*),[30] preserving their Entity, their Faith, their Language, their Schools and living under their own Laws and Customs administered by their own Patriarchs. THESE ARE NOW IN VERY GRAVE DANGER.

Surely the efforts of this Committee to preserve such a People, to bring peace, happiness and stability to their land, and to make them loyal and contented citizens of the Kingdom of Iraq, are worthy of support? Together with their fellow Semites, the Jews, who still preserve their pedigrees and trace their lineage to the Princes and Prophets of Judah, and with the proffered co-operation of the Yezidis, there can, through the medium of the League of Nations, be built up within the Kingdom of Iraq, and to its material benefit, a prosperous and law-abiding Community, the existence of which will form in these lands that guarantee for peace which is now so sadly lacking.

Donations

Donations are urgently required for the expenses of following up and completing this good work, and the expenses of travelling and for the maintenance of the Committee's representatives at Geneva and elsewhere during the next four months will be heavy.

A. HORMUZD RASSAM, *Chairman*,
Captain (late City of London Regt. Royal Fusiliers)
H. SEYMOUR HALL, *Trustee and Hon. Treasurer*
Paymaster Rear-Admiral (Retired)
W. B. LANE, *Trustee*, Lieutenant-Colonel, I.M.S. (Retired)
H. E. HOLLANDS, *Secretary*.

1 October 1931
13, Powis Square, London, W.11

Donations will be gratefully received and acknowledged by the Hon. Treasurer. Cheques and Postal Orders should be made out to the IRAQ MINORITIES RESCUE COMMITTEE and crossed, Barclays Bank, 160, Piccadilly.

---

[30] Term that designated non-Muslim communities under Ottoman rule, particularly Christians and Jews who enjoyed an autonomous status in the management of religious and communal affairs.

4.5 From the *Javid-nameh* of Muhammad Iqbal, 1932[31]

From the Islamfiche *project*

Preface

More than any other Muslim intellectual in modern times, Sir Muhammad Iqbal approaches the stature of the polymaths in earlier Islamic societies—a sort of 'Renaissance Man' of Islam. Born in the Sialkot in 1877, then a north-west province in India, Iqbal began his education in Lahore, before traveling to England to study philosophy and law at Cambridge University. He completed a doctorate in Munich in 1907 with a dissertation on the development of metaphysics in Persia. Returning to Lahore the following year, he taught philosophy, practised law, and engaged in political work as a member, and later president, of the Muslim League of India. In addition to these activities, he wrote prolifically in Urdu, Persian, and English, in subjects ranging from economics, politics, and law, to philosophy, religion, and poetry. In fact, if Iqbal the political figure is hailed as the father of modern Pakistan, Iqbal the writer made his greatest contributions as a poet. Drawing on the Persianate legacy of Indo-Muslim culture, he addresses contemporary issues in traditional forms, a combination which deeply affected the educated Indian Muslims of his day. At the same time, he was instrumental in hastening the maturity of Urdu poetry and the abandonment of the Persian language in favor of Urdu by Indian Muslim poets. The study of Iqbal by Pakistani and Indian Muslims is still relatively active and a testament to his cultural importance to the Muslims of South Asia.

In the selection presented here, Iqbal translates his thoughts on the possibilities of an Islamic revival into a poetry that is heavily indebted to traditional models. He moves from the relation between the individual Muslim and the Islamic community, to the relation of both these and the world as a whole. Surveying the current decadence of the Islamic world and its exploitation by the West, he places the blame squarely on the shoulders of the individual Muslim. For Iqbal, the regeneration of Islam starts with the individual believer, who must replace the lax practice of his faith with fervor and enthusiasm.

Iqbal's arguably greatest poem, the *Javid-nameh* ('The Epic of Javid'—Javid being the name of Iqbal's son), was written in Persian and pays homage to Islamic and Persian tradition. Indeed, the decision to write verse in Persian (as well as in Urdu) was motivated by a pan-Islamic idealism. The poem is written in the form of a *mi'raj*, an imaginary ascent through the heavenly spheres (and inspired by the actual journey,

---

[31] *Javid-Nama*, trans. A. J. Arberry (London: Allen & Unwin, 1966), 53–71.

according to Muslim tradition, of the Prophet Muhammad through the heavenly spheres from the Dome of the Rock in Jerusalem), in which the author is guided by the greatest of all Persian mystical poets, Jalal al-Din Rumi (d. 672AH/1273CE). On the way, Javid converses with various figures of classical and modern Islamic history, but the grand culmination is a meeting 'beyond the spheres' with the German philosopher Friedrich Nietzsche. The scene reflects the degree of Nietzsche's influence on Iqbal's thought. Although Iqbal was especially fond of the more extreme Islamic mystics, such as Al-Hallaj (d. 309/922), whom he saw as his predecessor in reviving the Muslim world, under Nietzsche's influence he decried the influence of Platonism, with its exaltation of the universal, on Islamic thought. He accorded the greatest importance to the individual personality; God Himself was the supreme individual, Whose proper name was Allah.

In 'The Sphere of Mercury', Iqbal, under the pen-name of Zendeh-Rud ('Living Stream'), meets two other prominent figures of the Islamic modernist movement, Jamal al-Din Afghani (d. 1897) and Said Halim Pasha (d. 1914). Al-Afghani in particular is Iqbal's mouthpiece for his criticism of almost all existing social structures—capitalism, communism, west European democracy, and medieval monarchy. He also sets forth Iqbal's ideal of an Islamic democracy free from the 'death of the heart' which he sees in Western democracies. Said Halim Pasha, an Ottoman figure who preached Islamic unity along with Al-Afghani, praises the Turkish leader Mustafa Kemal Atatürk (d. 1938) for his efforts at reform, but decries his slavish imitation of the West.

Text

The Sphere of Mercury

Visitation to the Spirits of Jamal al-Din Afghani and Said Halim Pasha

> A handful of dust so carried forward its task
> to the contemplation of its own manifestations:
> either I fell into the net of being and existence
> or existence became a prisoner in my net!
> Have I made a chink in yon azure curtains?
> Am I of the skies, or are the skies of me?
> Either heaven has taken my heart into its breast
> or it is my heart that has seized heaven.
> Is this external then internal? What is it?
> What manner of thing is it the eye sees? What is it?
> I beat my wings towards another heaven,
> I see another world rising before me,
> a world of mountains and plains, seas and dry land,

a world far more ancient than our earth,
a world grown out of a little cloud
that has never known the conquest of man—
images as yet unlimned on the tablet of existence
where no critic of nature has yet been born.

I said to Rumi, 'This wasteland is very fair,
very fair the tumult of the waters in the mountains.
I find no sign here of any living thing,
so whence comes the sound of the call to prayer?'
Rumi said, 'This is the station of the saints,
this heap of earth is familiar with our dust.
When the father of mankind departed out of Eden
he dwelt in this world for one or two days;
these expanses have felt the burning of his sighs,
heard his lamentations in the hour of dawn.
The visitors to this honourable station
are themselves pious men of lofty stations,
pious men such as Fudail and Bu Said,
true gnostics like Junaid and Ba Yazid.[32]
Rise up now, and let us pray together,
devote a moment or two to burning and melting.'

I went on, and saw two men engaged in prayer,
the acolyte a Turk, the leader an Afghan.
The Sage of Rum, in rapture continually,
his face radiant with an ecstasy of joy,
said, 'The east never gave birth to two better sons—
the plucking of their nails unravelled our knots:
Mawlana Jamal, Sayyed of all Sayyeds,[33]
whose eloquence gave life to stone and sherd,
and passionate Halim, commander of the Turks
whose thoughts matched the loftiness of his station.
To offer prayer with such men is true devotion,
a labour else whose hoped-for wage is Paradise'.

The recitation of that vigorous elder,
the Chapter of the Star in that silent plain—
a recital that to move Abraham to ecstasy,
to enrapture the pure spirit of Gabriel;

---

[32] Fudail, Bu Saʿid, Junaid, Ba Yazid—four famous Persian mystics.

[33] Mawlana is an honorific title, meaning 'Our Master'; Sayyeds are Muslims claiming descent from the family of the Prophet Muhammad.

the heedful heart becomes restless in the breast,
the cry 'No god but God' rises from the tombs;
it imparts to smoke the quivering of the flame,
bestows on David ardour and intoxication;
at his recital every mystery was revealed,
the Heavenly Archetype[34] appeared unveiled.

After prayer I rose up from my place
and kissed his hand in all humility.
Rumi said, 'A mote that travels the skies,
in its heart a whole world of fire and passion!
Only upon himself he has opened his eyes,
yielded his heart to no man, is utterly free;
swiftly he paces through the expanse of Being—
jestingly, I call him Zendeh-Rud.'

Al-Afghani
Zendeh-Rud, tell us of our terrestrial world,
speak to us of our earth and sky.
A thing of dust, you are clear-eyed as the Holy Ones—
give us some tidings of the Mussulmans!

Zendeh-Rud
In the heart of a people that once shattered the world
I have seen a conflict between religion and country.
The spirit is dead in the body through weakness of faith,
despairs of the strength of the manifest religion;
Turk, Persian, Arab intoxicated with Europe
and in the throat of each the fish-hook of Europe;
and East wasted by the West's imperialism,
Communism taken the lustre from religion and community.

Al-Afghani
Religion and Country
The Lord of the West, cunning from head to toe,
taught the people of religion the concept of Country.
He thinks of the centre, while you are at discord—
give up this talk of Syria, Palestine, Iraq![35]
If you can discriminate between good and evil
you will not bind your hearts to clods, stones, bricks.
What is religion? To rise up from the face of the dust

---

[34] The original of the Qur'an.
[35] An allusion to European colonization of the former Ottoman territories after World War I.

so that the pure soul may become aware of itself!
He who has said 'god is He' is not contained
within the confines of this dimensioned order.
A grass-blade is of the earth, and yet rises from the earth;
alas, if the pure soul should die in the dust!
Although man sprang out of water and clay,
from water and clay rose-like drew colour and sap,
alas, if he wanders forever in water and clay,
alas, if he soars not higher than this station!
The body says, 'Go into the dust of the roadway';
the soul says, 'Look upon the expanse of the world!'
Man of reason, the soul is not contained in dimensions;
the free man is a stranger to every fetter and chain,
the free man rails against the dark earth
for it beseems not the falcon to act like a mouse.

This handful of earth to which you give the name 'country',
this so-called Egypt, and Iran, and Yemen—
there is a relationship between a country and its people
in that it is out of its soil that a nation rises;
but if you look carefully at this relationship
you will descry a subtlety finer than a hair.
Though it is out of the East that the sun rises
showing itself bold and bright, without a veil,
only then it burns and blazes with inward fire
when it escapes from the shackles of East and West;
drunk with splendour it springs up out of its East
that it may subject all horizons to its mastery;
its nature is innocent of both East and West,
though relationship-wise, true, it is an Easterner.

Communism and Capitalism
The author of *Das Kapital* came of the stock of Abraham,
that is to say, that prophet[36] who knew not Gabriel;
since truth was implicit even within his error
his heart believed, though his brain was an infidel.
The Westerners have lost the vision of heaven,
they go hunting for the pure spirit in the belly.
The pure soul takes not colour and scent from the body,
and Communism has nothing to do save with the body.
The religion of that prophet who knew not truth

---

[36] Karl Marx (1818–83), author of *Das Kapital*.

is founded upon equality of the belly;
the abode of fraternity being in the heart,
its roots are in the heart, not in water and clay.

Capitalism too is a fattening of the body,
its unenlightened bosom houses no heart;
like the bee that pastures upon the flower
it overpasses the petal, and carries off the honey,
yet stalk and leaf, colour and scent all make up the rose
for whose selfsame beauty the nightingale laments.
Surpass the talisman, the scent and colour,
bid farewell to the form, gaze only upon the meaning.
Though it is difficult to descry the inward death.
call not that a rose which in truth is clay.

The soul of both is impatient and intolerant,
both of them know not God, and deceive mankind.
One lives by production, the other by taxation
and man is a glass caught between these two stones.
The one puts to rout science, religion, art,
the other robs the body of soul, the hand of bread.
I have perceived both drowned in water and clay,
both bodily burnished, but utterly dark of heart.
Life means a passionate burning, an urge to make,
to cast in the dead clay of the seed of a heart!

Said Halim Pasha
East and West
For Westerners intelligence is the stuff of life,
for Easterners love is the mystery of all being.
Only through love intelligence gets to know God,
love's labours find firm grounding in intelligence;
when love is companioned by intelligence
it has the power to design another world.
Then rise and draw the design of a new world,
mingle together love with intelligence.
The flame of the Europeans is damped down,
their eyes are perceptive, but their hearts are dead;
they have been sore smitten by their own swords,
hunted down and slaughtered, themselves the hunters.
Look not for fire and intoxication in their vine;
not into their heavens shall rise a new age.
It is from your fire that the glow of life comes,
and it is your task to create the new world.

Mustafa Kemal, who sang of a great renewal,
said the old image must be cleansed and polished;
yet the vitality of the Kaʿba cannot be made new
if a new Lat and Manat[37] from Europe enter its shrine.
No, the Turks have no new melody in their lute,
what they call new is only the old tune of Europe;
no fresh breath has entered into their breast,
no design of a new world is in their mind.
Turkey perforce goes along with the existing world,
melted like wax in the flame of the world we know.
Originality is at the roots of all creation,
never by imitation shall life be reformed;
The living heart, creator of ages and epochs,
that soul is little enamoured of imitation:
if you possess the spirit of a true Mussulman
examine your own conscience, and the Qur'an—
a hundred new worlds lie within its verses,
whole centuries are involved in its moments;
one world of it suffices for the present age—
seize it, if the heart in your breast grasps truth.
A believing servant himself is a sign of God,
every world to his breast is as a garment;
and when one world grows upon his bosom,
The Qur'an gives him another world!
The barque of us terrestrials has no helmsman,
no one knows where the Qur'an's world lies.

Al-Afghani
It is a world lost now in our breast,
a world awaiting yet the command 'Arise!'
A world without distinction of race and colour,
its evening is brighter than Europe's dawn;
a world cleansed of monarchs and of slaves,
a world unbounded, like the believer's heart,
a world so fair, that the effluence of one glance
planted the seed of it in ʿUmar's[38] soul.
Eternal it is, the impact of it ever new,

---

[37] Ancient Arabian gods, implying that Atatürk has succumbed to the 'new god' of the Western nation-state.

[38] Second caliph of Islam (13/634–23/644), whose opposition to the new religion had been transformed suddenly to loyal adherence.

ever new the leaf and fruit of its sure foundations;
inwardly it is anxious not of change,
outwardly, every moment is revolution.
Behold, that world lies within your own heart;
now I will tell you of its firm foundations.

The Foundations of the Qur'anic World
1. *Man, God's Vice-regent*
In both worlds, everywhere are the marks of love;
man himself is a mystery of love.
Love's secret belongs not to the world of wombs,
not to Shem or Ham, Greece or Syria:
a star without East and West, a star unsetting
in whose orbit is neither North nor South.
The words *I am setting* tell his destiny,
their exegesis reaches from earth to heaven.
Death, grave, uprising, judgment are his estates,
the light and fire of the other world are his works;
himself is Imam, prayer and sanctuary,
himself the Ink, himself the Book and the Pen.
Little by little what is hidden in him becomes visible;
it has no boundaries, its kingdom no frontiers.
His being gives value to contingent things,
his equilibrium is the touchstone of contingent things.
What shall I declare of his sea without a shore?
All ages and all times are drowned in his heart.
That which is contained within man is the world,
that which is not contained within the world is man.
Sun and moon are manifest through his self-display;
even Gabriel cannot penetrate his privacy.
Loftier than the heavens is the station of man,
and the beginning of education is respect for man.

Man alive in heart, do you know what thing life is?
One-seeing love that is contemplating duality:
man and woman are bound one to the other,
they are the fashioners of the creatures of desire.
Woman is the guardian of the fire of life,
her nature is the tablet of life's mysteries;
she strikes our fire against her own soul
and it is her substance that makes of the dust a man.
In her heart lurk life's potentialities,
from her glow and flame life derives stability;

she is a fire from which the sparks break forth,
body and soul, lacking her glow, cannot take shape.
What worth we possess derives from her values
for we are all images of her fashioning;
if god has bestowed on you a glance aflame
cleanse yourself, and behold her sanctity.

You from whose faith the present age has taken all fire,
now I will tell you openly the secrets of the veil.
The joy of creation is a fire in the body
and society is lightened by that light,
and whosoever takes any portion of that fire
watches jealously over his private passion;
all the time he fixes his gaze on his own image
lest his tablet should receive any other image.
Mohammad chose solitude upon Mount Hira
and for a space saw no other beside himself;
our image was then poured into his heart
and out of his solitude a nation arose.
Though you may be an unbeliever in God,
yet you cannot gainsay the Prophet's glory.
Though you possess a soul illumined as Moses,
yet without solitude your thoughts remain barren;
by isolation the imagination becomes more vivid,
more vivid, more questing, more finding.
Science and passion are both stations of life
both take a share of the impact of events.
Science derives pleasure from verification,
love derives pleasure from creativeness.
Display is very precious to the verifier,
to the creator solitude is very precious.
The eye of Moses desired to behold Being—
that was all part of the pleasure of verification;
thou shalt not see Me[39] contains many subtleties—
lose yourself a little while in this sea profound.
On all sides life's traces appear unveiled,
its fountain wells up in the heart of creation.
Consider the tumult that rages through all horizons;
inflict not on the Creator the trouble of display—
solitude is the protection of every artist,

---

[39] God's reply to Moses when he prayed for the Beatific Vision (Qur'an 7: 138).

solitude is the bezel in the artist's ring.

2. Divine Government
The servant of God has no need of any station,
no man is his slave, and he is the slave of none;
the servant of God is a free man, that is all,
his kingdom and laws are given by God alone,
his customs, his way, his faith, his laws are of God,
of God his foul and fair, his bitter and sweet.
The self-seeking mind heeds not another's welfare,
Sees only its own benefit, not another's;
God's revelation sees the benefit of all,
its regard is for the welfare and profit of all.
Just alike in peace and in the ranks of war,
His joining and parting are without fear and favour;
when other than God determines the aye and nay
then the strong man tyrannises over the weak;
in this world command is rooted in naked power;
mastery drawn from other than God is pure unbelief.

The tyrannical ruler who is well-versed in power
builds about himself a fortress made up of edicts;
white falcon, sharp of claw and swift to seize,
he takes for his counsellor the silly sparrow
giving to tyranny its constitution and laws,
a sightless man giving collyrium to the blind.
What results from the laws and constitutions of Kings?
Fat lords of the manor, peasants lean as spindles!

Woe to the constitution of the democracy of Europe!
The sound of that trumpet renders the dead still deader;
those tricksters, treacherous as the revolving spheres,
have played the nations by their own rules, and swept the board!
Robbers they, this one wealthy, that one a toiler,
all the time lurking in ambush one for another;
now is the hour to disclose the secret of those charmers—
we are the merchandise, and they take all the profits.
Their eyes are hard out of the love of silver and gold,
their sons are a burden upon their mother's backs.
Woe to a people who, out of fear for the fruit,
carries off the very sap from the tree's trunk
and, that the plectrum wins no melody from its strings,
slays the infant yet unborn in its mother's womb.
For all its repertory of varied charms

I will take nothing from Europe except—a warning!
You enchained to the imitation of Europe, be free,
clutch the skirt of the Qur'an, and be free!

3. *The Earth is the Lord's*

The history of man throughout East and West
is a tale of wars, battles, revolts, for 'land';
one bride there is, and we are all her husbands,
that enchantress is without all and with all withal.
Her blandishments are nothing but guile and trickery,
she belongs neither to you nor to me either.
These stones and rocks have nothing in common with you;
they are the stuff of stiffness, you are on a journey.
How can the sleeper and the wakeful mix together?
What has the planet to do with the fixed star?
God has called the earth simply our 'enjoyment',[40]
this valueless 'enjoyment' is gratis, gratis.
You landowner, take a wise hint from me:
take from the land your food and grave, but take it not.
How long will its company last? You are, it is not;
you are a living being, it is a lifeless show.
You are an eagle, therefore get you about the skies,
open your wings and pinions, rise clear of the earth.
'The Earth is the Lord's':[41] the inward meaning is plain,
and he who sees not this plain is an infidel.

I do not say, desert utterly dwelling and lane;
this world of colour and scent is your empery—
grain by grain gather the jewels from its soil,
falcon-like seize your prey out of its skies,
smite your axe against its mountain-ranges,
take light from your self and set it all afire.
Have nothing to do with the ancient ways of Azhar[42]
but hew out a new world to your own desire!
Yield not your heart to colour and scent, dwelling and lane;
the heart is His sanctuary, yield it only to Him.
Death without substance, without tomb and winding-sheet
is to lose oneself in riches, children and wife;
but he who has the words 'One God' by heart

---

[40] Qur'anic term for earthly possessions (cf. 7: 23).   [41] Qur'anic expression (cf. 65: 26).
[42] Al-Azhar is the pre-eminent madrash of Eqypt. Reforms and radicals often characterize this institution as 'out of touch' and focused on ritual rather than relevant theology.

can lose within himself a world entire.
What is the poverty of hunger, dancing, nakedness?
Poverty is true kingship; what is monkery?

4. *Wisdom is a Great Good*

God has declared, *Wisdom is a great good*;[43]
wherever you may see this good, seize it.
Science gives pinions to words and sounds,
 bestows purest substance on things without substance;
science finds a way even to heaven's zenith
to pluck the sight out of the sun's own eye.
Its transcript is the commentary of the cosmos,
the fate of the cosmos hangs upon its determining;
it says to the desert, 'Bubble up!' and it bubbles,
to the sea, 'Produce a mirage!' and it produces it.
Its eye beholds all the events in creation
that it may see the sure foundations of creation;
if it attaches its heart to God, it is prophecy,
but if it is a stranger to God, it is unbelief.
Science without the heart's glow is pure evil,
for then its light is darkness over sea and land,
its rouge renders the whole world black and blind,
its springtide scatters the leaves of all being,
sea, plain and mountain, quiet garden and villa
are ravaged by the bombs of its aeroplanes.
It is the fire that burns the heart of Europe,
from it springs the joy of raiding and robbing;
it turns topsy-turvy the course of the days,
despoils the peoples of their capital.
Its power becomes the faithful ally of Satan;
light becomes fire by association with fire.
To slay Satan is indeed a difficult task,
since he is hidden within the depths of the heart;
better is it to make him a true Mussulman,
better to smite him dead with the sword of the Qur'an.
God save us from majesty that is without beauty,
God save us from separation without union!
Science without love is a demonic thing,
science together with love is a thing divine;
science and wisdom without love are a corpse,

---

[43] Based on Qur'an 2: 272.

reason is an arrow that never pierced the target.
With the vision of God make the blind to see,
convert Abu Lahab into an impetuous Haidar![44]
You have displayed the foundations of the Book of God,
yet is yonder world still veiled in a shroud.
Why does it not strip off the veil from its face,
why does it not issue yet out of our hearts?
Before us lies a whole world wasting away,
a nation quietly reposing in its own dust;
the heart's ardour of Tartar and Kurd is vanished—
either the Mussulmans are dead, or the Qur'an is dead.

Said Halim Pasha

The religion of God is more shameful than unbelief,
because the mullah is a believer trading in unfaith;
in our eyes this dew-drop of ours is an ocean,
to his eyes our ocean is a dew-drop.
At the elegant graces of that Qur'an-vendor
I have seen the Trusty Spirit[45] himself cry out!
His heart is a stranger to what lies beyond the sky,
for him the Archetype of the Book is but a fable;
having no share of the wisdom of the Prophet's religion,
his heaven is dark, being without any star.
Short of vision, blind of taste, an idle gossip,
his hairsplitting arguments have fragmented the Community.
Seminary and mullah, before the secrets of the Book,
are as one blind from birth before the light of the sun.
The infidel's religion is the plotting and planning of Holy War;
the mullah's religion is corruption in the Way of God.
The man of God is the soul of this dimensionate world;
say from me to him, who has gone into solitude,
'You whose thoughts are life itself to the believer,
whose breaths are confirmation to the Community,
having the sublime Qur'an by heart is your rite,
your religion the publishing of the Word of God.
You with whom God speaks, how long will you hang your head?
Come, bring forth your hand out of your sleeve!
Speak of the history of the "white" people,[46]

---

[44] The first was one of Muhammad's worst enemies; the second is a nickname for 'Ali, the Prophet's cousin, son-in-law, and fourth caliph (35/656–40/661).   [45] The archangel Gabriel.

[46] Those who shared the miracle of the White Hand (Qur'an 20: 23).

speak to the gazel [unreadable] ... vastness of the desert.
Your nature is illumined by the Chosen One,[47]
so declare now, where is our station?'

The man of God takes not colour and scent from anyone,
the man of God receives colour and scent from God;
every moment there is in his body a fresh soul,
every moment he has, like God, a new labour.
Declare the secrets to the believer,
declare the exposition of the mystery of *Every day*.
The caravan has no halting-place but the Sanctuary,
the caravan has naught but God in its heart;
I do not say that its road is different—
it is the caravan that is different, different its regard.

Al-Afghani
Have you any acquaintance with the Traditions of the Chosen One?
'God's religion came a stranger into the world.'[48]
I will tell you the meaning of this virgin saying.
The 'strangerhood' of religion is not the poverty of God's remembrancers;
for the man who is truly a researcher
'strangerhood' of religion refers to the scarceness of its verses.
The 'strangerhood' of religion every time is of a different kind;
ponder well this subtlety, if you have eyes to see.
Fasten your heart again to the perspicuous Verses
that you may seize a new age in your lasso.
No man knows the inner secrets of the Book;
Easterners and Westerners alike twist and turn this way and that.
The Russians have laid down a new design;
they have taken bread and water, and jettisoned religion.
Behold truth, speak truth, seek only truth;
speak one or two words from me to the people.

Al-Afghani's Message to the Russian People
One thing is the goal and sum of the Qur'an,
other the rite and ritual of the Muslim;
in his heart there is no burning fire,
the chosen One is not living in his breast.
The believer has not eaten the fruit of the Qur'an,
in his cup I have seen neither wine nor beer.

---

[47] Title for Muhammad (in Arabic, Mustafa).   [48] Saying attributed to Muhammad.

He broke the magic spell of Caesar and Chosroes
and himself sat on the throne of empire;
when the young shoot of power gathered strength,
his religion took on the shape of empire.
But empire changes the gaze entirely,
reason, understanding, usage and way alike.

You who have laid down a new plan,
and disengaged your heart from the ancient system,
like us Muslims you have broken
the bone of imperial rule in this world.
So that you may like a lamp in your heart
take a warning from our past history;
set your foot firm in the battle,
circle no more about this Lat and Hubal.
This aged world requires a nation
that shall be both bearer of good tidings and adviser.
Return again to the peoples of the East;
your 'days' are bound up with the 'days' of the East.[49]
You have kindled a new flame in the soul,
your heart houses a new night and day.
The rite and religion of the Franks have grown old;
look no more towards that ancient cloister.
You have finished now with lords;
pass on from 'no', march onwards to 'but'—[50]
pass on from 'no', if you are a true seeker,
that you may take the road of living affirmation.
You who desire a new world-order,
have you sought for it a firm foundation?

You have expunged the ancient tale chapter by chapter;
illumine your thoughts from the Archetype of the Book.
Who gave the black man the White Hand?
Who gave the good news of no Caesar, no Chosroes?
Transcend the many-coloured splendours,
find yourself by abandoning Europe!
If you are apprised by the Westerners' cunning
give up the wolf, take on the lion's trade.
What is wolfishness? The search for food and means;
the Lion of the Lord seeks freedom and death.

[49] 'Days'—famous victories of the Arabs; by extension, the spread of Islam.
[50] Alludes to the Muslim creed, 'there is *no* god *but* God . . .'

Without the Qur'an, the lion is a wolf;
the poverty of the Qur'an is the root of empire.
The poverty of the Qur'an is the mingling of meditation and reason—
I have never seen reason perfect without meditation.
Meditation? To school pleasure and passion;
this is the affair of the soul, not the affair of lip and palate.
From it arise the flames that burn the breast,
it does not accord with your temperament yet.
Martyr of the delicate beauty of reason,
I will tell you of the revelations of reason!

What is the Qur'an? Sentence of death for the master-man,
succour for the slave without food and destitute.
Look not for good from the money-grubbing manikin—
You will not attain piety, until you expend.
What pray is born of usury? Tumults!
No one knows the pleasure of 'a good loan'.[51]
Usury darkens the soul, hardens the heart like a stone,
makes man a ravening beast, without fangs and claws.
It is lawful to draw one's sustenance from the soil—
this man's 'enjoyment', the property of God.
The believer is the trustee, God is the possessor;
whatever you see other than God is perishing.[52]
God's banner has been beaten down by kings,
their entry has reduced townships to misery.[53]
Our bread and water are of one table;
the progeny of Adam are *as a single soul.*[54]
When the Qur'an's design descended into this world
it shattered the images of priest and pope;
I speak openly what is hidden in my heart—
this is not a book, it is something other!
When it has entered the soul, the soul is transformed;
when the soul has been transformed, the world is changed.
Like God, it is at once hidden and manifest,
living and enduring, yes, and speaking.
In it are the destinies of East and West—
realise then the lightning-like swiftness of thought!

---

[51] Iqbal alludes both to the frequent Qur'anic injunctions against taking interest on loans, and to such Qur'anic passages as 2: 246, which enjoin the believer to lend to God 'a good loan', i.e. of obedience and good works, which God will recompense many times over.   [52] Cf. Qur'an 28: 88.
[53] Cf. Qur'an 27: 34.   [54] Cf. Qur'an 31: 27.

It told the Muslim, 'Put your life in your hands;
give whatever you possess beyond your needs.'[55]
You have created a new law and order;
consider it a little in the light of the Qur'an
and you will understand life's heights and depths,
you will comprehend the destiny of life.
Our assembly is without wine and cupbearer,
yet the melodies of the Qur'an's instrument are immortal;
if our plectrum now strikes without effect,
Heaven houses thousands of excellent strummers.
God's remembrance requires not nations,
it transcends the bounds of time and space.
God's remembrance is apart from the remembrance of every
remembrancer—
what need has it of Greek or Syrian?
If God should remove it from us
He can if He will transfer it to another people.
I have seen the blind conformity and opinionated-ness of Muslims
and every moment my soul trembles in my body;
I fear for the day when it shall be denied to them,
And its fire shall be kindled in quite other hearts.

The Sage of Rum bids Zendeh-Rud intone a song
The Sage of Rum, that man filled wholly with ecstasy and passion,
I know what affect these words had on his soul;
he drew from his breast a heart-rending sigh,
his tears ran redder than the blood of martyrs.
He, whose arrows pierced only the hearts of heroes,
turned his gaze upon Al-Afghani, and spoke:
'The heart must throb with blood like the twilight,
the hand must be thrust into the saddle-straps of God;
hope moves the soul to flow like a running river,
the abandonment of hope is eternal death.'
He looked at me again, and said: 'O Zendeh-Rud,
with a couplet set all being afire.
Our camel is weary and the load is heavy;
more bitter must be the song of the caravanner.[56]
The proving of holy men is through adversity,
it is right to make the thirsty yet more athirst.
Like Moses depart from the River Nile,

[55] Cf. Qur'an 9: 112; 2: 216–17.   [56] Used to urge the camels to keep going.

stride out like Abraham towards the fire.
A melody of one who catches the scent of the Beloved
bears a people onwards even to the Beloved's street.'

The Song of Zendeh-Rud
You say that these roses and tulips are permanent here;
no, they are travellers all, like the waves of the breeze.
Where is the new truth which we seek, and do not find?
Mosque, school and tavern, all alike are barren.
Learn a word from your own self, and in that word burn,
for in this convent all lack Moses' fire.
Speak not of the striving for purity of these monastery-dwellers,
they are all dishevelled of hair, blankets unwashed.
What temples they have fashioned within the Sanctuary,
these Unitarians[57] of one thought, but all split in two!
The problem is not that the hour of feasting has passed,
the problem is that they are all without sweetmeats and
boon-companion![58]

[57] 'Unitarian' here is a translation of 'muwahhidun' or believes in the unity of God—not to be confused with the Unitarian Universalist Church.

[58] Usual accompaniments to wine as a symbol of spiritual fervor.

4.6 Reporting the news with an Islamic revivalist twist: excerpts from *The Banner of Islam*, 1946
Camron Michael Amin

Preface

As the press organ of the radical Islamist movement known as the Fedayan-e Eslam (Devotees of Islam), *Parcham-e Eslam (The Banner of Islam)* provides a window on the development both of 'political Islam' and of the press in Iran. From its inception in the mid-nineteenth century, the press in Iran had fulfilled a didactic function, propagating official and intellectual wisdom to the masses and relying on subventions from official or private backers to survive. However, the pursuit of commercial success in the press meant constant innovation in coverage and format in an effort to increase readership and advertising dollars. Commercialism in the Iranian press was increasingly evident in the 1920s, which saw the arrival of Iran's main daily, *Ettelāʿat* ('Information') in 1926. Two other dynamics influencing the press were state censorship (starting in the 1850s) and the rise of mass politics in the 1890s. Beginning in the late nineteenth century, more Iranians began to pursue journalism, and defined themselves as voices of the people and public watchdogs. During Iran's 'experiment with democracy', from the Allied ousting of Reza Shah in 1941 to the CIA–MI6 engineered coup against Prime Minister Mosaddeq in 1953, state censorship was less consistent and the Iranian press churned with political activism, commercial opportunism, and journalistic competition. It was into this fast-paced environment that *The Banner of Islam* was born.

The sections quoted here represent an editorial practice that became widespread in the Iranian press in the 1940s: ongoing editorial commentary on the day's news and letters to the editor. In this way, the press could be in an apparent dialogue with its readers, responding to and reflecting a constituency of some sort. In reality, of course, most editors were trying to create a sense of fellowship with readers to boost circulation, by pandering to public sentiment in their editorial responses and, occasionally, by fabricating 'letters to the editor'. For ideologically committed newspapers like *The Banner of Islam*, explicit propaganda could be married to a sense of journalistic integrity and public activism. It is important to note that the selections quoted here are accompanied by direct commentary, but not all of the news briefs came with direct commentary and the number of direct commentaries could vary from 30 to 70 per cent from week to week. Furthermore, most of the content of *The Banner of Islam* consisted of social commentary, Islamic education, and feature-length calls for Islamizing political and social institutions.

The *Banner of Islam*'s logo depicted a hand clasping a banner with the Qur'anic verse, 'help from God and victory near at hand' (Q. 61: 13, *The Ranks*). The flag is about to be planted on a globe covered with the words

'Ignorance', 'Mercilessness', and 'Materialism'. The paper did not announce its affiliation with the Fedayan-e Eslam but did print the platform of a group calling itself 'The Muslim League' (*jami'at-e jame'eh-e moslemin*), and stood against Western influence, socialism, moral corruption, but also for the rule of Islamic law, economic nationalism, education, and support for Iran's poor. This is a similar platform to the one later adopted by the founder of Iran's Islamic Republic, Ayatollah Khomeini, who advocated 'Islamic Government' with clerical leadership and with an expressed concern for Iran's 'dispossessed' (*mosta'zafin*).[59] In the 1940s and 1950s it appears that while some ranking clerics were willing to loosely affiliate with the Fedayan-e Eslam, most kept their distance or were hostile to them. *The Banner of Islam* was banned briefly in June 1946 for inciting demonstrations against unveiled women, but resumed after a short while and continued publishing until February 1947. The Fedayan continued to propagandize in print (in the form of leaflets and books) and were held responsible for an assassination attempt against Mohammad Reza Shah in 1949 and the assassination of the left-leaning Prime Minster Razmara in 1951. Their efforts to forge alliances with the political cleric Ayatollah Kashani and join the government of Mohammad Mosaddeq were unsuccessful. Their leadership was executed in 1956 as part of a fresh crackdown by the Pahlavi state against them and the communist Tudeh Party.

Texts

1. 10 May 1946[60]

National and World News

Prison Review: The Ministry of Health reviewed the condition of prisons this week and sent the prison some free medicine that was received by the prison pharmacy.

The Banner of Islam: It would be good if you [in authority] interested the inmates in [religious] principles and God using a skilled preacher so that they would not be involved in crimes and criminality in the future. It has been overheard that, in accordance with the recommendations of the prison review, the Prime Minister is considering setting up a mosque and making it available to the inmates. We are pleased by this recommendation.

The Iraqi Government: The Iraqi government circulated a communiqué this week rejecting the report of the [UN] Special Committee on Palestine and announced that this report will cause bloodshed and disorder in the Middle East and that accepting conditions that would permit 100,000 Jewish immigrants to Palestine would be a gross violation of Arab rights.[61]

---

[59] For more on this comparison, see Amir H. Ferdows, 'Khomeini and Fedayan's Society and Politics', *International Journal of Middle East Studies*, 15: 2 (May 1983), 241–57.

[60] *The Banner of Islam*, 1: 7 (20 Ordibehesht 1325, 8 Jumada II 1365/10 May 1946), 1 and 4.

[61] From 1946 to 1948 Jewish settlers and Palestinian militias waged a struggle against the British Mandate in Palestine and against each other for control of Palestine. The British, unable and

The Banner of Islam: The Middle East is the plaything of rulers of the world. If the people of the Middle East do not see after the rights of their own societies, they will be [subject] to the games and pretexts of others.

2. 27 June 1946[62]

National and World News

Road Construction: According to the Ministry of Roads, 16 million rials [$280,000 in 1946] of the earnings of the Iranian Railroad, pending approval from the Ministry of the Treasury, will be spent from public funds on road construction.

The Banner of Islam: Owing to the hunger and extraordinary poverty and difficult circumstances of the people, it is appropriate that the government quickly generate work and repair roads and complete half-finished buildings and provide work to thousands of unemployed construction workers, craftsmen, stone cutters, laborers and engineers.

Helping Khorramshahr:[63] So far, the government has sent 2 million rials[64] in aid to the Ahvaz Treasury for relief expenditures resulting from damage to Khorramshahr.

---

unwilling to resolve the conflict, sought to end their Mandate in Palestine (in effect since 1920). While the fighting was going on, a United Nations Special Committee on Palestine was established to make recommendations for the resolution of the Jewish–Palestinian conflict. Settler forces had largely defeated Palestinian militias by 1947, and this set the stage for the widening of the conflict in 1948, when neighboring Arab states sought to reverse the gains of the settlers when they declared an independent state of Israel in May. The Iranian reading public followed the conflict in the press, but only the Fedayan-e Eslam attempted to recruit fighters for Palestine in the pre-independence phase of the war. In this, they were similar to the Sunni Muslim Brotherhood in Egypt, and appear to have been influenced by their example.

[62] *The Banner of Islam*, 1: 14 (6 Tir 1325, 27 Rajab 1365/27 June 1946), 1 and 4.

[63] Khorramshahr and Ahwaz are in south-western Iran, near Iran's first and most exploited oil-fields. Khorramshahr is also a major port along the Shatt al-ᶜArab waterway that leads to the Persian Gulf. During World War II the US Army Corps of Engineers expanded the ports facilities to help support the resupply of the Soviet Union. During the height of its activities Khorramshahr became the third busiest port in the world. 'The organization had engaged in construction work valued at $100 million and allowed for the transshipment of four and a half million long tons of materiel, almost 5,000 airplanes, and 184,000 vehicles to the Soviet Union' <http://www.hq.usace.army.mil/history/vignettes/Vignette_64.htm>. But these activities ended rather abruptly with the war, closing officially as a 'Russia-aid' port on 1 June 1945. This might have generated a 'boom–bust' cycle for the port town. Khorramshahr also fell victim to a tribal assault in January 1946, but the attack was repelled, so it is not clear exactly what prompted the need for aid to Khorramshahr in the spring of 1946. See T. H. Vail Motter, *The Persian Corridor and Aid to Russia* (Washington DC: Office of the Chief of Military History, Department of the Army, 1952), and 'Iranian Repulse Nomads of Iraq', *New York Times*, 13 Jan. 1946, p. 4; and 'Final Unit Arrives From Persian Gulf', ibid., 24 Jan. 1946, p. 4. I also would like to offer my thanks to Dr Michael J. Brodhead at the Office of History for the US Army Corps of Engineers for helping to research these details.

[64] This is the equivalent of approximately US$35,000 in 1946.

The Banner of Islam: At this time, as a result of foreign and local carelessness, great harm has been done to Khorramshahr. This has rendered people helpless and desperate. It is fitting that the wealthy follow the government's example and rapidly fulfil their duty to their suffering brothers and sisters and provide a little help and encouragement lest they be caught up in a force of nature one day, become desperate and make no profit.

3. 22 November 1946[65]

National and World News

Illness: His Grace Ayatollah Hajj Aqa Hosayn Qommi is unfortunately afflicted with pneumonia. Fortunately, according to reports, the danger [to him] has been averted by penicillin injections.

The Banner of Islam: We pray to the Divine Threshold for the speedy recovery of the Ayatollah and ask that You grant health and success to all the proofs of Islam, especially the ayatollahs Hajj Aqa Hosayn Qommi, Hajj Aqa Hosayn Borujerdi-Tabataba'i and Hajj Muhammad Kazem Shirazi.[66]

Ayatollah Kashani: Ayatollah Kashani has still not been released.[67] The news of his [pending] release that we reported last week based on reliable sources has not

[65] *The Banner of Islam*, 1: 32 (30 Aban 1325, 28 Dhu^cl Hijja 1365/22 Nov. 1946), 1 and 2.

[66] In the Twelver Shi^ci branch of Islam, believers are expected to rely upon a 'source of imitation' (*marja^c al-taqlid*), a cleric of reputation and rank, to guide them in Islamic law until the return of the Twelfth Imam (who has been out of contact since his 'greater occultation' in 945 CE) as the *mahdi* (or 'rightly guided one'), who will usher in justice under his rule and begin the sequence of events leading to the Day of Judgement. Since the late eighteenth century influential clerics were recognized by their peers (and the community of believers) with the rank of *ayat allah*, or 'sign of God'. From this select group came those recognized as 'sources of imitation'. Of the ayatollahs listed here, Isfahani (1867–1946), Qommi (1865–1947), and Borujerdi-Tabataba'i (1875–1962) succeeded each other as 'sources of imitation' in Iran. Khomeini became a 'source of imitation' after Borujerdi. Muhammad Kazem Shirazi was probably from a prominent family of Iranian clerics, though his relationship to another Muhammad Shirazi, who was recognized as a 'source of imitation' in Iraq and was killed in an uprising against the British in 1920, is not clear. The political activism of Twelver clerics in southern Iraq in the 1920s seems to have influenced the activism of clerics against the Pahlavi regime in Iran and Ba^cathist regime in Iraq later on. See Moojan Momen, *An Introduction to Shï¨i Islam* (New Haven: Yale University Press, 1985), 310–23.

[67] Ayatollah ^cAbd al-Qasem Kashani (1882–1962) was an overtly political cleric who, after his religious training in southern Iraq, devoted himself to a number of political causes including the Iraqi revolts against the British, the rise of the Pahlavi Dynasty (as a member of parliament he voted to replace the Qajars), and the rise and fall of Prime Minister Mosaddeq. His loose affiliation with two groups, the Mojahedin-e Islam (not to be confused with today's cultic, Islamic-Marxist Mojahedin-e Khalq) and the Fedayan-e Eslam, gave him power inside and outside of parliament, but also gave the government cause to act against him. Kashani was imprisoned in the town of Arak in 1943 for conspiring with the Axis powers to resist the Allied occupation of Iran during World War II. He was freed in 1945, but was arrested again by the Iranian prime minister Qavam on 17 July 1946 for his role in protesting press crack-downs by Qavam's government and possibly instigating unrest in the province

been acted upon. [The report was] that the Prime Minister had notified Salar Mansur, the owner of the village of Behjatabad (near Qazvin) of [Kashani's] release. But the officer in charge reports apologetically that he has not received an official order and that, for now, the illustrious *sayyed*,[68] this old man who has sacrificed for religion and nation, remains incarcerated in the aforementioned village. Reports are that his heart condition has become more grave, that he has asked for a doctor, but that, according to our information, no change has occurred in his situation. [Kashani] remains incarcerated in a small village and his heart is ailing him.

The Banner of Islam: It is the public's expectation that the Prime Minister will quickly issue orders to officials for his release.

Funeral Service and Telegraphs: Mr ʿAzizollah Naʿim, a Jewish rabbi, has held a funeral service at the Jewish synagogue and a large number of Jews expressed their sorrow and grief for the death of Ayatollah Esfahani. Also, the leader (*khalifeh*) of the Armenians of Iran and India, Mr Vahan, sent a telegraph of condolence for the [passing of] the Ayatollah to the Friday prayer leader and expressed grief and sorrow to the Muslim congregants.

The Banner of Islam: If the believers in Judaism and Christianity recognize and accept the truth of the religion of Islam, and the death of an Islamic leader causes them grief, we do not know what the source of disagreement and confusion in belief is and why they do not now become honored [to convert] to the Abrahamic religion (*din-e hanif*)[69] of Islam. Should we not consider such actions [i.e. the sending of condolences] to be merely political?

Foreign News

Palestine: According to the news from Cairo, the conflict of Palestinian Arabs and Jews has become calmer than before and the probability is that, in the near future, most of the people of Palestine, Arab and Jew, will establish an agreement.

The Banner of Islam: The ill-timed and inappropriate interference of foreigners in the affairs of Middle Eastern countries has caused murder, bloodletting,

of Khorasan. For a fuller biography and appraisal of Ayatollah Kashani, see Yann Richard, 'Ayatollah Kashani: Precursor of the Islamic Republic?', in Nikki R. Keddie (trans. and ed.), *Religion and Politics in Iran: Shīʿism from Quietism to Revolution* (New Haven: Yale University Press, 1983), 101–24.

[68] In Shiʿi Iran, the Perso-Arabic term *sayyed* denotes descent from the family of the Prophet Muhammad through his daughter Fatima.

[69] In classical Islamic historiography, the term 'hanif' denotes those who were monotheists in the tradition of Abraham before the Prophet Muhammad received his first revelation in 610. They were neither Jews nor Christians. Muhammad himself is described as a 'hanif' and is depicted in an uneasy relationship with the pagan beliefs of his fellow Meccans even before his prophetic career. The translation of the word as 'Abrahamic' here follows the work of M.G.S. Hodgson, *The Venture of Islam*, 3 vols. (Chicago: University of Chicago Press, 1975).

poverty, and empty-handedness. We even have the firm belief that discord and duplicity and disagreement that exists among Iranians is solely due to the interference of foreigners in Iranian affairs. Unless we Muslim and patriotic Iranians take heed and distance ourselves from foreigners, our future will be darker and our lives more difficult.

4.7 The Committee for Public Morality in Saudi Arabia, 1957
Guido Steinberg

Preface

After two failed attempts to rule the Arabian Peninsula, the Saudi state re-emerged in 1902 under the reign of King ᶜAbd al-ᶜAziz ibn ᶜAbd al-Rahman, the famous Ibn Saᶜud (*c.*1880–1953). The Saudi state had come into existence when its first ruler, Muhammad ibn Saᶜud (d. 1765), entered into an agreement with a puritan religious reformer, Muhammad ibn ᶜAbd al-Wahhab (d. 1792). Ibn ᶜAbd al-Wahhab's aim was to reform Najdi (i.e. Central Arabian) society along the lines of an idealized vision of the community of the early Muslims in Mecca and Medina, the so-called pious forefathers (*al-salaf al-salih*). The Wahhabiya, as this movement has usually been called, tried to rebuild this ideal state in eighteenth- and nineteenth-century Central Arabia (Najd). In their realm, the Wahhabis enforced a puritanical code of conduct, prohibiting smoking, music, and laughter, obliging Muslims to attend the communal prayers five times a day. More importantly for their neighbours, they led a jihad against all Muslims not following the Wahhabi interpretation of the faith.

From the 1740s, the Wahhabiya entered into a symbiotic relationship with the Saᶜud family in which the Saudi state relied on the religious legitimacy provided by the Wahhabi religious scholars, the ᶜulama (sing. *'alim*). The Saudi rulers posed as defenders of the true faith and thereby established three consecutive states, from 1744/45 to 1818; from 1824 until 1891; and a third one, which continues to the present day. On their side, the Wahhabi scholars greatly profited from this alliance. It gave them the opportunity to enforce their vision of an Islamic society with all the coercive mechanisms of this emerging state. This relationship proved to be so essential for the political survival of the two partners on the Arabian scene that they have preserved it until today.

One important aspect of this partnership was the so-called 'Committees of Enjoining Good and Forbidding Evil' (*Hay'at al-amr bi-l-maᶜruf wa-l-nahy ᶜani al-munkar*), or religious police. The Wahhabi scholars based their efforts to purge the Najdi cities on a rather general Qur'anic injunction to enjoin good and forbid evil. According to Wahhabi thought, every single Muslim was obliged to control the moral and religious conduct of his fellow citizens. In reality, mainly the Wahhabi ᶜulama, their students, and other religiously motivated persons patrolled the streets, threatening offenders with long wooden sticks. In order to control and canalize their religious fervor, the Saudi rulers from the nineteenth century embarked upon a process of institutionalization, which culminated in the foundation of the 'Committees of Enjoining Good and Forbidding Evil' in Najd in 1918/19 and in the Hijaz in 1926.[70] In both cases, the religious police served in order to advance state control of Bedouin troops (the so-called *Ikhwan*—see Sec. 1.10) in the cities on the one hand, [*sic*] and to force the urban populations to adhere to the Wahhabi tenets. The committees were placed firmly under the control of the ᶜulama from Riyadh. This form of control was especially important in the Hijazi cities, where the population rejected the new rulers and their Wahhabi puritanism. Thereby, Saudi rulers and Wahhabi scholars cemented their alliance once more, by establishing an institution that could be used as an instrument both of political and religious discipline. In the following decades, the activities of the religious police became a mirror of the ᶜulama's influence and their attitude towards the state.

During the early 1940s the religious police was confronted with a challenge of a new kind. With the production of oil in commercial quantities after 1938, Americans and other non-Muslim foreigners entered the country in large numbers for the first time. The Wahhabi ᶜulama and their followers rejected the influx of Westerners, fearing the corrupting influences of their lifestyle. At first, they could not hinder the king from pursuing his policy. However, after Ibn Saᶜud's death in 1953, and the accession of his son Saᶜud (r. 1953–64), the ᶜulama gained influence and the religious police became their primary instrument in the combat against foreign influences on Saudi Arabian culture and Islam.

In many documents of the 1950s available today in the US National Archives, American officials in the oil-rich Eastern province complained about the encroachments by the religious police on Americans and the facilities belonging to the Arab American Oil Company (ARAMCO) in the area. The document presented below is the first example of a Western official trying to grapple with this phenomenon. It is valuable for the student of Saudi history, as it addresses exactly the political questions overlooked by Saudi sources on the religious police.

Various American documents of this period treat the ᶜulama's influence in Saudi society as a passing phenomenon that will eventually have to give way to (secular) modernity. In reality, the ᶜulama have retained a strong, if secondary, position in the Saudi state until today, and the religious police-force remains a valuable instrument in domestic politics. Furthermore, the idea of the individual Muslim being responsible for the moral and religious conduct of his brethren has spread all over the Muslim world. Some countries, such as Afghanistan under the Taliban, established formal religious police units. Religious vigilantes, however, appear throughout the Muslim world, and they all refer to the duty of 'enjoining good and forbidding evil'.

---

[70] The Hijaz is a region in Western Arabia. Its most important cities are Mecca, Medina, and Jiddah.

Text

The Committee for Public Morality and its Influence in Saudi Arabia, 1957[71]

The Committee for Public Morality is one of the most influential and regressive of Saudi Government organizations. The function of the Committee is to ensure a rigorous and strict compliance by the Saudis with the precepts of Islam as interpreted by the doctrine of Muhammad Abdul Wahhab. It is important because its narrow puritanical outlook coupled with its power is one of the principle deterrents to progress in Saudi Arabia.

The name 'Committee for Public Morality' is a free translation of the Arabic *hayat al-amr bil ma'ruuf wal nahi 'an al-munkar [sic]*, which literally means 'the society for ordering virtue and forbidding vice'. Its members are known locally as *Mutawwi'in* (those whom one obeys). The origins of the Committee are obscure. Some say it is an outgrowth of a guild which was formerly responsible for the 'maintenance of order during the Pilgrimage. It appears that it was institutionalised in its present form by the late King Abdul Aziz, and was introduced in the Hejaz shortly after Abdul Aziz gained control there in 1926.

In this despatch the term 'Committee for Public Morality' refers to the organization as a whole, which consists of individual committees in the various towns of the Kingdom. The head of the Committee is Shaikh ʿAbd al-Malik ibn Ibrahim ibn ʿAbd al-Latif Al al-Shaikh, al-Nejdi. *Al-Bilad al-Saudiyah* No. 1247 of 2 November 1952 refers to Shaikh ʿAbd al-Malik as head of the Committees in Jiddah, Medina, and Taif, but *Umm al-Qura* No. 1606 of 2 March 1956 refers to him as the head of all the Committees of the Kingdom.[72] The Al al-Shaikh family, whom some say are descendants of Abdul Wahhab the eponymous founder of the Wahhabi sect, are prominent in Muslim religious organizations in Saudi Arabia.[73] Shaikh ʿAbd al-Malik's brother, Shaikh Muhammad Ibn Ibrahim ibn ʿAbd al-Latif Al al-Shaikh is the Mufti of Saudi Arabia and the latter's son Shaikh ʿAbd al-Aziz is principal of the Riyadh Institute.[74] Another brother, Shaikh ʿAbd al-Latif is head of the Bureau of

---

[71] United States National Archives, Washington, DC: C0052 (886A.413/4–2757): Houghton to Department of State, Jiddah, 27 Feb. 1957. 'The Committee for Public Morality and its Influence in Saudi Arabia.' Irregular transliterations are in keeping with original English text.

[72] These were Saudi Arabian newspapers. *Umm al-Qura* furthermore had the function of an official gazette.

[73] The Al al-Shaykh (the family of the Shaykh) are the descendants of Muhammad ibn ʿAbd al-Wahhab, *the* Shaykh. They dominated Saudi religious policy, education and the administration of justice until the end of the 1960s and retain important positions until today.

[74] Grand Mufti Muhammad ibn Ibrahim Al al-Shaykh (d. 1969) was one of the most influential Wahhabi scholars of the twentieth century. He dominated Saudi religious policy during the 1950s and 1960s.

Institutes and Colleges. At least twelve other members of the Al al-Shaikh family are members of the ulema (religious teachers). A few others are in the offices of cadis (judges) in the Hejaz. Reportedly most of the members of the various Committees for Morality are Nejdis, one of the reasons the *Mutawwi'in* are not popular in the Hejaz.

The Committee is a Government organization and is under the administrative control of the Presidency of the Judges. As far as policy is concerned, it apparently reports directly to the King. Its members are government officials and paid as such. They are appointed by Shaikh ᶜAbd al-Malik or his deputies and the Shaikh has 'absolute' power of dismissal. Committees according to Government regulations are formed in each city. In towns where there is an airport or seaport, a member of the committee must be stationed permanently in customs 'in order to inspect the goods and to forbid the entry of whatever is forbidden within the jurisdiction of the Committee.'

The Committees have relatively wide police powers. Although they are encouraged to use counsel and education to achieve their ends, they can and do administer corporal punishment and inflict short periods of imprisonment on offenders. According to their regulations, they can administer a maximum of ten lashes plus one week's imprisonment. These punishments, however, cannot be carried out unless approved by two or more members of a Committee. No judgment may be rendered unless it is supported by verses from the Qur'an and the Sunna (books containing sayings and customs of the Prophet) supported unanimously by the ulema. The Committees have the right to raid or inspect any place they suspect, except the place occupied by women which cannot be inspected unless the approval of the Chief of the Committee is obtained and the inspection takes place in the presence of the mayor of the quarter and a 'sufficient number of soldiers.'

To assist it, each Committee has a certain number of policemen assigned to it. These policemen work only for the Committees and are paid by them. In addition, the Director of Public Security and the Director of Police must instruct their policemen to comply with any demands of the Committee whether the policemen involved are assigned to the Committee or not.

The function of the organization is to maintain public morality by compelling people to perform their religious duties and to punish actions violating the precepts of Islam. To prevent contamination from the outside world, the Committee members stationed at the various customs ports ensure that customs inspectors do not permit the entry of dolls, liquor, phonographs, film, records or other forbidden items. During the five prayer periods, Committee members patrol the streets and make sure shops are closed and people are praying. The Committee patrols are probably most active at night, when they are on the lookout for drinking, music, dancing, and other forms of Saudi vice.

As examples of their work, they or the ulema (some members of the Committees are also members of the ulema) were responsible for the recent regulation prohibiting the representation of the human form on merchandise sold in Saudi Arabia. Such was the power of the Committee, that the Government instead of informing the Committees that such a regulation would be impractical, enacted the regulation and then resorted to various devices to nullify its effect.

The Committee is also considered responsible for holding up the installation of the dial system in Jiddah because it would give too much freedom to women.

Neither the Embassy nor Aramco is bothered by the Committees although a Committee member is stationed in each of Aramco's camps. They did try, unsuccessfully, to prevent Aramco from having movies in Jiddah and succeeded in prohibiting Saudi employees from wearing steel helmets. The reason for this injunction is apparently a saying of the prophet Muhammad against wearing the clothes of non-Muslims.

Although most active in Riyadh where one is barely permitted to smoke, the Committees have a strong influence on Jiddah society. There is no question that they are feared by the Jiddahwis who appear reluctant even to talk about them except in the most general terms. The more progressive dislike them because the Committees are a regressive force. Most hate them because they practice a double standard in the exercise of their duties. According to reports, they seldom molest the rich or the powerful.

The King's attitude towards this organization is not clear. Some say he fears it. Being a sincerely religious Muslim and protector of the Holy Places, he has to support the Committee which, whatever its effects, stands for the purity of the Muslim religion. However, there is evidence that the King is not dominated by them. In the past year the Directorate of Press, Radio and Publications has introduced music over the radio and pictures in the papers. The Director General of the Directorate, Abdullah Balkhair, is also a Secretary of the King and reports directly to him.

Comment: In the struggle between the forces of progress and reaction in Saudi Arabia, this organization is among the leaders of the latter group. It is probably at least partially responsible for the absence of public movies, the backwardness of the educational system, the caution with which the Saudis associate with foreigners, and in general, the more puritanical features of the Saudi social life.

Robert B. Houghton
Second Secretary of the Embassy

4.8 Twelver Shi^cism and revolutionary Islam in Iran: from ^cAli Shari^cati's, *Approaches to the Understanding of Islam*, 1968[75]
From the Islamfiche *project*

Preface

^cAli Shari^cati was born in 1933 to a provincial Iranian family with a long tradition of religious leadership. His father, Mohammad Taqi Shari^cati, was deeply committed to winning the increasingly secular intelligentsia back to Islam. Instead of following the family tradition of becoming a cleric, Mohammad Taqi became a teacher and dressed in Western clothing, in an attempt to appeal to young intellectuals. As a teenager, ^cAli, who alternated between being a studious loner and an extroverted wisecracker, suffered a crisis of faith which nearly drove him to suicide. His reflections on mysticism saved him, and later he considered mysticism, equality, and freedom as essential for the ideal man. He began his career as a high-school teacher at the age of 18 and simultaneously attended a teacher-training college. Soon after graduating he began to write, becoming involved with a series of radical political organizations. In 1959 he went to France for graduate study at the Sorbonne. Shari^cati's ideas were controversial among politicians and clerics in Iran. For example, he preferred the representations of many Islamic figures and stories as told by non-Shi^cite, even non-Muslim scholars. From 1959 until 1964, while in France, most of his political and journalistic involvements were aimed against the regime of Mohammad Reza Shah (r. 1941–79). When Shari^cati returned to Iran in September of 1964, he was arrested at the border. On this occasion his imprisonment lasted a month and a half. In 1967 he acquired a job teaching Islamic history at the University of Mashhad, which provided him with a platform from which to spread his ideas. He stressed the importance of intellectuals understanding Islam to the success of their attempts to solve socio-political problems. In 1971 Shari^cati was sent from Mashhad to Tehran, where he began to lecture at the Hosayniyeh Ershad. While holding this position, he gave a speech entitled 'The Responsibility of

---

[75] *Ravish-e Shinakht-e Eslam.* The Persian text of these lectures is available in Book 6 of Shari^cati's collected works (*Majmu^ceh-e Asar*, published in 35 volumes since the early 1980s by the Office for the Editing and Compiling of the Martyred Teacher ^cAli Shari^cati). For a full translation, see *An Approach to Understanding of Islam*, trans. Venus Kaivantash (Tehran: The Shari^cati Foundation, and Hamdami Publishers, 1979). Our translation comes from Herbert Bodman's *Islamfiche* project. For online translated excerpts of ^cAli Shari^cati's other works, go to <http://www.iranchamber.com/personalities/ashariati/ali_shariati.php>. For a glimpse at the continuing interest in his works, go to <http://www.shariati.com/wwwboard1.html>.

being a Shi'i', in which he laid out conditions which suggested that true Shi'ism was incompatible with the Shah's regime. Eventually the Hosayniyeh Ershad was shut down and Shari'ati went into hiding. He eventually surrendered himself in September 1973, after the authorities had held his father and brother-in-law in custody for one month to ensure his arrest. Eighteen months later, in March 1975, Shari'ati was released without ever having stood trial. He left Iran in May 1977, intending to emigrate to the United States, but was found dead in London on 19 June. The official cause of death was a heart attack, but many speculated that the Shah's secret police, SAVAK, were responsible. In any case, Shari'ati had received word the day before that authorities in Iran were detaining members of his family, who were on their way to join him in London.

Shari'ati belongs to a long tradition of Muslim reformers who have tried to reconcile their Islamic heritage with the best of Western thought and technology. From the time of Jamal al-Din Asadabadi 'al-Afghani' (d. 1897) and Muhammed 'Abduh (d. 1905) at the turn of the twentieth century, such intellectuals have attempted, with varying degrees of success, to utilize Western scientific concepts within an Islamic framework.

In Iran, as in other Middle Eastern countries, 'modernization' has been tied to Western economic and political control. The struggle of the Iranian people against autocratic rule and foreign domination has always had a dual national and Islamic character. During the reign of the last shah the political role of the clergy was strengthened because the secular, nationalist opposition was driven underground. Militant Islamic-Marxist groups like the *Cherikeh-ha-ye Feda'i-e Khalq-e Iran* (the Iranian People's Devoted Guerillas) and the *Mojahedin-e Khalq* (the People's Holy Warriors) drew on Shari'ati's formulations, but he distanced himself from these groups as he came under closer state scrutiny.

Presented here is the second of two lectures on the need to reinterpret Shi'i Islamic traditions to facilitate social and political activism.

Text

My topic concerns different approaches to the knowledge and understanding of Islam. 'Different approaches' constitutes a precise and important scientific concept, and it denotes methodology for the understanding of Islam.

The question of methodology is of extreme importance in history, and particularly in the history of science. The correct cognitive method for the discovery of truth is more important than philosophy, science or the possession of mere talent.

We know that in the Middle Ages, Europe spent a millennium in the most appalling stagnation and apathy, and that immediately after the end of this period, the stagnation and apathy gave way to a multi-faceted and revolutionary awakening in science, art, literature, and all areas of human and social concern.

This sudden revolution and burst of energy in human thought resulted in the birth of the civilization and culture of today's world. We must now ask ourselves, 'Why did Europe stagnate for a thousand years, and what happened to cause a sudden change in direction, so that in the course of three centuries, it discovered truths it had failed to perceive in a whole millennium?'

This is an extremely important question; it may, indeed, be the greatest and most important question that science must answer.

Without doubt, numerous factors caused the stagnation of Europe in the Middle Ages, and various causes suddenly awakened Europe from its sleep, setting it on the course of swift and dazzling progress in every respect.

We must point out here that the fundamental factor in the stagnation of thought, civilization and culture that lasted for a millennium in medieval Europe was the Aristotelian method of analogical reasoning. When this way of looking at questions and objects changed, science, society and the world also changed, and as a result of that, human life too. We are concerned here with culture, with thought and scientific movement, and it is for this reason that we regard the change in methodology as the fundamental factor in the Renaissance. At the same time, it is true from the sociological point of view that the main factor in this change was the transformation of the feudal system into that of the bourgeoisie; this was caused, in turn, by the breaching of the wall that separated the Islamic East from the Christian West, the breaching brought about by the Crusades.

Method is then of far-reaching importance in determining progress or decline. It is the method of investigation, not the mere existence or non-existence of genius, that brings about stagnation and apathy or motion and progress. For example, in the fourth and fifth centuries before Christ, numerous great geniuses existed who cannot be compared with the geniuses of the fourteenth, fifteenth and sixteenth centuries. Aristotle was without doubt a greater genius than Francis Bacon, and Plato a greater genius than Roger Bacon.[76] But what enabled the two Bacons to become factors in the advancement of science, despite their inferiority in genius to men like Plato, while those geniuses caused the millennial stagnation of medieval Europe? In other words, why should a genius cause stagnation in the world, and an average man bring about scientific progress and popular awakening? Because the latter has discovered the correct method of reasoning, by means of which even a mediocre intellect can discover the truth, while the great genius, if he does not know the correct method of looking at things and reflecting on problems, will be unable to make use of his genius.

---

[76] Roger Bacon (1220–92) was a Franciscan philosopher who advocated (though he seems not to have practised) experimental science well before the scientific method caught on in Western academia, but he also was drawn to mystical strains in Christianity. Sir Francis Bacon (1561–1626) was a lawyer, statesman, and philosopher whose contribution to modern science was his insistence that a rational and collaborative method of advancing knowledge was best for humankind.

It is for this reason that we see in the history of Greek civilization tens of geniuses gathered in a single place in the fourth and fifth centuries. The history of mankind has remained under their influence down to the present. But the whole of Athens was unable to invent a wheel, whereas in modern Europe, an average technician who cannot even understand the writings of Aristotle and his pupils has made hundreds of inventions.

The best example of this is provided by Edison, whose general principle was inferior to that of the third-class pupils of Aristotle, but who at the same time contributed more to the discovery of nature and the creation of industry than all the geniuses who have been trained in the Aristotelian school during the past 2,400 years. He made more than a thousand inventions, great and small. Thinking correctly is like walking. A person lame in one foot and unable to walk fast, if he chooses the right path, will reach his destination sooner than the champion runner who takes a rocky and winding path. However fast the champion may run, he will arrive late at his destination, if he reaches it at all; whereas the lame person who chooses the right route will attain his destination and goal.

The choice of correct method is the first matter to be considered in all the different braches of knowledge—literary, social, artistic and psychological. The first task of any researcher must therefore be the choice of the best method of research and investigation.

We must make full use of the experiences of history, and we must consider ourselves obliged, as the followers of a great religion, to learn and know Islam correctly and methodically.

Today is no time for the worship of what we do not know. The educated, in particular, have a heavier responsibility for acquiring knowledge of what is sacred to them; this is not merely an Islamic duty, but also a scientific and a human one. A person's character may be judged in accordance with his degree of knowledge concerning his beliefs, for the mere holding of a belief is no virtue in itself. If we believe in something that we do not fully know, it has little value. It is the precise knowledge of that in which we believe that may be counted a virtue. Since we believe in Islam, we must acquire correct knowledge of it and choose the correct method for gaining that knowledge.

The question now arises, what is that correct method? In order to learn and know Islam, we must not imitate and make use of European methods—the naturalistic, psychological or sociological methods. We must be innovative in the choice of method. We must of course learn the scientific methods of Europe, but we do not necessarily need to follow them.

Today, scientific methods have changed in all branches of knowledge, and new approaches have been discovered. In the investigation of religion as well, new paths must be followed and a new method must be chosen.

It is obvious that a single, unique method cannot be chosen for the study of Islam, since Islam is not a one-dimensional religion. Islam is not a religion based solely on the mystic intuition of man and restricted to the relationship between man and God; this is merely one dimension of the religion of Islam. In order to study this dimension, a philosophical method must be followed, because man's relation to God is discussed in philosophy, in the sense of general and unfettered metaphysical thought. Another dimension of this religion is the question of man's life on earth. In order to study this dimension, use must be made of the methods that have been established in the human sciences of today. Then, too, Islam is a religion that has built a society and a civilization; in order to study these, the methods of history and sociology must be used.

If we look at Islam from only one vantage point, we will have seen only one dimension of this multi-faceted phenomenon; even if we see it correctly, this will not suffice for a knowledge of the whole. The Qur'an itself is a proof of this. It is a book that has many dimensions, some of which have been studied by great scholars throughout history. For example, one dimension comprises the philosophical and creedal themes of the Qur'an that the philosophers and theologians of today would do well to reflect upon. A further dimension of the Qur'an, one which has remained more obscure than all the others, is its human dimension, comprising historical, sociological and psychological matters. The reason for this dimension's remaining unknown is that sociology, psychology and the human sciences are far more recent than the natural sciences. Similarly, the science of history is the most recent science to have appeared in the world; it is something different from historical data or the books of history that are among the oldest books in existence.

Historical passages concerning the fate of nations, their relations with each other, and the causes for their decline and fall, occur frequently in the Qur'an; they must be studied by the historian with a historical and scientific approach. The sociologist must examine them according to sociological method. Cosmological matters and questions relating to the natural sciences and natural phenomena must be examined and understood according to the methodology of the natural sciences.

Since my area of study and specialization is history and sociology, I assume the right to set forth what has occurred to me in this connection as a plan or design. I will set forth two methods, both of them relating exclusively to the vantage point of sociology, history and the human sciences. In order to make my meaning clearer, I will compare religion to an individual.

Only two ways exist in which to acquire knowledge of a great personality, and both of these ways must be pursued simultaneously in order to yield the final result—the knowledge of the great man in question.

The first way consists of studying and investigating the intellectual, scientific and written works of the individual, his theories, his speeches, his lectures and his books. Knowledge of the ideas and beliefs of a person is an indispensable preliminary to understanding him. But our investigation of these will not suffice for a complete understanding of the person, because many things will exist in his life that are not reflected in his works, his writings and his pronouncements, or, if reflected there, may be difficult to discern. The second way, which complements the first and makes possible a complete understanding of the person, is to study his biography and to seek an answer to such questions as: where was he born? to what family did he belong? what was his race and what was his country? how did his childhood pass? how was he educated? in what environment did he grow up? where did he study? who were his teachers? what events did he confront in the course of his life? what were his failures and his successes?

There are, then, two fundamental methods for gaining knowledge of a person, and both must be followed: first, the investigation of his thoughts and beliefs; and second, the examination of his biography from beginning to end.

A religion is like a person. The ideas of a religion are concentrated in its book, its 'scripture', the very foundation of the school of thought to which it summons men. As for the biography of a religion, it is its history.

There are, then, two fundamental methods for learning Islam correctly, precisely and in accordance with contemporary methodology. First, the study of the Qur'an, taking it as the compendium of the ideas and the scientific and literary output of the person known as 'Islam'; and second, the study of Islamic history, taking it as the sum total of the developments undergone by Islam from the beginning of the Prophet's mission down to the present.

These are the two methods, but unfortunately the study of the Qur'an and the study of Islamic history are very weak, as they now exist in our corpus of Islamic studies; in fact, they exist on the fringe of those studies. Fortunately, however, as a result of the awakening that has taken place in Muslim society in our age, Muslims are paying increased attention to the study of the Qur'anic text and to the analytical study of Islamic history.

In his book *The Night of Imperialism*, Farhad ʿAbbas says that the social awakening of the countries of North Africa—Morocco, Algeria, and Tunis—began on the day that Muhammad ʿAbduh[77] came to North Africa and began teaching the interpretation of the Qur'an, a subject that had not customarily been taught in the circles of religious learning.

We see that the author of the book—who was not himself religiously oriented—regards the beginning of awakening and religious development in

---

[77] Egyptian scholar (1849–1905), one of the first modern Muslim thinkers to try to reconcile religion with Western science and technology.

the countries of North Africa as having occurred when the Muslims and their religious scholars laid aside the study of the various religious sciences and made it their chief concern to go back to the Qur'an and study its text.

The knowledge and understanding of the Qur'an as the source of the ideas of Islam, and the knowledge and understanding of Islamic history as the record of the various events that have occurred at different times—these are the two fundamental methods for attaining a precise and scientific knowledge of Islam.

If today the Muslims of Iran are transforming their mosques into centers of activity and are drawing up plans for the instruction of the masses, on the twin bases of the Qur'an and history, they will have laid the firmest foundation possible for a great Islamic intellectual expansion and development.

Another method exists for gaining knowledge and understanding of Islam—the method of typology. This method, which many sociologists believe effective, consists of classifying topics and themes according to type and then comparing them on that basis.

Based on this approach, which is used in Europe in research on certain topics pertaining to the human sciences, I have established a method that can be applied to every religion. It consists of the identification of five distinguishing aspects or characteristics of every religion, and then comparing them with the corresponding features in other religions:

The god or gods of every religion; i.e., the entity worshipped by the followers of the religion.

The prophet of each religion; i.e., the person who proclaims the message of the religion.

The book of each religion; i.e., the foundation of the law proclaimed by the religion, to which it invites men in faith and obedience.

The circumstances of the appearance of the prophet of each religion and the audience to which he addresses himself; for each prophet proclaims his message in a different fashion. One will address himself to people in general (*al-nas*), another to princes and the nobility, and still another to the learned, philosophers and the elect. One prophet will thus seek to draw near to established power, while another sets himself up as an adversary and opponent to established power.

Those choice individuals each religion nurtures and produces—the representative figures it has trained and then presented to society and history. In just the same way that the best method for assessing a factory is to inspect the goods it produces, and for assessing a plot of land is to examine the harvest it yields, so too religion may be regarded as a factory for the production of men, and the men nurtured by each religion constitute the goods it produces.

According to this method, in order to learn and know more of Islam, one must first know God or Allah. Various ways exist for gaining knowledge of God, such as gazing and meditating upon nature and the methods of philosophy, illumination and gnosis [...] But the method I wish to propose is that of typology. We examine the type, concept, features and characteristics of the God discussed in Islam. For example, we ask whether He is wrathful or merciful. Is He exalted above all being? Is He commingled with man? Does His compassionate aspect predominate over His wrathful aspect, or is the reverse the case? In short, what 'type' of God is He?

In order to correctly recognize the characteristics of God, we must refer to the Qur'an and the words of the Prophet, as well as the elite among those whom he trained. For the divine attributes have been clearly set forth in the Qur'an, and the Prophet and those whom he trained have referred to them in their pronouncements. Then we can compare Allah with the figure depicted in other religions as God—Ahuramazda, Yahwa, Zeus, Baal,[78] and so forth.

The second stage in knowing and learning Islam consists in knowing and learning its book, the Qur'an. One must also understand what kind of a book the Qur'an is, what topics it discusses, and what areas it emphasizes. Does it speak more of the life of this world or more of the hereafter? Does it discuss questions of individual morality more, or social questions? Is it concerned more with material or with abstract objects? Is it more interested in nature or in man? In short, what matters does it treat and in what fashion?

For example, with respect to proving the existence of God, does it recommend to man that he should refine his soul in order to know God? Or does it instruct us to attain knowledge of God through the study of the particulars of creation, the external and internal worlds? Or should we follow both paths?

Having answered these questions, we should proceed to a comparison of the Qur'an with other religious texts, such as the Gospels, the Torah, the Vedas, the Avesta, and so on.

The third stage in acquiring knowledge of Islam is learning the personality of Muhammad ibn ʿAbdullah. To know and understand the Prophet of Islam is extremely important for the historian, for nobody has played in human history the same role as the Prophet. The role of the Prophet in the events he occasioned is an extremely powerful and positive one. When we speak of the personality of the Prophet, we mean both his human attributes and his relationship with God, with the particular spiritual strength he derived therefrom. In other words, we are concerned both with his human and his prophetic aspects.

For example, with the human dimension of the Prophet, we must study the way in which he spoke, worked, thought, smiled, sat and slept; we must study the nature of his relations with strangers, with enemies, with friends and family. We must also examine his failures and his triumphs and the manner in which he confronted great social problems. One of the basic and fundamental ways of

---

[78] Respectively, the Zoroastrian, Judaic, Greek, and Canaanite gods.

learning the original essence, spirit and reality of Islam is, then, learning about the Prophet of Islam and comparing him with the other prophets and founders of religions, like Moses, Jesus, Zoroaster and the Buddha.

The fourth stage consists of examining the circumstances under which the Prophet of Islam appeared. Did he, for example, appear without any preliminary? Was anyone waiting for him? Did he himself anticipate his mission? Did he know what his mission was to be? Or was it that a sudden and powerful blow descended upon his spirit, an extraordinary current of thought began to flow through his mind, totally changing his manner of speech and personality, in such fashion that he initially found it difficult to bear? How did he confront men when he first proclaimed his mission? To what class did he pay particular attention, and against what class did he struggle? All of these are matters that aid us in the understanding of the Prophet of Islam and the circumstances of his appearance.

If we compare the circumstances under which the Prophet of Islam appeared with those under which other prophets appeared—whether true or false—such as Jesus, Abraham, Moses, Zoroaster, Confucius, Buddha and so forth, we reach the following remarkable conclusion: all the prophets, with the exception of those of the Abrahamic line, turn immediately to the existing secular power and seek association with it, hoping to propagate their religion and message in society by means of that power. At the very outset of his mission, Abraham begins destroying idols with his ax; he strikes against the supreme idol of his people in order to proclaim his opposition to all the idols of his age. The first sign of the mission of Moses is when he enters the court of the Pharaoh in his shepherd's garb, with his staff in hand, and declares war on pharaonism in the name of monotheism. Similarly, Jesus struggles against the power of the Jewish priesthood, since it is allied with Roman imperialism. And the Prophet of Islam, at the very beginning of his mission, starts the struggle against the aristocracy, the slaveowners and the merchants of Quraysh,[79] the owners of the orchards in Ta'if.[80] The comparison of the two groups of prophets—the Abrahamic and the non-Abrahamic—helps us to understand the essence, spirit and orientation of the various religions in question.

The fifth stage in the learning and understanding of Islam consists in studying the outstanding examples, the finest goods that these factories for the production of men have delivered to humanity, society and history.

If, for example, we choose to study Aaron in the religion of Moses, St Paul in the religion of Jesus, and ⁽Ali, Husayn or Abu Zarr[81] in the religion of Islam, as

---

[79] The Meccan tribe to which the Prophet Muhammad belonged.

[80] A hillside town in Arabia, near Mecca.

[81] In Arabic, Abu Dharr al-Ghaffari, an early convert to Islam who became a critic of the third caliph, ⁽Uthman (r. 644–56), and later the Ummayads. For Shari⁽ati, Abu Zarr was more than a good Shi⁽i Muslim, he was the embodiment of a fusion between Islamic and socialist ideas of social

outstanding specimens of each of the religions, this will facilitate for us the understanding of the religions.

An exact, clear knowledge of those persons will, from the scientific point of view, resemble the knowledge of a factory through the knowledge of the goods it produces, because religion is a factory engaged in the production of men.

Let us tonight take Husayn as the example of one trained and nurtured by the religion of Islam, in order to discover what kind of man it is who believes in God, the Qur'an and the Prophet.

The life of Husayn is well known, as are the principles for which he fought. His sensitivity with respect to social matters and the destiny of the people, his devotion and self-sacrifice—these, too, are well known. It is well known, further, when the truth and what he believed in were threatened, how easily he renounced and sacrificed all that a man is attached to in the course of his worldly life. He was, in short, such a person that we can designate Husayn the son of Ali as an outstanding example for the purposes of our study.

In addition to learning and acquiring a knowledge of the life, ideas, and characteristics of Husayn, another method also presents itself to us. This is to compare Husayn with Abu ᶜAli, Ibn Sina and Husayn b. Mansur Hallaj, who were Muslim but trained and nurtured by philosophy and Iranian Sufism respectively.

The comparison of these three individuals will help us to gain a vivid comprehension of the differences between the schools of philosophy, Sufism and Islam, as well as their common features.

Ibn Sina was a great philosopher, scholar and genius, a source of pride to the whole history of science and philosophy in Islamic civilization. But this great and profound man, who was so outstanding as a philosopher and scholar, was content, from the social point of view, to place himself in the service of rank and power, and he never showed any concern with the destiny of man and the fate of his society. He saw no connection between his own fate and that of others. His sole concerns were the investigation of scientific matters and scholarly research. The outer form of his life was a matter of indifference for him; whoever granted him money and position was acceptable to him.

As for Hallaj, he was a man aflame. A man that is on fire has no responsibility; it is his function simply to burn and to cry out. Why was Hallaj burning? From the passionate love of God. He had taken his head between his hands and run through the streets of Baghdad proclaiming, 'Split open this head, for it has rebelled against me! Deliver me from this fire that is burning within me! I am nothing, I am God!' By this he meant, 'I no longer exist, God alone exists!'

justice. Shariᶜati's first publication was a translation/reworking of a book on Abu Dharr by Egyptian Jowdat al-Sahhar, which Shariᶜati published under the title *Abu Zarr Ghiffari: The God Worshipping Socialist* in 1955. See Ali Rahnama, *An Islamic Utopian: A Political Biography of Ali Shariati* (London: I. B. Tauris, 1998, 2000), 57–60.

Hallaj was constantly immersed in the burning invocation of God, and this was a source of true exaltation for him. But imagine if Iranian society were to consist of 25 million Hallaj's. It would be nothing but a vast lunatic asylum, with everyone running into the streets proclaiming, 'Come, kill me! I can endure it no longer! I have nothing! There is naught in my cloak but God!'

Such instances of burning passion and immersion represent a kind of spiritual or mystical lunacy, and if all the members of society were like Hallaj—or, for that matter, like Ibn Sina—the result would be wretchedness and destruction.

But now imagine a society in which only one Husayn son of ʿAli exists, together with several Abu Zarrs. That society would have life and liberty, thought and learning, power and stability; it would be capable both of defeating its enemies and of truly loving God.

4.9 Israel at fifty: the cultural war in the pages of *Ha'aretz* and the *Jerusalem Post*, 1998[82]
Danny Ben-Moshe

Preface

Israel's fiftieth anniversary in 1998 was designed to celebrate the Zionist movement and the accomplishments of the State of Israel. Under the jubilee theme, 'Together with pride, together with hope', a week of festivities was planned, but the events became a focus for divisions within Israeli society.

In Jerusalem, the Bat Sheva Dance Company was scheduled to perform a dance for the main ceremony, which involved undressing to their underwear to a song from the Passover holiday. The religious political parties protested that it was inappropriate to have a dance that would offend the religious public at a national event, as religious law demands modesty. The non-Orthodox public responded that this was religious coercion, that the Orthodox minority was imposing its values on the non-Orthodox majority and hence limiting the secular community's freedom of expression.

This dispute threatened to bring down the government as the religious parties, Shas, United Torah Judaism, and the National Religious Party, held the balance of power with fourteen seats in the 120-member parliament (Knesset). Demands were made that their coalition partner, Prime Minister Netanyahu, cancel the dance. The Israeli Artists Union declared that if this were to occur, all performers would withdraw from the event, hence threatening to turn the highlight of the jubilee into a farce. Ultimately, the Bat Sheva dancers did not perform, but other artists did.

A few days later angry students protested against the visit of National Religious Party ministers to a jubilee reception at the Diaspora Museum, located on the Tel Aviv University campus. The ministers required police protection as demonstrators protested against what they regarded as theocratic tendencies in Israel.

The jubilee also revealed differences within the religious community. While the modern Orthodox—the National Religious Party—is Zionist, the ultra-Orthodox are not. Some sections of the ultra-Orthodox community refuse to recognize Israel as a Jewish state. They argue that such a state will only be established when the Messiah comes, and regard Jewish political nationalism as heresy. In the ultra-Orthodox stronghold of Mea She'arim in Jerusalem, a black flag was flown at one Yeshiva (seminary) and Israeli flags were ripped from passing Israeli cars.

---

[82] These press excerpts have been made available to Professor Ben Moshe and MMESP by special permission from *Ha'aretz* and the *Jerusalem Post*. The editors are grateful for this unique support.

The jubilee also became a focus for divisions between the political left and right, with counter-demonstrations in the Har Homa suburb where the government of Prime Minister Benjamin Netanyahu was seeking to establish settlements on disputed territory in Jerusalem.

Other differences were also present, with Israel's Arab population unable to identify with the festivities and the state's Jewish character. The Palestinian Authority described how Israel's independence had led to a Palestinian tragedy.

The issue of Orthodox/non-Orthodox relations has been a significant one in Israel, pre-dating its inception. The Zionist movement was never monolithic, offering a range of ideas, from Orthodox to secular-liberal. There was much debate and difference of opinion about the content of the 1948 Declaration of Independence. It defines Israel as a Jewish and democratic state, but different sides of Israeli society gave different interpretations of this, with others recognizing an inherent contradiction in this concept.

While the nature of Israel's identity as a Jewish state was always an important issue, it was secondary to Israel's fight for survival, a fight which kept Israel unified. It is important to note that these events took place between the Oslo Accords of 1993 and the beginning of the second Palestinian intifada in 2000, when a 'peace process' was still in place and Israelis could, in theory, worry about their future without the prospect of continuing warfare with the Palestinians. The jubilee was a battle in Israel's *kulturkampf* or cultural war.

The Declaration of Independence ensures freedom of religion, but Orthodox/non-Orthodox relations have been guided from independence to the present by the Status Quo agreement reached between Israel's first prime minister, David Ben-Gurion, and the ultra-Orthodox political party Agudat Yisrael.

While the Status Quo was once accepted by most sectors of the Israeli population and practised in the spirit of accommodation, the ultra-Orthodox have, since the 1980s, become more narrow and militant in their interpretation and enforcement of the agreement. Demands have been made that places of entertainment such as cinemas be closed on the Sabbath and roads in religious areas be blocked so that non-Orthodox cannot drive through them. Religious law forbids driving and commercial entertainment on the Sabbath.

One condition of the Status Quo agreement is that religious courts, for all respective faiths, administer personal matters such as marriage and divorce. However, as Israeli society has become more Western, the rabbinical judges have become more uncompromising, leading to resentment of the Orthodox supervision of these matters. This trend was compounded by the arrival of 1 million immigrants from the former Soviet Union in the 1990s, many of who were not Jewish in accordance with Halacha (religious law). However, the religious courts demonstrated little flexibility in facilitating their conversion to Judaism, reflected in their attempt to change the law on the 'Who is a Jew' issue in 1997. As this affected non-Orthodox Jews in the Diaspora it also became a major issue in Israel–Diaspora relations.

Another aspect of the Status Quo agreement is the exemption of ultra-Orthodox from the otherwise compulsory national military service. While the exemption was originally envisaged for a few hundred religious men, it now extends to tens of thousands and is a cause for resentment. As religious parties have increased in their political representation and strength, they have acquired more social welfare benefits for their constituents, which in the absence of national service for this segment of society has become a cause of tension and resentment for others.

Although the peace process stalled in 2000, religious–secular relations remain an issue of ongoing concern. A range of responses has been offered. These include attempts at reaching an understanding between Orthodox and non-Orthodox to the 'secular revolution' which the then prime minister Ehud Barak planned to launch in 2000. Concern in certain sectors regarding the modern Orthodoxy's militant direction led to the expanded activities of Meimad, a left-wing religious group. Efforts have been made to introduce ultra-Orthodox military service. Some moderate religious leaders, such as Rabbi David Hartman, call for the separation of religion and state in Israel, believing that the politicized nature of religion alienates the non-Orthodox from Judaism. The status of Judaism in the Jewish state will be a contentious issue in any attempt to write an Israeli constitution.

Any change to Israel's electoral system is likely to lead to the reduced, but still significant, parliamentary influence of religious parties. Polls at the time of Israel's jubilee revealed that 80 per cent of Israelis think Orthodox/non-Orthodox tensions would lead to violence. Orthodox Jews constitute 6 per cent of the population as a whole, numbering 300,000. However, as 30 per cent reside in Jerusalem, their influence is particularly felt in the capital's politics. The balance of ultra-Orthodox/non-Orthodox will be affected by the much higher birth-rate of the former.

The texts below are from two of Israel's important daily newspapers, *Ha'aretz* and *the Jerusalem Post*. They illustrate the range of issues that collided on Israel's fiftieth birthday, and the choices Israelis had to make about how best to commemorate this milestone in Israeli history.

Texts

1. Jubilee Bells Ring Discord

(*Ha'aretz*, Sunday, 3 May 1998, by Dalia Shehori and Amira Segev, *Ha'aretz* Correspondents and Agencies)

Some 300 demonstrators greeted Education Minister Yitzhak Levy and Transportation Minister Shaul Yahalom, both of the National Religious Party, on

Friday morning at Tel Aviv's Diaspora Museum with chants of 'good morning, Iran' and 'We are not the light unto the nations, we are darkness.'

The demonstrations were prompted by demands from religious parties that the Batsheva Dance Company, which had been scheduled to perform at the Jubilee Bells gala show Thursday night, change a segment in its routine in which dancers strip to their underwear. Religious legislators called it offensive and pressed Jubilee officials to cut it from the show. The company pulled out from the gala after its dancers rejected a proposed compromise negotiated by President Ezer Weizman in which they would have worn long underwear under their clothes. The compromise had been endorsed by the company's management and board of directors.

Friday's demonstration outside the Diaspora Museum, where the ministers were scheduled to attend a Jubilee reception for leaders of the country's artistic and cultural institutions, was loud and rowdy. Protesters, including some of Israel's best-known entertainment personalities, booed and whistled at the two ministers, who were surrounded by police cordons.

Taunting the religious ministers, several protesters took off their shirts before they were dragged away by police. Levy announced he has established a forum composed of leading artists and representatives of the cultural department of his ministry. The forum will discuss issues of contention and will attempt to bridge differences. Referring to the Batsheva non-performance as a 'mishap,' Levy said, 'This was not just another artistic performance, but a state ceremony; we wanted everyone to be able to view it.'

2. University Students Attack Levy

(*Ha'aretz*, Friday, 8 May 1998, by Relly Sa'ar, *Ha'aretz* Education Correspondent)
About 50 students from Tel Aviv University yesterday burst into the office of the education minister to protest the preferential treatment accorded to ultra-Orthodox yeshiva students, as detailed in the State Comptroller's Report released Tuesday.

The students, who demanded free tuition for all undergraduates, refused to leave the Tel Aviv office of Rabbi Yitzhak Levy (National Religious Party) until he met them.

Before storming Levy's office, the students blocked traffic on a busy Tel Aviv street and painted a white line on themselves to dramatize their complaint that 'the state draws the line at students.'

Levy told student representatives that he supports their goal and would meet with them soon.

He said he would 'be a partner' to the fight for lower tuition fees provided 'the struggle is not directed against yeshiva students.'

The chairman of the Tel Aviv University student union, Erez Eshel, noted that yeshiva students 'are freed from the burden of having to support themselves and therefore they have time to think about ideology and formulate a cohesive worldview.' University students, in contrast, 'are always scurrying between lectures and work, and because they have to work to pay tuition, they don't have a minute's leisure to think.'

3. A Splintered Jubilee

(*Ha'aretz*, Tuesday, 5 May 1998, by Ran Kislev)

One of the bad jokes connected with Israel's Jubilee year celebrations was their central slogan: 'Together with pride, together with hope'. The national mood during these celebrations was primarily somber, not proud or hopeful; however, the most ridiculous element in this slogan is the word 'together'. With the possible exception of the traditional *mangal* (barbecue) at the Independence Day picnics, there was precious little in the Jubilee celebrations to justify the use of the word 'together.' The scandal surrounding the decision not to include the Batsheva Dance Company's 'Anaphase' in Thursday's Jubilee Bells program, and the stormy demonstration by artists against the National Religious Party cabinet ministers the following day, constituted together the most prominent—but certainly not the only—illustration of this fact. Here are some other examples: A number of bereaved parents acted in an unruly manner in order to prevent Deputy Construction and Housing Minister Meir Porush (United Torah Judaism) from representing the government in this year's Memorial Day ceremony at the Holon military cemetery, because he represents the ultra-Orthodox Jewish community, which, in their opinion, displays a contemptuous attitude to Israel's fallen soldiers. When author S. Yizhar tried to address the audience at a Memorial Day ceremony at Tel Aviv University, his words were disrupted by several bereaved parents because he referred to the assassination of Prime Minister Yitzhak Rabin and, in their view, thereby turned the ceremony into yet another skirmish between the left and the right in Israel. Here as well, other bereaved parents tried to defend the speaker, but, as in Holon, their efforts were unsuccessful.

These two events were not isolated incidents but rather are part of a much broader context. That same week, vandals, apparently residents of Jerusalem's ultra-Orthodox Mea She'arim quarter, desecrated a temporary memorial set up at the Bnei Akiva youth center on the outskirts of the neighborhood to honor Israel's fallen soldiers. Deputy Education Minister Moshe Peled (Tzomet) left the Independence Day assembly at his own kibbutz, Beit Hashita, in angry protest at the fact that Rabin's name was mentioned at that gathering.

The lighting of the torch on Mount Herzl in Jerusalem on the night ushering in Independence Day traditionally symbolizes national unity, but this was not the case during our Jubilee year. The ceremony itself was held in an atmosphere of controversy: President Ezer Weizman absented himself because Prime Minister Benjamin Netanyahu had elbowed his way in to light the Jubilee Torch. Furthermore, while the torches were being lit on Mount Herzl, leftists held their own alternative torch-lighting ceremony opposite the Prime Minister's Office, on the spot where left-wing demonstrator Emil Grunzweig was killed by a right-wing fanatic.

On Independence Day, two demonstrations were held at Har Homa: one was organized by the right to lay the cornerstone for the Jewish neighborhood scheduled to be built there, while the other was organized by the left to protest the establishment of the neighborhood in the first place. At their demonstration, the right-wingers referred to Rachel's Tomb, which is situated on the outskirts of Bethlehem and which can be seen from the Har Homa site. At their demonstration, the left-wingers referred to the grave that Netanyahu is digging for peace. At both demonstrations, the participants sang the national anthem, but they did not do so in unison.

This is admittedly a partial list; however, it does convey an accurate picture of the character of this year's Independence Day celebrations. In order to fix these celebrations within 'Jewish parameters,' no 'external' events connected with Israel's creation were included, such as the Nakba (Catastrophe) rallies organized by Israeli Arabs to mark the disaster that Palestinians feel was brought upon them with the establishment of the Jewish state in 1948. Nor did the celebrations include another 'external' event: the detonation of an explosive device at the entrance to an apartment occupied by three female Arab university students in Jerusalem's Musrara quarter.

This list is also sufficient proof to demonstrate the fact that Israeli society is not united and that fragmentation characterizes the major areas of life in this country. There is no national unity, nor can there ever be, over the issue of peace; in fact, even the very word 'peace' has become a political concept that arouses very different emotions, depending on which segment of society you are referring to. The Rabin assassination is a political issue, because it symbolizes the split in Israeli society, and this point was articulated by Deputy Minister Peled's behavior in his own kibbutz and by some bereaved parents at Tel Aviv University's Memorial Day ceremony.

There is no national unity, nor can there ever be, in the long-standing cultural war over the character of the State of Israel as it enters its next half-century of existence. This war is being conducted between, on the one hand, the defenders of a theocratic state who are members of Israel's ultra-Orthodox community and, on the other hand, the secular members of Israeli society who are the champions of a secular, enlightened state. The Batsheva dance company affair and one's attitude towards the bereavement connected with

Israel's fallen soldiers are but two expressions of this cultural war, which is no longer a potential threat but which is rather being conducted in our very midst at full throttle.

This fact is regrettable, but one must face reality. And no slogan will ever be able to change that reality.

4. Row Erupts Over 'Immodest' Dance

(The *Jerusalem Post*, *International Edition*, week ending 9 May 1998, by Liat Collins, Helen Kaye, and Sarah Honig)

Celebrations of Israel's jubilee were marred last week by an eruption of religious–secular acrimony over the decision by the Batsheva Dance Company not to perform Thursday night on the grounds that religious coercion was restricting its artistic freedom.

The company, directed by Ohad Naharin, won a round of applause for not performing at the Jubilee Bells event. Naharin also reportedly resigned, but was subsequently said to have retracted his resignation.

The controversy surrounded an excerpt from the company's *Anaphase* in which the dancers gradually take off most of their clothing to the words and tune of the song from the Haggada: 'Who Knows One?'

Although the piece had passed through the committee's approval procedure, questions were raised after religious members of the audience at the dress rehearsal objected. The objections were officially raised by Jerusalem Deputy Mayor Hairn Miller.

Among the proposed compromises were that the group would wear long underwear instead of briefs.

Meanwhile, following a decision by Tel Aviv Mayor Ronni Milo, Batsheva performed the disputed sequence in Tel Aviv later in the week, which was televised live.

Labor Party chairman Ehud Barak said he sees the incident as, 'the final collapse of the status quo on religious affairs, and as a capitulation to religious coercion.'

Yet Barak also condemned the fact that artists and actors heckled education Minister Yitshak Levy, calling him 'a dirty Jew' at a protest at the Diaspora Museum last Friday.

The Likud issued a statement accusing Labor and the left of seeking 'to make political capital in the most cynical way possible out of an incident which was the result of a simple oversight by the producers of Jubilee Bells, who should not have included a controversial dance in an officially-sponsored celebration.

'This was the wrong item in the wrong place and that is all it was,' the statement said.

Levy argued that 'to accuse us of censorship and of curbing the right to free expression is a gross manipulation of the truth. No one prevents anyone including Batsheva from putting on whatever act they wish in any auditorium they hire. But this is something to which the state invites guests to celebrate an event which has meaning to more than one segment of society. Not all those invited share the same tastes.'

4.10 Osama bin Laden's use of history: an audiotape released in early 2004
Benjamin C. Fortna

Preface

On 4 January 2004 Al-Jazeera satellite television aired an audiotape allegedly recorded by Osama bin Laden [Usama bin Ladin] (b. 1957), leader of the Al-Qaʿida terrorist network. The next day various news sources reported that an unnamed official of the United States Central Intelligence Agency had confirmed that the tape was likely that of bin Laden. The recording refers to several events that had recently occurred in late 2003, such as the capture of Saddam Hussein [Husayn] by US forces and the unveiling of an unofficial diplomatic solution to the Israeli–Palestinian impasse in Geneva.

Perhaps more interesting than the recent provenance of the tape was the way it drew upon long-past historical events and images to justify its argument for the continued resistance to the US occupation of Iraq in the aftermath of the second Gulf War and against the stance of those regimes deemed to be playing into the hands of the Western powers. The Americans are likened to both the Crusaders and the Romans, and the local regimes are compared with the Ghassanids, a buffer state for the Byzantine (or Eastern Roman) Empire against the tribes of Arabia, and the Lakhmids, an Arab tribe allied with Byzantium's regional rivals the Sasanian Empire of Persia.

Also worthy of interest are Osama bin Laden's rhetorical flourishes. Qur'anic language runs through the text, by turns chastizing and exhorting. Altogether, the combination of historical and recent events, the use of antiquated and contemporary language, and the fact that this mixed chronological message was conveyed via satellite television, and (presumably) subjected to the latest in voice-recognition software thousands of miles away from the Gulf, presents the historically engaged reader with a fascinating text.

Text

(Source: Al-Jazeera TV, Doha, in Arabic 2000 gmt 4 Jan. 04/BBC Monitoring/©BBC)
From Osama Bin Laden to his brothers and sisters in the entire Islamic nation: May God's peace, mercy and blessings be upon you.

My message to you concerns inciting and continuing to urge for jihad to repulse the grand plots that have been hatched against our nation, especially since some of them have appeared clearly, such as the occupation of the crusaders, with the help of the apostates, of Baghdad and the house of the caliphate, under the trick of weapons of mass destruction.

There is also the fierce attempt to destroy the al-Aqsa Mosque [in Jerusalem] and destroy the jihad and the *mujahidin* in beloved Palestine by employing the trick of the roadmap and the Geneva peace initiative.

The Americans' intentions have also become clear in statements about the need to change the beliefs, curricula and morals of the Muslims to become more tolerant, as they put it.

In clearer terms, it is a religious-economic war.

The occupation of Iraq is a link in the Zionist-crusader chain of evil.[83]

Then comes the full occupation of the rest of the Gulf states to set the stage for controlling and dominating the whole world.

For the big powers believe that the Gulf and the Gulf states are the key to controlling the world due to the presence of the largest oil reserves there.

O Muslims: The situation is serious and the misfortune is momentous.

By God, I am keen on safeguarding your religion and your worldly life.

So, lend me your ears and open up your hearts to me so that we may examine these pitch-black misfortunes and so that we may consider how we can find a way out of these adversities and calamities.

The West's occupation of our countries is old, yet new.

The struggle between us and them, the confrontation, and clashing began centuries ago, and will continue because the ground rules regarding the fight between right and falsehood will remain valid until Judgement Day.

Take note of this ground rule regarding this fight. There can be no dialogue with occupiers except through arms.

This is what we need today, and what we should seek. Islamic countries in the past century were not liberated from the crusaders' military occupation except through jihad in the cause of God.

Under the pretext of fighting terrorism, the West today is doing its utmost to tarnish jihad and kill anyone seeking jihad.[84]

The West is supported in this endeavour by hypocrites.[85]

This is because they all know that jihad is the effective power to foil all their conspiracies.

Jihad is the path, so seek it.

[83] Bin Laden's 1998 'declaration of jihad' against the United States elaborates on this Zionist-crusader formulation and warned of an American agenda to spread 'international kufr' (denial of God, the state of being an 'infidel'). See <http://www.meij.or.jp/new/Osama%20bin%20Laden/jihad1.htm>.

[84] There are echoes here of the Muslim Brotherhood's Sayyid Qutb (d. 1966) and other militant revivalists who argued that the notion that jihad was more about personal struggles against temptation and error than a militant resistance to infidels was essentially Western imperialist propaganda designed to weaken the resolve of Muslims.

[85] The term 'hypocrites' originally refers to those in Medina who gave their allegiance to the prophet Muhammad and Islam in 622 but clandestinely conspired with his pagan enemies among the Quraysh tribe of Mecca to undermine the morale and military defences of the Muslims.

This is because if we seek to deter them with any means other than Islam, we would be like the one who goes round in circles.

We would also be like our forefathers, the al-Ghasasina [i.e. the Ghassanids, noted in the preface to this text].

The concern of their seniors was to be appointed officers for the Romans[86] (and to be named kings in order to safeguard the interests of the Romans by killing their brothers, the Arabs of the peninsula).

Such is the case of the new al-Ghasasina; namely, Arab rulers.

Muslims: If you do not punish them for their sins in Jerusalem and Iraq, they shall defeat you because of your failure.

They will also rob you of land of the al-Haramayn [Mecca and Medina].

Today [they robbed you] of Baghdad and tomorrow they will rob you of Riyadh and so forth unless God deems otherwise.

Sufficient unto us is God.[87]

What then is the means to stop this tremendous onslaught?

In such hard times, some reformers maintain that all popular and official forces should unite and that all government forces should unite with all their peoples.

Everyone would do what is needed from him in order to ward off this crusader-Zionist onslaught.

The question strongly raised is: Are the governments in the Islamic world capable of pursuing this duty of defending the faith and nation and renouncing allegiance to the United States?

The calls by some reformers are strange.

They say that the path to righteousness and defending the country and people passes though the doors of those rulers.

I tell those reformers: If you have an excuse for not pursing jihad, it does not give you the right to depend on the unjust ones, thus becoming responsible for your sins as well as the sins of those who you misguide.

Fear God for your sake and for your nation's sake.

God does not need your flattery of dictators for the sake of God's religion.

The Gulf states proved their total inability to resist the Iraqi forces.

They sought help from the crusaders, led by the United States, as is well known.

How can these states stand up to the United States?

In short, these states came to America's help and backed it in its attack against an Arab state which was bound to them with covenants of joint defence agreements.

---

[86] Byzantium was known as 'Al-Rum'.

[87] Likely a reference to Qur'an 3: 173 (*The 'Imrans*): 'Those to whom the people said: Surely men have gathered against you, therefore fear them, but this increased their faith, and they said: "God is sufficient for us and most excellent is the Protector." '

These covenants were reiterated at the Arab League just a few days before the US attack, only to violate them in full.

This shows their positions on the nation's basic causes.

These regimes wavered too much before taking a stand on using force and attacking Iraq.

At times they absolutely rejected participation and at other times they linked this with UN agreement.

Then they went back to their first option.

In fact, the lack of participation was in line with the domestic desire of these states.

However, they finally submitted and succumbed to US pressure and opened their air, land and sea bases to contribute toward the US campaign, despite the immense repercussions of this move.

Most important of these repercussions is that this is a sin against one of the Islamic tenets.[88]

Most important and dangerous in their view was that they feared that the door would be open for bringing down dictatorial regimes by armed forces from abroad, especially after they had seen the arrest of their former comrade in treason and collusion with the United States when it ordered him to ignite the first Gulf war against Iran, which rebelled against it.[89]

The war consumed everything and plunged the area in a maze from which they have not emerged to this day.

They are aware that their turn will come.

They do not have the will to make the difficult decision to confront the aggression, in addition to their belief that they do not possess the material resources for that.

Indeed, they were prevented from establishing a large military force when they were forced to sign secret pledges and documents long ago.

In short, the ruler who believes in some of the above-mentioned deeds cannot defend the country.

[88] In the First Gulf War in 1990–1 Syria, Egypt, Saudi Arabia, and other Arab states actively supported the US-led United Nations forces to oust Iraq from Kuwait. In the more recent war support was much more tepid, even from ostensible US allies like Saudi Arabia. In addition to highlighting this hypocrisy in terms of pan-Arab ideals, Bin Laden invokes the Islamic expectation of unity in the face of outside threats.

[89] Here Saddam Hussein is portrayed as a US agent who launched a war against Iran in 1980. Iraq's offensive came in the wake of the Islamic Revolution of 1979, which ended the pro-US Pahlavi Dynasty in favor of an Islamic republic under the 'supreme leadership' of Ayatollah Khomeini. During the war, which lasted until 1988, Iraq received its principle backing from the USSR but also from France and the USA. These links would subsequently come back to haunt men such as Jacques Chirac and Donald Rumsfeld, whose visit to Saddam Hussein in 1983 on behalf of Ronald Reagan proved particularly embarrassing during the second Gulf War.

How can he do so if he believes in all of them and has done that time and again?

Those who believe in the principle of supporting the infidels over Muslims and leave the blood, honor and property of their brothers to be available to their enemy in order to remain safe, claiming that they love their brothers but are being forced to take such a path—of course this compulsion cannot be regarded as legitimate—are in fact qualified to take the same course against one another in the Gulf states.

Indeed, this principle is liable to be embraced within the same state itself.

Those who read and understood the history of kings throughout history know that they are capable of committing more than these concessions, except those who enjoyed the mercy of God.

Indeed, the rulers have practically started to sell out the sons of the land by pursuing and imprisoning them and by unjustly and wrongly accusing them of becoming like the al-Khawarij sect who held Muslims to be infidels and by committing the excesses of killing them.[90]

We hold them to be martyrs and God will judge them.

All of this happened before the Riyadh explosions in Rabiᶜ of this year [12 May 2003].

This campaign came within a drive to implement the US orders in the hope that they will win its blessings.

Based on the above, the extent of the real danger, which the region in general and the Arabian Peninsula in particular, is being exposed to, has appeared.

It has become clear that the rulers are not qualified to apply the religion and defend the Muslims.

In fact, they have provided evidence that they are implementing the schemes of the enemies of the nation and religion and that they are qualified to abandon the countries and peoples.

Now, after we have known the situation of the rulers, we should examine the policy which they have been pursuing.

Anyone who examines the policy of those rulers will easily see that they follow their whims and desires and their personal interests and crusader loyalties.

Therefore, the flaw does not involve a secondary issue, such as personal corruption that is confined to the palace of the ruler.

[90] In their efforts to combat militant Islamic insurgencies, Arab nationalist regimes like those in Egypt accused militant groups of being like the Kharijites who broke from the two major sects of Islam—Sunnism and Shiᶜism—after the Battle of Siffin in 657. Until their evolution into the ᶜIbadi sect of Islam (which now prevails in Oman), Kharijites warred against other Muslims on the basis of the doctrine that to be a 'bad Muslim' was to be an apostate and an outlaw to be fought. This differed from the more widely accepted view in Islamic law that a bad Muslim was still a Muslim and that apostasy was something that had to be explicitly asserted before bloodshed was called for. In essence, then, modern militant Islamic groups, which make frequent references to the lessons of early Islamic history, were likened to this prototypical Islamic militant group in the seventh century.

The flaw is in the very approach.

This happened when a malicious belief and destructive principle spread in most walks of life, to the effect that absolute supremacy and obedience were due to the ruler and not to the religion of God.

In other countries, they have used the guise of parliaments and democracy.[91]

Thus, the situation of all Arab countries suffers from great deterioration in all walks of life, in religious and worldly matters.

We have reached this miserable situation because many of us lack the correct and comprehensive understanding of the religion of Islam.

Many of us understand Islam to mean performing some acts of worship, such as prayer and fasting.

Despite the great importance of these rituals, the religion of Islam encompasses all the affairs of life, including religious and worldly affairs, such as economic, military and political affairs, as well as the scales by which we weigh the actions of men—rulers, ʿulama (clerics) and others—and how to deal with the ruler in line with the rules set by God for him and which the ruler should not violate.

Therefore, it becomes clear to us that the solution lies in adhering to the religion of God, by which God granted us pride in the past centuries and installing a strong and faithful leadership that applies the Qurʾan among us and raises the true banner of jihad.

The honest people who are concerned about this situation, such as the ʿulama, leaders who are obeyed among their people, dignitaries, notables and merchants should get together and meet in a safe place away from the shadow of these suppressive regimes and form a council for Ahl al-Hall wa al-ʿAqd [literally those who loose and bind; reference to honest, wise, and righteous people who can appoint or remove a ruler in Islamic tradition] to fill the vacuum caused by the religious invalidation of these regimes and their mental deficiency.

The right to appoint an imam [leader] is for the nation [of Muslims, i.e. the *umma*].

The nation also has the right to make him correct his course if he deviates from it and to remove him if he does something that warrants this, such as apostasy and treason.

This temporary council should be made up of the minimum number of available personnel, without [word indistinct] the rest of the nation, except what

---

[91] Despite the high hopes placed in them, most democratic experiments from the Ottoman Constitution of 1876 and the Iranian Constitution of 1906 and 1907 onwards have resulted in autocratic coups or further Western imperialist encroachment in Middle Eastern/Islamic counties. These results have led some sceptics of political reform to conclude that democratic institutions in the Middle East, like other adaptations from contemporary Western societies, served as a 'Trojan horse' to further Western world hegemony. Another feature of many regimes in the Middle East was the use of rigged referendums, elections and rubber-stamp parliaments to provide a democratic gloss to authoritarian rule.

the religion allows in case of necessity, until the number is increased when the situation improves, God willing.

Their policy should be based on the book of God [the Qur'an] and the Sunna [tradition] of his Prophet [Muhammad], God's peace and blessings be upon him.

They should start by directing the Muslims to the important priorities at this critical stage and lead them to a safe haven, provided that their top priority should be uniting opinions under the word of monotheism and defending Islam and its people and countries and declaring a general mobilization in the nation to prepare for repulsing the raids of the Romans, which started in Iraq and no one knows where they will end.

God suffices us and he is the best supporter.[92]

[92] See n. 87.

Selected bibliography

ABBAS, S. G., *Dr Mohammad Iqbal: The Humanist. A Reassessment of the Poetry and Personality of the Poet-Philosopher of the East* (Lahore: Iqbal Academy, 1997).

AKBAR ALI, SHAIKH, *Iqbal, His Poetry and Message* (New Delhi: Deep & Deep Publications, 1988).

AL-RASHEED, MADAWI, *A History of Saudi Arabia* (Cambridge: Cambridge University Press, 2002).

BARBIR, KARL, *Ottoman Rule in Damascus, 1708–1758* (Princeton: Princeton University Press, 1980).

BATATU, H., *The Old Social Classes and Revolutionary Movements of Iraq*, Book 1, Part 1 (Princeton: Princeton University Press, 1978).

BEN MOSHE, DANNY, 'The True Meaning of the Rabin Assassination', *Israel Affairs*, 2/2 (1995), 136–41.

BERGEN, PETER L., *Holy War, Inc.: Inside the Secret World of Osama bin Laden* (New York: Free Press, 2001).

CHAMBERLAIN, MICHAEL, *Knowledge and Social Practice in Medieval Damascus, 1190–1350* (Cambridge: Cambridge University Press, 1994).

COOK, MICHAEL, *Commanding Right and Forbidding Wrong in Islamic Thought* (Cambridge: Cambridge University Press, 2000).

EZRAHI, YARON, *Rubber Bullets: Power and Conscience in Modern Israel* (New York: Farrar, Straus & Giroux, 1997).

ETZIONI-HALEVY, EVA, *The Divided People: Can Israel's Break Up Be Stopped?* (New York: Lexington Books, 2002).

FARHANG, MANSOUR, 'Resisting the Pharaohs: ʿAli Shariʿati on Oppression', *Race and Class*, 21/1 (Summer 1979), 31–40.

FUCCARO, N., *The Other Kurds: Yazidis in Colonial Iraq* (London: I.B.Tauris, 1999).

GAMMER, MOSHE, *Muslim Resistance to the Tsar: Shamil and the Conquest of Chechnya and Daghestan* (London: Frank Cass, 1994).

GIBB, H. A. R. and HAROLD BOWEN, *Islamic Society and the West*, 2 vols.(Oxford: Oxford University Press, 1957).

HABIB, JOHN S., *Ibn Saʿuds Warriors of Islam. The Ikhwan of Najd and Their Role in the Creation of the Saʿudi Kingdom, 1910–1930* (Leiden: Brill, 1978).

HANSON, BRAD, 'The "Westoxication" of Iran: Depictions and Reactions of Behrangi, Al-e Ahmad, and Shariʿati', *International Journal of Middle East Studies*, 15/1 (Feb. 1983), 1–23.

HAZONY, YORAM, 'The "Jewish State" at 100', *Azur*, 32 (Spring 1997), 17–18.

HOURANI, ALBERT, 'The Fertile Crescent in the XVIIIth Century', in *A Vision of History: Near East & other Essays* (Beirut: Khayats, 1961).

—— 'Aspects of Islamic Culture', in Thomas Naff and Roger Owen (eds.), *Studies in Eighteenth-Century Islamic History* (Carbondale: Southern Illinois University Press, 1977).

JOSEPH, J., *The Nestorians and their Muslim Neighbours: A Study of Western Influence on Their Relations* (Princeton: Princeton University Press, 1961).

KLEIN HALEVI, YOSSI, 'Israel at 50: An Israeli Perspective', in *American Jewish Year Book*, 98 (New York: American Jewish Committee, 1998).

KOSTINER, JOSEPH, 'On Instruments and their Designers: The *Ikhwan* of Najd and the Emergence of the Saudi State', *Middle Eastern Studies* 21/3 (1985), 298–323.

—— *The Making of Saudi Arabia: From Chieftaincy to Monarchical State 1916–1936* (New York and Oxford: Oxford University Press, 1993).

KYLE, KEITH, and JOEL PETERS (eds.), *Whither Israel? The Domestic Challenges* (London: I. B. Tauris, 1993).

LAYISH, AHARON, '"Ulama and Politics in Saudi Arabia', in Metin Heper and Raphael Israeli (eds.), *Islam and Politics in the Middle East* (London and Sydney: Croom Helm, 1984).

LEVTZION, N. and J. O. VOLL (eds.), *Eighteenth-Century Revival and Reform in Islam* (Syracuse, NY: Syracuse University Press, 1987).

LIEBMAN, CHARLES, AND ELIHU KATZ (eds.), *The Jewishness of Israelis: Responses to the Guttman Report* (SUNY Series in Israeli Studies: New York, 1997).

MAHK, HAFEEZ (ed.), *Iqbal: Poet-Philosopher of Pakistan* (New York: Columbia University Press, 1971).

MANGO, ANDREW, *Atatürk* (London: John Murray, 1999).

MARCUS, ABRAHAM, *The Middle East on the Eve of Modernity: Aleppo in the Eighteenth Century* (New York: Columbia University Press, 1989).

MASTERS, BRUCE, *The Origins of Western Economic Dominance in the Middle East: Mercantilism and the Islamic Economy in Aleppo, 1600–1750* (New York: New York University, 1988).

MATTHEWS, D. J., *Iqbal: A Selection of the Urdu Verse* (London: SOAS, The University of London, 1993).

MUNAWWAR, MOHAMMAD (ed.), *Iqbal Centenary Papers* (Lahore: Department of Iqbal Studies, University of the Punjab at Lahore, 1982).

MUNTASIR, MIR (trans. and ed.), *Tulip in the Desert: A Selection of the Poetry of Mohammad Iqbal* (London: C. Hurst & Co., 1990).

NORTHEDGE, F. S., *The League of Nations, its Life and Times* (Leicester, 1986).

OMISSI, D., 'Britain, the Assyrians and the Iraq Levies, 1919–1932', *Journal of Imperial and Commonwealth History*, 17/3 (1989), 301–22.

RAFEQ, ABDUL-KARIM, *The Province of Damascus: 1723–1783* (Beirut: Khayats, 1966).

—— 'Changes in the Relationship Between the Ottoman Central Administration and the Syrian Provinces from the Sixteenth to the Eighteenth Centuries', in Thomas Naff and Roger Owen (eds.), *Studies in Eighteenth-Century Islamic History* (Carbondale: Southern Illinois University Press, 1977).

—— 'City and Countryside in a Traditional Setting: The Case of Damascus in the First Quarter of the Eighteenth Century', in Thomas Philipp (ed.), *The Syrian Land in the 18th and 19th Century* (Stuttgart: F. Steiner, 1992).

RAHNAMA, ALI, *An Islamic Utopian: A Political Biography of Ali Shari'ati* (London: I. B. Tauris, 1998).

RASHID, AHMAD, *Taliban: Militant Islam, Oil and Fundamentalism in Central Asia* (New Haven: Yale University Press, 2000).

RAYMOND, ANDRÉ, *The Great Arab Cities in the 16th–18th Centuries: An Introduction* (New York: New York University Press, 1984).

ROSEN-ZVI, ARIEL, 'State and Religion: Changing Status Quo?', *Institute of the World Jewish Congress, Policy Forum No. 11* (1996).

SCHIMMEL, ANNEMARIE, *Gabriel's Wing: A Study into the Ideas of Sir Mohammad Iqbal* (Leiden: E. J. Brill, 1963).

SEGEV, TOM, *Elvis in Israel: Post-Zionism and the Americanization of Israel* (New York: Metropolitan Books, 2002).

SHAMIR, SHIMON, 'Asᶜad Pasha al-Azm and Ottoman Rule in Damascus (1743–58)', *Bulletin of the School of Oriental and African Studies*, 26/1 (1963), 1–28.

SCHILCHER, LINDA, *Families in Politics: Damascene Factions and Estates of the 18th and 19th Centuries* (Stuttgart: F. Steiner, 1985).

SILBERSTEIN, LAURENCE J., *The Postzionism Debates: Knowledge and Power in Israeli Culture* (New York: Routledge, 1999).

SLUGLETT, P., *Britain in Iraq 1914–1932* (Oxford: Oxford University Press, 1976).

'Special Issue: The Americanization of Israel', *Israel Studies*, 5/1 (Spring 2000).

TAMARI, STEVE, 'Biography, Autobiography, and Identity in Early Modern Damascus', in Mary Ann Fay (ed.), *Auto/Biography and the Construction of Identity and Community in the Middle East* (New York: Palgrave, 2001).

—— 'Ottoman Madrasas: The Multiple Lives of Educational Institutions in 18th-Century Syria', *Journal of Early Modern History*, 5/2 (2001), 99–127.

TUCKER, JUDITH, *In the House of Law: Gender and Islamic Law in Ottoman Syria and Palestine* (Berkeley: University of California Press, 1998).

VAHID, S. A., *Iqbal: His Art and Thought* (Lahore, 1944; enlarged edn., London: Murray, 1959).

VASSILIEV, ALEKSEI, *The History of Saudi Arabia* (London: Saqi, 1998).

VOLL, JOHN, *Islam: Continuity and Change in the Modern World* (London: Longman, 1982).

WAHBA, SHEIKH HAFIZ, *Arabian Days* (London: Arthur Barker, 1964).

YOUSEFI, NAGHI, *Religion and Revolution in the Modern World: ᶜAli Sharīᶜati's Islam and Persian Revolution* (Lanham, Md.: University Press of America, 1995).

ZAID, ABDULLAH S., 'The Ikhwan Movement of Najd, Saudi Arabia 1908–1930', Ph.D thesis, University of Chicago (1989).

ZELKINA, ANNA, *In Quest for God and Freedom: The Sufi Response to the Russian Advance in the North Caucasus* (New York: New York University Press, 2000).

<users.skynet.be/terrorism/html/laden.htm>

<www.pbs.org/wgbh/pages/frontline/shows/binladen/>

5

Modern identities

Introduction

The documents in this section reveal some of the various ways in which identities can be created, emphasized, and re-evaluated in the modern period. Indeed, a principle component of modernity involves the rethinking of established notions of belonging and identity, both on a group and an individual level.

In most respects modern identities are no different in the Middle East from those in the rest of the world. As in other places, the preponderance of scholarly attention paid to the question of modern identities has been political in nature. There are good reasons for such a political emphasis; over the course of the nineteenth and twentieth centuries the relationship between the individual and the state in which he or she lived intensified in unprecedented fashion. Whereas in the eighteenth century and before, the state remained largely an abstraction, often at a considerable geographical distance from most of its subjects, in the modern period it became increasingly present and important in their daily lives. The modernizing states of this period gradually abandoned the more *laissez-faire* approach of the pre-modern period, expanding their reach into areas traditionally beyond their grasp.

Over the course of the nineteenth century Middle Eastern states created an array of new ministries to deal with a wide variety of new activities. Increasingly, centralizing governments were interested in and capable of dictating important aspects of their subjects' lives, ranging from education to health-care to commerce and local government. All of these changes inevitably increased the visibility of the state and affected the ways in which the subjects viewed it. In many cases the simultaneous increase in contacts with other states, especially but not exclusively those in the West, invited comparisons that often led to a readjustment of political expectations. With the break-up of the Ottoman Empire in the aftermath of World War I, many new states were created in the region, each of which brought the business of government closer to more of its subjects. That new proximity, combined with the displacement created by the war itself, the rise of telegraphic and print communication, and the fact that many of these states were controlled by Western powers through the mechanism of the Mandate system, meant that political awareness was rapidly increasing. As a result, political identities were progressively more contested; many of the defining moments, as these documents indicate, were ones that were heavily freighted with nationalist significance. The theme of anti-colonial or anti-*ancien régime* political identification is one of the loudest to be heard in this period. Likewise, most of the new states and those created subsequently, such as Israel, relied heavily on creating national identity and historical myth to construct something approaching a cohesive national polity.

Yet, as the documents in this and other sections (such as those devoted to Gender and Society, Religion and Society, and Economic Change) reveal, political identities were hardly the only ones that mattered in the modern period. While the political questions have long dominated the historical agenda, in recent decades attention has turned to the ways in which other sorts of identities were being formed. Although seldom unrelated to larger political issues, areas such as socio-economic, religious, and sexual identity-formation have been increasingly recognized by historians as important in their own right. The changes of the nineteenth and twentieth centuries have been so rapid and so profound that in many cases there now exist new identities that were not even dreamed of a few generations before, such as an Egyptian feminist or an Israeli nationalist. In other instances, established, older identities have been given radically new dimensions and roles: an Iranian mullah who holds a major political office, for example.

The documents in this and related sections have no single profile or least common denominator. In some, a case is being made for inclusion in or exclusion from a larger group; while in others, a sense of belonging is assumed and underpins the whole discussion.

5.1 On justice towards peasants: from Rifaᶜa Rafiᶜ al-Tahtawi's *Paths of Egyptian Minds in the Delights of Modern Culture*, 1869
Juan R. I. Cole

Preface

The Egyptian reformer and educator Rifaᶜa Rafiᶜ al-Tahtawi (1801–73), a major figure of the Arab Renaissance of the mid-nineteenth century, was born in the small town of Tahta in Upper Egypt. He rose to become one of Egypt's great landlords, and a pillar of the establishment in Ottoman Egypt under the khedives. One might have expected him to disdain the poor and workers, as, in fact, many among the Egyptian notables did. Despite a strong element of paternalism in his views he is remarkably sympathetic to the working poor. He was sent to study at Al-Azhar seminary in 1817 on his father's death, following in the footsteps of many of his uncles. In 1822 he began teaching at Al-Azhar, and in 1824 his mentor Hasan al-ᶜAttar nominated him as the preacher for one of Muhammad ᶜAli Paşa's newly formed military units. In 1826, again on Al-ᶜAttar's initiative, he was appointed one of four prayer leaders for an educational mission to Paris. While in France until 1831, he completed a rigorous course of university studies. On his return in 1831, Ibrahim Paşa granted him thirty-one *feddans* of land as a reward for his accomplishments, and he became a French teacher at the medical school. Throughout the 1830s and 1840s he busied himself as a translator and promoter of language-learning, and by 1846 was promoted to the civil rank of *miralay* and given a substantial grant of land. In 1850–4 he was exiled to Khartoum in the Sudan by ᶜAbbas I, but was permitted to return to Cairo by Saᶜid Paşa, where he worked again as a translator, and subsequently as superintendent of the military academy in the Citadel until its closure in 1860.

By 1863 the government's financial woes had been assuaged by the Cotton Boom, and Ismaᶜil Paşa had come to the throne, appointing Al-Tahtawi head of a new Translation Bureau charged with rendering into Arabic the Napoleonic Code. In 1868 Al-Tahtawi's history of ancient Egypt, *The Glorious Lights of Divine Confirmation* (*Anwar Tawfiq al-Jalil*) was published, and in 1869 he brought out a long and very important book on political economy, *Paths for Egyptian Minds to the Delights of Modern Culture* (*Manahij al-Albab al-Misriyya fi Mabahij al-Adab al-ᶜAsriyya*), from which the translation below is drawn. The heady atmosphere of the Cotton Boom years (1862–6), as well as the class stratification, dislocations, high indebtedness, growing taxes, and spiraling population growth of the mid- to the late 1860s, are apparent in this book. After 1850 Egypt's population growth-rate also swelled; the number of Egyptians rose from about 5 million in 1848 to about 8 million in 1882, a very substantial increase that put pressure on the land and contributed to the fragmentation of peasant estates. The number of landless laborers grew during this period.

In the passages that precede the text below, Al-Tahtawi attempts to explain why private property in land arises and why peoples give up their natural indolence to labor in agriculture. He was influenced in his thinking on these matters by his knowledge of European political economy, but also by his experiences in the Sudan, where he saw pastoral nomads such as the Dinka in a state he presumed to be pre-agricultural. He argued that, over time, population growth makes it impossible to live off the land as nomads do, impelling peoples to begin actively cultivating the soil. This turn to agriculture for Malthusian reasons makes land a commodity that can be bought and sold in the market, further increasing its value and the value of agricultural labor. Because of his labor theory of value, Al-Tahtawi seeks a better deal for workers, without wishing to expropriate landowners or to denigrate government officials. The French utopian socialist movement known as Saint-Simonianism influenced his ideas on these issues. They also owed something, however, to his understanding of Islamic law, which he interprets in a highly progressive manner. It is unknown whether Al-Tahtawi attempted to put into practice his ideals by paying his own peasants better than did other landlords of the time.

Text

In the course of a people's progress, a civilized right emerges among them—the right to own land by occupying it and giving it life where it had been fallow. From this time, the land comes to have a value in and of itself, in addition to the value of the labor. The worker of the land then has a claim on it by virtue of ownership, even when he is not actively laboring on it [...] At that time, each individual in the society will practice farming as his profession, and labor therein, being compelled to hire himself out for tilling and planting, so that he might earn a living through his profession. He works for the owner of the land in the capacity of a hired laborer, and charges himself with spending all his time in the service of the land, without repose save for necessary intervals for eating, drinking, sleeping, praying, and so forth. Thus, the agricultural produce increases and grows day by day through an abundance of labor, and the laborer who at one time worked a small amount and spent his time in idleness, is now obliged to do a huge amount of work in the same time. He seeks to acquire a great deal of produce, in accordance with the increase in human power. That is to say, both the workers and the property owners strive in investigating ways to advance and facilitate work, and to save time doing it.

The laborer, by striving, will be able to accomplish three or four times as much work in a single day as he used to do, insofar as the worker has become freed, under these conditions, from idleness and is at liberty to work and perpetually train himself. The more he practices, the more complete his knowledge, whereby he can make his work excellent. The laborer, by perfecting agriculture, improves it and becomes more skilled in it. He develops his work, becomes versatile, and divides it up. He comes to know times, seasons, and hours, to know what pertains to the various sorts of agriculture and the improvements that will strengthen it. The value of labor rises with experience and excellence, and the laborer likewise comes to have knowledge of the peculiarities of the modern resources on which he depends, which facilitate his craft, such as air, water, and steam. These techniques, which make his work easier, will play the role for him of volunteer labor. Only the master of skills and of crafts can improve their use. When these perfected and beneficial techniques become widespread among farmers, the daily productivity of the workers will improve and the fruits of their labor will prove abundant. An image of the activities of this advanced sort of labor will by these means be impressed on the mirror of the mind of the agricultural community. They will become accustomed to undertaking agricultural tasks with energy, and the social benefits will gradually be renewed, beginning to increase infinitely. And by these popular benefits the wealth of the subjects and the prosperity of their way of life will increase.

It is, at the moment, the landowners alone who pick the fruits of these agricultural improvements and reap the benefits of this reform of farming—which is for the most part produced by labor and the use of the power of tools. They, and not those who practice the profession of agriculture, enjoy the greatest advantages. The land- and farm-owners are the ones who seize the general proceeds, and who obtain their benefits, until everyone else receives hardly anything from these yields. They only give to the people according to the service and labor of the latter, recompensing them for their hardships out of their magnanimity. This is to say that normally the owners enjoy the revenues of the labor, and pay, in exchange for an immense amount of work, an insignificant sum that does not requite this labor. What reaches the workers in return for their labor upon the farms, or makers of tools in return for crafting them, is a small thing in relation to the huge amounts yielded to the owners. The owner seizes most of the produce of the earth for himself, and after settling the accounts of agricultural expenses and all their costs, he takes their produce in its entirety as profit from the land, provender for livestock, and the cost of tools. He only gives an insignificant amount of it to those who perform the labor. He does not take into account that someone among these workers has improved agriculture through his work, and invented productive techniques for it, making great discoveries in causing agriculture to thrive and in multiplying its activities.

The right of ownership and possession of farms has permitted the owners to administer the affairs of their estates with complete liberty, and to give to the workers whatever they think is appropriate for them. The owners believe that they possess great rights because of their ownership, and that they themselves are the most deserving of the prosperity and riches accruing from the revenues of agricultural activity. They hold that none of the other people of the kingdom deserve any of the earth's produce, except in recompense for his service and the benefit he has been commissioned to render in respect to the land. In consequence, everyone who wants to make his living from service, which is labor, is compelled to work for whatever amount it is possible to get from the owners, depending upon their pleasure, even though this amount be extremely small and incommensurate with the labor. This is particularly so in areas where there are a great many workers, who then accept diminished wages and compete with one another in this, to the benefit of the landowners. This happens even though the earth's yields and fertility are only improved by the farming activity of these wage laborers whose wages have been cut. And just as the owners monopolize all the agricultural labor of the peasant stratum, in the same way they monopolize the products of all the crafts. For all the crafts strive and endeavor in tasks and activities that are called for by the needs of the farm-workers, such as smith-craft, carpentry, and all the crafts of trades that relate to agricultural affairs.

The result of all this is that if the fates do not aid someone to become the possessor of a strip of land, he will continue to share with the owner of the land in the agricultural profits which are obtained, but his enjoyment will be extremely deficient. For, he will receive from the agricultural produce only the amount that the owner grants to him in compensation for his services, his art and craft, and the price of the tools, instruments, and machines suitable to agriculture. If the owner of the land is liberal, generous, and open-handed, he will compensate him completely and be generous to the one by whose art he benefits. It has been the custom that the farm-worker is not requited according to the amount of his service and cultivation because of the famous rule, 'He who sows shall reap;' that is, the harvest belongs to the owner. And Muhammad said, 'The crop belongs to the sower.' However, the meaning here is that the seed and its fruit belong to whoever sows it, though he has to pay a rent—for instance for the land—not that that worker is to take a tiny wage for his labor. A narrative is found in the two books of *Sound Traditions* that Muhammad treated with the people of Khaybar by dividing into two the fruit and crops that they produced.[1] That is, he gave them half in recompense for their labor. And in another version, he gave the Jews of

---

[1] This is a reference to collections of Hadith (a report on the sayings and actions of the Prophet Muhammad) considered reliable by Islamic legal scholars. It is not clear which specific collection(s) Al-Tahtawi has in mind.

Khaybar the date trees, the earth, and materials in return for their labor, leasing, and farming. What pleased Muhammad were the forms of farming such as leasing (*musaqah*). The crop mentioned in the tradition was barley, as some have demonstrated, and like this above-mentioned crop are *mulukhiyya*,[2] okra, peaches, and apricots, and it is proper to cultivate these crops by lease. The seed for these crops comes from the landowner, unlike the case where the seed is from the labourer, which is a form of contracting (*mukhabara*) [for a mature form of the seed] and is also termed an agreement (*musharata*), which occurs in the case of grapes and peaches. In this instance, the owner provides land to the worker, who then sows it with his own seed, and likewise in the case of wheat. The incidence of contracting, although it is impermissible, is now greater in Egypt than that of [licit] leasing.

Thus the tradition, 'The crop belongs to the sower,' does not at all indicate that the owner is allowed to usurp the yield without compensating the worker. Nor can swindling the hired laborer be justified by holding that the owner has paid out his capital for the costs of the farming and taken upon himself its expenses, and thus is the one who most deserves to usurp the enormous yields, and most deserves to profit from his vast wealth, since he is the basis for profit-making, whereas the activity of the farm-workers is only secondary and is produced and improved by investment of capital. Such analyses are pure fallacies, however, since our discussion of the worker has already determined that he is the source of productive labor, without whom the land would not have yielded these great profits. The landowner's short-changing the worker by diminishing his wages is pure injustice against him. His owning the land and expending from his capital on agriculture do not necessitate that he grab up the major portion of the yield and injure the wage laborer, who is vulnerable because peasants are numerous, and are thus willing to take diminished wages and are bid down in competition with one another. This underpayment does not produce love for the owners on the part of the hired labor, and 'Grapes are not reaped of thistles.' In this lies mutual harm, which is forbidden in the revelation.

That it is forbidden is indicated by what Abu Hurayrah[3] related: 'The Messenger of God said, "Be not envious of one another, nor consider one another ritually

---

[2] The plant species *Corchorus olitorius*, also known as Jew's mallow. It is the prime ingredient in a traditional Arab stew of the same name (i.e *mulukhiyya*).

[3] He was an early convert to Islam from the Daws tribe, companion of the Prophet, and well-known narrator of Hadith. Quoting Abu Hurayrah here would emphasize the soundness of the Hadith to a nineteenth-century (and even a twenty-first-century) Muslim audience. Recently, the reliability of Abu Hurayrah has become the subject of criticism by Sayyid Muhammad al-Tijani al-Samawi in his book *Then I Was Guided* (2000). His critique of Abu Hurayrah has been interpreted as an attack on Islamic legal traditions and an attempt to win converts to either the Tijaniyya Sufi order or Shiʿism. For an online glimpse at the back and forth, see <http://www.al-islam.org/guided/> and http://www.ansar.org/english/answering.htm>.

polluted, nor hate one another, nor turn your backs on one another, nor sell another merchandise after he has contracted to buy it from someone else. Be brotherly servants of God. A Muslim is the brother of a Muslim, and does not transgress against him, nor abandon him, nor lie to him, nor despise him. Piety is right here." He pointed to his breast three times. "It is sufficient evil for a man to despise his Muslim brother. Every Muslim is forbidden to [take from] every other: his blood, his wealth, and his dignity." '

5.2 An official report on efforts to re-establish Ottoman control over Kuwait, 1870

Frederick Anscombe

Preface

Ottoman authority and interest in eastern Arabia were weak through long periods of the empire's existence. In 1550 the Ottomans seized control of Hasa, the region of eastern Arabia between Basra and Qatar, turning it into a forward base for its struggle to push the Portuguese out of the Persian Gulf. The Portuguese threat receded in the seventeenth century, and the Ottomans thus made no attempt to recover their position, following a determined campaign waged by the Arabian Banu Khalid tribe in 1670 to expel them. The following century saw significant migrations by tribes in Arabia, one result of which was the settlement of Kuwait by subdivisions of the ʿUtub, a tribe which migrated from the interior of Arabia to the west. Although the port town of Kuwait acknowledged allegiance to the Ottoman state, particularly in the early nineteenth century, when the ascendant power of the Saʿudi-Wahhabis posed an alarming threat, it generally retained its *de facto* independence. In the 1860s the Ottomans introduced reforms to the administration of Baghdad province, by which they tried to bring Kuwait under the empire's customs regulations. They gave up their hope of bringing this smuggling haven under control, however, when the idea provoked firm Kuwaiti opposition.

Events elsewhere in the Gulf changed this stand-off in 1870. The British, based in India, intervened in a dispute among members of the Khalifa family which ruled Bahrain. This dispute had led to violence not only in Bahrain but also on the Arabian mainland, in Qatar and Hasa. Worried about threats to maritime commerce, the British deposed the most recent successful claimant to the sheikhdom of Bahrain and installed their own preferred candidate, Shaykh ʿIsa (r. 1869–1923). This aggressive action caused alarm in Istanbul and Baghdad, and on the eastern Arabian mainland. Worried about British designs on their southern flank, the Ottomans wished to exert a clearer claim to frontier lands. They became willing to forgo the customs revenues that could have been levied in Kuwait, in return for the Kuwaiti shaykhs' explicit recognition of Ottoman suzerainty. With Kuwait's allegiance secured, the Ottoman governor of Baghdad, Midhat Paşa,[4] was

---

[4] Midhat was one of the leading figures of the Ottoman modernization era known as the *Tanzimat*. In the 1860s and early 1870s he introduced important administrative reforms in the provinces of the Danube, Baghdad, and Damascus. He was grand vizier in Istanbul at the height of the Eastern Question crisis of 1876–7, during which he was instrumental in introducing the first Ottoman constitution

able to launch an expedition to secure the coasts of Hasa and Qatar in 1871. The text below (Istanbul, Başbakanlık Osmanlı Arşivi, Usul-i İrade Dosya 77) is Midhat's report to Istanbul on the successful negotiations to bring Kuwait under the Ottoman flag.

Text

To the Illustrious Office of the Grand Vizier

My humble report is as follows:

[I report] as your excellency ordered. The place known as Kuwait is a merchant port of two or three thousand houses lying on the coast twenty-four hours south of Basra. While in the early days it was one of those areas attached to Basra, it later somehow gradually won the status of an independent community, because geographic barriers prevented its supervision and it thus was left on its own. The Franks considering it a 'Republic,' it is so marked on [their] maps and is recognized as completely separate and independent. The people of this place, an old part of the well-protected [Ottoman] domains, all belong to the Sunni *madhhab*[5] and, all of them being traders, they fly a special form of the Ottoman flag on most of their seven or eight hundred ships. Nevertheless, because they did not want to obey Basra in the past, it remained in an isolated and independent condition and administration. In spite of that, given the current condition of Bahrain under British domination and foreigners' schemes to send ships to seize the Hasa and Qatif[6] coasts lying between Kuwait and Bahrain, correspondence was initiated through various channels for the purpose of finding a means to bring Kuwait under control and administration. It is clear that, once foreigners become entrenched in the [Hasa–Qatif] coast, they will come in turn to Kuwait. Were we to bring this Kuwait under proper administration, it would smooth the way to saving the area beyond it through the naval force now being organized in Basra, and it is probable that a solution for even the Bahrain problem could then be found. Since the shaykhs of Kuwait have long had income from 150 measures (*kare*) of dates [from Faw], worth 50–60,000 *guruş*, this income was cut off, in order to ease the proposition [that Kuwait come under Ottoman control].

During my most recent trip to Basra, their shaykhs and elders were brought there. Regarding their comments and the wishes and desires which they showed,

and in placing Sultan Abdülhamid II on the throne. The conservative sultan later had the reformist Midhat sent into internal exile in the Hijaz, where he was later executed.

[5] A tradition of legal practice. In this case, Sunni practice is differentiated from that of the Shiʿi, of whom there were many in southern Iraq, Bahrain, and Hasa. Within the broad group of Sunnis, however, there were four specific schools of legal interpretation, also known as *madhhab*s: Hanafi (the tradition followed by the Ottoman state), Maliki, Shafiʿi, and Hanbali.

[6] A port on the Hasa coast close to Qatar and Bahrain.

[they said that] while they are proud to be subjects of the Sublime [Ottoman] State, their basic fear is to come under impositions such as customs duties and taxes. Since it is the case that the Sublime State in no way needs them, and its basic goal is [to establish its] patronage and protection, the requirements of the situation on this subject were explained to them at length. Then they drew up and submitted a protocol, which included the request that the current shaykh be given the title and office of *kaymakam*.[7] It also asked for the official appointment of judges with permission to exercise their authority as before according to the Shafi'i *madhhab*, since most of the people of the said town are followers of the Shafi'i practice (although there are also some followers of the Maliki and Hanbali *madhhab*s as well) and *shari'a* judicial authority is organized according to the Shafi'i school of law. The report requests also that imperial warrants be given to five *khutbi*[8] mosques from among the sacred mosques [of Kuwait]. The necessary decrees have been given in writing, and the matter of the letters of appointment and imperial warrants has been sent by telegraph to the Illustrious Interior Ministry. It has been decided in accordance with current needs that, in order to give that place a greater show of order, one hundred military gendarmes should be stationed there, with their salaries paid by them [the Kuwaiti leaders]. This, too, should be mutually agreed and brought into effect immediately upon the imminent return of the current *kaymakam*, who is at present in the Hijaz.[9] In this matter order and direction belong to him who has the power to command.

9 February 1870, from Baghdad

Governor of the Province of Baghdad, Midhat (seal)

---

[7] The governor of a *kaza*, which was the third level of provincial administration, below *vilayet* and *sancak*.

[8] A mosque in which Friday midday prayers and sermons were held, in the course of which the name of the ruler would be cited.

[9] The first *kaymakam* was 'Abd Allah al-Sabah (r. 1866–92). This proposal came to nothing, as the gendarmes were never stationed in Kuwait.

5.3 Nationalism, Ottomanism, pluralism, humanism: extracts from the Sufi writing of Abu'l-Huda al-Sayyadi, 1903
Thomas Eich

Preface

Abu'l-Huda al-Sayyadi was born in a small northern Syrian village in 1850. Although he was from a low social level, he soon climbed to the position of a close advisor of Sultan Abdülhamid II (r. 1876–1909). Documentary evidence reveals that Abu'l-Huda was consulted on issues concerning the dissemination of Abdülhamid's pan-Islamic propaganda beyond the boundaries of the Ottoman Empire, consisting mainly in the statement that the sultan was the rightly guided caliph of his time and thus all Muslims of the world should at least accept him as their religious leader. In these documents Abu'l-Huda argues for limiting such propaganda to a modest scale. Sayyadi was a prolific writer and published roughly sixty books starting in 1881, continuing until his death in 1909. Most of his books are about the Sufi *tariqa* (order of mystics, pl. *turuq*) of the Rifaʿiyya headed by Abu'l-Huda. Sufism rests on the premise that, besides studying the Qur'an and the sayings of the Prophet Muhammad, Muslims can come closer to God by particular ascetic practices and the regular reading of certain prayers in a ritualized way at weekly gatherings (the so-called *dhikr*). Abu'l-Huda devoted most of his writings to the description and definition of key terms, prayers, and rituals for the Rifaʿiyya. In addition, he encouraged the construction and renovation of Rifaʿiyya shrines all over Iraq and Syria, during a period that can be described as the renaissance in the history of the Rifaʿiyya.

This sudden success and expansion of the Rifaʿiyya soon led to polemical attacks from other mystical orders, especially the Qadiriyya. This *tariqa* has its center in Iraq, as did the Rifaʿiyya. The expansion of the latter immediately led to a loss of followers, income, and therefore influence of the Qadiriyya. The criticism directed against the Rifaʿiyya centred around two topics. First, it was doubted that the founder of the order, Ahmad al-Rifaʿi (d. 1182), was a descendant of the Prophet Muhammad (a so-called *sharif*). Consequently, the Rifaʿiyya would have had to be classified below the Qadiriyya, as its founder ʿAbd al-Qadir al-Jilani (d. 1166) had sharifian status. Second, the Rifaʿiyya is famous for its ecstatic rituals, practised during the *dhikr* where people in a trance walk over burning coals, drink poison, or push iron sticks through parts of their body without suffering any apparent harm. It was argued that these practices were un-Islamic innovations (*bida'*) and therefore this *tariqa* should not be followed. Most of Abu'l-Huda's writings in the late 1880s and the 1890s were devoted to defending the Rifa'iyya against these attacks. Among others, several books were produced about genealogy, in order to prove Ahmad al-Rifa'i's sharifian descent. They are the most frequently quoted works from Sayyadi's oeuvre. Obviously all of Abu'l-Huda's books were directed at the followers of the Rifa'iyya in the first instance. But, since they aimed at the expansion of the *tariqa* by winning over followers of other *turuq*, almost all Sufis of the Arab world at that time have to be included in his intended audience. It can be argued that Abu'l-Huda's writings targeted a mass audience, especially among the lower social classes where the Rifa'iyya was traditionally prevalent. Most probably the books were read aloud in Sufi lodges or at gatherings in the private homes of shaykhs, since the literacy rate was very low in the Ottoman Empire. The practice of reading books aloud in front of a bigger audience has a long history in the Middle East, as most teaching was oral until the twentieth century. Besides there is the tradition of reading tales aloud for the purpose of amusement in coffee-houses, which can be witnessed sometimes still today. The aiming of Abu'l-Huda's books at a mass audience can also be seen from a school-book by Sayyadi about the nature of Islam published in 1905.

The late nineteenth century was a time of rapid political and social change in the Middle East. The European colonial powers expanded their influence in the region, which led to the occupation of Egypt by Great Britain in 1882, among other things. In the late 1890s and after 1900, these powers increasingly supported the new ideology of nationalism in regions of the Ottoman Empire. This was a fundamental threat to the Ottomans, as their empire comprised a wide range of nationalities, whether it be those of the Balkans or Armenians, Kurds, and Arabs in what are today Syria, Iraq, and Turkey. From the 1890s onwards repeated rebellions and wars erupted in different parts of the Ottoman Empire, some of them leading to the separation of certain national communities from the Empire, particularly in the Balkans after 1900. Abu'l-Huda wrote several books after 1900 in which he addressed common themes of Sufi literature and linked them to the political reality he was experiencing. The translated passages below are from his two books *Hadiqat al-ma'ani fi haqiqat al-rahim al-insani* ('The garden of the meanings concerning the truth of human kinship') and *Hadiqat al-bayan fi hukm nau' al-insan* ('The garden of the clear explanations about the reigning of the human species'), which were published around 1903. The latter book was printed on the empty margins of the former, a common technique in Arabic manuscripts. In this particular case this technique was most probably used because *Hadiqat al-bayan* was the summary of the contents of *Hadiqat al-ma'ani* and another book published in 1903 under the title *Ruh al-hikma* ('The essence of wisdom').

The following passages are relevant for the study of the modern history of the Middle East in two respects. First, among the ideological trends in the Arab world of the late nineteenth and the early twentieth centuries mainly nationalism and Islamic reformism have been studied. The presumably opposing trends have received only little attention. Abu'l-Huda is commonly depicted as one of the outstanding key figures of these presumably opposing trends. A reading of his writings is therefore a valuable contribution to complementing our understanding of what was happening in the Arab world around 1900, a time which proved to be formative for its intellectual developments during the twentieth century. Second, the following passages offer an insight into the ways Sufi thinking can turn into political thinking. It is often thought that Sufism usually serves as a metaphorical refuge for those seeking to withdraw from the harsh realities of this world. Abu'l-Huda reveals that, on the contrary, Sufis actively took part in the political discussions of the Arab world around 1900, employing common concepts and symbols of Sufi thought in political statements.

Abu'l-Huda writes somewhat vaguely of 'tyrants and oppressors', obviously referring to the colonial powers and their occupation of Tunisia and Egypt in the early 1880s. He finished the manuscript *Hadiqat al-bayan* in 1899, so it can be assumed that the two other books *Ruh al-hikma* and *Hadiqat al-ma'ani* were written shortly before that date. The immediate reason for its strong anti-colonial tone seems to lie in the war between Greece and the Ottoman Empire, which was prompted by the Greeks after a quarrel over the control of Crete. Greece was defeated swiftly by the Ottomans. In the aftermath of this victory, the European colonial powers intervened, forcing the Ottomans to accept humiliating conditions in the peace treaty. It became clear that the Christian European powers would never allow any kind of political success to a Muslim power.

Texts

1. Passages from Abu'l-Huda's *Hadiqat al-ma'ani fi haqiqat ar-rahim al-insani* ('The garden of the meanings concerning the truth of human kinship')

Everything has taken its share from God's justice. The secret of growing is that the one who causes this growing is one [i.e. God]. In spite of their different colors, these plants drink from the same water. And look at the mysterious arrangement of things. You see a beautiful garden, the beauty of its flowers, decorated by its dew. The red leaves [petals] of the rose differ from other leaves, which are green. Their mingling shows that the difference in color does not hinder them from mixing and making one common appearance. And this difference in color resembles the existence of different convictions (*haqa'iq*). It is all right if the owner of the garden can interfere and turn all flowers into one color. But if he did not succeed in doing that, would his common sense make him pluck out from the colorful roses all which he is not satisfied by? Would he destroy the order of the garden, meaning the order which has been existing and came into being by the creating hands of God? If he did so, he would be an idiot.

Each occurrence has something opposed to it and each created thing has something resembling it. The one to whom there is nothing contrary and nothing similar is *the one, the unique, who never gave birth and was not born* [Qur'an 112: 2; i.e. God]. Therefore to everything positive something negative came into being. To daylight there is night, to summer winter, to warm cold, to shadow heat. So everything pleasant has its opposite and to its side there is something similar to it. We mentioned that the reason for the existence of strife is that right is on the side of truth and wrong is on the side of vanity. An example for the right being on the side of truth is the case of the occurrence of the prophets in their respective communities to guide them on the right way, reform their morals, and lead them to the way which brings them profit in this and the next life. Then groups of infidels, tyrants, oppressors, and aggressors opposed them. For this reason there were some among them [i.e. the prophets] who fought and killed the others, some were killed themselves, some implored God to lead them the right way and others turned their backs on their communities. So the prophets fought for God. Their fight was for the spread of the word of God, not for earthly purposes. It was an expression of their obeisance to God, which meant worshipping, improving the basic situation, and bringing profit to mankind, regardless of race, religious school, and character. He who deviated from the order of God, deviated into the fire. The second reason [for the existence of strife], i.e. the wrong being on the side of vanity, is the greed of the sons of this world, who instead of worshipping the Creator, worship that which is created and succumb to this world's vanities. In this they follow the moods of their desires and place their own race over other races or, superciliously, their soul over other souls. Then this wrong encounters its equals and discord arises, not harmony. Maybe one wrongdoer attacks a truth he considers weak, so he wants this truth to be annihilated. But even if this truth appears to be obliterated it is harbored in the heart of the common people as well as the elite. It is hidden away and the assailants cannot pry it [from their hearts].

In all this turmoil every individual has to act according to his reason in everything he does and says. Then he has to clean the opinions derived by his reason from avarices and tendency towards greed, so that he may avoid the desires of the soul and its reign/superiority. He may quell its agitation by contemplation and the deduction of an opinion. So if he notices that he is an oppressor he will stop it and will treat his human brother fairly, with justice and kindness. And if he were oppressed he would try to be patient and forgive his oppressor. The evil which is done to him, he would reciprocate with good, and he would act according to the morals of the prophets. If he could not do so he would have to act according to the Qur'an: *If someone attacks you, pay him back in his own coin* [Qur'an 2: 194]. But fear God that the agitation of your desirous soul should not lead you astray in aggression to an extent which is greater than the one you were given. If you show more aggression than you have received, then you become an oppressor yourself.

You see a small nation (*umma*) eating a handful and thanking God for it, and you see another, very large nation. So the eyes of one man or a small group of men fall on the small nation burning in greed. They start making up false evidence and proofs out of mere tyranny and aggression. So this large nation rises with its horses and men and the other nation gets defeated. They subjugate and chain them after they had been free, and they take away their belongings, as if they were a kind of booty. If everyone in this attacking nation knew the right of mankind and the reign of humanity, and if they internalized the righteous morals, which would stop them at the limits defined by God, which have to exist as common sense shows, would the members of this large nation then agree on the word of a single man or a small group who are guided by greed to conquer and humiliate a small nation, which is part of mankind as well? No! If this nation understood the holiness of this rule and the wisdom of this truth, it would return the speech of this seducer into his face by asking: If you and your family were living on a small field, and people from a big field attacked your family, and took away your safety and your rights and scattered all that you, your family and many of your friends represent and own, would you accept that and stay peaceful or not?

So the best thing which man (*makhluq*) can save in order to come close to God, besides his firm belief in Him, is his loving care for the creation of God and his support for it. The worst people are those whose zeal is devoted to their particular nationality and language. They ignore their broader nationality, which is mankind. Each individual has to care for this broader nationality by respecting the rights of the human species. So if we see an Arab despising all other nations and languages, we judge him harshly, just as we would do with a Turk, Persian, European, or Chinese and every human being Eastern or Western. So, if he goes on harming people, destroying their rights and burning their homes, we know that he broke from the bond of humanity and his nature became like the one of an irrational animal.

2. Passages from Abu'l-Huda's *Hadiqat al-bayan fi hukm nau ʿal-insan* ('The garden of the clear explanations about the reigning of the human species')

By summing up the two books we mentioned at the beginning [i.e. his *Ruh al-hikma* and *Hadiqat al-ma ʿani*] we left aside their inquiries. We only mentioned the intention of the wise meanings of the two books, so that the condition of the species may be put in an order, which keeps with the necessity of humanity, preserves the rights of mankind, and supports the fundamental freedom, which is given in the created world to humans. In this respect, the one who deals according to this duty is not opposed by the Qur'anic saying: *If your God had liked, he would have created mankind as only one people* [Qur'an 11:118]; meaning their unity of feeling, conviction, race and language or as mankind as a whole. There is the old saying: *There is nothing imperfect in God's creation* [slightly wrong citation of Qur'an 67: 3: *You do not see anything imperfect in God's creation*]. This means you have to act according to the necessary right of mankind, which means that it is impossible to unite people on one speech because of their different convictions, and it is not possible to gather them all for a common cause, due to their different opinions. But concerning their fundamental nature the Westerner knows that the Easterner is created just like himself from one common soul and that they are united by their genealogy leading back to Adam and their human origin. And the Easterner is aware of that, too.

5.4 Excerpts from *Üç Tarz-i Siyaset* ('Three Kinds of Politics') by Akçuraoğlu Yusuf, 1904
Barak Salmoni

Preface

Akçuraoğlu Yusuf[37] was born in the southern Russian town of Simbirsk on the Volga in 1876. His father died when Yusuf was only 3 years old, forcing the family to emigrate to Istanbul, the capital of the Ottoman Empire. Yusuf Akçura was thus one of the 'Outside' Turks who arrived in the Ottoman Empire from Russian lands and went on to popularize new concepts of cultural and national identity among Ottoman intellectuals in the decades before World War I.

While in Istanbul, Akçura attended the military academies of Sultan Abdülhamid II (r. 1876–1909). It was here that he read the works of the Ottoman litterateurs who had first brought to light a cultural Turkishness. This spurred him on, not only to write early articles about the Turks of Russia, but also to associate with students and junior officers, who ultimately established the Committee of Union and Progress, called the Young Turks in Europe. Subsequent involvement in banned Young Turk publications led to Akçura's internal exile to Libya in 1897. Fleeing to Paris instead, however, he sought the company of Young Turk elements there.

In Paris, Akçura continued his higher education, which was to have a profound and lasting impact on his political and ideological attitudes. As a student at the French École des Sciences Politiques, he attended classes on mass psychology and nationalism theory taught by renowned French intellectuals, such as Sorel[38] and Boutmy[39]. He studied also at the Sorbonne,

---

[37] Otherwise known as Yusuf Akçura or Yusuf Akçorin.

[38] Albert Sorel (1842–1906) worked as a French diplomat, a career that gave him unique access to the archives of the foreign ministry. Subsequently, he became a diplomatic historian. His monumental *Europe et la Révolution française* (8 vols., 1895–1904) surveyed the influence of the French Revolution in Europe. Applying to diplomatic history Tocqueville's thesis of essential continuity between the *ancien régime* and Revolutionary France, Sorel focused on the inevitability of European struggle for supremacy and the continuity of nationalist interests from one regime to another in France. The introductory section of this work has been translated as *Europe under the Old Regime* (1947).

[39] In addition to comparative constitutional history, Émile Boutmy wrote on the political psychology and national bonds of the British. A key work is his *The English People: A Study of Their Political Psychology* (1904).

attending lectures by Durkheim[40] and Seignobos,[41] amongst others. These European intellectuals emphasized the importance of societal collectives and national units as the motive forces of modern history and the contemporary world. Combined with Akçura's studies in the field of nascent Turcology, these experiences reinforced his conviction that Turkishness was a geographically broad ethnic phenomenon with contemporary political importance.

The readiness of the pre-1908 Young Turk movement to incorporate non-Turkish elements into a non-racial, non-religiously based Ottomanism began to hold little attraction for Yusuf Akçura. In 1903 he returned to Russia, where he worked as a teacher in Turkish schools, and was involved, to some degree, in the Russian Revolution of 1905. After the Young Turk Revolution in Istanbul in 1908, he returned to Ottoman lands, becoming a central pan-Turkist organizer and ideologue. Throughout the next decade he contributed articles to most major periodicals whose purpose was to nurture a sense of Turkishness among his compatriots that went beyond the confines of the Ottoman state.

After the Ottoman defeat in World War I, Akçura joined the Anatolian resistance led by Mustafa Kemal (later Atatürk). Simultaneously, he abandoned political interest in Turks outside the emerging state of Turkey. As a gifted historian, emphasizing the antiquity and high civilization of the Turkish race, he suited the intellectual mood of the new political order and gained official support for his views. He served in the Turkish Parliament into the 1930s, and became the head of the Turkish History Commission in 1932, continuing his work until his death in 1935. During this period he taught university-level history, and assisted in the writing of the Turkish Republic's first series of new history texts for middle and secondary schools. Additionally, he was a leader of the Turkish Hearth Movement.

---

[40] Together with Max Weber, Émile Durkheim (1858–1917) is considered one of the chief founders of modern sociology. Educated in France and Germany, he taught social science at the University of Bordeaux and the Sorbonne. Influenced by the positivist philosophy of Auguste Comte, he argued that the methods of natural science could be applied to the study of society: to support his theories he drew extensively on anthropological and statistical materials. He held that the collective mind of society was the source of religion and morality, and that the common values developed in society (particularly in primitive societies) were the cohesive bonds of social order. In more complex societies, he suggested that the division of labor encouraged cohesion, but that the loss of commonly held values led to social instability and disorientation of the individual. His important works include *The Division of Labor in Society* (1893, tr. 1933), *The Rules of Sociological Method* (1895, tr. 1938), *Le Suicide* (1897), and *The Elementary Forms of Religious Life* (1912, tr. 1915).

[41] The French historian Charles Seignobos (1854–1942) taught at the University of Paris and wrote many works on French and European history and civilization, including contributions to the series edited by Ernest Lavisse and Alfred Rambaud. A number of these are used as textbooks in France. Seignobos's most outstanding book is his *Histoire politique de l'Europe contemporaine* (1897). Noted for his clear and unbiased narrative, Seignobos emphasized political history rather than social and economic change.

Akçura wrote *Üç Tarz-i Siyaset* in 1904, after his return to Russia. It was published in the Cairene *Türk* and soon sent to Istanbul, where it attracted substantial and controversial attention. On the one hand, Akçura was attempting to answer a question that had long troubled Ottoman intellectuals: how can the Ottoman polity be saved territorially and politically, and furthermore, what must be done to return it to its position as a global power equal to Europe? On the other hand, he was the first major thinker within the Ottoman-Islamic milieu to assess policies of civic Ottoman patriotism and Islamic collectivism and find them wanting. Moreover, Akçura's voice was the first to suggest ethnic-based Turkism as an alternative approach to preserving the Ottoman state, an opinion explained by his experiences in Russia of the policy of cultural Russification for the sake of national unity. Furthermore, he studied in Europe at a time when racial nationalism appeared vindicated by a newly unified Germany which had defeated France in the 1870–1 war over Alsace-Lorraine, thereby also defeating France's civic model of patriotism. Indeed, Akçura's ideas are informed by his consciousness of contemporary Europe, and demonstrate his earnest efforts to arrive at a political-cultural solution to the Ottoman state's most pressing problems. As such, *Üç Tarz-i Siyaset* is a central text of Turkish nationalism.

Text

Üç Tarz-i Siyaset ('Three Kinds of Politics')[42]

In the Ottoman realms, I believe three chief political paths have been conceived and pursued since the desire awoke to gain power and progress through enlightenment from the West. The first was to bring into being an Ottoman nation through the unification and representation of the different groups subject to the Ottoman government. The second was the political unification of all Muslims under the government's management by benefiting from the Caliphate being in the Ottoman ruler's possession (that which the French call *Panislamisme*). The third was to form a Turkish political nationality based on race.

Of these courses, the first two had an important influence on the Ottoman state's general policies for a while; as for the latter, it was seen only in some editorialists' writings. [...]

The formation of an Ottoman nation is the only solution for preserving the Ottoman domains within their current borders. However, does the true power of the Ottoman state lie in preserving its current geographical shape?

---

[42] Translated from Yusuf Akçura, *Üç Tarz-i Siyaset, Ali Kemal'in buna Cevabi ile Ahmed Ferid'in Ayni Mevzua Dair bir Mektubunu da Havidir* ('Three Kinds of Politics, Including the Response of Ali Kemal to this and a Letter by Ahmed Ferid Relating to the Same Topic') (Istanbul: Matbaa-i Kader, 1911).

In the event of the Ottoman nation's emergence, there would come into existence a heterogeneous nation established upon freedom and equality of rights, based on the state's subjects belonging to different religions and ethnicities. Since they would unite with the thought solely of homeland (the Ottoman lands) and nation (the Ottoman nation), religious disputes and national differences would not persist. In this process, like Greeks and Armenians, Turks and Arabs too would dissolve [into one nation]. The Ottoman Turks who founded the state would be satisfied merely with the spiritual benefits of attributing their first leader's name (Osman) to the homeland and nation, and especially by seeing that the empire, which had come into being through the efforts of their forebears, was no longer falling apart. Maybe they would even be led to abandon the Ottoman name: in this free state, through the desire of the majority—most of whom comprised the formerly subjugated (Muslim and non-Muslim) nations—the Ottoman title that demonstrated the old subjugation could even be discarded. [. . .]

To say that in the emergent Ottoman nation the power and influence of the Turks and Muslims would not increase does not mean that the Ottoman state's strength would decrease. Our fundamental concern, however, involves the state's strength. This strength certainly would increase; a nation that is orderly and well bonded—in essence, to use the fashionable expression, forming a bloc—is doubtless stronger than an anarchic state whose inhabitants are in continuous disagreement and conflict.

However, the fundamental and important issue is whether or not groups belonging to different religions and ethnicities, which suffer inherent conflicts and struggle, can now be joined and intermingled.

It was seen above that this kind of experiment concluded in failure. Henceforth, in order to understand whether or not success is possible, let us review in some detail the reasons for the previous experience's lack of success.

1. The Muslims and especially the Ottoman Turks did not want this combining and intermingling. Their six-hundred-year domination would have ended legally and they would have descended to the level of equality with *reâyâ* [non-Muslim subject classes] whom they had been accustomed to viewing as subordinate during these years. As the most immediate and material consequence of this, it would become necessary to enfranchise the *reâyâ* in the civil service and military, which [Muslims] had heretofore almost monopolized. [. . .]

2. Islam would not desire [an Ottoman nation]. Since it is a powerful religion protecting its adherents' true interests from an entirely material and worldly standpoint and not accepting the complete and true equality of Muslims and non-Muslims, Islam would always relegate *zimmîs* (non-Muslims) to second class. [. . .]

3. The non-Muslim subjects would not want [it], since each of them had its past, its independence, and a government now glorified through recent progress. Muslims, and the Turks especially, had ended that independence and destroyed those governments. According to [non-Muslim] claims, they had witnessed mostly oppression not justice whilst under Ottoman sovereignty, contempt rather than equality, and affliction instead of comfort. Their property, and even at times their personal dignity and honor, had been trampled.

The Christian nineteenth century on the one hand has taught these [groups about] their past and present condition, their rights, and their nationalisms; on the other hand, it weakened their rulers, the Ottoman state. Some of their partially subjugated friends had even been able to gain independence. [...]

Perhaps some [of these peoples'] interests indeed favored the formation of an Ottoman nation. Yet, rather than considered reasoning, these [people] too were subject to their excited emotions. No one at all was amenable to forming a new nation by mixing and fusing together with a people they considered the executioner of their past independence.

4. The Ottomans' great enemy Russia, along with the petty Balkan governments—[Russia's] servants and advanced guard—also did not want an Ottoman nation. Russia was in pursuit of possessing the Bosphorus Straits, Anatolia and Iraq, Istanbul, the Balkans, and the Holy Land, and by these means, of reaching its political, economic, national, and religious goals. By taking the Bosphorus Straits, the Russian fleet would obtain a large and protected port like the Black Sea, and could exit freely into the Mediterranean, considered one of the most important international commercial [sea] lanes. Later, by launching forth whenever it wanted from fortified ambush, and by confronting the commercial and naval vessels of Britain—our era's keeper and protector of India—it would cut off the road to the United Kingdom's richest colony. In brief, Russia furthermore would surround the western approaches to India, upon which it had long focused its attention. By possessing Anatolia, it would assume control of one of the world's most productive and fertile regions, and by swooping down as far as Iraq, just as it had taken all of Western Asia, it would come to press even more against India's western gates. Perhaps it would even disturb in its own favor the balance in the age-old competition between Russia and England for [control of] the Islamic collective and the sacred Islamic lands. As a result, by acquiring the Straits and an important portion of Ottoman Asia, Russia would obtain enormous political and economic profits. [...]

The easy attainment of these goals depends on the weakening of the Ottoman state and continuing strife and conflict amongst the Ottoman subjects. Based on this, Russia would never be amenable to the formation of an Ottoman nation.

As for the Serbian and Greek states, which in those times had only just gained political life,[43] they would want to increase external perception of 'their fellow nationals remaining under the Turkish yoke'. Because of this, the existence of Ottoman subjects in a state of [legal] disparity would be necessary to their interests, and they would work for this.

5. A segment of European public opinion also opposed [Ottoman nationality]. This is because some of those who created European public opinion were still influenced by the Muslim–Christian religious quarrel and the legends of the Crusader Wars. Consequently, they hoped to liberate Christians from Islamic sovereignty so as not to have the Cross—even a small corner of it—under the Crescent, and to drive and expel infidels from European territory, the Christian country. Some [others] reasoned solely from the perspectives of humanity and science. They wished to save 'European nations, capable of all types of progress, from the yoke of the semi-barbaric, oppressive Turanians who appeared to have no other skills aside from war and struggle' and to drive away these Asiatics to the Asian desert whence they had come. [. . .]

The obstacles mentioned above have not been eliminated; they have increased and developed. The policies of Abdülhamid fueled the strife and antagonism between Muslim and non-Muslim. By gaining more independence, one segment of the non-Muslim subjects has increased the ardent desires of the others. Because Russia has gradually augmented its power and might, its deleterious effects on the Ottoman state have grown. The Serbian, Greek, Bulgarian, and Montenegrin influences also have manifested themselves, and European opinion has turned even more against the Turks. France, one of the most powerful proponents of the Ottoman nation policy, has become Russia's accomplice by losing the greatness it possessed in the era of the Paris Treaty.[44] In sum, both within and beyond the state, an environment has emerged totally inauspicious to the policy [of Ottomanism]. Based upon this, I believe it is futile to strive to form an Ottoman nation.

Let us now examine whether or not the policy of Islamic Unification would be beneficial to, or capable of, implementation in the Ottoman state. As implied above, this policy's implementation would necessitate increased religious strife

---

[43] Greece obtained independence by 1829, after a revolt, Ottoman suppression, and European intervention. Serbia became independent in 1878, while Bosnia was ceded to Austria-Hungary in that year. After stages of autonomy, Rumania attained independence in 1878; Bulgaria achieved autonomy in 1878 and declared independence in 1908. Much of this was decided at the 1878 Berlin Congress following the 1876–8 Russo-Ottoman War.

[44] The Treaty of Paris, signed on 29 March 1856, marked the formal end of the Crimean War, in which France and Britain had defeated Tsarist Russia. It demonstrated the latter two countries' regional pre-eminence, as they acted as the defenders of Ottoman independence and territorial integrity.

and enmity among Ottoman subjects, the loss of non-Muslim subjects and parts of the country occupied predominantly by them, and consequently, the lessening of the Ottoman state's strength.

Aside from this, in general, the Muslim/non-Muslim difference would intrude upon Turks, and the brotherhood born of race would be fractured by religious disagreement.

However, as opposed to these dangers, the corpus of Muslims in the administration of the Ottoman state, and consequently the Turks, would unite very closely with an extremely powerful bond. They would thus form a collective, an Islamic collective, which would be closer-knit than the 'Ottoman Nation', composed of differing religions and races. Because of this, it would be stronger in spite of its limitations of wealth, land, property, and numbers.

More important, the union and gradual strengthening of all the world's Muslims would facilitate the creation of a religion-based power able to preserve [its] existence among the great powers which would emerge with the Anglo-Saxon, German, Slavic, Latin, and perhaps even Yellow race's union. [...]

However, is the successful implementation of this form of policy possible in the Ottoman state?

Islam is one of those religions attributing great importance to political and social matters; one of Islam's basic rules could be expressed as the principle that 'religion and nation are one'. Islam eliminates the ethnic and national identities of those who are believers as it works for the removal of their languages, and desires to make them forget their pasts and legends: 'Islam is a powerful mill, in that it grinds up the members of different races and religions, and produces Muslims who are one in terms of religion and ethnicity, have the same rights, and are undifferentiated from each other'.

At its emergence, Islam had a strong, ordered political organization. Its constitution was the Qur'an. Its official language was Arabic. It possessed an elected president and a sacred central ruler.

To a degree, however, Islam also witnessed those changes experienced in other religions throughout history. As a consequence of racial influences, the political unity that Islam constituted was partially broken. Not even a century had passed since the Hicret [the migration of the Prophet Muhammad and his followers from Mecca to Medina in 622 CE, *hijra* in Arabic], when the manifestation of the Arab and Persian nationalities' antagonism in the mutual aversion of the Ummayad and Hashimite [Abbasid] dynasties opened an irreparable split in Islamic unity, causing the immense Sunni–Shi°i conflict. [...]

Later, the Arab and Persian elements were diluted with Turks, Berbers, and other groups. In spite of Islam's intense concern with equality, unity, and representation, the unity of ideas and policy within Islam was further spoiled, since these [groups] partially preserved their national urges and particularities [...] Before long, the Islamic Caliphate itself was divided into two and even three. It lost the unity of its official and religious language as well, since Persian rose to claim its rights as much as Arabic.

A time came when the Islamic powers began to descend toward a lowest point. As a segment of the Islamic lands, gradually its majority, and then even more than three-quarters, passed under the sovereignty of the Christian nations, the unity of Islam was entirely sundered.

Recently, in spite of Islam's desire, the tribal and national zeal which it had not been able to erase completely began to show its head, even if a little, with the influence of Western thought.

In spite of so many events impairing its strength, Islam is still quite powerful. One could say that religious doubt, or worse, unbelief, is not at all experienced yet by the ranks of Muslims. Almost all adherents of Islam are obedient people stirred with religious excitement, who would undertake any sacrifice for the religion, and whose religiosity is complete.

Although some Muslim states' new laws diverge from Islamic law, their [these laws] basis is still portrayed as Islam. Arabic is still the sole religious language, so much so that for the Muslims of many places it is the scientific and literary language. Further, Islamic *madrasas*—with some exceptions—still maintain the same curriculum with the same (Arabic) language. In short, it may be said that Islamic civilization continues with its original unity.

Every Muslim, before stating, 'I am a Turk' or 'I am an Iranian', still says 'Praise to Allah, I am a Muslim'. The greater part of the Islamic world still recognizes the ruler of the Ottoman Turks as the Caliph of Islam. All Muslims still turn their faces towards Mecca the Venerable five times a day, and run from all corners of the globe, while enduring all sorts of tremendous longings with total excitement and ardor, all to prostrate themselves before the Ka῾batüllah and kiss the Black Rock.[45] It should be repeated without fear that Islam is still quite powerful. Therefore, in the implementation of the 'Unification of Islam' policy, the internal obstacles are easily surmountable. External obstacles, however, are extremely powerful. In truth, on the one hand all Islamic states are under the influence of the Christian states. On the other hand, notwithstanding one or two exceptions, all Christian states possess Muslim subjects. Because these states view even the strong spiritual bonds of subject Muslims to foreign political centers as quite

---

[45] Located in Mecca in modern Saudi Arabia, the Ka῾ba is the spiritual center of Islam, and the shrine to which pilgrimage is made as part of the hajj. At its center is a large black rock around which Muslims circumambulate. According to traditional belief, it was placed there by Ibrahim and Isma῾il (Abraham and Ishmael), the original monotheists.

contrary to their own interests, and consider their service of a broad idea [such as Islamic unity] to have potentially significant ramifications, these states would want to hinder its occurrence in every way. They would be able also to fulfil this desire thanks to their influence and power over all Islamic states. Consequently, Christian countries would oppose, perhaps successfully, even the attempt of the Ottoman state, the most powerful Islamic state of our time, to implement seriously the policy of 'Unification of Islam'.

When it comes to the benefits in the policy of 'Unification of Turks', the Turks within the Ottoman realms would unify quite tightly with both religious and racial bonds—more tightly than with just religious ones. And, even though they were originally not Turkish, the remaining Muslim elements which had been somewhat Turkified would be assimilated even more to Turkishness. Moreover, the groups that had not yet been assimilated at all, but did not have a national consciousness, could also be Turkified.

However, the principle benefit is that this would aid the unification of the Turks—who share language, race, customs, and even, for the most part, religion, and who are spread throughout the majority of Asia and Eastern Europe. Thus, the Turks' formation of a vast political nationality able to protect their existence among the other great nationalities would also occur. Likewise, in this large collective, the Ottoman state would play the most important role, because it is the most powerful, developed, and civilized of the Turkish groups. And, between the white-skinned and yellow-skinned worlds, which will be fully realized in the somewhat distant future and that recent events bring to mind, a world of Turkishness will come into being. In this intermediate world, the Ottoman state would take on the duty that Japan desires to fulfil in the yellow-skinned domain.

Set against these benefits are the disadvantages of the departure from Ottoman hands of the non-Turkish Muslim peoples who live in the Ottoman lands and whose Turkification is impossible, as well as the future cessation of Ottoman relations with non-Turkish Muslims, since Islam would split into Turkish and non-Turkish components.

In comparison to the policy of Islamism, there are greater internal difficulties for the policy to unite the Turks. Although the concepts of nationalism may have begun to enter the consciousness of the Turks through the West's influence, as stated above, this phenomenon is still quite new. The ideas of Turkishness, Turkish literature, and the idea to unify Turks—all this is still a newborn child. Turkishness has none of the powerful organization of Islam, none of its fullness of life, or fullness of passion. In sum, Turkishness has almost none of the materials and facilities to bring a firm union into being. Today the majority of Turks are in a state of forgetfulness regarding their past!

Yet it must not be forgotten that in our time the great majority of those Turks whose union is possible are Muslim. For this reason, Islam could be an important element in the formation of a great Turkish nationality. Indeed, some of those wishing to define 'nationality' look upon religion as a factor. In order for Islam to be able to perform this service in the unification of Turks it must change in a manner that accepts the emergence of nations within it, just as happened only recently in Christianity. This change is almost obligatory: the general trend of our era involves races. Religions, because they are religions, are gradually relinquishing their political importance and power, and freedom of conscience is taking the place of religious unity within societies. By ceding the role as society's manager of affairs, religion has undertaken the guidance and mentoring of hearts, and has become solely the conscientious bond between creator and creature. Therefore, it is only through the union of religions with race, and through religions as buttressing and even serving ethnic groups, that they can preserve their political and societal importance.

As for the external obstacles, they are weaker in comparison to those facing the Islamist policy, because of the Christian states only one, Russia, has Muslim Turkish subjects. Thus, as mandated by its interests, only this country would work against the unification of the Turks. When it comes to other Christian states, it is likely that they may even encourage this [Turkish] policy because it is detrimental to Russian interests.

From the preceding observations these results follow: even if the creation of an 'Ottoman nation' brings benefits to the Ottoman state, it cannot be implemented. [As opposed to this], the policy directed toward the unification of Muslims and Turks contains equal benefits and drawbacks for the Ottoman state. As regards the matter of their implementation, it would be as easy as it would be difficult.

In such a situation, which strategy should be pursued? When I heard the title of the newspaper *Türk*, I had hoped that finally I had found the answer to this question that had always been troubling me. Considering its name, I had also thought that the answer would be the policy of Turkishness. But, I saw that the 'Turk' whose rights would be defended, his mind improved, his thoughts activated, was not, as I had supposed, any Turk from the peoples of the great race covering an important section each of Asia, Europe, and Africa, from Peking to Montenegro, from the Timor peninsula as far as the lands of the black-skinned [peoples]. It was only a Western Turk of the Ottoman state's subjects. *Türk* only sees them, only knows them, and also knows them only since the fourteenth century CE—and then according to the French sources. Consequently, at this time it only desires the preservation of their [Ottoman Turks'] rights against external nations, as well as subject groups who, whether Muslim or non-Muslim, are of different ethnicities. For *Türk*, Turkishness's military, political, and cultural past is only made up of Hüdavendigârs, Fatihs, Selims, Ibn Kemals, Nafis, Bakis,

Evliya Çelebis, and Kemals. It does not reach as far as Oğuzlar, Cengizs, Timurs, Beys, Farabis, Ibn Sinas, Teftezat, and Nuvais. [...][46]

In sum, the question—which heretofore has occupied my mind, and for which I have not been able to find a convincing answer, and which is still planted in front of me—awaits an answer: of the policies of Islamicness and Turkishness, which is more beneficial and capable of implementation for the Ottoman state?

Zeviye Köyü (Russia), 15 March 1904

[46] The author here contrasts Turks in Ottoman realms to those in the larger Turkic world. The first group refers to military, political, or intellectual leaders from Ottoman lands, such as Sultan Mehmed II (r. 1451–81) and Sultan Selim I (r. 1512–20), who conquered Constantinople and the Arab lands respectively, as well as the key Ottoman litterateurs Nafi and Baki. The second group encompasses a similar group of elites whom he views as Turkish, yet who lived outside of Asia Minor or were not Ottomans. These include the Central Asian Oguz Turkish tribal confederacy, the Mongol Ghengiz (Çengiz) Khan, Tamerlane (Timur), in addition to Islamic thinkers Farabi and Ibn Sina (Avicenna), to whom some attribute Turkish ethnicity.

5.5 Pan-Asianism in the late Ottoman Empire, 1905–1912

Renée Worringer

Preface

Around the turn of the twentieth century, the Asian continent was witness to sweeping changes: European imperial powers competed with one another to seize areas of Asia and Africa for colonial purposes. The Ottoman Empire was not immune to this Western encroachment; foreign governments occupied Ottoman territories in North Africa (Algeria, Tunisia, and Egypt) and the Balkans, challenging the suzerainty of the Ottoman sultan. Increasingly, Europeans became involved in Ottoman domestic affairs, both financial and political. Sultan Abdülhamid II (r. 1876–1909) responded to such circumstances with an international plea for pan-Islamic resistance to the West under his authority as the caliph of all Muslims. Ottoman intellectuals, journalists, political activists, and statesmen before, during and after the sultan's deposition sought ways to repel foreign intrusion and to learn from the West in order both to guarantee the survival of the empire into the modern era and ensure their acceptance as equals among the Great Powers. As the following sampling of the late Ottoman press reveals, the pan-Asian current was felt across the political spectrum.

Following its victory in the Russo-Japanese War in 1905, Japan came to represent both the triumph of the East over the West among citizens in the Ottoman Empire and the possibility of reversing the power imbalance. For the average citizen, such as the barber depicted in the comical Arabic anecdote [excerpt 1] written by the Egyptian litterateur Mustafa Lutfi al-Manfaluti (1876–1924), the Japanese victory was a newsworthy event that came up in daily conversation. To another observer, Abdullah Cevdet, Japan's prowess on the battlefield inspired patriotism and a feeling of solidarity with distant Asian brethren, even as he wrote in French [excerpt 2].[10]

Still others in the Ottoman Empire considered Japan to embody a pan-Asian agenda of resistance to Western imperialism that coincided with Islamic solidarity. Tatar and Crimean Muslim exiles from Russia poured into the Ottoman capital, where they often became spokesmen for modernization and the liberation of Muslims under non-Muslim rule. One

[10] Abdullah Cevdet was an Ottoman intellectual and Young Turk refugee in Europe who was among the founding members of the Committee of Union and Progress nucleus in the Ottoman Medical Academy in 1889. The Committee of Union and Progress, or CUP, was the political organ of the Young Turk movement to reinstate the Ottoman constitution. In 1908 they succeeded in doing so. Ultimately, the CUP became an official political party and controlled the Ottoman government with the same level of centralization as the autocratic sultan it deposed.

of these activists, a Tatar Muslim named Abdürreşid İbrahim, spent time in various regions of Asia (including the Ottoman Empire and Japan), where he operated as a direct link between Muslims and Japanese. Rumors soon began to circulate in the Ottoman and Arabic press that the Japanese were about to convert to Islam and thus spiritually unite the two ends of Asia.[11] İbrahim tended to propagate this rumor wherever he could, whether through his travels across Muslim lands or in his writings in Ottoman newspapers. The Japanese, interested in cultivating a dependable relationship with the Islamic world in Asia for future use, further encouraged this belief. In 1909 İbrahim's involvement with a group of Japanese elites called the Black Dragons (*kokuryūkai* in Japanese) culminated in forming an organization in Tokyo called the 'Asia Defense Force' (in Ottoman Turkish, *Asya Kuvve-yi Müdâfaası*; in Japanese, *Ajia Gi Kai*). This organization published a journal called *Daito* in Japanese (*Greater Asia*, or *Maşrık-ı Aᶜzam* in Ottoman Turkish). In 1911 the Islamic modernist Ottoman Turkish newspaper in Istanbul, *Sırat-ı Müstakim*,[12] published the Ottoman translation of the 'Asia Defense Force' society's official statement of purpose [excerpt 3].

While İbrahim was on his return trip from East Asia to the Ottoman Empire in 1909, one of his travelling companions was a Japanese man named Yamaoka Kotaro,[13] who met up with İbrahim in Bombay, India, converted to Islam, took the Muslim name Ömer, and accompanied İbrahim on the pilgrimage to Mecca; incidentally, he sent detailed reports back to the Japanese government about what he observed in Islamic lands. After spending time in the company of prominent Muslim figures in Mecca and Medina,[14] the pair stopped in Damascus in 1910 while on their way to the Ottoman capital. In Syria, they delivered speeches to an enthusiastic audience in an Ottoman Committee of Union and Progress clubhouse.[15] Their words were published the next day in Muhammad Kurd ᶜAli's well-known Damascene Arabic newspaper, *Al-Muqtabas* (also known as *Al-Umma*) [excerpt 4].[16]

[11] As one Ottoman newspaper put it in 1907: 'If the Japanese convert to Islam, they will be brothers to forty million Kitay [Chinese] and eighty million Indian Muslims, to Java, Afghan, Central Asia, Iran, Ottoman and Egypt's Islamic peoples. And in this manner Japan will exert political influence all over the Asian continent.' *Balkan*, 121 (19 Jan. 1907), 2.

[12] Turkish poet Mehmed Akif [Ersoy] edited the journal (later renamed *Sebilürreşat*). This journal represented the views of a group of conservative intellectuals who had disliked Abdülhamid II's absolutism as much as they resented Young Turk secularism that granted equality to non-Muslims.

[13] Surnames precede first names in the Japanese language.

[14] Including Sharif Husayn of Mecca.

[15] In Ottoman Turkish, *nâdî ittihâd ve Terakkî*. These clubhouses were meeting places for opposition cells across the Empire in the pre-revolution period. After the Young Turk revolution, they were used to elicit support from the local population for CUP activities.

[16] The Ottoman authorities closed down *Al-Muqtabas* repeatedly for its politically dissident views, and thus it frequently resumed publication under various pseudonyms. At the time of Ibrahim and Yamaoka's visit to Damascus, it was operating under the name *Al-Umma*.

Abdürreşid İbrahim co-translated a text from Japanese to Ottoman Turkish that was written by a Japanese convert to Islam and contributor to *Daito* named Hatano. The translation of his pan-Asian pamphlet, entitled *Asia in Danger*, included graphic photographs of atrocities committed by Europeans against people in Asia. It was published in Istanbul in 1912 and distributed throughout major cities in the Ottoman Middle East [excerpt 5]. İbrahim later presided over the opening of the first mosque in Tokyo in 1938. He died in Japan in 1944 while producing Indonesia-bound war propaganda for the Japanese.

Texts

The Chatterbox Barber

(Mustafa Lutfi al-Manfaluti, 'Al-Hallaq al-Tharthar', *Al-Nazarat*, 3, 6th edn. (1932) (Arabic))

He says some of his friends told him about a man who entered the barbershop of a barber well known for his nonstop talking, in the days of the Russo-Japanese war. The man sat in front of the mirror while the barber cut strange shapes in his hair. After he finished, the barber turned to the others sitting in the shop and said, as if finishing an earlier conversation, 'For the sake of explanation and settling the dispute between us, I drew for you a map of the Russo-Japanese war on the head of the customer. Here's Tokyo, and here's Port Arthur. And here Russia was defeated! And here the Japanese were victorious! And in this line the Russian fleet passed! And in this site the two fleets gathered!' At this point he started speaking zealously of the courage of Japan, and he said 'And on this site the Japanese struck Russia decisively, demolishingly!!' And he hit the center of the customer's head with his hand. The man stood up screaming and howling at his exposed head, and dashed out cursing politics and politicians, and Russia and the Japanese, and the whole of humanity. Al-Manfaluti ends by saying: 'I did not know whether the storyteller was joking or serious; what I did know was that he made a good performance.'

Japan, Carrier of the Torch

(Abdullah Cevdet, 'Le Japon porteur de flambeau', *İçtihat*, 5 (April 1905), 77 (French))

Japan has become more and more conscious of its high civilizing mission in Asia. Not only does it know to take some fortresses and conquer some regions, it also knows to open some new horizons, a radiant horizon for the minds of Asians bruised by infamous despots and their loathsome obscurity. We read in *The Times* newspaper an excerpt from the speech of Japanese Parliament's ex-president Okuma. We are pleased to reproduce the following passage from it: 'It is incumbent upon us that we who hold the banner of Asian civilization have the sacred duty of tendering a helping hand to China, to India, to Korea, to all the nations of

Asian civilization. They wish us, as their powerful friends, to free them of the yoke that Europe imposed upon them, and to show the world that the Orient can have a confrontation with the West on the battlefield.'

Today it is precisely 'the standard of the battlefield' which measures success in science, industry, and in all intellectual domains. We remember a Japanese officer who said something a little like this: 'The question of instruction and of education is a hair which is attached to a thousand other things; the teacher is the primary auxiliary of the conqueror, the teacher alone assures and sustains the success of the army.'

One can hardly say it better and it is far from being a 'yellow peril.' [...] Japan is therefore the carrier of the sword and the torch: the sword, for the oppressors, for the insolent invaders: the torch for the oppressed, for those that shine unto themselves and die for lack of light and liberty.

An admirable example to follow!

In Japan: *Daito* and the Asia Defense Force Society's Declaration

('Japonya'da *Daito*' Mecellesi ve Asya Gi Kai' Cemiyetinin Beyânnamesi', *Sırât-ı Mûstakim*, 6: 133 (3.1327/1911), 42–4 (Ottoman Turkish))

ᶜ[...] Because of the importance for all Asians of the Ajia Gi Kai's official declaration, we translate exactly, the following:

"Asia, which we inhabit, is filled with high and sacred ideas comprising a most important position in the world. It surpasses all the other continents with the vastness of its lands, the greatness of its mountains and rivers, the number of its peoples, the abundance and blessings of its harvest.

"For these reasons were born the oldest civilizations in Asia, the greatest ideas, they spread from Asia. But, sadly, today Asians are ignorant of one another, they are even enemies of one another. These rifts are the real reason for the Westerners' invasion of the Orient. If this reason cannot be understood and made to disappear, we should surely fear for the future of Asians. Asians, whose morals are proper, whose customs are admirable, whose nature is peaceful, whose ideas are sound, will naturally strive to improve and evolve Asia only by trusting in themselves.[17] Although we are assured of good results based upon this, we founded the Ajia Gi Kai society and, having public recourse to Asians, we welcome participation and cooperation."

At the bottom of the declaration were written the names of the fourteen individuals who are the original founders of the society. We congratulate the Ajia Gi Kai society, which is established for the purpose of service to Asians' independence and prosperity, for the publishing success of our affiliate *Maşrık-ı Aᶜzam*, and we beseech God that it be able to achieve its noble intentions.

[17] The expression could also be translated as 'having self-confidence'.

General Information about the Society's Activities

The society shall occupy itself with the following principal issues in order to preserve the present conditions of the existing governments in Asia and to secure their progress: agriculture, education, economy, colonies established geographically, national relations, politics, and military affairs.

The society's findings shall be published by its own journal.

The society shall establish local branches gradually in China, Siam, India, Iran, Afghanistan, Turkey, and important centers in Asia.

The society, in order to know for certain the present circumstances of the various countries on the Asian continent, shall conduct investigations by means of members whom it dispatches.

Society Regulations

Article 1: The society shall be called Ajia Gi Kai.

Article 2: The society's central administration has been formed, and in the near future local branches shall be formed in important centers on the Asian continent.

Article 3: Individuals who want to be registered as members in the society must apply to the central administration or to one of the local branches with the recommendation of two [current] society members.

Article 4: There is one director of the society.

Article 5: The society's officers are as follows: one director; councilors, an executive committee, and the terms of these offices is three years. It is possible to re-elect the same official.

Article 6: The councilors will be appointed based upon the decisions given in executive committee meetings.

Article 7: The society shall appoint a secretary and other officers as required.

Article 8: Councilor meetings happen as needed at the request of the executive committee.

Article 9: Every month the society's activities are communicated to the members.

Article 10: Regulations about the activities of local branches shall be organized at a later date with a more complete and extensive statement.

Article 11: There are three types of members.

Honorary members: Those famous people whose membership in the society would be an honor to the organization, and members of notable families.

Permanent members: They have paid up membership equivalent to twenty years.

General members: Members giving annual dues of five yen in advance are registered.

Article 12: Cash donations given to the society shall be deposited in a suitable, reliable bank, and incomes and expenditures shall be disclosed in the journal.

Article 13: Members must register in the society's special ledger. Rather than being given a receipt for membership fees, a notice will be placed in the journal.

Article 14: The society distributes its own publications to individuals who are members according to Article 11.

Article 15: Additional regulations shall be organized as needed concerning rewards and admonitions that appear as a result of members' activities relating to the society.

Japan and Islam

('Al-Yaban wa'l-Islam', *Al-Muqtabas* [*Al-Umma*] (18 February 1910) (Arabic))

[...] Brother ʿUmar,[18] of the Japanese who had converted to Islam recently, spoke in English. His [real] name was Yamakawabara (*sic*).[19] Dr ʿAbd al-Rahman Effendi Shahbandar[20] translated his words into Arabic, and Al-Yüzbaşı[21] Khalid Effendi al-Hakim translated his words into Turkish. ʿAbd al-Rahman Effendi al-Shahbandar introduced him by leading with the words:

'The Japanese know ways to benefit from modern civilization. Thus they grasped its truth and they disregarded corrupt characteristics, and after they studied the true essence of the sciences their attention turned to material things only, except that some among them found that [material things] alone are not sufficient to improve their affairs. They must have some religion, and thirty-five men converted to Islam. Their [original] religion was Buddhism; among them is the former Director of Education in Japan. They found that true religion and virtuous character raises the level of development, and that mankind must have some form of religion. [...] They found that [Islam] is beneficial to them. [...]'

Yamakawabara (*sic*) spoke:

'[...] Why did Islam not spread to Japan until now? Japan, after obtaining its freedom forty years ago, started imitating Europeans by way of their modern civilization. Most Japanese at that time did not think of advancing patriotic feeling in the Japanese nation; rather they thought about procuring material gains. Oh Brothers, what do you think about this dangerous feeling which grows in the minds of the Japanese? That an example of this strong feeling, built on profit only, reduces the value of Japan and obliterates its future. The wise of the nation must find that religion is the best treatment for this material predilection. [...]'

---

[18] The Arabic transliteration of this name is used here because the newspaper excerpt is from Arabic.

[19] This is a misspelling of Yamaoka.

[20] Shahbandar was a noted secularist whose Ottomanist leanings eventually gave way to a more Arabist orientation. By 1915 he was forced to flee Ottoman lands after being accused of anti-Ottoman activities and complicity with the British. He later played a prominent role in Syrian Arab politics.

[21] Ottoman Turkish term for the military rank of captain.

Shahbandar said in closing (in English and in Arabic):

'The Ottoman Empire is an Islamic empire but that does not suggest that the Christians and Israelites and Druze are not Ottomans. On the contrary! It is similar to the official religion in the United Kingdom, which is Christianity, and it gathers under its banner the other religions. Thus the United Kingdom is like the Ottoman Empire. It gathers them all in a single word, and that is "Ottoman" [...] we do not want to unite with Easterners just for aggression against the Europeans; but rather to save humanity.'

Asia in Danger

(Hatano, *Asya Tehlikede*, trans. Mehmet Hilmi Nakawa and Abdürreşid İbrahim (Istanbul: Sebilürreşat, 1912), 12 and 17 (Ottoman Turkish))

[...] All of these [peoples of Asia] can each form an ability, a basis, for an Asian alliance. In that case Japan's government would without hesitation not miss the opportunity, and at first should immediately conclude a China–Japan agreement; afterwards it would strive for treaties with the Ottoman, Afghan, and Siamese states. Persia, as it learns of this unity, will extend its own hand and take refuge. Junior members of the Indian government will immediately begin to dispatch secret representatives, perhaps without hesitation, and take refuge. Coming to the East Indies (Java), there they too understand the aim; enlightened men are not few, they will extend a hand of co-operation immediately to us. In order to establish an alliance such as this, before all else, there must be a prudent and sagacious guiding leader. They will never at any time conclude a sound agreement when always in competition with other governments. The Triple Alliance, considered relatively sound, is under the administration of an efficient manager like [Kaiser] Wilhelm. As for the Triple Entente, it is not considered sound, because it does not possess a reliable leader [...]

A Japanese–Ottoman alliance possesses more significance than a treaty with China because Japan and the Ottomans are like two citadels on each of Asia's flanks. If these two states were to conclude a genuine agreement, they could prevent every type of European activity in Asia, in spite of the present state of affairs, where the Ottomans occupy distinctly a lower position in the view of Europeans.

The Ottomans have desired an association with Japan for some time. Although negotiations for a treaty have been conducted, unfortunately every time they remain subjected to the opposition of the Christian states who seek in others' misfortune their own benefits, and who especially do not desire any progress among Muslims.

Unfortunately Japan's diplomats who don hats[22] were mindful of this resistance, and they did not dare to negotiate an alliance, the Japanese state not

---

[22] This phrase is intended to indict the Japanese state for its willingness to appear Western at all costs.

wishing to hear of European objections. Had [Japan] wanted successfully to negotiate an alliance with the Ottomans based upon international law and not upon Capitulations, the Ottomans without hesitation would have agreed, and they would have restored the greatest power for the unity of Asia.[23] If we [Japanese] had considered our own advantages with our own heads, if we could have seen the task with our own minds, the Ottomans would have been able to provide assurance in our political life. When required, we [by means of the Ottomans] could preoccupy the Europeans, the English in the Mediterranean [for example]. Behold, because we could not think with our own heads, we were not able to benefit from opportunities like this.

[23] During diplomatic negotiations between the Ottoman state and Japan in the late nineteenth century and throughout the first decade of the twentieth century, the Japanese government continually insisted upon being granted Capitulatory privileges in the empire as a prerequisite to any official treaty. The Ottomans consistently rejected this request, and as a consequence no formal alliance was signed until after the establishment of the Turkish Republic.

5.6 Armenian and Iranian collaboration in the constitutional revolution: the agreement between Dashnakists and Majlis delegates, 1908

Houri Berberian

Preface

A semi-official agreement was reached between the Dashnaktsutiun (Armenian Revolutionary Federation, an Armenian political party), represented by Rostom, and the Iranian constitutionalists made up of six Majlis (parliament) members led by Sayyid Hasan Taqizadeh. Meetings took place from 30 December 1907 to 4 January 1908. The Dashnaktsutiun was founded in 1890 in Tbilisi (Georgia) by three Russian Armenians: Kristapor Mikayelian (1859–1905), Rostom (Stepan Zorian, 1867–1919), and Simon Zavarian (1866–1913). Its simultaneously nationalist and socialist agenda advocated political and economic freedom for Armenians in the Ottoman Empire; a variety of political and social reforms, including a popular democratic government; elections; and freedoms of speech, press, and assembly. The party did not advance the independence or separation of Ottoman Armenian provinces from the Ottoman Empire, unlike the other major Armenian political party of the same period, the Hnchakian party, founded in 1887. The party's tactics and strategies included propagating party ideas, organizing fighting groups for defensive purposes, as well as targeting government officials and establishments, traitors, and 'all kinds of exploiters'. Furthermore, the Dashnaktsutiun, like the Hnchakian party, also advocated collaboration with non-Armenian subjects of the Ottoman Empire, specifically Kurds, Assyrians, Yezidis, and Turks. Like the Hnchakian party, it failed to realize this aspiration in any effective or lasting way, although its association outside Ottoman territories with Iranian constitutionalists is its most successful attempt. Both parties, especially the Dashnaktsutiun, established branches in Iran, specifically the north-western Azerbaijan province in the 1890s; it used Iranian soil as a launching ground for small expeditions into Ottoman territory and was involved in the transfer of arms, revolutionary literature, and fighters.

In order to comprehend the reasons behind Armenian commitment to the Iranian movement and the activities of Armenians in the struggle, it is imperative to be aware of the process of Armenian politicization in the late nineteenth century in both the Ottoman and Russian Empires. The Ottoman provinces with a large Armenian population became the focus of the

Armenian revolutionary movement in the late nineteenth century, while the Russian-ruled Caucasus became the source of this nationalist and socialist revolutionary movement. Starting in the late nineteenth century, certain segments of Armenian communities in the Ottoman and Russian Empires experienced a rising political consciousness and activism as well as an increasing level of education, especially in the Caucasus, which contributed greatly to the intellectual, cultural, and political development of centuries-old Iranian Armenian communities, through teachers, activists, and ideas crossing borders.

The combination of factors, mainly the existence of an Iranian-Armenian community undergoing a process of intellectual and political transformation, and the inflow of Caucasian intellectuals, political activists, and revolutionaries, laid the foundation for future action. However, such factors were not sufficient to warrant or explain the commitment made by the Armenian parties to the Iranian Constitutional Revolution. Political, ideological, and even practical concerns had a considerable influence over both the initial decision to participate and the continued commitment to the revolution throughout its tenure. Among the most important reasons behind Armenia's participation in the Iranian Constitutional Revolution were Ottoman aggression toward Iran; the coup of the Young Turks and the restoration of the 1876 constitution in July 1908, which prompted Hnchakists and especially Dashnakists to cease activities against the Ottoman government and to redirect their focus, to some degree, away from operations in Ottoman Armenian provinces to Iran; the perception by both Armenian parties of the revolution as a struggle against the domination and exploitation by Russia, which sought to stop the constitutional movement—a perception fueled by Russian persecution of Armenians inside Russia; the re-evaluation of policy by both parties, which questioned their overt nationalism and opened the way to greater attempts at solidarity and the internationalist ideals of socialism; the perception and depiction of the Iranian Constitutional Revolution as a stage in the socialist struggle, which necessitated collaboration with progressive forces, that is, with Caucasian and Iranian socialists; the period between December 1906 to December 1907 in Iran highlighted by the debate over constitutional laws and the radicalization of Tabriz, which demonstrated a new Iranian political reality and a new atmosphere of insecurity, causing the parties to rethink neutrality; and the Russian crackdown on dissidents beginning in 1908, which forced many political activists to flee from Russia and the Caucasus to Iran, where they embraced a new cause—the Iranian Constitutional Revolution.

As indicated by their many collaborative efforts, it seems the Iranians recognized the importance of having Caucasian Dashnakist fighters on their side, for they brought with them a great deal of experience and knowledge, as did most Caucasian revolutionaries joining the constitutionalist forces. Iranian constitutionalists worked not only with Dashnakists and Hnchakists but also with social democratic Armenians who had no ties to either party.

Neither the Iranian delegates nor the Dashnaktsutiun signed the following pact. According to Rostom, because the delegates held 'public and political positions, they avoided signing an agreement which is sealed with the representative of a revolutionary party'. Rostom asserted that he too did not want to sign the agreement in consideration of the position held by some Dashnakist members against participation, and that both sides were 'morally bound' as well as constrained by future circumstances to fulfil their promises.[24]

Text (translated from the original French)[25]

Due to the violation of the Persian border by the government of the Sultan[26] and the exceptional gravity of the consequences that could result, Vosuq al-Dawleh[27] (vice-president of the Majlis), Mostashar al-Dowleh,[28] Haji Amin al-Zarb,[29] Haji Mo'in al-Tojjar,[30] Taqizadeh,[31] and Haji Mirza Ibrahim Aqa[32] (deputy of the Persian Chamber) met at a conference with the representative of the Eastern Bureau of the Armenian R[evolutionary] F[ederation]; after long deliberations in sessions from 30 Dec., 31 Dec. 1907, 2 January, 3 January and 4 January 1908, they arrived at the following accord:

Whereas the populations of Persia and Turkey are equally interested in seeing a constitutional regime established and maintained in both countries as an indispensable stage in realizing the principles of solidarity of nations and in safeguarding the interests of the working classes,

[24] Rostom to Western Bureau, 10 Jan. 1908, Archives of the Armenian Revolutionary Federation, Watertown, Mass., File 1729, Document 2. [25] Source: ibid., file 583, document 41.

[26] All mentions of 'sultan' in this document refer to Ottoman Sultan Abdülhamid II (r. 1876–1909).

[27] Vosuq al-Dawleh was Tehran delegate and vice-president of the first Majles and later foreign minister. In 1911 he was part of the cabinet of ministers that yielded to the Russian ultimatum requiring the dismissal of the American finance adviser, Morgan Shuster and also suspended the Majles, which stood opposed to Russian demands.

[28] Mostashar al-Dawleh was Tabriz delegate to the first Majles and part of the interim government before the second Majles elections.

[29] Mohammad Hosayn Amin al-Zarb, a wealthy merchant and financial supporter of strikers in the early period of the constitutional revolution, was the merchants' delegate.

[30] Mo'in al-Tojjar was a wealthy merchant and delegate to the first Majles.

[31] Sayyed Hasan Taqizadeh was one of the most influential delegates and constitutionalists. He was Tabriz delegate and co-founder and leader of the Democrat Party, one of the most important political parties of the constitutional period. He was also part of the committee that wrote the supplementary laws to the constitution.

[32] Mirza Ibrahim Aqa was Tabriz delegate and head of the revolutionary *anjomans* (councils).

Whereas the government of the Sultan aims by its aggressive acts to create international difficulties, to divert popular energy from the interior struggle, and to stop in this way the revolutionary movement gaining ground day by day,

Whereas the normal functioning of the constitution in a neighboring country and in a coreligionist people contributes greatly to the extension of the revolutionary movement in Turkey, and because of this the Ottoman monarchy will see the necessity to discredit and also to overthrow the constitutional regime in Persia,

Whereas consequently the progressive parties in the two countries have an imperative duty to combat the policies of the government of the Sultan in all its manifestations,

It is agreed.

The Armenian Rev[olutionary] Federation undertakes:

1. To carry out in Europe propaganda in the interests of the constitutional regime established in Persia.

2. To inquire into the views of the French government on the Persian question and communicate to the Majles the information acquired. Profiting from our relations with the influential members of the French Chamber, to do all that is possible for us to provoke the intervention of France in favor of the integrity and independence of constitutional Persia.

3. To pursue the establishment of amicable relations between Persia and Bulgaria[33] with the goal of co-ordinating the policy of these two countries regarding the government of the Sultan.

4. To organize active resistance of all the elements hostile to the present regime of Turkey and to accelerate general revolution.

5. To render a Turkish–Persian war unpopular in Turkey through the use of propaganda and demonstrations.

6. To gain neutrality of all Kurdish tribes which are in friendly relations with the Dashnaktsutiun.

7. To favor the attachment of Caucasian Muslim elements and organizations to the cause in Persia.

8. To assist the Majles in its project to engage officers, including Caucasian Muslim ones, for the Persian army.

[33] Starting in the mid-nineteenth century, following the example of the Greeks, who had gained their independence from the Ottoman Empire by 1829, other Ottoman subjects like the Bulgarians sought autonomy from the empire. Russia seized the opportunity to intervene, and in the Treaty of San Stefano in 1877 Bulgaria, as well as Montenegro, Rumania, and Serbia, received independence from the Ottomans. The European powers, fearing Russian gains, called for the Congress of Berlin in 1878, whereby, among other changes, Bulgaria was returned to the Ottomans until 1912, when it and its Balkan allies fought the Ottoman Empire and regained independence.

9. To establish wireless telegraph in regions of war operations.

10. To procure heliographs[34] and specialists to handle them.

11. To assist in the organization of medical/sanitary services in the Persian army.

During war:

To provide one or two competent officers to the staff of the general of the Persian army.

To place at the disposal of the Persian army some specialists to handle devices of explosive material.

In general, besides revolutionary acts of the Armenian Federation-Dashnaktsutiun, the central committee of Azerbaijan in the name of the Federation undertakes to organize detachments, which are voluntary and co-operative with the Persian army, for guerilla warfare.

The Persian friends undertook on their part:

To provide to the Dashnaktsutiun safe passage to Persia and, in particular, Azerbaijan for the free transport of men, arms, and munitions.

To bring from abroad, at the Dashnaktsutiun's expense, arms and munitions of this organization and books to Azerbaijan to designated persons;

To fund in Azerbaijan a cartridge factory. To sell at cost to the Dashnaktsutiun arms, cartridges, cannon powder, etc. from the arsenals of the government.

To bring together the Persian inhabitants of Turkey, up to limits of possibility, in the work of general revolution.

While respecting the national rights enjoyed by Armenians in Persia under the monarchical regime, to broaden in the future and legalize all democratic institutions based on said rights.

To reserve tillable land called 'Khalesseh'[35] in Salmas or in surrounding regions for Armenian refugees.[36]

To insist in all opportune circumstances, especially in international conferences, on the necessity of the establishment of a constitutional regime in Turkey, in general, and the realization of autonomy in the Armenian provinces, in particular.

During war:

Beside general actions, to provide during war to Armenian detachments operating in Azerbaijan arms, munitions, horses, and means of existence.

Note: The articles concerning the statements on war will be compulsory after a later meeting.

---

[34] A heliograph is a signalling apparatus that reflects sunlight with a movable mirror to flash coded messages.　　　　[35] 'Khalesseh' refers to *khaliseh*, which were government-owned lands.

[36] The mention of refugees may be a reference to those Armenians fleeing communal violence between Caucasian Muslims and Armenians, which began in 1905 and continued in varying degrees until 1907. The violent clashes resulted in the death and injury of thousands as well as the plunder of hundreds of villages.

5.7 Excerpts from Ahmet Ağaoğlu's *The Turkish World*, 1912–1913
A. Holly Shissler

Preface

Ahmet Ağaoğlu (1869–1939), a Turkish-speaking Shiᶜi Muslim and scion of a wealthy landowning family, was born in the town of Susha in the Nagorno Karabagh region of Russian-ruled Transcaucasia. As a boy, he received a traditional Islamic education at home, including the study of the Qur'an and classical Arabic and Persian literature, and later attended Russian middle and secondary schools. In 1888 he traveled to Paris, where he enrolled as a student of ancient Iranian language and literature at the newly founded École Pratique des Hautes Études. In 1894 he returned to Transcaucasia, ultimately settling in the booming oil town of Baku.

From the time of his return to Transcaucasia, Ağaoğlu was very active in the political life and cultural debates of the Muslims in Russia. He became an important figure in the great 'Azerbaijani Awakening', or cultural and political renaissance of that period, writing numerous articles and pamphlets on topics such as educational reform, constitutionalism, the question of the proper position of women in Islamic society, the training and role of religious leaders, Sunni–Shiᶜi relations, and Armenian–Turkish relations. Prominent both as a publicist and a political leader in the period of the Russian Revolution of 1905—during which he fiercely advocated the rights of the Muslim community of the Russian Empire, and particularly of Transcaucasia—he was forced to flee to the Ottoman Empire in 1909.

The first decades of the twentieth century in the Ottoman Empire were characterized by an atmosphere of crisis arising from substantial losses of territory, fiscal collapse, and constant threats to the integrity of the remaining parts of the empire both from separatist movements within its borders, and from foreign intervention and external aggression. At the same time, the 'Young Turk' Revolution of 1908 encouraged a mood of optimism and a sense of possibility with the reinstatement of the constitution and the easing of press restrictions. In this context, Ottoman intellectuals and statesmen engaged in passionate debate about how to save the empire. Their discussion focused on two large issues: first, the nature and prerequisites of 'progress', which was understood to refer to the acquisition of science and technology for military and industrial ends; second, the proper composition of the Ottoman polity and bases of legitimacy for the Ottoman state. The main subject for consideration was what types of political institutions to adopt, and how to engender popular loyalty to the

Ottoman state. Not surprisingly, many thinkers saw these two problems as interconnected.

In 1911 Ağaoğlu entered the debate and, together with other intellectuals, founded a cultural society, the Turkish Hearth, to promote Turkish culture and Turkish nationalist sentiment. This was a somewhat tricky proposition, as the Ottoman Empire contained a wide variety of ethnic and religious groups. Many Ottomans, even those of Turkish ethnicity, were not eager to think of themselves in such terms. Shortly after its creation, the Turkish Hearth established a journal, *Türk Yurdu* ('Turkish Homeland'), which rapidly became very influential and was widely circulated in both the Ottoman and Russian empires. The following extracts are from the sixth part in a series of eight articles entitled *The Turkish World*, written by Ağaoğlu and published in *Türk Yurdu* between 1912 and 1913. This journal was to contribute, in part, to the transformation of the once pejorative term *Türk* into a positive dynamic of cultural identity.

The series first discusses the geographical extent and history of the Turks, before addressing itself to the comparative weakness of the Turkish world vis-à-vis the West, and the various strategies for reform and renewal. Part 6 is particularly concerned with the political ideologies of Islamism and nationalism, and their relation to one another.

Text

The Turkish World: Part 6

(Ahmet Ağaoğlu, 'Türk Âlemi 6', *Türk Yurdu*, 1/10 (1328 AH; 1912/13 CE), 292–7)

1. In our last article we stated that the exponents of the Islamist current of thought are compelled to accept and acknowledge that the nationalist current is a very natural and legitimate actor. But at the end of the same article, we also wrote this sentence: 'Here there is a question that can be asked of yours truly on their part (that is on the part of the exponents of the Islamist current) that is quite important and justifiable. That question is this: "What if the nationalist current and feelings of racial solidarity[47] were to take on a form contrary to religion and to Islam?" ' We delayed answering that question until today. [...]

8. And so, now we will answer the above question. But in order that the views we set forth might be understood well and in detail, let us first define what nationalism is. Once this word, which is very important and at the same time very broad, has been understood, quite a number of misapprehensions can easily be eliminated. [...]

---

[47] 'Race' and 'racial' are used here in the broader nineteenth-century sense of a 'people' or 'nation', as in the 'English race', rather than in the later pseudo-scientific and color-based sense.

12. In our opinion, the French sage and famous writer Ernest Renan has put forward a meaning that explains the word 'nationalism' in the simplest and best way in his famous article, 'The Question of Nationality.'[48] [...]

15. Renan says: 'Nationalism is the result of the lullabies that people heard for the first time on their mother's lap; of the babble they uttered when first they began to speak; of the words they were unable to pronounce successfully having babbled away for many a long month; of the prayers and legends they eagerly listened to and learned from their nurses, grandfathers, great grandmothers and great grandfathers; of the prayers in which they bent their knee for the first time; of holidays they celebrated, having awaited them with burning anticipation; of the customs and traditions peculiar to their milieu; of the streets on which they grew up; of the games that they played; of the schools they successively attended; of the tableaux which their surroundings showed them; of the marks which these tableaux left on their minds; of the history that their forebears lived through; of the spiritual and material ties which bind them to other people in their milieu.' [...]

26. If this definition is summarized, it can be said that the essential factors [that contribute] to nationalism consist of these: first, language; second, religion, customs, and convictions; third, a common history, fatherland, and destiny. [...]

28. This means that religion is one of the most important foundations of nationalism. The reasons for this are quite simple and clear. For binding people to one another, especially in the days of nomadism,[49] religion is one of the largest and most effective forces; and indeed, after language, it is a unique factor. All the nations that are alive in the world, and that today have achieved the highest level of development in terms of nationalism, were constituted first of all on the basis of religion, on the basis of the unity of religion. Religion always plays the role of leaven in the formation and establishment of nationalities and ethnicities. Indeed, religion has a great effect, an effect of the first order, even on the establishment of the national language, of the national customs and convictions, of the national mode of thought, of the national way of life. That the nationality and ethnicity—the becoming one—of the French, who are today seen as atheists, were brought into being through the effects of the Catholic religion is beyond any question or doubt. There is no doubt that the Catholic religion was the first factor in creating a single entity by blending together the various and sundry nations inhabiting France, starting with the Greeks through to the Germans. Yes,

---

[48] The original author's note simply says: '*Question de Nationalité*—Er. Renan.' However, I have not been able to locate a work of this title by the French theologian and Philosopher Ernest Renan (1823–92), nor have I come across a passage that is substantially similar to this in his other works.

[49] Here Ağaoğlu is referring to the belief that human societies move through stages of development, from primitive hunter-gatherers, to nomadism followed by barbarism, concluding with civilization.

in later times, a number of other factors did also have an impact on the development and activities of the French nationality and ethnicity, but Catholicism was the primary leaven in this process. [...]

43. Now, let us turn to the Turks. The fate of the Turks in historical times has been inextricably and unbreakably bound up with the fate of the Islamic world. We are not going to give attention to the periods and civilizations of Karakorum and Baikal[50] here; it is difficult to talk about them in any case because, unfortunately, those periods are still cloaked in such uncertainty that it is not possible to advance any theory at all about them based on the limited information at our disposal. Only one thing is certain and incontestable: the history of mankind identifies the Turks most of all with Islam. Even we cannot imagine or picture ourselves any other way. From the day we erupted into western Asia we have identified ourselves with Islam: the former life has been forgotten by us. [...]

52. For the Turks, Islam has acquired a national, racial character in the fullest sense. Anyway, [the situation] with respect to time is this: Islam is still completing its thirteenth century [of existence], while the Turks, for their part, are completing their eleventh century as Muslims. The Turks did not surrender to the sword; [rather] they gained Islam thanks to victories and conquests. No Muslim commander, having vanquished the Turks, forced them to accept Islam. On the contrary, after they had conquered the Islamic peoples and lands, the Turks accepted Islam of their own inclination and wish. It is a common error accepted by history that Ghazan Khan[51] introduced the Turks to Islam: Islam had honored them before him. Ghazan Khan himself, having been drawn into this common stream, simply gave it an official character. Considerably prior to Ghazan Khan's appearance on life's stage, Turkish concubines had been introduced into the palace harems of the Abbasid Caliphs, and young Turkish warriors, brought from Turkistan for the protection of the Caliphs, defended the abode of the Caliphate from the attacks of the Samanids, the Tahirids,[52] and others. [...]

66. The first Turkish tribe to erupt into western Asia and therefore into the territories of the dominion of the Islamic Caliphate, having gathered around Mahmud of Ghazna, went all the way to India to spread Islam and enlarge its compass, and established Islam in India on a permanent footing. The Seljuk[53]

---

[50] The author here refers to the early history of the Turks in inner Asia.

[51] Ghazan Khan (r. 1295–1304), a member of the Ilkhanid Dynasty established in Iran as a result of the Mongol invasions, converted to Islam and was responsible for making it the state religion.

[52] The Tahirids ruled in Khorasan in the ninth century and the Samanids in Transoxiana from 875 to 998. Though nominally provincial governors of the Abbasids, in fact they functioned as independent dynasties.

[53] The Seljuks were a Turkish tribal confederation that entered the central Islamic lands early in the eleventh century and quickly carried all before them. The Seljuk Dynasty lasted from 1038 to 1194, and they entered the city of Baghdad in 1055.

period followed the Ghaznavid[54] era, giving solidity and luster anew to the Caliphate, which had fallen into disintegration and decline, and been reduced to petty kingdoms. On the one hand, in the east, they restored peace and tranquility and strengthened Islamic unity; on the other hand, in the west, (that is in Egypt and Asia Minor), they opposed the Crusader tide, and for centuries fought to protect and defend the Islamic world. Later, the Ottomans succeeded the Seljuks, that is to say, the same nation under two different names. [. . .]

77. It is a quite important and striking fact that, while the Turks were protecting and defending the Islamic world in Asia and Africa as well as—having advanced straight north-west—injecting Islam into the center of Europe, Islam, which existed at the other end of Europe and in a place the Turks would be unable to reach, namely in Spain, was completely wiped out by the Christians. So much so, that today there does not remain so much as a mark or a trace of Islam in that region. [. . .]

82. In short, during nine hundred years of the thirteen-hundred-year history of Islam, the Turkish nation has taken upon its own shoulders the duty of defending, guarding, protecting, and preserving the Islamic world. A nation that has made an idea, a principle, [or] a religion its polestar for so long, would have earned amply the right to label that idea, that principle, [or] that religion with its own national name: this is not only a right, it is at the same time an obligation. For the Turks, Islam is not merely a religion: it is, at the same time, a national, racial religion. If today the Germans can regard Lutheranism as an ethnic or national religion, and the English Anglicanism, and the Russians Orthodoxy, then a thousand times more justly can the Turks so regard Islam. [. . .]

91. That is to say, that among the Turks, like it or not there is no help for it, those who are caught up by the nationalist current are compelled to accept the Islamic current, albeit in the name of nationalism; they will deem Islam an immovable pillar of nationalism. [. . .]

94. Nationalism cannot remain merely an abstract idea or inclination; it also has an applied form, and the real nationalist current consists of those applications. The supporters of the nationalist idea naturally will want to give a national color and spirit to all the affairs of life, but whence will they draw the raw materials and inspiration for that national color and spirit? It is self evident that [these will be drawn from] the nation; and for this they will study the language and history of the nation, its natural social, political, and economic structures, its traditions, the literature and ideals of [its] common people. And so, in this way they will strive for the introduction of the national elements that are available

[54] The Ghaznavid Dynasty (977–1186) took its name from its capital city, Ghazna, located in modern-day Afghanistan. Its most famous ruler, Mahmud (998–1030), carried out many successful campaigns into the Indian subcontinent.

into all the business of life, and for the arrangement of the lives of the people on [the basis of] these materials and [sources of] inspiration. As we submitted above, however, there is no element pertaining to Turkish life but that it has been influenced and subjected to profound alteration by Islam. Whichever way we turn, we will find a strong imprint of Islam. It is strange, is it not, that today there remain among us no more than ten or fifteen names that are pure Turkish names, and women's names especially are very limited. This is a *fait accompli*. Even those who wish to study and understand the Turk first must study and understand Islam. Anyway, this has come to pass not amongst us alone; it is so amongst other nations as well. Those who are exponents of nationalism have almost always been exponents of religion. Those of our partisans of nationalism who have come out against religion have not studied and examined what nationalism is, at length and in depth; they are deceived in their own feelings, in their own way of thinking. He who repudiates the religion of a nation, its fundamental spirit and life, cannot be a partisan of that nation. Such people can be free thinkers, cosmopolitan, progress-loving, freedom-loving, and even patriotic, but they cannot be partisans of nationalism. To be a partisan of nationalism means accepting the nation as it is, that is, together with its language, its literature, its customs, its religion, its social, political, and economic structures. Just as it is not possible to be a partisan of a nation while repudiating the language, history, and customs of that nation, so it is not possible to be a partisan of that nation whilst repudiating its religion. In short, insofar as its character, a nation is a single unity, an indivisible whole: it cannot accept division or dismemberment [. . .] But, does accepting a nation's religion mean accepting the ignorant fanaticisms, silly customs, harmful usages, old wives' tales and legends which exist in the nation under the rubric of religion? [. . .]

125. We will give an answer to this question in our upcoming article.

5.8 Sephardic Zionism in the Ottoman Empire: 'The Time is Here', *Ha-Herut*, 1 April 1914[55]
Abigail Jacobson

Preface

The article 'The Time is Here' was published in the Sephardi Zionist newspaper *Ha-Herut* on 1 April 1914.[56] The author of the article is Haim Ben-Atar, the editor of the newspaper. *Ha-Herut* was published in Jerusalem between the years 1909 and 1917, and was closed down in April 1917 by the Ottoman government. Nonetheless, it was the only Jewish newspaper that was published in Palestine throughout most of World War I.[57] The early version of *Ha-Herut* was a Ladino[58] newspaper, *Al-Liberal*, which was published after the 1908 Young Turk Revolution.[59] *Ha-Herut* was not conceived as a newspaper aimed exclusively at the Sephardi community, but as a Zionist-national paper for the entire Jewish population in Palestine. It was obvious, however, that Ha-Herut's founders regarded the newspaper not only as a platform for the Sephardi community but also as a means for the expression of the community's political views and its participation in public life in Palestine. As such, the newspaper's writers represented the young intelligentsia in the Sephardi community of Jerusalem.[60]

Ha-Herut focused on several issues, among which were future relations between Jews and Arabs in Palestine and the question of loyalty to the Ottoman Empire. The newspaper usually expressed pro-Ottoman views, and encouraged foreign residents among the Jews in Palestine to become Ottoman subjects officially.[61] The discussion regarding loyalty to the

[55] This document is taken from a paper entitled 'Ashkenazim, Sephardim and Jewish–Arab Relations in Pre-World War I Palestine', which was written under the guidance of Professor Holly Shissler and Professor Rashid Khalidi from the University of Chicago.

[56] The Sephardi community was dominant among the old Jewish community in Palestine. It included Jews who immigrated to Palestine from Islamic countries, North Africa, the Balkans, Anatolia, and the former Andalusia, as well as indigenous Jews.

[57] Yitzhak Bezalel, 'On the Uniqueness of "*Ha-Herut*" and on Haim Ben Atar as its Editor', *Pe'amim*, 40 (1989), 134–5 (Hebrew).

[58] Ladino is a dialect of Spanish, combined with Hebrew words, which is spoken by Jews who originate from Spain and Portugal.

[59] The Young Turk Revolution (1908) marked the second constitutional period in the Ottoman Empire (1908–22). The revolution was led by the Committee of Union and Progress (CUP), which initially carried out reformist ideas for the future of the Ottoman Empire.

[60] Bezalel, 'On the Uniqueness', 127, 129.

[61] ibid. 137–9. Most of the European Jews who immigrated to Palestine since 1882 as part of the Zionist immigration waves (*Aliya*) kept their European citizenship. As foreign citizens they enjoyed various privileges that were granted to them by the Ottoman government (as part of the Capitulations system).

empire conveyed the complex identity of the Sephardi community in Jerusalem. Most of the Sephardi Jews were Ottoman subjects and thought of themselves as loyal to the Ottoman Empire. Alongside this Ottoman loyalty, the reading population of *Ha-Herut* was also defined by the editors as Zionist, Jewish nationalist.[62]

The article 'The Time is Here' addressed the question of the Ottomanization of recent Jewish immigrants to Palestine, and called for co-operation between Jews and Arabs in Palestine for the development of the country. The context of this essay was the Ottoman decision to ease the process of granting Ottoman citizenship to Jews who wished to immigrate to the Ottoman Empire. Previous Ottoman opposition to Jewish immigration to Palestine gradually became more moderate. The change in policy may be explained by the Ottoman defeat in the Balkan Wars and the empire's need of financial support from anyone, including Zionist and Jewish sources.[63]

Text

Selected excerpts from 'The Time is Here'

To date, our Arab enemies have claimed that the Jews immigrate to Palestine in order to exploit its inhabitants without adopting Ottoman citizenship.[64] Many Muslim leaders in Jerusalem expressed their fear of the foreign Jews who arrive in the country and remain [here] under the protection of foreign governments, do not adopt Ottoman citizenship, do not learn the language of the state and do not take part in the duties of the homeland. [. . .][65] But these people [who criticize the immigrants] forget that many [Jews] wished to adopt Ottoman citizenship but were prevented from doing so by the [Ottoman] government itself. [. . .]

Anyway, now we all have to be truly happy with the decision taken by our enlightened government, according to which the number of Jews who wish to become citizens here [in Palestine], and to work hand in hand with the inhabitants of the country for the development of the mutual homeland and its true success, will increase.

[62] Zionism is the movement of Jewish national revival and independence of the Jewish people in Eretz Yisrael (the land of Israel). Modern political Zionism originated in Russia, from which the first wave of immigration to Palestine began in 1882.

[63] Neville Mandel, *The Arabs and Zionism Before World War I* (Berkeley: University of California Press, 1976), 141–2.

[64] The words 'citizen' (*ezrach* in Hebrew) and 'subject' (*natin* in Hebrew) are used in the text interchangeably in relation to the legal status of the Jews in the Ottoman Empire and Palestine.

[65] The writer refers to Jewish immigrants who held foreign citizenship and were dependent on the protection of European consulates in Palestine under the privileges of Capitulations (see n. 61 above). It is also worth noticing the use of the word 'homeland' (*moledet* in Hebrew). The use of this word may allude to the ongoing discussion among the Young Ottomans regarding the question of *vatan*, Ottoman homeland.

Our government realized that Palestine could not become a true success as long as its gates are closed for the Jewish immigrants who are able to develop it.

Now it is time to fulfill the great duty [of serving the Ottoman Empire]. The destiny of our community is in our hands. It is not enough that the majority of the inhabitants in Palestine would be Jewish.[66] The important factor is that the number of Jews who live in Palestine would be Ottoman. This is the main basis for our settlement in the country, and the essence of our success, which can help us, our country, and all of its inhabitants. [...]

We have to show to all the Nashashibis, Husaynis and Khalidis[67] that we do not wish to exploit the people of the country [*am ha-Aretz*, in Hebrew. It can be understood in the context that the author means the Arabs who lived in the country]. [...] We wish to work and live side by side with our neighbors for the promotion of the economic conditions of our empty[68] country, and for the development of the culture and education in the country. [...]

[66] This is a strange sentence. The majority of the inhabitants in Palestine were not Jewish but Arab, and the Jews were the minority in Palestine during that period. It is not quite clear why Ben-Atar indicated that the Jews were the majority in Palestine.

[67] These are some of the elite Muslim families, which the Sephardi wished to convince of the good and sincere intentions of the Jews in Palestine.

[68] The word 'empty' here is probably used metaphorically, and means empty in the cultural, spiritual sense, not in the geopolitical sense of the word.

5.9 Interview with Boubeddi Ben Ayyad, a Moroccan World War II veteran of the French Army, 1999[69]

Moshe Gershovich

Preface

France's involvement in Morocco lasted forty-four years (1912–56), during which time, together with Spain, it was entrusted with the 'protection' of the North African kingdom. The unofficial French intrusion into and military conquest of Morocco began in 1907 and lasted twenty-seven years, ending in 1934 with the complete 'pacification' of the last ridges of the High Atlas Mountains.

The French conquest and subsequent occupation of Morocco's rural countryside relied heavily on the use of native Moroccans. All in all, the number of Moroccan soldiers enrolled within the ranks of the French Army between 1908 and 1962 surpassed 170,000. Many of them were dispatched outside their country and fought for the defense and liberation of France in World Wars I and II respectively, as well as in other theaters of operation where the tricolor had once flown. In resisting French colonialism as well as while fighting for its cause, Moroccan warriors demonstrated courage, endurance, and loyalty that won them the respect and trust of their former adversaries and subsequent comrades-in-arms.

Who were the men who tied their lot in with that of their country's colonial masters? Where did they come from? What led them to join the ranks of the French Army? How were they treated while wearing French uniforms? What circumstances led to their discharge? How were they reintegrated within Moroccan civil society? What effects did their military careers have on their lives and on their communities? The answers to these questions may be as numerous as the number of veterans questioned. Yet, some common denominators can be extracted when specific biographies are juxtaposed with others.

The life story of Boubeddi Ben Ayyad has much in common with those of other veterans interviewed in Morocco,[70] while revealing a unique

[69] While preparing this document I received the news that Mr Ben Ayyad had passed away in 2001. He had apparently moved to France, where he petitioned for naturalization. While there he went to the hospital to receive further treatment of his wartime wound. The doctors discovered some shrapnel remains in his stomach and decided to operate. Mr Ben Ayyad died during the operation. May this document serve as a modest memorial to his life, and to the thousands of Moroccans who shed their blood for France.

[70] My research project, entitled 'Serving the Tricolor: Moroccan Soldiers in French Uniforms' has been partially funded through a Fulbright Senior Scholar Grant in 1998–9. I wish to thank the

8. Mr Ben Ayyad, c.1999

quality that merits the selection of his account to represent the entire group. Mr Ben Ayyad was born in 1917 and served in the French Army between 1936 and 1942 as a rifleman (*tirailleur*). Almost half of his military service was passed in a German POW camp, an experience that he vividly recounts below.

My interview with Mr Ben Ayyad took place in September 1999 at his home in Khemisset, a mid-sized city on the eastbound route from Morocco's capital of Rabat to the interior cities of Meknes and Fez. My friend Brahim, an electrician at Al-Akhawayn University in Ifrane where I was teaching at the time, introduced me to Mr Ben Ayyad. While working on his professional degree, Brahim used to rent a room in Mr Ben Ayyad's house and developed a close relationship with him and his family. Upon hearing of my oral history project involving Moroccan war veterans of the French Army, Brahim insisted that I must come with him to meet his former landlord. Our interview lasted more than two hours, a significantly longer duration than the twenty–thirty minute sessions I would typically spend with other veterans. Mr Ben Ayyad had been blessed with a crisp memory and vivid presentation that became apparent as he was recounting his life story, particularly those agonizing years he had spent in captivity. Later, I arranged for the recorded interview to be fully transcribed and translated.[71] The text presented below is based on that transcription

Moroccan–American Commission for Educational and Cultural Exchange for its assistance during my stay in Morocco.

[71] I wish to thank my former student, Adil Serghini (MA, Al-Akhawayn University in Ifrane, 2001) for helping with the translation of the French-Arabic original text in to English. However, all responsibility for mistakes that may have occurred while translating the text rests with me alone.

with minimal editing and a few footnotes to facilitate the understanding of the text.

Text

Q: What can you tell us about your family and its contacts with French colonialism?

A: My family originates from the Ait Ourible tribe, the region of Khemisset. Nobody in my family liked the French or wanted them to stay. Some members of my family actively resisted them. My grandfather's brother and my father attacked the office of the local governor, Muhammad ben Tabesh. He was a Moroccan who had worked for the French in Khemisset. My father was caught and placed in jail for three months. It happened in 1938. I was in France at the time.[72]

Q: What did you know about the French and their army before you joined up?

A: I didn't know anything about them and I had never worked for them before joining their army. All I knew was that they were no good. Even though at the time they were not yet imprisoning or beating people, they were severe on us. They were asking for taxes, food and cattle to help France in its war. They would come to someone and ask him to give them a cow. Then they would go to another and ask him for two or three. If someone didn't agree to give it to them, they would force him to do so.

Q: Did you go to school and receive education?

A: Yes, I went to a primary school where we studied Arabic and French. I left school around the age of fourteen.[73]

Q: What made you join the French Army? How did it happen?

A: It happened in 1936 in Meknes. It was my own choice. I wanted to be a soldier so I volunteered.[74] I knew that the French were in need of men for the war with Germany. They used to come and announce it at the souk (market) of Khemisset. They told people they could earn a lot of money if they joined the French army. They had trucks with them and they took us to Meknes. There we signed contracts for four years of service. They gave us clothing and

[72] The date and some details concerning this incident may be questionable. Ben Ayyad stated that the purpose of the attack was 'to fight for independence and "kick out" the French'. It was, he added in response to 'King Muhammad V's claim of independence'. It is possible that Ben Ayyad combined several events that occurred at different points in time.

[73] Ben Ayyad is one of very few veterans I encountered who had acquired any level of education prior to enlistment. Most veterans were never presented with such an opportunity during and after their service in the French Army. They remained virtually illiterate.

[74] That may have been only part of the reason, however, since Ben Ayyad acknowledged he had no alternative occupation at the time. It may be noted that his enlistment coincided with the Great Depression that hit Morocco (and the rest of the world) during the 1930s.

some money: 120 *rials*. At the time you could buy two cows with that sum. I gave the money to my father.

Q: What can you tell us about your initial experience in the army?

A: We stayed in Meknes for six months for basic training. We learned how to use a gun; we trained for war. Then we left for Casablanca and took a ferry to Marseilles. We were stationed in a place called Sandier[75] where we stayed throughout 1937. Then we moved to Alsace and moved within various locations of the 'Maginot Line.'[76] We were there when the war started. I remember it well. Daladier (France's Premier at the time) declared war on the evening of September 3rd. We were in Alsace and people around us started crying; they were afraid of the war.

Q: What can you tell us about your combat experience?

A: Our officers told us to get ready. We wore our military uniforms and took our arms. Each one knew the post where he should be. My post was in transmission, but I nevertheless had arms on me. Every once in a while, I would move onto the battlefield. I worked with the commanders of the unit. There were many of them and I can't remember all their names. My captain's name was Poitreau. There was also a major named Disserie. Poitreau committed suicide when we were in Belgium and the Germans surrounded us. They were disguised as bushes. When Poitreau saw them he took his gun and shot himself. Then each one of us tried to defend himself and fight. Some chose to flee. The British planes helped us while the Italian planes backed the Germans. The Russians were fighting the Germans from the other side.[77]

We continued our way through Belgium. I'm not sure where we were at this point. By night there were fireworks and smoke, then many planes started bombing. The Germans bombed and destroyed roads, bridges, railroads and tunnels. They destroyed everything so the French would find no way to move. The French soldiers started to take off their uniforms and fled.

We arrived in Saint-Étienne, about 700 kilometers from Paris. The Germans were already in Paris. There was one General, the commander of the 43rd division, who had his arms and legs broken. He told his officers to drop their arms and stop fighting. There were three Moroccan officers with him. They told the General that they were not willing to give up and that they had worked for

[75] The pronunciation and hence transliteration of some minor place-names in this interview may be inaccurate. We have attempted to verify the information, but in some cases were unable to do so.

[76] The Maginot Line was a chain of state-of-the-art fortifications constructed by the French Army during the 1930s along the Franco-German border. The line was considered to be impenetrable. It was never put to the test, however, since the eventual German offensive in May 1940 targeted a sector of the border that was not covered by the line.

[77] The last statement may reflect Ben Ayyad's limited exposure to the realities of the war, or it could be attributed to failing memory. Italy entered the war nearly two weeks after the end of the Belgian campaign, while the USSR remained neutral until June 1941, when it was invaded by Germany.

France so they wouldn't stop till they died. The General then gave command to another Captain.

Q: What happened then?

A: After the new Captain took over, we went to the forest of Moronal. When we reached the forest we found the Germans waiting for us. A Moroccan lieutenant named Tèhaami (a native of Khemisset) told us not to be afraid to die. There were lots of wheat fields surrounded by barbed wire. We went in there and the Germans started firing on us with tanks. Many people fell dead. There were 200–300 Moroccans in the division. More than half died there, including a brother-in-law of mine. One friend of mine got killed next to me. We were hiding behind an apple tree. I was on the right side and he was on the left. Then they bombed us. The tree got split in two. I told my friend to stay still. He was very young and scared so he moved to another tree about three meters further away. Then they fired on him with a machine gun and split his head in two.

We went out of the wheat field and found some German soldiers dead as well. We arrived at a farm that belonged to a Frenchman. Four of us decided to go to the farm to bring water and ask about the news because they had a radio in the farm. Our commander asked the man in the farm about the news and only then did we learn that the Germans had already been in Paris.

There was another French officer, Lieutenant Marchal, who decided to divide us. One group went first to check the road and give us signs to move. The other group just followed. We would move through the forest by night because the Germans had planes that could locate people. By day we would hide. We stayed like that for three nights. When we came across some French farms we would ask them for something to eat. After the third night the planes had located us. That day Marchal went first as usual to check the road. He saw nobody and told us to advance. Suddenly, a German officer appeared, called us to stop, and asked who we were. Marchal told him that we were *tirailleurs*, but before he even finished his sentence the German officer had shot him. Then the Germans called for trucks that took us to prison. We came to a place where they gave us numbers. Mine was 44782. That camp was in France, but then they took us to Belgium. They had everything. In an instant they would encircle us with barbed wire and make an imprisonment camp.

Q: And then you were moved to Germany?

A: We arrived next at Stuttgart. The Germans had big tents; each would fit 300 people. We stayed in there for three months and eighteen days. They would give us one kilo of bread for four persons per day. In the mornings they would give us coffee with no sugar. People couldn't even stand up. We had no strength. One morning they told us to stand in a line and we thought they were going to kill us. They gave us one kilo of bread, one bottle of honey, and one chunk of butter per person. Then we went to the train station of Stuttgart.

The train had wagons for cattle. They put seventy prisoners in a wagon. We had two German soldiers per wagon guarding us. We stopped once in a while in a forest to eat for ten minutes. It took us three days. The train was going slowly and we finally arrived in a French city called Mont Argie. The Germans had occupied it. Some of us went off there; others continued to Chartres. They put us in buildings.

We stayed in Mont Argie where we used to receive parcels from Morocco. Each one of us would receive a parcel with Sultan Muhammad V's name on it from the Red Cross. The parcels contained things like couscous, sweaters, and socks. We were allowed to write letters to our families. I had not been married yet at that time, so I wrote to my parents to assure them I was still alive.

Q: Could you tell us more about the way the Germans treated you?

A: The Germans took us to work in farms. They paid us ten centimes per week. I used to work with the mayor of the town. The Germans used to assign us the places of work. Because it was too much for the Germans to feed us, they forced the employers to accept us and pay us. Each Sunday a German controller would come and ask the employers whether the Moroccans were well fed. The Germans were more lenient on us than on the French prisoners. They understood that the French were the ones who fought against them. We were only subordinates. The Germans would speak with us in French. We even used to joke and discuss things with them. I also learned some German, basic words like 'bread,' 'I want to eat,' etc.

Q: How did you regain your freedom?

A: I stayed at Mont Argie for a year and nine months working on that farm. Then the Germans started to set some prisoners free. I was released and returned to Morocco. We had to go through medical checking to see whether we were injured or something. Then they handed us over to the French who sent us to a hospital in Paris. We stayed there for a month. Then we were freed. They gave us papers and took us by train from Paris to Limoges. They counted us and gave us forty French francs. We had to take off the clothes with which we came from Germany. We took a shower and found new clothes. They organized a small party. We had drinks and cookies before we left for Morocco.

At the time of my release I was still hurt from a hand grenade that had hit me when we were with Lt. Marchal trying to escape from the Germans. My wound healed, but when I came to Morocco they re-opened the wound and took out a small piece of the grenade. The operation took place in Kenitra.[78] Last week I was in Casablanca to take some X-rays on my arm, because I still have some pieces left. There is a French doctor who takes care of the Moroccan veterans in a hospital in Casablanca.

---

[78] A city on the Atlantic shore, some 20 miles north of Rabat.

My return to Morocco coincided with the arrival of the Americans.[79] They were shooting in Kenitra when I came there. They did so to pretend that they had entered here by force. The Americans stayed in Morocco, before going on to Italy, then to France. They arrived in Morocco two or three days after I had returned.

Q: What did you do after you left the French Army?

A: After I left the hospital I got a job and worked as a forest guard with the Protectorate. I was given a house in the forest of Dar Salim near Sidi Yahya, not far from Kenitra. Later I went to Sidi Slimane and then to El-Housima[80] where I worked for the Spanish. I stayed there for five years. Then I returned to the interior of Morocco. I went through five different jobs in different locations before retiring in 1977. After I had retired, I went to the city of Orléans in France with my wife. I returned to Morocco in 1983 and settled back in Khemisset where I have lived since then.

[79] The Allied invasion of North Africa (Operation 'Torch') took place in November 1942.

[80] A city on the Mediterranean shore in northern Morocco, at the time part of the Spanish protectorate zone.

5.10 Iran and the National Front, a speech by Prime Minister Mohammad Mosaddeq, 27 September 1951[81]

Robert G. Landen

Preface

The political career of Mohammad Mosaddeq (1880–1967), aristocrat and liberal constitutionalist, came to a dramatic end on 20 August 1953, when a coup orchestrated by the British and American governments and executed by forces loyal to the king, Mohammad Reza Shah Pahlavi (1926–80, r. 1941–79) removed him from power as Iran's prime minister.[82] His colleagues in Iran's parliament (the *Majles*) had elected him prime minister in May 1951 after he successfully secured passage of a law nationalizing Iran's oil industry. The passage of the law put Mosaddeq in conflict with the British government, which sought to retain the Anglo-Iranian Oil Company's exclusive control over Iran's oil (established by the D'Arcy Concession of 1901: see Sec. 8.5). From May through September of 1951 the British positioned forces in the region to invade Iran, and covertly sponsored bids for power by Mosaddeq's political rivals, notably Sayyed Zia al-Din Tabataba'i.[83] Mosaddeq managed to outmanoeuvre Tabataba'i, and the Truman Administration brought British plans for an invasion up short.[84]

---

[81] *Speech of Prime Minister Muhammad Mossadegh on Baharestan Square, 27 September 1951* (Tehran: Foreign Ministry of Iran, 1951), 1–6.

[82] The coup began on 16 August. It failed initially when Mosaddeq loyalists got wind of the coup and tipped him off. Mosaddeq arrested the officer (Colonel Nasiri, later a head of the shah's secret police, SAVAK) sent to remove him from power. Pro-Mosaddeq forces filled the streets and the shah fled the country on 17 August. After Mosaddeq persuaded supporters to leave the streets, fresh anti-Mosaddeq riots broke out on the 19th, and troops loyal to the coup's leader, an ex-general and senator, Fazlollah Zahedi, besieged Mosaddeq's house. Mosaddeq fled to a neighbouring house that evening, and was arrested by Zahedi's forces on 20 August. Mohammad Reza Shah returned from his 'vacation' on 23 August. See Homa Katouzian, *Musaddiq and the Struggle for Power in Iran* (London: I. B. Tauris, 1999), 188–93.

[83] Tabataba'i had supported the coup that brought Reza Khan (later Reza Shah) to power on 3 February 1921. Backed by the British (as was Reza Khan), he served as Iran's prime minister for three months before being ousted by Reza Khan. Tabataba'i's failed effort to secure power in September was, in fact, his second contest with Mosaddeq. Back in May he had suffered the indignity of being informed of Mosaddeq's premiership while in the king's palace, expecting to be confirmed in the office himself. After Tabataba'i was out-manoeuvred, Ahmad Qavam (a cousin of Mosaddeq, whose own name also derived from a Qajar title, Qavam al-Saltaneh, 'Strength of the Monarchy'), made an unsuccessful bid for power in July 1952 with the support of the British and Mohammad Reza Shah. Qavam had served as prime minister before (1921–3, 1942, 1946–8).

[84] Mark J. Gasioworski, 'The 1953 Coup in Iran', *International Journal of Middle East Studies*, 19/3 (Aug. 1987), 264.

Nonetheless, under pressure from a British-led boycott of Iranian oil, the Mosaddeq government soon found itself in dire economic straits. The coalition of nationalists, leftists (excluding the communist Tudeh Party), and Islamic revivalists (excluding the radical *Fedayan-e Eslam*) that had brought him to power, known as the National Front (*Jebbheh-ye Melli*), fell apart over the course of 1952 and 1953. To consolidate his position, Mosaddeq resorted to rigging elections and forming closer relations with Iran's communists. It was the latter sin that drove America's new Eisenhower Administration to approve a covert plan (Operation Ajax) to overthrow Mosaddeq. The coup would not have succeeded without the help of supporters of the Pahlavi Dynasty. As a member of parliament in the 1920s, Mosaddeq (whose last name was derived from his old Qajar title, Mosaddeq al-Saltaneh, 'Affirmer of the Monarchy') had opposed the parliamentary vote in 1925 to replace the Qajar Dynasty (1797–1925) with the Pahlavi Dynasty. Indeed, Reza Shah (Mohammad Reza Shah's father) had kept Mosaddeq under house arrest for most of his reign (1925–41). It was the Allied invasion and occupation of Iran from 1941 to 1946 that allowed Mosaddeq to return to parliamentary politics, and he stood for election in 1943 (the first relatively free elections in Iran since the sixth *Majles* of 1924–6), to become the representative from Tehran in the fourteenth *Majles* (1944–6). During his premiership, from 1951 to 1953, Mosaddeq attempted to reduce the power of the monarchy by reducing its influence over the military. Furthermore, British and (later) American efforts to remove Mosaddeq depended on Mohammad Reza Shah's signing an order dismissing Mosaddeq from power (the Iranian constitution gave this power to the king), a move the young shah resisted until August 1953.

Mosaddeq made the speech reproduced below a week after his government had expelled British workers from Iranian oil facilities in Abadan. He was at the height of his domestic popularity and regional celebrity. Shortly after he delivered this speech, Mosaddeq travelled to the United States to defend Iran's position with respect to the AIOC at the UN Security Council and to lobby (unsuccessfully) for aid from the Truman Adminis-tration. On his return trip, he stopped in Egypt (which was in its final year of rule by a British-backed monarch) and was received enthusiastically by crowds there.[85] His government published the text of the speech (includ-ing the favorable editorial comments inserted within it). A master orator, Mosaddeq had a number of audiences, foreign and domestic, in mind.

Text

[I]n my opinion wherever a crowd is gathered of men of good will and patriotic feelings a true *Majles* is to be found there; and where a group of people opposed

[85] Katouzian, *Musaddiq*, 119. Under the leadership of Jamal ᶜAbd al-Nasir [Nasser] in 1956, Egypt engaged in its own costly confrontation with England and France in a bid to nationalize the Suez Canal.

to the interests of the country are assembled that place is not considered as a Majles.

My dear countrymen, you are well aware that we did our utmost for a peaceful settlement of the oil dispute through negotiations (*cheers of the crowd*). Dear countrymen, I openly declare that the Iranian people will not give up their rights through the exercise of force (*enthusiastic cheers of the crowd*). The Iranian people have realised very well how they have been oppressed for half a century and now will not give up their lawful rights (cheers of the crowd and shouts of 'long live Dr Mosaddeq'). A limited number of *Majles* deputies have imagined that through yielding to the desires of foreigners our people would give up their legitimate rights through pressure brought upon them. The Iranian people have come to know that by forming a ruling class separated from them they will not give up their rights [*enthusiastic cheers—Then the Prime Minister paused and produced a list and showed it to the people*]. My dear countrymen, according to official figures the former usurping company[86] has only paid us 110 million pounds during the forty years of its operations, i.e., since 1912 when the company started its exploitation activities it has only paid us 110,943,798 pounds in the way of royalties, taxes and dividends due to the Iranian Government for its twenty percent shares in the company.[87] Countrymen, we were prepared to keep the British technical experts in the South so as not to disturb the international peace; we were prepared to compensate the former Company for all losses arising out of the nationalization of its installations, and settle the whole issue on a sound basis, i.e., either to pay for the shares of the company according to their quoted value at the international markets, or alternatively to follow the practice of those countries who have nationalized their mineral resources, leaving the choice to the company to choose either one of the two ways which guarantees its interests best. We were prepared to put an end to all the claims of the company and the counter-claims of the Iranian Government, in a manner mutually satisfactory to both parties. We also declared our readiness to supply Great Britain yearly with its oil requirements on the basis of the average of the oil received by it during the last three years, and for a period of time which would be mutually agreed upon; furthermore we agreed to earmark fifty percent of the value of the oil given to them for the amortization of the claims of the former company as judged by one of the two above-mentioned standards. We also gave the British another

---

[86] A reference to the Anglo-Iranian Oil Company, (AIOC) renamed that National Iranian Oil Company.

[87] Originally, the Iranian government had a 16% share. From 1931 to 1933 the government of Reza Shah waged a campaign to rescind the D'Arcy Concession of 1901. Relying on 'gunboat diplomacy', the British government forced Reza Shah to back down. As part of the settlement between the Iranian government and the Anglo-Persian Oil Company (as it was then known), Iran's share was increased to 20%, but the sixty-year term of the concession was extended by another fifty years.

advantage, to transfer to them the quantities of oil bought by our other customers, provided they produced duly signed orders from them.[88] We showed our readiness to establish anew sincere relations between the two Governments; our main intention was simply to recover our legal rights, i.e., the profits of our oil resources from a cruel usurper, and to use the same for the amelioration of the lot of fifteen million poor people, to give them what is due to them in the way of health and education. [*At this moment loud applause and shouts were uttered by the audience accompanied by clapping which lasted for several minutes.*] The British Government did not show any willingness to accept our just and equitable proposals. [*The crowd shouted, 'Death upon the British, death upon the British'.*] I don't want to hear you utter any words like this 'Death upon the British'; but I admonish you to pray to God Almighty to lead the British to the path of justice to recognize our lawful rights; and that God may open their eyes to see our miseries. [*At this juncture the great multitude who were gathered in the Parliament Square started to weep.*]

My dear countrymen, there was a time when the British Government was following a laudable policy in Iran; and that was at the beginning of our constitutional movement. When the British Government realized that certain mean and treacherous elements in our population had become the tools of the despotic Government of the Czars of Russia, it immediately decided to back up the liberal movement in Iran, and consequently through great sacrifices of our liberty-loving people who gave their lives for this purpose a constitutional regime was established in our country.[89] This was a very wise role that was played by the British Government; but unfortunately as time went on, this laudable attitude was changed, and the British Government entered into partition agreements with the Government of the Czars based on zones of influence.[90] Then the First World War began and subsequently a communistic regime appeared in Russia. The British Government instead of backing the patriotic and liberal elements of this country (i.e., that portion of the population who had the preservation of our country's independence at heart), paved the way for the establishment of a dictatorial Government which deprived all the people of their human rights of freedom; not being content with this, the British Government before making the Coup d'État intended to impose upon the Iranian people a protectorate,[91] while taking advantage of the confused state of affairs in Soviet Russia which was at the

---

[88] Mosaddeq is summarizing a number of ideas floated by the Iranians and American diplomats. These negotiations, encouraged by the Americans, culminated in Prime Minister Attlee (of the Labour Party) sending a negotiating team to Tehran headed by Richard Stokes. Stokes left Iran on 22 August 1951. In the British general election the following month, the more hawkish Winston Churchill, leader of the Conservative Party, defeated Attlee. Churchill had made the defense of AIOC rights in Iran a major issue in the election.   [89] The Constitutional Revolution took place from 1905 to 1906.
[90] This would be in 1907.   [91] This is a reference to the failed Anglo-Persian Treaty of 1919.

time absorbed in its internal difficulties. This agreement did not materialise through your patriotic sentiments, my dear brothers. Furthermore the appearance of the U.S.S.R. as a new factor in world politics and also the declaration of the Government of the United States of America for the formation of a League of Nations through which the rights of the small nations were to be defended all combined to neutralise the proposed agreement. Dear countrymen, I have fought this imperialism during the life of the 14th *Majles* [*approval of the crowd*]. I have opposed the credentials of Sayyed Zia al-Din Tabataba'i, the employment of Dr Millspaugh and the Sadr Government,[92] and also the tri-party commission;[93] in short I have been a vigilant fighter against everything which endangered the freedom of our country and our people.

In the 14th *Majles* my countrymen were not so enlightened regarding these vital questions as they are now to come and help me in the passage of the new Electoral Bill submitted by me to the Parliament, and to show their persistence in achieving this goal.[94] My only aim has been to prevent the recurrence of a situation in which we would have no *Majles*; but on the other hand I have always desired to see in continued existence a center in which opinions could be expressed freely. Countrymen, political parties, patriots, I must declare that you were negligent in this affair; because during the last days of the life of the *Majles* some people decided to close this place, which was the refuge of the people, against the will of the Majority of the nation. Consequently the *Majles*

---

[92] From 1942 to 1944 the Iranian government employed Arthur Chester Millspaugh as a financial adviser. His term of employment was cut short by constant protests and accusations of corruption in the press and parliament. It was his second time in Iran, having served as a financial adviser in the 1920s. His efficient tax collection earned him many enemies among Iran's elite, but Reza Shah forced him out the first time when he attempted to impose some fiscal discipline on the Court. See A. C. Millspaugh, *Americans in Persia* (Washington DC: The Brookings Institution, 1946). During the 14th *Majles*, Mohsen Sadr, a very conservative ex-cleric and supporter of the Pahlavi Dynasty, was voted into power by a coalition of three conservative nationalist factions: the National Unionists (*Ettehad-e Melli*), the Patriots (*Mihanparastan*), and the Democrats (headed by tribal leaders, and not to be confused with Ahmad Qavam's later Democrat Party). As an independent, Mosaddeq led a parliamentary boycott of Sadr's government, walking out of sessions from June to September 1945, thus making it impossible for Sadr to confirm his cabinet choices and form a government. Sadr stepped down as prime minister in October 1945. See Ervand Abrahamian, *Iran: Between Two Revolutions* (Princeton: Princeton University Press, 1982),186–221.

[93] 'The Tri-Party Commission' refers to a discussion among the British, American and Soviet governments to create a 'world oil commission' to regulate oil development concessions, particularly with regard to the Middle East. The point became moot when the Iranian government rejected initial Soviet proposals for an oil concession on 17 October 1944. See 'Anglo-American Oil Talks', *The Times*, 6 June 1944, p. 3; and Fakhreddin Azimi, *Iran: The Crisis of Democracy, 1951–1953* (New York: St Martin's Press, 1989), 141–2.

[94] Mosaddeq opposed measures that would restrict universal male suffrage in Iran, but failed to support women's suffrage, despite the pressure of an active women's suffrage campaign (led by feminists and the Tudeh Party) from 1943 to 1946.

was dissolved and a period of uncertainty followed.[95] What should not have been done was done by those who brought about this situation; to mention one case, the budget deficit of 3,000 million *rials* is the outcome of the unlawful activities of the Government during the period at which the Parliament was closed.

When the new Elections for the 15th *Majles*[96] started in Tehran my political friends and myself took refuge in the Imperial Court to secure the non-interference of the Government in the National elections, but we were met with a negative reply. A few days after we left the Imperial Court somebody came and told me, 'Do you know that the British Embassy was behind this movement of your taking refuge in the Imperial Court.' My reply was of course a resolute 'no'; but I added if the British Embassy had written to me to go and take refuge in the Imperial Court for securing the freedom of the National Elections I, for one, would not have refused. Suppose the British Embassy had told me to observe my religious fasting; do you think I should have refused to do so because the utterance was made by the British Embassy? On the contrary I should have observed my religious injunctions irrespective of the source which reminded me to do so. Then I enquired as to the identity of the person who made you think that the British Embassy was at the back of our movement of taking refuge in the Imperial Court? In reply he said, 'Because they had told the Soviet Russians that if the Tehran Elections were free from interference the returns might not be helpful to the passage of the proposed mixed Irano-Russian Oil Company agreement.'[97]

Therefore the elections should be under the control of the Government; so that neither the Tudeh Party could send any members nor those who intended to oppose the above-mentioned agreement.

When the Elections for the 16th *Majles* started I was totally disappointed because all our efforts during the 14th and 15th *Majles* elections were futile;[98] but

[95] This could be a reference to the beginning of Ahmad Qavam's term as prime minister in January 1946. Elected by the most narrow of parliamentary majorities (one vote), he stalled on seeking approval of his cabinet while negotiating with the Soviets over their withdrawal from Azerbaijan. His supporters prevented the *Majles* from reaching a quorum until the last meeting of the session (11 March 1946), thus helping Qavam to avoid formal parliamentary scrutiny. Abrahamian, *Iran*, 222–3.

[96] This would be in the late autumn of 1947—the elections were so clearly rigged by Prime Minister Ahmad Qavam that the Tudeh Party boycotted them and Mosaddeq himself 'retired' from politics in protest of the results.

[97] As part of the effort to negotiate a Soviet withdrawal from Iran following World War II, the government of then Prime Minister Ahmad Qavam had offered the Soviets oil and gas concessions in northern Iran in late 1946. According to the former Iranian constitution, the Iranian *Majles* was required to ratify such agreements before they could become effective. The pro-Soviet demeanour of the next session of the Iranian *Majles* would therefore have been important to the passage of the concession. The *Majles* did not ratify the agreement with the Soviets.

[98] Parliamentary elections were supposed to be held every two years. The elections for the 16th *Majles* would be conducted in the Fall of 1949, with the new session running from spring 1950 until spring 1952.

when the time came for the Tehran elections I said to myself let us do our best, may the desired goal be achieved. Hence I requested many of you, dear countrymen, to assemble before the Imperial Court to obtain our rights of free franchise. You responded to my call and showed your national maturity in a very admirable manner. [*At this moment the Premier was overcome by his feeling and the drops of tears appeared on his cheeks, which made everybody cry.*] My dear countrymen, your opponents who were waiting for any disturbance were dismayed, because they had in mind to put under arrest anybody who broke the peace of the audience as a rioter and inflict upon him all sorts of punishment.

But fortunately nothing of the sort happened and peace was preserved. A few of us only went to the Court with a plea to have the Minister of Interior, Dr Eqbal, removed from his office; as our request was not complied with we left the Court. Instead of that we entered into a fearful campaign to succeed in the elections. As a result of this campaign myself and a few members of the National Front (whom you all know well) were elected; and because of the continuation of our campaign in the *Majles*, while being in the minority *we took the reins of the Government*. Who has ever heard of an opposition that has taken the Government in its hands![99] [*To this remark one of the people retorted with a shout: 'You were the Majority and not the opposition.'*]

The coming into power of the opposition was only due to the backing of you, my dear countrymen, who are the well wishers of our fatherland. For our part I must say that we accepted the responsibilities of the Government for the sole purpose of recovering the lost rights of the Iranian people; we accepted the heavy duties of the Government in order to put an end to the exploitation of our people by others. It is quite surprising that a handful of persons try in vain to show that your sentiments are aroused through the intrigues of the Government. Do tell me frankly, has any member of the Government ever given you any instruction or even spoken to any of you? [*The reply was 'Never, never.'*] The fact that the opposition has come into power is good proof that your sentiments are genuine. It came to my knowledge that the British Ambassador had called on His Excellency Taqizadeh, the President of the Senate, three days ago; and had expressed his surprise at the fact that an Opposition had come into existence in the *Majles*, while such an opposition did not exist in the senate. He had furthermore explicitly stated that as long as Dr Mosaddeq is in power the British Government is not ready to enter into negotiations with the Iranian Government.[100] [*At this juncture*

[99] Mosaddeq was never formally part of the National Front. He valued his independence. Support for his premiership in the *Majles* in May 1951 transcended party affiliations on the strength of support for Mosaddeq's call for the nationalization of Iran's oil industry.

[100] Sayyed Hasan Taqizadeh was one of the original Social Democrats in the first session of Iran's *Majles* from 1907 to 1909. Over time, his enthusiasm for both radical Westernization and the primacy of the parliament waned. He was an early supporter of Reza Shah Pahlavi, but ran afoul of the shah due

the multitude showed their sentiments towards the Prime Minister by saying, 'Long live Dr Mosaddeq and long live his Government.' A bouquet was presented to him by one of the audience; the Premier put the flowers on his head and then returned them to the person who had made the offer. The Premier then went on and said,] His Excellency Mr Taqizadeh gave the appropriate reply to the said Honourable Ambassador stressing the fact that no foreign intervention is permissible in the internal affairs of Iran.

Now I want to tell you, my dear countrymen, that it is impossible for the present Government to take any steps contrary to your welfare; and as long as a vote of no-confidence is not given by both houses this Government shall continue its fight with all severity and persistence to recover your rights. *[While great roars of applause were rending the air in the Baharestan Square, the Premier went back to the Majles and thence returned to his residence.]*

to his handling of negations with Britain during Iran's 1930s bid to end the D'Arcy Concession. He wisely stayed outside the country for the duration of Reza Shah's reign, but was rehabilitated under Mohammad Reza Shah, receiving a Senate seat when that body was finally convened in 1950. Although the Iranian constitution called for the creation of a Senate (some of whom were to be appointed by the king, resembling in a sense, the British House of Lords), it was not until the monarchy truly felt threatened by the power of parliament that it was brought into being. Here, Mosaddeq praises Taqizadeh's responses to a British effort to use its influence in the *Majles* (including the newly formed Senate) during the summer and early autumn of 1951.

5.11 Anwar al-Sadat's speech to the Israeli Knesset, 1977[101]
From the Islamfiche project

Preface

The family of Anwar al-Sadat was of the landed peasantry, and his father was an early village recipient of Western education. From the age of 7, al-Sadat lived in Cairo, where he was painfully aware of the humiliations inflicted upon native people by the British occupiers. He became a nationalist, and at age 18 entered the military academy, which was then an important avenue for upward mobility for the Egyptian lower middle class. There he met Gamal Abdel Nasser (Jamal ʿAbd al-Nasir) and other future members of the Free Officers Corps, which overthrew the corrupt king, Farouk (Faruq), in 1952. From the time of the coup, al-Sadat held numerous positions in the government. His excellent connections to Islamic religious nationalists led to his 1955 appointment as the first secretary-general of the Islamic Congress, a group devoted to pan-Islamic unity. On the death of Nasser in 1970, al-Sadat became president of Egypt, a position he consolidated through a purge of left-wing rivals in 1971. He led Egypt in the October War of 1973 after his repeated calls for a negotiated settlement with Israel were ignored. On the evening of Saturday, 19 November 1977, the day before ʿId al-Adha (the Day of Sacrifice signalling the end of the pilgrimage to Mecca),[102] al-Sadat became the first Arab leader to make an official visit to Israel, and in 1979 he signed the United States-sponsored Camp David Accords establishing mutual recognition and relations between Israel and Egypt in return for Israeli withdrawal from the Sinai Peninsula.

Although until 1977 no Arab leader granted official recognition to Israel, the people of the Arab world were certainly aware of its presence. Periodic border skirmishes and raids, intermittent full-scale warfare (1948, 1956, 1967, 1973), and the presence of the Palestinian refugees and

---

[101] Anwar Al-Sadat, 'Speech to the Israeli Knesset on November 20, 1977', in *In Search of Identity: An Autobiography* (New York: Harper & Row, 1978), 330–43. (Original Source: the *New York Times*.) Original Arabic Source: *Al-Sadat fi khitabihi al-taʿrikhi amam al kiniysit*, *Al-Ahram* (Cairo), 21 Nov. 1977, p. 6.

[102] On 9 November Sadat had declared before the Egyptian People's Assembly that he would even be willing to go to the Israeli Knesset in pursuit of peace. Israel's Prime Minister Begin invited him to Israel on 15 November. Mohamed Ibrahim Kamel, *The Camp David Accords: A Testimony* (London: Routledge & Kegan Paul, 1986), 14–17. Since May of 1977, secret negotiations taking place around the issue of Sadat visiting Israel had been mediated by President Nikolai Ceauşescu of Romania and King Hasan II of Morocco. Kirk J. Beattie, *Egypt During the Sadat Years* (New York: Palgrave, 2000), 226–8.

guerrillas ensured popular knowledge of the Israeli state. However, the native Arab people of Palestine consistently refused to accept the loss of their ancestral homeland, and nationalists throughout the Arab world considered Israel a final colonial insult to Arab national integrity. In spite of the strength of anti-Zionist sentiment in the Arab world, truces had been negotiated with Israel after each war, and both King Husayn (Hussein) of Jordan and his grandfather King ʿAbd Allah had extensive contacts with various Israeli leaders. Egypt, as the biggest Arab state bordering on Palestine, had borne much of the brunt of the permanent conflict with Israel. From at least 1971, al-Sadat was searching for a respectable way to disengage from the conflict. The minimal requirements—a complete return of conquered Egyptian territory and at least nominal progress toward a Palestinian state—were attained after long and hard bargaining in the Camp David Accords of 1979. Egypt's participation in a separate peace treaty with Israel under America's aegis led to its isolation from the rest of the Arab and Muslim world, which strongly opposed the treaty. It also left other direct parties to the conflict (that is, those with territorial disputes with Israel)—the Palestinians, Jordan, and Syria—without a viable scenario for a comprehensive peace plan.

The speech before the Israeli Knesset (parliament) is directed to a diverse audience. Sections of it are clearly addressed to Arab public opinion, while others are meant to appeal to the West. The visit to Israel and the subsequent Camp David Accords did result in greater Western economic and military aid which offset Egypt's regional isolation, but also fuelled the opposition of religious extremist groups (some factions of the Muslim Brotherhood, Takfir waʾl-Hijra, the Islamic Group, and Islamic Jihad) to al-Sadat and did nothing to help Egypt's ailing economy, which had not responded to al-Sadat's attempt in the mid-1970s to open Egypt to foreign trade and investment (a program known as the *infitah*, or 'opening'). Sadat's efforts to counter and contain domestic opposition included such conflicting measures as recognizing long-suppressed and recently revived political parties (the New Wafd, the Socialist Labor Party), creating a new political party of his own (the National Democratic Party, replacing the Egyptian Arab Socialist Party) in 1978, to 'Islamizing' Egypt's constitution by inserting a clause recognizing the *shariʿa* (Islamic Law) as the main source of legislation in May 1980, and changing the constitutional requirement that a president serve for a limit of two terms.[103] Spurred on by concerns over religious opposition to the fulfilment of the Camp David Accords in April 1982 (at which time the Israelis would completely withdraw from the Sinai Peninsula), al-Sadat cracked down on radical Islamic groups on

[103] Beattie, *Egypt*, 261–2. al-Sadat's move to the religious right might also have been an effort to get ahead of the radical Islamicist political tide that had removed from power the Shah of Iran, Mohammed Reza Pahlavi. Under al-Sadat, Egypt became the final refuge for the Shah, where he died in 1980.

2 September 1981. These arrests, and a scheduled parade celebrating the Egyptian offensive across the Suez Canal in the 1973 Yom Kippur War with Israel, set into motion a plot among junior officers who were members of the Islamic Group to kill al-Sadat. Planning began on 23 September and the plot was carried out on the parade grounds on 6 October 1981.[104]

Whether al-Sadat is seen as a casualty of the peace process, authoritarian politics, or the resurgence of religious political extremism, it was this speech (of all the dozens recorded and published by the Egyptian State Information Service) that may stand as his most important and provocative political act.

Text

Speech to the Israeli Knesset on 20 November 1977

In the name of God, Mr Speaker of the Knesset, ladies and gentlemen, allow me first to thank deeply the Speaker of the Knesset for affording me the opportunity to address you.

As I begin my address I wish to say, peace and the mercy of God Almighty be upon you and may peace be with us all, God willing. Peace for us all, of the Arab lands and in Israel, as well as in every part of this big world, which is so beset by conflicts, perturbed by its deep contradictions, menaced now and then by destructive wars launched by man to annihilate his fellow men.

Finally, amidst the ruins of what man has built among the remains of the victims of mankind there emerges neither victor nor vanquished. The only vanquished remains always a man, God's most sublime creation. Man, whom God has created, as Gandhi,[105] the apostle of peace puts it, to forge ahead, to mold the way of life and to worship God Almighty.

I come to you today on solid ground to shape a new life and to establish peace. We all love this land, the land of God, we all, Muslims, Christians and Jews, all worship God.

Under God. God's teachings and commandments are: love, sincerity, security and peace.

I do not blame all those who received my decision when I announced it to the entire world before the Egyptian People's Assembly. I do not blame all those who received my decision with surprise and even with amazement—some gripped even by violent surprise. Still others interpreted it as political, to camouflage my intentions of launching a new war.

I would go so far as to tell you that one of my aides at the presidential office contacted me at a late hour following my return home from the People's

[104] For an interesting account of the plot, see Mohamed Heikal, *Autumn of Fury: The Assassination of Sadat* (London: André Deutsch, 1983), 241–55.

[105] Mahatma Gandhi (1869–1948), the Indian nationalist leader and advocate of non-violence.

Assembly[106] and sounded worried as he asked me, 'Mr President, what would be our reaction if Israel actually extended an invitation to you?'

I replied calmly: 'I would accept it immediately. I have declared that I would go to the ends of the earth. I would go to Israel, for I want to put before the people of Israel all the facts.'

I can see the faces of all those who were astounded by my decision and had doubts as to the sincerity of the intentions behind the declaration of my decision. No one could have ever conceived that the President of the biggest Arab state, which bears the heaviest burden and the main responsibility pertaining to the cause of war and peace in the Middle East, should declare his readiness to go to the land of the adversary while we were still in a state of war.

We all still bear the consequences of four fierce wars waged within thirty years. All this at the time when the families of the 1973 October war are still mourning under the cruel pain of bereavement of father, son, husband, and brother.

As I have already declared, I have not consulted as far as this decision is concerned with any of my colleagues or brothers, the Arab heads of state or the confrontation states.[107]

Most of those who contacted me following the declaration of this decision expressed their objection because of the feeling of utter suspicion and absolute lack of confidence between the Arab states and the Palestine people on the one hand and Israel on the other that still surges in us all.

Many months in which peace could have been brought about have been wasted over differences and fruitless discussions on the procedure of convening the Geneva Conference.[108] All have shared suspicion and absolute lack of confidence.

But to be absolutely frank with you, I took this decision after long thought, knowing that it constitutes a great risk, for God Almighty had made it my fate to assume responsibility on behalf of the Egyptian people, to share in the responsibility of the Arab nation, the main duty of which, dictated by responsibility, is to exploit all and every means in a bid to save my Egyptian Arab people and the pan-Arab nation from the horrors of new suffering and destructive wars, the dimensions of which are foreseen only by God himself.

After long thinking, I was convinced that the obligation of responsibility before God and before the people make it incumbent upon me that I should go to the far corners of the world—even to Jerusalem to address members of the Knesset and acquaint them with all the facts surging in me, then I would let you decide for yourselves.

Following this, may God Almighty determine our fate.

[106] The Egyptian parliament.

[107] The Arab countries directly involved in the conflict with Israel: Egypt, Jordan, and Syria.

[108] From 1973 an on-again, off-again international conclave in Geneva, Switzerland, aiming at a comprehensive solution to the Arab–Israeli conflict.

Ladies and Gentlemen, there are moments in the lives of nations and peoples when it is incumbent upon those known for their wisdom and clarity of vision to survey the problem, with all its complexities and vain memories, in a bold drive toward new horizons.

Those who like us are shouldering the same responsibilities entrusted to us are the first who should have the courage to make determining decisions that are consonant with the magnitude of the circumstances. We must all rise above all forms of obsolete theories of superiority, and the most important thing is never to forget that infallibility is the prerogative of God alone.

If I said that I wanted to avert from all the Arab people the horrors of shocking and destructive wars I must sincerely declare before you that I have the same feelings and bear the same responsibility toward all and every man on earth, and certainly toward the Israeli people.

Any life that is lost in war is a human life, be it that of an Arab or an Israeli. A wife who becomes a widow is a human being entitled to a happy family life whether she be an Arab or an Israeli.

Innocent children who are deprived of the care and compassion of their parents are ours. They are ours, be they living on Arab or Israeli land.

They command our full responsibility to afford them a comfortable life today and tomorrow.

For the sake of them all, for the sake of the lives of all our sons and brothers, for the sake of affording our communities the opportunity to work for the progress and happiness of man, feeling secure and with the right to a dignified life, for the generations to come, for a smile on the face of every child born in our land—for all that I have taken my decision to come to you, despite all the hazards, to deliver my address.

I have shouldered the prerequisites of the historic responsibility and therefore I declared on 4 February 1971, that I was willing to sign a peace agreement with Israel. This was the first declaration made by a responsible Arab official since the outbreak of the Arab–Israeli conflict. Motivated by all these factors dictated by the responsibilities of leadership, on 16 October 1973, before the Egyptian People's Assembly, I then called for an international conference to establish permanent peace based on justice. I was not heard.

I was not in the position of a man pleading for peace or asking for a cease-fire. Motivated by the duties of history and leadership, I later signed the first disengagement agreement,[109] followed by the second disengagement agreement in Sinai.

Then we proceeded, trying both open and closed doors in a bid to find a certain road leading to a durable and just peace.

[109] Compromises engineered by American Secretary of State Henry Kissinger in 1973 and 1974 to provide for Israeli pullbacks from the Sinai Peninsula.

We opened our heart to the peoples of the entire world to make them understand our motivations and objectives and actually to convince them of the fact that we are advocates of justice and peacemakers. Motivated by all these factors, I also decided to come to you with an open mind and an open heart and with all conscious determination so that we might establish permanent peace based on justice.

It is so fated that my trip to you, which is a journey of peace, coincided with the Islamic feast, the holy Feast of the Sacrifice when Abraham—peace be upon him—forefather of the Arabs and Jews, submitted to God, and, not out of weakness but through a giant spiritual force and by free will, sacrificed his very own son, thus personifying a firm and unshakable belief in ideals that have had for mankind a profound significance.

Ladies and gentlemen, let us be frank with each other. Using straightforward words and a clear conception with no ambiguity, let us be frank with each other today while the entire world, both East and West, follows these unparalleled moments which could prove to be a radical turning point in the history of this part of the world if not in the history of the world as a whole.

Let us be frank with each other, let us be frank with each other as we answer this important question:

How can we achieve permanent peace based on justice? Well, I have come to you carrying my clear and frank answer to this big question, so that the people of Israel as well as the entire world may hear it. All those devoted prayers ring in my ears, pleading to God Almighty that this historic meeting may eventually lead to the result aspired to by millions.

Before I proclaim my answer, I wish to assure you that in my clear and frank answer I am availing myself of a number of facts which no one can deny.

The first fact is that no one can build his happiness at the expense of the misery of others.

The second fact: never have I spoken, nor will I ever speak, with two tongues; never have I adopted, nor will I ever adopt, two policies. I never deal with anyone except in one tongue, one policy, and with one face.

The third fact: direct confrontation is the nearest and most successful method to reach a clear objective.

The fourth fact: the call for permanent and just peace based on respect for United Nations resolutions has become the call of the entire world. It has become the expression of the will of the international community, whether in official capitals where policies are made and decisions taken, or at the level of world public opinion, which influences policymaking and decision-taking.

The fifth fact, and this is probably the clearest and most prominent, is that the Arab nation, in its drive for permanent peace based on justice, does not proceed from a position of weakness. On the contrary, it has the power and stability for a sincere will for peace.

The Arabs' declared intention stems from an awareness prompted by a heritage of civilization, that to avoid an inevitable disaster that will befall us, you, and the whole world, there is no alternative to the establishment of permanent peace based on justice, peace that is not swayed by suspicion or jeopardized by ill intentions.

In the light of these facts which I meant to place before you the way I see them, I would also wish to warn you, in all sincerity I warn you, against some thoughts that could cross your minds.

Frankness makes it incumbent upon me to tell you the following:

First, I have not come here for a separate agreement between Egypt and Israel. This is not part of the policy of Egypt. The problem is not that of Egypt and Israel.

An interim peace between Egypt and Israel, or between any Arab confrontation state and Israel, will not bring permanent peace based on justice in the entire region.

Rather, even if peace between all the confrontation states and Israel were achieved in the absence of a just solution of the Palestinian problem, never will there be that durable and just peace upon which the entire world insists.

Second, I have not come to you to seek a partial peace, namely to terminate the state of belligerency at this stage and put off the entire problem to a subsequent stage. This is not the radical solution that would steer us to permanent peace.

Equally, I have not come to you for a third disengagement agreement in Sinai or Golan or the West Bank.

For this would mean that we are merely delaying the ignition of the fuse. It would also mean that we are lacking the courage to face peace, that we are too weak to shoulder the burdens and responsibilities of a durable peace based upon justice.

I have come to you so that together we should build a durable peace based on justice to avoid the shedding of one single drop of blood by both sides. It is for this reason that I have proclaimed my readiness to go to the farthest corner of the earth.

Here I would go back to the big question:

How can we achieve a durable peace based on justice? In my opinion, and I declare it to the whole world, from this forum, the answer is neither difficult nor is it impossible despite long years of feuds, blood, faction, strife, hatreds, and deep-rooted animosity.

The answer is not difficult, nor is it impossible, if we sincerely and faithfully follow a straight line.

You want to live with us, part of the world.

In all sincerity I tell you we welcome you among us with full security and safety. This in itself is a tremendous turning point, one of the landmarks of a decisive historical change. We used to reject you. We had our reasons and our fears, yes.

We refused to meet with you anywhere, yes.

We were together in international conferences and organizations and our representatives did not, and still do not, exchange greetings with you. Yes. This has happened and is still happening. It is also true that we used to set as a precondition for any negotiations with you a mediator who would meet separately with each party.

Yes. Through this procedure, the talks of the first and second disengagement agreements took place.

Our delegates met in the first Geneva conference without exchanging a direct word, yes, this has happened.

Yet today I tell you, and I declare it to the whole world, that we accept to live with you in permanent peace based on justice. We do no want to encircle you or be encircled ourselves by destructive missiles ready for launching, nor by the shells of grudges and hatreds.

I have announced on more than one occasion that Israel has become a *fait accompli*, recognized by the world, and that the two superpowers have undertaken the responsibility for its security and the defense of its existence. As we really and truly seek peace we really and truly welcome you to live among us in peace and security.

There was a huge wall between us which you tried to build up over a quarter of a century, but it was destroyed in 1973. It was the wall of an implacable and escalating psychological warfare.

It was a wall of the fear of the force that could sweep the entire Arab nation. It was a wall of propaganda that we were a nation reduced to immobility. Some of you had gone as far as to say that even for fifty years to come, the Arabs would not regain their strength. It was a wall that always threatened with a long arm that could reach and strike anywhere. It was a wall that warned us of extermination and annihilation if we tried to use legitimate rights to liberate the occupied territories.

Together we have to admit that that wall fell and collapsed in 1973. Yet, there remains another wall. This wall constitutes a psychological barrier between us, a barrier of suspicion, a barrier of rejection; a barrier of fear, of deception, a barrier of hallucination without any action, deed or decision.

A barrier of distorted and eroded interpretation of every event and statement. It is this psychological barrier which I described in official statements as constituting 70 percent of the whole problem.

Today, through my visit to you, I ask you why don't we stretch out our hands with faith and sincerity so that together we might destroy this barrier? Why shouldn't our and your will meet with faith and sincerity so that together we might remove all suspicion of fear, betrayal, and bad intentions?

Why don't we stand together with the courage of men and the boldness of heroes who dedicate themselves to a sublime aim? Why don't we stand together with the same courage and daring to erect a huge edifice of peace?

An edifice that builds and does not destroy. An edifice that serves as a beacon for generations to come with the human message for construction, development, and the dignity of man.

Why should we bequeath to the coming generations the plight of bloodshed, yes, orphans, widowhood, family disintegration, and the wailing of victims?

Why don't we believe in the wisdom of God conveyed to us by the wisdom of the proverbs of Solomon:

'Deceit is in the heart of them that imagine evil: but to the counselors of peace is joy.'

'Better is a dry morsel, and quietness therewith than an house full of sacrifices and strife.'

Why don't we repeat together the Psalms of David the Prophet:

'Unto Thee will I cry, O Lord. Hear the voice of my supplications. When I cry unto Thee, when I lift up my hands towards thy holy oracle.

'Draw me not away with the wicked, and with the workers of iniquity, which speak peace to their neighbors, but mischief in their hearts.

'Give them according to their deeds and according to the wickedness of their endeavors.'

Ladies and gentlemen, to tell you the truth, peace cannot be worth its name unless it is based on justice and not on the occupation of the land of others. It would not be right for you to demand for yourselves what you deny to others. With all frankness and in the spirit that has prompted me to come to you today, I tell you, you have to give up once and for all the dreams of conquest and give up the belief that force is the best method for dealing with the Arabs.

You should clearly understand the lesson of confrontation between you and us. Expansion does not pay. To speak frankly, our land does not yield itself to bargaining, it is not even open to argument. To us, the nation's soil is equal to the holy valley where God spoke to Moses. Peace be upon him.

We cannot accept any attempt to take away or accept to seek one inch of it nor can we accept the principle of debating or bargaining over it.

I sincerely tell you also that before us today lies the appropriate chance for peace. If we are really serious in our endeavor for peace, it is a chance that may never come again. It is a chance that if lost or wasted, the resulting slaughter would bear the curse of humanity and of history.

What is peace for Israel? It means that Israel lives in the region with her Arab neighbors in security and safety. Is that logical? I say yes. It means that Israel lives within its borders, secure against any aggression. Is that logical? And I say yes. It means that Israel obtains all kinds of guarantees that will ensure these two factors. To this demand, I say yes.

Beyond that we declare that we accept all the international guarantees you envisage and accept. We declare that we accept all the guarantees you want from the two superpowers or from either of them or from the Big Five or from some of them. Once again, I declare clearly and unequivocally that we agree to any guarantees you accept, because in return we shall receive the same guarantees. In short then, when we ask what is peace for Israel, the answer would be that Israel lives within her borders, among her Arab neighbors in safety and security, within the framework of all the guarantees she accepts and which are offered to her.

But, how can this be achieved? How can we reach this conclusion which would lead us to permanent peace based on justice? There are facts that should be faced with courage and clarity. There are Arab territories which Israel has occupied and still occupies by force. We insist on complete withdrawal from these territories, including Arab Jerusalem.

I have come to Jerusalem, the city of peace, which will always remain as a living embodiment of coexistence among believers of the three religions. It is inadmissible that anyone should conceive the special status of the city of Jerusalem within the framework of annexation or expansionism. It should be a free and open city for all believers.

Above all, this city should not be severed from those who have made it their abode for centuries. Instead of reviving the precedent of the Crusades, we should revive the spirit of ʿUmar ibn al-Khattab[110] and Salah-al-Din [Saladin],[111] namely the spirit of tolerance and respect for right.

The holy shrines of Islam and Christianity are not only places of worship but a living testimony to our interrupted presence here. Politically, spiritually and intellectually, here let us make no mistake about the importance and reverence we Christians and Muslims attach to Jerusalem.

Let me tell you without the slightest hesitation that I have not come to you under this roof to make a request that your troops evacuate the occupied territories. Complete withdrawal from the Arab territories occupied after 1967 is a logical and undisputed fact. Nobody should plead for that. Any talk about permanent peace based on justice and any move to ensure our coexistence in peace and security in this part of the world would become meaningless while you occupy Arab territories by force of arms.

---

[110] (ʿUmar ibn al-Khattab') the second Muslim caliph (*khalifa*, lit. successor).

[111] Saladin (Salah al-Din): the famous fifth/twelfth-century Muslim ruler, born in Iraq of Kurdish origin, who not only defeated the European crusaders and retook Jerusalem, but also ended Fatimid rule in Egypt and reinstated Sunni Islam.

For there is no peace that could be built on the occupation of the land of others, otherwise it would not be a serious peace. Yet this is a foregone conclusion which is not open to the passion of debate if intentions are sincere or if endeavors to establish a just and durable peace for our and for generations to come are genuine.

As for the Palestine cause—nobody could deny that it is the crux of the entire problem. Nobody in the world could accept today slogans propagated here in Israel, ignoring the existence of a Palestinian people and questioning even their whereabouts. Because the Palestine people and their legitimate rights are no longer denied today by anybody; that is, nobody who has the ability of judgment can deny or ignore it.

It is an acknowledged fact, perceived by the world community, both in the East and in the West, with support and recognition in international documents and official statements. It is of no use to anybody to turn deaf ears to its resounding voice, which is being heard day and night, or to overlook its historical reality.

Even in the United States of America, your first ally, which is absolutely committed to safeguard Israel's security and existence and which offered and still offers Israel every moral, material, and military support—I say, even the United States has opted to face up to reality and admit that the Palestinian people are entitled to legitimate rights and that the Palestine problem is the cause and essence of conflict and that so long as it continues to be unresolved, the conflict will continue to aggravate, reaching new dimensions.

In all sincerity I tell you that there can be no peace without the Palestinians. It is a grave error of unpredictable consequences to overlook or brush aside this cause.

I shall not indulge in past events such as the Balfour Declaration[112] sixty years ago. You are well acquainted with the relevant text. If you have found the moral and legal justification to set up a national home on a land that did not all belong to you, it is incumbent upon you to show understanding of the insistence of the people of Palestine for establishment once again of a state on their land. When some extremists ask the Palestinians to give up this sublime objective, this in fact means asking them to renounce their identity and every hope for the future.

I hail the Israeli voices that called for the recognition of the Palestinian people's right to achieve and safeguard peace.

Here I tell you, ladies and gentlemen, that it is no use to refrain from recognizing the Palestinian people and their right to statehood as their right of return. We, the Arabs, have faced this experience before, with you. And with the reality of the Israeli existence, the struggle which took us from war to war, from

[112] The brief statement issued by Britain's foreign secretary, A. J. Balfour, in 1917, favoring the development of a Jewish homeland in Palestine, thus setting a precedent for British support for Zionist activity in the Mandate territory from 1920 to 1948.

victims to more victims, until you and we have today reached the edge of a horrible abyss and a terrifying disaster unless, together, we seize this opportunity today of a durable peace based on justice.

You have to face reality bravely, as I have done. There can never be any solution to a problem by evading it or turning a deaf ear to it. Peace cannot last if attempts are made to impose fantasy concepts on which the world has turned its back and announced its unanimous call for the respect of rights and facts.

There is no need to enter a vicious circle as to Palestinian rights. It is useless to create obstacles, otherwise the march of peace will be impeded or peace will be blown up. As I have told you, there is no happiness [based on] the detriment of others.

Direct confrontation and straightforwardness are the shortcuts and the most successful way to reach a clear objective. Direct confrontation concerning the Palestinian problem and tackling it in one single language with a view to achieving a durable and just peace lie in the establishment of that peace. With all the guarantees you demand, there should be no fear of a newly born state that needs the assistance of all countries of the world.

When the bells of peace ring there will be no hands to beat the drums of war. Even if they existed, they would be stilled.

Conceive with me a peace agreement in Geneva that we would herald to a world thirsting for peace. A peace agreement based on the following points:

Ending the occupation of the Arab territories occupied in 1967.

Achievement of the fundamental rights of the Palestinian people and their right to self-determination, including their right to establish their own state.

The right of all states in the area to live in peace within their boundaries, their secure boundaries, which will be secured and guaranteed through procedures to be agreed upon, which will provide appropriate security to international boundaries in addition to appropriate international guarantees.

Commitment of all states in the region to administer the relations among them in accordance with the objectives and principles of the United Nations Charter. Particularly the principles concerning the nonuse of force and a solution of differences among them by peaceful means.

Ending the state of belligerence in the region.

Ladies and gentlemen, peace is not a mere endorsement of written lines. Rather it is a rewriting of history. Peace is not a game of calling for peace to defend certain whims or hide certain admissions. Peace in its essence is a dire struggle against all and every ambition and whim.

Perhaps the example taken and experienced, taken from ancient and modern history, teaches that missiles, warships and nuclear weapons cannot establish security. Instead they destroy what peace and security build.

For the sake of our peoples and for the sake of the civilization made by man, we have to defend man everywhere against rule by the force of arms so that we may endow the rule of humanity with all the power of the values and principles that further the sublime position of mankind.

Allow me to address my call from this rostrum to the people of Israel. I pledge myself with true and sincere words to every man, woman, and child in Israel. I tell them, from the Egyptian people who bless this sacred mission of peace, I convey to you the message of peace of the Egyptian people, who do not harbor fanaticism and whose sons, Moslems, Christians, and Jews, live together in a state of cordiality, love and tolerance.

This is Egypt, whose people have entrusted me with their sacred message. A message of security, safety, and peace to every man, woman, and child in Israel, I say, encourage your leadership to struggle for peace. Let all endeavors be channeled toward building a huge stronghold for peace instead of building destructive rockets.

Introduce to the entire world the image of the new man in the area so that he might set an example to the man of our age, the man of peace everywhere. Ring the bells for your sons. Tell them that those wars were the last of wars and the end of sorrows. Tell them that we are entering upon a new beginning, a new life, a life of love, prosperity, freedom, and peace.

You, sorrowing mother, you, widowed wife, you, the son who lost a brother or a father, all the victims of wars, fill the air and space with recitals of peace, fill bosoms and hearts with the aspirations of peace. Make peace a reality that blossoms and lives. Make hope a code of conduct and endeavor.

The will of peoples is part of the will of God. Ladies and gentlemen, before I came to this place, with every beat of my heart and with every sentiment, I prayed to God almighty. While performing the prayers at the Al-Aqsa[113] mosque and while visiting the Holy Sepulcher[114] I asked the almighty to give me strength and to confirm my belief that this visit may achieve the objective I look forward to for a happy present and a happier future.

I have chosen to set aside all precedents and traditions known by warring countries. In spite of the fact that occupation of Arab territories is still there, the declaration of my readiness to proceed to Israel came as a great surprise that stirred many feelings and confounded many minds. Some of them even doubted its intent.

Despite all that, the decision was inspired by all the clarity and purity of belief and with all the true passions of my people's will and intentions and I have chosen this road, considered by many to be the most difficult road.

---

[113] Al-Aqsa (*al-masjid al-aqsa*, lit. the further mosque), a famous Jerusalem mosque associated with the Prophet Muhammad's night voyage from Mecca to Jerusalem (Qur'an, 17: 1) and therefore one of the holiest sites in Islam.

[114] The Jerusalem church first built by the emperor Constantine in the fourth century CE to mark the site where Christ was buried and rose from the dead, therefore a major Christian pilgrimage site.

I have chosen to come to you with an open heart and an open mind. I have chosen to give this great impetus to all international efforts exerted for peace. I have chosen to present to you in your own home, the realities, devoid of any scheme or whim. Not to maneuver, or win a round, but for us to win together, the most dangerous of rounds embattled in modern history, the battle of permanent peace based on justice.

It is not my battle alone. Not is it the battle of the leadership in Israel alone. It is the battle of all and every citizen in all our territories, whose right it is to live in peace. It is the commitment of conscience and responsibility in the hearts of millions.

When I put forward this initiative, many asked what is it that I conceived as possible to achieve during this visit and what my expectations were. And as I answer the questions, I announce before you that I have not thought of carrying out this initiative from the precepts of what could be achieved during this visit. I have come here to deliver a message. I have delivered the message and may God be my witness.

I repeat with Zacharia: Love, right and justice. From the holy Qur'an I quote the following verses: 'We believe in God and in what has been revealed to us and what was revealed to Abraham, Ishmael, Isaac, Jacob and the thirteen Jewish tribes. And in the books given to Moses and Jesus and the prophets from their Lord, who made no distinction between them.' So we agree, Salam 'Alaykum— peace be upon you.

Selected bibliography

ABU HAKIMA, AHMAD, *The Modern History of Kuwait, 1750–1965* (London: Luzac, 1983).

ABU-LUGHAD, JANET L., *Rabat: Urban Apartheid in Morocco* (Princeton: Princeton University Press, 1980).

ABU MANNEH, BUTRUS, 'Sultan Abdülhamid II and Shaikh Abulhuda al-Sayyadi', *Middle Eastern Studies*, 15 (1979), 131–53.

ADAMS, ISAAC, *Persia By a Persian* (Washington DC: Published by author, 1900).

AFARY, JANET, *The Iranian Constitutional Revolution, 1906–1911: Grassroots Democracy, Social Democracy, and the Origins of Feminism* (New York: Columbia University Press, 1996).

AL-HAJ, MAJID, *Education, Empowerment and Control: The Case of the Arabs of Israel* (Albany: State University of New York Press, 1995).

ALTSTADT, AUDREY L., *The Azerbaijani Turks: Power and Identity Under Russian Rule* (Stanford, Calif.: Hoover Institution Press, Stanford University, 1992).

ANDERSON, LISA, 'Qaddafi's Islam', in John L. Esposito (ed.), *Voices of a Resurgent Islam* (New York: Oxford University Press, 1992).

ANSCOMBE, FREDERICK, *The Ottoman Gulf: The Creation of Kuwait, Sa'udi Arabia, and Qatar* (New York: Columbia University Press, 1997).

ANTONIUS, GEORGE, *The Arab Awakening* (London: Hamish Hamilton, 1938).

ARAI, MASAMI, *Turkish Nationalism in the Young Turk Era* (Leiden: Brill, 1992).

AVRUCH, KEVIN W., *American Immigrants in Israel: Social Identities and Change* (Chicago: University of Chicago Press, 1981).

BERBERIAN, HOURI, 'The Dashnaktsutiun and the Iranian Constitutional Revolution, 1905–1911', *Iranian Studies*, 29/1–2 (Winter/Spring 1996), 7–33.

——*Armenians and the Iranian Constitutional Revolution of 1905–1911: 'The Love for Freedom Has No Fatherland'* (Boulder, Col.: Westview Press, 2001).

BERKES, NIYAZI, *The Development of Secularism in Turkey* (Montreal: McGill University Press, 1964).

BEZALEL, YITZHAK, 'On the Uniqueness of "*ha-Herut*" and on Haim Ben Atar as its Editor', *Pe'amim*. 40 (1989) (Hebrew).

BIDWELL, ROBIN, *Morocco Under Colonial Rule: French Administration of Tribal Areas* (London: Cass, 1973).

BILL, JAMES A. and WILLIAM ROGER (eds.), *Musaddiq, Iranian Nationalism and Oil* (Austin: University of Texas Press, 1988).

BIMBERG, EDWARD L., *The Moroccan Goums: Tribal Warriors in a Modern War* (New York: Greenwood Press, 1999).

BRAND, GILA and DEVORAH HAKOHEN, *Immigrants in Turmoil: Mass Immigration to Israel and its Repercussions in the 1950s and After* (Syracuse, NY: Syracuse University Press, 2003).

CHAQUERI, COSROE (ed.), *Armenians in Iran: The Paradoxical Role of a Minority in a Dominant Culture: Articles and Documents* (Cambridge, Mass.: Center for Middle Eastern Studies of Harvard University, 1998).

—— 'The Role and Impact of Armenian Intellectuals in Iranian Politics 1905–1911', *Armenian Review*, 41/2 (Summer 1988), 1–51.

CLAYTON, ANTHONY, *France, Soldiers and Africa* (London Brassey's Defense Publishers, 1988).

COLE, JUAN R. I., *Colonialism and Revolution in the Middle East: Social and Cultural Origins of Egypt's ʿUrabi Movement* (Princeton: Princeton University Press, 1993).

DAWISHA, ADEED, *Arab Nationalism in the Twentieth Century: From Triumph to Despair* (Princeton: Princeton University Press, 2003).

DAWN, C. ERNEST, *From Ottomanism to Arabism: Essays on the Origins of Arab Nationalism* (Urbana, Ill.: University of Illinois Press, 1973).

DESHEN, SHLOMO A., *The Predicament of Homecoming: Cultural and Social Life of North African Immigrants in Israel* (Ithaca, NY: Cornell University Press, 1974).

DIBA, FARHAD, *Mohammed Mossadegh: Political Biography* (London: Croom Helm, 1986).

EICH, THOMAS, *Abu l-Huda as-Sayyadi: Eine Studie zur Instrumentalisierung genealogischer Kontroversen und sufischer Netzwerke im spätosmanischen Reich* (Berlin: Klaus Schwarz Verlag, 2003).

—— 'Abu l-Huda, the Rifaʿiya and Shiism in Hamidian Iraq', *Der Islam*, 80 (2003), 142–52.

—— *Netzwerke der Macht, Macht der Genealogie: Aufstieg und Fall des Abu l-Huda as-Sayyadi* (forthcoming).

EICKELMAN, DALE, *Knowledge and Power in Morocco: The Education of a Twentieth-Century Notable* (Princeton: Princeton University Press, 1985).

ELIAV, MORDECHAI, 'Inter-Communal Relations in the Jewish *Yishuv* in Erets Israel in the Nineteenth Century', *Peʿamim*, 11 (1982) (Hebrew), 118–34.

EL-KIKHIA, MANSOUR, *Libya's Qaddafi: The Politics of Contradiction* (Gainesville, Fla.: University Press of Florida, 1997).

ELM, MOSATAFA, *Oil, Power, and Principle: Iran's Oil Nationalization and Its Aftermath* (Syracuse, NY: Syracuse University Press, 1992).

FARAH, CAESAR E., 'Reassessing Sultan Abdülhamid II's Islamic policy', *Archivum Ottomanicum*, 15 (1995–6), 191–212.

FIRST, RUTH, *Libya: The Elusive Revolution* (Harmondsworth: Penguin Books, 1974).

GAZIT, MORDECHAI, 'Egypt and Israel—Was There a Peace Opportunity Missed in 1971?', *Journal of Contemporary History*, 32/1 (Jan. 1997), 97–115.

GEORGEON, FRANÇOIS, *Aux Origines du Nationalisme Turc: Yusuf Akçura, 1876–1935* (Paris: ADPF, 1980).

—— *Des Ottomans aux Turcs: Naissance d'une Nation* (Istanbul: Isis, 1995).

GERSHOVICH, MOSHE, *French Military Rule in Morocco: Colonialism and its Consequences* (London: Cass, 2000).

GORNY, YOSEF, *The Arab Question and the Jewish Problem* (Tel Aviv, 1985) (Hebrew).

HANIOĞLU, M. ŞÜKRÜ, *The Young Turks in Opposition* (New York: Oxford University Press, 1995).

HOISINGTON, WILLIAM A. Jr., *Lyautey and the French Conquest of Morocco* (Basingstoke: Macmillan, 1995).

HOURANI, ALBERT, *Arabic Thought in the Liberal Age, 1798–1939* (Oxford: Clarendon Press, 1962).

HOURANI, ALBERT, *Arabic Thought in the Liberal Age, 1798–1939*, 2nd edn. (Cambridge: Cambridge University Press, 1983).

—— 'How Should We Write the History of the Middle East?', *International Journal of Middle Eastern Studies (IJMES)*, 23 (1991), 125–36.

Immigration and Settlement in Israel, Israel Pocket Library, Keter.

JANKOWSKI, JAMES P. and I. GERSHONI, *Rethinking Nationalism in the Arab Middle East* (New York: Columbia University Press, 1997).

JONES, CLIVE, *Soviet Jewish Aliyah, 1989–92: Impact and Implications for Israel and the Middle East* (London: Frank Cass, 1996).

KARAWAN, IBRAHIM A., 'Sadat and the Egyptian–Israeli Peace Revisited', *International Journal of Middle East Studies*, 26/2 (May, 1994), 249–66.

KARPAT, KEMAL (ed.), *Ottoman Past and Today's Turkey* (Leiden: Brill, 2000).

KATOUZIAN, HOMA, *Musaddiq and the Struggle for Power in Iran* (London: I. B. Tauris, 1990).

KAYALI, HASAN, *Arabs and Young Turks: Ottomanism, Arabism, and Islamism in the Ottoman Empire, 1908–1918* (Berkeley: University of California Press, 1997).

KELERMAN, AHARON, *Society and Settlement: Jewish Land of Israel in the Twentieth Century* (Albany: State University of New York Press, 1993).

KELLY, JOHN, *Britain and the Persian Gulf, 1795–1880* (Oxford: Clarendon Press, 1968).

KHALIDI, RASHID, *et al.* (eds.), *The Origins of Arab Nationalism* (New York: Columbia University Press, 1991).

LANDAU, JACOB M., *The Politics of Pan-Islam: Ideology and Organization* (Oxford: Oxford University Press, 1990).

—— *Pan-Turkism: From Irridentism to Cooperation* (Bloomington: Indiana University Press, 1995).

The Latin-American Community of Israel (New York: Praeger, 1984).

LIPPMAN, THOMAS W., *Egypt After Nasser: Sadat, Peace and the Mirage of Prosperity* (New York: Paragon House, 1989).

LIVINGSTON, JOHN W., 'Western Science and Educational Reform in the Thought of Shaykh Rifaa Tahtawi', *International Journal of Middle East Studies*, 28/4 (Nov. 1996), 543–64.

MAHMOOD, ZAHID, 'Sadat and Camp David Reappraised', *Journal of Palestine Studies*, 15/1 (Autumn 1985), 62–87.

MANDEL, NEVILLE, *The Arabs and Zionism Before World War I* (Berkeley: University of California Press, 1976).

MAOZ, MOSHE (ed.), *Studies on Palestine During the Ottoman Period* (Jerusalem: Magnes Press, 1975).

LEWIS, BERNARD, *The Emergence of Modern Turkey* (London: Oxford University Press, 1968).

OFER, DALIA, *Escaping the Holocaust: Illegal Immigration to the Land of Israel, 1939–1944* (Oxford: Oxford University Press, 1999).

PENNELL, C. R., *Morocco Since 1830* (New York: New York University Press, 2000).

PORCH, DOUGLAS, *The Conquest of Morocco* (New York: Knopf, 1983).

POULTON, HUGH, *Top Hat, Grey Wolf and Crescent* (New York: New York University Press, 1997).

RAPOPORT, LOUIS, *Redemption Song: The Story of Operation Moses* (New York: Harcourt, 1986).

SADAT, ANWAR, *In Search of Identity, A Biography* (New York: Harper & Row, 1978).

SALEM-BABIKIAN, NORMA, 'The Sacred and the Profane: Sadat's Speech to the Knesset', *Middle East Journal*, 34/1 (Winter 1979), 13–24.

SHAW, STANFORD J., and EZEL KURAL SHAW, *History of the Ottoman Empire and Modern Turkey. Vol. II: Reform, Revolution, and Republic: The Rise of Modern Turkey, 1808–1975* (Cambridge: Cambridge University Press, 1977).

SHULEWITZ, MALKA HILLEL (ed.), *The Forgotten Millions: The Modern Jewish Exodus from Arab Lands* (New York: Continuum, 2001).

SUNY, RONALD GRIGOR (ed.), *Transcaucasia, Nationalism and Social Change: Essays in the History of Armenia, Azerbaijan, and Georgia* (Ann Arbor: University of Michigan Press, 1996).

SWEARINGEN, WILL D., *Moroccan Mirages: Agrarian Dreams and Deceptions, 1912–1986* (Princeton: Princeton University Press, 1987).

SWIETOCHOWSKI, TADEUSZ, *Russian Azerbaijan, 1905–1920: The Shaping of National Identity in a Muslim Community* (New York: Cambridge University Press, 1985).

TER MINASSIAN, ANAHIDE, *Nationalism and Socialism in the Armenian Revolutionary Movement (1887–1912)* (Cambridge, Mass.: Zoryan Institute, 1984).

VANDEWALLE, DIRK (ed.), *Qadhafi's Libya, 1969–1994* (Basingstoke: Macmillan, 1995).

WEINTRAUB, DOV, *Immigration and Social Change: Agricultural Settlements of New Immigrants in Israel* (Tel Ariv: Israel Universities Press/Humanities Press).

ZAMERET, ZVI, *Melting Pots in Israel: The Commission of Inquiry Concerning the Education of Immigrant Children During the Early Years of The State* (Albany: State University of New York Press, 2002).

ZENKOVSKY, SERGE A., *Pan-Turkism and Islam in Russia* (Cambridge, Mass.: Harvard University Press, 1960).

ZIRINSKY, MICHAEL P., 'Harbingers of Change: Presbyterian Women in Iran, 1883–1949', *American Presbyterians: Journal of Presbyterian History*, 70/3 (1992), 173–86.

——'A Panacea for the Ills of the Country: American Presbyterian Education in Inter-War Iran', *Iranian Studies*, 26/1–2 (1993), 119–37.

——'American Presbyterian Missionaries at Urmia During the Great War', *Proceedings of the International Roundtable on Persia and the Great War*, Tehran, 2–3 March 1997 (forthcoming).

ZÜRCHER, ERIK J., *Turkey: A Modern History* (London: I. B. Tauris, 1993).

6

Views of the world

Introduction

One of the great misconceptions about the Middle East in the modern era is that it was always in a state of being forcibly surprised by world events and Euro-American progress and power. This was certainly not the case among the educated elites in the eighteenth century who were charged with formulating a response to these changes, and, with the spread of modern communication and transportation systems in the nineteenth century, the circle of informed Middle Easterners only grew. It was during the nineteenth century that increasing numbers of Middle Eastern merchants, students and diplomats made their way to the West as visitors, and, as the century progressed, many from more humble origins began to seek opportunities by emigrating to Europe and the Americas. There was also increased regional travel within the greater Middle East and an influx of Western diplomats, military personnel, colonial officials, missionaries and technical personnel. Such contact produced a variety of reactions by Middle Easterners and the foreigners in their midst. There was hostility and 'orientalist/occidentalist' stereotyping to be sure, but also many more subtle observations that testify to an increasing familiarity and intimacy between these two complex societies. And not just between these two. Middle Easterners kept track of each other's experiences and those of East Asian societies as well. The documents in this section provide windows on these many emerging 'views of the world' generated by Middle Easterners and visitors to the Middle East.

6.1 Letters from Nader Shah to the Ottoman Court, 1736
Ernest Tucker

Preface

The following two documents are letters written in 1736 by Nader Shah
to the Ottoman Sultan Mahmud I (1730–54) and his grand vizier.[1] Nader
sent the letters to Istanbul with a three-man delegation to reciprocate the
Ottoman mission that had witnessed Nader's accession to the Iranian
throne in March 1736. He had begun his career as a common Safavid
soldier. As his military abilities began to be recognized, he was swiftly
promoted to the position of Shah Tahmasp II's main general by the end
of the 1720s.

In 1732 Nader deposed Tahmasp, increasingly seen as weak and vacillating,
and made Tahmasp's young son ʿAbbas III a figurehead ruler. By 1736
Nader had been so successful as a commander that he was emboldened to
take the throne himself. To legitimize this act, he assembled nomadic and
sedentary leaders from all over Iran at Mughan in northern Azerbaijan.
Nader's official history stated that they proclaimed him shah in a ceremony
referred to as a *quriltay*. Among the Mongols, *quriltay* meant a ruling
family's conclave on the steppe to elect a new leader or khan. Since the
Safavids had scarcely held *quriltay*s since the fifteenth century, Nader's
1736 Mughan assembly was unprecedented. He wanted to show the
support of as many Iranian leaders as possible for his seizure of the throne
from the Safavids, who had claimed divine sanction for their control
of it since 1501.

These letters from Nader to the Ottoman court presented his plan to
establish lasting peace between the two empires in the wake of his accession. The Safavids had fought intermittently with the Ottomans since the
fall of Isfahan to the Afghans in 1722. Nader believed that this situation
could be ended by the resolution of longstanding disputes between Sunni
and Shiʿi Muslims, because conflict between them could be legitimized
by the fact that they considered each other apostates. Nader wanted to
have Twelver Shiʿi Islam, the official religion of Iran, recognized as a fifth
legal school of Sunni Islam with the same status as the traditional four
Sunni legal schools. Iranian practices regarded by Sunnis as heretical,
such as the ritual cursing of the first three caliphs—Abu Bakr, ʿUmar,
and ʿUthman—would be abolished, while distinctive Shiʿi practices
not considered heretical by the other four schools, such as the veneration

---

[1] There was also a third letter addressed to the Ottoman *Shaykh al-Islam*, but as it is very similar to
the grand vizier's letter, it is not included here.

of Shi'i Imams' tombs as great holy sites, would be continued. Although Nader continued to promote this plan until the mid-1740s, the Ottomans never accepted it, as it flew in the face of many centuries of Muslim tradition and legal interpretations. The Ottoman sultan had much less interest than Nader in upsetting the Islamic world's status quo in 1736.

Nader's reign has mostly been remembered in Iran as tyrannical and bloody. He fought several costly campaigns against the Ottomans, taxed his subjects heavily, and terrorized local political elites as he tried to secure control over his domains. Partly in reaction to Nader, subsequent Iranian rulers like the Qajars became strong champions of Iran's Shi'i identity as a mark of separation from the larger Sunni world community. Despite its failure, however, Nader's plan helps mark the beginning of modern Iran, since it is a key element of one of the first episodes in the modern debate on the proper relationship between religion and government that persists today.

Text

Copy of a letter from Nader Shah to the Exalted Sultan

(Başbakanlık Arşivi, Istanbul, *Name-i Hümayun Defteri* 3)
In the name of God, the Merciful, the Compassionate!

Unrestrained thanks and praise, along with appropriate care and concern, belong to God without limit, because just sultans have been chosen according to the phrase 'We have placed you on the earth in order to improve the situation and provide for peace and the refuge of mankind.'[2] In order to stop disputes and fighting between groups of men, 'Remember the blessings of God, since you had been enemies and he put your hearts together in love, so that by His grace, you became brethren.'[3] The night chamber of conflict and obstinacy has been transformed with the rising of the true dawn of authority. A crown has been placed on the head, no, golden crowns that bind have been placed on those who need the forgiving God, and the door has been opened for all.

It is proper to praise beyond thought or comparison the pure spirit and luminous grave of the messenger without equal [Muhammad]. His good news to all nations is decorated by a valuable earring—the choice hadith: 'Blessed be the righteous who recite the word.'[4] It is a clear guide on the high road to correct argument between one branch of the prophet's followers and other branches. [The Qur'an] is the unique great jewel of being, the pole of the God-worshipping heaven, the signet sun of that throne which came from the seal of all the prophets,

---

[2] Qur'an 10: 14.   [3] Qur'an 3: 103.
[4] A hadith is the report of Muhammad's words or deeds.

Muhammad, may the blessings of God be upon him and upon his blessed family, the wise caliphs, and noble companions![5]

Now then, raised up to his excellency [the Ottoman sultan]'s lofty sun-high imperial view and his mind that shines in heaven and is filled with friendliness, to that man at the celestial level with the Pleiades, Saturn, Jupiter, Mars, the Sun, Venus, Mercury, and the Moon, that [ruler] with the glory of Solomon, the grace of Alexander, the justice of Anushirvan, the man verified by the Just Sultan [God], that shadow of God, he who is the living expression of kindness upon God's people, the greatest sultan of the world, the grandest khan of the era, receiver of the crowns of greatness and regal dignity, the adornment of sultanic and powerful fortune, that is, the second Alexander, the cream of the dynasty of the family of Osman [the Ottomans][...]sultan of the lands, *khaqan* of the seas, servant of the two holy places,[6] the second Alexander of the two horns, a star in the spheres of power, glory, greatness, succession, mercy, kindness, acting justly, and nobly doing good, Sultan Mahmud Khan son of Sultan Mustafa Khan (may God prolong his reign and power!) is the fact that from the time when God, whose help we seek, created time and established the world, this is the real meaning of the true statement that we were created by Him with being and soul. Obedience to the prophet's [words] gave us mercy and was required of us. As long as we followed the people of the Sunna we benefited with joy.[7]

The appearance of Shah Esma'il Safavi caused fanaticism to come from questioning and controversial behavior, which turned some groups of Muslims and the *community* of the Leader of prophets towards heresy. So God produced this humble supplicant of the divine court [Nader] to bring order to the vast areas and roads of Iran and to benefit the affairs of Muslims. Because of this, in the middle of the blessed month of Ramadan [i.e. March 1736], this well-wisher [Nader] assembled all the great lords, blessed ʿolama,[8] praiseworthy eminent men, commanders of provinces, and venerable leaders of the tribes and *uymaqs* of Iran on the Mughan steppe.[9] The reasons and justification for the true *madhhab* were given to them in the writings of that eminent, model minister, magnificent counselor, the respected pole of world order, fulfillment of the

---

[5] Muslims generally revere Muhammad, his family, his caliphs or successors as ruler, and his companions as exemplary human beings.

[6] Khan and *khaqan* are both variations of the Mongol word for 'leader'. 'The two holy places' is a traditional way to refer to Mecca and Medina. Note the blending of Central Asian images ('khan'), Islamic images ('servant of the two holy places'), and classical images ('second Alexander') in this passage

[7] 'Sunna' refers to the sayings and practices of Muhammad, considered by Muslims to be verified by God. 'Sunni Muslim' therefore, simply means 'a Muslim who follows the Sunna'.

[8] ʿ*Olama* ('scholars') are experts in Islamic law and theology.

[9] *Uymaq*, in Turkish and Persian, means 'tribal group'.

important affairs of mankind: the *shaykh al-Islam* (may his usefulness continue!).[10]
In their hearts and on their tongues, all of them gave up works of innovation
[*bid'a*], accepting and submitting to the sublime Sunna of his Excellency
[Muhammad], the best of humanity (upon him be the best of blessings and
peace!).[11] In order that this good building be kept safe and guarded from disturbance and damage and that there be no alteration or change in the strong
foundations of this path, they stopped following the Safavid dynasty and chose
[Nader,] supplicant of the provident God's court, to be Iran's *king*.

Then his Excellency, the esteemed minister and valued counselor of the exalted
Ottoman state, Hajj 'Ali Pasha, the governor of Qaraman (May God increase
his greatness!), was chosen from among the notables of the lofty [Ottoman] realm
and sublime sultanate to negotiate peace. Upon this, [Nader,] refuge of leadership and nobility, exalted embodiment of nobility and courage, sent 'Abd al-Baqi
Khan Zanganeh, governor of Kermanshahan, an esteemed Iranian leader, [Nader's]
trusted follower, and a supplicant of the Creator (may He be glorified!), on this
embassy with a letter to promote good government, tranquility, and welfare.
That eminent essence of the lords and great ones—best of the nobles and the
great—the prime minister Mirza Abu al-Qasim—along with Molla 'Ali Akbar,
most intelligent and thoughtful exemplar of the learned and the 'olama's leader,
one of the great lords and excellent leaders, religious teacher of Khorasan, [Nader's]
imam, and a supplicant of God the Judge's endless goodwill, to accompany his
excellency the ambassador 'Abd al-Baqi Khan on a journey to the imperial
[Ottoman] court, vast as the heavens, threshold of the shadow of God, and a
royal axis.[12] Thus, just as they have been charged to do, they will show the agents
of the exalted [Ottoman] sultanic state and associates of this good khedival
kingdom that (God be praised!) [Nader,] supplicant of the [divine] court that
created heaven and earth has worked hard and taken trouble to follow the clear
faith and evident religion correctly—to free it from disparagement.[13] This affair
can be completed and end well with the highest effort, along with the expression
of burning desire and exalted innermost intention, on the part of the [Ottoman]
khedive at the level of the Pleiades—this *monarch* of heavenly grandeur—God
(may He be exalted!) willing, so that a response is given that will be accepted and
approved by the prophet (may God bless him and give him peace!) at the end

[10] A *madhhab* is one of the schools of Islamic legal interpretation. The *shaykh al-Islam* is the head
of the 'Ulama.

[11] *Bid'a* means 'innovation in religious belief or practice'. This is a major sin because God alone
has ordained correct religious belief and practice in the Qur'an.

[12] Imam here means 'prayer leader'.

[13] Note that 'khedive' and 'khedival', usually used in the West to refer to the nineteenth-century
rulers of Egypt, were common titles of Islamic rulers in many countries. I have chosen to retain them
to suggest the wide scope of their use.

of time and will not require any justification. Since these words have been stretched and prolonged beyond good manners, the explanation of these circumstances is contained in the letters to his excellency the grand vizier and the most valued counselor, the leader of the ʿolama: the *shaykh al-Islam*.[. . .]

A Letter from Nader Shah to his Excellency the Esteemed Grand Vizier

In the name of God, the Merciful, the Compassionate!

His high excellency, the grand vizier (God, may He be exalted, elevate his dignity and double his prosperity with unlimited glories from the khedive and honors from the king!), is honored and revered as the refuge of dignity, fortune and administration, the hand of dignity, greatness, and glory, vigilant in bravery and courage, highly-placed model of great viziers, leader of dignified commanders, organizer of affairs with correct opinion, administrator of important community affairs whose thoughts penetrate, trusted by the exalted *khaqani* state, faithful servant of the splendid sultanic power, well-organized vizier with correct counsel, realm-ordering conscience, most valued and dignified order, and great center of world order.[. . .] With this, the kingdom-decorating opinion knows that it is clear and obvious to observe that dispute and quarrel has arisen between the Muslims of Rum [the Ottoman Empire] and Iran. It began when Shah Esmaʿil Safavi emerged with a heavenly claim, based on corrupt motives and in order to establish his power, creating the basis for this sort of sedition, corruption, killing, and stubbornness among groups of Muslims, who are all part of the *community* of one prophet—followers of one book and one *qebleh*.[14] The effects of this have continued to the present.

At this time, our leader, in order to heal the religious community that seeks truth and to spread the true faith that is the inheritance of the people of Iran and to remove the dispute and quarrel, assembled all the great commanders, ʿolama, notables, nobles, leaders of the regions and tribes of Iran in the middle of Ramadan on the Mughan steppe. To confirm his most holy, divine excellence [Muhammad] and the secret thoughts of his holiness, the refuge of prophecy, the veil of doubt and difference has been removed from the face of the *madhhab* of truth. We proclaimed to all the people of Iran with explanations, proofs, and demonstrations that these false and useless issues had been created by the corrupt designs of the Safavid dynasty that are against the words of the chosen messenger [Muhammad], the great companions, and the pure Imams. All [those present] accepted these words, lest following the Safavid dynasty would bring fresh corruption and immeasurable chaos. Our royal leader was chosen to be

---

[14] Shah Esmaʿil was the first Safavid monarch, who ruled from 1501 to 1524. The *qebleh* (Arabic *qibla*) is the niche in the front of any mosque that points in the direction of Mecca for prayer.

shah and monarch: the inheritance of the great Turkman *il* [tribe].[15] After his Excellency the esteemed minister [. . .] ʿAli Pasha, the governor of Qaraman sent by the noble and exalted Ottoman state to discuss peace, had talked with his excellency [Nader], he needed to explain these matters to the glorious guardians of the Ottoman state.

We therefore ordered him to bring this joyful news to the heaven-orbiting sultan's [Ottoman] court. However, this esteemed minister hesitated since he did not have permission to return to the blessed Excellency of the Ottoman state. Yet, since the conclusion of this affair with good result would have great benefits for this state [Iran] in this world and the next, the aforementioned [ambassador] was sent to the celestial sultanic court accompanied by [. . .]ʿAbd al-Baqi Khan Zanganeh, the governor of Kirmanshahan, his Excellency, the essential leader [. . .] Mirza Abu al-Qasim, and the most knowing and understanding master of the ʿolama [. . .] Molla ʿAli Akbar, the teacher of Khorasan [. . .] in order to strengthen the clear faith and establish the religion that sees, so that with the passage of time, through the power and strength of the forgiving God, the pillars and laws [of Islam] will not become weak until the end of time.

If God the Benefactor wills, the carpet of friendship will be spread with the help and love of the Spreader, since He is without fault. Recognition of this situation, which now has been advanced and put into final form through the endeavors and efforts of our auspicious regent [Nader], requires for this reason that the people of loosing and binding [the rulers] and well-wishers of that eminent [Ottoman] state establish the acceptability [. . .] of the Jaʿfari [*mazhab*] as the fifth *mazhab* with the [other] four and confirm their place in the Holy Mosque [of Mecca] alongside other Muslims by erecting a pillar for them in the holy House of God.[16] Every year an Iranian amir would be sent to guide the Iranian hajj group to the noble precincts of the Holy House in order to visit the shining tombs of his excellency, the best of men (may God bless him and give him peace!) and those of the rightly guided caliphs (may God be pleased with them!).[17] A trusted representative of the sublime Ottoman seat in the capital of Iran and from this side, in exchange, a trusted representative in the great Ottoman capital would reside, so that the signs of togetherness and unity would

---

[15] This unusual use of the word 'Turkman' recalls the historical position of Turkic peoples (i.e. groups who speak languages similar to modern Turkish) as rulers of Iran and other parts of the Middle East for many centuries.

[16] Jaʿfari refers to the fifth Shiʿi Imam Jaʿfar al-Sadiq, long regarded as the greatest legal scholar among the Shiʿis and therefore commensurate with the founders of the other Islamic legal scholars (*mazhab*s).

[17] Each of the four schools of Sunni Islam had its own hajj pilgrimage caravan, which was led by an *amir al-hajj*, which is what Nader is proposing that the Iranians also be allowed to do. It is worth noting that regularizing the Iranian hajj caravan might have had important economic benefits, because so much commerce took place each year in the context of the hajj.

be apparent. Every Iranian captive in the vast Ottoman provinces who had wanted to get married would be allowed to keep his marriage contract. For those who did not want to be married, in accordance with the holy law of the prophet, an official decree would be issued that wherever they were, they would be released to be able to go back to their homelands. This side [Iran] would carry out the same action. Other issues and affairs have been left to the representatives [of this embassy], which God willing they will communicate orally and in detail. Since the delegates have gone to the heaven-built threshold to promote religion and faith, the definite achievement of goodwill between both sides is their goal. They will all join in sharing the benefits of this great proposal. May the days of governing and having fortune, glory, prosperity, and pomp continue!

6.2 Ottoman–Iranian marriage and the Ottoman legal code, 1822–1926

Karen M. Kern

Preface

During the last quarter of the nineteenth century, after a long period of administrative reform known as the *Tanzimat* (1839–76), the Ottoman Empire entered into a period of renewed attention to the Sunni religious foundations of the empire and expanded its involvement in the minutiae of the daily lives of its subjects. These activities resulted in a growing concern among Ottoman officials over the large numbers of Iranian Shiᶜis who lived in the empire. The Iranian community was composed primarily of non-Ottoman subjects and included diplomats, merchants, and craftsmen who had settled in the larger cities of the empire, as well as Iranian subjects living in border regions of Iraq who, for centuries, had traveled between Iran and Iraq for seasonal trade, or for study in the Shiᶜi shrine cities in Iraq. This group was the largest non-Ottoman Muslim community in the Ottoman Empire. The four documents translated below reveal increased government attention to this community, including its attempt to regulate marriages between Ottoman Sunni women and Iranian Shiᶜi men.

As early as 1512, shortly after the establishment of the Shiᶜi Safavid[18] state on the Ottoman's eastern border, various Ottoman *şeyhülislams*[19] issued *fetva*s (religious opinions) denying the legality of marriages between Ottomans and *kizilbaş* (*qezelbash*) who were considered heretics by the religious establishment. Although classical Sunni Islamic law was generally inclusive and did not prohibit Sunni–Shiᶜi marriages, rare exceptions were made in the case of persons considered followers of the most serious heresies. In spite of the inclusiveness of classical Islamic law, the Ottoman government, and the senior religious officials who issued these *fetvas*, included both Ottoman and non-Ottoman members of the Shiᶜi community in the prohibition. Periodically throughout the sixteenth and into the early seventeenth century, the prohibition of such marriages continued to be proclaimed by *fetva*. Although no evidence has come to light detailing the position of the central religious authority on the question of Shiᶜi marriages for the eighteenth century, on the local level a judge in Damascus prohibited marriages between Ottomans and Iranians travelling on the

---

[18] The Safavid state was established in 1501 by Shah Esmaᶜil.

[19] Chief Ottoman religious official and member of the Ottoman bureaucracy responsible for matters of canon law.

hajj,[20] who were often forced to wait in the region for long periods before joining caravans to the holy sites.

The central administration of the Ottoman government once again considered the question of Sunni–Shi'i marriages in 1822 during the reign of the reforming sultan Mahmud II (1808–39). The *Buyruldu-i Âli* (Imperial Order) 'Concerning the Prohibition of Marriage with Iranians', in the first translation printed below, was produced directly from the office of the sultan himself. The prohibition, which had been reaffirmed and enforced by religious authorities for centuries, was now under the jurisdiction of the executive branch of government. By the time of this proclamation, Sultan Mahmud had embarked on a reform program whereby he attempted to modernize the administrative structures of the empire. His reforms brought him into confrontation with the most powerful institutions in the empire, including the religious establishment. Nevertheless, his policies were to provoke a process of reorganization of the administration and of the legal system, the *Tanzimat*.

During these decades of reform, legislation modeled on European codes of law was enacted in areas of commercial and civil law. Matters once confined to the jurisdiction of *şeriat* (Islamic law) courts were introduced into the secular system. This codification of law known as *Mecelle-i ahkam-i adliyye* was the first such codification by a Muslim country, and was drawn up in 1877 as the Ottoman Civil Code. The *şeriat* was not officially abandoned, however, and maintained its authority in matters of marriage, divorce, and inheritance. Ultimately, these questions of personal status were not included in the civil code.

During the years following the prohibition of Ottoman–Iranian marriages in 1822, the Ottomans and Iranians sought to formalize relations between their two empires on the model of Ottoman relations with European states. For example, the Iranian state finally achieved recognition as an independent entity, something the Ottomans had never formally accepted. Iranians were also allowed capitulatory rights over their citizens in the Ottoman Empire similar to the rights that had long been accorded to European states. However, during these decades the Ottomans and Iranians also continued to struggle for influence in the Ottoman province of Iraq with its vast wealth and resources. Since Iraq had a large mixed population of Sunnis and Shi'is, the question of marriages between the sects became an important issue for the Ottomans.

In 1874, during the reign of Sultan Abdülaziz, a law was passed banning marriages between Ottoman Sunnis and Iranian Shi'is. Now the justification for the prohibition of these marriages was based on a long-established tradition in *fetva* literature and by executive mandate. The law 'Protecting the Prohibition of Marriages between Ottoman and Iranian Citizens',

---

[20] One of the five pillars of Islam: a religious pilgrimage to Mecca and Medina incumbent upon all Muslims once during their lifetime.

the second document translated below, reaffirmed the 1822 prohibition of these marriages. By this time, however, a new Ottoman nationality law, based on the French model, had been enacted as part of the legal reforms of the *Tanzimat*. The 'Law of Ottoman Nationality' of 1869 permitted Ottoman women to marry foreigners, but upon marriage Ottoman women immediately acquired the citizenship of their husbands, thereby losing Ottoman citizenship. The children of these marriages also took the citizenship of their father. The only exception to the provision of the Ottoman nationality law concerning the nationality of Ottoman women who married foreigners was Article 3 in the 1874 law prohibiting Ottoman–Iranian marriages. In this law Ottoman women who married Iranians remained Ottoman subjects, as did their children.

The 1874 law was reaffirmed and clarified on a number of occasions throughout the reign of Abdülhamid II (r. 1876–1909). During this period, government ministries were questioned on the validity of the prohibition by the various provinces. Legal advisers to various ministries continued to remind Ottoman officials that the prohibition was still in force.

In 1914 the Iranian Embassy in Istanbul requested a cancellation of the prohibition by arguing that Iranian citizens should be accorded the same rights to marry Ottoman women that were granted to Muslim citizens of other foreign states. The third entry included below represents the response of the legal advisors to the Interior Ministry explaining the reasons for the original prohibition and their interpretation of the need for its continuation.

During World War I, and in the years immediately following the end of the war, Ottoman officials recognized that this law had little meaning, especially considering that Iraq had come under foreign control. Yet any movement to cancel the prohibition met with little success: not until the last sultan had been overthrown and a secular republic established did Turkish officials abolish it. In 1926, without fanfare or memorandum of intent, the prohibition of Ottoman–Iranian marriages was annulled by law. This law, entitled 'Concerning, the Preservation of the Prohibition of Marriage between Iranian and Turkish Citizens', is the fourth translation below.

Texts

1. *Buyruldu-i Âli* (Imperial Order): 'Concerning the Prohibition of Marriage with Iranians', 1822

All Muslims are obliged to know the religion of Islam and to learn matters concerning belief, but some people of ignorance who deviate from these obligatory principles marry or cause [others] to marry by undertaking acts not suitable to the dogma of religious precepts and sacred observances of Islam [and if] people of ignorance, may God forbid, change Muslim schools (*mezhep*) [they] will be subject to disappointment in this world and the next.

In the matter of contracting marriages to persons of some unknown lineage, most sons and grandsons cannot inquire into the origins of the person's descendants. [Therefore] it is the obligation of the neighborhood imam, who draws up the contract, to make the marriage contract free from doubt by investigating the family origins of the person, in order not to go against the beloved Islamic faith, or to be surprised by making marriage contracts between persons of unknown origin and school.

Also in this matter, those who contract and cause to contract marriage of Sunni women with Iranians will be investigated and, if it is proven, [will be] arrested.

With respect to this matter, from this time onward the religious authorities of Istanbul and its environs who absolutely do not investigate, or are negligent and do not pay attention, as well as the neighborhood imams who give permission, contract marriage, or who dare to cause [these marriages] to occur, by allowing people to marry [those] who are inclined to ignorance, Shiʿis, heretics, persons of unknown lineage, and many Iranians, will be punished with the strongest punishment.

For the judges of Istanbul, Egypt, and Üsküdar, the matter of the Imperial Decree is clear. The neighborhood imams who perform marriages in these categories will be strongly punished. The strongest punishment is declared [also] for those who give and take girls to these persons of unknown origins, and may God forbid situations like this henceforth.

2. Başbakanlık Osmanlı Arşivi (BOA), *Ecnebi Defterleri*, 43/1, 11 Rebiülahir 1237 (5 January 1822), 36–7: 'Law Protecting the Prohibition of Marriages between Iranians and Ottoman Subjects'

1. Marriage between Ottoman and Iranian subjects, as in olden times, is strongly prohibited.
2. Those [officials] who are authorized to perform marriages, [and] who act against the prohibition, will be held responsible.
3. [If] a woman who is an Ottoman subject marries an Iranian subject against the prohibition, both the woman and her children will be considered Ottoman subjects and liable for conscription, military tax and all other financial obligations.

3. BOA, *Ecnebi Defterleri*, 43/1, 25 Şaban 1291/24 Eylül 1290 (7 October 1874), 17: 'Response of the Legal Advisors to the Interior Ministry'

Since ancient times, marriage between Ottoman Muslim women and Iranians was prohibited, even as far back as [the time of] Yavuz Sultan Selim I,[21] [when]

---

[21] Ruler from 1512 to 1520.

because of the administrative system in use in the Ottoman State, Shi°ism was not widespread.

The *ferman* dated 11 Rebiülahir 1237 of Sultan Mahmud II[22] states: ʿAs a result of the marriage with Iranians and persons of unknown lineage who are inclined to Shi°ism [and] heretical *mezheps* [. . .] the *ferman* was issued, one by one, to the *kadi*s in Istanbul, Egypt, and Üsküdar and [. . .] to neighborhood imams. Those imams who contract the marriages and those [. . .] who take or give [their daughters] to these persons of unknown lineage will be liable for serious punishment, so that these [marriages] will not occur after this time. After the *Tanzimat*, the [need for] the prevention [of these marriages] was understood since many Ottoman Muslim women, especially in Iraq and some other districts, married Iranians in order to release their sons from military service. The system of conscription of male children who are born as a result of these marriages between *mezheps* was adopted.[. . .]

The law dated 27 Şaban 1291/24 Eylül 1290,[23] strengthening the aforesaid prohibition, was enacted. The Iranian embassy, in an official note, requested the cancellation of the aforesaid prohibition, asking permission for citizens of Iran to have the same rights of marriage as Muslim citizens of other foreign states. With respect to the cancellation of the aforesaid prohibition, the regulations in the law are clearly set forth and strengthened. If marriages of Ottoman women and Iranians occur in contravention of the prohibition, both the women and their children are in every case counted as Ottoman citizens and are liable for military service, and all other tax obligations as written in Article 3.

The aforesaid prohibition will continue in view of the fact that [there are] 100,000 Iranians who, if they marry Ottoman women as they please, as a result of [these] marriages it is expected that thousands of sons will possess foreign status. [We are] giving careful attention to the non-multiplication of foreign citizens in the [Ottoman] state.

4. BBA, HR.HM .ISO, 7–1/1, 2 Teşrinisani 1331/15 November 1915: 'Law of 26 April 1926, "Concerning the Preservation of the Prohibition of Marriage between Iranian and Turkish Citizens" '

Article 1. The prohibition concerning marriages of Iranians with Turkish women is abolished.

Article 2. After this [time], all formalities that arise from these kinds of marriages are subject to public laws.

---

[22] 5 January 1822.

[23] 9 October 1874. Since this refers to the 'Law Protecting the Prohibition of Marriages between Ottoman and Iranian Subjects' of 7 October 1874, this date must be incorrect.

Article 3. With respect to the rules in force as a result of the prohibition, all matters such as citizenship, which have been concluded up until now, are valid.

Article 4. This law is valid from the date of publication.

Article 5. Officials of the Ministries of Justice, Interior, and Foreign Affairs are commissioned to carry out the provisions of this law.

6.3 The journals of an Ottoman student in England, July 1829 to January 1830
Paul Sedra

Preface

Joseph Hekekyan was a Renaissance Man, and the proof is in his papers. The journals he kept while studying in England range in subject from hydraulic engineering to ancient Egyptian chronology to the moral status of prostitution. In tone, he shows a similar range of rhetorical skill, from the abstract and esoteric to the impassioned and personal, and indeed ranging in language from English and French, to Armenian and Ottoman Turkish, to Greek and Arabic. His writings expose the complexities and layers of identity and vision in the nineteenth-century Ottoman world that would be lost in the twentieth century as empire fragmented into nation-states, forcibly separating nineteenth-century compound identities, such as Ottoman Arab, Ottoman Armenian, and Ottoman Greek.

Having lived between worlds—the Istanbul of his childhood, the England of his adolescence, and the Egypt of his career—Hekekyan, as an historical figure, resists straightforward classification. Born in Istanbul in 1807 to Armenian parents, his childhood was a frenetic one, with frequent shifts from tutor to tutor and school to school. His father, a civil servant in the administration of Mehmed Ali [Muhammad ʿAli], Egypt's Ottoman *vali* or viceroy, sent Hekekyan, at age 10, to England to continue his education. His parents had, perhaps rather curiously, dubbed their son the 'little Englishman' prior to his departure, given his predilection for English manners. Hekekyan lived up to the label, embracing the values of the mythical 'English gentleman' and striving fiercely to embody them, despite the fact that he never quite gained recognition as such. During his studies in England, at Clapham Academy and Stonyhurst College, he rubbed shoulders with the sons of the 'respectable' (native British) folk whose approval he sought, and he gradually lost whatever facility he had once enjoyed in the languages of his childhood. After the death of the boy's father in Cairo, Mehmed Ali undertook responsibility for Hekekyan's maintenance, with the understanding that the Armenian—like several young Ottoman students dispatched to Paris by the *vali*—would ultimately come to Egypt, equipped to help the viceroy realize ambitious reform aims in such fields as the military, agriculture, industry, and education. In September 1830 Joseph Hekekyan finally landed in Egypt, a land whose 'improvement' had long remained the object of his studies—and yet a land to which he was altogether foreign.

His relationship with Egypt, the Egyptians, and their ruler would remain ambiguous throughout his career. Profoundly influenced by the

English improvement ethic, fiercely devoted to the rationalization of government and the extension of commerce, Hekekyan respected Mehmed Ali's efforts to develop an efficient administration and to secure trade routes through Egypt. However, each time he travelled through the country, visiting towns and villages and chatting with the common people, he lamented the extraordinary brutality with which that administration was 'reformed.' For instance, the journals of his numerous expeditions in search of coal record in minute detail the sufferings of Egypt's peasants and Bedouin, as the administration of Mehmed Ali and his successors as viceroy coerced participation in public works—the construction of canals, factories, and, of course, palaces.

When in the company of the numerous doubters of his loyalty to Mehmed Ali, Hekekyan would proclaim himself an 'Egyptian'—yet he admitted that he was always most comfortable in the company of Cairo's European community. The journals of his adolescence mount fierce attacks upon Christian missionary activity in Muslim lands—however, at the Egyptian court he would express his profound resentment of the bigotry he experienced as a Christian among his Muslim peers.

The extracts from his early journals, a few of which are assembled here, aim to give an impression not only of the world-view that would inform Hekekyan's efforts at reform in Egypt, but further, of the struggles involved in straddling worlds, both practically and intellectually. They reveal the fact that reform, in Ottoman eyes, was never a matter of blind imitation of European practice—and they call into question the whole notion of the 'native' informant, forcing historians to face the question of just who an Ottoman Armenian might be in an Ottoman imperial and Egyptian provincial context.

Text

[Roads and civilization]

In Turkey I should deem a distance of 205 miles to be quite a journey—in the first place requiring a previous arrangement of affairs and of making one's will—in the next arming from head to foot. In England on the contrary we appoint the very place and time when, for instance from London to Edinburgh, 400 miles or more, we are to dine with a friend—and the business is done as quietly as if we were only going to take a short walk for taking the fresh air—and without any preparation but that of taking a shirt or two, with the toilet materiel in a bag under the arm—and plenty of money in our pockets—for in England we cannot move a yard without expense.

The greatest care is taken of the roads; men are seen working on the roads all over the empire—and in all directions there are commodious conveyances for the service of the public. Good roads, canals, railroads and ships are of the first necessity for the civilization of a country. For as knowledge and good laws together with their strict observance comprehend in a great measure civilization, it is evident that facility of intercourse promotes the collection of the former— and the easy administration of the latter—for if one portion of mankind be divided from another by insurmountable barriers the same law will not be able to be administered to both—and they will vary in points of legislation. By means of easy conveyance property becomes valuable, and the country becomes so much the richer; thus advancement in knowledge, good laws, and the wealth of a nation go hand in hand.

A country cannot be rich without being well governed, and no great improvements in learning can be made in a country where there are no good laws— consequently a country cannot be wealthy without it being governed with good laws. Concerning the laws which should govern the people of any country I have one point to insist upon—and that is—unless those laws be made by the people themselves they will never be enforced without many coercive measures on the part of the despots being had recourse to; and this circumstance tends more to the debasement of a people than their subversion by foreign arms.[24]

[The problem of English labour]

The English workmen come and leave the works whenever they please and there is no power held over them. Whenever they get any money they run and spend it in drinking—and for a day or two after their course of drunkenness they are unwilling to come to their work—hence it is an ordinary circumstance that on Mondays few men can be mustered in the Manufactories and other works—for, having abused the day of rest with debauchery they are not fit to exert themselves on the following day, and they find themselves obliged to drink a little more to reanimate them.[25]

[A Sunday in Newcastle]

I went to the principal church with Mr Giles.[26] It is very old—and as for the architecture of it, the great impression it made on me was the ingenious contrivance of making the whole superstructure appear as if it would fall and crush me to death. Devils and monkeys' heads carved out of the woodwork, in various ludicrous postures had the delightful effect of making me laugh. The Parson, a young man with a tremendous head of hair which was curled and adjusted in all manner of ways, except that in which it would incline naturally, read prayers in a solemn and grave tone of voice. His smooth face was forced into certain wrinkles so that he might appear dignified and totally bent upon prayer, and his

---

[24] British Library, Hekekyan Papers, Additional MS 37,448, Volume 1, Journal of July 1829 to January 1830, pp. 32–3.   [25] Vol. 1, p. 64.

[26] Hekekyan had entered the service of Mr Giles in September 1828, to study hydraulic engineering.

manner of delivery seemed to be studiously contrived that the congregation might listen to his reading with admiration. The Clerk, just below him, was a fat man; his hair was brushed down very flat on his forehead, and he delivered his responses in the tone of some street criers who sell fish and cabbages. After prayers were over, we had a sermon delivered by a Parson much older than the one who read Prayers—this being had a nose tipped with red and otherwise much swollen so that whenever he shook his head once, his nose vibrated three times at least; it would have repaid the most lethargic person to have made a journey from London to Newcastle upon Tyne, to have heard this worthy man pronounce the words 'mortification,' 'abstinence' and 'watching' while he showed all the outward marks of 'debauchery,' 'indulgence' and 'sloth.'

Respecting Sundays—the population of England may be divided into three grand classes. The most numerous get drunk, the second neither get drunk nor pray but remain idle the whole day, the third and least are composed of such people who really pray to God and think of their salvation. The drunkards form, generally speaking the labourers and mechanics—the idlers, comprehending sleepers, dressers, drivers and women oglers, are generally Clerks in Public Offices, Counting Houses and other establishments. The sleepers are those who after being obliged to attend to their business early, during the week days, lie in bed on Sundays till two or three in the afternoon, and employ the rest of the day in reading accounts of murders, fires, accidents, and war. The dressers are those who, whilst in their counting houses, meditate upon which of certain two waistcoats they each may have, to put on—they in despair often decide to put on both. The drivers are those who, despising their stomachs, put on false whiskers and rattle about in sorry vehicles drawn by horses as starved as themselves—they are seen to make frequent bows to people in carriages that pass them, and to shake their heads at somebody in a crowd—they pass for personages who have extensive acquaintances. As for the women oglers, they are too contemptible for me to take any further notice of. Yet I may remark that they form that great number of men who being hated by individuals of the sex, imagine they are generally admired by the petticoat public.

Those who do really pray may be divided into many species—for instance, people who are condemned to be hung—many who have just lost a near relation or are in apprehension of losing them—people who have just had a leg or an arm broken, or who labour under sickness—old women and old men being forsaken by their less aged friends and no longer capable of enjoying the pleasures of this life, turn to Heaven and read their Bibles furiously—very ugly young women are often driven to lead an exemplary life of devotion—and many others which I cannot mention—for, a volume might be filled with them.[27]

[27] Vol. 1, pp. 76–7.

[A weekend with friends]

I took a Cabriolet to the Elephant and Castle Coaching House—from thence a contrivance with a canvas covering took me down to Streatham for a trifle.[28] Omer was, happily for me, at home; I found him in his study surrounded by huge volumes, maps, sabers and enveloped in tobacco smoke.[29] On the sofa sat the four young Turks just arrived from Liverpool. They were dressed in the English costume. They recollected having seen me whilst in quarantine.[30] They talked with loud voices—very quick and with violent gestures; quite different from English lads. I could not understand a word of what they said and Omer was kind enough to stand interpreter. We spent the day in reading Shakespeare and smoking cigars.[31]

[Altercation in Glasgow]

A drunken young Scotchman came and took me by my elbow as I was standing on the bridge, and shook me as if I had been asleep and told me I was blocking up the passage: I turned round and gave him a well lodged kick just below one of his knees and made him reel. Some of the passers by hissed at me; some called me a b——y foreigner; and some praised my conduct. Kicking is not considered fair play—but then how should a young gentleman dirty his hands by fighting a regular battle with a blackguard, drunk and covered with filth. When a dog assails a man, he kicks it—and does not strip off his coat and begin to square his fists.[32]

[28] Elephant and Castle and Streatham are neighborhoods in south London.

[29] Hekekyan had met Omer Effendi, an officer of Mehmed Ali's son Ibrahim, in October 1826. Omer was part of a contingent of officers dispatched to England to study the language and various arts and sciences.

[30] Quarantines were public-health measures deployed at ports to prevent the spread of contagious diseases from ship to land, by keeping arriving passengers in isolation for a prescribed period.

[31] Vol. 1, pp. 84–5.   [32] Vol. 1, p. 136.

6.4 The young Ottoman: Namık Kemal's 'Progress', 1872[33]
Robert G. Landen

Preface

Born into an old Ottoman official family—his father was the court astronomer—Namık Kemal (1840–88) entered the bureaucracy at the age of 17 with a post in the Translation Bureau. He soon drifted into the circle that founded the Young Ottoman movement, becoming one of the group's major literary spokesmen and, over time, an embarrassment to the government. In 1865 his writings and increasingly radical editorship of the *Tasvir-i Efkâr* ('Illustration of Opinion') forced him to flee to Paris, where he edited the opposition newspaper *Hürriyet* ('Liberty'). Thereafter, he lived in and out of exile, some of it internal, before his premature death in 1888.

For Kemal, a man at home with symbols and abstractions, the three ideas of 'progress', 'liberty', and 'the fatherland' were central to his philosophy. Although he had great faith in reason, and believed that the deliberations of a representative assembly would halt the disintegration of the Ottoman Empire, his influence can be traced in large part to the emotional appeal in his writings, which glorified ancient Ottoman greatness. They show the signs of both Ottoman classical and Western European influence, and Kemal was equally familiar with the verses of Ottoman poets and the writings of the philosophers. Şerif Mardin aptly subtitles his chapter devoted to Namık Kemal 'The Synthesis'.

Kemal's writing was free of much of the Arabic and Persian phraseology still used by his contemporaries. Thus he was a pioneer in developing the modern Turkish idiom and is still read with appreciation by Turks. Today his influence rests largely on his popular reputation as a founder of Turkish nationalism; it would be more accurate, however, to describe him as a proto-nationalist, a transitional figure whose consciousness was inspired more by a multinational Ottoman patriotism and by reformist Muslim ideals than by the more exclusive ideals of secular Turkish nationalism.

Text

Progress

What necessity is there to travel through all civilized countries? If one only visits London with observant eyes, the wonders one will see will amaze one. If all the

[33] *Terakki* ('Progress'), editorial in *İbret*, 45 (Istanbul, Nov. 1872), trans. in Wells, Charles, *The Literature of the Turks: A Turkish Chrestomathy* (London: Bernard Quartich, 1891), 156–61.

improvements in the world were photographed in a picture, the whole civilized world could only show as much as London. It is no exaggeration to say that London is a type of the world. Therefore we have chosen it as a sample (of the civilized world).

This city is generally enveloped in a black mist, like the happiness of mankind is involved in clouds of doubt and uncertainty, and its houses are as deeply covered with black as its very stones and trees are affected by the habits of civilization. But if we look behind that dark veil, the beauty of civilization is revealed to us in such splendour and majesty that an intelligent man must be smitten by it.

If anyone who is in London wishes to see the principles of justice in full play, before all things, there is that gigantic House of Parliament, which was the cradle of many of the constitutions (rules of politics) which we see in the world. If one looks at its construction, it seems as if the power and resistance of public opinion with regard to the administration had been embodied, and that that tremendous body had been turned to stone, to show, as it were, that it is protected from destruction by any shock. If one enters it, he sees three or four hundred representatives, the most distinguished men of a nation (composed of one hundred and eighty millions of members) which, if not the first of all civilized nations, is one of the first, every one of whom explains, with extraordinary eloquence, the wishes of the people and the wants of the future, and displays all possible skill in expounding the principles of justice and the secrets of progress.

This distinguished body has, as its basis and support, political assemblies, each one as extensive as a town, which consists of forty or fifty, or sometimes, a hundred, or a hundred and fifty thousand people, who have all agreed about a common object. When they meet, not only is there no disorder or turmoil, but very often, except for the polite discussions which are going on, not even a cough is to be heard. So many men meet together in one place; some of them speak, and their defects are listened to in silence and then, at once, they go candidly and politely to their government, and explain what they need. Ninety out of a hundred of their demands are granted, as they are consistent with right and supported by overwhelming force.

Judges in the Court of Justice, appointed in accordance with the principles laid down by the Parliament, are to be seen, whom all parties trust even more than the indulgence of their own fathers. These judges are helped and controlled by a body called the 'jury,' who swear to do their utmost to investigate the truth, and who are themselves the friends and neighbours of the two litigants. There are lawyers to state clearly both sides of the question in the presence of the Jury, who (some of whom) would prefer gaining a deserving case to a lap full of gold.

Behold, this is the state justice is in, but education is still more perfect. If you go into any school, children ten or twelve years of age are accustomed to order and education only to be found amongst men of twenty and thirty [elsewhere]. There are higher schools where the pupils study three or four languages, and know six or seven sciences.

Twenty, or five-and-twenty-children, ten or twelve years of age, will go to a garden [park]. Either they have a newspaper in their hand and try to make themselves acquainted with what is going on in the world, or they sit in a corner and enjoy the pleasantness of the air, and freshness of the trees, which they survey with an intelligent glance. In their ships, crews are to be found who study the most abstruse mathematical questions, like the laws of gravitation. In the shops clerks are to be found who will discuss the ideas of the *savants* of Germany about the philosophy of rights.

There is a Zoological Garden. When all the animals in the cages pass before one's eyes, one by one, one fancies that Noah's Ark has just arrived there saved from the Flood, and all in it just landed.

If you enter their libraries, there are two or three millions of books, in all languages, and hundreds of librarians, who deserve to be called 'Universal Geniuses,' to help you find them. There are never less than eight hundred readers, and, amongst them, there are professors ninety years of age, and girls of eighteen.

Well! in the Museum Library, if any one wants a printed book, in no matter how outlandish a language, they must give it to him, or if they have not got it, they must send for it as quickly as possible.

There is a library in the House of Parliament to which one lord alone bequeathed thirty thousand volumes.

If one goes to a 'refined place of amusement,' he can see experiments in difficult matters connected with chemistry and natural philosophy which, if they were made in China, would be considered miracles.

If one sees the jewels and precious things in the shops, one thinks that the hidden treasure of nature, and the wealth of the world, have been plundered and brought there.

The traffic is such that in every street the rapid and continual circulation is like a whirlpool of men, which flows from one end to another without cessation.

In the town, besides more than forty thousand private carriages, there are more than thirty-five thousand hired vehicles, and more than fifteen thousand omnibuses. At the centre of the railways of the town, for fourteen hours every day there is a train with sixty carriages every two minutes. Nevertheless, it often happens to any one that he has to wait his turn to get into a train or an omnibus, and sometimes, in a crowded part of the town, he can find no vehicle.

There is one place in the town where three trains run one above the other by means of bridges; and there is a park, in which, at promenade times, fifty or sixty thousand carriages circulate.

When one goes to the warehouses on the banks of the River Thames, and looks at the exports and imports every day, he thinks that the tide, which causes the river to rise and fall every day, casts all the productions of the world here, and that all the manufactures made by man go from here to be distributed.

If one goes to the factories here, his hair stands on end! He thinks the thing at work is not a machine, but an iron monster as big as a piece of a mountain, who spouts forth fire from his mouth, and every member of whom, when it moves gives out a terrible cry, and that he is continually working without repose, day and night, to carry out the orders of 'King Intellect,' who has made him his prisoner.

There are printing-machines, which print in one hour, two hundred and fifty thousand copies of a newspaper eight times as large as the *İbret* (the Istanbul newspaper in which this editorial appeared). In one printing office fifty thousand workmen are employed, and in one beer brewery they have fifteen thousand carthorses.

There are hotels one mass of gilding, ornamented in a way to make palaces envious, where three thousand people can sleep, and four thousand persons can dine at their tables. There is a tailoring establishment where sufficient clothes are to be seen to dress all the people in our town of Scutari (Üsküdar), from seven to seventy years of age; and there are seven to eight hundred shopmen, and five or six hundred shopwomen, to show the goods to customers.

There are regular markets under the river, and splendid bridges up in the air!!!

There is a place of amusement called the 'Mirror Palace' [Crystal Palace], which owing to all the colours of the rainbow sparkling on it from the reflection of the light, on a sky-blue ground, looks, from a distance, like a mountain of diamonds.

In the daytime the water from the fountains forms steeples of light! In the evening, when the gardens are flooded with gas [light] and moonlight one thinks it is day, and one can see from one end of them to the other. These gardens are such that it is doubtful whether anyone who was capable of visiting Paradise could produce any better imitation of it in this world of affliction.

To see the military strength of their government, it is sufficient to go down to the banks of the river, or to the old castle of the town [the Tower]. There are ironclad vessels to be seen which are like a big city made of iron.

If you wish to know what the people can do, you need only look at the lists of subscriptions in the newspaper.

One widow lady presents three hundred thousand pounds to an orphan asylum!

A blacking manufacturer, in his will, leaves twenty thousand pounds to the poor!

It is very wonderful that one sees no other signs of such a powerful government in public but the police, who are employed only in preserving public order.

As regards the police, their work consists in the daytime of such things as seeing that carriages do not collide, and stopping the greatest people of quality with a sign, if they wish to go out of their turn before some ordinary individual: and at night, in quelling a few drunken squabbles, examining the doors of shops and houses to see if they are closed, and windows to see if they are fastened, and such like things connected with order and justice.

Although the people are so opulent, the greatest millionaire will go to his shop when he is eighty, and work till evening, like a shopman.

By continual effort and knowledge they have produced a world of opulence, compared to which, all the golden palaces and jewelled castles, and splendid flower gardens which the imagination of the Persian poets described in the most exaggerated way in India and China, are as nothing.

Well, we know it is impossible in a few years to make Istanbul like London, or Roumelia [Ottoman Europe] like France. But, as Europe has got into this condition in two centuries, and they had to discover the means of progress, whereas we find those means ready to our hands, if the work be properly taken in hand, there is no doubt that in two centuries, at any rate, we shall be able to get into a condition to be counted one of the most civilized nations. And as regards two centuries, are they more than a twinkling of an eye in the life of a community?

6.5 The West through the eyes of an Iranian Qajar monarch: Naser al-Din Shah's first trip to Europe, 1873[34]

Robert G. Landen

Preface

Naser al-Din Shah Qajar had one of the longest reigns in Iranian history, from 1848 to 1896. He oversaw a number of modernization campaigns— all ambitious and many abortive—that drew upon two main strategies: state-led modernization, and state-granted development concessions to foreign entrepreneurs. He was also notoriously corrupt and unfocused in his efforts, earning him the contempt of many among a younger generation of bureaucrats (charged with executing his modernization efforts) and intellectuals. Naser al-Din Shah inherited the long-standing problem of maintaining central authority in the provinces and among the many tribal groups upon which the government depended for military power. In addition, he inherited the uniquely nineteenth-century problem of fending off the imperialist attentions of both Russia and Britain, Iran's two largest trading partners. To these twin challenges he offered the same strategy: playing competing interests off against one another, playing for time while seeking room to maneuver.

Although Iranian aristocrats, merchants, students, and adventurers had travelled west since the late eighteenth century (with some earlier isolated cases), Naser al-Din Shah was the first Iranian monarch to travel to Europe. The purpose of the trips was to court foreign investment from a country other than Russia or Britain, if possible. European governments, keen to soften up the Qajar monarch for their concession-seeking subjects, generally showed the king a good time. This initial trip led to a pattern of foreign travel that was increasingly seen as an unnecessary extravagance on the part of the Qajar court. Indeed, each of his three trips (1873, 1878, and 1889) resulted in at least one concession, usually to a British or Russian concessionaire. During Naser al-Din Shah's reign the pace of moderniza- tion was overshadowed by concerns over European imperialism, worsening economic conditions, and frustrations with monarchical rule. The policies of his own modernization programs provoked agitation. For example, the London-based newspaper *Qanun* ('The Law') was published in the 1890s by the disgruntled bureaucrat, Mirza Malkom Khan, who had been trained in the elite Dar al-Fonun school founded by Naser al-Din Shah in 1851. Protests against Naser al-Din Shah's granting of a tobacco concession to a

---

[34] Naser al-Din Shah, *The Diary of H.M. The Shah of Persia During His Tour Through Europe in A.D. 1873*, trans. J. W. Redhouse (London: John Murray, 1874), 96–7, 140–2, 183, 229–30, 236–7.

British company in 1890 spread from city to city, facilitated by a telegraph network that he himself had hoped would increase government control over the provinces.

In 1896 Mirza Reza Kermani assassinated Naser al-Din Shah outside Shah ᶜAbd Al-ᶜAzim cemetery. Kermani was linked both to the pan-Islamic activist Jamal al-Din Al-Asadabadi 'Al-Afghani' (who was languishing under house arrest in Istanbul) and the intellectual voice of Iranian 'renewalism' or, *tajaddod-parvari*, Mirza Aqa Khan Kermani (no relation to the aforementioned Kermani), who clamored for a revived sense of Iranian nationalism and constitutional limits on monarchical authority. Al-Afghani died of cancer in 1897, but both Mirza Reza (who was captured) and Mirza Aqa Khan Kermani (who was extradited from the Ottoman Empire) were executed in 1897 for their role in the assassination of Naser al-Din Shah. Less than ten years later, a revolution in 1905–6 imposed a constitution on the Qajars.

This travelogue can be seen as being in the same tradition as other Qajar travelogues in the late eighteenth and nineteenth centuries, in that it provided an account of the advances and faults of the European world—a form of expertise termed 'Occidentalism' by today's scholars. Unlike other travelogues, it also served as a form of propaganda for the Qajar state by highlighting the diplomatic skills and modernity of the king himself.

Text

[Germany]

[. . .] At an hour to sunset we arrived at the works of M. Krupp, who came himself to the railway (to meet us). He is a tall, thin old man. He has himself, in a certain space of time, created the whole of these works. The cannon of every government does he furnish from hence. Guns of every description, such as large cannon for forts, cannon for ships, and cannon for field use in campaigns, are all manufactured here. His plant and workshops, of which steam is the motive power, resemble a mighty city. He employs 15,000 workmen, for the whole of whom he has erected houses and lodgings, paying them salaries and wages. After deducting his expenditure, his own yearly income amounts to 800,000 *tumans* (£320,000).

We went to the shop of the steam hammers. They are singular hammers like mountains; and, worked by steam, fulfill the office of forging cannons. They make these of any pattern they desire. When the hammer strikes the gun, the earth floor of the workshop emits a sound and trembles. It was a marvelous thing. We went all over the works, and they turned out some large and some small cannon. We then went to a house which he had prepared, and there we dined. He gave us an excellent dinner. In the conservatory of this house we saw a tree, the leaves of which were two ells (seven feet) long, and half an ell (twenty-one inches) wide. The steam-hammers, in spite of their great distance from this room, made the earth shake here as though in an earthquake. M. Krupp made us a present of a most magnificent breech-loading six-pounder cannon, with all its appliances.

[Britain]

[. . .] We returned to our train, and took our seat in a carriage with the self same personages. We started. Everywhere we passed over the bosoms of mountains and across valleys, traversing numerous tunnels ('holes in the mountain'), of which two were about a quarter of a league in length, very dark and suffocating.

The country of England had no resemblance to that in other territories. It has much forest, large trees, population without interval, and enormous cultivation. The wealth of the English is famous throughout the world; there is no need to describe it [here].

We passed by the town and outlying districts of Chiselhurst, the abode of Napoleon III, and where he died.[35] His tomb is also there. The train travelled at so furious a rate that it was impossible for one to distinguish any place. From the rapidity of our motion fire came out of the wheels, and one carriage caught fire. It wanted but little for all to be burnt. They stopped the train, got down, and extinguished the fire. All was right, and again we went on until we reached the beginning of the city of London. Again it is impossible to describe the prosperity, the populousness, the extent of the city, the numbers of lines of railway over which incessantly the trains come and go in every direction, the smoke of manufactories, and the like. We traveled over the exteriors of the roofs of the houses; and thus we reached the station and stopped.[. . .] The population of the city is said to be over eight crores (four millions)[36] of souls. It has most lovely women. The nobleness, the greatness, the gravity and sedateness of the women and men shine out from their countenances. One sees and comprehends that they are a great people, and that the Lord of the Universe has bestowed upon them power and might, sense and wisdom, and enlightenment. Thus it is that they have conquered a country like India, and hold important possessions in America and elsewhere in the world. Their soldiers are strong of frame and beautifully attired; their armour-wearing household cavalry are very strong and handsome young men, exquisitely dressed, like the cavalry of Russia. Their horses are very fine and strong, but their number is few. They are but four regiments, each of four hundred men.[. . .]

The city of Manchester, by reason of its exceeding number of manufactories, has its houses, doors, and walls, black as coal. So much so, that the complexions, visages, and dresses of the people are all black. The whole of the ladies of that place at most times wear black clothing, because, no sooner do they put on white or colored dresses, than lo! they are suddenly black.

---

[35] Charles-Louis-Napoléon Bonaparte was the president of the Second Republic (1850–2) and then emperor (until 1871), as 'Napoleon III'. [36] One *korur*=500,000.

[France]

[. . .] We and the Marshal [MacMahon, president of France][37] took seats in a carriage, went into the gardens of Versailles, and drove about. They have many basins and fountains of water, the source of which, like that of the fountains at the Crystal Palace of London, is derived from a steam-engine. They had opened the sources and let the water on in the fountains. There was a lake below the basins and fountains, very beautiful and spacious avenues, forest trees, the heads of which were all intertwined so as to form a kind of roof, with every here and there a circular open space of grass with trees around, having in the centre a large basin with a fountain of great altitude. It is a very charming place.

One spot was formed into a kind of artificial mountain, with a cascade falling from the mountain. Several marble statues were placed behind the cascade—one, a group named Apollo, who was the specific deity of manly beauty, of light, and of poetry. He is adorning (himself), the others round him are holding a mirror, flowers, or implements of the toilet. It was so beautiful a piece of statuary that one could not even imagine it. I formed the desire to go up near to these statues under the cascade. The Marshal and General Arture said it would be very difficult to go there, as the path was altogether precipitous, of rocks and steep. I said I would go; I alighted from the carriage, and went up. It is true that the way was disagreeable; but to us, who had seen and traversed much worse paths in the hunting grounds of Persia it offered no difficulty. When we had arrived near the statues, General Arture came (also); but, meeting with a fall, all his clothes were bemired, and his sword was either bent or broken. The Marshal likewise came up; but with great difficulty, and with the assistance of several persons. But this manner of getting up there by a Marshal and a general of France is in no way derogatory to their firmness and courage. Well; the statues were very beautiful, though somewhat soiled, and covered with cobwebs.[. . .]

The celebrated Rothschild,[38] a Jew also, who is exceedingly rich, came to an audience, and we conversed with him. He greatly advocated the cause of the Jews,

---

[37] Marie-Edmé-Patrice-Maurice MacMahon, Comte de, Duc de Magenta (1808–93). After a distinguished military career in Europe and the Middle East (at least, from the French perspective—the Italians, Ottomans, and Algerians were likely not very keen on him), he became President of the Third Republic from 20 November 1873 to 28 January 1879. He was a good twenty years older than the Iranian shah and 65 years old at the time they met.

[38] The patriarch of the French branch of the Rothschild family, Baron Edmond de Rothschild (1845–1934), appears to have supported assimilation to proto-Zionism in the early 1870s when this meeting with Nader al-Din Shah occurred, but had a change of heart in the mid-1870s after viewing a play by Dumas. Zionist associations, collectively known as Hovevêi Zion ('Lovers of Zion'), began to form in the late 1870s. After an 1882 meeting with a Hovevêi Zionist organizer of the first *aliyah* ('going up' [to Israel]), Rothschild became an important but anonymous (at the time) supporter of Zionist immigration to Palestine. Howard M. Sachar, *A History of Israel* (New York: Knopf, 1991), 16 and 30–2.

mentioned the Jews of Persia, and claimed tranquility for them. I said to him: 'I have heard that you, brothers, possess a thousand crores of money. I consider the best thing to do would be that you should pay fifty crores to some large or small State, and buy a territory in which you could collect all the Jews of the whole world, you becoming their chiefs, and leading them on their way in peace, so that you should no longer be thus scattered and dispersed.' We laughed heartily, and he made no reply. I gave him an assurance that I do protect every alien nationality that is in Persia.

M. Lesseps, so well known, who has joined the Mediterranean to the Red Sea—i.e., a large company having been formed, has, through the exertions of this personage, opened that canal, and by this means shortened for commerce the passage to India, Persia, China, etc. and, from Europe, by about two thousand leagues—came to an audience, together with his son, a youth.[39] He has now a fresh scheme in his head—that of making a railway from the town of Orenburg in Russia to the city of Samarqand, and thence on to Peshawar in British India. But this is a notion very remote (from reason) and distant (from practicability).

---

[39] Ferdinand-Marie, Vicomte de Lesseps (1805–96), was the French diplomat, engineer, and entrepreneur who oversaw the development of the Suez Canal, securing a concession in 1854 and managing its construction from 1859–69. He also facilitated the British Government's acquisition of the Egyptian shares of the Suez Canal in 1875, when the khedival government in Egypt went bankrupt.

6.6 The battle for British public opinion on Turkey and the Eastern Question: two documents, 1876 and 1904

Nazan Çiçek

Preface

William Ewart Gladstone (1809–98), the Liberal prime minister of Great Britain between 1868 and 1874, lost the general election in November 1874 to the Conservative leader Benjamin Disraeli. Having announced in January 1875 his resignation from the leadership of the Liberal Party as well as his withdrawal from active political life, Gladstone devoted his time to an agitation campaign against Turkish measures to suppress the Christian insurrection in Bulgaria, and before long he re-emerged as a dominant figure in British politics.

The revolt in Bulgaria, which was organized by the Bulgarian Revolutionary Committee, started at the beginning of May 1876 and, having been countered by Turkish irregular forces, eventually turned into a bloody civil war. Gladstone's publication of the pamphlet *Bulgarian Horrors and the Question of the East*[40] in September 1876 caused a strong reaction against the Turks in British public opinion and sold 200,000 copies within a month. In the pamphlet Gladstone not only censured the Ottoman administration and the Turks as a nation but also questioned the traditional British policy regarding the Eastern Question. Throughout the nineteenth century British decision-makers believed that the Ottoman Empire, which had seemed on the brink of dissolution, had to continue to exist because it was a necessity for the balance of power in Europe and a *sine qua non* for British interests in the eastern Mediterranean, as well as in India. Therefore the maintenance of the integrity and the independence of the Ottoman Empire became the guiding principle of official British foreign policy, which manifested itself in the Anglo-Turkish alliance in the Crimea against Russia. While supporting the Sublime Porte against external threats, a series of Whig, Tory, and Liberal British governments also attempted to strengthen the empire from inside and undertook a project of impressing on the Ottomans the urgent need to set about reforming their entire governmental structure.

However, despite the enthusiasm of Tanzimat-era statesmen and the large number of reform decrees, the Ottoman Empire did not succeed in carrying out the modernization task that would mould Turkey along European lines. Thus the failure of the Ottoman reformation became

---

[40] W. E. Gladstone, *Bulgarian Horrors and the Question of the East* (London: John Murray, 1876).

almost indisputable in the eyes of British observers towards the end of the nineteenth century, and the revolts of Christian subjects in the European part of the Empire, which broke out one after another, afforded anti-Turkish circles in Great Britain the opportunity to challenge the traditional British policy with respect to the Eastern Question. Gladstone's *Bulgarian Horrors* in this context marked the manifestation of Liberal-Radical opposition to official British support for the Ottoman Empire. Although Gladstone was accused of partisanship by Conservatives for sacrificing the higher interests of the British Empire to his liberal populist politics, after *Bulgarian Horrors* became a bestseller the Disraeli cabinet felt obliged to make some concessions in the official British attitude towards the Ottoman Empire. Moreover, the success of Gladstone's pamphlet paved the way to a flurry of inflammatory publications against Turks in Great Britain.

During the reign of Abdülhamid II (r. 1876–1909), anti-Turkish propaganda in Britain—produced overwhelmingly by Radical-Liberal circles—reached its peak with Gladstone's *Bulgarian Horrors*. The most widely circulated Victorian periodicals published articles censuring the Turks more severely than ever. The Christian uprising in Bosnia and Herzegovina in 1875, the outbreak of a second revolt in Bulgaria in 1876, the Russo-Turkish war of 1877–8, and the Congress of Berlin in 1878 gave the Radical-Liberal Victorian middle and upper classes the opportunity to discuss the features of Ottoman rule in Europe in a wider context.

This political agitation against Turks, which accelerated towards the end of the nineteenth century, prompted Ottoman officials to undertake a project of 'image management'. A department of the Foreign Ministry was charged with following the foreign press and classifying the news and articles relating to the Ottoman Empire. In accordance with counter-propaganda, a range of pamphlets and articles in English as well as in Turkish was sponsored by the Sublime Porte to contain the damage done to the Turkish image by inflammatory anti-Turkish publication in Britain. The second text, *A Study in English Turcophobia*,[41] has been chosen in order to give an example of the Ottoman attempt to influence European public opinion through counter-propaganda during Sultan Abdülhamid II's reign. The text in question claimed to be the translation of an anonymous Turkish pamphlet and was published in England by the London Pan-Islamic Society in 1904. Despite the claim of the publisher, however, there is no evidence to suggest that this text was really based on an original Turkish pamphlet rather than produced by a member of the Pan-Islamic Society in English. Nevertheless, both the style of the text and the arguments contained within it prove that the pamphlet, either written originally in Turkish or in English, was officially inspired and appeared as a product of

---

[41] Anon., *A Study in English Turcophobia* (London: Pan-Islamic Society, 1904).

Ottoman 'image management'. Moreover, unlike some other publications in the same vein, the pamphlet under examination was written not only to explain and justify the Ottoman response to certain events but also to initiate a lengthy polemic against the whole Radical-Liberal discourse.

Texts

1. Bulgarian Horrors and the Question of the East, 1876

By a slow and difficult process, the details of which I shall presently consider, and through the aid of newspaper correspondence, and partly of the authorised agent of a foreign state, but not through our own Parliament, or Administration, or establishments abroad, we know now in detail that [there] have been perpetrated, under the immediate authority of a Government to which all the time we have been giving the strongest moral, and for part of a time even material support, crimes and outrages, so vast in scale as to exceed all modern example, and so unutterably vile as well as fierce in character, that it passes the power of heart to conceive, and of tongue and pen adequately to describe them. These are the Bulgarian horrors; and the question is, what can and should be done, either to punish, or to brand, or to prevent? [. . .]

The authors of the crimes are the agents, the trusted, and in some instances, the since-promoted servants of the Turkish Government. The moral and material support, which during the year has been afforded to the Turkish Government, has been given by the Government of England on behalf of the people of England. In order to [have] a full comprehension of the political question at issue, it will be necessary to describe the true character and position of the Turkish Power, and the policy, as I think it the questionable and erroneous policy, of the British Administration.

Let me endeavour very briefly to sketch, in the rudest outline, what the Turkish race was and what it is. It is not a question of Mahometanism [i.e. Islam] simply, but of Mahometanism compounded with the peculiar character of a race. They are not the mild Mahometans of India, nor the chivalrous Saladins of Syria, nor the cultured Moors of Spain. They were, upon the whole, from the black day when they first entered Europe, the one great anti-human specimen of humanity. Wherever they went, a broad line of blood marked the track behind them; and, as far as their dominion reached, civilisation disappeared from view. They represented everywhere government by force, as opposed to government by law. For the guide of this life they had a relentless fatalism; for its reward hereafter, a sensual paradise. [. . .]

But although the Turk represented force as opposed to law, yet not even a government of force can be maintained without the aid of an intellectual element, such as he did not possess. Hence there grew up, what has been rare in the history of the world, a kind of tolerance in the midst of cruelty, tyranny, and rapine. Much of Christian life was contemptuously let alone; much of the subordinate functions of government was allowed to devolve upon the bishops; and a race of Greeks was attracted to Constantinople, which has all along made up, in some degree, the deficiencies of Turkish Islam in the element of mind, and which at this moment provides the Porte with its long known and, I must add, highly esteemed Ambassador in London. Then there have been from time to time, but rarely, statesmen whom we have been too ready to mistake for specimens of what Turkey might become, whereas they were in truth more like *lusus naturae*, on the favourable side; monsters, so to speak, of virtue or intelligence; and there were (and are) also, scattered through the community, men, who were not indeed real citizens, but yet who have exhibited the true civic virtues, and who would have been citizens had there been a true polity around them. Besides all this, the conduct of the race has gradually been brought more under the eye of an Europe, which it has lost its power to resist or to defy; and its central government, in conforming perforce to many of the forms and traditions of civilisation, has occasionally caught something of their spirit.

This, I think, is not an untrue description of the past, or even of the present. The decay of martial energy, in a Power which was for centuries the terror of the world, is wonderful. Of the two hundred millions sterling which in twenty years it borrowed from the credulity of European Exchanges, a large part has been spent upon its military and naval establishments. The result is before us. It is at war with Servia [*sic*], which has a population, I think, under a million and a half, and an army which is variously stated at from five to eight thousand; the rest of those bearing arms are a hitherto half drilled militia. It is also at war with the few scores of thousands of that very martial people, who inhabit the mountain tract of Montenegro. Upon these handful of our race, an empire of more than thirty millions discharges all its might; for this purpose it applies all its own resources, and the whole of the property of its creditors; and, after two months of desperate activity, it greatly plumes itself upon having incompletely succeeded against Servia [*sic*], and less doubtfully failed against Montenegro. Shades of Bajazets, Amuraths, and Mahmouds!

Twenty years ago, France and England determined to try a great experiment in remodelling the administrative system of Turkey, with the hope of curing its intolerable vices, and of making good its not less intolerable deficiencies. For this purpose, having defended her integrity, they made also her independence secure; and they devised at Constantinople the reforms, which were publicly enacted in an Imperial Firman or Hatt-i Humayoum [*sic*]. The successes of the Crimean War, purchased (with the aid of Sardinia) by a vast expenditure of French and English life and treasure, gave to Turkey, for the first time perhaps in her blood-stained history, twenty years of a repose not disturbed either by herself or by any foreign Power. The Cretan insurrection imparted a shock to confidence; but it was composed, and Turkey again was trusted. The insurrection of 1875 [. . .] [has] disclosed the total failure of the Porte to fulfil the engagements, she had contracted under circumstances peculiarly binding on interest, on honour, and on gratitude. Even these miserable insurrections, she had not the ability to put down. In the midway of the current events, a lurid glare is thrown over the whole case by the Bulgarian horrors. The knowledge of these events is, whether by indifference or bungling, kept back from us, but only for a time. The proofs are now sufficiently before us. And the case is this. Turkey, which stood only upon force, has in the main lost that force. [. . .] Power is gone, and the virtues, such as they are, of power; nothing but its passions and its pride remain.

It is time, then, to clear an account which we have long, perhaps too long, left unsettled, and almost unexamined. In the discussion of this great and sad subject, the attitude and the proceedings of the British Government cannot possibly be left out of view. Indeed, the topic is, from the nature of the case, so prominent, and from the acts done, so peculiar, that I could hardly be excused from stating in express and decided terms what appear to me its grave errors; were it only that I may not seem, by an apparent reserve, also to insinuate against them a purposed complicity in crime, which it would be not only rash, but even wicked, to impute. The consequences of their acts have been, in my view, deplorable. But as respects the acts themselves, and the motives they appear to indicate, the faults I find are these. They have not understood the rights and duties, in regard to the subjects, and particularly the Christian subjects, of Turkey, which inseparably attach to this country in consequence of the Crimean War, and of the Treaty of Paris in 1856. They have been remiss when they ought to have been active; namely, in efforts to compose the Eastern revolts, by making provocation against the terrible misgovernment which provoked them. They have been active, where they ought to have been circumspect and guarded. It is a grave charge, which cannot be withheld, that they have given to a maritime measure of humane precaution the character of a military demonstration in support of the Turkish Government. They have seemed to be moved to little by an intelligent appreciation of prior obligations, and of the broad and deep interests of humanity, and too much by disposition to keep out of sight what was disagreeable and might be inconvenient, and to consult and flatter the public opinion of the day in its ordinary, that is to say, its narrow, selfish, epicurean humour. [pp. 11–18]

A few months ago, the new Sultan served the turn, and very well. Men affirmed that he must have time. And now another new Sultan is in the offing. I suppose it will be argued that he must have time too. Then there will be perhaps new constitutions; firmans of reforms; proclamations to commanders of Turkish armies, enjoining extra humanity. All these should be quietly set down as simply equal to zero. At this moment we hear of the adoption by the Turks of the last and most enlightened rule of warfare; namely, the Geneva Convention. They might just as well adopt the Vatican Council, or the British Constitution. All these things, are not even the oysters before the dinner. [p. 45]

Do not let us ask for, do not let us accept, Jonahs or scapegoats, either English or Turkish. It is not change of men that we want, but a change of measures. New Sultans or ministers among Turks, new consuls or new ambassadors in Turkey, would only in my opinion divert us, at this moment, from the great practical aims in view. Besides if we are to talk of changing men, the first question that will arise will be that of our Ministers at home, to whose policy and bias both Ministers and subordinate officers abroad always feel a loyal desire as far as may be to conform. [. . .]

We come now to consider the objects we should desire and seek for through our Government.[. . .] It is not yet too late, but it is very urgent, to aim at the accomplishment of three great objects, in addition to the termination of the war, yet in my view inseparably associated with it.

To put a stop to the anarchical misrule[. . .], the plundering, the murdering, which, as we now seem to learn upon sufficient evidence, still desolate Bulgaria.

To make effectual provision against the recurrence of the outrages recently perpetrated under the sanction of the Ottoman Government, by excluding its administrative action for the future, not only from Bosnia and the Herzegovina, but also, and above all, from Bulgaria; upon which at best there will remain, for years and for generations, the traces of its foul and bloody hand.

To redeem by these measures the honour of the British name, which, in the deplorable events of the year, has been more gravely compromised than I have known it to be at any former period.[. . .]

I may be asked, either seriously or tauntingly, whether there is not also a fourth to be added, namely, the maintenance of the 'territorial integrity of Turkey.'

Now as regards the territorial integrity of Turkey, I for one am still desirous to see it upheld, though I do not say that desire should be treated as of a thing paramount to still higher objects of policy. For of all the objects of policy, in my conviction, humanity, rationally understood, and in due relation to justice, is the first and highest. My belief is that this great aim need not be compromised, and that other important objects would be gained by maintaining the territorial integrity of Turkey.[. . .] [pp. 48–50]

It would not be practical, even if it were honourable, to disguise the real character of what we want from the Government. It is a change of attitude and policy, nothing less. We want them to undo and efface that too just impression which, while keeping their own countrymen so much in the dark, they have succeeded in propagating throughout in Europe, that we are the determined supporters of the Turk, and that, declaring his 'integrity and independence' essential to 'British interests', we have winked hard, and shall wink, if such be, harder still, according to the exigencies of the case, alike at his crimes and at his impotence. We want to place ourselves in harmony with the general sentiment of civilised mankind, instead of being any longer, as we seem to be, the Evil Genius, which dogs, and mars, and baffles it. We want to make the Turk understand that, in conveying this impression by word and act to his mind, the British Government have misunderstood, and therefore, have misrepresented, the sense of the British people.[. . .] [p. 57]

An old servant of the Crown and the State, I entreat my countrymen upon whom far more than perhaps any other people of Europe it depends, to require, and to insist, that our Government, which has been working in one direction, shall work in the other, and shall apply all its vigour to concur with the other States of Europe in obtaining the extinction of the Turkish executive power in Bulgaria. Let the Turks now carry their abuses in the only possible manner, namely by carrying off themselves. Their Zaptiehs and their Mudirs, their Bimbashis and their Yuzbachis, their Kaimakams[42] and their Pashas, one and all, bag and baggage, shall I hope, clear out from the province they have desolated and profaned. This thorough riddance, this most blessed deliverance, is the only reparation we can make to memory of those heaps on heaps of dead; to the violated purity alike of matron, of maiden, and of child; to the civilisation which has been affronted and shamed; to the laws of God or, if you like, of Allah; to the moral sense of mankind at large. [p. 61]

2. A Study in English Turcophobia, 1904

It is perhaps not known to so many persons in England that the Turks are a people of extraordinary patience. They can treat with dignified forbearance even the most irritating provocations. But there is a limit to all human endurance. It is simply out of respect for the gratifying remembrance of one or two historic events, which united Turkey and England as allies, that the Turks have tried to ignore all the abuse piled upon them. But the attacks which have been made upon the national honour and religion of the Turks by a section of the British press and by a large number of political and clerical agitators in England during the last quarter of a century are now becoming too outrageous to be left without a reply.

The practice of abusing and slandering the Turks is resorted to more especially by those politicians and journalists who claim to defend the cause of freedom; and it must be on account of their love of freedom that these persons indulge so freely in vulgar invective. The anti-Turkish crusaders of what was originally the Gladstonian school have of late won over many followers from among the ranks of politicians who used to exhibit signs of friendship towards Turkey, especially in

[42] *Zaptiye* was the term designating the police force in the Ottoman Empire. Yüzbaşı and Binbaşı were the names for higher ranks in the Ottoman army. *Kaymakam* was the name for the administrative head of a district.

the days when that country was more ready to allow herself to be used as a buffer state against Russia, and when the occupation of Egypt was not yet accomplished.

The crusade to which we have just alluded assumes much more violent proportions whenever Turkey finds herself face to face with grave international troubles. Her detractors in England seem to have no sense of the decorum of impartiality. [. . .] The agitation on the Macedonian question which is now being carried on in England is the latest instance of this Turcophobia, and indeed so much malice is now exhibited in this connection that we feel constrained to defend the impugned honour of the nation to which we ourselves belong. In writing these lines we not only intend to refute the changes which are systematically and persistently brought against us by our detractors, but we also wish to discuss the true character of the humanity by which they pretend to be prompted in their campaign.

We are truly loathe to write this pamphlet in such forcible terms; but, judging by the excessively violent nature of their attacks, we think that our enemies neither deserve considerate treatment, nor understand the etiquette of criticism so necessary in international disputes. We do not however wish for a single moment to imitate the reprehensible ways of these individuals by making a counter-attack upon the English nation, although they cast such sweeping and indiscriminate aspersions upon us. A sense of decency prevents us from insulting any nation [. . .] Certainly a great people, like the British, which has contributed so largely to the progress and welfare of mankind is deserving of our respect. [pp. 3–4]

We will first consider the case of free-lance journalists and amateur politicians of Turcophobe tendencies.[. . .] The former is generally sent out as a correspondent to the disturbed provinces of Turkey by anti-Turkish papers, notably Radical journals. The latter, if he cares to go out to the East to study the 'real situation', can sent [*sic*] out on his own account, and for the purpose of making his name known in the political circles of his country as an authority on crucial Eastern problems; he does not require the pecuniary assistance of any paper. As they are both well aware of the extraordinary credulity with which the majority of Christian Englishmen receive any story concerning the Turkish Moslems, they both represent us in England in the same malicious light.

They both make wise suggestions to the obtuse Powers of Europe as to the best possible solution of the Eastern embroglios [*sic*]—suggestions which chiefly consist in wresting the affairs of our own country from us and appointing Christian governors who no doubt, would be endowed by Providence with peculiar administrative genius.[. . .] These gentlemen abuse the methods of administration of our best trained officials, whose hands are fettered by capitulations and who have to discharge their duties in the face of the wily intrigues of *agents provocateurs*, while thwarting the interference of the European powers. In reading their productions we sometimes wonder why the British public did not discover the existence among them of these remarkable gentlemen before the beginning of the South African War. These men might then have save[d] England from mobilizing nearly three hundred thousand men, from spending nearly three hundred million sterling, and from struggling for three years to bring the Boers to submission. It is not astonishing that the marvellous talent of these [English] critics of the Turkish 'maladministration' should not be made use of by their own country men in reorganizing the war and other offices in England, where the administrative chaos is reported by Englishmen themselves as deplorable [. . .]

As the result of careful enquiries we found that if they [the all-knowing journalists and politicians who visit our country] had been at any university at all they had preferred to spend the time of their university course in enjoying the sports and pastimes so well-known in English universities. It therefore appeared to us that they must have accumulated their vast stores of knowledge on every subject by reading novels and newspapers and other such light productions.[. . .] [pp. 5–6]

The fact is that our friend, the learned politician, is in reality a *charlatan*[. . .] If he were to spend his time and money on researches and publish an account of them, the production would not sell, or at any rate, it would not be largely read. It is therefore wise of him to concern himself with politics, and write books or long articles to the Turcophobe papers on the 'intolerable position of the Christians' in Turkey. If he cannot earn money in this way he can at least make his name better known.

The English language is not largely spoken in the near East. The question therefore arises, how do these amateur authorities on Eastern affairs study the real situation. [. . .] It is needless to say that these Turcophobe diatribists do not speak the language of the Turks whom they are so ready to criticise.[. . .] So they are bound to depend upon Armenian or Bulgarian or any other trustworthy cicerones of the Eastern Question nationality. If their interpreters happen to have been educated or 'civilised' by missionaries, woe to the truth seeking Englishman who tries to form an accurate opinion on Eastern matters by reading the productions of these authorities! for their assertions are mainly based upon the information supplied to them by such cicerones.[. . .]

Bona fide consular reports may be published, and they may contradict the fiendish stories of these atrocity mongers. They may moreover mention that the provocations given to the Turks by revolutionary bandits were beyond human endurance. But the mind of the atrocity-monger is incapable of any sense of shame, when his stories are thus officially shown to be false. Besides he can console himself with the reflection that the mischievous impression created by his falsehoods on the public mind cannot be easily obliterated by the subsequent publication of the official reports. If possible, he avoids mentioning, or at any rate detailing the outrages of revolutionary bandits, but if they are too flagrant to be overlooked [. . .] then the correspondent will try to excuse the anarchical acts of his friends, [. . .] by characterizing them as 'simple madness', and their perpetrators as desperate through misfortune. But this tenderness of treatment and restraint of language are not shown to the Turkish soldiers and people when he attributes to them many ghastly crimes the mere reading of which is enough to fill the heart of any Turk with abhorrence, and cause him to wonder how the mind of such a 'civilised being' could evolve these calumnious fictions. [. . .] Supposing that one of those long-suffering Turks were to come over to England, [. . .] with the object of accomplishing a mere work of revenge, such, for instance, as blowing up St. James's or Exeter Hall at the time when the clerico-Radical agitators were holding one of their usual anti-Turkish demonstrations, would the Turcophobe journalist treat of such a crime with the same restraint of language? Would they not become still louder in crying out for a European crusade to wipe the whole Turkish nation from the face of earth? [. . .] [pp. 7–9]

The hostile and malicious misrepresentation of all things Turkish nowadays is not only practised by the Radical papers, but also by certain organs of the extreme jingo party. The anti-Turkish diatribes of which even surpass those of the Radical press. Egypt is now under British control, and there is no other spot in the map of the Ottoman Empire which (to use the words of an English paper) could be 'painted with the British red', while Germans are completely ousting the British in the markets of Turkey. Why then should the organs of these self-interested jingoes remain any longer friendly towards the Turk? [. . .] They call the outrageous conduct of our assailant 'patriotism', but when we are provoked to take up arms to defend our country against aggressions they style this 'Muhammedan fanaticism'. [. . .] They deny that we have any instinct of patriotism. They criticise the old policy of their country alleging that if England had not prevented the formation of the 'Big Bulgaria' of the San Stefano Treaty [in 1878] 'the terrible deeds of the Turks' would not now be happening in Macedonia. [. . .] What natural ties bind Bulgarians to the English we fail to see. Should Russia engage in a struggle with the English in any part of Asia these wily Bulgarians, [. . .] would very likely volunteer on the Russian side. [pp. 11–15]

Among the Radical politicians of the Turcophobe school there are not a few who, like the founder of the school, have in their time been friends of our country. Why they turned into such deadly enemies is incomprehensible to most of our compatriots. As we are not sufficiently advanced to understand the delicacy of political morality in vogue in over-civilised lands, we made enquiries of some of our friends in Europe as to the cause of the change of front so frequently made by their politicians. We were informed that in civilised countries all politicians are more or less opportunists. A change in circumstances affects their policy, and they will denounce today the principle which they yesterday pledged their honour to maintain.[. . .] This being the case it is not correct to say that our old friends became our enemies because they were disgusted with the hopelessness of Turkish misrule: They were perfectly aware of the part played by the officious Powers of civilised Europe in causing and perpetuating that misrule.

It is palpable fallacy for these old friends to say that we do not want to reform our country. Reforms, if not productive of a new *imperium in imperio*, i.e., of a new autonomy in a given part of Turkey,—a new blow at the Ottoman sovereignty and at the rights of Mussulman inhabitants,—but on the contrary conducive to the prosperity and well-being of our countrymen at large, would be heartily welcomed by us. These Turcophobe politicians actually say that we are opposed to reform a country every inch of which was won at the cost of the blood of our ancestors[. . .] The reforms which we need, but which we are never allowed by Europe to carry out in peace, and the reforms which the politicians in question are so ardently trying to impose upon us, are two different things. We know too well the meaning of their benevolent offers. These politicians, moreover, talk of our incapacity to apply any reforms. We should like to challenge any of these theorizing politicians to come forward and administer the affairs of a Turkish province better than the average Turkish governor under the same singular disabilities and intrigues, and in face of the international obstacles which always exist in Turkish dominions.[. . .]

They make mention of the disabilities under which the Christians of Turkey are supposed to suffer, disregarding the circumstance that Turkey is actually employing Christians of all nationalities under her rule as ambassadors, ministers, conculs [*sic*], governors, judges and civilian officials in various posts. What shall we say about the political disabilities of the Mussulmans whose territories have been seized by the Christian Powers? Take as an example the most highly civilised and most liberal of these Powers: We do not see that the Mussulmans under her rule are able to take any proportionate share in the administration of their native country, to say nothing of their absolute disability to take any part[. . .] in the administrative and the other offices of the government to which they are subject.[. . .] [pp. 16–18]

According to the Radical Turcophobes, a province which has once been severed from the Turkish rule is excellently governed as soon as its administration is handed over to Christians and a crown-seeking European prince made its ruler. It is true that when this change [is] accomplished, the element of strife is either partially or wholly suppressed in the freed province.[. . .] At first its Muhammedan population is got rid of smoothly and methodically.[. . .] It is certainly governed in comparative peace; international intrigues no longer reign there; and as a favour to their freed Christian brethren the European powers give up, totally or partially, the capitulations or extraterritorial privileges of their subjects in the liberated country[. . .] [pp. 19–20]

What can be done to obviate the mischief periodically wrought by the Turco-phobes in England is a difficult question. There are some Young Turks who are inclined to think that this Turcophobia is caused by the faulty regime of the present Sultan.[. . .] We do not believe that the rule of the Sultan, however bad it may be, is the cause of the prevailing Turcophobia. If our enemies hate the Sultan, they do so not simply because he is an unworthy ruler, but more especially he is the Turkish sovereign. If we had the best sovereign imaginable they would still carry on their anti-Turkish agitation; they might indeed hate us the more if they saw us living in peace and prosperity under a better ruler.

These Young Turks moreover complain that the Sultan has completely suppressed our national energy, so that the people cannot raise their voice in self-defence against the slanderous charges brought against them in Western Europe by the Turcophobe agitators. The chief step they suggest for the contradiction of these charges is to enlighten public opinion independently of the Sultan's government. This is a futile hope. We cannot find means and opportunity for contradicting the fabrications of the numerous Turcophobe journalists. Moreover we cannot wipe out the evil impressions always produced on the public mind by the members of anti-Turkish associations, such as the Anglo-Armenian Committee, the Balkan Committee, and the Byron Society [. . .]

With all these facts and possibilities facing us it seems to us folly to expect to succeed in our attempt to correct the wrong ideas and prejudices prevailing against us in Western Europe. [. . .] We can only find our salvation in defending our country with the usual Turkish fortitude and determination. A nation which has been fighting for centuries the combined forces of several European states cannot be lacking in vitality. If Christendom is trying to crush the Mussulman power she must be made to see that the Turk will die, not like a 'sick man', but like a man struggling to defend his race and faith with unparalleled determination. [pp. 29–30]

6.7 Ismail Gaspirali and Tatar emigration from Russia to the Ottoman Empire, 1902–1903
Brian Glyn Williams

Preface

Between 1774 and 1783 the Russians conquered the Crimean Tatars, a Turkic-Muslim ethnic group descended from the Mongol Golden Horde and other ancient Turkic nomadic confederations. After the annexation of their state, known as the Crimean Khanate, by Imperial Russia this Muslim people began a series of migrations from the Crimean Peninsula (in present-day Ukraine) to the Islamic Ottoman Empire. The Western political construct of nationalism, which glorifies ethnic groups' histories, cultures, languages, and links to natal territories (usually defined as 'Fatherlands' or 'Homelands'), had not yet spread to the Muslim world at this early stage. Seen in this context, it is not surprising that this community of Muslims, who still defined themselves in religious, not modern ethno-national terms, chose to abandon their home villages in the Russian (Christian) dominated Crimea in order to live in the *Dar al-Islam* (Land of Islam).

In a process known as *hijra* (religious migration), hundreds of thousands of Crimean Tatar Muslims emigrated from the Crimea to the Ottoman Empire. In the process, the Crimean Tatars gradually became a minority in their own homeland as Slavic settlers took their place. By the late nineteenth century the remaining Crimean Tatar community of just 200,000 in the Russian Empire faced the real risk of extinction as a separate ethnic group. Far from rallying in defense of their rights to the Crimea in the face of this development, the religiously defined Crimean Tatar Muslims of the nineteenth century usually followed their conservative village mullahs' advice to abandon the lands of the infidel and migrate to the lands of the Ottoman caliph, which were seen as sacred Islamic lands (in Tatar the lands of the Ottoman caliphs were known as *ak topraklar*, i.e. white or sacred lands).

By the nineteenth century, however, the Turkic-Muslim peoples inhabiting the Russian Empire (such as the Volga Tatars, Kazakhs, Azerbaijanis, Uzbeks, Crimean Tatars, etc.) experienced a significant process of cultural modernization that came, in part, as a response to their perceived position of inferiority with regard to their Christian Russian rulers (the various Muslim peoples of the Russian Empire had been conquered between the sixteenth and nineteenth centuries). This process of confronting the elements of conservative Islam in Russian Muslim society led to a reshaping of these peoples' basic world-view and promoted a secularization process that was to see many of the Russian Muslims' Islamically-based traditions attacked by modernist reformers. The modernist movement of the Russian Turkic-Muslims was to witness the various Turco-Muslim peoples of the world constructing themselves as ethno-nations with secularly defined homelands (*vatanlar*) based on the Western principles of nationalism instead of religion.

One of the first great reformers in this movement was a Crimean Tatar newspaper editor and educational reformer named Ismail Gaspirali (Gaspirinsky in Russian). Gaspirali had a profound impact on the various Turkic-Muslim peoples of the Russian Empire, not only through his reform schools, which spread throughout the empire, but also his modernist newspaper (the first of its kind among the Muslims of the Russian Empire) known as *Tercuman* ('The Translator'). In the pages of this newspaper Gaspirali, who had been exposed to modern Western culture in his studies in Moscow and Paris, patiently spoke out for women's rights, described the cultural progress of the Christian West, fought against the religious obscurantism and conservatism of the entrenched mullahs, and introduced new ways to define his people (i.e. all Turkic-Muslims in the Russian Empire) based not on religion, but on a previously latent sense of ethnicity and common language.

Gaspirali's ambition was to unite the various Turkic-speaking Muslims of the Russian Empire into one nation that could then resist the cultural stagnation that had overwhelmed them. He actively promoted his motto, 'Unity in Language, Thought and Deed' (*Dilde, Fikirde ve İshte Birlik*) in the pages of his newspaper and tried to encourage the construction of a Pan-Turkic nation in the Russian Empire.

In addition to his work establishing ethnicity, as opposed to religion, as the primary marker of group identity for the Crimean Tatars and other Russian Muslims, Gaspirali also contributed to the forging of the Crimean Tatar nation by working tirelessly to halt the emigration of Crimean Tatars to the Ottoman Empire. This emigration to the Muslim Ottoman Empire was, to a considerable extent, due to the fact that the Crimean Tatars did not define themselves as a territorialized nation in the modern secular sense. Rather, they saw themselves as Muslims abandoning the *Dar al-Harb* (the Land of War with the infidel) for the *Dar al-Islam* (i.e. the realm of the Ottoman caliph). They certainly did not construct the Russian-dominated Crimea as a 'Fatherland' in the Western nationalist sense.

When a new move towards migration to the Ottoman Empire broke out among the Tatars in the Crimea in 1902, Gaspirali began a regular series of articles in *Tercuman* entitled 'On Migration', in which he fought to prevent the departure of his Turkic countrymen to the lands of the sultan. The following excerpts from this series of articles demonstrate both his rhetorical style and ideological priorities.

Texts

1902

My dear friend Ali-Jaffer ['Ali-Ja'far], you have decided to resettle in Turkey. You have decided this is what you want to do; and God be with you! May God grant you everything good. But permit me to be to you a sincere friend who frequently prays for your well being and weeps over your fate—since you are a good, simple man take this brotherly advice.

Dear Ali-Jaffer, you may depart now, you may leave in spring or next year—you are allowed to go; nobody will detain you—but do not hurry in this fashion, God does not love haste. At present it is winter, and cold; the earth is covered with snow and here you are preparing to go somewhere. Everything living is in its burrow; all things living are hiding from the frigidity and cold. Who is driving you, my dear, that you throw yourself with your family and baby in this cold time on a journey across the stormy sea? Why, my dear, do you subject the children of your blood to the misery of a winter voyage? Consider, will it not be a sin to subject them to such suffering? After winter comes spring; after the cold warmth. Once you have decided to abandon the blessed Crimea, would it not be better to prepare to travel in the spring, when it will be warm, and then proceed on the road you will travel? Surely now, you will not see the land on which you dwell for it is covered with snow.

Courageous Ali-Jaffer, remember your distant ancestors were brave knights, the praise of whom resounded half way around the world, your close fathers were universally known as honest, kind, patient people, worthy of a better fate and greater fortune. Do not throw your little ones into the embraces of the cold, or even perhaps starvation. It is true that God will provide for everything, but remember the children and the family, He has entrusted them to us.[43]

March 1903

Here is an evident fact: not long ago the relative of the famous master Selim Usta, Maksumadzhi Khalil, left from Bahçesaray. He (Selim Usta) received a tearful letter which he conveyed to the editor. The emigrant (to Turkey) complains that no one remained in Constantinople, and that they were transported to the Asiatic side (of the Bosphorus). Here they left them without any assistance, letting each get settled as he was able and capable. As to requests for allotting land, the local authorities require an acceptance certificate for resettlement. Those who do not possess such a certificate are coldly asked—'Were you really driven from Russia or is perhaps someone calling you here?' The aforementioned Khalil states further that emigrants on the steppe set up tents from torn felt, clothing, and other trash. Thank Allah, that the warm spring sun allows such an existence, otherwise death would arrive soon.[44]

May 1903

We have heard rumors that in one or another Tatar village people are selling their land and cattle, having in mind resettlement in Turkey. If this is true, then we

[43] Ismail Gaspirali, *Tercuman*, 43 (11 Nov. 1902), 65.

[44] Id., 'Pis'mo Emigranta', *Tercuman*, 10 (14 Mar. 1903), 37.

must pity these people for they know not what they do. To leave one's homeland one must have some sort of reason, to go to a new place one must have true, exact knowledge of that place, otherwise it will not be resettlement but senseless wandering. Any senseless, unfounded move will lead to poverty, destruction, and ruin.

We do not at this time wish to go into the living and working conditions of our people in Turkey, but wish to caution those inclined to wander to do the following; do not sell anything, do not undertake anything until it is positively known that the government will allow resettlement; a passport to travel abroad costs 10–15 rubles and therefore it does not make much sense to waste such a huge sum. [. . .] You will just be throwing your money away.

Those who exhaust their means will live in poverty there and then live in poverty here, as often happens when they return to the Crimea. Everyone should think twice before selling everything and setting off on an unknown journey with children and elderly. There is no land of milk and honey over there. Anywhere and everywhere one must work diligently, skillfully and untiringly for his daily bread. The rules of life are the same in the Crimea as they are in Turkey and in Japan.[45]

September 1903

Last year in a series of articles we proved to our countrymen all the absurdity and disastrous nature of emigration to Turkey. [. . .] The results of this rashness are now becoming visible to all. Hundreds have written reporting the deaths of whole families and massive illness among emigrants. As the living witnesses to the calamities, those having the possibility to return to the Crimea arrive with every steamship, having grown older over the year and, of course, having been ruined. The victims of the emigration mania are so eloquent that seeing and listening to them is heartbreaking. There is a hope that the emigration, which is already calming down, will die permanently. Thank God since there were no causes for emigration and there still are none. It is necessary to simply sit down and engage in work with zeal.[46]

[45] Id., 'Ob Emigratsiia', *Tercuman*, 17 (7 May 1902), 3.
[46] Id., *Tercuman*, 36 (15 Sept. 1903), 155.

6.8 Conceptualizing modernity in late Ottoman times: Japan as a model nation, 1902–1913
Renée Worringer

Preface

In the nineteenth century, domestic circumstances, as well as international challenges posed by European Powers, led various sectors of Ottoman society to the conclusion that drastic changes had to be initiated to prevent the destruction of the Ottoman Empire. A transformation of the Ottoman polity had ensued as a consequence of its incorporation into the world economic system; the former Ottoman-Islamic ideology binding this heterogeneous empire together was giving way to new ideas of constitutionalism and parliamentary government, shared national consciousness and a duty to one's homeland, secular rationalism, and Islamic modernism[47]—all of which contributed to a discourse on becoming 'modern' in the Ottoman Empire at this time. As one response to this transformation, some Ottoman thinkers during and after the reign of Ottoman Sultan Abdülhamid II (r. 1876–1909) looked east, to Meiji Japan, as a pattern for the kind of technological modernization and socio-political reform that would rescue the empire from its potentially disastrous fate.[48] Discussions of virtually every aspect of Japanese state and society appeared in newspapers, journals, and longer monographs; Ottoman government communiqués between officials pointed out the achievements of modern Japan that made it a powerful nation-state rivalling Europe; conferences were held in the Ottoman capital in an attempt to explicate the secrets of Japanese success.[49] Japan seemed to have reversed racial/cultural hierarchical schemes influencing the global order as it modernized state structures and societal mechanisms. As a result, the modern Japanese nation had become the first non-Western great power: it promulgated a constitution in 1889, launched a compulsory education program and undertook a system of universal military conscription. It was able to negotiate internationally binding alliances (the Anglo-Japanese Alliance of 1902) and win wars that guaranteed

---

[47] Islamic modernists in the empire argued that the proper assimilation of 'true' Islam (indigenous Muslim culture) with the beneficial aspects of Western material civilization should be the new basis for society. See Şerif Mardin, *The Genesis of Young Ottoman Thought* (Princeton: Princeton University Press, 1962) and David Dean Commins, *Islamic Reform: Politics and Social Change in Late Ottoman Syria* (New York: Oxford University Press, 1990).

[48] The newspaper was frequently the forum in which to disseminate most efficiently the new platforms, policies, or ideas of citizens anxious for the empire's survival in the contemporary modern world.

[49] See e.g. the published proceedings: Comte Léon Ostrorog, *Conference sur la Renaissance du Japon* (Istanbul: 1911).

influence and colonies in Asia (Sino-Japanese War, 1894–5; Russo-Japanese War, 1904–5). Japan's history, its national culture and heritage, its political organization, and its economy were just a few of the topics examined in order to enlighten the Ottoman Empire in a quest for its own particular style of modernity.

The sultan's statesmen (such as the author of the first excerpt) directly experienced the confrontation with, and the intellectual currents underlying, Western imperial power. They sought to modernize the empire in order to catch up with Europe, without necessarily threatening the sanctity of the Ottoman throne. For them, modernity was contingent upon technological progress; participating in certain ritual demonstrations of power between states signified modern nationhood and acceptance as equals by the 'civilized world'.

For the Young Turk opposition, many of whom were educated in and/or exiled to Europe in the period prior to 1908, the deposition of Sultan Abdülhamid II and the reinstatement of the Ottoman constitution were antecedents for reordering society according to their particular ideological outlooks. The Young Turk movement, comprised as it was of a myriad of political figures and intellectuals who adhered variously to secularism, Social Darwinism, elitism, capitalism, and nationalism, ultimately witnessed their revolution in 1908. As the second excerpt shows, the metaphor of modern Japan figured dramatically in the rhetoric of prominent Young Turk activists and political exiles like Ahmed Rıza. His version of modernity was determined by certain politicized, social criteria represented in the Japanese nation and lacking in the current Ottoman state. The last excerpt, penned by an Ottoman Arab official years after the Young Turk revolution and delivered originally as part of a lecture in Istanbul, reflects the sentiments of an intellectual still awaiting the realization of Ottoman modernity in 1913, and his prescription for how this must be undertaken. Believing in cultural determinism—shared Ottoman-Islamic heritage as integral to an enduring Ottoman patriotic spirit that transgressed religious and ethnic identities—Japan represented the best balance of indigenous character combined with Western material civilization.

Texts

1. A view of Japan from Ottoman ruling circles

(Memorandum from the Ottoman Consul-General in Singapore to the Ottoman Foreign Minister, Ottoman Prime Ministry Archives, BBA YA.HUS 430/46, June 1902. Ottoman Turkish)[50]

I was invited via telegram by the Japanese Consul to Singapore, Malakka, and Penang stationed in Singapore to visit the Japanese war-cruiser called *Mikasa*

---

[50] Report on Prince Komatsu's stopover in Singapore en route to attend a British coronation ceremony in London.

which carries 50 cannon, a crew of 313, whose bulk equals 15,200 tons, and which is under the command of Captain Hayasaki, who will voyage to Japan after several days, having come from London on 29 April. Your humble servant accepted the invitation to ride with the Japanese Consul and the Consul's Chancellery aboard a small steamboat that was ready at the pier to take us to the warship around 16:00. Upon my arrival at the steamship, I was received very cordially by the Commander and we entered the salon. After performing the official introductions, the Honorable Captain stated how very pleased he was with our visit and that Japan has the utmost affection and friendship with the eternal Ottoman state and that he himself would see to it that we enjoyed the tour of the ship. After Your humble servant responded with expressions of gratitude for the tour, I offered in the appropriate manner that our affection and friendship were sincere, that I would present an air of comportment and hospitality showing proper grace in accepting [this] on behalf of my sovereign government, that in the recent past His Majesty the Sultan's imperial frigate *Ertuğrul* had been dispatched by royal decree to Japan's capital bearing many precious gifts, and that this was indeed great proof of our affection and friendship. After this, the Honorable steamship commander himself accompanied us as we toured from start to finish; I added that I remained grateful for the pleasure and kindness of having witnessed such feats of organization and perfection, and I came back ashore aboard the small steamboat that had been readied. The afore-mentioned cruiser had been over-hauled in the London shipyard this time, and had been outfitted with the latest technical advances and systems in an extremely elegant and sturdy manner; two days later it would depart for Japan. I obtained detailed information about another steamship. Various gifts were sent to London from Japan aboard the German postal steamer *Koenig Albert* on 5 May for His Majesty the King's official coronation; notable among them were a pair of large vases, inside of which was gold, that were handcrafted by thirty skilled and capable Japanese artisans who completed them after five years of continuous work. They were preferred to the rest of the gifts because of their value and exquisiteness. His Majesty Prince Komatsu, who carried these very gifts, arrived in Singapore via the German postal steamer for the purpose I put forth above. Your humble servant, having received another invitation from the Japanese Consul the next day, learned that it was possible to have an audience with His Majesty in an informal manner if I wished. Because your humble servant had learned that the afore-mentioned Prince had recently visited the imperial capital (Istanbul) and that the Sublime state had shown kindness, I immediately responded to the invitations, indicating that I would accept. At 11:00 when the steamer arrived, I entered the presence of His Majesty the Prince with his intermediary, the Japanese Emperor's Chief Master-of-Ceremonies Mr. Inoue. After the official introductions, which showed quite a great deal of refine-ment where I was concerned, I offered that the Ottoman state had established a Consulate in a place like Singapore that was near Japan, that [the State] was pleased with this, and that soon, under the progressive auspices of His Majesty the Sultan, [the State] even hoped to place an ambassador in Japan. [. . .] At 15:00, His Excellency the governor of Singapore and all of the Consuls arrived at the steamship; the steamer left at 15:30, headed for London, after an official sendoff for the Prince. His Majesty the Prince will head from here to Rome by way of Naples in order to meet His Royal Highness the King of Italy, and afterwards to France to meet with His Excellency the President, and from there he will head to London in order to attend the official coronation. As for his return trip, it is known in addition that he will go back to Japan by way of St. Petersburg and from there to Harbin [in China]. The Japanese government has been in a progressive state of mind these last few years; reportedly next year with the official support of Great Britain it will dispatch 2,000 Japanese to the Cape of Good Hope where they will settle and find work. Because the Japanese state works to advance [itself] from every angle, in every particular, and they strive to the utmost degree, currently they are undertaking regular services to America, Europe, China, and neighboring ports with big, beautiful steamers and postal ships. Easy and efficient transports, they almost rival the European postal and cargo steamers. Right now, even under the progressive auspices of His Majesty the Sultan, it is evident that we, the Imperial Ottoman state, will in a short time be left quite behind, not only by the Japanese, but also by the most civilized nations. Your humble servant received a written invitation dated yesterday from His Excellency the Spanish Consul, that I have been invited to a banquet that will be held in honor of the coronation of His Majesty the King of Spain on the sixteenth of this coming May.

2. A Young Turk exile's comparison of Japan and the Ottoman Empire: 'Turkey and Japan'

(Ahmed Rıza, 'Turquie et Japon', *Mechveret Supplément Français*, 149 (15 March 1904), 1–2. French.)[51]

What an imposing spectacle—and at the same time heartrending for our patriotism—that is what we are offered by Japan! Behold a people that, 50 years past was considered a horde of noble savages, at most exciting the literary curiosity of some eccentric writers. Europe assessed their vases, their fans and their silks in fanciful drawings. And that was just about all. Now, silently, in the fever of a lofty national conception and nobly ambitious aspirations, a magnificent evolution is at work. Bounding ahead, so to speak, this people found its way through the disdain or the simple arrogance of the Western Powers and reached the level of

[51] This Young Turk political activist and Comtean positivist lived in exile in Paris, where he published the principle organ of the Committee of Union and Progress (CUP), *Mechveret* ('Consultation'), and its French supplement. Ahmed Rıza later became president of the Ottoman Chamber of Deputies after the 1908 revolution to reinstate the constitution.

modern civilization. This miracle was owing to the extraordinary will of the Japanese to be counted among the Great Powers from three points of view: intellectual, commercial, and military.

The campaign against China[52]—China with 500 million souls—has already proven in a triumphant way that Japan was irreducibly possessive of its integrity and its national prestige. The present war is the most vivid demonstration.[53] Russian politics, politics of monopolizing and of oppression, politics eternally simmering in the 'pot' of which V. Hugo speaks, found the expeditious Japanese prompted to retaliate. And all sympathies go out to this people who, for their rightness and renown, drew swords against the enemy without by any means worrying about [Russia's] appellation 'the colossus of the North.'

As for this example of vitality and valiance, this lesson of ardent patriotism given by a nation so recently regenerated, what could be the impression of Sultan Abdülhamid? The question appears naive on our part. But considering the men among the Japanese who lead, how not to wonder about those august Ottoman monarchs, ancestors of the spineless coward who [now] governs us, who governed with a powerful and faithful hand, castigating the insolence of those who dared to carry out an attack upon the honor of the homeland?

How not to wonder that the people, that the Turkish soldiers themselves remained the same, honest, generous, and brave; that they are ready to defend their country against pirates, bandits, and excessive desire for wealth, if a strong and respected leader gave them the legitimate signal? Meanwhile this [Ottoman] people, this army, has only at their head one for whom their unspeakable sacrifices are all made to satisfy his immeasurable selfishness. While thanks to the cowardice of its ruler, the Empire is torturing itself, it is in tatters; the tiniest threat of a [foreign] Power makes us turn pale; there are not worse humiliations to which we have yet to be subjected in order not to trouble the digestion of such a sovereign. One has only to want: we yield. One has only to tender the hand: we give. The awful despotism of Abdülhamid has reduced us to a nation of ghosts whose sons are no longer even held by him, but by foreign hands.

And, while the cannon thunders over there, the Japanese steadily torpedoing and demolishing the fleet of their enemies, here in our Empire, the work of destruction continues by us and against us. The reason for this is very simple: all those who cherished their country and had demonstrated this love were eliminated, struck down by ostracism, or in part by annihilation. Indeed, the depletion of patriots—the hope and shield of the Homeland—is frightening. Those who pronounce the word Constitution—this Constitution, which is precisely what made Japan what it is today—understand; some who start to speak are stifled and

---

[52] The campaign referred to here is the Sino-Japanese War of 1894–5.

[53] This is a reference to the Russo-Japanese War of 1904–5, in which the Japanese proved victorious.

disappear. Officials, officers, and *softas*[54] suspected of any degree of liberalism are sent to populate the fortified enclosures in faraway provinces. The hand that makes a gesture of impatience is wrenched; the voice that whispers a truth is suppressed; the head that rises up in need of independence is placed into a noose. The immense city is desolate, silent. More cheerful are our flourishing cemeteries on the shores of the sea or stretching along hillsides, with white stones under cypresses, the singing of streams or the consoling chirping of birds. How not to wonder at it all?

And, in order to continue the cruel parallel between Japan and Turkey, what do we have, as opposed to the devoted men who surround the Mikado and work with such sincere abnegation to boost the country? A collection of wretched courtiers who, by their speech, their connections, their threats, terrorize the Sultan, hold him in their claws, isolate him in perpetual horror. Why? Through him fly money and favors. Now the pain has become chronic, he has gangrene in all his being. Like a leper [with] his wounds, he is made to rot where he lives and outside of it he can no longer survive. And presently, that which he sees in this beautiful and unhappy capital is a deep misery, it is fear, and, upon word of an order coming out of Yıldız Palace, it is abandonment, it is all treachery and all depravity. Under this cursed regime, it is the terrible recession into chaos. And so have been dispersed—[only] for the moment, we hope—the patriotic seed of a famous group of men who, in order to bring back life to the country, have judged that it was not too much to make a sacrifice of their own lives.

It is a glory and a consolation for us to venerate the memory of these pure and noble hearts who were called Midhat, Mustafa Fazıl, Kemal, Odian, and who, at least as refugees in death, do not see a criminal monarch putting the country that they had ardently beloved into such a dishonourable situation.[55] As for some of those patriots whom death spared, they had to leave the native soil. From afar, as they had done of near, they put their devotion and their tireless activity into the service of Turkey and, with the aid of pen and deed, they say to the Ottoman people by what means, by what efforts they can reinstate the Constitution of 1876, which is their sole salvation. At this moment, their voices may be covered by the clamours of battles and the deafening growl of politics, possessing the next lightning strikes. What is important [in this]? They acted for us, upholding

[54] This is a term for students in Islamic schools, called in Ottoman Turkish a *medrese*, who receive a traditional education. In early May 1876 riots took place in Istanbul among these theological students, who demanded the resignation of Grand Vizier Mahmud Nedim Paşşa and sought a constitutional regime.

[55] These are the names of some prominent Ottoman figures who were involved with the Young Ottoman movement which demanded representative government in Ottoman lands as a response to the authoritarian nature of the Tanzimat reforms. Midhat Paşşa, the Ottoman grand vizier in 1876, is credited with facilitating the promulgation of the Ottoman constitution of 1876.

good, and good will be upheld. Because we do not believe in depriving ourselves of the assurance that the Ottomans, following the dramatic events unfolding in the Far East with an avid interest—and it is never too late to do good!—will find superiority [enough] to induce revolt in the presence of all the acts of banditry that are perpetrated in Turkey, against Turkey, permitting the suffocation of their patriotic cry!

Note this happy symptom, and encourage it.

3. Another opinion on the Ottoman future: 'Japan and the Japanese'

(Sati Al-Husri, 'Japonya ve Japonlar' [lecture originally given at the East Theater in Istanbul], published in *Büyük Milletlerden Japonlar, Almanlar*, Konferans Kütüphanesi (Istanbul: 'Kader' Matbaası, 1329AH/1913CE), 34–7. Ottoman Turkish)[56]

These explanations that we gave about the general lines of Japanese history show that the course of action which the Japanese pursued for progress was very evident and plain: the Japanese imitated Europeans and Americans in order to progress; they borrowed European and American theoretical and practical sciences and techniques, administrative and legal structures and laws; they demonstrated a great efficacy and an intense sense of perseverance in the matter of imitation and borrowing, in particular they attributed a great significance to borrowings and renewal (modernization) relating to [national] prosperity and cultural refinement. This course of action, which brought the Japanese out of a state of being a medieval community and into completely modern nation-hood in the space of thirty years, serves as a very powerful warning through example for us.

We—like the Japanese—remained unversed in European civilization for a period of centuries. We—like the Japanese—just started, after having become distant from Europeans, to appreciate the need to borrow and imitate that civilization.

In fact, we have not been living in a country far from Europe and closed to Europeans, like the Japanese; on the contrary—we have been right next to Europe; clashing with Europeans for centuries, we have seen a lot of foreigners in our commercial ports for centuries. Nevertheless, it is as though there has come to be a virtual wall of China or a great ocean between us and the Europeans who used to stand so close to us, and even among us, so that for a period of centuries we passed the time unaware, and without our gaining a share

---

[56] Al-Husri, a Syrian Arab by birth, grew up in the Ottoman system and served in the Ottoman Ministry of Education. A staunch believer in Ottomanism until the demise of the empire in 1918, he subsequently reoriented himself around the notion of a pan-Arab nation and again utilized the Japanese example to support his arguments for Arab unity in the twentieth century.

of the intellectual, industrial, political, and social advancements and revolutions which occurred in the civilized world.

We decided thirty years before the Japanese to come out of this virtual isolation and to share Europeans' developments: we promulgated the Beneficent Tanzimat Decree thirty years before the Mikado's auspicious Charter Oath.[57] Although this is the case, we have not yet been able to advance like the Japanese; still we have not been able to present ourselves to the civilized world as a 'contemporary nation'.

Because—in regard to progress and renewal—in the course of borrowing and imitating European civilization—we do not behave in earnest, with consistency. In particular, we have ignored [the country's] prosperity and cultural refinement, occupying [ourselves] with political and administrative issues above all else. We behave like a sick person that frequently changes the doctor's treatment and the method of care, and does not adopt any medical regime and treatment unless a crisis happens or recurs. [. . .] However, because of our many contacts and material intermingling with Europe, we have experienced a lot of harm due to this lack of firmness and earnestness; we resemble not a person trying to walk and swim among the floods of civilization, [but] as [someone] stricken, meeting a fate of being dragged behind the current's whims while we want to stop motionless in these torrents; because we do not want to satisfy the demands of the century by our own free will, we have suffered vicissitudes caused by the force and pressure of events. Therefore naturally, we could not remain as we were, but also we could not advance much. [. . .]

From now on, the 'history of Japanese progress' will show us with great clarity what kind of course of action it is that is necessary for us to pursue for 'true progress': to try to borrow and emulate European civilization, to attribute great importance to procedures and reforms connected to prosperity and culture, and to demonstrate perseverance and efficacy in these matters. [. . .]

These have to be the most significant convictions that the history of Japan's progress will give us. This history has to give us another very important conviction besides this: however backward a nation may remain in the matter of progress, if it shows a sufficient level of earnestness, it has to be made to believe that it will be able to make good the time that it has lost.

---

[57] The 'Beneficent Tanzimat Decree' refers to the 1839 Ottoman Rescript of Gülhane. It proclaimed protection of private property, equality among all Ottoman citizens regardless of religion, the abolition of tax-farms, universal conscription, and the guarantee of fair trial for the criminally accused. The Japanese Charter Oath of 1868 pronounced the new Meiji government's ideological and reform program, which included a dismemberment of the Confucian class system, the right of assembly, the provision for representative government, discarding harmful customs of the past, and the active procurement of knowledge from throughout the world.

After paying close attention to the general course of this history, henceforth we must not even doubt that it is possible to make up for the time that we lost with regard to progress and civilization, no matter how much nor how valuable it was. The thing that is necessary for us, in order for this, is to strive. To struggle; with determination, to endeavour with earnestness, materially, spiritually, without tiring; without giving up hope, to strive. [. . .]

Behold our life and salvation's only means. [. . .]

6.9 The Ottoman home front, a German correspondent's remarks, 1917[58]
Robert G. Landen

Preface

Dr Stuermer, a correspondent for the *Koelnische Zeitung* stationed in Istanbul during 1915–16, left an interesting account of the internal situation within the Ottoman Empire during World War I. Wartime attempts to curb inflation and to reform the Ottoman monetary system were symptomatic of the severe financial strains which the conflict brought. The hardships experienced by Ottoman subjects during the war are difficult to overestimate. Shortages of food and spiralling inflation marked daily life in the capital, problems continually exacerbated by waves of refugees arriving there from the shrinking provinces. By 1917 the empire was in a very weak state; lack of food and medicines was as rampant among the civilian population as among the troops.

The war stimulated the growth of Turkish nationalism to the point where even the German allies of the Ottoman Empire were subjected to the inconveniences arising from a wholesale Turkification campaign.

Text

On the financial side, apart from Turkey's enormous debt to Germany, the wonderful attempt at a reform and standardization of the coinage in the middle of May 1916 is worthy of mention. The reform, which was a simplification of huge economic value of the tremendously complicated money system and introduced a theoretical gold unit, must be regarded chiefly as a war measure to prevent the rapid deterioration of Turkish paper money.

This last attempt, as was obvious after a few months' trial, was entirely unsuccessful, and even hastened the fall of paper money, for the population soon discovered at the back of these drastic measures the thinly veiled anxiety of the Government lest there should be a further deterioration. Dire punishments, such as the closing down of money-changers' businesses and arraignment before a military court for the slightest offence, were meted out to anyone found guilty of changing gold or even silver for paper.

In November 1916, however, it was an open secret that, in spite of all these prohibitions, there was no difficulty in the inland provinces and in Syria and Palestine in changing a gold pound for two or more paper pounds. In still more

---

[58] Harry Stuermer, *Two War Years in Constantinople*, trans. E. Allen (New York: George H. Doran, 1917), 121–4, 154–7.

unfrequented spots no paper money would be accepted, so that the whole trade of the country simply came to a standstill. Even in Constantinople at the beginning of December 1916, paper stood to gold as 100 to 175.

The Anatolian population still went gaily on, burying all the available silver *medjidichs* and even nickel piastres in their clay pots in the ground. [. . .] The people, too, could not but remember what had happened with the 'Kaime' [a paper-money issue] after the Turko-Russian war, when thousands who had believed in the assurances of the Government suddenly found themselves penniless. In Constantinople [İstanbul] it was a favorite joke to take one of the new pound, half-pound, or quarter-pound notes issued under German paper, not gold, guaranteed and printed only on one side and say, 'This (pointing to the right side) is the present value, and that (blank side) will be the value on the conclusion of peace.'

Even those who were better informed, however, and sat at the receipt of custom, did exactly the same [. . .]; no idea of patriotism prevented them from collecting everything metal they could lay their hands on, and, in spite of all threats of punishment—which could never overtake them!—paying the highest price in paper money for every gold piece they could get. Their argument was: 'One must of course have something to live on in the time directly following the conclusion of peace.' In ordinary trade and commerce, filthy, torn paper notes, down to a paper piastre, came more and more to be practically the only exchange. [. . .]

As early as the summer of 1915, there were clear outward indications in the streets of Constantinople of a smouldering nationalism ready to break out at any moment. Turkey, under the leadership of Talat Bey, pursued her course along the well-trodden paths, and the first sphere in which there was evidence of an attempt at forcible Turkification was the language. Somewhere toward the end of 1915 Talat suddenly ordered the removal of all French and English inscriptions, shop signs, etc., even in the middle of European Pera. In tramcars and at stopping-places the French text was blocked out; boards with public police warnings in French were either removed altogether or replaced by unreadable Turkish scrawls; the street indications were simply abolished. The authorities apparently thought it preferable that the Levantine public should get into the wrong tramcar, should break their legs getting out, pick flowers in the park and wander round helplessly in a maze of unnamed streets rather than that the spirit of forcible Turkification should make even the least sacrifice to comfort.

Of the thousand inhabitants of Pera, not ten can read Turkish; but under the pressure of the official order and for fear of brutal assault or some kind of under-hand treatment in case of non-compliance, the inhabitants really surpassed themselves, and before one could turn, all the names over the shops had been painted over and replaced by wonderful Turkish characters that looked like decorative shields or something of the kind painted in the red and white of the national colors. If one had not noted the entrance to the shop and the look of the window very carefully, one might wander helplessly up and down the Grand Rue de Pera if one wanted to buy something in a particular shop.

But the German [. . .] was highly delighted in spite of the extraordinary difficulty of communal life. 'Away with French and English,' he would shout. 'God punish England; hurrah, our Turkish brothers are helping us and favoring the extension of our German language!'

The answer to the pan-German expansion of politicians and language fanatics, whose spiritual home was round the beer tables of the 'Teutonia,' was provided by a second decree of Talat's some weeks later when all German notices had to disappear. A few, who would not believe the order, held out obstinately, and the signs remained in German till they were either supplemented in 1916 on a very clear hint from Stamboul [İstanbul], by the obligatory Turkish language or later quite supplanted. [. . .]

Then came the famous language regulations, which even went so far—with a year of grace granted owing to the extraordinary difficulties of the Turkish script—as to decree that in the offices of all trade undertakings of any public interest whatsoever, such as banks, newspapers, transport agencies, etc., the Turkish language should be used exclusively for bookkeeping and any written communication with customers. [. . .] Old and trusty employees suddenly found themselves faced with the choice of learning the difficult Turkish script or being turned out in a year's time. The possibility—indeed, the necessity—of employing Turkish hands in European businesses suddenly came within the range of practical politics—and that was exactly what the Turkish Government wanted. [. . .]

6.10 Muslim state participation in UN human rights debates, 1946–1966

Susan Waltz

Preface

In 1946 the new United Nations resolved to establish a standard for internationally recognized human rights. Two years later UN members adopted the Universal Declaration of Human Rights (UDHR).[59] In 1966 they voted to approve the text of two companion human rights treaties and open them for ratification. The International Covenant on Civil and Political Rights (ICCPR) and the International Covenant on Economic, Social, and Cultural Rights (ICESCR) accrued sufficient individual ratifications to enter force in 1976.[60] States that ratify the treaties are known as State Parties, and for these two treaties they include Algeria, Egypt, Iran, Iraq, Israel, Jordan, Kuwait, Lebanon, Libya, Morocco, Syria, Tunisia, and Yemen. The covenants are legally binding as instruments of international law.

The process of negotiating these three human rights instruments spanned twenty years, and despite changes in government, ideology, and national policies, accredited diplomats from the Arab Middle East participated throughout. From 1946 to 1949, Omar Lotfi [ʿUmar Lutfi] (Egypt) served on the Human Rights Commission that was charged to draft the UDHR, and its clearest expression of universal application can be traced to his intervention. Charles Malik,[61] an Arab Christian from Lebanon, was the Commission's rapporteur. In the autumn of 1948 he was elected chair of the General Assembly's Third Committee and in that capacity he guided UN delegates through an article-by-article scrutiny of the draft UDHR. Eighteen years later, when the time came to confirm the final text of the Covenants, the Third Committee was presided over by Morocco's Halima Embarek Warzazi. Every Middle Eastern[62] country voted in favor of the text of the two treaties, both in the Third Committee and in the General Assembly's plenary session.

Unfortunately, the extent of Middle Eastern engagement with the human rights covenants is not well known or appreciated. Eighteen years earlier, on 10 December 1948, Saudi Arabia abstained from the General Assembly's

---

[59] Link to full text of UDHR, <http://111, hrewb.org/legal/udhr.html>.

[60] Link to each of these to the same page, <http://www.hrweb.org/legal/undocs.htm>.

[61] For more on him, please link to <http://www.un.org/ga/55/president/bio13.htm>.

[62] The list of Middle Eastern signatories to the UDHR include Afghanistan, Algeria, Indonesia, Iran, Iraq, Israel, Jordan, Kuwait, Lebanon, Libya, Malaysia, Mauritania, Morocco, Pakistan, Saudi Arabia, Somalia, Sudan, Syria, Tunisia, Turkey, United Arab Republic [Egypt], and Yemen.

historic plenary vote on the UDHR. That single item is the best-known fact about the Arab world's participation in the UN debates on human rights, and popular awareness of the 1948 abstention has served to obscure many other interesting facts. Saudi Arabia was the only UN member state to have continuous representation by the same delegate throughout the entire period of UN discussion and debate on these instruments. Jamil Baroody voted to abstain from the UDHR, but in 1966 he cast Saudi Arabia's votes *in support of* the two legally binding covenants. As an extension of that vote, Saudi Arabia gave tacit assent to provisions for gender equality (joint Article 3) that had been introduced by Bedia Afnan, delegate from Iraq.

Twenty years is a long time to negotiate a treaty. Over that period, diplomats rotated in and out of the process, and new member states joined the discussion at the UN. In the Middle East, the governments and policies of some states changed mid-course. Egypt, for example, was a monarchy when the process began in 1948, and at the time when the covenants were approved in 1966 it was joined in political union with Syria, as the United Arab Republic. The relatively long time-span complicates efforts to generalize, but some broad observations about the participation of Middle Eastern governments can be made.

Delegates from the Middle East and Muslim world participated throughout the proceedings. A steady stream of new states (such as Tunisia, Morocco, Israel, and Yemen) joined the debates, but no Middle Eastern state dissociated itself from the proceedings.

Opinions and positions were not always uniform across the region, and sometimes delegates from the region openly argued with each other. Delegates expressed opposing views about gender rights, and differed on interpretations of religious freedom in Islam. All the same, it can be said that Middle Eastern delegates tended to pay close attention to the same issues—even when they disagreed or changed positions on them.

Like diplomats from other parts of the world, Middle Eastern delegates were inclined to focus their attention and energy on a relatively small set of issues, and tended to be most vocal when those issues made their periodic appearance on the agenda. Middle Eastern delegates argued about the interpretation of religious freedoms. They engaged deeply in debates about rights pertaining to the family and the place of socio-economic rights, and they spearheaded a successful campaign to include the right to self-determination in the covenants. As a means of opposing colonial rule they championed the universality of human rights, and delegates from some Middle Eastern countries were early and outspoken advocates of strong measures of implementation for the covenants, though eventually they would reverse this position.

When debate stalled—as it frequently did over twenty years—diplomats eventually looked for ways to accommodate their colleagues from other cultures and those who held dissimilar interests, while clever phrasing sometimes allowed difficult issues to be finessed. This was the tactic used to win Saudi Arabia's support for the covenants after its 1948 abstention from the UDHR vote; the UDHR phrase asserting 'freedom to change or maintain' religious beliefs was altered in the ICCPR, with the new text assuring 'freedom to have or adopt' beliefs. The change assuaged the concerns voiced by the Saudi Arabian delegation, and in 1966 they voted alongside other Middle Eastern delegations in favor of the full text of the treaties.

Below is a sampling of contributions by Middle Eastern and Muslim delegates to the UN debates on human rights instruments. Most of these interventions arose in proceedings of the UN General Assembly's Committee on Social, Humanitarian, and Cultural Questions (known as the Third Committee), which meets every autumn for a session of several months (sometimes extending into January or February). In sessions of the Third Committee, accredited diplomats reviewed, amended, and approved the text of the documents as the smaller Commission on Human Rights transmitted them. In 1948, when the UDHR was being examined, the Third Committee spent a full two months on the text. The Third Committee began its examination of the covenants in 1950, inviting delegates to offer general commentary. In subsequent years it debated a few politically sensitive questions (for example, whether to include a right of self-determination) and then it carried out an article-by-article review of the texts of the two treaties. Once the Third Committee approved the texts, they were forwarded to a plenary session of the General Assembly, for a final vote and accompanying speeches. In some years the plenary speeches were registered verbatim, though in most years they were recorded in summary form, with a clear effort to capture the intent, and flavor, of a delegate's speech. Interventions in the Third Committee were recorded in summary form. All passages below are quoted directly from UN records and are presented here organized into five distinct (but related) topics. It is worth remembering that the delegates are representing the official positions of their governments in these discussions.

Texts

1. On social and economic rights

Mr Baroody (Saudi Arabia) said he had voted for the Syrian amendment because it conformed to Islamic law, under the terms of which 'social justice' had a broader and more comprehensive meaning than 'social security.' In Saudi Arabia, the institution of *zakat*, a voluntary tax levied for the purpose of assisting the poor and unemployed, was one of the five pillars of Islam. Social security was a recent historical development in Western society, while *zakat* had been an article of faith in actual operation in Muslim communities for almost fourteen centuries.

[*Official Records of the United Nations General Assembly Third Committee, 1948, during debate on the draft UDHR*]

Azmi Bey (Egypt) regretted the absence of articles on economic, social and cultural rights [in the initial draft covenant], as those rights had become an essential part of the structure of civilized society. Although his country had already made great strides in that field, it would have wished to see such rights included as a guide, an example and a stimulus to its own activities.

[*Official Records of the United Nations General Assembly Third Committee, 1950, during a discussion on the desirability of including articles on economic, social, and cultural rights*]

Mrs Afnan (Iraq) believed that to distinguish economic and social rights from other fundamental human rights was merely academic. They should all find a place in the covenant, as they had in the Declaration. Any right acquired by any human being should be acquired by all human beings. [. . .] The right to life meant nothing concrete unless it was supplemented by the guarantee of health, work, and education—the means toward living. No great harm would be done if some countries used the inclusion of articles on economic, social and cultural rights as a pretext not to ratify the covenant. The very practical result of their inclusions would be that the peoples of those countries would find in them a stimulus to bring pressure to bear upon their governments to pass legislation in line with the provisions of the covenant and thus finally to ratify it.

[*Official Records of the United Nations General Assembly Third Committee, 1950, during a discussion on the desirability of including articles on economic, social, and cultural rights*]

Mr Baroody (Saudi Arabia) [. . .] [said], We still maintain that human rights and freedoms, whether civil and political on the one hand or economic, social, and cultural on the other hand, are so interconnected and interdependent that their separation into two documents would be artificial and arbitrary. Indeed, any human rights covenant which does not explicitly safeguard economic, social and cultural rights would, at best, be no more than an affirmation of civil and political rights which are to be found in almost all national constitutions and in the statute laws of Member States. [. . .]

Most of those who have been advocating two separate covenants seem to overlook the lessons of history and brush aside the climacteric changes which have everywhere been convulsing in recent times. The world today is in the midst of a colossal social and economic revolution which, if not met with prompt reforms, may easily pave the way for dictatorship and consequent global wars and conflicts. More than one-half of the world's population today is destitute, and millions upon millions are living on the brink of starvation. Meanwhile, the leaders of highly developed countries [. . .] speak of evolutionary progress and counsel patience. Patience is a luxury in which only the satiated can complacently indulge. [. . .] We in the United Nations can afford to be patient because we belong to the satiated class, regardless of our political affinities. In so far as our personal welfare is concerned, it does not matter much one way or the other if one covenant or two covenants are separately or simultaneously presented for signature. But what about the one billion or more people in the world who are clamouring against an endemic state of hunger and disease? What about those intransigent millions amongst them who have started to revolt when they discovered that merely raising their voices was not enough to secure for them even man's elemental birthright of food, shelter and clothing, let alone social and cultural rights. [. . .]

In the nature of man's existence and in his relationship to society all these rights are an indivisible whole. Try to split them and the result would be a human explosion [. . .] [requiring] a dictator to stem it. [. . .] Such situations lead to a state of emergency being declared everywhere. The exercise of civil and political rights becomes jeopardized in consequence and, should war be declared, most of these rights would be suspended, not only for the duration of the conflict but for several years afterwards. All this has happened, not only in ancient history, but within our own lifetime. Two major wars, interspersed by sporadic and quite often prolonged states of emergency, do not seem to have been enough to jolt us into the consciousness that economic stringency has been to a large extent at the root of abnormal and frequently suicidal behavior in the international field. The indigenous people of the world will no longer be soothed or calmed down by being presented with documents which promise them protection of life by law without adequate food, which promise them freedom from servitude without the security of work, which promise them, in other words, a multitude of political and civil rights without those economic and social conditions without which liberty and the sanctity of life become mere words.

[*Official Records of the United Nations General Assembly Plenary Meetings, 1952, during a debate in the full General Assembly on key political questions, including the indivisibility of rights and their universal application*]

2. On family rights and gender equality

Mrs Ikramullah (Pakistan) said all civilized countries could accept article [16], which she thought was designed to prevent child marriage and marriages contracted without the consent of both parties, and also to ensure protection of women after divorce and the safeguarding of their property. [. . .] Unfortunately, she could not support the [Saudi Arabian] amendment, as she feared it would enable countries with laws discriminating against women to continue to apply them.

[*Official Records of the United Nations General Assembly Third Committee, 1948, during article-by-article examination of the draft UDHR*]

Sayed Ahmad Zebara (Yemen) said that his delegation had carefully studied the text of the first eighteen articles of the covenant and felt, like the delegation of Saudi Arabia, that, as they stood, those articles completely disregarded a number of circumstances peculiar to the Arab and Muslim countries. Under Article [2], paragraph 2, the States' parties to the covenant undertook to take the necessary steps to adopt such legislative or other measures as might be necessary to give effect to the rights recognized in the covenant [. . .] Article [23] did not take into consideration the differences between the laws of the various countries in particular with regard to marriage, divorce and inheritance. [. . .] It would be impossible to force a State to abandon traditional legislation which it had applied for centuries and which was known to be in conformity with the aspirations and needs of the people.

[*Official Records of the United Nations General Assembly Third Committee, 1950, during a period of commentary by state delegates on the general adequacy of the initial 18 articles of the draft covenant*]

Mr Hendraningrat (Indonesia) thought that in any effort to modernize marriage practices the greatest caution should be exercised, so as not to offend unnecessarily those who accepted long-established customs and traditions. [. . .] Although he had withdrawn his amendment to article [23], he still had misgivings about the reference in paragraph 3 to 'the free and full consent of the intending spouses.'

[*Official Records of the United Nations General Assembly Third Committee, 1962, during article-by-article review of the draft covenant*]

Mr Baroody (Saudi Arabia) said that he would like to know the exact meaning, in the amendment, of the word 'ensure.' Did it mean the same as 'guarantee'? Secondly, it was difficult to speak of equality in connection with rights and particularly in connection with responsibilities, since men and women could not have rights and obligations that were quantitatively and qualitatively identical.

[*Official Records of the United Nations General Assembly Third Committee, 1962, during article-by-article review of the draft covenant*]

Mrs Fekini (Libya) said her delegation attached the utmost importance to article [23], bearing in mind that this article concerned the interests of an institution—namely the family—which was universally recognized as the cornerstone of all societies. [. . .] [The text] must be formulated in such a way as to guarantee the equality of the rights and responsibilities of the spouses, without prejudicing existing family relationships and in conformity with the principles of the Charter of the United Nations. [. . .] The objections regarding equality of rights so far as property and its administration were concerned did not affect the women of Muslim countries for they enjoyed those rights in full. She expressed the hope that in other parts of the world such discriminatory practices would soon be brought to an end.

[*Official Records of the United Nations General Assembly Third Committee, 1962, during article-by-article review of the draft covenant*]

Mrs Afnan (Iraq) expressed strong support for the objectives of Article [23] [. . .] Since marriage was being considered in the context of founding a family, the categorical requirement of the free and full consent of the intending spouses in paragraph 3 was essential; but she objected to the extreme vagueness of the term 'marriageable age' in paragraph 2. To place the emphasis on free and full consent without specifying a minimum age was illogical, for consent could not be valid unless the intending spouses had the minimum maturity necessary to give or withhold it.

The difficulties which had arisen in connection with paragraph 4 [and the question of whether states should be obliged to ensure gender equality] were understandable, seeing that discrimination against women was not confined to one race or culture [. . .] Different opinions had been expressed concerning the principle of equality of rights and responsibilities, especially the latter. In her view, the essence of equality was a balance between rights and responsibilities. In the family, equality meant a division of responsibilities, which had varied from society to society and from period to period: the essential thing was the equality of men and women before the law. Although, under Islamic culture, women were not legally treated as minors, the corruption of the social system and the excessive protection of women had led, in the end, to their segregation; that was why many women were willing to exchange privileges for equality.

[*Official Records of the United Nations General Assembly Third Committee, 1962, during article-by-article review of the draft covenant*]

3. On the right to self determination and universal application of human rights

Badawi Bey (Egypt). Members of the Committee all recognized that the General Assembly should adopt, at the current session, a resolution concerning the declaration of human rights. That was to be recommended for two reasons. On the one hand, the declaration of human rights would, for the first time, be put on an international level. On the other hand, the declaration would be effective, not only in States Members of the United Nations, but also in territories over which they had jurisdiction. It was perhaps in that respect that the declaration might mark the greatest progress.

[*Official Records of the United Nations General Assembly Third Committee, 1948, during introductory statements on the draft UDHR*]

Mr Pazhwak (Afghanistan) said that his delegation regarded colonialism as a flagrant violation of the most sacred rights of the individual. In depriving peoples of their rights to govern themselves, colonial powers often violated the right to life and liberty and many other fundamental rights of the individual. There was no greater or more iniquitous injustice than that of enslaving a country [. . .] The covenant on human rights could not be universal if its provisions did not apply to all peoples.

[*Official Records of the United Nations General Assembly Third Committee, 1950, during a discussion on the desirability of including special articles on the covenants' applicability to federal states and non-self-governing and trust territories*]

Mr Baroody (Saudi Arabia). [. . .] when I speak on this right of self-determination, I am speaking on the part of millions who should be sitting in this General Assembly. A lot of water, so to speak, has flowed under the bridge since a request was made for the insertion of an article on self-determination in the covenant. The anguished cry for freedom and liberation from the foreign yoke in many parts of the world has risen to a very high pitch, so that even those who had been compelled to block their ears with the cotton wool of political expediency can no longer deny that they can hear it. [. . .] The pressure on the gates of freedom has increased and millions and millions of people trying to break through have been kept at bay with bayonets and with tanks and machine guns. So great has been the pressure that those in the front rows have fallen as martyrs of freedom, while thousands taken into custody languish in prison depths and thousands more live in hiding, driven from the comfort of their homes. There are also those who, from fear of being killed or impounded, have fled their native land and now live as exiles in foreign climes just because they could articulate more eloquently their burning desire and that of their fellow men for freedom and self-determination.

What we are asking here is that the people living in the Non-Self-Governing Territories should be free. They cannot enjoy any human rights unless they are free, and it is in a document like the covenant that self-determination should be proclaimed. As I have no further time left in which to speak, I will end by saying that I support all of those who have spoken in favour of inserting an article on the right of peoples to self-determination.

[*Official Records of the United Nations General Assembly Plenary Meetings, 1952, during a debate in the full General Assembly on key political questions, including the indivisibility of rights and their universal application*]

4. On implementation

Mr Savut (Turkey) [. . .] The United Nations was a family widely scattered over the earth and whose members had lived under various and widely differing social and legal systems. [. . .] The intention was to make a law for such a world with all its nations. That of course did not mean that such a law should also cover some of the more reprehensible practices found in primitive societies. The draft covenant should contain only the very highest standards. It should however be drafted in terms sufficiently general and pliable to render it acceptable to all nations, whatever their stage of development. Moreover, it should be drafted in such terms as to allow for development; it would be undesirable to make it too rigid for the sake of attaining legal precision. Those conditions were not easy to achieve, but they were nonetheless attainable; and if they were attained, no nation could refuse to accept the draft covenant on the grounds that it was against its own established system.

[Official Records of the United Nations General Assembly Third Committee, 1950, during a period of commentary by state delegates on the general adequacy of the initial 18 articles of the draft covenant]

Mr Kayali (Syria) remarked that Part II of the covenant, which dealt with implementation, was the most important section. It was the measures of implementation rather than the preceding articles that should enable the United Nations to ensure that human rights were respected in all parts of the world. Domestic experience of States had shown that a good law was not enough; there must be adequate means to enforce it. The same was true on the international plane. [. . .] He supported the Swedish representative's suggestion that the right of petition or complaint of violation of human rights should be given not only to States, but also to individuals and groups of individuals.

[Official Records of the United Nations General Assembly Third Committee, 1950, during a discussion of the adequacy of initially proposed measures of implementation]

Azmi Bey (Egypt) observed that States which signed the covenant in good faith need have no fear of any form of control; consequently, the Egyptian delegation was ready to accept the establishment of a permanent human rights committee, a court to sanction the committee's findings, or any other provision that might seem necessary.

[Official Records of the United Nations General Assembly Third Committee, 1950, during a discussion of the adequacy of initially proposed measures of implementation]

Mr Atassi (Syria) said that [. . .] the text of the Covenant itself [could not include] a clause granting individuals the right to submit petitions against States, because the human rights committee, however impartial it might be, would necessarily have to judge petitions from a political standpoint. Most complaints by individuals against the State of which they were nationals would be of a partisan nature, or even artificially concocted, and might disturb international peace and security.

[Official Records of the United Nations General Assembly Third Committee, 1966, during the final debate on articles of implementation]

5. On freedom of religion, Islam and human rights

Mr Baroody (Saudi Arabia) urged that the reference to the individual's right to change his religion should not be retained in article [18]. He asked the French

representative whether his Government had consulted the Muslim peoples of North Africa and other French territories before accepting the text, or whether it intended to impose it on them arbitrarily.
[*Official Records of the United Nations General Assembly Third Committee, 1948, during debate on the draft UDHR*]

Sir Mohammed Zafrullah Khan (Pakistan). The few observations his delegation wished to make in connection with the declaration concerned article [18] which dealt with freedom of conscience, including freedom to change one's religion. When the latter question was discussed in the Third Committee, its whole scope had not been understood; for that reason he thought it necessary to set out very clearly his delegation's position as to that part of article [18]. Pakistan was an ardent defender of freedom of thought and belief and of all the freedoms listed in article [18]. There could be no doubt on that point, and if that question only had a political aspect, the declaration he had just made would have been sufficient. But for the Pakistan delegation the problem had a special significance as some of its aspects involved the honour of Islam. [. . .] The teaching of Islam was based on the Qur'an which contained the oral revelations made to the prophet Muhammad; the Qur'an was, therefore, the very word of God for Muslims. It stated that neither faith, nor conscience which gave birth to it, could have an obligatory character. The Qur'an expressly said, 'Let he who chooses to believe, believe, and he who chooses to disbelieve, disbelieve'[63] and it formally condemned not lack of faith, but hypocrisy.
[*Official Records of the United Nations General Assembly Plenary Meetings, 1948, in final debate prior to formal UNGA vote on the UDHR*]

Azmi Bey (Egypt) stated that his country had given proof on many occasions of its great respect for human rights and had enthusiastically welcomed adoption of the Universal Declaration of Human Rights. [. . .] The first 18 articles [of the draft ICCPR] were, generally speaking, acceptable in principle. [. . .] However, Article [18] proclaimed the unquestionable right of everyone to freedom of thought, conscience and religion. The article went on to state, quite logically, 'this right shall include freedom to change his religion or belief, and freedom, either alone or in community with others, to manifest his religion or belief in teaching, practice, worship, and observance.' It was, however, to be kept in mind that the draft covenant was not simply a declaration of principles but a legally binding document which, as such, had to be ratified by governments in accordance with their constitutional procedures. Attitudes in national legislatures varied from extreme liberalism to extreme reaction and he feared that the

---

[63] This is a rather loose rendering of Qur'an 2: 256: 'There is no compulsion in religion; truly the right way has become clearly distinct from error; therefore, whoever disbelieves in Satan and believes in God he indeed has laid hold on the firmest handle, which shall not break off, and God is Hearing, Knowing.'

retention of the words 'freedom to change his religion or belief' [. . .] might make it difficult for many governments to secure ratification. He would therefore suggest deletion of the words in question.

[*Official Records of the United Nations General Assembly Third Committee, 1950, during a period of commentary by state delegates on the general adequacy of the initial 18 articles of the draft covenant*]

Mrs Afnan (Iraq). The question of religion had been raised. If all nations lived in accordance with the spirit and the letter of their religion there would be no need for a covenant of human rights. No covenant could, in any case, demand so much in respect of human rights as Islam did.

[*Official Records of the United Nations General Assembly Third Committee, 1950, during a period of commentary by state delegates on the general adequacy of the initial 18 articles of the draft covenant*]

Mr El-Erian (Egypt/UAR)[64] stressed that under the constitutional and statutory provisions in force in his country everyone had the right to freedom of thought, conscience, and religion. [At an early session of the Commission on Human Rights, the Egyptian delegate had submitted two amendments for improvement of the text of the UDHR.] He had informed the Commission at its 319th meeting that in Egypt a person could not be discriminated against for changing his religion, but he could change it only after three conversations with a minister of the religion that he wished to renounce. If, as the representative of France had said, the Commission on Human Rights had amended the text in a spirit of compromise, it was to be hoped that the Third Committee would be able to follow that example and make the necessary changes in article 18 so that it could be unanimously adopted.

[*Official Records of the United Nations General Assembly Third Committee, 1960, during article-by-article review of the draft covenant*]

Mr Pazhwak (Afghanistan) said that [. . .] in principle, all the draft articles were acceptable to his delegation, but article 18 of the draft covenant on civil and political rights was unacceptable in the form in which it stood. He was wholly in accord with the principle embodied in that draft article, as it was consistent with Afghan law and tradition. [. . .] All the fundamental human rights were principles of the Islamic religion, so that no Muslim Government could vote against any fundamental human right embodied in the covenants. Accordingly, he wished to explain quite clearly why his delegation opposed the reference to change of religion in draft article 18.

---

[64] In 1952 Egypt experienced the 'Free Officer' Revolt that replaced a British-supported monarchy with the Revolutionary Command Council, a group driven by pan-Arabist and socialist sentiments. The ultimate leader within the RCC became Jamal ᶜAbd al-Nasir (d. 1970), who assumed the presidency of Egypt and engineered a merger with Syria that lasted from 1958 to 1961, known as the United Arab Republic. Egypt maintained the name UAR even after the split with Syria.

The question had sometimes been asked why Muslims permitted non-Muslims to become Muslims but did not allow Muslims to leave Islam. Islam never repulsed any non-Muslim who expressed a sincere desire to become a Muslim; it received him. But there was a great difference, from the Islamic point of view, between repulsion and the failure to give permission to change a religion. Any religion that gave an individual permission to change his religion might, from that point of view, be considered to be interfering with his beliefs, whereas the right to hold beliefs without interference was a fundamental human right. The freedom of religious belief could be achieved if the individual was left free to maintain the belief that he had freely accepted. That was the positive approach.

Freedom to change religion was a negative approach. If an individual who had freely accepted a certain religion was told that he was free to change it, the idea was put into his mind that he was believing in something which he could change if given the right to do so. Doubt would be instilled and his belief damaged. That would be tantamount to interference with his freedom of thought and conscience. The right to old opinions without interference was stated in article 19, which became superfluous once the right to change religion had been stated. The Afghan delegation intended to propose amendments which would make those draft articles generally acceptable, once the philosophy of the Muslim countries had been grasped.

[*Official Records of the United Nations General Assembly Third Committee, 1954, during a period of general commentary by state delegates on a new draft of the ICCPR*]

Mrs Anegay (Morocco) said that [. . .] religions were not intended to divide the world but to unite it, and they were all based on the same principles. She therefore hoped that the Committee would be able to reach agreement on a text which would take into account all beliefs as well as the lack of belief.

[*Official Records of the United Nations General Assembly Third Committee, 1960, during article-by-article review of the draft covenant*]

6.11 The Lebanese community of Dearborn, Michigan, 1975–2000
Ronald R. Stockton

Preface

The first Lebanese immigrant arrived in the Detroit area in 1898. By the 1970s the inner-ring city of Dearborn had a small Lebanese community, mostly Shiᶜis from the southern part of the country. Many worked in the automobile industry or in small businesses. Conforming to a typical immigrant pattern, most were clustered in two neighborhoods. Two decades later Dearborn had a very substantial Lebanese population and was being touted as the nation's Arab population center. This surge in immigration began during the 1975–6 Lebanese Civil War, and accelerated after the first Israeli invasion of Lebanon in 1978, and again after the massive 1982 invasion. Most of these refugees came from towns that bordered on Israel. Many fled first to Beirut, before emigrating when the war spread to the city. Places such as Bint Jbail and Tibnin were particularly represented in the migration; the former remained within the so-called Israeli Security Zone until May 2000, when the Israeli army withdrew as the military situation deteriorated.

The impact of the influx on Dearborn was considerable. By 2000 a third of the population was of Arab ancestry, mostly Lebanese, but also of Yemeni and Iraqi extraction. Over half of the school population was Arab. The schools had to move quickly to meet the needs of their new student body and to create a major bilingual program to help students adjust to their new language and country. The reallocation of resources and hiring priorities produced inevitable tensions, as did efforts to accommodate Muslim holidays and practices.

The numbers of students in the bilingual education program reflect the changing situation. The two-year Lebanese Civil War produced a 50 per cent increase, but the 1978 Israeli invasion produced nearly a one-year doubling, then another doubling, then another 30 per cent increase. By the time of the second Israeli invasion in 1982, the number of students in bilingual education had increased 700 per cent over the 1976 figure. By the mid-1990s, the influx had stabilized (see Table 6.1).

A second phenomenon coincided with an influx of Lebanese Shiᶜi students—a rise in Islamic identity. The Iranian Revolution of 1979 produced a significant shift in consciousness. Conservative imams, trained in Iraq's Najaf seminary during the 1970s (when the Ayatollah Khomeini was in exile there), began to arrive, as did other Khomeini-era imams. While the Muslim community had always been culturally conservative, these imams began to encourage an Islamic consciousness. For females,

TABLE 6.1. Children in bilingual education, Dearborn Public Schools

Year	Number of children	Significant events
1976–7	218	Lebanese Civil War begins in 1975
1977–8	317	
1978–9	582	First Israeli Invasion in 1978
1979–80	1,103	
1980–1	1,400	
1981–2	1,481	
1982–3	1,560	Second Israeli Invasion in 1982
1983–4	1,720	
1984–5	1,675	
1985–6	1,644	

Note: While a few students spoke other languages, the figures reflect the Arab influx.

TABLE 6.2. Arab female students, Dearborn Fordson High School

Year	Total Arab females graduating in class	Number covered with headscarf
1980	25	0
1985	52	1
1990	73	6
1995	73	12
2000	152	52

this included covering the head (see Table 6.2). In Dearborn's Fordson High School, where 89 per cent of the 2,000 students at the turn of the century were of Arab heritage, the school photographs illustrate the change.

In 1986 Dearborn's popular two-term mayor retired and the city held an open election. There were two candidates, both members of the city council. One was the Council president, so designated because she was the top vote recipient in the previous election. She had a good working relationship with the Arab community (many of whom did not vote), and soon took an early lead in the polls. Then a whispering campaign began referring to her as 'the Arab princess', although she was not of Arab ancestry. Prior to the election, her opponent put out a tabloid newspaper with the bold headline, 'Let's Talk About The "Arab Problem" '. This changed the dynamic of the race, giving him the victory. It also created a breach between the new mayor and the Arab community, a breach that took a decade to heal.

Wafa Unis Shuraydi graduated from Fordson High School in 1979 and from the University of Michigan-Dearborn in 1984. She married a local professor and became a teacher in the Dearborn school system, continuing her education until she received a doctorate. Her description of her experiences, first published in 1986 in the *Michigan Alumnus*, became required reading for new teachers during the district orientation program.

Text

Wafa Unis Shuraydi, 1984

The Lebanese Civil War started in 1975. Until then, Lebanon was just a small, beautiful country located on the Mediterranean. No one thought that this peaceful nation, the jewel of the Middle East, was on the verge of becoming a land of furious crimes and terrorist acts.

My family, five girls, two boys, Mom and Dad—are Muslim Shiʿi. I was born in Christian-controlled East Beirut and had lived there all my life. By 1976, Beirut was a divided city and Muslims in the East feared for their lives. My family fled the city, abandoning all our possessions, and went to our new home village in the South. A few months later, when Israel began bombing southern villages, we fled back to Beirut, this time to the West.

But in Beirut, death was everywhere, its stamp on every house: day and night shelling devastated the city. My family's economic status deteriorated. Savings put aside for college education were spent on everyday needs. In 1978, Dad decided reluctantly that the best solution was to emigrate for the United States.

For us, leaving Lebanon was not a choice; it was a decision made and acted upon quickly with no room for sentiment or reconsideration. This seventeen-year-old girl's dreams were buried under the rubble of war, death machines, and spilt blood. Even though going to America was a joy and a blessing, our departure was charged with vigorous emotions tearing my thoughts apart. It was hard leaving my hometown and birthplace, throwing aside childhood memories. I suppressed my feelings as we left, but stepping into Detroit Metropolitan Airport, I sensed that I would never go back to Lebanon. A sudden storm of tears filled my eyes and washed over the coldness of that place.

We settled in Dearborn, Michigan. Our first few months were unbearable. My father, who had been a respected and well-paid professional dye blender in Lebanon, had to settle for a low-paying job in a meat company. His income was so little the family barely survived.

Along with my brother and sister, I enrolled in a nearby high school. I did not know one word of English, but after three months in a bilingual program, had learned enough to enter regular classes. However, the language problem was minor compared with the cultural gaps. My first shock was seeing girls and boys hugging each other in public. I had never seen such a thing in Lebanon, which had not experienced a sexual revolution. Moreover, most of my time had been spent reading or hiding from bombs in underground shelters, and there was little room for love among the ruins.

A second shock occurred when I went to gym class where I was told to swim with boys. Coming from a traditional Muslim Shiʿi background such a thing was not permissible. My gym teacher could not understand my abstention from swimming and I ended up dropping the class.

The psychological agony immigrants go through is an agony no Westerner can fully comprehend. Many Americans expect the newcomer to adjust miraculously in no time. We are often told such things as: 'You live in America, this is not Lebanon'; 'Speak English'; 'Go back to your country'. Frequently we are called 'camel jockey' and described in other, similarly derogatory terms. People expect us to eradicate our traditions, religion, customs, and native language, and cast them aside like an old shoe. At the same time, our parents keep reminding us of our religion and customs. From them we hear: 'You are Muslim'; 'You cannot date, that is shameful'; 'Speak Arabic; we do not understand English'; 'Marriage is the protector of a girl's dignity; what are you going to do with a college degree?'; 'No one will marry you after the age of twenty', and so on.

The new culture requires drastic deviation on our part from our roots and traditions. Our original culture demands obedience and attachment to customs that are considered old-fashioned in this country. Individuals—especially girls—are caught in the middle of this struggle; no one asks what they want or think. Most of us live two lives, one that is influenced by openness and westernization, the other that is drowned in conservatism and fear of shame and guilt.

In a sense, our world becomes schizophrenic. Boys can date, have a girlfriend, and ultimately live on their own. At the same time, brothers will not allow their sisters to date or move into an apartment. Contradictions. Our world is full of contradictions.

Often girls are pressured into early marriages, believing they will no longer be deprived of their freedom if they marry. All too frequently, however, the reality is that the woman finds herself constrained by children and responsibilities, or divorced two years later. Those who choose to continue their education are in a minority. They face antagonism and are constantly reminded that a woman's place is in the kitchen. My dream since first arriving in the United States was to attend The University of Michigan-Dearborn. I graduated from high school with a good grade point average and was able to achieve that dream. But attending the University was the challenge of my life. I had doubts about my abilities and about the ability of my family to pay for my education. Fortunately, many people helped and encouraged me.

I think for any immigrant living in the United States, adjusting to its culture is not easy. But for a Shiʿi Muslim, no matter how much we adjust and how happy we are, we are still considered foreigners. We are reminded of this every time an act of terrorism occurs. We are stereotyped as 'terrorist', 'barbarian', 'backward' and 'ignorant'. This is the tax we have to pay as long as we live here, no matter how much we assimilate.

Over the years, the thought of going back to Lebanon vanished. I am an American now, both in my citizenship and my thinking, and am here to stay. My father's aim was to see his children educated and respected. He has succeeded in that endeavor. I no longer have to worry about war and death. My family and I can aim toward a better life in the land that provided us with the peace we were never allowed in Lebanon.

Selected bibliography

ABRAHAM, NABEEL, and ANDREW SHRYOCK (eds.), *Arab Detroit: From Margin to Mainstream* (Detroit: Wayne State University Press, 2000).

ABU-LUGHOD, IBRAHIM, *The Arab Rediscovery of Europe* (Princeton: Princeton University Press, 1963).

ALLWORTH, EDWARD, *Tatars of the Crimea: Return to the Homeland* (Durham; Duke University Press, 1998).

AMANAT, ABBAS, *The Pivot of the Universe: Nasir al-Din Shah and the Iranian Monarchy,1831–1896* (Berkeley: University of California Press, 1997).

AUSTIN, ALFRED, *Tory Horrors or the Question of the Hour: A Letter to the Right Hon, W. E. Gladstone* (London: Chatto & Windus, 1876).

BAKHASH, SHAUL, *Iran, Monarchy, Bureaucracy and Reform Under the Qajars, 1858–1896* (London: Ithaca Press for the Middle East Centre, St Antony's College, 1978).

BERKES, NIYAZI, *The Development of Secularism in Turkey* (Montreal: McGill University Press, 1964).

CLEVELAND, WILLIAM, *The Making of an Arab Nationalist: Ottomanism and Arabism in the Life and Thought of Satiᶜ Al-Husri* (Princeton: Princeton University Press, 1971).

COMMINS, DAVID DEAN, *Islamic Reform: Politics and Social Change in Late Ottoman Syria* (New York: Oxford University Press, 1990).

CORNISH, J. E. and JOHN HEYWOOD, *Bulgarian Horrors and England's Duty: An Appeal* (Manchester: A. Ireland & Co., 1876).

DERINGIL, SELIM, *The Well Protected Domains: Ideology and the Legitimation of Power in the Ottoman Empire 1876–1909* (London and NewYork: I. B. Tauris, 1998).

DOUMANI, BESHARA, *Rediscovering Palestine: Merchants and Peasants in Jabal Nablus, 1700–1900* (Berkeley: University of California Press, 1995).

FAHMY, KHALED, *All the Pasha's Men: Mehmed Ali, His Army and the Making of Modern Egypt* (Cambridge: Cambridge University Press, 1997).

FAROQHI, SURAIYA, *Approaching Ottoman History: An Introduction to the Sources* (Cambridge: Cambridge University Press, 1999).

FISHER, ALAN, *The Crimean Tatars* (Stanford, Calif: Hoover Institute, 1979).

FORTNA, BENJAMIN C., *Imperial Classroom: Islam, the State, and Education in the Late Ottoman Empire* (Oxford: Oxford University Press, 2002).

GERSHONI, ISRAEL, and JAMES JANKOWSKI, *Egypt, Islam, and the Arabs: The Search for Egyptian Nationhood*, 1900–1930 (New York: Oxford University Press, 1986).

[GLADSTONE, W. E.] *Mr. Gladstone's Resolutions and Speeches on the Eastern Question in the House of Commons, May 7, 1877* (published for the Eastern Question Association, London: Cassel Petter & Galpin, 1877).

GLENDON, MARY ANN, *A World Made New: Eleanor Roosevelt and the Universal Declaration of Human Rights* (New York: Random House, 2001).

HANIOĞLU, M. ŞÜKRÜ, *The Young Turks in Opposition* (New York: Oxford University Press, 1995).

—— *Preparation for a Revolution* (New York: Oxford University Press, 2001).

Harris, David, *Britain and the Bulgarian Horrors of 1876* (Chicago: University of Chicago Press, 1939).

Heyworth-Dunne, J., *An Introduction to the History of Education in Modern Egypt* (London: Luzac & Co, 1939).

Hourani, Albert, *Arabic Thought in the Liberal Age, 1798–1939* (Cambridge: Cambridge University Press, 1983).

Islamouğlu-İnan, Huri (ed.), *The Ottoman Empire and the World Economy* (Cambridge: Cambridge University Press, 1987).

Jenkins, Roy, *Gladstone* (London: MacMillan, 1995).

Johnstone, Henry Butler, *Bulgarian Horrors, and the Question of the East: A Letter Addressed to the Right Hon. W. E. Gladstone* (London: William Ridgway, 1876).

Kayali, Hasan, *Arabs and Young Turks: Ottomanism, Arabism, and Islamism in the Ottoman Empire, 1908–1918* (Berkeley: University of California Press, 1997).

Kazemzadeh, Firuz, *Russia and Britain in Persia, 1864–1914* (New Haven and London: Yale University Press, 1966).

Keddie, Nikki R., *Sayyid Jamal al-Din 'al-Afgani': A Political Biography* (Berkeley: University of California Press, 1972).

Khalidi, Rashid (ed.), *The Origins of Arab Nationalism* (New York: Columbia University Press, 1991).

—— Lisa Anderson, Muhammad Muslih and Reeva Simon (eds.), *The Origins of Arab Nationalism* (New York: Columbia University Press, 1991).

—— 'Arab Nationalism: Historical Problems in the Literature', *American Historical Review*, 96/5 (Dec. 1991), 1363–73.

Kirimli, Hakan, *National Movements and National Identity Among the Crimean Tatars* (Leiden: E. J. Brill, 1997).

Lauren, Paul Gordon, *The Evolution of Human Rights: Visions Seen* (Philadelphia: University of Pennsylvania Press, 1998).

Lewis, Bernard, *The Emergence of Modern Turkey* (London: Oxford University Press, 1961).

Lockhart, Laurence, *Nader Shah* (London: Luzac & Co., 1938).

Mardin, Şerif, *The Genesis of Young Ottoman Thought: A Study in the Modernization of Turkish Political Ideas* (Princeton: Princeton University Press, 1962; repr. Syracuse, NY: Syracuse University Press, 2000).

Masters, Bruce, *Christians and Jews in the Ottoman Arab World: The Roots of Sectarianism* (Cambridge: Cambridge University Press, 2001).

Matthew, H. C. G., *Gladstone 1809–1898* (Oxford: Oxford University Press, 1997).

Millman, Richard, *Britain and the Eastern Question, 1875–1878* (New York: Clarendon Press, 1979).

Mitchell, Timothy, *Colonising Egypt* (Berkeley: University of California Press, 1988).

Morsink, Johannes, The *Universal Declaration of Human Rights: Origins, Drafting, and Intent* (Philadelphia: University of Pennsylvania Press, 1999).

Mustafa, Ahmed Abdel-Rahim, 'The Hekekyan Papers', in P. M. Holt (ed.), *Political and Social Change in Modern Egypt* (London: Oxford University Press, 1968).

Nakash, Yitzhak, *The Shiahs of Iraq* (Princeton: Princeton University Press, 1994).

ORGA, IRFAN, *Portrait of a Turkish Family* (London: Victor Gollancz, 1950; repr. Eland, 1988).

PARTRIDGE, MICHAEL, *Gladstone* (London: Routledge, 2003).

ST. CLAIR, S. G. B., *Bulgarian Horrors! And Mr. Gladstone's Eastern Policy* (London: Blanchard & Sons, 1876).

SEDRA, PAUL, 'Modernity's Mission: Evangelical Efforts to Discipline the Nineteenth-Century Coptic Community', in Eleanor H. Tejirian and Reeva Spector Simon (eds.), *Altruism and Imperialism: The Western Religious and Cultural Missionary Enterprise in the Middle East* (New York: Middle East Institute, Columbia University Occasional Papers 4, 2002).

SMITH, GOLDWIN, 'England's Abandonment of the Protectorate of Turkey', *Contemporary Review* (31 Feb. 1878), 603–19.

SOUSA, NASIM, *The Capitulatory Regime of Turkey: Its History, Origin and Nature* (Baltimore: Johns Hopkins University Press, 1933).

SULLIVAN, SIR EDWARD, *Party and Patriotism, Being the Letters Addressed to the* Morning Post *on September 6th, 18th and 28th* (London: Ranken & Co., 1876).

TAVAKOLI-TARGHI, MUHAMMAD, 'Imagining Western Women: Occidentalism and Euroeroticism', *Radical America*, 24 (July–Sept. 1990 [1993]), 72–87.

TOLEDANO, EHUD, *State and Society in Mid-Nineteenth-Century Egypt* (Cambridge: Cambridge University Press, 1990).

TUCKER, ERNEST, 'Nader Shah and the Jafari *Mazhab* Reconsidered', *Iranian Studies*, 27/1–4 (1994).

——'The Peace Negotiations of 1736: A Conceptual Turning Point in Ottoman–Iranian Relations', *Turkish Studies Association Bulletin*, 20/1 (Spring 1996).

WALBRIDGE, LINDA, *Without Forgetting the Imam: Lebanese Shi'ism in an American Community* (Detroit: Wayne State University Press, 1997).

WALLERSTEIN, IMMANUEL, *The Modern World-System*, 3 vols. (New York: Academic Press, Inc., 1974, 1989).

WALTZ, SUSAN, 'Reclaiming and Rebuilding the History of the Universal Declaration of Human Rights', *Third World Quarterly*, 23 (June 2002), 437–48.

——'Universal Human Rights: The Contribution of Muslim States': under review for publication, available from author at<swaltz@umich.edu>.

WILLIAMS, BRIAN, *The Crimean Tatars: The Diaspora Experience and the Forging of a Nation* (Leiden: E. J. Brill, 2001).

——'*Hijra* and Forced Migration from Russia to the Ottoman Empire', *Cahiers du Monde Russe*, 41/1 (Jan.–Mar. 2000).

WOODS PASHA, ADMIRAL, *Blackmailing the Sultan: Refutation of the Calumnies in Osman Bey's Anonymous Pamphlet* (London: n. pub., 1890).

WRIGHT, DENIS, *The Persians Among the English* (London: I. B. Tauris, 1985).

ZARCONE, THIERRY, and FARIBA ZARINEBAF-SHAHR (eds.), *Les Iraniens d'Istanbul* (Paris: Institut Français de Recherches en Iran, Institut Français d'Études Anatoliennes, 1993).

ZÜRCHER, ERIK J., *Turkey: A Modern History* (London: I. B. Tauris, 1993).

7

Redefining tradition

Introduction

A remarkable feature of the modern period in the Middle East is the extent to which existing traditions have assumed new roles, responding to the changing circumstances of the time. Documents in this section highlight the extent to which older institutions, genres, and styles have been reappropriated and adapted to modern contexts. Indeed it is tempting to say that it is the interplay between the traditional and the modern which gives such vitality to much of this period and thus to the sources we have chosen to represent it in historical fashion.

On one level, it is the persistence of tradition in the face of modernity which is remarkable. Traditional forms of poetry (including that of the *qasida*, which has endured since pre-Islamic times), architecture, consultation with religious scholars, military uniforms, and long-standing traditions of governance all proved adaptable to changing needs and aesthetics.

At the same time, the documents in this section highlight the novelty and in some cases the radical change involved in the modern period. In this sense the historical material included here reflects not only new adaptations of older forms but also completely new ways of thought, novel social and political categories, and unprecedented possibilities for individual and collective consciousness. In other words, it is not just the mention of an invention such as the telephone or the appearance of Hitler's and Mussolini's names in a Yemeni poem that is striking; after all, we might well expect such novelties to be incorporated into the production of historical sources of the day. Rather, it is the novelty of imagination involved in reforming an entire language, emigrating to the New World, or revamping institutions that had endured for centuries that stands out as perhaps the ultimate expression of the modern period.

7.1 A late Ottoman style of architectural poetry: *Tevarih-i manzume*, 1796
Shirine Hamadeh

Preface

In the Ottoman poetic tradition, *tevarih-i manzume* (sing. *tarih-i manzume*) were a genre of versification with a purpose: that of chronicling important events. The term literally means histories in rhyme, or rhymed chronograms. These compositions, whose origin can be traced back to the medieval Muslim world, consisted of a single hemistich. The letters it contained had to add up to the date of the event celebrated according to the system of numeration of the Arabic alphabet. These challenging little arithmetical exercises were composed to commemorate important moments in the history of the Ottoman Empire, like the enthronement of a monarch, a princely birth or wedding, a military victory, or the consecration of an imperial mosque. Frequently, the chronogram was appended to a fully fledged poem, usually in the form of a panegyric (*qasida*), which was also referred to as *tarih-i manzume*.

Rhymed chronograms began to flourish extensively from the beginning of the eighteenth century onward. Unlike earlier periods, when they were hardly represented in individual poets' anthologies (*divan*), they started filling a substantial section of the *divan* alongside the more 'elevated' forms of panegyrics and lyric poetry (*gazel*). In particular, chronograms composed in praise of a new or restored building, or garden, gained unprecedented popularity among court poets in Istanbul. Most notable among these poets were Nabi, Nedim, Nevres, Seyyid Vehbi, Enderunlu Fazıl Bey, Sünbülzade Vehbi, and Süruri, the most prolific chronogrammatist of all time. In the anthologies of chronograms (*mecmūʿa-i tevarih*), which began to be compiled in the eighteenth century, 'architectural chronograms' formed a separate section titled 'Monuments of Benefactors'. It was divided into several chapters, each corresponding to a different building type, such as mosques, colleges, bridges, public fountains, baths, libraries, shops, pavilions, kiosks, waterfront palaces, waterfront residences, gardens, and promenades.

Contrary to their earlier counterparts, eighteenth-century building chronograms were not simply panegyric devices composed in praise of the building patron. While the opening and closing verses of the poem were sometimes devoted to an encomium for the patron, longer and longer sections were dedicated to praise and depictions of the building itself, including valuable insights on a largely lost architectural world and contemporary canons of aesthetic appreciation. Partly as a result of the innovations that penetrated Ottoman poetry in the eighteenth century, notably by the increasing use of simple diction and colloquial idioms, these chronograms achieved a sense of immediacy uncharacteristic of those from earlier periods. Traditional poetical conceits and erudite metaphors, accessible only to those with considerable literary fluency, blended with tangible images of the building's form, design, color, texture, and architectural features, that could be easily understood by reference to the subject.

These compositions, often witty and amusing, sometimes silly, but generally delightful in their imagery, were intended primarily as building inscriptions. On the completion of a building, poets were invited to compete in conjuring up the most appropriate one-liner, to which a poem was later attached. It was together with its poem that the most successful chronogram would be selected for the inscription. The trend for poetic inscriptions quickly caught on, replacing the simple foundation inscription, and became an integral part of the eighteenth-century outdoor iconographical program of both religious and secular buildings. Used on the exterior walls of mosques, libraries, public fountains, palaces, and more modest residences, poetic epigraphy was a new venue for the public dissemination of court poetry, which traditionally had been confined to select literary salons.

The huge popularity of building chronograms among eighteenth-century court poets was largely a reflection of the intensive building and restoration activity that was taking place in the Ottoman capital, especially along the suburban shores of the Bosphorus and the Golden Horn. Countless palaces, kiosks, pavilions, fountains, libraries, mosques, and colleges, sponsored by members of the ruling elite and individuals from various segments of society, were celebrated in chronograms, and it was not uncommon for a poet to compose several odes about the same building. The chronogram below is one of seven poems written by Enderunlu Fazıl (d. 1809) in celebration of the pavilion of Neşatabad,[1] built in 1793 at Defterdar Burnu, on the European shore of the Bosphorus, as an extension to the century-old palace of the monarch's sister, Hatice Sultan. Commissioned from the Lorrainian artist and architect Melling, the pavilion of Neşatabad inaugurated a new phase of imperial building commissions granted to resident European architects from the reign of Sultan Selim III (r. 1789–1808) onward. Antoine-Ignace Melling had arrived in Istanbul in 1784 under the protection of the Russian Embassy, and remained in the city until 1802. Although he is better known today for his magnificent drawings of architectural monuments in Istanbul,[2] he was then mostly recognized for his active involvement in the building and restoration of various foreign ambassadorial residences. It was one of these residences,

[1] In Persian, neshatabad (TK. neşatabad) literally means the Abode of Joy. In the eighteenth century it became fashionable to endow Ottoman imperial palaces with Persian names, in the fashion of Safavid imperial palaces.

[2] These were collected in 1819 in *Voyage pittoresque de Constantinople et des rives du Bosphore*, along with a text by Lacretelle.

9 Detail of engraving by Melling showing the pavilion of Neşatabad at Defterdar Burnu, with the old palace of Hatice Sultan in the background. (Source: Antoine-Ignace Melling, *Voyage pittoresque de Constantinople et des rives du Bosphore* (Istanbul, 1819)

that of the Danish Baron de Hübsch, at Büyükdere, that earned him the admiration of Hatice Sultan and the commission of Neşatabad in 1793. Fazil's chronogram on the pavilion of Neşatabad is dated h. 1210 (1795–6).[3]

Text

Chronogram for the new pavilion, which is a European building, in the felicitous waterfront residence of Neşatabad

Come and see the heavenly view from this pavilion of Neşatabad,
Especially from this newly created innovative design!
The Truth is, colorless, in that monochrome garment.[4]
This new edifice makes the old canon looks crude.
It is a smooth-cheeked beauty, well-proportioned
Whose symmetrical body is more delightful than a box tree
It is reflected in the sea as the sea is reflected on its wall.
This one is silver mirror, that one, [a mirror] of steel.[5]
Its ornamented form is as though cast out of a mould,
It is beyond the reach of the most skillful master.
I believe that skillful architect used to
Draw, [watching] from the observatory, maps of the constellations of stars.[6]
On the bases of their patterns he laid out the [pavilion's] plan.
None of the previous masters had ever seen such a design!
He came and laid out this invention in form
The masters from among the ancients never envisioned its design
[Beyond] its design, the new colors and novel ornamentation
Were never seen by Mani, or even Behzad.[7]

[3] Enderunlu Fâzıl. *Divân-ı Fâzıl Enderun* MS. Topkapı Sarayı Müzesi Kütüphanesi, H. 906, fols. 67b–68a: *Târikh berâ-yı ʿasr-ı cedid fireng teşyiddir der sahilhâne-i Neşâtâbâd maʿmurbâd* (h 1210 AH). Born in the provincial Arab town of Safad, Fazil moved to the capital at an early age and received his education at the imperial palace. There he remained, in his capacity of a court poet, until 1784. It was in the following two decades, however, while he served in various official positions in and outside of Istanbul, that Fazıl wrote his best-known narrative poems, *Defter-iʿAşk* (the Book of Love) and *Hubânnâme ve Zenânnâme* (Book of Men and Book of Women), under the patronage of a high-ranking bureaucrat of the central administration, Ratib Efendi.

[4] This may refers to the polished white surface of Melling's pavilion. Unlike contemporary princely palaces and pavilions, which were built of wood and always painted a dark red hue, Neşatabad was built of stone.

[5] A possible allusion to the sturdiness of the building, as, unlike steel mirrors, silver mirrors were not prone to rust.

[6] By suggesting that Melling must have been fluent in the sciences of astrology and astronomy, here Fazıl indirectly points to the architect's far-sightedness and creativity.

[7] Behzad was the legendary Persian painter, and Mani his Chinese equivalent and founder of the Manichean religion. Their role as witnesses to Ottoman artistic splendors is an old trope in Ottoman poetry.

There is no need for a description of its design and ornament.
I have heard so many verses singing their praise by Fazil, the master poet.
I asked about the palace of Shirin created by Ferhad,
and then about the garden of Iram, adorned by Sheddad.[8]
I have not seen a place resembling the pavilion of Neşatabad.
It was revealed to me in this form by the guidance of the mirror.[9]
In luck and prosperity may it truly endure!
May it be protected from the gaze of the envious eyes!
As long as the noble mood of the exalted and honorable Sultan
alights from the favorable breeze of this site,
may God preserve it from feast to feast until the Day of Judgement!
May its garden seasons be filled with the flowers of merriment!
May Neşatabad remain full of joy until the Day of Resurrection,
with the visits of the benevolent Sultan,
the Honorable Sultan Selim, in whose reign
fortune repented of the sins of this world.
Praise be to God! In his empire, every place turned into a garden of Iram.
With this loving friend, truly, the just world became paradise.
O Fazil! It is time for your poor heart to pray
for the Honorable Sultan, the exalted sovereign of the world.[10]
May the sun and the moon always [shine] over these times of bliss!
May the Lord preserve [us from] the reverses of unjust fate!
May his merciful, noble disposition never cease
to help the depraved of the world.
May such jeweled chronograms[11] be always produced!
Come and look at the abode of happiness from the roof of Neşatabad![12]

[8] Ferhad is one of the heroes of the famous romance in verse, *Hüsrev ü Shirin* (in Persian, *Khosraw va Shirine*), composed by the twelfth-century Persian poet Nizami and first translated into Ottoman in the fifteenth century. The Garden of Iram is said to have been built by the legendary king Shaddâd bin Şâd in emulation of the garden of paradise.

[9] The mirror here is a reference to the Bosphorus water channel in which the pavilion is reflected, and hence to the proximity of the pavilion to the shore; it may also be an allusion to divine beauty, according to the mystical conception that mirrors reflected the beauty of God.

[10] This is the point at which the poet begins his encomium and prayer for the building patron, in this instance Sultan Selim III.

[11] Unlike the 'full' chronogram, in a 'jeweled' chronogram only the dotted letters are counted to add up to the date of the event celebrated.

[12] As in the opening verse, this closing verse praises the virtues of the pavilion's location and the visual prospects it afforded.

7.2 Imams in the reformed army of Mahmud II: uniform regulations from Ottoman military archives, c.1827
Halil İbrahim Erbay

Preface

The Ottoman sultans Selim III (1789–1807) and his cousin Mahmud II (1808–39) are credited with initiating the transformation of the Ottoman Empire, enabling it to survive against the great powers of the West. Inspired by the European style of state-building, Sultan Mahmud II managed to take further steps towards restructuring the empire and creating a centralized state.

Like his predecessors and successors, Mahmud II gave priority to military matters in his reform program. This was largely due to the defeats of the Ottoman armies by the 'infidels' and the territorial losses of the empire. However, major changes in the military establishment had always been difficult. Even before he came to power Mahmud had had the chance to witness the failure of Selim's attempts at establishing a modern army distinct from the Janissary corps, which was regarded as the main obstacle to reform. Consequently, Mahmud's solution was more radical than that of Selim: he sought the abolition of the old and the establishment of the new. In 1826 he destroyed the entire Janissary corps, replacing it with a new army, *Asakir-i Mansure-i Muhammediyye* (the Victorious Soldiers of Muhammad).

Ultimately, Mahmud's reforms were aimed at creating a centralized state. To this end the central government was reshaped to fulfil the requirements of the new situation, leading the traditional-style governing body to convert to a 'modern' bureaucratic structure. The old departments of the Sublime Court (*Bab-ı Âli*) gradually transformed into new ministries with new uniforms for their personnel, initially unfamiliar to Ottoman society. These reforms were to reach their peak in the *Tanzimat Fermanı*, or Gülhane Decree of 1839, issued by Abdülmecid, Mahmud's successor, although the latter prepared its infrastructure.

Throughout Ottoman history, the ulema held a vital role and stood alongside the ruling elite. The most important tasks of members of the ulema] were the articulation of the religious law, the operation of the Muslims' judicial system, and teaching in elementary schools and *medreses*, the Islamic colleges where Islamic sciences such as Arabic grammar, jurisprudence, and Qur'anic exegesis were studied. The ulema also developed a professional hierarchy unique in terms of its complexity, which allowed its members the power to justify or undermine imperial policies.

Mahmud's achievement in the reform movements was due to his success in maintaining the ulema as an ally. Occasionally, the latter's desire to support the reforms went even further than Mahmud's.

The document presented below from the Başbakanlık Osmanlı Arşivi (Prime Ministerial Ottoman Archives) in Istanbul reflects the relations between the ulema and the state, in other words, between the reforms and the religious establishment. It might, therefore, serve to indicate some clues about the official perception of Islam in the age of reform. This document concerns the provision of special clothes to the imams employed in the newly established *Mansure* Army, the style these clothes should take, and their introduction into the ranks of the ulema. The imams were assigned the task of leading daily prayers and instructing soldiers in Islamic principles. Interestingly, some officials suggest that the imams wear special uniforms similar to those worn by soldiers, despite the fact that imams as members of the ulema profession already had their own dress code. Additionally, they began to be paid a regular monthly salary even though imams were normally living on the income from religious endowments. It is also interesting to note that the state, complaining that applications for the posts were coming from the poor and students, tried to attract candidates from the higher strata of the ulema instead.

The document contains three parts, which appear in reverse order to the sequence in which they were written: the first is the imperial decree indicating the decision of the sultan; the second part is the opinion of the commander-in-chief (*Serasker*) of the *Mansure* Army; and the third is that of the minister (*nazır*) on the subject. Although there is some mention of another statement as supplementary to the decree, which belongs to the Şeyhülislam, it is missing from the document. Although the document is undated, it is known that the dress code of the imams in the *Mansure* Army was set in January 1827.[13] It is quite possible therefore that the decree was also issued around this date.

Text

The Imperial Decree—17318

The official statement of the Commander-in-Chief [*Serasker*] and the aforementioned Minister [*Nazır*] and the meanings of the memorandum of our well-wishing master [i.e. the Şeyhülislam] became known to my imperial Majesty. Our master mentioned the abundance of judges in Anatolia and Rumelia,[14] [but] he never mentioned their efficiency or their lack of efficiency and the reasons for this abundance. In spite of the fact that it is evident that the members of the profession will despair of the entrance of a hundred men to the profession at the same

---

[13] Avigdor Levy, 'The Ottoman Ulema and the Military Reforms of Sultan Mahmud II', *Asian and African Studies*, 7 (1971), 26.   [14] The name of the European part of the Ottoman Empire.

time, it is necessary to know how many men enter the hierarchy of Anatolia and Rumelia, how many men have appointments from the Council, and how many men have their appointments renewed through favoritism. It has become known to my imperial Majesty that this matter was carried out by issuing orders related to dealing with [it] in various places during [12]13–[12]14.[15] Let a copy of [the issued orders] be extracted and submitted to my imperial Majesty from the records. After that it is necessary to deal with their implementations according to their requirements and necessity. Since the imams of this place [i.e. Istanbul] have had their monthly salaries raised by thirty *kuruş* to sixty *kuruş*[16] then, let the salaries of the imams in the provinces be increased by thirty *kuruş* to sixty *kuruş* in the same way and let their clothes be arranged as indicated below. However, it is not necessary for those who are from the *şürefa*[17] to wear black cloth on their turbans. Let those who are from the *şürefa* wear green [cloth on their turbans and let] the rest wear either white or black as they wish. On the matter of the turban, it is suitable to leave them [free to choose] according to their character.

The joint statement of your servants the Commander-in-Chief and the Minister
They [i.e., the Commander-in-Chief and the Minister] recommended that if the imam efendis, whom they are sending, are given a suit of special clothes, as given to others [i.e. military officers], in the beginning of their assignment and each year in the day of *Hıdır*[18] (the beginning of the summer season), and [also] are granted a rank in the *ilmiye* profession which is suitable for their status after having served for seven or twelve years, this will instil ambition both to those currently serving and to those who are to be registered from now on.

As the matter has been inserted through the correspondence with the well-wisher [and] munificent Şeyhülislam Efendi in his one-piece statement sent in that respect, the fact is that due to the abundance and overpopulation of men of the profession, anyone of them is subject to [waiting for] twelve or fifteen years to obtain a rank.

Especially considering that it is not possible even for the men of the profession, who are under his [i.e. the Şeyhülislam's] office, to live on and to have welfare with the judicial revenue, it is obvious that he [i.e. the Şeyhülislam] cannot administer the profession as a whole if another eighty to one hundred ranks from the regions Anatolia and Rumelia are granted to persons from the imams of the *Mansure* Army who have completed twelve or seven years of service. As the aforementioned well-wisher Efendi [i.e. the Şeyhülislam] pointed out, it does not suit to grant

[15] 1799–1800 CE.   [16] Piaster.
[17] A term which used to refer to the descendants of the Prophet Muhammad through his daughter Fatima and her husband ʿAli. For more details, see article 'Shurafa' in *The Encyclopaedia of Islam*, new edn. (London: Brill, 1960–86).
[18] Fortieth day after spring equinox, first day of summer.

them a grade from the *ilmiye* profession [i.e. religious scholarship], and as your Excellency knows, the monthly salary of the Istanbul regiments' imams has recently been raised from thirty to sixty *kuruş* due to the thirty *kuruş* [being given] to cover the cost of cloth.

Likewise, at the moment, the idea to allocate salary [to the provincial regiments' imams] in another way has been changed because the monthly salary of the provincial regiments' imams has been increased to sixty *kuruş* in accordance with the Istanbul regiments' imams, [so they were] provided means of maintenance and welfare. However, as your servants, the aforementioned Commander-in-Chief and the Minister, communicated in this statement, both the Istanbul regiments' imams and the provincial ones will be given a suit of clothes on their assignments and in the day of *Hıdır* (the beginning of the summer season). [Despite this], it is necessary for them to be differentiated and separated from other people, but, as indicated by your servant the aforementioned governor of Çirmen[19] who wrote that imams be given a round wrapped cap. If all of them are required to wear the round wrapped cap, it would not be suitable for these to wear the round cap like soldiers due to their being imams. [Because of this], it would be suitable to establish a regulation for both the Istanbul and provincial regiments' imams, for the sake of separation, to wear the turban, and to wrap black muslin band cloth [around their turbans], regardless of whether they are from the *şürefa* or not. If [this practice] is regarded as suitable to the decree of your imperial Majesty, it will be carried out by appending to the imperial law, and sending certificates to your servants the indicated Commander-in-Chief and the aforementioned Minister and the provincial officials as well as the essential places, it is known to your imperial Majesty that the abovementioned statement of your aforementioned well-wisher has been presented and submitted for the consideration of your imperial Majesty.

The command and the order unto Him to whom all commanding belongs

Although the salary of the imams of The Victorious Soldiers of Muhammad in Istanbul, which was thirty *kuruş*, has been increased to sixty *kuruş* by adding thirty *kuruş* as the cost of cloth in accordance with the imperial decree of his Majesty, which came out latterly, and in that respect it has been appended to the imperial law, they cannot arrange their clothes in order to be recognised as the imams of the aforementioned Army because the well-wisher efendis, willing to be imams and recruited by exam until now, are from the groups of students and the poor. Further, because they do not have a kind of ambition for the future and because all the officers and private soldiers of the aforementioned Army are provided a suit of clothes in the beginning of their assignment and every year in the beginning of summer while the imam efendis are deprived, [this situation]

---

[19] A town (*sancak*) in the province of Edirne in the nineteenth century, now in Greece.

is making the current ones feel sad and causing many of the people who are qualified and concerned [about the imam posts], not to be ambitious. The [posts of]
imam in most of the [Army] divisions are not filled yet, and if those who are
qualified and concerned are assigned carelessly, it is clear then that the right aim
cannot be achieved.

Since, if these [i.e. the provincial regiments' imams] are also granted from the
protection and generosity of his Majesty, like others, a suit of clothes in the beginning of their assignment and also every year in the summer, and a post suitable to
their situation from the *ilmiye* profession after serving for seven or twelve years,
[this] will be the cause of eagerness and desire for those who are already assigned
and also those who will be assigned from now on, and [this] will also bring about
some benefits. For example, it will be easy to fill [the posts] soon, the required
services will be performed as desired, and each of them will be recognised and
distinguished from other people. The [following] matters immediately came to
these humble servants' minds that all the imam efendis of the aforementioned
Army should be given [the following items] in the beginning of their assignment
as well as every year in the day of *Hıdır*; a quilted *molla* turban in a lasting color,
a green turban for *şürefa* and a black one for non-*şürefa*, a broadcloth robe
without clasped belt in the shape of long jacket without sleeves (*çepken*) and
Manisa[20] [style] or a similar kind of waistcoat, high broadcloth boots, two shirts
and undershirts, red-edged shoes, boots every November, wool-quilted raincoats
every year and when damaged, a suitable officer-sword, a bag, a metal water bottle,
a tight Circassian style[21]-broadcloth cloak every three years in the colour of the
military division to which each imam belongs; and that the matter of rank assignments should be arranged by transferring [it] to the Şeyhülislam.

Additionally, it has been mentioned in the content of the letter dispatched by the
governor of the province of Çirmen, the kind Esad Paşa, that although the imams
of the two divisions of the [Army of] Victorious Soldiers of Muhammad in Edirne
are paid thirty *kuruş* monthly salary as required by the imperial law, they will not be
able to afford [the cost of] their clothes. And there is nothing on their clothes to
indicate that they are the imams of the aforementioned Army, [so that] it will be
good to arrange their clothes and dress in a suitable way. [Therefore] if their clothes
are orderly arranged by providing every year a round wadded cap made of green
broadcloth without ribbons, an Egypt-style long robe made of the green broadcloth of officer uniforms, a loose dress, *çakır* style[22] trousers, a girdle of Moroccan
wool, a stout coarse woollen raincoat, a pair of yellow travelling clothes and a pair
of boots, this will cause, through driving away their need of clothes, them to carry
on eagerly in their service, to act and to desire the good prayers.

---

[20] A town in Western Anatolia.   [21] With a tight-fitting body and full skirt.
[22] Secured round the waist in folds and sewn to light leather boots at the ankles.

Your servants in the İzmir regiment have written that because two imams who were assigned to the aforementioned division heard that the salary of imams of the aforementioned Army in Istanbul has been increased, they also demand an increase in their salary like Istanbul [imams] and that a few [imams] applied for vacation. If this matter is approved in the opinion of the guardian of the benefactions [i.e. Mahmud II] and the matter of which type of clothes is agreed by your imperial Will among those which, as mentioned above, came to these humble servants' mind and have been offered by the aforementioned [i.e. the provincial governors], [its] implementation will be necessary not only for the Istanbul regiments' imams but also for all the imams in Anatolian and Rumelian provinces. In that respect, about sending the certificates (*ilmühaber*) to the place of these humble servants, to the provincial places and to the other essential places, by appending to the imperial law, the command and the order belongs unto Him to whom commanding belongs.

[Stamped] Hüseyin[23]   [Stamped] Saib[24]

---

[23] Ağa Hüseyin Paşa (1776–1849) was the first commander-in-chief of the *Mansure* Army between 16 June 1826 and 8 May 1827.   [24] Saib İbrahim Paşa was the first minister of the *Mansure* Army.

7.3 Science in religious education: a fatwa from Cairo, 1888

Indira Falk Gesink

Preface

In 1888 the khedive[25] of Egypt, Tawfiq Pasha, asked a *qadi*[26] to decide whether it was permissible to introduce 'practical' studies, including advanced mathematics and natural sciences, into the curriculum at Al-Azhar Mosque-Madrasa[27] in Cairo. This question was not as simple as it might seem; in fact, it was loaded with political and religious significance.

At the time of Tawfiq Pasha's request, Al-Azhar was one of the most prestigious schools of Islamic jurisprudence. Established in 972 CE, Al-Azhar was considered to be the oldest functioning college in the world, attracting scholars from across the globe. These scholars taught a range of subjects relating to religion and religious law, including the Arabic language, recitation, and interpretation of the Qur'an, Hadith (reports about the sayings and actions of the Prophet Muhammad and his early community), and the texts of the four main Sunni legal schools.[28] Al-Azhar's graduates were employed at all levels of society: as Qur'an teachers for elementary students; as prayer leaders at mosques; as clerks for the government; as college-level professors; as lawyers; and as upper-level legal specialists (*muftis* and *qadis*). Such employment often required the graduates to function as ethical and religious guides for the communities they served. Consequently, the students at the mosque needed to learn not only the texts of religion and law, but also the nature of such intellectual or spiritual dilemmas as might divert ordinary Muslims from 'the straight path' of Islam. At the higher levels of study, students learned about legal and religious controversies, including those 'heresies' that in the past had threatened to fragment the unity of the Islamic community.

By the mid-nineteenth century, however, some of those associated with Al-Azhar had begun to doubt that the traditional range of subjects was sufficient to prepare graduates for future employment. According to these reformers, the world had changed, and the main ethical and religious

---

[25] 'Khedive' was a title used to designate the hereditary governors of Egypt under the Ottoman Empire from the 1860s until Egypt's independence.

[26] A *qadi* is a judge in the Islamic legal system.

[27] *Madrasa* is the Arabic for school. Before the twentieth century, *madrasa*s were schools for the study of the Islamic legal tradition and were commonly associated with a large mosque and supported by charitable endowments (plural *awqaf*, singular *waqf*).

[28] These were the Hanafi, Maliki, Hanbali, and Shafiʿi schools of legal interpretation. Al-Azhar was unique in maintaining teachers in all four schools; most schools only offered instruction in the predominant school in the region where they were located.

dilemmas that Muslims were likely to face arose no longer from the controversies of the past, but rather from the military and economic power of the West, and the intellectual challenge of new scientific theories. Various scholars and government bureaucrats began to consider whether the students should be adding the study of contemporary mathematics and sciences to their legal studies.

Therein lay a problem. Many of the most recent advances in the applied and theoretical sciences had been made by Europeans, who had also acquired some degree of control, either economic or political, over much of the Middle East. In fact, Egypt had been under British occupation since 1882. Thus, the study of 'science' at Al-Azhar might be understood to imply acceptance of European domination, European thought, and perhaps even European cultural superiority.

Tawfiq Pasha was himself implicated in the acceptance of European domination of Egypt, as he owed his authority in part to Europeans. His predecessor, Ismaᶜil, had run up a large debt (calculated in 1879 to be £98.4 million sterling) to finance the 'modernization' of Egypt, a program of reforms influenced by Western models. Many aspects of the reforms benefited the Egyptian population, such as new schools and the completion of the Suez Canal. However, they also included a number of expensive but superficial projects intended to impress European rulers and investors, such as the construction of wide streets and French-style buildings in major Egyptian cities, and a lavish celebration of the opening of the Suez Canal in 1869. By 1876 Egypt was bankrupt, and Egyptian finances were placed in the hands of French and British controllers, acting as representatives of the European creditors to whom Egypt owed money. In 1879 European pressure persuaded the Ottoman sultan to depose Ismaᶜil and replace him with his son, Tawfiq.

Tawfiq Pasha's dependence on European support continued throughout his term in office. In 1881 his rule had been challenged by a coalition of Egyptian army officers, landowners, and religious scholars who were opposed to European domination of the government and demanded constitutional rule in Egypt. The slogan of this movement, which was called the ᶜUrabi Revolt after its leader, Colonel Ahmad ᶜUrabi, was 'Egypt for the Egyptians!', and it engendered a fear amongst the European creditors that the constitutionalist rebels might decide to repudiate Egypt's debt. There were concerns, moreover, for the safety of Europeans and native Christians living in Egypt, although Colonel ᶜUrabi had issued a statement in conjunction with the Al-Azhar shaykhs[29] affirming co-operation between the Muslim and Christian communities. As tensions increased, European residents began to panic and evacuate to British ships anchored in the harbor of Alexandria. In June a riot broke out in Alexandria, and in the chaos, Tawfiq

---

[29] 'Shaykh' is a title given to religious scholars, mystics, headmen, elders, and others deserving of respect.

Pasha sought refuge aboard those same ships. The British subsequently occupied the country in the name of restoring Ottoman authority, initiating a period of Egyptian history known as the 'Veiled Protectorate' (1882–1914), during which Ottoman-appointed khedives ruled nominally, but British officials undertook the actual business of government.

It was during the period of the Veiled Protectorate that the question arose as to the ability of Al-Azhar's graduates to function in a world dominated politically, economically, and even intellectually, by Europeans. Compelled by circumstances to address the question of how Al-Azhar should adapt its curriculum—even its understanding of religion—to the challenges of this new era, Tawfiq Pasha petitioned his *qadi*, Muhammad Bayram, for a *fatwa* on the issue of introducing 'practical' subjects into the school's curriculum.[30] Some Azhari professors thought that the reform of Al-Azhar was not the khedive's business, however, as Egypt's religious institutions had traditionally been independent of the government (whether it be that of the khedive himself, or the method of government practised by the British in Egypt). Therefore, as the khedive's question was especially controversial, Muhammad Bayram referred it to higher authorities than himself: to Shaykh Muhammad al-Inbabi, a mufti of the Shafiʿi legal school and head of Al-Azhar Mosque, and Muhammad al-Banna', Egypt's chief mufti and a member of the Hanafi legal school. In response, the two scholars issued fatwas.[31]

The Qur'an had commanded Muslims to seek knowledge, especially with regard to religion. The quest for knowledge was considered a duty incumbent on the community, which could be fulfilled by scholars on its behalf. Schools such as Al-Azhar existed in part to help the community meet its obligation to seek religious knowledge, and Bayram asked if that obligation also applied to fields of knowledge not explicitly related to religion. As the instrumental sciences, those that were 'tools' to acquire further knowledge—such as the Arabic language and grammar—were already taught at Al-Azhar, might the other disciplines not be permitted under the same rationale?

The contents of the petition and fatwa, printed below, invite further questions. Why, for example, might sciences such as astronomy, chemistry, or biology be seen as a challenge to nineteenth-century Islamic doctrines? Why might those who were employed in law, education, and legal guidance need to know these sciences? Why was it controversial for Khedive Tawfiq

[30] A *fatwa* is a non-binding legal opinion. Anyone who needs advice on legal or religious matters may petition a mufti (a jurisconsult, or a specialist in legal advice) for a fatwa. The petitioner is not, however, required to follow the advice contained in the fatwa.

[31] The text of the petitions and fatwas was reprinted by Muhammad Bayram's son, the reformer Mustafa Bayram, in *Tarikh al-Azhar: Kalima ʿan al-muʾtamar al-thalith ʿashar min muʾtamarat ʿulamaʾ al-lughat al-sharqiyyah, al-munʿaqid bi-madinat Hamburg fi awaʾil shahr September sanat 1902* ('History of Al-Azhar: A Speech Delivered at the Thirteenth Conference of Eastern Language Specialists, Hamburg, Germany, September 1902'), 27.

to initiate this type of reform? How did Shaykh al-Inbabi justify his answer? Considering the potential controversy of the *fatwa*, note how Shaykh al-Inbabi signed it. Why would a mufti ask for forgiveness, and from whom?

This exchange of legal advice led to heated debates in the Egyptian press, which generated public interest in reforming Al-Azhar. In 1896 the subjects of study in question were officially incorporated into the curriculum, and by 1911 had gained general acceptance amongst the students.

Texts

1. Petition by Muhammad Bayram, *qadi* for the Khedive Tawfiq

Is it permissible for the Muslims to learn mathematical subjects such as geometry, arithmetic, astronomy, natural sciences, and the composition of parts that is known as chemistry, and other than these among the remaining [topics of] learning, especially those upon which may be built increased strength in the nation [*umma*], and considering the need to keep up with contemporary nations, according to the Qur'anic command that we be prepared to defend the faith?

Indeed, are these subjects incumbent upon a part of the nation, in the sense that they are a duty that some must fulfill on behalf of the community as a whole, as mentioned by Imam Hujjat al-Islam al-Ghazali[32] in the *Revival of the Religious Sciences*, and agreed to by the Hanafi religious scholars? And if the ruling is in favor of this, then is it permitted to teach [these sciences], as it is permissible to teach the instrumental subjects [*ʿulum al-ʿaliyya*], such as grammar and others that are currently widespread, in Al-Azhar Mosque and the Mosques of Al-Zaytuna and Al-Qarawiyin?[33]

2. Fatwa issued by Shaykh Muhammad al-Inbabi, Shafiʿi mufti and head of Al-Azhar Mosque

It is permissible to study the mathematical subjects such as arithmetic, geometry, and geography, because nothing in them contradicts religious matters. Indeed, it is our duty to learn what [these subjects] contribute to the benefit of religion

[32] Al-Ghazali (1058–1111) was one of the most famous scholars in Islam. Born in Iran, he showed early evidence of brilliance and taught as a young scholar at a *madrasa* in Baghdad. Early in his professional career, doubting the validity of the information he was conveying to his students, he sought the best means of acquiring true knowledge. In the process, he became an expert in Islamic jurisprudence, theology, philosophy, and Sufism (Islamic mysticism). He stopped teaching for eleven years while living as a mystic, and drew the conclusion that the mystical path should be combined with adherence to Islamic ritual and legal adherence to produce a deeper and more personal commitment to religion. His writings, including the *Revival of the Religious Sciences* mentioned here, became extraordinarily influential, and Islamic reformers throughout history often referred back to Al-Ghazali's ideas to support their arguments.

[33] The Zaytuna Mosque in Tunis and the Qarawiyin Mosque in Fez, Morocco, were the most famous *madrasa*s of the Maghrib (North-West Africa).

or worldly affairs on behalf of the community, just as we are obliged to learn the science of medicine, as Al-Ghazali advised us in the passages of *The Revival*.[34] Furthermore, it is beneficial to teach those subjects that increase one's ability to undertake this duty. But, one must not undertake the study of astronomy, seeking out the shapes of stars, planets, and their orbits for the purpose of astrology, seeking to infer from celestial movements the events of the netherworld. This is forbidden, as Al-Ghazali mentioned [. . .][35]

[. . .] The study of natural sciences [is permitted], that is, the description of bodies and their characteristics and how they transform and change, as in *The Revival*, in the second chapter of the 'Book of Knowledge.' If the research is done according to the methods of the legal specialists, there is no prohibition of it. Likewise, the learned Shihab al-Din Ahmad bin Hajar al-Haythami advised us in a part of his book, *Fatawa al-jami*ʿ, of several important issues at that time, such as familiarity with the characteristics of metals and plants for use in medicine, and knowing the workings of tools that may benefit the welfare of the worshipers. But, if it is done according to the methods of the philosophers, it is forbidden, because it leads to falling into doctrines that contradict the *shariʿa* [. . .][36]

[. . .] There is no harm in teaching the mathematical subjects as the instrumental subjects are taught, and the same is so for natural sciences and the science of the composition of parts [chemistry], as long as they are taught in a manner that cannot be immediately understood to oppose the legal tradition, as with the remaining rational studies, such as logic, discursive theology, and argumentation. Indeed, it is incumbent upon us to know these three subjects to the extent required to defend religious doctrines.

1 Dhu al-Hijja 1305 H
Muhammad al-Inbabi, Servant of Knowledge and the Poor, at Al-Azhar. May he be forgiven.[37]

---

[34] Geography was considered a 'mathematical' subject because of the calculations of latitude and longitude used in navigation, and because of its use by travelers in estimating the direction of Mecca for prayer. Shams al-Din al-Inbabi, *fatwa* dated 1 Dhu al-Hijja 1305 (1888), in Muhammad Bayram, *Tarikh al-Azhar*, 27.

[35] Many Muslim reformers sought to distinguish between 'valid' forms of knowledge and 'invalid' or corrupt forms. The difference between astronomy and astrology was often used as an example. Astronomy, or the study of stars and planets and their orbits, was legitimate knowledge. Astrology, or the use of astronomical knowledge to predict the future or to divulge information about the 'unseen world', was considered to be superstition. Many nineteenth-century Islamic reformers categorized astrology with practices of folk religion (such as attributing special powers to saints and saints' tombs), which they considered to be 'backward' and 'extra-Islamic', having originated not from Islamic sources, but rather from pre-Islamic cultures.   [36] *Shariʿa* is the Islamic legal tradition.

[37] Seventeen days after Shaykh al-Inbabi issued his *fatwa*, the Hanafi Mufti Shaykh Muhammad al-Banna' issued his, agreeing with Inbabi's opinion. Muhammad al-Banna', Grand Mufti of Egypt, *fatwa* no. 171 (17 Dhu al-Hijja 1305 [1888]), cited in Bayram, *Tarikh al-Azhar*, 29.

7.4 A memorial to a young Assyrian refugee, 1922
Eden Naby

Preface

On 23 January 1923 a letter arrived at the rooming house where Anni and Ludiya Shimmon were staying in Milwaukee, Wisconsin. The sisters had been sent by their father, the Reverend (Qasha)[38] Babilla Shimmon, to the United States to escape the dangers of refugee life in Tabriz, Iran. The letter took six months to arrive, having been posted on 31 May 1922. The young women, both in their early twenties, had managed to survive wartime atrocities perpetrated against the Assyrians during World War I by taking shelter with the American missionaries in Urmia, in the province of Azerbaijan in Qajar Iran.[39] Their mother Maryam died in 1918, together with thousands who fell victim to hunger, typhoid, dysentery, cholera, and shots randomly fired into the missionary compounds by local Muslims.[40] Most were buried in mass graves dug in the large American missionary compounds that comprised the hospital, schools, and residence areas of the missionaries in Urmia. No stones mark these graves. In later years the small percentage of Assyrian families allowed to return to Urmia attempted to raise commemorative stones to their lost family members.

In the case of Yoash Shimmon, the 18-year-old recent graduate of Urmia College, the American Boys' School, his father memorialized the death of

[38] The members of this particular Assyrian family were Presbyterians and the title does not reflect a rank in the Assyrian Church of the East.

[39] The controversy concerning Ottoman massacres during World War I has focused on the question of genocidal operations against the empire's Armenian population. However, Pontic Greeks and Assyrians were also victims of Ottoman wartime atrocities. Assyrians from Anatolian towns (Harput, Mardin, Diyarbekir, Adana, and others) and northern Syrian villages of Tur Abdin, fled to Urmia (Urmia) and Salmas in north-western Iran in 1915. In addition to tensions with local Assyrians (which may have been aggravated by confessional differences—Assyrian Church of the East, Uniate, and various Protestant denominations—among the Assyrians), the new arrivals had to contend with the hostility of Muslim Azeri Turks in the urban areas and Kurds in the rural areas. Interestingly, the Assyrians referred to all Muslims as 'Afshars'. The Afshars were a Turkish nomadic tribal group with a long history in the Iranian Plateau—the peak of their political power was from 1736 to 1747, during the reign of Nader Shah Afshar.

[40] The exact relationship of local Muslim violence against the Armenians to the broader conflicts of World War I is still under study. The Ottomans, Russians, and British all tried to influence rural Turkish and Kurdish tribal groups to participate in the war on their side. This involved arming and funding tribal leaders, such as the Kurdish leader Ismaᶜil Simko, which tended to fuel their local territorial ambitions and embolden them to settle ethnic and religiously based scores with other groups. It is also possible that the Iranian Qajar government, in an attempt to reduce Russian influence in its territories, may have followed the Ottoman example and encouraged violence against the Assyrians.

his son by writing a commemorative document on paper (15 × 17 inches) which he treated as if it were a traditional Middle Eastern tombstone of the nineteenth century. The paper, folded in half, resembles two sides of a stone with one side inscribing the qualities of the deceased and the other, more decorative, repeating the salient features of his life and death in a larger, more elaborate style of writing. The Shimmon family, one of many Assyrian Christian families that had taken advantage of the educational opportunities offered through the presence of American missionaries who had arrived in Urmia in 1834, lived in the large and prosperous village of Gugtapa, just south of Urmia. Like many others native to the area of Iran located between Lake Urmia and the Zagros mountain chain that divided Iranian and Ottoman domains (Afshar Turks, Assyrians, and Armenians), the Shimmon family owned vineyards and orchards, by means of which they led a relatively prosperous rural life. Kurds, who now live in many of the over seventy Assyrian villages in the area since the middle of the twentieth century, had lived a semi-pastoralist existence in the more mountainous western region of Iranian Azerbaijan. Jews, also speaking a dialect of Aramaic close to that spoken by the Assyrians, lived in the town of Urmia itself rather than the countryside.

Qasha Babilla, whose father and grandfather had received their education at the same American Boys' School from which his son Yoash had graduated in 1918 (one of four graduates, a number only one-third that of earlier classes during peaceful times), had advanced degrees from American institutions. He had returned to his home in Urmia prior to World War I. In 1918, believing in a promise by British forces that they would send military reinforcements to help against the Ottoman Turks poised to overrun north-west Iran in pursuit of the Assyrians, Qasha Babilla and his three sons joined other Assyrian men who headed south-west to meet the British forces. He left his three daughters and wife in Urmia. No British help ever arrived. The desperate Assyrians scattered and died in flight. The fortunate few, such as the Shimmon family, despite the loss of several family members, managed to reunite in Tabriz. The father's connections in Milwaukee allowed him to send his remaining daughters to the United States as soon as they graduated from Fiske Seminary, the girls' school dubbed 'Mount Holyoke in Urmia' due to the origins of the school in 1838 as an extension of the first American college for women in the United States. Due to the dangers in Urmia from 1914 through 1923, Fiske Seminary resumed its skeleton teaching activities in Tabriz after the surviving Assyrians of Urmia were allowed to find security in Tabriz. Due to the atrocities, the Assyrian community in Urmia, which, thanks to the American missionary presence and its own resolve, had become the centre of Assyrian cultural renaissance in the Middle East, deteriorated into a backwater after World War I. The Assyrian Diaspora begins in this period, as Assyrians gradually fled their homeland for refuge in Europe, Australia, and the Americas.

Text

The Memorial to Yoash, son of Qasha Babilla Shimmon

Yoash, the son of Qasha Babilla and Rabi[41] Maryam of Gugtapa, was born on August 22, 1900 (*alap-sade*)[42] in the vineyards of the village. He grew up a healthy child and complete in faith. At seven years of age he entered the village school. At fourteen (*yud-delat*) he enrolled in Urmia College and graduated that academy but in that same year, on July 9 (*yud-yeth*) he fled with his father. On the road to Bijar, he contracted dysentery. When they got to Bijar, all help possible was provided him. But it was futile. After nine days of illness, he went to his Lord on August 1918 (*alap-sad-yud-Khet*) in Bijar.

The other thing that needs to be said is this: he said, 'Father, my life's telephone wire[43] has been cut and I am going to my Savior.' He was buried in Bijar at the foot of a hill, under an almond tree. He is awaiting the Resurrection to share in the joy of His Master.

Tribute to the fine character of this young man:

1. He was obedient and he would never talk back.
2. He was truly faithful. He never acted against his conscience.
3. He was active and never wasted time.
4. He was humble and pure of heart, in action and work.
5. He honored his parents.
6. He prayed and read the Scriptures.
7. He loved life and was happy.

He never knew of his mother's death because he was far [away]. He left a heart's sorrow to his wandering father and his brothers and sisters.

'My days are like a shadow that declineth; and I am withered like grass.' Psalms 102: 11 (*qap-bet-yud-allap*).[44]

---

[41] This honorific was used for educated men and women, although it literally means, 'teacher'.

[42] Traditionally, the Syriac/Assyrian alphabet is used to represent numbers: a similar system is employed in later Semitic writing such as Hebrew and Arabic, and in alphabet systems derived from the latter, such as Persian and Ottoman Turkish.

[43] The meaning of this use of the word 'telephone' (*telipun*—taw-lammat-pe-waw-nun) is not obvious. The family believes the intended meaning here is 'my life has ended'.

[44] This biblical passage, unlike the rest of the memorial is written in classical Syriac.

7.5 The Brigadier and the Imam: two commemorative poems from Iran, 1928 and 1989
Paul E. Losensky

Preface

For over a thousand years, Persian poetry has been one of the primary mediums of social and political discourse in Iran. Composed for occasions such as military victories, coronations, or the death of public leaders, commemorative poems tell us less about what happened than about what it means. By integrating current events into the time-honored language and symbolism of the literary tradition, this poetry strives to give an enduring significance to the contingencies of political life, to create myth and history from the news of the day, and to bestow legitimacy on the ideology and power of the governing regime. The poems below memorialize two of the formative events in modern Iranian history, drawing on many of the same images to create two radically different versions of Iran's past and future.

From his exile in Germany, the poet and scholar Ebrahim Pur-e Da⁀ud wrote the first of these poems in 1928 to celebrate the replacement of the Qajar Dynasty by the Pahlavi Dynasty of Reza Khan/Shah in 1925. This praise poem (or *madh*) begins by decrying the Turkic origins of the Qajar tribe, which had ruled Iran since the end of the eighteenth century, and depicts the tyranny of their rule as the logical outcome of foreign usurpation.[45] Overtaxed villages haunted by owls, desolate fields, thorns, jackals, and snakes—Pur-e Da⁀ud draws on a repertoire of images that had been developed by generations of poets to represent governmental corruption and oppression. Reza Shah, by contrast, is introduced as the 'son of the land', and the promise of his dynasty is associated with the splendor of the pre-Islamic heritage of Persia. The ancient Zoroastrian god Hormoz guards the 'new social order' of Iranian nationalism.

Reza Shah's new social order, however, lasted little more than fifty years, and it becomes the force of tyranny depicted in the first half of the eulogy (*marsiyeh*) composed by Parviz ⁀Abbasi-Dakani on the death of the Imam Khomeini on 4 June 1989. Scorched fields, serpents, and thorns now

---

[45] The anti-Turkic and anti-Arab strains of modern Iranian nationalism were sharpened by nineteenth-century intellectuals like Mirza Fath ⁀Ali Akhundzadeh (d. 1878) and Mirza Aqa Khan Kermani (d. 1897) and found a home in the Iranian chauvinism of some literary figures like Sadeq Hedayat (d. 1951) and the general tenor of state ideology and education during the Pahlavi Dynasty, most notably perhaps in Reza Shah's attempt to purify Persian of Arabic and Turkish loan-words in 1934. Ironically, he got the idea after a visit to Turkey in the summer of 1934, where he witnessed the efforts of Kemal Atatürk to purify Turkish of Arabic and Persian loan-words.

become symbols of the police terror of the Pahlavi Dynasty, and nationalist ideology is condemned as the 'secularist night'. The lore of pre-Islamic Iran is reduced to the legendary king Zahhak, who literally fed off the lives of his subjects. ᶜAbbasi-Dakani instead places Khomeini in the sacred history of Islam, stretching from Ishmael to the martyrs of Kerbala. The image of the sun heralds a new beginning at the end of both poems. Pur-e Daᶜud summons Hormoz, often represented as a solar disc in the sacred iconography of ancient Persia, to guard the new shah. For the poet of the Islamic Republic, death transforms Khomeini into a spiritual sun that replaces all 'false mirrors' and even the mundane physical laws of astronomy. Reinterpreted in the light of contrasting ideologies, a single symbol serves to legitimate two historical occasions in terms of the perennial cultural values embodied in literary form.

Texts

1. The Fall of the Reign of the Qajar Dynasty by Ebrahim Pur-e Daᶜud[46]

> Now listen! Tidings have come! Ahmad Shah
> of Iran[47] has tumbled down from the throne,
> the throne purged, wiped clean of evil demons—
> the Turkmen bandits of the Qajar house.
> Give thanks to the Almighty for this news.
> We've escaped again this shameful disgrace.
>
> One hundred and fifty years we endured
> this disgrace, constant misery and grief
> and fevered sighs. Helpless, impotent,
> at wit's end, our path blocked at every turn:
> The stranger held dominion over us,
> a Tatar raider on Jamshid's[48] throne.
>
> Abject dynasty of Aqquyunlu[49]
> come from Mongol yurts like ill-natured ghouls—
> their depredations sowing confusion,

[46] The text of the poem is taken from Ebrahim Pur-e Daᶜud, *Purandokht-nameh*, with English translations by D. J. Irani (Bombay: Iranian Zoroastrian Anjoman, 1928), 86–8. This new translation was prepared with reference to those of D. J. Irani and Hadi Hasan, *A Golden Treasury of Persian Poetry* (Delhi: Publications Division, Ministry of Information and Broadcasting, Government of India, 1966), 222–3.   [47] The last ruler of the Qajar Dynasty who ruled from 1909 to 1925.

[48] Jamshid is the mythical founder-king of Iran who invented the basic tools of civilized life and established the legendary ancient Kayanian monarchy.

[49] Pur-e Daᶜud here links the Qajars with the Aqquyunlu, another tribal confederation of Turkish descent, which ruled over parts of Iran in the fifteenth century.

a band of traitorous thieves made camp,
ran pell-mell over Shapur's[50] land, and plunged
the brilliant sun of the Zand[51] into night.

The leader of this cruel band of robbers
of evil stock and bad temper, ill-willed
and ill-omened, made the whole land a sea
of human blood, and he swam rapacious
in that sea till he cast anchor near Rayy[52]
folded and packed his black tents and held court.

The seven kings of this Turkish tribe turned
ancient Iran into a ruined heap.
The cry of owls rose from earth to heaven.
Its people all senseless, homeless, lifeless,
emaciated, forlorn, distracted,
dejected—the bounty of Qajar rule!

Only taxes come from alien rule;
Only stings come from scorpions and snakes.
What do you expect from brigands and thieves?
A lion's strength cannot come from jackals,
nor the splendor of Parviz[53] from Qajars.
Roses come from roses, and thorns from thorns.

This dynasty undermined existence;
the beams of our homes sagged under the load.
Everywhere were idleness, foolishness,
drunks boasting, begging—an ugly stupor—
Sufism, materialism, egotism,
stealing, lying, cheating, murder and hate.

Name a single king from this House who was just.
Name one capable, wise, illustrious.
In a plundered land, where's the silver and gold,
the guns, the troops, armor, helmets and shields?
In an arid, parched land, where are the green fields,
harvest and fruit, granaries full of wheat?

[50] Shapur is the name of two famous Sasanian kings (r. 242–72 and 309–79 CE), both of whom led successful wars against the Roman Empire.

[51] Springing from Iranian tribal stock, the short-lived Zand Dynasty (1747–94) is often regarded as a golden age of enlightened rule before its overthrow by the Qajars.

[52] Rayy is a medieval city located south of Tehran where the Qajars established their capital.

[53] Known for his military prowess, Khosrow Parviz (r. 591–622 CE) was the last great ruler of the Sasanian empire before the coming of Islam.

What once grew from the earth was all destroyed,
what was raised from the land, crushed and laid low,
men of means rendered destitute and poor.
Outsiders in control, we were abased—
honor brought only infamous disgrace,
leaving behind Qajar toadies and clowns.

Sardar Sepah[54] swept out the aliens.
This son of the land soothed his bereaved mother.
He struggled like a man and charged from all sides
and threw the Qajar from the Peacock Throne.
He established a new social order:
May the Creator Hormoz[55] protect him!

The flag of the Constitution now flies.
The messenger brings tidings of freedom.
Wasps no more infest their citadel nest,
the country relieved of tyranny's sting.
And let's hope tomorrow this storm will tear
the cloaks and turbans from deceitful shaykhs.

Ancient Iran regains youthful strength.
Let its body breathe with a new spirit,
a hidden radiance shine from its heart
and recall the Kayanian splendor.
Let it be washed clean of the dust of time,
of the Qajar pollution and disgrace.

2. Parviz ᶜAbbasi-Dakani, 'Believe in the Exodus of the Sun'[56]

Life then was just the wilting of a leaf,
a loitering in the alleys of death,
brains filling the cups of the new Zahhaks,[57]
flames engulfing fields of comprehension.
Thorns had sprouted from the earth of the faith,
and serpents from the shoulders of rancor.
Floods swept the stronghold of indirection,

[54] The army commander: this was one of Reza Khan's positions before he was made shah in 1925.

[55] Another name for Ahuramazda, the principal god of the good in Zoroastrianism, the religion of ancient Iran.

[56] *Sugnameh-e Imam* ('Book of Mourning for the Imam'), ed. Mahmud Shahrokhi and ᶜAbbas Moshveq-Kashani (Tehran: Sorush, 1369/1990), 262–5. Special thanks to the *Journal of the Society for Iranian Studies* for permission to reproduce Paul Losensky's translation.

[57] Zahhak was a legendary king of ancient Iran. The ultimate symbol of injustice and political terror, he had two serpents growing from his shoulders that had to be fed with human brains.

existence a mirror of fetid swamps.
Tulips at the brink of death's agonies,
and two well-known words—the wall and the noose.
Stalks of grass thirsting in the desert sleep;
flowers prisoner to the sickles' onslaught.
In every street ran rumors of the noose,
night's terror, fear of denunciation.
Flight, and everywhere the sword of danger:
our footsteps walked alongside destruction.
Without the moon's lamp on the circling roads,
our footsteps beat out an unmeasured verse:
anxieties on the streets of madness,
in our cups, wine the color of bruised blood.
Like chaff fallen into churning whirlpools,
the corpses of dead fish hung from the hooks.
Hobgoblins' twilight, secularist night,
triggers of resentment cocked and fired.
Wheels of exhaustion were spinning blindly,
and roads stretched out as far as death's crossing.
They decked the road with barricades and walls.
They demanded taxes on our presence.
Human footsteps were strangers to these roads.
Love went insane at the touch of madness.
Rain's spite knew the secrets of the leaves' sleep.
Highways stretched to the far outskirts of death.
The final stop on a one-way transit:
nullity's line blotting out being's script.
The road, a mirror, comrade of my tears;
lump in the throat, an antique legacy.
I have seen the scars on the minutes' back.
I have seen a garden of poppies' blood.

*

He came from suns, from luminosities.
He'd brought the scent of love from distant lands.
In time of thirst, he was the rain's essence.
He gave drink to a parched generation.
His hands warmer than the sun; in his words,
the smell of roses, the sound of water.
He came from beyond earth, from destiny.
With you, he rewrote this age completely.

It was a new chapter in unity.
His fealty was like that of the sun.
His voice was the cry of centuries of pain
from the sons of Cain to the Brigadier.[58]
His shoulders bore wounds Cain had inflicted,
Ishmael's secret was lodged in his throat.
Upon his body, a plain, simple shirt—
his hands were the banner of detachment.
He had a smiling poem on his lips,
and his smile joined in the songs of love.
His hands were the sun of winter's season,
love's equator in the latitudes of pain.
We gathered in the flames of his presence.
We learned about love from his majesty.
He talked of the flowering of springtime
and with the desert, of the taste of rain.
With autumn's painful onslaught, the garden
died. Exhaustion encamped in my belief.
His death is the death of my every word.
His scar is on every page of our hearts.
He leaves along a path of buttercups
toward blossoming's verdant night, to the Lord.
He departs, but his voice remains behind.
He has led his tribe from the vale of night.
His hands let us smell the scent of the sea.
His words breathe with perfumes of tomorrow.
We are now crossing the streets of the night.
We speak with the voice of Muhammad's people.[59]
In the attacks of planes, missiles, and smoke,
we learn a history of love and song.
The roots of our history reach beyond.
Our hearts are Karbala's geography.[60]
We have found lordship in humility.
We have found divinity in loving.

[58] A reference to Reza Khan Pahlavi (1878–1944), who ruled Iran from 1925 to 1941. He began his march to power by participating in a coup against the Qajars in 1921. At that time he was a colonel in the Persian Cossack Brigade.

[59] This verse can also be translated: 'We speak together with Al-e Ahmad', referring to the writer Jalal Al-e Ahmad (1923–69). His critique of Iranian society during the Pahlavi era, *Gharbzadegi* ('Plagued By the West'), exercised a powerful influence during the Islamic Revolution.

[60] Karbala is the site in present-day Iraq where Husayn [Hussein] ibn ʿAli was killed on the tenth of Muharram in the year 61 (10 October 680). Husayn's martyrdom was the defining moment in the history of Shiʿi Islam and is memorialized each year in the ceremonies of ʿAshura.

The tulips are lanterns lighting our path.
Phoenixes hold the secret of our fire.
Yet, my heart is driven mad with sorrow,
my tired eyes have become an ocean.
Come, come! Let us begin to weep. Let us
believe the exodus of the sun.
Its setting has exiled the false mirrors—
O sun, do not rise in the east again!

7.6 Three poems on British involvement in Yemen, from the Yemeni press, 1937
Flagg Miller and Ulrike Freitag

Preface

The three poems printed below represent a battle of words over the crucial question of the future of Hadhramaut, a region halfway between Aden and Oman that is today a province of Yemen. In 1937, when the first *qasidah* was composed by Salah al-Ahmadi, a Hadhrami mercenary in Hyderabad,[61] Sultan Salih bin Ghalib al-Quᶜayti had just concluded an advisory treaty with Britain. Although his country had been under British protection since 1888, this step was heavily criticized by al-Ahmadi, who felt that such an alliance with a Christian power differed from the kind of external alliances with Muslim neighbors that Hadhrami rulers had often sought to strengthen their positions. Al-Ahmadi's poetic opponent is most likely Muhammad bin Hashim, a journalist, teacher, and government advisor who had spent some twenty years in Indonesia and had returned to the Kathiri sultanate in the interior of Hadhramaut, in order to promote internal reform. Against the background of ongoing problems between the Quᶜayti and Kathiri sultanates, Ibn Hashim expresses the hopes of a significant number of Hadhrami merchants and scholars that, with European 'help', Hadhramaut might be pacified and its people made beneficiaries of lasting prosperity.

The rhetorical contours of the exchange reveal some of the political fault-lines dividing Hadhrami society at the time. Some members of the Diaspora, like Ibn Hashim, who had experienced the benefits of stable government and modernization under colonial rule abroad, believed that co-operation with the British could bring rewards. Others felt that Wahhabi Islam, as practised in Saudi Arabia, was best suited to solve the internal problems. For the latter, European rule—symbolically represented by immoral, immodest women—implied submission to unbelievers who introduced non-Islamic innovations. Descent-based status, as well as profession, often informed political allegiances: Al-Ahmadi was a tribesman and warrior, Ibn Hashim was an urban intellectual and a *sayyid*, an individual who claimed descent from the Prophet and rejected the tribal custom of bearing arms.

The poems also attest to the close relations between Diaspora and homeland. As it happened, Harold Ingrams (see n. 66) ultimately established peace and introduced many reforms. However, soon after World War II opposition began to mount from a new generation of Arab nationalists. Shortly after the British retreated from Aden and the Protectorate areas of Yemen in 1967, Hadhramaut became part of the People's Democratic Republic of Yemen.

[61] Hyderabad was an Indian princely state until Indian independence in 1947.

Although Hadhramis were represented in high office from Zanzibar to Singapore, their country did not possess a printing-press or radio station. In view of the illiteracy of most of the population, poetry proved a powerful means of mobilizing public opinion.

The three poems are composed in the *qasida* genre, widely recognized as the oldest and most prestigious genre of poetry in the Middle East. Although *qasidas* can be composed in classical Arabic, using quantitative metrical schemes that were standardized by Arab scholars as early as the eighth century CE, they are also frequently composed in vernacular Arabic and set to meters drawn from popular folk-song. The *qasidas* featured here adhere roughly to the *rajaz* meter, one of the most common meters in folk-song. While the poets drew from a rich oral song tradition, however, they also composed these *qasidas* in writing, in a format known in southern Yemen as *bid wa jiwab* ('initiation and response'). In this quintessentially epistolary format, one poet composes a *qasidah*, and the second poet responds with his own *qasida* that matches the former in meter and rhyme. While used for exchanging greetings and news, *bid wa jiwab* poetry is often also political in content, addressing both local and trans-local issues. As in much political Yemeni poetry, the poets in this case use their talents to try to seek common ground on pressing issues of political authority in their homeland.

By committing their verses to writing and addressing one another across considerable distances, *bid wa jiwab* poets adapt the conventions of oral poetic composition to pen. Alleviated from mnemonic constraints, such *qasidas* are often longer than most orally composed *qasidas*. In this case, moreover, while both poets model their *qasidas* on an aggressive oral invective style (*hija'*) familiar to tribal poets throughout the Arabian Peninsula, they also frame their *qasidas* with Qur'anic supplications to God, both in the initial and final verses, and are careful to mention the written mediation ('O Messenger of script' and 'A *qasida* came to him, threaded together like a string of pearls'), that facilitates their communication. Where traditional political legitimacy was attached not only to the literate authority of religious elites (*sada*) but also to non-literate tribal leadership (*qaba'il*), both poets bolster their arguments by deliberately writing their compositions for multiple audiences.

Text

1. *Bid* from al-Ahmadi[62]

Note: * All names marked by an asterisk refer to Hadhrami clans, tribes, or prominent members thereof. Many of the references evoke specific historical figures or events.

---

[62] This poem, although perhaps initially sent to Hadhramaut in written form, has been transmitted orally. Hence a number of slightly varying versions are in circulation. We have generally followed the one reprinted in ʿAbd al-Khaliq al-Batati, *Ithbat ma laysa mathbut min tarikh Yafiʿ fi Hadhramawt* (Jeddah, 1989), 101–8. Slightly different versions have been printed in Ghalib bin Awadh al-Quʿayti, *Taʿammulat ʿan tarikh Hadramawt qablaʾl-Islam wa-fajrihi maʿa mash ʿamm ʿan hijra wa-nataʾij ʿalaqat al-hadarima ʿibraʾl-azmina bi-shuʿub janub sharq Asiya*, (n.d., n.p), 160–71, and ʿAbdallah al-Nakhibi,

1   I have begun with Thee and call Thee, O Most Sublime, Thou whose generosity is unsurpassed!
Welcome O Everlasting, who unshackles the ankles from chains,

2   I ask Thee Thy forgiveness, when I brood alone in the tombs!
Al-Qu͏ᶜayti[63] said: throughout my long night, I was not blessed with sleep,

3   No worldly worry, nor any yearning for long-curled maidens,
Aged, at ninety, facing the dwelling of eternity.

4   Perhaps my home will be found in Paradise near the Pond of Gathering;[64]
I am short of nothing, and the Sultan does not press me for money,

5   Living in Deccan, the land of ᶜUthman, sultan of the Indians,[65]
Sultan, son of sultan, son of sultan, who drives off the coward.

6   Yet how I was affected by the waning of honor after ascendancy,
[when] I acquired news that does not ease the heart, from the land of plateaus:

7   The land of al-Ahqaf [Hadhramaut] has been lost, like an ax-mangled
    piece of meat, abandoned in the cold;
It went with the *sahib*[66] for no price, and with no soldiers in his train.

8   They built churches and barracks for the soldiers there.
Ah, my homeland! What shame upon the graves of my ancestors!

9   How I shouted, how I called! I spoke of it before it occurred.
But I am excused. As a single stick, I produce no fire.

10   Where are the rulers, al-ᶜAbdallah,* and Hamdan,* the lions?
Where is Ibn Mutlaq,* where is Rubᶜah,* where is the son of Salem, ᶜAbud?*

11   Where is the Quᶜayti?* Where is Yafiᶜ,* who sallies well into the deltas?
Those who repel the flood, sending its course back up its slopes,

12   Those who have the most eminent customs of ᶜAd or Thamud,[67]
Where is al-Tamimi* and the Manahil?* Where is Bin ᶜAbd al-Wadud?*

13   Where are the Shanafir?* Where are the Nahd* who bear the heavy loads?
Where are the Jaᶜidi?* Where are the Kindah,* whose war-cry is 'Bin Kunuud'?

14   The ᶜAwbathani* and Sayban,* the guardians of borders,

---

al-Kawkab al-lamiᶜ fima uhmila min tarikh Yafiᶜ (Jeddah, 1999), 113–23. We would like to thank Sultan Ghalib b. ᶜAwadh al-Quᶜayti for generously sharing with us his own translation of, and annotations to, the poems, which we have used extensively.

[63] Al-Quᶜayti is a clan of the Yafiᶜ, from which both the poet's sub-clan and the ruling family of the major Hadhrami sultanate stemmed. Here, the poet refers to himself.

[64] The Pond of Gathering is said to be located in the highest firmament of paradise, where the Prophet Muhammad will be and where the Muslim *umma* will gather after the Judgement.

[65] The reference is to Hyderabad, a major destination of Hadhrami migrants, many of whom enrolled in the service of the ruler of Hyderabad.

[66] In India, 'sahib' meant 'master'. The reference is to Harold Ingrams, the British colonial official who, together with Hadhrami notables, peacefully arranged for a truce among the warring tribes of Hadhramaut and who was instrumental in the conclusion of the advisory treaties.

[67] ᶜAd and Thamud are Arabian tribes that existed before Islam.

Where is Ba Surrah* and Bin Salih Muhammad, the ᶜAmudi?*

15   Where are those who said we protected it with the walls of our ancestors?

They were a party to the contract, they were its witnesses.

16   They will assail the *madrasas*, mosques, and prayer,

Wine in the markets, it will delight the sons of the Jews [i.e. Christians],

17   While women expose their sweet cheeks in the market,

What bitterness inside me, what a life of ignominy. O rancorous spleen!

18   It is better to depart, and to make one's abode in the land of the Zaydis,[68]

Or else in Mecca, in the care of Faysal Bin Saᶜud.[69]

19   Son of the Imam of justice, the savior, despite his rancor,

And be close to the Kaᶜba, and visit Mustafah, the Pride of Creation.[70]

20   Upon him God's prayers, as many as the thunderous heavens.

2. *Jiwab* from Muhammad b. Hashim[71]

1   I have begun with God, with the most glorious of giving, O Befriender!

O Opener of doors, O Generous One, you shower us in generosity!

2   Forgive us our faults and cover our mistakes, and grant us our goals;

And two thousand of God's prayers upon the Guide of mankind, the light of
   creation

3   Then said he, who lingered, thoughts spinning, without the arrival of sleep;

A *qasida* came to him, threaded together like a string of pearls.

4   Bin al-Ahmadi, shaykh of the tribe who dwelled in the land of the Indians,

He rails at Yafiᶜ and at Hamdan and the aged ᶜAbud.

5   Upset by the flood that has covered the lowlands and highlands alike,

[But that] showed mercy on Wadi al-ᶜAjal, which dances and bristles in
   the cold,

6   Joy there has multiplied, and the lovely cheeks have relaxed;

Care has prevailed, affliction has dissipated, and justice stands upon pillars.

7   The land has submitted and improved from Najran to the tomb of Hud;

Safety abounded, the traveller spends the night alone with his purse.

8   After he had [once] been frightened of overwhelming tyranny,

Injustice had spread and evil gathered, and no-one honoring promises,

9   Their tribes were spoiled, they betrayed and trifled with oaths;

How many a parent strives for his family, with a chill in the world.

10   He orphaned his children, widowed his wife, and stayed awake in his grave,

---

[68] Land of the Zaydis: Northern Yemen, where the predominant confession is Zaydi Shiᶜism, and where a religious/political Imam ruled.

[69] Faysal, son of ᶜAbd al-ᶜAziz bin Saᶜud, was viceroy of the recently conquered Hijaz.

[70] Mustafa: another term for the Prophet Muhammad.

[71] There were rumours at the time that Ingrams suggested that Ibn Hashim respond to the popular poem by al-Ahmadi.

Atrocious conditions, repulsive and dark, which make the hair on the skin stand on end.

11   Your treachery has even exposed to Satan the sacred realms of the heart;
Whosoever has benefited or mended only stoked the conflict with kindling.

12   The ways ahead may perhaps bring black neglect;
[Yet] a way will be found, even if a stick in Wadi Bin Rashid strikes another stick.

13   Who will repel the flood? Is there a powerful state that will protect?
If there is any fury, it will be restricted. Rather, there will be an outcry of Thamud.

14   What is one to think of you, you stupid and obstinate shaykh of Yafiᶜ?
You loathe our security and the salvation that riled the envious.

15   Long live Ingrams, from whom the mountains of the earth shudder from fright!
Through prestige he amended it, without ruler[72] or any soldier leading,

16   He chained its wolves and will rule by shackling the panthers;
He revived Islamic law, vanquished in support of justice, and wards off evil.

17   And al-Kaf Bu Saqqaf[73] commands, he who produced a good deed,
Writer and orator, conflict became quashed through his efforts.

18   Do not deny people their favor, the lowest of qualities is denial;
The flood sweeping through Europe: see how it is linked to the mountains?

19   If this has not happened [yet] then it will happen, if the delegations multiply,[74]
The one I know is better than the Lord of Ethiopians, may he not return.

20   As for that which you mentioned, my friend, about the government of Bin Saᶜud,
It is a pretension. If it were true, the nose of the envious would quash you.

21   Ask the trustworthy in the Mother of Villages [Mecca] about it, and those who have settled in Zarud.[75] No one loathes justice, Father of ᶜUmar, except the Jews.

22   You praised ᶜUthman, and in lauding him, you surpassed the limits;
Does he have the power to bring water back once its channels are restored?

23   You mentioned Yafiᶜ and Midhhij,* and also Hamdan the lion's;
Judicious words, but what you said occurred in an age of the ancients.

24   The strands of the nest have vanished; they have left behind only a handful of Bani Kindah,[76]

[72] *Awla*: possibly a misspelling of *dawla* (state or ruler), or *Eawla* (which would translate as 'attack').

[73] The reference is to Sayyid Abu Bakr bin Shaykh al-Kaf of Tarim, who belonged to a major merchant family with branches in Singapore and Java and was one of the major supporters of British intervention.

[74] This could refer to both the growing number of European visitors to Hadhramaut and the increasing Hadhrami calls for outside help in solving internal problems.

[75] Zarud: a quarter of Mecca. This is a reference to the large Hadhrami contingent in Mecca.

[76] A reference to the migrations, in which—according to the poet—the worthiest men left the country.

Pretty figures, but merely camel skin stuffed with straw.

25 No one kicks when retreating, [especially] in an age when they are brought up to sell rice-bags;[77]

Fifty years have gone by, according to the document and witnesses,[78]

26 The old man ᶜAwadh [al-Quᶜayti] confirms it, he who would defend honor;

That is your answer in rhyme, Salah Ahmad the stray.

27 If you add more [then] I shall add more, and if you respond then we will talk and review;

The conclusion is to the Guide,[79] peace rests in my resurrection and sitting [in heaven].

27 May God's mercy, by his honor, bring the lord [Muhammad] to eternal Heaven.

3. *Jiwab* from Al-Ahmadi

1 Glory to Him who forgave us [our sins], the creations and thunder glorify Him;

God is eternal, God is the vanquisher of rebellious Satan.

2 That is a section, (now) greetings and welcome as many (times) as the number of creations,

With verses from a concealed poet, a falcon on the crags of mountains,

3 They have reached us, [though] we know not whether from friend or envier;

He speaks of Yafiᶜ and Hamdan, the beams and supports.

4 Arise, O Messenger of script, [go] from Hyderabad, the land of good fortune,

Land of prosperity, justice, mercy, and the acquisition of money

5 From its abundance everyone fills his bag and sets off for the [Hadhrami] highlands;

They became sultans, and established government, what a strange dream during slumber!

6 They have loosened the halter[80] and transformed it, these people of greed and false oaths;[81]

This is the way of Deccan, and this is its excellence, O how excellent!

7 These are true words, the resolute enemy will attest to them.

---

[77] *Furud* normally means pistol in Hadhrami Arabic. However, according to a witness of the period, *furud* also referred to rice bags imported from the USA for a while during this period. The substitution of local staples by rice was a result of changing food habits.

[78] This is a reference to the Protectorate Treaty of 1888 between the Quᶜayti sultan and the British, to which ᶜAwadh b. ᶜUmar al-Quᶜayti agreed. [79] Another term for the Prophet Muhammad.

[80] A variant of the text reads: '*arrakhu khatmaha, hawwaluha*'. It seems that the printed version represents a misspelling.

[81] A reference to Arab military leaders in Hyderabad who had contributed to the worsening of the security situation by pursuing their own aims, instead of serving the Nizam loyally.

Avaunt! Who will criticize ᶜUthman or Bin Saᶜud?

8   He who sets off for Mecca, and established justice and the 'limits'[82] there,
O arranger of verses, whose sword is laid in its sheath,

9   Ease up on the camel a little, don't spill over or dismount in the fire;
You repudiated my warning about Hamdan and the aged ᶜAboud.

10   See who is next to you, [and] do not abuse. Be alerted, the signal brings responses;
You understood some of [my] aims, but you overstepped the boundaries of others.

11   All your words about the tribes are true, I do not deny;
Their courage was debased, they abandoned their Mausers[83] and pistols.

12   And the others fell, as if they were in ignorance and paralysis,
Going in circles with a claim that has no proof or witnesses to it.

13   If anything remains, leave its place concealed, Bin Hamoud;[84]
The village leader does not loathe justice, whoever lies does not return to [his lie].

14   What you said about my children is a wound to which no poultices can be brought;
I do not deny some of your assertions, but disagree with some of your exaggerations.

15   A harsh wind[85] has blown over al-Ahqaf [Hadhramaut] that will desiccate every stick;
What disgrace upon the affluent and elders, amongst whom are leaders!

16   But alas, I am in my nineties, on my cane with my eyes feeble;
The guest who came to you is comparable to [only] a pulse in the veins.

17   There is no haunch or thigh-meat, only hideous bones wrapped in skin;
Your entire homeland is a patch of sterile earth, abandoned in the mountains.

18   The food of its people is yellow, red and black corn, and you spend the night hungry;
No kernel in the storeroom, not even *khumsiyyah* coins[86] in the pocket.

19   Islamic law, my friend, is hidden in the graves;
The young man will slip, as will slip the fair cheeked-ones.

20   Kisses on the forehead will be stolen, and breasts squeezed;
That is the biggest catastrophe. With the 'Padre',[87] marriage contracts will be nullified.

21   He who digs a hole for others will fall back into its maw;

---

[82] This refers to the Islamic punishments in Islam.   [83] A common type of rifle.

[84] Al-Ahmadi here plays on the root h-m-d, which forms the basis of Muhammad, both his opponent's name and that of the Prophet, from which Muhammad b. Hashim claimed descent.

[85] *Nafla* could be either a hot or cold wind.   [86] Small, locally used coins, often of copper.

[87] Al-Ahmadi was familiar with Catholic priests and missionaries in India. Here, he uses their image to highlight the dangers to proper Islamic comportment and morality emanating from Europeans.

You say in your poetry and composition that Salah Ahmad is astray,

22   You erred in your composition: Mt Sayban is not a give-away;

Only God knows who rolled up his bed and set off early in the cold.

23   If you shared my opinion, what power you would have had to thwart the aggression!

But from neglect, flames prevailed as the lions fled.

24   He who abandons his pride, abandoned to failure, spends the night fettered;

If the flood is not regulated, it will carry away [vainly] into the mud-flats.

25   Woe unto me! Tell him [how is it] that Bal-Harith resembled lions;[88]

How strange it is that you said Bin Talib is like Ba Rabud.[89]

26   If Bu Ghalib [al-Quᶜayti] had remained alive, the lions would not have been obliterated;

During his day, if he had told us to summon the peaks, they would have been summoned!

27   And al-Kaf,[90] Bu Saqqaf, his sea-deep mind cannot be measured by instruments,[91]

If anyone sought rice, his house would never empty of delegations.[92]

28   He who raises an argument strikes at the issue, by dint of his efforts;

God knows all secrets, consciences, and intentions.

29   I think that it came, discarded [like a] clay-dish sent forth over from London;

Hitler and Mussolini commissioned them, to fortify the borders.

30   The order has been executed, indeed, its support has grown at the fringes;

Hope is still with God, O poet, and Saleh[93] is still here.

31   Also, do not forget ᶜAli [bin Saleh al-Quᶜayti].[94] To his worthiness, the world attests;

If only [his] maneuvers would repair the lapses on the day of resistance.

32   He has a sharp mind that extracts the embattled at the time of bloodletting;

He and ᶜAli Mansur[95] are in the same course, and agree on the meaning.

33   The brother of Jaᶜfar, known for his wisdom, unravels the knots;

Enquire about Hamid al-Mihdhar:[96] tell him that the counsel will reconvene.

---

[88] Bal-Harith: a tribe just north of the Hadhrami boundaries, which is associated with Bayhan.

[89] Bin Talib was a famous tribal leader who had made a significant fortune in Singapore, while Ba Rabud came from a menial, non-tribal background, but had risen to some fame in the Hyderabad police.   [90] The 'wa-lakan' of the Arabic text is a typographic error.

[91] *Bulud* is an instrument for measuring heights and depths.

[92] A reference to Sayyid Abu Bakr bin Shaykh al-Kaf's widely reputed, and enjoyed, generosity.

[93] Sultan Salih b. Ghalib al-Quᶜayti, who ruled 1936–56 and was widely appreciated as a reformer.

[94] ᶜAli b. Salah al-Quᶜayti was the second cousin of Sultan Salih and, for some time, his deputy and governor of Shibam.

[95] Sultan ᶜAli b. Mansur al-Kathiri (r. 1929–38). His brother was Jaᶜfar b. Mansur al-Kathiri.

[96] Sayyid Hamid b. Abu Bakr al-Mihdhar, the Quᶜayti chief minister and brother-in-law of Sultan Salih.

34   Between me and him is a pact and good men fulfill promises;
If he wants to meet with me, if he has any interest, I am not begrudging.
35   May [God] forgive his sins that were written in the accounts;
I conclude. God's prayers on our deliverer on the Day of Appearance.
36   Eternal prayers to the Chosen One in my prostrations and worship.

7.7 Taha Husayn: revolt against tradition, from *Al-Ayyam* (*The Days*), 1939

From the Islamfiche *project*

Preface

The publication in 1939 of the second volume of Taha Husayn's auto-biography, *The Days*, followed by one year the appearance of his profound and influential essay, *On the Future of Culture in Egypt*. From the auto-biographical depiction of Husayn the youthful student in *The Days*, it becomes clear that the ideas put forward by Husayn the mature educator and writer of *On the Future of Culture in Egypt* were the product of lifelong concerns and first-hand experience.

Taha Husayn (1889–1973), who received the first doctorate awarded by the first secular university in Egypt, was the son of a sugar-refinery worker in Upper Egypt. Despite the fact that he lost his sight as a child, he made his way through the traditional Qur'an school and was sent to Al-Azhar in Cairo at the age of 13 to continue his religious studies. He remained there for eight years, but as he became more and more dissatisfied with the traditional system of education, he was drawn into the intellectual world of the secular reformers who had recently founded the Egyptian University. Completing his studies there, Husayn went on to earn a second doctorate at the Sorbonne in Paris and returned to Egypt to establish himself as a leading writer, educator, and reformer.

Among Husayn's writings are novels, literary essays, historical studies, and political and social commentaries, but his best-known and most-loved work is probably his three-volume autobiography, *The Days*. The first volume, undertaken when Husayn was approaching his fortieth year and dictated to his wife in a matter of days, recalls his early childhood in Upper Egypt. The second volume, which appeared a decade later, covers the Al-Azhar period, from his arrival as a bewildered, blind 13-year-old, to his decision eight years later to remove himself in all but formal terms. Al-Azhar had been the seat of traditional Islamic learning since its founding in the fourth/tenth century, but by 1902, when Husayn arrived, its curri-culum and teaching methods were under questioning and criticism from religious and secular reformers alike. The students were also drawn into these conflicts and lined up behind their favorite shaykhs in support of one side or another. As Husayn became aware of these deep currents of rivalry and discontent, his respect for Al-Azhar was eroded. The ambivalence of his later years there was reflected in his daily routine: he continued to attend lectures at Al-Azhar in the mornings, but in the afternoons traveled to the Egyptian University for a taste of secular learning along European lines.

The following excerpts combine vignettes of life at Al-Azhar with a record of Husayn's growing distance from it. The directness of the narrative tends to focus the attention of the reader on the situation of the young student Taha Husayn (who is referred to throughout as 'he' rather than 'I'). But it should be kept in mind that the narrator is Taha Husayn, the educator and writer, who now recounts his experiences with the hindsight of personal growth and historical change.

Text

Chapter III

The third phase of his existence was the one he loved best of all. In his own room he endured all the pains of exile. It was like a foreign country to him, and he never became familiar with its contents, except perhaps those nearest to him. He did not live in it in the same sense that he had lived in his country home or in other familiar rooms where nothing was unknown to him. He passed his days there in exile from people and things alike, and in such anguish of heart that the oppressive air he breathed there brought him no rest or refreshment, but only heaviness and pain.

Nor was there any doubt of his preferring these hours in Al-Azhar to the agitated journey back and forth, whose hazards drove him almost to despair. It was not only his steps that were confused and unsteady; his very heart was overwhelmed by that unnerving perplexity which perverts a man's purposes and drives him blindly onwards, not only along the material road which he needs must follow, but also along the free paths of the mind, feckless and without a plan. Not only was he distracted by the hubbub and tumult that eddied around him. He was also distressed at the unsteadiness of his walk and the impossibility of harmonising his own quiet, faltering steps with the firm and even brutal pace of his companion.

It was only in the third phase of his day that he found rest and security. The fresh breeze that blew across the court of Al-Azhar at the hour of morning prayer met him with a welcome and inspired him with a sense of security and hope. The touch of this breeze on his forehead, damp with sweat from that feverish journey, resembled nothing so much as the kisses his mother used to give him during his early years, when he chanted verses from the Qur'an to her, or entertained her with a story he had heard at the village school; or when, as a pale, delicate infant, he abandoned the corner in which he had been reciting the litany from the Sura Ya-Sin to go and carry out some household task or other.

Those kisses revived his heart and filled him not only with tenderness, but also with hope and confidence. The breeze that welcomed him in the court of Al-Azhar, no less, brought rest after weariness, calm after tumult, a smile after gloomy looks. However, he as yet knew nothing of Al-Azhar, and had not the least idea what he would find there. But it was enough for him to brush with his bare feet the ground of that court, to feel on his face the caress of its morning breeze, and to realise that around him Al-Azhar was preparing to awake from its drowsiness, that its inertia would soon give place to activity. He began to recover consciousness of himself, as life returned to him. He felt the conviction of being in his own country, amongst his own people, and lost all sense of isolation, all sadness. His soul blossomed forth, and with every fibre of his being he yearned to discover . . . well, what? Something he was a stranger to, though he loved it and felt irresistibly drawn towards it—knowledge. How many times had he heard this word, and longed to find out its hidden meaning! His impression of it was vague enough, to be sure; but of this he was convinced, that knowledge had not limits and that people might spend their whole lives in acquiring a few drops of it. He too wished to devote his whole life to it and to win as much of it as he could, however little that might be. His father and the learned friends who came to visit him had spoken of knowledge as a boundless ocean, and the child had never taken this expression for a figure of speech or a metaphor, but as the simple truth. He had come to Cairo and to Al-Azhar with the intention of throwing himself into this ocean and drinking what he could of it, until the day he drowned. What finer end could there be for a man of spirit than to drown himself in knowledge? What a splendid plunge into the beyond!

All these thoughts suddenly thronged into his young spirit, filling it and taking possession of it, blotting out the memory of that desolate room, of the turbulent, twisty road, and even of the country and its delights. They convinced him that it was no mistake or exaggeration to be consumed with love for Al-Azhar as well as with regret for the country.

The boy paced on with his companion until he had crossed the court and mounted the shallow step which is the threshold of Al-Azhar itself. His heart was all modesty and humility, but his soul was filled with glory and pride. His feet stepped lightly over the worn-out mats that were laid out across the floor, leaving a bare patch here and there, as if on purpose to touch the feet which passed over them with something of the benediction attached to that holy ground. The boy used to love Al-Azhar at this moment, when worshippers were finishing their early-morning prayer and going away, with the marks of drowsiness still in their eyes, to make a circle round some column, or other, and wait for the teacher who was to give a lecture on tradition or exegesis, first principles of theology.[97]

At this moment Al-Azhar was quiet, and free from the strange intermingled murmurs that filled it from sunrise until evening prayer. You could only hear the whispered conversations of its inmates or the hushed but steady voice of some

---

[97] These are among the primary subjects of the traditional Azharite courses (see introduction).

young man reciting the Qur'an. Or you might come upon a worshipper who had
arrived too late for the common service, or had gone on to perform extra prayers
after completing the statutory number. Or maybe you would hear a teacher
beginning his lecture in the languid tone of a man who has awakened from sleep
and said his prayers but has not yet eaten anything to give him strength and
energy. He starts in a quiet, husky voice: 'In the name of God, the merciful,
the compassionate: Praise be to God, father of the worlds. May His peace and
blessing be upon our lord Muhammad, the most noble of the prophets, upon his
family and his companions. These are the words of the author of the Book, may
God rest his soul and grant us the fruits of his learning. Amen!'

The students listened to the lecture with the same quiet languor in which it was
given. There was a striking contrast between the different tones the shaykhs used
at the early-morning and midday lectures. At dawn their voices were calm and
gentle, with traces of drowsiness in them. At noon they were strong and harsh,
but fraught too with a certain sluggishness induced by the lunch they had just
eaten, the baked beans and pickles and so on which made up the usual fare of an
Azharite at this time. At dawn the voices seemed to beg humbly for favour from
the great authorities of the past, while by noon they were attacking them almost
as if they were adversaries. This contrast always astonished and delighted the boy.

On he went with his friend up the two steps leading into the *liwan*.[98] There
beside one of those sacred pillars, to which a chair was bound by a great chain,
our friend was deposited by his companion, who left him with these words:
'Wait there and you will hear a lecture on tradition; when mine is over I will
return and fetch you.' His companion's lecture was on the first principles of
Islamic law, given by Shaykh Rady, God rest his soul. The textbook was the
Tahrir[99] of Al-Kemal Ibn al-Humam. When the boy heard this sentence, every
word filled him at once with awe and curiosity. First principles of law? What
science was this? Shaykh Rady? Who could he be? Tahrir? What was the meaning
of this word? Al-Kemal Ibn al-Humam? Could there be a more wonderful pair of
names? How true it was that knowledge is a boundless ocean, full of unimagin-
able benefit for any thoughtful being who is ready to plunge into it. The boy's
admiration for this lecture especially grew deeper every day as he listened to his
brother and his brother's friends studying their lesson beforehand. What they
read sounded very strange, but there was no doubt of its fascination.

As he listened the boy used to burn with longing to grow six or seven years older,
so that he might be able to understand it, to solve its riddles and ambiguities, to be
master of the whole subject as those distinguished young men were, and to dispute
with the teachers about it as they did. But for the present he was compelled to

[98] Colonnade surrounding the central court of the mosque.
[99] 'Correct Reformulation' (of the first principles of law). The work was written in the fifteenth
century.

listen without understanding. Time and again he would turn over some sentence or other in his mind on the chance of finding some sense in it. But he achieved nothing by all this, except perhaps a greater respect for knowledge and a deeper reverence for his teachers, together with modesty as to his own powers and a determination to work harder.

There was one sentence in particular. How many sleepless nights it cost him! How many days of his life it overcast! Sometimes it tempted him to miss an elementary lecture—for he had understood his first lessons without difficulty— and so led him on to playing truant from the shaykh's lecture on tradition, in order to speculate on what he had heard from the lips of those older students.

The sentence which took possession of him in this way was certainly a remarkable one. It would fall echoing in his ears as he lay on the threshold of sleep, and drag him back to a wakefulness which lasted all night through. This was the sentence: 'Right is the negation of negation.' What could these words mean? How could negation be negated? What might such negation be? And how could the negation of negation be right?[100] The sentence began to whirl round in his head like the ravings of delirium in a sick man's brain, until one day it was driven out of his mind by one of Al-Kafrawi's *Problems*.[101] This problem he understood at once and was able to argue about. Thus he came at last to feel that he had begun to taste the water of the boundless ocean of knowledge.

The boy sat beside the pillar, toying with the chain and listening to the shaykh on tradition. He understood him perfectly, and found nothing to criticise in his lesson except the cascade of names which he poured forth on his listeners in giving the source and authorities for each tradition. It was always 'So-and-so tells us' or 'according to so-and-so.' The boy could not see the point of these endless chains of names, or this tedious tracing of sources. He longed for the shaykh to have done with all this and come down to the tradition itself. As soon as he did so the boy listened with all his heart. He memorised the tradition and understood it, but showed not the slightest interest in the shaykh's analysis, which reminded him too well of the explanations given by the imam of the mosque in his country village and the shaykh who used to teach him the elements of law.

While the shaykh proceeded with his lesson Al-Azhar began gradually to wake up, as if stirred out of its torpor by the voices of the teachers holding forth, and by the discussions which arose between them and the students, amounting sometimes almost to quarrels. The students came closer, the voices rose higher, the echoes intermingled and the shaykhs raised their voices again, so that the students might be able to hear them, ever higher and higher, up to the final climax

[100] As the context is legal, the sentence means: 'Property is a counter-claim against a counter-claim', or the assertion of a right against all comers. In a different context the words might well mean: 'Truth is the refutation of refutation', or the rebuttal of scepticism.

[101] An Azharite grammarian of the eighteenth century.

of the words 'God is all-wise.' For meanwhile other students had come up to wait for a lecture on law by another shaykh, or maybe the same one; so he had no choice but to end the early-morning lecture and begin the next. Then the boy's companion would return, take him by the hand without a word and drag him all ungently to another place, where he dumped him like a piece of luggage and abandoned him again.

The boy realised that he had been transferred to the law class. He would listen to this lecture until it came to an end and both shaykhs and students went off. Then he would stay rooted to the spot until his friend came back from Sayyidna al-Husayn, where he had been attending a lecture on law given by Shaykh Bakhit, God rest his soul.

Now Shaykh Bakhit was prolix in the extreme, and his students used to harass him with objections. So he never finished the lessons until the middle of the morning. Then the boy's companion would return to where he was, take him by the hand without a word and lead him out of Al-Azhar. And back he went through the second phase along the road between the Al-Azhar and his lodgings into the third and final phase, where he was left alone in his place in the corner of the old carpet stretched out over a rotten worn-out mat.

Chapter XII

Such was the building in which the boy settled and the surroundings in which he lived. In all probability the experience of life and of human character which he gained there at first hand were at least as beneficial to him as the progress he made at the Azhar in grammar and logic, law and theology.

Two or three days after he arrived his brother handed him over to a shaykh who had won his degree that same summer and was to begin teaching for the first time in his life by taking a class of boys. He was a man round about forty, with a reputation for soundness and intelligence. He had wrestled with fortune and won. It was not, to be sure, a victory equal to his merits, for though he had done well to pass and be placed in the second class, he was thought extremely unlucky not to have got into the first. His intelligence was limited to book learning. When he ventured on practical affairs he showed himself more of a simpleton than anything else. He was known among his friends, teachers and students alike, as a man passionately addicted to material pleasures, to which he was drawn not so much by vice or perversion as by a natural extravagance of impulse. He was a notoriously big eater, with an insatiable craving for meat. Not for one single day could he restrain that colossal appetite, however great the demands it made upon him.

Apart from this he had a most extraordinary voice, at once tremulous and jerky. He tried to cut off one syllable from another, but they would persist in getting jumbled together again, though he opened his lips much wider than he should have done. No one could talk to him for long without laughing, and sooner or later you were bound to start aping the tremors and jerks of his voice and the way in which he mouthed his words.

He had scarcely taken his degree before he rushed off to buy the insignia, including the doctor's gown, which he started to wear immediately. In the normal way the shaykhs never wore it until some time after they had earned their degrees, when they had already built up a certain reputation and found themselves in easier circumstances.

But this fellow took to a gown straight away, much to the amusement of his friends, both shaykhs and students. They laughed all the more sarcastically in that, although he wore a gown, he went as barefoot as a beggar—inside his shoes. He never wore socks, either because he couldn't afford to, or for abstinence's sake. In the streets he affected a ponderous stride and a lofty academic air, but as soon as he had stepped over the threshold of Al-Azhar all his gravity vanished and he broke into an undignified trot.

The boy recognised his step before he heard his voice. Arriving for this first lecture with the usual shambling gait, he tripped over the boy and almost fell; his sockless ankles touched the boy, and their coarse skin scratched his hand. He went on and sat down, propping his back for the first time where he had for so long yearned to put it, against the lecturer's column.

This shaykh, like many of his contemporaries, was at once highly accomplished in the sciences of Al-Azhar and severely critical of the traditional method of teaching. He had been much influenced by the teachings of the imam, but had not really taken it to heart. He was neither a genuine reformer nor yet a die-hard, but something between the two. This was enough to make the shaikhs look askance at him and regard him with a certain anxiety and mistrust. At the very beginning of his first lecture on sacred law he announced to his class that he had no intention of reading with them the book which beginners were usually started on, *Maraqi-l-Falah ʿala Nur al-Idah*,[102] but that he would give them lessons of his own, which would be well up to the level of *Maraqi-l-Falah*. Their job was to listen carefully, make sure that they understood and take what notes they needed. He then began his lecture, which proved extremely useful and interesting. He followed the same method in his grammar lectures. He neither read Al-Kafrawi's *Commentary*,[103] nor taught the nine ways of reciting 'Bismillah al-Rahman al-Rahim'[104] and the syntax of its inflexions. He gave them a solid grounding in grammar, defining the word and the sentence, the noun, the verb and the particle. This lecture too was both clear and interesting.

---

[102] *Steps to Success* from *The Light of Clarity*, a Hanafite textbook dating from the eleventh century.

[103] This book and Khalid's are the two most valued commentaries on the fourteenth-century *Ajurrumi* [Ajurrumiyya], the main elementary grammar in use at Al-Azhar to this day.

[104] 'In the name of God, the Merciful, the Compassionate'—the opening words of the Qur'an.

At tea-time that afternoon the boy was asked what he had been told at his law and grammar lessons. When he repeated what he had heard to his brother and the rest of the group they were pleased with what he told them about the shaykh and approved his method of teaching. So the boy continued to attend these two lectures every weekday, for how long he cannot remember. He was continually wondering when he would be admitted to Al-Azhar as a regular student and have his name inscribed on the registers. As yet he was merely a boy attending no more than two lectures in a regular, organised way. He went to one other, the lecture on tradition after the dawn prayer, but that was only to fill in the time till his brother came away from his lecture on first principles, which was when the law lesson began.

At last the great day came. After the lecture on law the boy was told to present himself for a test in the recitation of the Qur'an, which was to qualify him for entry to Al-Azhar. He had not been notified beforehand and so had not prepared for the examination at all. If he had been given notice he would have gone through the Qur'an once or twice by himself before the test, but it had not occurred to him to recite the Qur'an since the day of his arrival in Cairo. So when he was told that he was to be examined in an hour's time his heart began to throb with anxiety. He hurried off to the scene of the examination at the Chapel of the Blind in a state of extreme nervousness and trepidation. However, as soon as he came face to face with the examiners his fear suddenly left him and gave place to the bitterest distress: Something happened then which he was never to forget. He had been waiting for the two examiners to finish with the student before him when suddenly he heard one of them call him in words which fell cruelly on his ears and seared his heart with anguish: 'You next, blind boy.'

It would never have occurred to him that these words were addressed to himself if it had not been for his brother, who without saying a word seized him none too gently by the hand and led him in front of the examiners. He had been used to great consideration on this point from his family, who avoided mentioning the affliction in his presence. He appreciated this delicacy on their part, though he never forgot his blindness and was always brooding upon it. Despite this shock he sat down in front of the examiners, who asked him to recite the *sura*(h) of the Cave. But he had scarcely started on this before he was told to turn to the *sura*(h) of the Spider, and after a few verses of that one of the examiners said 'That's enough, blind boy, you're admitted.'

The boy was scandalised by this examination, which had no sense in it at all and was no test of memory whatever. He had been expecting at the very least that the board would examine him on the grammar which his father used to test at home. He went off very pleased with his success but furious with the examiners, whose negligence he found inexcusable. Before he left the Chapel of the Blind, however, his brother drew him off to one side, where a servant took his right arm and put a token round his wrist consisting of a piece of thread connected by a leaden seal. 'That's all,' said the man. 'Congratulations!'

The boy did not understand the meaning of this token. But his brother explained that he must keep it on his wrist for a full week until he had seen the doctor, who would examine his health, estimate his age and vaccinate him against smallpox.

The boy had reason to be excited over this bracelet, since it was the token of his success at the qualifying examination. The first lap, then, was over; except that he was still haunted by the brutal words with which the examiner had summoned and dismissed him. The week ran its course in the usual way. He woke at the sound of Uncle Hajj ᶜAli's voice; left for Al-Azhar at dawn and came back after the lecture on law; returned to Al-Azhar again at noon for the lecture on grammar, then stayed still in his corner until night. Next morning he would be off to Al-Azhar as soon as he heard the muezzin cry, 'Prayer is better than sleep.'

The day of the medical examination arrived and the boy turned up for it in a state of trepidation; he was afraid that the doctor might summon him in the same way as the examiners had done. Nothing of the sort, however; there was no summoning this time at all. The boy's brother piloted him to the doctor, who took his arm and made the necessary incisions. 'Fifteen,' he said and that was all. So now the boy was on the list of students at Al-Azhar, though he had not yet reached the age mentioned by the doctor and required by the regulations. He was only thirteen. However, the bracelet was taken off his wrist and he went back home full of misgivings as to the good faith of the examiners and of the doctor. He scarcely knew whether to laugh or to weep.

Chapter XV

The most obvious practical change was that he left his place in the corner of the room on that old carpet spread over a tattered, worn-out mat. He scarcely used it any more except when he sat down to lunch or supper and when he retired to bed at nightfall. Almost the whole of his day was spent at Al-Azhar and in the other mosques nearby where lectures might also take place. When he came back to the tenement he only slipped into the room to take off his coat, and then went outside again to sit with his companion on a strip of felt mattress which was spread out in front of the door and took up more than half the passage, so that there was no space for more than one or two people to walk past.

The two boys passed their time either talking or, more frequently, reading. They broke off now and again to attend to anything interesting which occurred on the floor below. One would listen to the conversation while the other watched what was going on and described what he saw to his companion.

In this way the boy got to know the building a great deal better than before. He learnt much more about its occupants' affairs and listened to many more of its conversations. He came out of his seclusion and began to live a much freer life. However, the most fruitful and interesting hours of his life after this friend's arrival were spent neither in his room nor in the block, but within Al-Azhar itself. The boy was able to rest in his room after the dawn lecture until it was time for the lecture on law. Thus he listened with his friend every morning to the stammering prayers of the shaykh with the obsession, which before that he had only been able to relish once a week, on Fridays.

When the time came for the lecture to begin he went off with his companion towards Al-Azhar by the route he used to take with his brother; only now they would talk excitedly or joke together all the way. They often avoided the filthy, bat-ridden alley and went down Shariᶜa Khan Gafar [Jaᶜfar], which was much cleaner but also brought them out into Shariᶜa Sayyidna-l-Husayn. Another change was that, after his friends' arrival, the boy acquired a habit of never passing the Mosque of Sayyidna-l-Husayn, much less going inside, without saying a Fatiha. The custom, which he learnt from his friend, soon became ingrained. The years passed by and his mode of life changed, but he cannot recall ever passing this mosque without saying over to himself the hallowed words of the first chapter of the Qur'an.[105]

For their meals the boy's brother allowed him and his companion an extremely small sum of money, with the right to claim his own ration of bread, consisting of four loaves, from the Hanafite section[106] every morning. They ate two of the loaves for lunch and kept the two others for supper. Though their money allowance was minute in the extreme—no more than one piastre a day—they learned how to lay it out economically so as to enjoy a fair number of the delicacies they hankered after. Some days they even got up with the birds, passed through the narrow opening in the still locked door and picked their way towards Al-Azhar. On the road they would stop at a *balila*[107] shop and each take a large helping. They adored *balila*, for they were used to eating quantities of it in the country. They loved the sugar which was poured over it to mix with the big grains and melt in the boiling broth. No sooner did it touch their lips than the last traces of sleep disappeared; a delicious warmth spread through their mouths and stomachs, and primed their whole bodies with energy. It was a splendid preparation for the law lecture. Now they could listen to what the shaykh was saying with a sense of well-being in body and mind alike.

[105] The Fatiha is said here as a prayer for the soul of Husayn, who was killed defending his claim to the Prophet's succession.

[106] There are twenty-six sections in Al-Azhar into which students pass according to their rite or place of origin. A section is strictly the space between two pillars, and might perhaps be rendered 'house'. The Hanafites, belonging to one of the four rites of orthodox Islam, have a section of their own. Another section, the Fashnite, caters for students from Middle Egypt.

[107] Boiled maize or wheat: a very sweet concoction, often eaten with milk or butter.

Nor were they too poor to turn aside in Shariᶜa Sayyidna-l-Husayn and sit down on the narrow wooden bench outside one of the food shops. There might or might not be a strip of mat on the hard wood, but in any case it seemed to them as soft as down to sit on as they waited in blissful anticipation for bowls of soaked figs to be brought to them. They eagerly swallowed these and drank down the juice, then stayed quiet for a while chewing the raisins which were left at the bottom.

They even had enough money, on their way home in the morning or the afternoon, to stop at a sweetshop and indulge their harmless passion for *harissa*[108] or *bassbussa*[109] without spoiling their appetite for lunch or supper.

Lunch was a simple affair. It meant going to one of the shops which sold boiled beans, and eating them with two of the four loaves. Two portions of *ful* [beans] cost two and a half milliemes; and they bought a bunch or two of leeks for half a millieme. The shopkeeper brought them a big bowl of soup with beans swimming in it and a little oil to taste. They dipped their bread in the soup and chased the beans out with it as best they could, using the other hand to help themselves to leeks. By the time they had finished the bread and the leeks they had had enough to eat, and in fact almost too much: but there was still some broth left in the bowl. The boy was ashamed to accept it at first, but when his cousin laughed at him for this and held out the bowl for him to finish he finally drank up the soup and gave the bowl back clean to the proprietor.

Thus their lunch cost them not more than three milliemes—not to mention what they had eaten before lectures began. It only remained for them to go back to Al-Azhar and fill their brains as they had filled their bodies. The boy was very careful never to miss his law and grammar lectures with the shaykh who was half-reformer and half-conservative, not only out of obedience to his brother but also for his own personal satisfaction. But he was also extremely anxious to hear other lecturers and savour other subjects. This he could now do without any difficulty, thanks to the lectures which were given late in the morning when students came back from their lunch. The two friends determined to attend a lecture on Al-Kafrawi's *Commentary* which was given every day at this time by a shaykh who had only just qualified, though he had been connected with Al-Azhar for a very long time. He was already quite old and had spent many years studying for his degree. When at last he achieved it he began in the usual way by reading Al-Kafrawi's *Commentary*.

The boy had heard a good deal of adverse criticism of this book both from his teachers and from his brothers' friends. But the more they decried it the more interested he became. He could not be deterred from going to the first lecture

---

[108] *Harissa* is a sweetmeat made with flour or butter.

[109] *Bassbussa* is a nut-cake of Syrian origin.

and learning the nine ways of reciting 'Bismillah al-Rahman al-Rahim,' case-endings and all. In fact he quite fell in love with this branch of learning, and he and his companion became as regular attendants at this grammar lecture as they were at the other. Nevertheless he realised that it was at the other lecture that he learnt his grammar; here he only learnt to laugh. This new lecture was a genuine source of amusement, because of the unending inflexions which the commentator insisted on citing, and above all on account of the shaykh himself, who read the text and the commentary in an extraordinarily laughable voice. He did not so much read as sing it, and the sounds did not come up from his chest but down from his head. His voice combined two contradictory qualities; it was at once dull and rich, muffled and full.

He was an Upper Egyptian, from the furthest south, and had kept the dialect of his province without any modification either in speaking, recitation or chanting. He had a fiery temperament and whether he was reading, asking questions, or answering objections, his manner was uniformly harsh. He was easily provoked to anger, and to question him was to earn an insult. Anyone who persisted in an inquiry was liable to have his ears boxed if he was close up, or get a shoe thrown at him if he was sitting further away. The shaykh's shoe was as big as his voice was loud, and every bit as rough as his clothes—he did not wear an overcoat, but only a coarse cloak—and its sole was studded with nails to protect it against wear and tear. One can imagine, then, what it was like to be hit in the face, or anywhere else for that matter, by so formidable a shoe.

The result was that students were afraid to ask questions, and whether the shaikh was reading, explaining, criticizing, or chanting they never interrupted. So he never wasted either his own time or that of his students. He began the academic year with Al-Kafrawi's *Commentary* and before the end he had finished Shaykh Khalid's book as well. In this way his students read two books in a single year, while the other shaykhs' classes had looked at no more than one. As for our conservative-liberal, he with his tiny group of students had not gone beyond the first few chapters of the grammar.

All this had its influence on the boy's grammatical experience, if such an expression may be allowed. When he came back to Cairo after his summer holiday he found the conservative-liberal had gone. So he followed the normal course for an Azharite; in law he attended a lecture on Taᶜy's commentary on the *Kanz*,[110] and in grammar one on Al-Attar's notes to the commentary on *Al-Azhariya*.[111] But it is better not to anticipate events but to go back to the boy's first year.

---

[110] *Kanz al-Daqa'iq* ('Treasury of Extracts') is a Hanafite law-book by the thirteenth-century Persian jurist Al-Nasafi. Taᶜy lived in Egypt in the eighteenth century.

[111] Short title for *The Azharite Introduction to Arabic Studies*. Al-Attar (1766–1834?) was rector of Al-Azhar from 1828 until his death.

After the late morning lesson he used to go off to the midday lecture and then return home with his cousin to read over the material for the next day's lectures, as all really serious students did, or to pick out passages from various books, whether he understood them or not. As the sun moved towards its setting the two friends turned their minds to supper, in a mood which varied from gloom to exaltation according to the amount of money they had left. If they still had half a piastre they would split it in two and buy with one quarter some *halawa*[112] and with the other a little Greek cheese. This made a really luxurious supper. They took a piece of cheese and piece of *halawa* together in one mouthful, and considered this strange combination extremely palatable. But if they had spent some of their money on *balila* or figs then there would only be a quarter of a piastre left them. In this case they bought a little sesame paste[113] and poured on it some of the black or white honey which they had from the country. This would not be too rich a supper, but it might well have been worse.

Sometimes, however, what with *balila* or figs or both of them together, they had spent all their money and had nothing left at all. No matter: they had kept the two loaves and there were two reserve tins in the room, one containing black honey to dip the two loaves in, and make do with that instead of luxuries like *halawa* and cheese and sesame paste. They even contrived to give a relish to these iron rations by dipping their bread alternately in the white honey and the black.

Now the sun was lowering towards the west and soon the muezzin would be climbing his minaret. The two boys must be off to Al-Azhar at once. Like the older students they attended a lecture after evening prayer. It was a course on logic, and the text used was Al-Akhdari's *Sullam*.[114] The lecturer was a shaykh who considered himself learned, but whose title to learning Al-Azhar had never recognised. He went on studying year after year and persisted in trying for a degree, but without success. He never despaired, and was never satisfied with the examiners' verdict; so in the end they found him not only tedious but provoking as well. He bored them by his constant attendance at lectures and his annual reappearance at the examination. But what really infuriated them was his practice of sitting down beside one of the columns after evening prayer, surrounded by a circle of students, and reading a book on logic to them just as if he were an eminent shaykh. For logic was a subject which only the most distinguished of the doctors would venture upon.

Certain it is that this student shaykh was remarkable neither for learning nor for teaching ability. His ignorance and incapacity were obvious even to these beginners. He too came from the furthermost part of Upper Egypt, and his speech remained exactly as it had been before he came up to Al-Azhar. Nothing

---

[112] *Halawa tihiniya* is a thick sticky sweet made of sesame paste, sugar, almond oil, and almonds.

[113] Sesame paste, one of the ingredients of *halawa*, is a sort of sticky flour consisting of the dregs of sesame oil. [114] The *Stairway* is a treatise written in ninety-four verses, around the year 1534.

was changed either in his way of talking or of reading. Moreover he was easily provoked and violent in his anger. Not that he ever insulted the students or knocked them about; he did not dare to intrude on the privileges of the genuine doctors, who acquired a licence to such things when they took their degrees.

All this might be true, and the two boys had been told about it by the others. But that did not prevent them from attending regularly at this lecture, so that they might be able to tell themselves that they were learning logic and visiting Al-Azhar between sunset and nightfall, just as the advanced students did.

The first year sped by like a flash and it seemed no time before the law and grammar courses were over. Soon the students would be saying goodbye and going off to spend the summer in their native towns and villages. Ah, how the boy had longed for this holiday, and how homesick he had been for the country! But now that the holiday had actually arrived here he was hoping the journey would be put off so that he could stay in Cairo. Was he sincere in this attitude, or did he have other reasons for taking it? Yes and no.

He was sincere in that he loved Cairo and hated leaving it now that he knew it so well. Moreover he never liked travelling. But he also felt obliged to stay by the fact that his brother used to spend most of his holidays in Cairo and thus earned the approval of his people, who considered this a sign of the most praiseworthy diligence. The boy wished to do as his brother did, so as to be equally well thought of. But all this self-denial was of no use. One day he and his companion were packed off in a gharry with their clothes tied up in a pair of bundles. At the station they were provided with tickets and deposited in a crowded third-class carriage. The train moved off and had barely passed a couple of stations before they had forgotten all about Cairo and Al-Azhar and the building they lived in. They could only think of one thing and that was the country with all its promise of happiness and delight.

Selected bibliography

CACHIA, PIERRE, *Taha Husain: His Place in the Egyptian Literary Renaissance* (London: Luzac, 1956).

CATON, STEVEN, *Peaks of Yemen I Summon* (Berkeley: University of California Press 1990).

CHAMBERS, RICHARD L., 'The Ottoman Ulama and the Tanzimat', in Nikki R. Keddie (ed.), *Scholars, Saints and Sufis: Muslim Religious Institutions in the Middle East Since 1500* (Berkeley and London: University of California Press, 1972).

CRONIN, STEPHANIE, *The Making of the Modern Iran: State and Society Under Riza Shah Pahlavi, 1921–1941* (London, New York: Routledge Curzon, 2003).

FINDLEY, CARTER V., *Bureaucratic Reform in The Ottoman Empire: The Sublime Porte, 1789–1922* (Princeton: Princeton University Press, 1980).

—— *Ottoman Civil Officialdom: A Social History* (Princeton: Princeton University Press, 1989).

FREITAG, ULRIKE, 'A Poetic Exchange About Imperialism', in Lutz Edzard and Christian Szyska (eds.), *Encounters of Words and Texts: Intercultural Studies in Honor of Stefan Wild* (Hildesheim, Zürich, and New York: Georg Olms Verlag 1997).

—— and WILLIAM G. CLARENCE-SMITH (eds.), *Hadhrami Traders, Scholars and Statesmen in the Indian Ocean, 1750s–1960s* (Leiden: E. J. Brill, 1997).

GHANI, SIRUS, *Iran and the Rise of Reza Shah: From Qajar Collapse to Pahlavi Rule* (London and New York: I. B. Tauris, 1998).

GIBB, E. J. W., *A History of Ottoman Poetry*, 4 (London, 1967).

HAMADEH, SHIRINE, 'The City's Pleasures: Architectural Sensibility in Eighteenth-Century Istanbul', Ph.D thesis, MIT (1999).

HANAWAY, WILLIAM, 'Five Mystical Ghazals by the Ayatollah Khomeini', *Iranian Studies*, 30/3–4 (Summer/Fall, 1997), 273–6.

HEYD, URIEL, 'The Ottoman Ulema and Westernization in the Time of Selim III and Mahmud II', *Scripta Hierosolymitana*, 9, *Studies in Islamic History and Civilization*, edited on behalf of the School of Oriental Studies by Uriel Heyd (Jerusalem: The Hebrew University, 1961).

HUSAYN, TAHA, *The Future of Culture in Egypt*, trans. Sydney Blazer (Washington, D.C.: American Council of Learned Societies, 1954; repr. New York: Octagon Books, 1975).

INGRAMS, HAROLD, *Arabia and the Isles*, 3rd edn. (London: John Murray, 1966).

KARPAT, KEMAL, 'The Land Regime, Social Structure, and Modernization in the Ottoman Empire', in William R. Polk and Richard L. Chambers (eds.), *Beginning of Modernization in The Middle East: The Nineteenth Century* (Chicago: Chicago University Press, 1968).

—— (ed.), *Ottoman Past and Today's Turkey* (Leiden and Boston: Brill, 2000).

—— *Studies on Ottoman Social and Political History: Selected Articles and Essays* (Leiden: Brill, 2002).

KURAN, APTULLAH, 'Eighteenth Century Ottoman Architecture', in T. Naff and R. Owen (eds.), *Studies in Eighteenth-Century Islamic History* (Chicago: University of Chicago Press, 1977).

LEVY, AVIGDOR, 'The Ottoman Ulema and the Military Reforms of Sultan Mahmut II', *Asian and African Studies*, 7 (1971).

LEWIS, BERNARD, *The Emergence of Modern Turkey*, 2nd edn. (London: Oxford University Press, 1968).

LOSENSKY, PAUL E., 'Elegies for a Lost Leader: Six Poems on the Death of Khomeini', *Iranian Studies*, 30/3–4 (Summer/Fall, 1997), 277–89.

MILLER, W. FLAGG, 'Metaphors of Commerce: Trans-valuing Tribalism in Yemeni Audiocassette Poetry', *International Journal of Middle East Studies*, 34:1 (2002), 29–57.

MOIN, BAQER, *Khomeini: Life of the Ayatollah* (London and New York: I. B. Tauris, 1999).

PORTERFIELD, AMANDA, *Mary Lyon and the Mount Holyoke Missionaries* (New York: Oxford University Press, 1997), 68–86.

RODIONOV, MIKHAIL, 'Poetry and Power in Hadramawt'; *New Arabian Studies*, 3(1996).

SERJEANT, ROBERT B., *Prose and Poetry from Hadhramawt*, 1st edn. (London: Taylor's Foreign Press, 1951).

SHAW, STANFORD, AND EZEL KURAL SHAW, *History of the Ottoman Empire and Modern Turkey*, Volume II: *Reform, Revolution, and Republic: The Rise of Modern Turkey, 1808–1975* (Cambridge: Cambridge University Press, 1978).

SHIMMON, PAUL, *Massacres of Syrian Christians in N.W. Persia and Kurdistan* (London: Wells Gardner, Darton & Co., 1915).

WERDA, JOEL E., *The Flickering Light of Asia: Or, the Assyrian Nation and Church*, 2nd edn. (Chicago: Assyrian Language and Culture Classes, 1990).

8

Economic change

Part 1: Economic data
Michael Twomey

Introduction

An important complement to the historical study of a geographical region is knowledge about the quantitative aspects of the region's growth and development. The purpose of the tables in this chapter is to present and review several main economic and social indicators for the countries in the Middle East, North Africa, and the Indian subcontinent. Our principal goal is to familiarize the reader with the sort of information that is available. This involves considerations of how far back in time a certain variable can be measured, as well as for what countries coverage can be found. Some comments are presented at the bottoms of the tables, while others of a more general type are presented in the 'Comments' section following the tables.

In most cases, the data in the tables have been reported by international agencies such as the United Nations and the World Bank, which in turn have relied on national sources, usually governments, for most of their information. The presentation of the tables proceeds from social to economic variables; from population and vital statistics to national income, then on to sectoral groupings—agriculture, foreign trade and investment, petroleum and railroads—before ending with migration, within the region, and towards Europe. It is inevitable that the selection of items to include reflects the professional inclinations of an economist who looks to historians for insights about contemporary problems.

It will become clear that the coverage in most tables begins during the twentieth century, and for at least half of these tables the data begin after mid-century. In general, the longest series are available for Egypt, Turkey, and India, reflecting the greater care that was taken to collect statistics in these areas, as well as the closer attention they have received from empirically oriented social scientists.

Our longer-term goal is to encourage and facilitate further work, either extending chronologically the various series, or the construction and analysis of cross-country comparisons. The work of Şevket Pamuk on Turkey has been an especially fruitful example of the first type of exercise, while that of Angus Maddison currently defines the state of the art of cross-country comparisons. Both authors are well represented in the bibliography.

List of Tables

TABLE 8.1. Population, 1900–2000 (millions)

	1900	1950	1975	2000
Algeria	5.0	8.9	16.1	31.1
Bahrain	—	0.1	0.3	0.6
Bangladesh	—	45.6	76.3	130.4
Egypt	10.0	21.2	37.0	70.5
India (3)	280.0	*454.9*	*771.5*	*1,274.7*
India	—	369.9	620.5	1,002.7
Iran	10.0	16.4	33.4	66.0
Iraq	2.3	5.2	11.1	22.7
Israel	—	1.3	3.4	5.8
Jordan	0.3	0.6	1.8	5.0
Kuwait	—	0.1	1.0	2.0
Lebanon	0.5	1.4	3.1	3.6
Libya	0.8	1.0	2.6	5.1
Morocco	5.0	9.3	17.7	30.1
Oman	0.4	0.5	0.9	2.5
Pakistan	—	39.4	74.7	141.6
Qatar	—	<0.05	0.2	0.7
Saudi Arabia	2.5	3.9	7.2	22.0
Sudan	6.0	8.1	16.1	35.1
Syria	1.8	3.5	7.4	16.3
Tunisia	1.5	3.5	5.7	9.6
Turkey	14.0	21.1	40.5	65.7
UAE	—	0.1	0.5	2.4
West Bank and Gaza	—	1.0	1.1	2.6
Yemen	3.0	4.8	7.9	17.5
Palestinians	0.5	*1.5*	*3.5*	*7.7*
Gulf States	0.2	*0.3*	—	—
Ottoman Empire	25.0	—	—	—

Note: 'India (3)' includes post-Partition Bangladesh, Pakistan, and India.

Source: Column 1 from McEvedy and Jones (1978). Columns 2–4 from US Bureau of the Census website, *International Data Base* <http://www.census.gov/ipc/www/idbnew.html>, downloaded May 2003; data for West Bank and Gaza from Maddison (2001). Author's calculations in italics. The datum for the Gulf States in 1950 is the sum of the individual countries. The series on Palestinians uses the McEvedy and Jones datum for 1900, and interpolations from Abu-Lughod (1995, 411) for 'Arabs of Palestinian birth or descent'. That author estimated that in 1992 60% of Palestinians lived outside of Mandatory Palestine, and 21% outside of Palestine, the East Bank, Lebanon, and Syria. McEvedy and Jones (1978) estimated the Gulf Coast population in 1950 at 0.5 million; and that for Palestine in 1950 as 2.25 million.

TABLE 8.2. Population growth, 1950s and 1990s (%)

	Population growth rate		Birth rate		Death rate		Max. population growth	
	1950s	1990s	1950s	1990s	1950s	1990s	rate	Year
Algeria	2.6	1.6	51	19	24	4	3.2	1983
Bahrain	3.6	3.6	—	21	—	3	5.2	1980
Bangladesh	—	1.4	—	31	—	10	2.6	1985
Egypt	2.4	2.1	44	28	19	7	2.6	1965&1983
India	1.3	1.7	41	26	24	9	2.3	1966
Iran	2.4	1.5	33	19	10	6	3.7	1984
Iraq	3.1	2.7	49	37	22	10	3.3	1987
Israel	3.8	2.5	35	22	7	6	3.2	1972
Jordan	3.1	2.9	45	28	21	3	3.6	1996
Kuwait	2.4	3.9	45	20	11	2	5.7	1992
Lebanon	2.8	2.0	20	20	7	5	3.0	1962
Libya	1.5	2.1	48	19	23	3	4.5	1981
Morocco	1.9	1.7	50	19	26	4	2.8	1986
Oman	—	2.4	51	35	32	4	5.4	1981
Pakistan	1.4	2.3	50	38	28	11	3.2	1973
Qatar	—	2.0	—	20	—	2	9.4	1970
Saudi Arabia	—	3.5	51	25	32	3	5.6	1982
Sudan	—	2.1	45	36	26	12	3.0	1981
Syria	4.2	2.8	47	31	21	4	3.6	1983
Tunisia	1.4	1.3	30	17	10	6	2.7	1984
Turkey	2.7	1.5	45	23	18	7	2.5	1983
UAE	—	—	—	16	—	4	17.6	1975
West Bank and Gaza	—	3.8	—	42	—	5	—	—
Yemen	—	3.5	51	22	32	7	4.0	1979

Earlier data:

	1920–4		1938	
	Egypt	India	Egypt	India
Birth rate	43	33	43	33
Death rate	26	27	26	24

Source: Population growth, birth rates, and death rates for the 1950s from UN *Statistical Yearbook, 1960*, and those for Libya and Sudan, UN *Demographic Yearbook 1979*. Population growth rates for 1995–2000 from UN *Demographic Yearbook 2000*; for Israel and Pakistan from UN *Statistical Yearbook 1999*. The maximum rate of population growth was obtained using three-year averages of the data on the *World Development Indicators* CD-Rom for 2002. Earlier birth and death rates for Egypt and India from UN *Statistical Yearbook 1952*.

TABLE 8.3. Vital statistics, 1950–2000

	Total fertility rate		Infant mortality (per 1,000 live births)		Life expectancy at birth (years)	
	Late 1960s	Late 1990s	1950s	Late 1990s	Early 1950s	Late 1990s
Algeria	7	3	80	35	43	68
Bahrain	5	3	—	9	—	73
Bangladesh	7	3	—	79	38	58
Egypt	7	4	130	29	42	67
India	6	3	126	73	41	62
Iran	8	3	108	33	42	68
Iraq	7	5	97	92	43	59
Israel	4	3	47	6	72	78
Jordan	7	5	107	—	43	—
Kuwait	7	4	33	9	56	—
Lebanon	6	2	13	20	54	73
Libya	7	4	80	18	43	70
Morocco	7	3	149	17	43	67
Oman	7	6	—	27	35	71
Pakistan	7	5	124	95	39	59
Qatar	7	—	—	10	—	—
Saudi Arabia	7	6	—	20	35	71
Sudan	7	5	94	86	34	55
Syria	8	4	40	27	44	71
Tunisia	7	2	74	26	44	71
Turkey	5	3	153	37	48	—
UAE	7	3	—	8	—	75
West Bank and Gaza	—	6	—	24	—	71
Yemen	7	3	—	74	33	59

Earlier periods:

	1920–4	1938
Infant mortality in Egypt (per 1,000 live births)	141	163

Notes: The total fertility rate is the average number of children that would be born alive to a hypothetical cohort of women, if throughout their reproductive years, the age-specific fertility rates for the specified year remained unchanged. As such, it is an indirect measure of how many children would be born throughout her lifetime, to an average woman in that reference year.

Source: Various issues of the UN *Demographic Yearbook* and the UN *Statistical Yearbook*, and author's calculations. Generally, the data for the first reference year was taken from the *Demographic Yearbook* for 1979, which provided historical data. For some countries, the first year benchmark years, for infant mortality were, after 1950: Morocco, 1962; Tunisia, 1960; Iran, 1972; Libya, 1972; Kuwait, 1960; Pakistan, 1968; Turkey, 1967. For Israel, the first reference year on life expectancy was 1961. Earlier data for Egypt from the UN *Statistical Yearbook 1952*. The data for Algeria in 1950 were calculated as a weighted average for data on Europeans and Muslims, from UN *Statistical Yearbook 1952*.

TABLE 8.4. Other social measures

	Illiteracy rate (%)			HDI		Index of freedom			
						1972–3		2001–2	
	1950s	1970s	2000	1975	2000	P	C	P	C
Algeria	83	74	33	0.50	0.70	6	6	6	5
Bahrain	87	60	12	—	0.83	6	5	6	5
Bangladesh	—	74	59	0.34	0.48	2	4	3	4
Egypt	75	62	45	0.44	0.64	6	6	6	6
India	81	67	43	0.41	0.58	2	3	2	3
Iran	87	64	24	0.56	0.72	5	6	6	6
Iraq	89	76	44	—	—	7	7	7	7
Israel	—	12	5	0.79	0.90	2	3	1	3
Jordan	—	46	10	—	0.72	6	6	5	5
Kuwait	66	40	18	0.75	0.81	4	4	4	5
Lebanon	—	37	14	—	0.76	2	2	6	5
Libya	87	50	20	—	0.77	7	6	7	7
Morocco	86	79	51	0.43	0.60	5	4	5	5
Oman	—	81	28	—	0.75	7	6	6	5
Pakistan	81	79	57	0.35	0.50	3	5	6	5
Qatar	—	42	19	—	0.80	6	5	6	6
Saudi Arabia	—	67	24	0.59	0.76	6	6	7	7
Sudan	88	85	42	0.35	0.50	6	6	7	7
Syria	—	60	26	0.54	0.69	7	7	7	7
Tunisia	84	62	29	0.51	0.72	6	5	6	5
Turkey	68	40	15	0.59	0.74	3	4	4	5
UAE	—	44	24	—	0.81	7	5	6	5
West Bank and Gaza	—	—	14	—	—	—	—	6	5
Yemen	—	86	54	—	0.48	—	—	6	6

Regional totals

	Illiteracy		HDI
	1970	2000	2000
Middle East and North Africa	70	35	0.65
East Asia and Pacific	44	14	0.73
Latin America and Caribbean	26	12	0.77
Sub-Saharan Africa	72	39	0.47
South Asia	68	45	0.57
High-income OECD	—	—	0.93
World	—	—	0.72

Note: The Human Development Index (HDI) is a measure that attempts to capture a broader vision of human development than, for example, per capita GDP. The HDI is scaled; its values range from 0 to 1, incorporating data on life expectancy, adult literacy, school enrolment ratios, and GDP per capita. For the year 2000 its values ranged from 0.942 (Norway) to 0.275 (Sierra Leone). The Index of Freedom attempts to measure Political Rights (P) and Civil Liberties (C). It is measured on a scale from 1 to 7, lower numbers indicating more freedom. The table's reference year for the West Bank and Gaza was 1995–6; since then these areas have been disaggregated into Israeli- and Palestinian-administered; for the year 2000 the former received scores of 6, 5, while the latter scores were 5 and 6, respectively.

Source: Illiteracy for years around 1950 from UNESCO *Statistical Yearbook* (1963), and UN *Statistical Yearbook* 1952; for 1970s the UNESCO *Statistical Yearbook* (1981) and *World Development Indicators* for 2000 from the UN *Statistical Yearbook* 46. For the West Bank and Gaza for the year 2000, from the World Bank's website <http://www.worldbank.org/data/countrydata/aag/wbg_aag.pdf/>. For HDI: United Nations Human Development Programme, *Human Development Report*, 2002. The Index of Freedom was downloaded from the website of the Freedom House <http://www.freedomhouse. org/ratings/>, a private-sector research group in Washington, DC, in April 2003. No HDI data were reported for Iraq, nor for West Bank and Gaza.

TABLE 8.5. Gender issues: ratio of indicators for females to males, in per cent

	Labour force Participation			Adult illiteracy		Persistence to fifth grade education	
	1950	1970	1995	1970	2000	1975	1995
Algeria	18	24	33	130	180	97	101
Bahrain	4	6	32	164	192	—	101
Bangladesh	68	73	77	137	147	—	—
Egypt	29	36	42	155	168	92	—
India	55	56	50	153	173	—	—
Iran	21	24	33	142	183	—	—
Iraq	18	20	23	141	157	99	—
Israel	28	44	65	207	239	—	—
Jordan	14	16	28	236	327	98	—
Kuwait	6	11	48	159	127	—	—
Lebanon	12	23	37	205	250	—	—
Libya	23	22	28	197	346	92	—
Morocco	37	46	53	135	168	100	97
Oman	3	7	18	139	193	—	100
Pakistan	25	30	38	134	170	—	—
Qatar	3	6	29	143	86	99	103
Saudi Arabia	3	6	19	165	195	97	105
Sudan	35	36	40	151	176	57	98
Syria	28	31	35	201	337	90	102
Tunisia	23	30	45	144	212	91	101
Turkey	85	63	58	225	360	—	—
UAE	3	8	27	153	83	102	101
West Bank and Gaza	—	—	18	—	288	—	—
Yemen	33	36	39	134	230	—	—

Source: Author's calculations, based on: labour force participation data in International Labour Organisation, *Economically Active Population 1950–2010*, 4th edn.; data on illiteracy and persistence to fifth grade education in the World Bank, *World Development Indicators 2002* (CD-Rom). Data on the West Bank and Gaza from the website of the Palestinian Bureau of Statistics <www.pcbs.org/inside/selcts/>.

TABLE 8.6. Urban population as a percentage of total population, 1950–2000

	1950	1975	2000
Algeria	22	40	57
Bahrain	64	79	92
Bangladesh	4	10	25
Egypt	32	43	43
India	17	21	28
Iran	27	46	64
Iraq	35	61	68
Israel	65	87	92
Jordan	36	58	79
Kuwait	59	84	96
Lebanon	23	67	90
Libya	19	61	88
Morocco	26	38	55
Pakistan	17	26	33
Qatar	64	83	93
Saudi Arabia	16	58	86
Sudan	6	19	36
Syria	31	45	51
Oman	2	20	76
Tunisia	31	50	66
Turkey	21	42	66
UAE	24	65	87
Yemen	6	17	25

Regional averages:

	1950	1975	2000
Near East	22	41	56
East and Southeast Asia	16	26	42
Latin America	42	61	75
Sub-Saharan Africa	9	19	32
Industrial countries	62	74	78
World	30	38	47

Source: FAO data bank FAOSTAT, downloaded in April /2003 from the FAO website <http://apps.fao.org/default.htm>. Bharier (1971, 25–7) provides the following estimates of urban percentages in Iran: 1901, 21%; 1934, 21%; and 1950, 28%. The government of Turkey's *Statistical Indicators* divides the population by residence into two categories, cities and villages; in 1927 cities were 24% of the total population, and 25% in 1950. Illustrating the sensitivity of the definition of the term 'urban', Hansen (1991, 41, n. 4) mentions two studies on Egypt, which variously put the urban percentage in 1927 at 17% or 27% of the total population. Hansen states that urbanization in Egypt was not pronounced until after World War II.

TABLE 8.7. Real GDP/capita, 1913–1998 (1990 International $)

	1913	1920	1930	1940	1950	1973	1998
Algeria	*1,104*	*1,280*	*1,397*	—	1,365	2,356	2,688
Bahrain	—	—	—	—	2,104	4,377	4,620
Bangladesh	—	—	—	—	540	497	813
Egypt	732	—	—	732	718	1,022	2,128
India (3)	673	635	726	696	*613*	*827*	*1,672*
India	—	—	—	—	619	853	1,746
Iran	—	—	—	—	1,720	5,445	4,265
Iraq	—	—	—	—	1,364	3,753	1,131
Israel	—	—	—	—	2,817	9,646	15,152
Jordan	—	—	—	—	1,663	2,389	4,113
Kuwait	—	—	—	—	28,834	26,674	11,273
Lebanon	—	—	—	—	2,429	3,157	3,445
Libya	—	—	—	—	—	8,169	*4,757*
Morocco	807	*927*	*1,040*	—	1,455	1,694	2,693
Oman	—	—	—	—	622	3,278	7,267
Pakistan	—	—	—	—	643	954	1,935
Qatar	—	—	—	—	30,520	43,859	7,304
Saudi Arabia	—	—	—	—	2,231	11,040	8,225
Sudan	—	—	—	—	821	780	880
Syria	—	—	—	—	2,409	4,018	5,765
Tunisia	822	*1,003*	*1,164*	—	1,115	2,221	4,190
Turkey	*1,370*	785	*1,304*	2,017	1,818	3,753	6,552
UAE	—	—	—	—	15,694	24,908	13,857
West Bank and Gaza	—	—	—	—	950	2,236	5,671
Yemen	—	—	—	—	976	1,757	2,298
Palestine, of which	—	*431*	*589*	*847*	*1,993*	—	—
Jews	—	*841*	*1,435*	*1,463*	*3,144*	—	—
Arabs and others	—	*382*	*421*	*584*	*949*	—	—
Regional totals:							
West Asia (15 nations)	679	—	—	—	1,855	4,972	5,407
Africa	585	—	—	—	852	1,365	1,368
Asia excluding Japan	640	—	—	—	635	1,241	2,936
Latin America	1,511	—	—	—	2,554	4,531	5,795
United States+	5,257	—	—	—	9,288	16,172	26,146
Western Europe	3,473	—	—	—	4,594	11,534	17,921
World	1,510	—	—	—	2,114	4,104	5,709

Note: 'United States+' is the average for the USA, Canada, Australia, and New Zealand, as calculated by Maddison. 'India (3)' combines part-Partition Bangladesh, India, and Pakistan. The first year in the table for Algeria, Morocco, and Tunisia is 1910. The year corresponding to the second year in Turkey is 1923, and 1922 for Palestine and its sub-aggregates. Libya was not included in Maddison, nor is its GDP presented in recent IMF *International Finance Statistical Yearbooks*. The data in the table is from the UN *Statistical Yearbook* 45 (1998), and was converted using market exchange rates. The total for Palestine in 1950 uses the rough approximation of combining Maddison's totals for Israel, West Bank and Gaza. Maddison estimates the following per capita income levels for 1870, in 1990 international dollars: Asia excluding Japan 543, Latin America 698, 'United States+' 2,431, Western Europe 1,974, and the world average at 867. His estimate of Indian GDP/capita in 1870 is 533. Using Amin (1996), Algeria's GDP / capita level in 1880 would have been 1,028. Hansen and Marzouk (1965, 3) argue that Egypt's per capita income in 1939 was the same as in 1913. Maddison (1995, 139) argued that the per capita income level of Anatolian Turkey in 1913 was the same as the level it had reached in 1929. As a rough order of magnitude, this is compatible with treatments in Hansen (1991, 308) and Pamuk (2000). The 1990 international dollars, also known as 1990 purchasing power parity (ppp) dollars, convert from domestic currency into US dollars using a synthetic, non-market exchange rate, which attempts to estimate an average exchange rate linking prices of both traded and non-traded goods.

Source: Maddison (2001) and Maddison (1995), and author's calculations for Algeria, Morocco, Tunisia using Amin (1966), for Egypt using Hansen and Marzouk (1965), for Palestine Metzer (1998), and for Turkey the Turkish government's *Statistical Indicators*. Results from author's calculations indicated by italics.

TABLE 8.8. Total real GDP, 1913–1998 (000 million 1990 International $)

	1913	1920	1930	1950	1973	1998
Algeria	6.8	7.3	9.0	12.1	35.8	81.9
Bahrain	—	—	—	0.2	1.0	2.9
Bangladesh	—	—	—	24.6	36.0	101.7
Egypt	8.9	—	—	15.2	36.2	140.5
India (3)	204.2	194.1	244.1	272.2	598.7	2,065.9
India	—	—	—	222.2	494.8	1,072.7
Iran	—	—	—	28.1	171.5	274.7
Iraq	—	—	—	7.0	39.0	24.6
Israel	—	—	—	3.6	30.8	85.5
Jordan	—	—	—	0.9	4.0	18.3
Kuwait	—	—	—	4.2	23.8	21.6
Lebanon	—	—	—	3.3	8.9	12.1
Libya	—	—	—	—	18.3	25.4
Morocco	3.6	4.7	6.7	13.6	28.8	78.4
Oman	—	—	—	0.3	2.8	17.2
Pakistan	—	—	—	25.4	67.8	261.5
Qatar	—	—	—	0.8	6.2	5.1
Saudi Arabia	—	—	—	8.6	73.6	171.0
Sudan	—	—	—	6.6	11.8	29.5
Syria	—	—	—	8.4	27.9	96.1
Tunisia	1.7	2.1	2.8	3.9	12.1	39.3
Turkey	18.1	16.6	29.1	38.4	144.5	423.0
UAE	—	—	—	1.1	9.7	31.9
West Bank and Gaza	—	—	—	1.0	2.5	14.8
Yemen	—	—	—	4.4	12.4	37.7
Palestine, of which	—	0.3	0.6	4.6	—	—
Jews	—	0.1	0.2	3.5	—	—
Arabs and others	—	0.3	0.3	1.1	—	—
Regional totals:						
West Asia (15 nations)	27	—	—	110	559	1,236
Africa	73	—	—	195	529	1,039
Asia excluding Japan	593	—	—	825	2,633	9,953
Latin America	122	—	—	424	1,398	2,942
United States +	586	—	—	1,635	4,058	8,456
Western Europe	906	—	—	1,402	4,134	6,961
World	2,705	—	—	5,336	16,059	33,726

Note: 'United States+' is the average for the USA, Canada, Australia, and New Zealand, as presented by Maddison.'India (3)' combines part-Partition Bangladesh, Pakistan, and India. The first year for Algeria, Morocco, and Tunisia is 1910. The year corresponding to the second year is 1923 in Turkey, and 1922 for Palestine and its sub-aggregates. Libya was not included in Maddison, nor is its GDP presented in recent IMF *International Financial Statistical Yearbooks*. The data for Libya taken from the UN *Statistical Yearbook* 45 (1998), and converted into1990 international dollar using market exchange rates. The total for Palestine in 1950 uses the rough approximation of combining Maddison's totals for Israel, West Bank and Gaza. According to Metzer's estimates, the fraction of output generated by Jews in Palestine was: 21% in 1922, 40% in 1930, 54% in 1947, and was 76% of the 1950 total calculated by Maddison for Israel, West Bank and Gaza. Maddison's estimate for Indian GDP in 1870 is 134,882. The 1990 international dollars, also known as 1990 ppp dollars, convert from domestic currency into United States dollars using a synthetic, non-market exchange rate, which attempts to estimate an average exchange rate linking prices of both traded and non-traded goods. For example, the market exchange rate for Turkey in 1993 (from the *International Financial Statistics Yearbook*) was 10,985 Lira/US$, while the exchange rate that Maddison used, from the purchasing power parity calculations, was 5,139 Lira/US$ (Maddison 2001, 217). Another relevant example would be Egypt in 1985, which experienced multiple exchange-rates in a situation of severe exchange-rate controls. In Egyptian pounds per US dollar, the exchange rates ranged from 0.7 to 1.55, and the purchasing power parity exchange rate for that year was 0.2828 (Maddison 1995, 179).

Source: Maddison (2001) and author's calculations for Algeria, Morocco, Tunisia using Amin (1966), for Egypt using Hansen and Marzouk (1965), for Palestine Metzer (1998), and for Turkey the Turkish government's *Statistical Indicators*. Results from this author's calculations are indicated by italics.

TABLE 8.9. Average annual inflation rates by decade, 1910s–1990s (%)

	1910s	1920s	1930s	1940s	1950s	1960s	1970s	1980s	1990s
Algeria	—	—	—	28	4	—	8	9	17
Bahrain	—	—	—	—	—	—	12	2	1
Bangladesh	—	—	—	—	—	—	—	—	5
Egypt	9	−3	0	9	0	4	9	16	9
India (3)	10	−3	−3	11	—	—	—	—	—
India	—	—	—	—	2	6	8	9	9
Iran	—	—	—	15	7	2	12	17	22
Iraq	—	—	—	14	1	2	2	—	—
Israel	—	—	—	—	11	5	35	65	9
Jordan	—	—	—	—	—	—	11	7	3
Kuwait	—	—	—	—	—	—	8	4	2
Lebanon	—	—	—	14	2	—	—	—	—
Libya	—	—	—	—	—	5	6	—	—
Morocco	—	—	—	27	5	2	8	7	4
Oman	—	—	—	—	—	—	—	—	0
Pakistan	—	—	—	—	8	4	12	7	9
Qatar	—	—	—	—	—	—	—	3	2
Saudi Arabia	—	—	—	—	—	2	12	0	1
Sudan	—	—	—	9	4	3	16	33	57
Syria	—	—	—	—	2	2	10	20	6
Tunisia	—	—	—	—	4	3	7	9	4
Turkey	43	0	−1	12	9	6	27	38	57
Yemen	—	—	—	—	—	—	—	—	26
Palestine	—	−5	0	10	—	—	—	—	—

Note: Not all decades have all ten years. 'Indian(3)' Combines part-Partition Bangladesh, Pakistan, and India. A value of 0 indicates that the absolute value of the calculated number was less than one half. As frequently happens at the end of wars, the immediate post-war period sees a decline in prices. This cyclical behavior of prices was more extreme in Turkey, where a small overall change in prices during the 1920s hides an initial period of post-war inflation, followed by the deflation that began before 1929, and continued into the 1930s.

Source: Author's calculations, using price data from IMF *International Financial Statistics Yearbook*, Mitchell (1998), *World Development Indicators 2002* CD-Rom, Pamuk (2000).

TABLE 8.10. Agricultural land, 1913–2000 (1,000 ha)

	Arable land and orchards							Irrigated land		
	1913	1927	1938	1950	1961	1980	2000	1961	1980	2000
Algeria	5,013	6,607	6,401	5,820	7,066	7,509	8,195	229	253	560
Bahrain	—	—	—	—	3	6	6	1	1	4
Bangladesh	—	—	—	—	8,880	9,158	8,484	426	1,569	4,187
Egypt	3,227	3,491	2,234	2,445	2,568	2,445	3,291	2,568	2,445	3,291
India	—	—	—	16,760	160,986	168,255	169,700	24,685	38,475	54,800
Iran	—	—	—	2,338	15,271	13,713	16,326	4,700	4,948	7,500
Iraq	—	—	—	352	4,700	5,439	5,540	1,250	1,750	3,525
Israel	—	—	—	480	397	413	418	136	203	194
Jordan	—	—	—	—	294	337	401	31	37	75
Kuwait	—	—	—	—	1	1	10	0	1	7
Lebanon	—	—	—	280	262	301	332	41	86	104
Libya	—	—	—	2,499	1,970	2,080	2,150	121	225	470
Morocco	—	3,103	7,270	8,150	6,970	8,030	9,734	875	1,217	1,305
Oman	—	—	—	—	23	41	80	20	38	62
Pakistan	—	—	—	—	16,881	20,300	21,960	10,751	14,680	18,090
Qatar	—	—	—	—	1	5	21	1	3	13
Saudi Arabia	—	—	—	20	1,170	1,962	3,785	343	600	1,620
Sudan	—	—	—	717	10,845	12,460	16,433	1,480	1,800	1,950
Syria	—	1,520	1,566	3,536	6,381	5,684	5,352	558	539	1,211
Tunisia	3,170	3,288	3,564	3,803	4,250	4,701	5,014	100	243	380
Turkey	—	—	9,555	15,260	25,167	28,479	26,672	1,310	2,700	4,500
UAE	—	—	—	—	8	23	247	—	—	—
Yemen	—	—	—	—	1,337	1,463	1,669	—	—	—

TABLE 8.10. (*Continued*)

	Arable land and orchards							Irrigated land		
	1913	1927	1938	1950	1961	1980	2000	1961	1980	2000
Regional totals (million ha):										
Near East					78	83	91	15	18	27
East and Southeast Asia					73	84	97	10	14	20
Latin America and Caribbean					102	139	159	8	14	19
Africa South of Sahara					119	140	161	3	4	5
South Asia					190	202	205	36	56	79
Industrialized countries					379	395	386	26	37	43
World					1,346	1,432	1,497	139	210	272

Egypt	1900	1925	1950
Cultivated	2,197	2,276	2,382
Cropped	3,008	3,449	3,878

Sources: 1913–50, various issues of FAO *Production Yearbook*, and its predecessor publications; 1961–2000, the FAOSTAT data-bank from the FAO website, <http://apps.fao.org/default.htm>. The 1937–50 data for Morocco refer to French Morocco. The data for Syria in 1927 and 1938 include Lebanon. The first year for Israel is 1953, and that for Jordan is 1947. The FAO *Production Yearbook* for 1954 reported Jordan's arable land in 1953 to have been 893,000 ha; presumably that included some of what is now referred to as the West Bank, which is the reason for using the datum for 1947. The FAO *Production Yearbook* 1949 reported Palestine's 1947 total of arable land and orchards as 697,000 ha, which is compatible with *A Survey of Palestine* (1946), i. 320, where the reported 1945 cultivated area (i.e. not including fallow) was 578,000 ha. It would appear that neither the World Bank nor the FAO report annual data of agricultural production in the West Bank and Gaza, which would not be surprising given the current political climate. The Palestine Central Bureau of Statistics (website <www.pcbs.org/inside/selets.htm>) reports total cultivated area at 184, 000 ha in 1999/2000 (over half in fruit trees!), which compares with the data in the *Statistical Abstract of Israel* 2001 on crop areas in Jewish localities in Judea, Samaria, and Gaza of only 2,600 ha. The *Statistical Abstract of Israel* for 2001 reports total land cultivated in Israel 1949/50 at 240, 000 ha. For various year during the period 1961–82 Gharaibeh (1985, 61) reports cultivated areas declining from 200,000 to 159,000 ha. using sources from Jordan, the West Bank, and Israel. The data on cultivated and cropped land in Egypt is from Radwan (1974, 270), and indicate the importance of multi-cropping in that country, whereby more than one harvest is achieved on a given piece of land in a twelve-month period.

TABLE 8.11. Agricultural production index numbers, 1910–2000 (1989–1991 = 100)

	1910	1920	1930	1930s*	1952	1961	1980	2000
Algeria	51	60	71	70	73	63	72	128
Bahrain	—	—	—	—	—	47	156	122
Bangladesh	—	—	—	—	—	59	81	137
Egypt	25	23	29	33	37	43	75	148
India	—	—	—	—	34	47	67	131
Iran	—	—	—	—	21	31	60	150
Iraq	—	—	—	—	22	50	79	71
Israel	—	—	—	—	16	38	89	112
Jordan	—	—	—	—	—	77	67	145
Kuwait	—	—	—	—	—	22	91	183
Lebanon	—	—	—	—	—	37	67	156
Libya	—	—	—	—	17	22	83	141
Morocco	—	15	21	24	33	31	57	7
Oman	—	—	—	—	—	22	60	157
Pakistan	—	—	—	—	26	32	62	146
Qatar	—	—	—	—	—	18	36	168
Saudi Arabia	—	—	—	—	—	15	27	91
Sudan	—	—	—	—	36	59	102	158
Syria	—	—	—	—	27	35	97	154
Tunisia	12	16	22	30	36	34	73	130
Turkey	—	8	16	19	34	43	77	118
UAE	—	—	—	—	—	14	48	568
Yemen	—	—	—	—	—	53	77	138

Regional aggregates:

	1961	1980	2000
Near East	42	75	133
East and Southeast Asia	38	73	132
Latin America and the Caribbean	45	79	134
Africa south of the Sahara	52	75	131
South Asia	46	68	132
Industrialized countries	61	91	114
World	50	79	125

Notes: * Mid-1930s.

Sources: 1961–2000, from the FAO database FAOSTAT <http://apps.fao.org/default.htm>, downloaded May 2003; earlier years from the author's calculations using Amin (1966), Hansen and Wattleworth (1978), the official Turkish *Statistical Indicators*, and various issues of the FAO *Production Yearbook* and the United Nations *Statistical Yearbook*. The first year for Turkey is 1923. Using Amin, the corresponding datum for Algeria in 1880 would be 29; according to the Hansen/Wattleworth index (Table IV), the output index for Egypt in 1887 would be 14. Unfortunately, professional opinion is divided about the pre-Partition experience of agriculture in India: see Guha (1992).

TABLE 8.12. Freshwater availability and use, late 1990s (meters³ per person per year)

	Natural availability	Desalination	Use	% into agriculture
Algeria	460	2	181	52
Egypt	830	0	1,055	82
Bangladesh	8,444	0	133	86
India	1,822	0	592	92
Iran	1,900	0	1,122	92
Iraq	3,111	0	2,478	92
Israel	265	—	287	54
Jordan	169	0	255	75
Kuwait	10	122	306	60
Lebanon	1,220	0	400	68
Libya	109	10	870	84
Morocco	936	0	399	89
Oman	364	15	658	94
Pakistan	2,812	0	1,382	97
Saudi Arabia	111	42	1,056	90
Syria	1,541	0	844	90
Tunisia	577	1	312	86
Turkey	3,344	0	558	73
UAE	56	327	896	67
Yemen	206	1	253	92

Sources: The World Resources Institute, *World Resources 2002–04*, and author's calculations. Freshwater availability includes the annual flow of rivers and the recharge of aquifers (groundwater), including flows originating outside a country. Disregarding errors of measurement, in countries where the amount of water used is greater than the sum of natural availability and desalination, there is a drawing down of aquifers, which is a process that cannot continue indefinitely. The ultimate source for this data is the AQUASTAT database maintained by the Food and Agricultural Organization of the United Nations; the first publication of this series provided estimates for the middle and late 1970s.

TABLE 8.13. Foreign trade—dollar values, 1913–2000 (1,000 million current US $)

	1913	1929	1938	1950	1960	1975	1990	2000
Algeria								
Export	0.097	0.152	0.162	0.333	0.39	4.70	12.93	—
Import	0.129	0.230	0.143	0.434	1.26	6.01	9.78	—
Bahrain								
Export	—	—	—	0.137	0.19	1.20	3.76	5.70
Import	—	—	—	0.119	0.18	1.20	3.71	4.63
Bangladesh								
Export	—	—	—	—	—	0.33	1.67	4.69
Import	—	—	—	—	—	1.32	3.62	8.36
Egypt								
Export	0.157	0.250	0.147	0.504	0.57	1.40	4.96	4.69
Import	0.137	0.264	0.184	0.619	0.67	3.93	16.78	14.01
India(3)								
Export	0.828	1.168	0.614	2.000	1.73	5.64	25.26	56.10
Import	0.643	0.906	0.576	1.730	2.91	9.87	34.61	70.94
India								
Export	—	—	—	1.312	1.34	4.36	17.97	42.38
Import	—	—	—	1.280	2.26	6.38	23.58	51.29
Iran								
Export	—	0.133	0.140	0.701	0.84	20.21	19.31	28.35
Import	—	0.740	0.079	0.302	0.56	10.34	20.32	14.30
Iraq								
Export	—	0.020	0.068	0.122	0.47	8.30	—	—
Import	—	0.036	0.046	0.105	0.39	4.21	—	—
Israel								
Export	—	0.008	0.029	0.035	0.22	1.94	11.58	31.40
Import	—	0.035	0.056	0.302	0.56	6.09	2.60	31.40
Jordan								
Export	—	—	0.003	0.004	0.01	0.15	1.06	1.90
Import	—	—	0.006	0.030	0.12	0.73	2.60	4.54
Kuwait								
Export	—	—	—	—	0.96	9.18	7.04	19.44
Import	—	—	—	—	0.24	2.39	3.97	7.16
Lebanon								
Export	—	—	—	—	0.04	1.12	0.49	0.72
Import	—	—	—	—	0.29	2.05	2.53	6.23
Libya								
Export	—	—	0.006	0.011	0.01	6.84	13.23	10.25
Import	—	—	0.047	0.020	0.17	3.54	5.34	3.75
Morocco								
Export	0.073	0.048	0.043	0.190	0.35	1.54	4.27	6.96
Import	0.045	0.100	0.063	0.328	0.41	2.57	6.92	11.53
Oman								
Export	—	—	—	—	—	1.44	5.51	5.51
Import	—	—	—	0.006	0.02	0.77	2.68	5.04

TABLE 8.13. (*Continued*)

	1913	1929	1938	1950	1960	1975	1990	2000
Pakistan								
Export	—	—	—	0.693	0.39	1.06	5.62	9.03
Import	—	—	—	0.455	0.65	2.17	7.41	11.29
Qatar								
Export	—	—	—	0.022	0.13	1.81	—	7.06
Import	—	—	—	0.007	0.03	0.41	1.70	2.50
Saudi Arabia								
Export	—	—	—	—	0.89	29.68	44.42	77.58
Import	—	—	—	0.115	0.23	4.21	24.07	30.24
Sudan								
Export	—	0.032	0.030	0.095	0.18	0.44	0.37	1.81
Import	—	0.033	0.032	0.078	0.18	1.03	0.62	1.55
Syria								
Export	—	0.020	0.022	0.082	0.11	0.93	4.21	19.26
Import	—	0.057	0.037	0.211	0.24	1.69	2.40	16.71
Tunisia								
Export	0.034	0.055	0.039	0.114	0.12	0.86	3.70	5.85
Import	0.028	0.078	0.045	0.147	0.19	1.42	5.31	8.57
Turkey								
Export	—	0.075	0.115	0.264	0.32	1.40	12.96	26.57
Import	—	0.124	0.119	0.311	0.47	7.70	22.30	53.50
UAE								
Export	—	—	—	—	—	6.96	23.54	—
Import	—	—	—	—	—	2.69	11.20	38.14
Yemen								
Export	—	—	—	0.119	0.18	0.18	—	4.08
Import	—	—	—	0.127	0.23	0.62	—	2.23
Ottoman Empire								
Export	0.104	—	—	—	—	—	—	—
Import	0.176	—	—	—	—	—	—	—

Note: 'India (3)' continues post-Partition Bangladesh, Parietal, and India.

Sources: Several issues of *International Financial Statistics*, UN *Statistical Yearbook*, the League of Nations *Statistical Yearbook*, and for 1913 Woytinsky (1955) and Lamartine Yates (1959). Sum of North and South Yemen, 1950 through 1975.

TABLE 8.14. Trade quantum index numbers, 1910–2000 (1980=100, unless otherwise noted)

	1910	1930	1938	1950	1960	1970	1980	1990	2000
Algeria									
Exports (1960 = 100)	54	101	—	99	100	—	—	—	—
Imports (1960 = 100)	14	26	—	38	100	—	—	—	—
Exports GS	—	—	—	—	114	96	100	151	207
Imports GS	—	—	—	—	68	40	100	80	72
Bangladesh									
Exports GS	—	—	—	—	54	72	100	256	749
Imports GS	—	—	—	—	27	66	100	190	357
Egypt									
Exports	52	50	60	67	80	70	100	—	—
Imports	82	99	88	142	134	109	100	—	—
Exports GS	—	—	—	—	38	50	100	160	244
Imports GS	—	—	—	—	22	43	100	87	114
India									
Exports	—	—	—	51	54	82	100	167	478
Imports	—	—	—	34	55	62	100	149	454
Iran									
Exports GS	—	—	—	—	—	—	100	259	289
Imports GS	—	—	—	—	—	—	100	108	53
Israel									
Exports	—	—	—	2	13	26	100	161	412
Imports	—	—	—	9	14	25	100	172	442
Jordan									
Exports	—	—	—	—	13	26	100	251	409
Imports	—	—	—	—	14	25	100	118	210
Morocco									
Exports	—	14	24	54	82	93	100	177	204
Imports	—	18	23	35	40	62	100	124	119
Pakistan									
Exports	—	—	—	—	—	30	100	208	311
Imports	—	—	—	—	—	22	100	125	173
Saudi Arabia									
Exports GS	—	—	—	—	16	52	100	—	—
Imports GS	—	—	—	—	2	6	100	—	—
Sudan									
Exports	—	—	35	38	64	100	—	—	—
Imports	—	—	25	34	68	100	—	—	—
Syria									
Exports	—	—	—	44	80	105	100	184	337
Imports	—	—	—	19	33	32	100	75	164

TABLE 8.14. (*Continued*)

	1910	1930	1938	1950	1960	1970	1980	1990	2000
Tunisia									
Exports GS	15	34	38	49	49	73	100	98	134
Imports GS	3	7	11	13	19	30	100	110	132
Turkey									
Exports	—	70	88	100	—	—	—	—	—
(1950 = 100)									
Imports	—	—	69	100	—	—	—	—	—
(1950 = 100)									
Exports GS	—	—	—	—	—	90	100	500	1,005
Imports GS	—	—	—	—	—	59	100	294	582

Note: GS of goods and services.

Sources: Author's calculations, based on data on exports and import quanta from UN *International Trade Statistical Yearbook*, and the UN *Statistical Yearbook*. Exports and imports of goods and services, from the *World Development Indicators* CD-Rom. Pre-1950 data for Algeria, Morocco, and Tunisia from Amin (1966), and for Egypt from Hansen and Lucas (1978). No series could be formed for: Bahrain, Iraq, Kuwait, Lebanon, Libya, Oman, Qatar, United Arab Emirates, West Bank, and Yemen. The difference between 'Exports' and 'Exports GS' is the value of services, which can include items like tourism, exports processing, or business services. Generally speaking, trade in services has grown faster than trade in goods, necessitating the separate treatment of the two series. The last year's observation for Morocco and Tunisia was 1994, for Syria it was 1997, and for Turkey it was 1999. The second reference year for Syria was 1952. The first reference year for Turkey was 1929.

TABLE 8.15. *Middle East crude oil production, 1920–2000* (million barrels per year)

	1920	1930	1940	1950	1960	1970	1980	1990	2000
Algeria	—	—	—	0	68	376	405	429	458
Bahrain	—	—	7	11	17	28	18	15	14
Egypt	1	2	7	16	23	119	218	319	273
Iran	12	46	66	242	386	1,397	608	1,127	1,349
Iraq	—	1	24	50	354	570	920	745	938
Israel	—	—	—	—	1	32	0	0	0
Kuwait	—	—	—	126	594	1,090	606	429	759
Libya	—	—	—	—	7	1,209	654	502	515
Oman	—	—	—	—	—	121	104	250	354
Qatar	—	—	—	12	63	132	173	148	269
Saudi Arabia	—	—	5	200	456	1,387	3,623	2,340	3,067
Syria	—	—	—	—	—	29	61	142	191
Tunisia	—	—	—	—	—	34	40	34	29
Turkey	—	—	—	0	3	25	17	73	53
UAE	—	—	—	—	—	284	625	773	864
Yemen	—	—	—	—	—	—	0	70	161
MENA/ World total (%)	—	—	6	17	27	41	37	32	37

Note: MENA = Middle East and North Africa.

Source: Twentieth Century Petroleum Statistics (until 1980) and US Department of Energy website: <http://www.eia.doe.gov/emeu/international/petroleu.html#IntlProduction.>. Libya's first year of production was 1961, which is shown here as 1960. The MENA/World datum for 1940 refers to 1938. The 'Neutral Zone' between Kuwait and Saudi Arabia produced 50 million barrels in 1960; from 1970 its production is split evenly between Kuwait and Saudi Arabia. Israel's total includes production from Sinai fields in 1970.

TABLE 8.16. World crude oil prices, 1913–2000, nominal and real (US $ per barrel)

	1913	1920	1930	1940	1950	1960	1970	1980	1990	2000
Nominal price	0.95	3.07	1.19	1.02	1.71	1.90	1.80	35.69	23.81	26.24
Prices in 1999 US$	16.06	25.70	11.94	12.17	11.89	10.74	7.75	72.40	30.35	26.88

Source: Data from US Department of Energy website <http://www.eia.doe.gov/emeu/international/petroleu.html#IntlPrices>, downloaded April 2003. The initial source of the data and calculations was a series (up to 1999) from British Petroleum. The real price for 2000 was updated using the nominal price and the US GDP deflator. Prices refer to US petroleum through 1940, and Saudi Arabia and Dubai prices thereafter.

TABLE 8.17. Export product diversity, 1938–2000 (%)

	1950					2000				
	Agriculture	Mining	Fuels	Chemicals	Manufacturing	Agriculture	Mining	Fuels	Chemicals	Manufacturing
Algeria	90	9	0	0	1	0	0	98	1	1
Bahrain	—	—	—	—	—	0	4	70	2	23
Bangladesh	—	—	—	—	—	9	0	0	1	90
Egypt	93	1	0	0	0	17	1	37	8	33
India	40	6	0	0	46	14	2	4	10	67
Iran	14	0	86	0	2	4	0	89	1	6
Iraq	66	0	0	0	33	—	—	—	—	—
Israel	66	0	0	0	33	4	1	1	12	82
Jordan	2	0	98	0	0	14	10	0	21	53
Kuwait	82	6	0	0	13	0	0	91	6	2
Lebanon	82	6	0	0	13	22	3	0	14	61
Libya	93	6	0	0	1	0	0	95	3	2
Morocco	71	28	1	0	0	23	7	4	12	54
Oman	—	—	—	—	—	3	0	82	1	13
Pakistan	100	—	—	—	—	15	0	1	52	32
Qatar	—	—	—	—	—	0	0	88	6	6
Saudi Arabia	0	0	100	0	0	1	0	91	5	2
Sudan	100	0	0	0	0	81	0	0	0	19

Syria	93	0	0	0	7	13	1	76	0	9
Tunisia	79	21	0	0	0	9	1	12	10	67
Turkey	87	6	0	1	4	14	1	1	4	80
Yemen	—	—	—	—	—	34	0	6	10	47

1938

	Agriculture	Mining	Fuels	Chemicals	Manufacturing
Algeria	93	7	0	0	1
Egypt	98	2	0	0	0
India	61	4	0	0	21
Iran	22	0	74	0	4
Sudan	100	—	—	—	—
Turkey	94	5	0	0	0

Note: Agriculture, includes livestock, fishing, and forestry.

Sources: Author's calculations, using data in various issues of UN, *International Trade Statistics Yearbook*. Conceptually, there often is not a clear division between categories such as agriculture and industry; important cases are sugar, seed oils, or fuels and chemicals with various by-products of petroleum. Data for 2000 are expressed in standardized categories as presented by the UN. Much of the earlier data were not so presented, and had to be assigned by this author. For several countries the disaggregated estimates did not sum up to the total as provided in the source; this may be due to government exports, exports going over land, or other such problems. For Kuwait in 1950 the value of petroleum exports was not given, but was instead approximated by applying to Kuwait's exported volume that year's price in Iraq.

TABLE 8.18. Foreign investment, 1888–1970; nominal total, and real per capita

	Nominal total	Per capita levels (1913 US$)		
	(million $)	Total	Business	Government
1888				
Egypt	628	129	25	104
India	635	3	2	1
Ottoman	672	31	4	27
1913				
Algeria	219	40	13	28
Egypt	1,008	86	44	43
India (3)	2,258	8	2	5
Iran	97	9	—	—
Morocco	12	3	1	2
Ottoman	1,053	52	18	34
1938				
Algeria and Tunisia	197	11	4	7
Egypt	513	18	15	4
India (3)	2,774	4	2	2
Iran	197	7	7	0
Iraq, Syria, and Palestine	137	9	—	—
Morocco	284	24	7	17
Turkey	597	20	19	1
1970				
Algeria	1,150	16	3	13
Egypt	1,890	11	1	11
India	10,777	4	1	3
Iran	4,212	29	6	22
Iraq	482	10	4	6
Israel	2,339	151	8	144
Jordan	144	19	3	15
Lebanon	164	12	7	5
Morocco	1,225	16	3	12
Pakistan	3,931	12	2	10
Syria	311	4	0	4
Tunisia	774	24	5	19
Turkey	3,047	17	2	15

Note: India (3) for 1938 excludes Burma and Ceylon, includes, post-partition Bangladesh, Pakistan, and India.

Sources: Author's calculations, for 1888 using Crouchley (1936, 139, 147) for Egypt, Pamuk (1987) for the Ottoman Empire, and Stone (1999, Table 5) for India. The 1913 per capita totals are from Pamuk (1987, 145), shares from Pamuk and Twomey (2000); 1938 from Lewis (1948), 1971 from OECD (1973) and *World Debt Tables*. For 1888, the domestic £ data were reflated by 15% (the average price increase in Britain), as a very rough indicator of price changes between 1888 and 1913. The 1913 exchange rate used was 5US$/£. For the Ottoman Empire, the estimated population in 1888 was 25 million, slightly higher than the total for 1913, reflecting territorial changes. For 1938 and 1970, the original US$ data were deflated by a US price index, the US GDP deflator taken from *The Statistical Abstract of the United States*. The separation of foreign investment into categories such as business and loans to governments has been subject to much debate; contemporary categories are not very useful in analyzing pre-World War I data. The government–private sector dichotomy is questionable in discussing enterprises such as Anglo-Iranian Oil, infrastructure products, of which railroads were very important, or transfers from the metropolitan budget to private enterprises in the colony. The foreign–domestic dichotomy is not helpful in treating French colonial investment in Algeria, and one suspects that the high total of per capita foreign investment in Egypt also includes funds generated by resident foreigners. This table's separation of Pamuk's totals for foreign investment in 1913 for Algeria and Morocco uses the results in Twomey (2000). For 1938, the separation relied on the descriptions in Lewis (1948), while these data for 1970 identify debt with government loans, and FDI with business investment. Woodruff (1967, 154) reported estimates of total foreign investment in 1913 in Egypt at $700 million, in French North Africa at $200 million, and in the Ottoman Empire of $1,200 million. Bharier (1971, 163) reported the value of total fixed assets of the Anglo-Iranian Oil Company in 1915 at £1.6 million. The market value of the Suez Canal Company fluctuated between E£15 and E£20 million during 1883–1933 (Crouchley 1936, 105) or about $100 million, and is included in this table with business investment in Egypt. By the latter date the company was essentially a financial firm headquartered in Europe, whose value had nothing to do with that of the canal itself, which indeed had been built using corvée labor a half-century earlier. The datum in Lewis for Algeria does not include settlers' investment financed locally. Morard (1948) presented a total value of French assets in Algeria pre-World War II that is five times as large as that reported by Lewis (1948), but without providing supporting data; that number can only be considered an informed guess.

Table 8.19. International finance: foreign direct investment (FDI) and debt, 1970 and 2000

	Accumulated stocks (million US$)				Ratios to GNP (%)			
	1970		2000		1970		2000	
	FDI	Debt	FDI	Debt	FDI	Debt	FDI	Debt
Algeria	210	940	3,441	25,002	4	19	6	47
Bahrain	140	182	5,772	85,609	—	—	72	1,074
Bangladesh	—	—	980	15,169	—	—	2	33
Egypt	88	1,802	20,845	28,957	1	23	21	29
India	1,650	8,920	18,916	99,098	3	14	4	22
Iran	930	3,282	2,474	7,953	8	28	2	8
Iraq	185	297	—	—	5	8	—	—
Israel	120	2,219	21,450	43,970	2	41	19	40
Jordan	25	119	1,510	8,226	4	19	18	99
Kuwait	650	198	527	—	23	7	1	—
Lebanon	100	64	1,084	10,311	7	4	7	63
Libya	1,400	113	—	—	35	3	—	—
Morocco	240	985	6,141	17,944	6	25	18	54
Oman	80	50	2,480	6,267	31	20	12	32
Pakistan	524	3,407	6,896	32,791	5	34	12	55
Qatar	100	65	1,920	—	33	22	13	—
Saudi Arabia	890	371	25,963	—	17	7	15	—
Sudan	35	385	1,396	15,741	2	18	12	137
Syria	35	276	1,699	21,657	2	13	10	128
Tunisia	175	599	11,451	10,610	12	42	59	55
Turkey	300	2,747	9,335	116,209	2	15	5	58
UAE	246	144	1,836	—	16	10	4	—
West Bank and Gaza	—	—	306	—	—	—	7	—
Yemen	—	—	888	5,615	—	—	10	66

Sources: 1971 FDI from OECD (1973), debt from OECD (1973) and *World Debt Tables*; 2000 FDI from *World Investment Report* and debt from *Global Development Finance*. Debt in 2000 for Bahrain and Israel (in italics) from IMF *International Financial Statistics Yearbook*. The GNP data are from the *World Debt Tables* and *Global Development Finance*. Under current usage, the two major sub-categories of foreign investment are loans and foreign direct investment (FDI); the latter is defined as purchase of a controlling share of the equity of a business enterprise. Loans are made to governments and also to businesses, but in many contexts loans to businesses are guaranteed by their governments, making them essentially government loans. Thus the identification of 'debt' as loans to governments, and 'direct investment' as business investment, is useful, although imprecise. Bahrain's high level of debt relative to GNP reflect its role as a financial intermediary; both its external assets and liabilities are more than ten times GNP. In fact, Bahrain is a net lender to international markets; one might expect that to be the case for other Gulf oil exporters, but data are lacking.

TABLE 8.20. Railways, total length and length per capita, 1880–1990

	Length (km.)					km. per capita				
	1880	1913	1925	1950	1990	1880	1913	1925	1950	1990
Algeria	1,310	3,315	4,207	4,379	4,293	313	571	701	492	169
Bangladesh	—	—	—	2,611	2,746	—	—	—	57	25
Egypt	1,510	4,538	4,555	5,625	7,736	190	373	325	265	138
India (3)	14,478	55,822	62,087	66,011	73,868	56	184	194	149	68
India	—	—	—	54,845	62,367	—	—	—	153	74
Iran	0	9	250	2,652	4,847	0	1	21	162	87
Iraq	—	—	1,218	1,660	1,721	—	—	406	322	95
Israel	—	—	—	303	573	—	—	—	237	127
Lebanon	—	—	—	417	417	—	—	—	307	135
Libya	—	—	230	342	342	—	—	256	356	90
Morocco	0	427	1,733	1,695	1,893	0	73	289	182	77
Pakistan	—	—	—	8,555	8,755	—	—	—	217	65
Saudi Arabia	0	0	0	402	1,036	0	0	0	104	66
Sudan	—	2,411	2,781	3,247	4,756	—	372	397	403	179
Syria	—	—	1,402	852	1,752	—	—	425	244	139
Tunisia	—	1,825	2,060	2,093	2,475	—	975	898	596	302
Turkey	—	3,000	3,957	7,671	8,429	—	196	314	363	150
Palestine	—	—	1,121	—	—	—	—	1,045	—	—
Ottoman Empire	1,637	5,438	—	—	—	68	194	—	—	—

Notes: '0' means that the datum is zero, while — indicates that the data are not available, which could be because they are zero. India (3) is the sum of pre-Partition Bangladesh, India, and Pakistan.

Sources: Railways, from Mitchell (1998). Population from McEvedy and Jones (1978) and Maddison (2001). In 1860 the length of Indian railroads was 1,349 km.

TABLE 8.21. Inward and outward stocks of non-national populations and workforce, in the Gulf States and Israel (populations in 000s)

(a) *Arab labor exporters: to the GCC*

	1975			1997		
	Total pop.	Overseas pop.		Total Pop.	Overseas pop.	
		000.	%		000.	%
Egypt	36,950	620	2	64,824	1,635	3
Jordan	1,800	503	28	4,322	410	9
Lebanon	3,090	53	2	—	—	—
Oman	913	57	6	—	—	—
Sudan	16,050	65	0	32,594	250	1
Syria	7,410	105	1	16,138	265	2
Tunisia	5,700	52	1	—	—	—
Yemen, Rep.	—	—	—	15,857	500	3
Yemen AR	5,037	608	12	—	—	—
Yemen, PDR	1,660	123	7	—	—	—

(b) *Labor-importing countries: the GCC*

	1975			1994		
	Total pop.	Non-nationals	% Non-nationals	Total pop.	Non-nationals	% Non-nationals
Bahrain	267	58	22	550	205	37
Kuwait	1,027	555	54	1,620	949	59
Oman	846	136	16	2,049	538	26
Qatar	180	127	71	532	403	76
Saudi Arabia	7,334	1,398	19	18,180	5,127	28
UAE	551	351	64	2,150	1,522	71
Total	10,204	2,625	26	25,082	8,744	35

(c) *Arabs in non-national workforce, GCC*

	1975	1985	1996
% non-nationals in GCC workforce	51	72	70
% non-national population in GCC	31	33	38
% Arab in non-national population in GCC	72	56	31
Estimated number of non-national Arabs in GCC	2,022	3,105	3,305

Table 8.21. *(Continued)*

(d) *Labor imported into Israel*

	1970	1990	2002
Israel: Domestic labor force	963	1,492	2,284
Workers from West Bank and Gaza	21	108	30
Workers from elsewhere	0	3	247

Note: GCC = Gulf Co-operation Council. Serageldin *et al.* (1983, 61) also records Libya with 501,000 non-nationals in 1975, or 19% of its population. Birks and Sinclair (1980, 134) report that almost three-fourths of Arab migrant workers in Libya in 1975 were Egyptian (229,000 out of 310,000). The number of Tunisian workers in Libya they estimated as 38,000, which is the equivalent of half the number of Tunisian workers reported by the OECD in France. The ESCWA table indicated the following percentages of non-national residents in these labor-exporting countries in 1975: Egypt 1%, Jordan 7%, and Syria 4%. ESCWA provided no data on non-nationals for Iraq and Lebanon. The results of Serageldin and his co-authors (Birks, Stocknat, Li, and Sinclair) went through several revisions, some of which were used by Kapiszewski (2001). The latter author does not specify the sources for his estimates of the non-national ('expatriate') communities in 1997; no breakdown by country of the non-national labour forces in the GCC is presented. Amin and Awny (1985), Feiler (1986), Hansen (1991, 28), Roy (1991, 551), and Sell (1987) review the various estimates of the number of Egyptians living overseas. This number had grown from the half million in our table to somewhere between 2 and 4 million in 1984, with Iraq accounting for 40%, and Saudi Arabia for 27%. The number of overseas workers may well have been between 1 and 2 million, representing over 10% of the domestic labor force. These numbers were to decline subsequently, especially with regard to Egyptians in Iraq. An indirect measure of the importance of overseas workers is the ratio of workers' remittances to GDP; calculations using *World Development Indicator* data indicate that this ratio for Egypt peaked in 1983. In gross terms, Egypt may once have been the country with the highest number of citizens resident overseas, but that position is now held by Turkey. The economically active labor force in the West Bank and Gaza was 695,000 in 2000, according to the PCBS website <www.pcbs.org>. The number of people from the West Bank and Gaza working in Israel without registration has been estimated at 60,000. The fraction of non-nationals in the working population was typically higher than the fraction of non-nationals in the total population, because of disincentives for (predominantly young male) workers to bring their families.

Sources: Labor importers:1975 from Serageldin *et al.* (1983, 61); 1994, ECSWA *Survey* (1995, 133). Labor exporters: 1975 Serageldin *et al.* (1983, 59), population from *World Development Indicators*; 1997 Kapiszewski (2001, 65), population from Maddison (2001). Percentages for 1975–96 from Kapiszewski (2001, 37, 62, 69, 71). Israeli data downloaded from Israel Central Bureau of Statistics site <www.cbs.gov.il/engindex.htm>.

TABLE 8.22. Immigrants in Europe from Maghreb countries and Turkey, 1921–1999
(a) *Total number of foreign born in Europe, by home country (000s)*

	1921	1936	1946	1954	1962	1982	1999
Algeria	—	—	—	—	—	813	504
in France	36	73	22	222	350	805	478
Morocco	—	—	—	—	—	638	1,144
in France	—	—	16	11	33	493	504
Tunisia	—	—	—	—	—	244	198
in France	—	—	2	5	27	213	154
Turkey	—	—	—	—	(small)	1,935	2,639
in Germany	—	—	—	—	—	1,581	2,054

(b) *Ratio of foreign-born to home population, (%)*

	1921	1936	1946	1954	1962	1982	1999
Algeria	—	—	—	—	—	4.0	1.6
in France	0.6	1.0	0.3	2.3	3.2	4.0	1.5
Morocco	—	—	—	—	—	3.2	3.9
in France	—	—	0.2	0.1	0.3	2.1	1.7
Tunisia	—	—	—	—	—	3.6	2.6
in France	—	—	0.1	0.1	0.6	3.2	1.6
Turkey	—	—	—	—	—	4.1	4.0
in Germany	—	—	—	—	—	3.3	3.1

(c) *Number of overseas workers in Europe, by home country (000s)*

	1921	1936	1946	1954	1962	1982	1999
Algeria	—	—	—	—	—	287	245
in France	—	—	—	—	224	287	237
Morocco	—	—	—	—	—	174	493
in France	—	—	—	—	20	145	227
Tunisia	—	—	—	—	—	72	118
in France	—	—	—	—	12	71	84
Turkey	—	—	—	—	—	781	1,637
in Germany	—	—	—	—	18	652	1,290

TABLE 8.22. (*Continued*)

(d) *Ratio of overseas workers to home labor force* (%)

	1921	1936	1946	1954	1962	1982	1999
Algeria	—	—	—	—	—	5.5	2.5
in France	—	—	—	—	6.8	5.5	2.4
Morocco	—	—	—	—	—	2.4	4.4
in France	—	—	—	—	0.4	2.0	2.0
Tunisia	—	—	—	—	—	3.1	3.2
in France	—	—	—	—	0.9	3.1	2.3
Turkey	—	—	—	—	—	3.9	5.4
in Germany	—	—	—	—	0.1	3.3	4.2

Sources: Population and immigrant workers in France from Algeria, Morocco, and Tunisia, 1921–62, Talha (1989) reporting French census data; other totals and numbers in France and Germany from various years of *Trends in International Migration*, with author's calculations of some totals based on itemized listings for several important countries. Workers from Turkey in Germany in 1962 from Martin (1991, 21). Population from McEvedy and Jones (1978) and Maddison (2001); home labor force (economically active population) from *World Development Indicators*. The reader is reminded that there are many distinct definitions of 'foreign-born', typically varying by country. The country specific data (Algeria–France, Turkey–Germany) are more reliable than the European totals. Germany and other European countries instituted policies to attract guest-workers around 1960; the link between France and Algeria was of course longer and embedded in a colonial relationship. There were no other massive south–north migrations of workers before World War II, although the dissolution of the Ottoman Empire, and subsequent fighting inside Anatolia, did lead to very sizeable refugee flows: Collinson (1994, 36–7).

Comments on the tables

Population, and population growth, and vital statistics (Tables 8.1–3)

The table on total population (Table 8.1) serves as the introduction to the subject, indicating absolute—and therefore relative—sizes, across countries and over time. Important explanations of the chronological trends are presented in the table on population growth (Table 8.2). For almost all countries, the growth rate of population increased from the 1950s (and, we infer, from earlier times) until the late 1970s or 1980s, after which it has declined rather steeply. The immediate explanation for this is the behaviour of birth rates and death rates (Table 8.3), for abstracting from international migration, the population growth rate is the difference between the birth rates and the death rates. Death rates decline due to improvements in medicine and health care, which can be seen especially in the decline in infant mortality. In contrast, the explanation of birth rates is more complicated, as these respond both to economic variables (growth of per capita income) and to social factors. In general, birth rates peaked in the 1960s, resulting in a period of one or two decades during which the decline in birth rates was outweighed by the decline in death rates, so that population growth rates continued to rise.

Gender comparisons (Table 8.5)

In its annual *Yearbook* the ILO defines 'economically active population' as 'all persons of either sex who furnish the supply of labor for the production of goods and services'. It would appear that what is being measured is the provision of labour outside the home. One striking finding is that Turkey started out with relatively equal labor force participation rates, and that the ratio has fallen, in contrast to all other countries. A closer look at the data sources would be needed to see if the strong increase in the Gulf States includes or excludes immigrants. The raw data indicate an increase in literacy among both men and women, so that the increasing differential between the sexes with regard to literacy results from a slower growth of literacy among women. The scattered observations for the late 1990s reveal that more young women are staying in school than their male counterparts, which will presumably eliminate the differential in literacy over time.

Urbanization (Table 8.6)

In spite of the difficulties of specifying empirically what is meant by the term 'urban', there is no doubt of the acceleration of this phenomenon during the second half of the twentieth century. This is generally true throughout the world, as the regional data indicate.

GDP and GDP/capita (Tables 8.7–8)

The growth of real GDP is a major indicator of the size of an economy, and therefore of its change over time. The data on total GDP (Table 8.8) suggest rather stagnant levels of GDP during the first half of the century, followed by acceleration, especially among oil exporters.

There are two intriguing trends to note in Table 8.7 (GDP/capita). Some of the oil exporters had extraordinarily high levels even before the oil-price increases in the 1970s. Secondly, the decline in the real price of oil after 1980 resulted in dramatic reductions in measured GDP/capita, such as have seldom been observed in world history.

Two other noteworthy results in Table 8.7 are the decline in living standards in Turkey, as a result of the break-up of the Ottoman Empire and the destruction accompanying World War I and the internal unrest that followed. Secondly, attention is drawn to the rise in per capita incomes in Mandatory Palestine, of both its Jewish and non-Jewish residents.

One of the pitfalls in this type of analysis is the selection of the exchange rate that is used to convert values from national currencies to some international standard. The tables presented here use a synthetic, non-market exchange rate, called a purchasing power parity (PPP) converter, which is an estimate of an average exchange rate linking prices of both traded and non-traded goods. Research on the best method of calculating these exchange rates has been continuing at the University of Pennsylvania, the European Union, and the World Bank. Although this type of calculation is still somewhat controversial, it is the case that Maddison's work defines the current state of the art of historical comparisons of output across countries. The examples given at the bottom of Table 8.8 indicate that the PPP converter often yields dollar estimates of incomes that are two or three times as high as those resulting from the use of nominal exchange rates.

Inflation (Table 8.9)

The table indicates a wide range of values for inflation. There was a marked cyclical behaviour of inflation before and after World War I, rather high amounts of inflation during World War II, and frequent bursts of inflation subsequently. Perhaps noteworthy are the prolonged experience of inflation in Turkey, almost as bad in Syria and Sudan, and the elimination of even higher inflation in Israel. The low-population Gulf States have had little inflation, due to the oil bonanza, while the experiences of Iran and Iraq have been somewhat intermediary, as well as can be determined by the available data.

Agricultural land (Table 8.10)

Land obviously plays a central role in the history of these countries; of interest to us are the expansion of land under cultivation, and the growth of irrigated land.

The historical series are longest for those countries where European colonialism was most important, and we have less quantitative information about the early twentieth century experience in the ex-Ottoman territories.

Agricultural production (Table 8.11)

Comparisons with the other regional aggregates reveal that the growth of agricultural production in the Middle East and North Africa was about as rapid as elsewhere during the second half of the twentieth century. The data for earlier periods may be especially useful in identifying shorter phases of more rapid growth, for example, in Algeria and Egypt before 1900, and Turkey before 1950.

Freshwater availability (Table 8.12)

This table is based on the FAO database that provides one of the few credible measures of sources and uses of water for a large number of countries. A convenient benchmark of water needs is the 'Falkenmark level', of 1,000 cubic metres per person per year. Most countries in the region are short of water by this measure. A fuller analysis would take notice of the high fraction of water that is used in farming, and consider the possibilities of maintaining water availability for houses and domestic use by restricting agricultural production, or encouraging economizing efforts. Any effort at gaining an historical perspective on water scarcity quickly runs up against a general unavailability of data for the period before 1970 for all but a few countries. In addition, the orderly presentation of data on water availability should not hide the possibility that shared water resources—in rivers or in underground aquifers—might lead to economic and political conflicts. The major rivers that cut across national boundaries are the Nile, the Tigris and the Euphrates, and the Jordan.

Trade-dollar values (Table 8.13)

This data should be useful for comparisons across countries or over time. The reader is cautioned that exports and imports are not the only uses made for foreign exchange, although more complete tables of balance of payments are not generally possible until the 1970s. An important element in them would be profits (or management fees) for multinational oil companies, workers remittances, and loans.

Trade quantum index numbers (Table 8.14)

Foreign trade is a key ingredient in the determination of a country's growth and welfare. The reader is reminded that these index numbers imperfectly reflect these influences, as they abstract from changes in international prices, and are less valid when there are dramatic changes in the composition of the basket of goods exported, both of which are important in our case with petroleum. For most of the countries for which series are not available, an export quantum could be approximated by the data on petroleum exports, but this would still leave open the question of how much was purchased with those petro-dollars.

Middle East oil production (Table 8.15)

The outline of the story described by these data is generally familiar. The picture could be filled out with information on natural gas, without altering the basic messages about timing and which countries were important fuel exporters.

World crude oil prices (Table 8.16)

The increase in the nominal price of oil by a factor of twenty between 1970 and 1980 is unique for a product of its importance in world trade. Even adjusting for other price increases, the real price rose almost ten times. Furthermore, it fell by more than half subsequently, due to increased production and greater efficiency by consumers.

Export diversity (Table 8.17)

Two obvious shifts of fundamental importance are that from agriculture to fuels, and a subsequent diversification from fuels to chemicals and manufacturing. It is the case that the profile of imports did not change significantly, at least in ways that could be captured in the data at hand.

Early foreign investment (Table 8.18)

The size of foreign investment relative to population was at its peak in Egypt and Turkey/the Ottoman Empire before World War I. The subsequent decline represented expanded productive capacities of domestic entrepreneurs, who displaced the foreigners, as well as conscious political decisions to force out the foreigners, using market or non-market means. In addition, there was less international lending from the traditional European sources, which devoted their energies to domestic reconstruction, while the United States and Japan sent their overseas funds to Latin America and East Asia, as well as Europe. In the Middle East, counteracting those trends, which we might refer to as nationalistic, was the expansion of direct investment in oil production for export, which accelerated in the 1920s, and again in the 1950s. The table indicates that this was not accompanied by an expansion of lending to the governments.

International finance, 1970–2000 (Table 8.19)

Capital flows may be into a country, which increase its foreign liabilities, or out from a country, contributing to its external assets. Less information is available about assets; some Third World countries, like South Korea and Taiwan, have a positive net position. The data are available in the International Financial

Statistics for Bahrain, Israel, Jordan, Tunisia, Turkey, and Yemen, and indicate that only Bahrain has a positive net asset position, although one would expect a similar situation to hold for some other Gulf States, which might explain why they have no debt totals available. The table indicates a widespread increase in the relative size of both foreign direct investment (FDI) and debt after 1970, although several oil-producing countries bought out the foreign owners of those industries, lowering their ratio of FDI to GNP. Several of the countries with large debt/GNP ratios, such as Sudan, Syria, and Turkey, have been forced to undergo stabilization programmes to preserve creditworthiness.

Transport (Table 8.20)

The expansion of railroads was a key element in the growth of many of today's industrial countries. When viewed in relative terms (i.e. km. per capita) the table generally reveals an inverted U curve, peaking around 1925. The subsequent decline responds to several factors, the most important of which are the exhaustion of new profitable routes, and displacement of railroad transportation by motor vehicles. This decline would be earlier and sharper if the indicator were Railroad km. /GNP, as argued in Twomey (2000). Given that many railroads were foreign-owned, this relative decline is an important contributor to a decline in foreign investment.

Migration (Tables 8.21–22)

These tables analyse the size and growth of the overseas populations in the labor-receiving and labor-exporting states. Three separate cases are depicted, that of the flow of workers around the Gulf States, of Palestinians into Israel (Table 8.21), and that of the export of workers to Europe (Table 8.22). With the exception of Algerians in France, these movements became sizeable only after 1950. Egypt and Turkey had the largest number of people overseas, although relative to their local populations out-migration was larger in Jordan and the Occupied Territories. Perhaps most noteworthy is the dominance of foreigners in the populations of several of the Gulf States, and especially the recent stagnation of the number of Arab migrant workers there, as the host countries turned to immigrants from East Asia, for both economic and socio-political motives. Jordan and North and South Yemen underwent the strongest declines, for reasons having to do with political alignments that formed during the conflict in Kuwait in 1991. Similarly, significant numbers of residents of the West Bank and Gaza began to work in Israel after the 1967 war, but political events during the late 1990s led the Israeli government to look elsewhere for workers.

One indicator of the importance of overseas workers is the share of national income represented by the workers' remittances. Using balance-of-payments data from the International Monetary Fund, this can be calculated to have been about 16 per cent in Jordan, between 1976 and 1995, and in Yemen the ratio reached 21 per cent in 1995. For Egypt and Morocco it was over 5 per cent, while for Algeria, Sudan, Tunisia, and Turkey it was less than 5 per cent during this period. For the West Bank and Gaza at the end of the 1990s, workers' remittances from Israel were also of the order of one-sixth of Gross National Income, according to Palestinian CBS data. For the labor-importing countries, the ratio of (outward) remittances to GDP grew to be over 10 per cent in the late 1990s in Bahrain, Oman, and Saudi Arabia, and was less than 10 per cent in Kuwait.

Selected bibliography

ABU-LUGHOD, JANET LIPPMAN (1995), 'The Displacement of the Palestinians', in Robert Cohen (ed.), *The Cambridge Survey of World Migration* (Cambridge: Cambridge University Press).

AMIN, GALAL A., and ELIZABETH AWNY (1985), *International Migration of Egyptian Labour: A Review of the State of the Art* Manuscript Report IDRC-MR 108e, Ottawa[?]: International Development Research Centre.

AMIN, SAMIR (1966), *L' Économie du Maghreb: la colonization et la décolonization* (Paris: Les Éditions de Minuit).

BHARIER, JULIAN (1971), *Economic Development in Iran 1900–1970* (Oxford: Oxford University Press).

BIRKS, J. S., and C. A. SINCLAIR (1980), *International Migration and Development in the Arab Region* (Geneva: International Labour Office).

COLLINSON, SARAH (1994), *Europe and International Migration* (London: Printer Publishers for the Royal Institute of International Affairs).

CROUCHLEY, A. E. (1977[1936]), *The Investment of Foreign Capital in Egyptian Companies and Public Debt* (Arno Press reprint of Ministry of Finance, Egypt, Technical Paper No. 12).

FEILER, GIL (1986), 'The Number of Egyptian Workers in the Arab Oil Countries, 1974–1983: A Critical Discussion', Working Paper at the Dayan Center for Middle Eastern and African Studies, Tel Aviv University.

Food and Agriculture Organization of the United Nations [FAO] (annual), *Production Yearbook*. Published earlier by the Institut International d'Agriculture as *International Yearbook of Agricultural Statistics*, and *Annuaire International de Statistique Agricole*.

GHARAIBEH, FAWZI A. (1985), *The Economies of the West Bank and Gaza Strip*, (Boulder and London: Westview).

GUHA, SUMIT (2002), *Growth Stagnation or Decline? Agricultural Productivity in British India* (Delhi: Oxford University Press).

HENSEN, BENT (1991), *The Political Economy of Poverty, Equity, and Growth: Egypt and Turkey* (Oxford: Oxford University Press).

—— and EDWARD F. LUCAS (1978), 'Egyptian Foreign Trade, 1885–1961: A New Set of Trade Indices', *Journal of European Economic History*, 7: 2–3, pp. 429–60.

—— and G. A. MARZOUK (1965), *Development and Economic Policy in the U.A.R. (Egypt)* (Amsterdam: Horth-Holland).

—— and MICHAEL WATTLEWORTH (1978), 'Agricultural Output and Consumption of Basic Foods in Egypt, 1886/87–1967/68.' *International Journal of Middle Eastern Studies*, 9: 4 (November), 449–69.

International Labor Organization (1997), *Economically Active Population 1950–2010*, 4th ed. (two computer diskettes).

International Monetary Fund [IMF] (annual), *International Financial Statistics Yearbook*.

KAPISZEWSKI, ANDRZEJ (2001), *Nationals and Expatriates: Population and Labour Dilemmas of the Gulf Cooperation Council States* (Reading: Ithaca Press).

LAMARTINE YATES, P[AUL] (1959), *Forty Years of Foreign Trade* (London: George Allen & Unwin).

LEWIS, CLEONA (1948), *The Unites States and Foreign Investment Problems* (Washington, DC: Brookings).

McEVEDY, COLIN, and RICHARD JONES (1978), *Atlas of World Population History* (New York: Penguin Books).

MADDISON, ANGUS (1995), *Monitoring the World Economy 1820–1992* (Paris: OECD).

—— (2001), *The World Economy: A Millennial Perspective* (Paris: OECD).

MARTIN, PHILP L. (1991), *The Unfinished Story: Turkish Labour Migration to Western Europe* (Geneva: International Labour Office).

METZER, JACOB (1998), *The Divided Economy of Mandatory Palestine* (Cambridge: Cambridge University Press).

MITCHELL, B. R. (1998?), *International Historical Statistics: Africa, Asia, and Oceania 1750–1993*, 3rd ed. (London: Macmillan Reference).

MORAD, L. (1948), 'Algérie et Sahara', in *Encyclopédie Coloniale et Maritime* (Paris).

Organisation for Economic Co-operation and Development [OECD] (annual), *Development Cooperation*.

OECD (annual), *Trends in International Migration*. Earlier version published as *SOPEMI, Continuous Reporting System on Migration*.

PAMUK, ŞEVKET (1987), *The Ottoman Empire and European Capitalism, 1820–1913: Trade, Investment and Production* (Cambridge: Cambridge University Press).

—— (2000), *500 years of Prices and Wages in Istanbul and Other Cities* (Ankara: State Institute of Statistics), in Turkish and English.

RADWAN, SAMIR (1974), *Capital Formation in Egyptian Industry and Agriculture 1882–1967* (London: Ithaca Press).

ROY, DELWIN A. (1991), 'Egyptian Emigrant Labour: Domestic Consequences', *Middle Eastern Studies*, 551–82.

SELL, RALPH R. (1987), 'Gone for Good? Egyptian Migration Processes in the Arab World', *Cairo Papers in Social Science*, 10:2 (Summer).

SERAGELDIN, ISMAIL et al. (1983), *Manpower and International Labor Migration in the Middle East and North Africa* (New York: Oxford University Press).

State Institute of Statistics, Prime Ministry, Republic of Turkey (annual), *Statistical Indicators* (Ankara), in Turkish with English translations of titles of tables.

STONE, IRVING (1999), *The Global Export of Capital from Great Britain, 1865–1914* (Houndsmills: Macmillan Press).

A Survey of Palestine (1946; repr. 1990), 3 vols. (Palestine: Government Printer).

TALHA, LARBI (1989), *Le Salariat immigré dans la crise: la main d'œuvre maghrébine en France (1921–1987)* (Paris: Editions du Centre National de la Recherche Scientifique).

Twentieth century petroleum statistics (annual), business publication sponsored by Dallas, DeGlolyer and MacNaughton.

TWOMEY, MICHAEL J. (2000), *A Century of Foreign Investment in the Third World* (London: Routledge).

United Nations (annual), *Demographic Yearbook*.

United Nations (annual), *International Trade Statistics Yearbook*.

United Nations (annual), *Statistical Yearbook*.

United Nations Conference on Trade and Development [UNCTAD] (annual), *World Investment Report*.

United Nations Development Programme (annual), *Human Development Report*, (Oxford: Oxford University Press).

United Nations Economic and Social Commission for Western Asia [ESCWA] (annual), *Survey of Economic and Social Developments in the ESCWA Region*.

United Nations Educational, Scietific and Cultural Organization [UNESCO], (annual), *Statistical Yearbook*.

WOODRUFF, W. (1967), *Impact of Western Man: A Study of Europe's Role in the World Economy 1750–1960* (New York: St Martin's Press).

World Bank, (annual), *Global Development Finance*; Previously titled *World Debt Tables*.

World Development Indicators, 2002. CD-Rom distributed by the World Bank.

WOYTINSKY, W. S. and E. S. (1955), *World Commerce and Governments: Trends and Outlook* (New York: Twentieth Century Fund).

World Resources Institute, *World Resources* 2002–4 (New York: Oxford University Press).

Part 2: The cultural impact of economic change

Introduction

While statistical data is vital in understanding the economic transformation of modern Middle Eastern society, qualitative information can provide a window on how these changes were noticed, interpreted, and negotiated over time. Quantitative information, gathered in a systematic and comprehensive way, becomes much harder to come by as we examine the economic history of the Middle East before the twentieth century. For earlier periods, economic historians have had to mine other sorts of records for economic information.

While the quantitative information obtained in this fashion is sometimes patchy, it comes with a wealth of cultural baggage to be unpacked. The documents in this section offer glimpses into the politics and cultural significance of traditionally constructed 'classes', state-led modernization, foreign debt, trade concessions, and land reform.

8.1 The barber of Damascus: Ahmad Budayri al-Hallaq's chronicle of the year 1749
Steve Tamari

Preface

The following excerpt comes from the chronicle of Ahmad Budayri al-Hallaq, a barber of eighteenth-century Damascus, the capital of modern-day Syria. Budayri's chronicle is remarkable for its representation of the voice of the common people. The bulk of the sources for Islamic history prior to the modern period represent elites, particularly the educated elite of scholars, known as the *ᶜulama*. However, for reasons that have yet to be explained, a number of Syrian commoners—including soldiers, court clerks, priests, a merchant, a farmer, and our own barber—wrote chronicles during the eighteenth century. Unlike the formal genres of history-writing that dominate Islamic historiography, the chronicle allowed the writer more latitude to describe people and events that were of interest to the lower and middle classes.

Ahmad Budayri was born in the Qubaybat neighborhood, one of the rough-and-tumble areas south of the city's walls. We know very little about his life outside of the chronicle itself. He began his chronicle in the year 1741 and it ends just over twenty years later, in 1762. He was married, had two sons and a daughter, and apparently worked as a barber for his entire career. The fact that he wrote a chronicle indicates that he was literate and not without literary ambitions.

Budayri's chronicle covers two key decades in the history of Ottoman Syria. The Ottomans had ruled Syria and most of the Arabic-speaking world since the early sixteenth century. Profound changes in the administration of the Arab provinces took place during the eighteenth century as the Ottoman central authorities in Istanbul depended increasingly on local political and military leaders to rule these territories. The rise of localism—as historians have since termed this phenomenon—is marked in Damascus by the coming to power of a succession of members of the ᶜAzm family, a family of Syrian origin. The key to ᶜAzm control over geographical Syria was their appointment as emirs, or guardians, of the annual Muslim pilgrimage from Damascus, where pilgrims from the northern and eastern reaches of the Islamic world convened to caravan across the treacherous Syrian and Arabian deserts. Management of the hajj brought the city—not to mention its rulers—considerable prestige and wealth.

The ᶜAzms reached the pinnacle of their power during the reign of Asᶜad al-ᶜAzm (also known as Asᶜad Paşa), who ruled the province of Damascus for an unprecedented fourteen consecutive years from 1743 to 1757. In addition to the provincial capital, the province of Damascus included the

major cities of modern-day Syria, Lebanon, Jordan, and Israel/Palestine.
As'ad's power was gradually challenged by elements on the periphery of his
domain, including Druze notables in Mount Lebanon, the renegade Zahir
al-ʿUmar in the Galilee and along the Palestinian coast, and Bedouins of the
Syrian desert.

This selection from Budayri's chronicle covers the year 1749. By this
time, Asʿad Paşa exerted complete control over the city's economy as well
as its politics. In addition to acquiring property for himself, he initiated the
biggest building boom in Damascus's history since the medieval period. In
1750 he began construction of a palace, which remains a landmark in the
centre of the walled city.

Budayri is a close observer of the economic consequences of these developments. He is a meticulous observer of changes in the prices of staple
commodities like wheat and bread. A *ratl* is a measure of weight that corresponds, roughly, to 6 pounds; a *wuqiya* equals about a half a pound. The
qirsh, the larger denomination of the silver currency then in use, equaled
forty *masari*.

This translation is based on a manuscript that has a story of its own.
Sometime during the late nineteenth century a prominent member of the
Damascene ʿulama acquired Budayri's original text and revised it, replacing
many of the author's colloquialisms with more formal usage. The original
subsequently disappeared and the first printed edition was based, instead,
on the nineteenth-century version. This translation is based on the printed
edition. In a final twist, Budayri's original manuscript was recently uncovered in a Dublin library.[1]

Text

The Year 1162 AH (1749 CE)[2]

The first of Muharram landed on a Saturday. This year was destined by God to
be a blessed one for us and for all our fellow Muslims. As for now, however, the
common people continue to suffer under the weight of the high cost of living.

---

[1] Dana Sajdi, 'Peripheral Visions: The Worlds and Worldviews of Commoner Chroniclers of the
18th-Century Ottoman Levant', Ph.D dissertation, Columbia University (2002), 31, 38 n. 112, 66–7;
id., 'A Room of His Own: The History of the Barber of Damascus (fl.1762)', *MIT Journal of Middle
East Studies*, 3 (Fall 2003), 19–35. <www. Mit. edu/cis/www/ mitlejmes/ intro. htm>.

[2] The Muslim calendar begins with the migration (*hijra*) of Muhammad and his earliest followers to
Medina from Mecca in 622 CE. This selection from Budayri's chronicle covers the year 1162 AH (*anno
hegirae*) which began on 22 December 1748 of the Gregorian calendar which Westerners and much of
the world use today. The Muslim calendar is a lunar calendar with twelve months: Muharram (1), Safar
(2), Rabiʿ al-Awwal (3), Rabiʿ al-Thani (4), Jumadi al-Ula (5), Jumadi al-Akhira (6), Rajab (7), Shaʿban
(8), Ramadan (9), Shawwal (10), Dhu al-Qaʿda (11), and Dhu al-Hijja (12). I have noted some additional
Gregorian dates in later footnotes for those who wish to keep track. To convert other dates from Hijri
to Gregorian (and vice versa) go to <http://www.rabiah.com/convert/convert.php3>.

However, it must be a positive omen that the year opened with heavy rains. Our collective optimism was expressed by the poet of al-Sham,[3] Shaykh ʿAbd al-Rahman al-Bahlul:

> We anticipate from God this year
> A bounty of happiness and good cheer
> He enriches us with His benevolence
> This, I predict, will be a year of affluence.

On Monday the 2ⁿᵈ of Muharram, Shaykh Ismaʿil al-Ajluni, the pre-eminent hadith scholar in all of al-Sham, indeed, the seal of hadith scholars, died.[4] He had been a teacher under the central dome at the Umayyad Mosque. Everyone in Damascus, young and old, attended his funeral. He was buried in the Shaykh Arslan Cemetery, may God be pleased with him.

During the same period, Ibrahim Agha, commander of the imperial guards, who had been relieved of his duties only a few months earlier, died. He was pious and humble and observed the Friday prayers at the Umayyad Mosque without fail. May God have mercy on him.

On the 27ᵗʰ of Muharram, the official messenger of the hajj caravan arrived in town and, three days later, the carrier of letters from the pilgrims also arrived. On a Thursday night, the 5ᵗʰ of Safar, the caravan itself finally arrived in town. The next day, Friday, a promising youth from two famous scholarly and pious families died. Shaykh Bakri b. Mustafa b. Saʿd al-Din was scion of both the Saʿdiyya Sufi order on his father's side and of the al-Sadiqiyya family on his mother's.[5] May God have mercy on him.

At the beginning of the month of Safar, a house in the Uqayba neighborhood collapsed on a group of people, killing seven of them. A man named Saʿid b. al-Shakush and his wife were rescued.

On the 10ᵗʰ of Rabiʿ al-Awwal, a bitter cold snap gripped the city. Folks started selling coal by the basket-full, carrying it on their heads. The *ratl* ran for five *masari*. They roamed the markets and neighborhoods.

On the 17ᵗʰ of Rabiʿ al-Awwal,[6] an official messenger from Istanbul arrived to call upon Asʿad Paşa al-ʿAzm, the emir of the hajj and the governor of Damascus. It appeared that this message came directly from the imperial palace so he ordered a fireworks display to mark the occasion. Imperial guards and regular forces raced toward the governor's palace. The people of Damascus thought that a skirmish had taken place so the town shut down. The governor was informed

---

[3] Al-Sham is a popular term for Damascus. Bilad al-Sham (the Land of al-Sham) refers, roughly, to geographic Syria.

[4] This is the scholar whose writings are featured in Sec. 4.1 above. *Hadith* are reports of the words and deeds of the Prophet Muhammad and are central to the elaboration of Islamic law.

[5] The 'b' between names stands for 'ibn', which translates as 'son of'.   [6] 7 March 1749.

and responded, 'Fire the cannon and light the fireworks once again.' The order was filled and the common folk calmed down and opened their shops. During these days, some of the Turkish imperial guards got drunk and four locals were injured and died some days later from their wounds. No inquest was made on behalf of these unfortunates.

High prices continued to mount. A *ratl* of the most inferior kind of bread cost six *masari*, the medium quality eight *masari* and the best quality twelve. A *wuqiya* of clarified butter cost seven *masari* and the same measure of oil cost two. The common people were in deep distress.

During the month of Rabic al-Awwal, news reached Damascus of severe flooding in Tripoli. This happened because the town's river overflowed its banks and inundated the town, drowning more than 500 people not to mention all manner of livestock and the destruction of property. May God protect us.

Meanwhile, Zahir al-cUmar, the ruler of Tiberius, and his henchmen wreaked havoc on the surrounding countryside plundering and looting. The reason for these hostilities was the presence of Arabs and Turkomen in his territory.[7] Ascad Paşa, the governor of Damascus, had previously launched an attack on these unruly elements killing a number and confiscating their livestock and property. The governor was thus able to dominate the market for meat with the confiscated herds with the result that prices rose dramatically, up to five times higher. During this month, the cost of a *ratl* of bread rose from nine *masari* to twelve, sweet breads to seventeen *masari*, a *ratl* of garlic to twenty-four *masari*, a sack of wheat to fifty *qirsh* and a sack of corn to forty-eight, two eggs for one *masari*, a *ratl* of rice for fifteen *masari* and a *ratl* of coal for six *masari*. The price of everything increased much beyond its just worth. During the month of Rabic al-Thani, Ascad Paşa killed three members of a Shici band and the leader of a group of bandits who promptly fled the city.

On Monday the 4th of Jumadi al-Akhira,[8] the newly appointed *qadi* of Damascus, al-Sayyid Muhammad Efendi Bashmaqji, arrived in town. I learned recently that Hamid al-Imadi, the *mufti* of Damascus,[9] had been hoarding wheat like all the other bigwigs [10] who don't fear God.

Those responsible for regulating weights and measurements came to the mufti and said, 'We sell wheat for fifty *qirsh* a sack.' He said in return, 'Take it easy. Perhaps the price will rise . . .' If our own Muslim *mufti* has no compassion for his fellow man, how can he possibly be fair?

---

[7] In this context, Budayri uses the term 'Arab' to refer to nomadic Arab tribes.

[8] 21 May 1749.

[9] The *qadi* was the chief judge of the province, who was usually of Turkish origin. The *mufti*, or jurisconsult, was usually from one of the most elite local families.

[10] This is a slightly whimsical translation of *al-akabir wa'l-cayan*. It literally means 'the great and notable persons', but this folksy touch seemed more suitable here.

A council was called by As'ad Paşa to discuss the increase in public immorality, particularly the gathering of female prostitutes in the alleyways and marketplaces and the fact that these women were sleeping in shops, bakeries, and coffee shops. In the end, the council broke up and no action was taken.

The rise in prices in Bilad al-Sham continued unabated. It reached us the *ratl* of bread in Tripoli cost ten *masari*, and in Gaza and Ramla twenty-five *masari*. Thus, the misfortune and subjugation of the common people continued.

At the same time, As'ad Paşa bought an immense amount of real estate including homes, gardens, mills, and the like. This happened before he built his palace. On the 8th of Jumadi al-Akhira, the new barley harvest reached market. Brown barley bread sold for four *masari* a *ratl* and white bread for six. Two days later, the town crier announced that wheat bread was going for four *masari* and the white for six. But none of this was of benefit to the poor for every day there was a new price. All is in the hands of God.

On Wednesday the 11th of Jumadi al-Akhira, the new wheat harvest reached market. A sack of wheat sold for forty-five *qirsh*. Earlier, it had been selling for fifty-two. So, the crowds cried foul and rose up attacking bakeries and demanding that the *ratl* of bread sell for three and four *masari*. So, the merchants began to sell at these prices, a fact which was welcomed by the populace who proceeded to celebrate.

Meanwhile, As'ad Paşa was in the garden of his father in the area of the al-Aqsab Mosque where he was enjoying a picnic accompanied by the town's bigwigs.[10] When he heard news of the popular unrest, he fell into a furious rage and ordered Mahmud Tafakji Paşa to take his infamous band of ruffians to roam the city and its markets and to warn the bakers that those who dare to sell white bread for anything less than six *masari* and brown for anything less than four will be beaten. So, the situation returned to the way it had been originally. Luckily, by the 16th of the month, the sack of wheat had fallen to twenty-six *qirsh* and the *ratl* of bread to three *masari* so there was finally relief to the people's misery thanks to the grace of God.

News reached Damascus that 'Abdallah Agha b. Hamza and Kamal Khalil, both heads of bands of outlaws who had been expelled from Damascus, had been captured and killed by Zahir al-'Umar, the lord of the citadel of Tiberius. Zahir had their severed heads sent to Sidon. The ruler of Sidon then forwarded them to Istanbul. Zahir sent a message to Istanbul demanding an order to ban As'ad Paşa from the territories under Zahir's control and from collecting taxes there.

On Monday the first of Rajab, As'ad Paşa began an effort to ban coffee and tobacco consumption in the city. He ordered that anyone disobeying this order would be executed. The consumption of coffee and tobacco had become a calamity affecting men, women, and even girls.

On the 3rd of Rajab, the bakers announced that the *ratl* of inferior bread cost four *masari*, the better quality five, and that mixed with barley or corn two. The people of Damascus, particularly the poor, were so overcome with joy that many began to cry with happiness. They began to decorate the market places throughout the city. On that day, the sack of new wheat or barley sold for eight *qirsh*. God graced his worshippers with blessings and generosity.

On Friday the 2nd of Sha^cban, Khalil Agha and Ahmad Agha, sons of Ibn al-Durzi, entered town and headed for the home of the deputy governor of Damascus who gave them a warm reception. They carried a letter of introduction from As^cad Paşa whom they had met through Shaykh Ibrahim al-Sa^cdi al-Jabawi, may God bless him and his ancestors. Khalil and Ahmad were fleeing Bedouin raiders when As^cad Paşa promised them refuge.

Two days before the beginning of Ramadan, the *qadi* of Damascus, Muhammad Efendi Bashmaqji, spent the day in al-Sahliyya with his entire household, including his wife. Late in the day, he was seen heading back to town and the central court carrying a pistol and wearing only one shoe. It appeared he was drunk.

However, I investigated this rumor and found it to be false. In fact, he was not drunk but was caught in a violent rage. Apparently, he was so infatuated with one of his female servants that he was willing to divorce his wife on her behalf. Here's what happened. Realizing her husband was in love with another, his wife decided to make the *qadi*'s life unbearable. One day some guests of the servant came to pay her a visit. So, she planned a lavish feast in al-Salihiyya. But the jilted wife conspired to thwart her plans. When the guests arrived and were left without food or drink, the servant started to cry. The *qadi* was so obsessed with this woman that he immediately divorced his wife on her account. He told his entourage to return to the city and he demanded his shoes. One shoe was missing so he descended himself with only one shoe on and rode all the way to the court in this unkempt and agitated manner. His enemies seized the opportunity to accuse him of drunkenness and his wife went as far as lodging a complaint with the central state. An official decree followed which ordered the banishment of the unfortunate *qadi* to Cyprus and the confiscation of his assets which were to be turned over to the wife. She promptly sold these for a sum of almost eight bags of gold coins. By this time, people began to sympathize with the *qadi* except for those who had held a grudge against him for his uprightness and humility. He was so generous that he regularly opened his pantry during Ramadan and gave away enormous quantities of clarified butter and rice and other staples and even meat. More than thirty people would eat at his place nightly during Ramadan. Because he refused to accept bribes or take sides in legal disputes, there were unscrupulous people in our town who were only too happy to join with his wife against him.

On Sunday the 15th of Shawwal[11] an armed retinue guarding tribute headed for Istanbul from Egypt arrived in Damascus. On the 16th, the ceremonial litter led by the emir of the *hajj*, As^cad b. Isma^cil al-^cAzm, departed Damascus. This was the seventh caravan to be led by As^cad Paşa. His father Isma^cil had led six. Two days after the departure of the *hajj*, the deputy governor executed two members of a band of robbers which had been responsible for a recent spate of robberies. The two, one of whom was named Shaykh al-Takiyya, were finally caught stealing from a private home.

Four days after the Syrian *hajj* caravan left town, al-Sayyid Yunis, one of As^cad Paşa's business partners, left town with another large caravan. They caught up with the main caravan at Muzayrib.

During the course of this year, As^cad Paşa paid for the renovation of the second storey of the college built by his father in the Tailors' Market. He also provided renewed funding for the college's charitable functions including feeding the poor and purchasing copies of the Qur'an.

On the 9th of Dhu al-Qa^cda,[12] the aforementioned *qadi* departed for Sidon on his way to exile in Cyprus. A few bigwigs saw him off. On the 15th of the month, three individuals accused of forgery were publicly humiliated by being paraded through town riding backwards on donkeys with their faces blackened. One was Kurdish and the other Daghistani.[13]

On the same day, the paşa ordered prostitutes to leave the city. It appears he wanted to banish them to other cities. So, it was announced to neighborhood headmen that they should turn in any suspicious women. Then the town crier announced that all women—save those of the governor's household and that of his chief lieutenant—should not veil. The paşa's men then began a round of inspections that got progressively intrusive and provoked public outrage. Within only a few days, the 'ladies of the night' had returned to their usual haunts in the alleyways and market places. In the end, the governor imposed a tax on them such that each had to pay ten *qirsh* to be collected and regulated by an official of the court.

On Tuesday Sa^cd al-Din Paşa, brother of As^cad Paşa al-^cAzm, entered Damascus at the head of the official *hajj* litter because he was the head of the military unit responsible for provisioning the returning caravan, a post he had assumed the previous year.

[11] 27 September 1749.   [12] 21 October 1749.
[13] Daghistan is a Turkish-speaking area in the Eastern Caucasus near the Caspian Sea. The Russian Empire conquered the area from the Ottomans in the ninteenth century.

8.2 Six Ottoman documents on the power of guilds in the Balkans, 1760s
Frederick Anscombe

Preface

In the eighteenth century, Arnavud Belgrad (known today as the city of Berat, Albania) was one of the leading towns of the Albanian provinces of the western Balkans. It served as the administrative center of the province of Avlonya (Vlora, today the leading city and port of southern Albania). The population of the town, estimated to be around 15,000 in 1770, included Christians and Jews, but was predominantly Muslim. The town's economy and society were both closely tied to a very well-developed system of craft guilds, of which there were twenty-two by the middle of the century. The most important of these were the tanners and other guilds that worked with leather, such as the cobblers. Among the remaining guilds were some devoted to metalworking, such as the kettle-makers and the silversmiths jewelers corporations, while yet other guilds, including the tailors and the silk-makers, dealt in textiles. The economic and social strength of the guilds derived in part from various tax exemptions granted by the sultans, beginning with Mehmet II (r. 1451–81), who rewarded these corporations for extraordinary services rendered, primarily military in nature. Such services were best performed by young, unmarried men, and bachelors seeking craft training and admission into the guilds formed a noticeable part of the town population: six inns offered lodging to bachelors in 1670, for example, and a mosque erected in 1827–8 came to be known as 'the Bachelors' Mosque'.

The 1760s was a decade of increasing turbulence and economic difficulties in many parts of the Ottoman Empire, including the western Balkans. Powerful guilds in some Albanian towns used their strength to compete aggressively for economic and, increasingly, political advantage. The best-known example of this trend was the case of İskenderiyye (now Shkodra, northern Albania), where the town's guilds formed factions to support rival families competing for the governorship of that province. Some of the guilds in Arnavud Belgrad seem to have acted similarly at the beginning of the decade, recruiting young men to strong-arm the courts, intimidate rivals, and even engage in occasional banditry outside the town. Perhaps inevitably, they clashed with the governor of Avlonya, Velabishtli Ismail Paşa, a member of a leading local family who was also struggling to strengthen his authority over the region. The translated documents given below are selections from a series of orders issued by the central government to the authorities in Arnavud Belgrad, and from a report sent to Istanbul by two imperial officials sent to investigate the dispute. It appears that Ismail sought to win Istanbul's backing for his attempt to break the independent strength of the guilds by appealing to the central government's interest in raising much-needed revenue and in preventing banditry and other unrest. While his tactic succeeded at first, he overplayed his hand by removing the law court and the market from the town center to an outlying village, which also happened to be Ismail Paşa's home. Once he had passed away, the guilds sought a reversal of Ismail's actions. As a result, Istanbul rescinded the most severe punishments imposed upon the guilds and townspeople, including the relocation of the court and the market, as well as the imposition of a financial surety for good behavior.

Texts

I. Order to the governor of Avlonya, Ismail Paşa, and to the judges of Avlonya province[14]

When the ships of the unbelievers attacked the fort of Avlonya on the coast,[15] six hundred [and fifty] Muslims from the traders [and the guilds of the] tailors, tanners, and slipper-makers of Arnavud Belgrad gave assistance [in the fort's defense]. In return for their services, it was recorded in the imperial registers that they would be excused and exempt from *avarız-i divaniye* and *tekalif-i örfiye*.[16] With the passage of time, the aforementioned people, exceeding the bounds of appropriate behavior, have inscribed in their registers Muslims and *reaya*[17] from villages of the district who have no [skill in the guild's] trade and have gathered such men, known as bachelors, in their shops and meeting rooms, all for the purpose of each guild raising their flag and engaging in banditry. Holding [guild membership] documents from the guild *kethudas*[18] and claiming exemption and prohibition of payment of imperial revenue, not only do they use these as excuses and causes to suspend imperial revenues and to disregard my imperial commands, judicial orders, and governors' decrees, but also to spread this sort of foul behavior and shameless acts to others [. . .]

Late December 1761

[14] This order is found in: Istanbul, Başbakanlık Osmanlı Arşivi, Mühimme 162, p. 336/1.

[15] It is unclear to which Christian attack upon Avlonya this refers. The most recent such significant attack on Avlonya occurred in 1715 during the last Ottoman war with Venice.

[16] 'Extraordinary' and customary taxes which formed a significant part of the revenue due to Istanbul. Muslims resident in the Arnavud Belgrad citadel had enjoyed tax exemptions for such service since the Ottoman conquest, but the exemptions granted specifically to guild members may well have come later.

[17] A term for the taxpaying subjects of the empire, which in the eighteenth century came to refer most often to Christians.

[18] One of the chief administrative officers of a guild who usually represented the corporation in contacts with representatives of the government, often translated as 'steward'.

II. Order to the Governor of Avlonya, Vizier Ismail Paşa, and the Judge of Arnavud Belgrad[19]

To you, the aforementioned vizier: you have been charged by imperial command to carry out the shaping of a sound order in Arnavud Belgrad and the cleansing of bandits from the city, but the court in that town lies beyond the guilds. Villagers coming to plead suits according to the Şeriat pass by the aforementioned guilds on their way to and from the court. It is the [guild members'] practice to have [the suit] appointed to themselves. You wrote and requested in a letter the issuing again of an imperial order to stop and expel the court from its current location, for it to be moved to another quarter of the city, Verabishte[20], and for *şeriat* judgements to be carried out there, in order to negate these sorts of tricks and stratagems of the guilds. In light of all of this, it is decreed that the said court is to be moved from its old location to the said quarter, which is deemed appropriate [. . .]

End June/beginning July 1762

III. Order to the Governor of Avlonya and the Assistant Judge of Arnavud Belgrad

People of known name, residents of Arnavud Belgrad and members of the three guilds of tanners, slipper-makers, and tailors, made [the following] declaration in court. 'We have acted wrongly for a long time, have collected the worst sort of bandits under our command and engaged in acts of sedition leading to public disorder, fought with each other in the name of the guilds of tanners, slipper-makers and tailors, been insubordinate and fought against our judges and governors, and have prevented the collection of imperial revenues. Because our banditry became intolerable, before this an exalted order was issued by the imperial *divan*[21] regarding the ending and prevention of our banditry and the shaping and bonding of the people of the city to a strong, worthy order. The command was sent and executed by a suitable representative of the imperial court, Al-Hajj Hasan (may his glory increase), formerly confidential messenger of the Grand Vizier. Upon his arrival, the following leaders of the bandit groups were expelled from our city: Hasan, Muhsin, Molla Ibrahim, Said, Little Hasan, Mehmed Gorija, Salih Kavach, Ali Gorija the Bachelor, Rasul Katoja, Yegor Ibrahim Sakayla, Omar Sok, Hüseyn the Janissary, his brother Ibrahim, Hussein Ajar,

---

[19] This and the following documents are found in: Istanbul, Başbakanlık Osmanlı Arşivi, Cevdet Dahiliye 14561.

[20] While Verabishte/Velabisht was one of the quarters of Arnavud Belgrad, it lay well outside the centre and was more rural than urban.

[21] The high council of the state, chaired by the grand vizier.

Sinan Evsiye, Doku Chalo, Mosqo the Voyvode,[22] Ahmed Beh, Islam Kaloda, Chavush Ertitas,[23] Abdi Hoja Shusha, Aziz the Kethuda, Abdülaziz the Kethuda, Hasan Zaira, Hasan Zitum, Abdullah Bezdan, Arslan Kirshiyan, Osman the Dizdar,[24] Hajji Abdullah, Abdul Avar, Malo Zal, Omar Tarya, Muhzirbashi Ebu Bekir,[25] and Mustafa Keshova. Furthermore, the houses of five [leading] bandits were destroyed. From today, [the conditions of the strong, firm order are:] we are not to become involved in sedition which will lead to public disorder; the expelled bandits are not to visit the city, and if any of them come secretly, they are to be approached and seized immediately and delivered to the judges and governors, and their punishments arranged; no claim to be guildsmen shall be made by any of us who are not artisans or by any people entered in the guild registers who come from villages outside the city; sheep-tax collectors shall not be hindered from collecting imperial revenue by [guild] *kethuda*s claiming that 'tailors, tanners and slipper-makers are exempt'; we shall not interfere with the collection of other imperial revenues, with the execution of imperial orders issued [in Istanbul], and with governors and judges acting on judicial matters; we shall not block and turn away by force any who come from neighboring villages to make a claim of rights from the guilds in their meeting rooms; we shall not hold court in our [guild] meeting rooms and shops and investigate claims with witnesses; we shall not set out to fight with each other; we shall not plunder possessions and goods from the homes of the poor and the *reaya*; we shall not take up banditry in the regions of Tırhala,[26] Karlı İli, Agrafa[27] and Yenishehir;[28] we shall not pillage caravans and their attendants which pass near the city; we shall not fight in the weekly market held in the city or plunder the goods of the market people; we shall not keep in our shops and meeting rooms any bachelor from the villages who has no [guild craft] skills and no guarantor; we shall not raise flags and standards and horse-tails[29] like pashas do; and we shall not exceed the 650 men from the three guilds specified in the imperial order assigning us to the defense [of the fort of Avlonya].' If someone dares to oppose the new order, he is to be exiled to another province. In future, if any action arises which contravenes the conditions of this agreement as written, they have accepted and undertaken to pay to the imperial treasury a bond of 50,000 *gurush*[. . .] [The governor and assistant judge are now to make these people understand that,

[22] An agent entrusted with the collection of revenues due to a high official based in Istanbul or elsewhere in the provinces.

[23] *Çavuş* was a title with many meanings. In this case it might imply an officer of the local gendarmerie or 'police'.   [24] The commander of the local military garrison.

[25] An officer of the lawcourt, roughly equivalent to a bailiff.

[26] Today: Trikkala, central Greece.

[27] Today, both Karlı İli and Agrafa are in western Greece.   [28] Today: Larissa, eastern Greece.

[29] A pasha was permitted to raise horse-tails in the manner of a military standard, the number depending upon his rank.

should this agreement be broken, the government would not be content with taking the 50,000 *gurush* surety. It would not only demand a sum several times larger, it would also mete out the necessary legal punishments through the court.]

8 August 1762

IV. Order to the Deputy Judge of Arnavud Belgrad

Previously, due to reports of the bad behavior of some residents of Arnavud Belgrad, an imperial order was issued to the governor of Avlonya province, the late Ismail Paşa, according to which the people whose bad behavior was reported asked pardon in court for the previous crimes. But the bandit ringleaders among the people of the city, Hasan and others whose names were written down, were expelled and driven from the said city. It was recorded that the testimonial [concerning the conditions that those expelled not visit the city upon pain of arrest and punishment, and the posting of the 50,000 *gurush* surety] was registered in the imperial treasury in early July 1762. But now people of the said city have come to the Seriat court [and testified]: Hasan (may his goodness increase)—*devr-i khan* and *khatib*[30] in the holy mosque of the blessed Sultan Mehmed in the said city, known for his learning and his excellence, diligently and modestly occupied with teaching—was set upon and abused in contravention of the Seriat, because the unspecific name 'Hasan' was reported to the Sublime Porte as one of those aforementioned people driven out of the city and forbidden to return. Because the deputy judge of Arnavud Belgrad, Mevlana Dervish Hasan (may his knowledge increase), has reported that [the people] have petitioned for the issuance of an imperial order that the said Hasan not be set upon and abused in future, [an official will be sent to investigate the case].

October–November 1764

V. Order to the Judge of Arnavud Belgrad

Previously, due to reports of the bad behavior of some residents of Arnavud Belgrad, an imperial order was issued to the governor of Avlonya province, the late Ismail Paşa, according to which the people whose bad behavior was reported asked pardon in court for the previous crimes. It was recorded that the testimonial [concerning the conditions that the guilds not accept unqualified members or attempt to hinder the collection of revenue, and the posting of the 50,000 *gurush* surety] was registered in the imperial treasury in early July 1762. Now, people of the said city have come to the şeriat court [and testified]: the tanners Mehmed Gorija, Ali Gorija, and Salih Kavach, and the tailors Ibrahim Iskila and Hasan Zitum, residents of the said city, while behaving properly and plying their crafts, were previously falsely accused by the aforementioned deceased

---

[30] Qur'an reader and preacher of the sermon delivered at the midday Friday prayers.

[governor] out of spite. [These townspeople] testify to their good character and petition for the issuance of an imperial order forgiving them for their previous sins [and punishments]. [It is ordered that an official will be sent to investigate the case.]

October–November 1764

VI

[In response to the petitions forwarded to Istanbul by the deputy judge of Arnavud Belgrad, two officials came to the city to investigate. Upon their making inquiries], a large and numerous group of people—the learned, the just, the imams, the preachers, the elders of the three guilds, and others—came to [them] and made the following statement. As was written, from the beginning the afore-mentioned deceased [governor of Avlonya] bore spite, hatred, and enmity towards the said people [listed in document V]. He was not content with sending false reports, intending to act on pure spite, betray [us] and cause [us] damage, and assessing and registering the [50,000 *gurush*] surety. In order to inflict further damage on the market and bazaar, he moved the court and the market, which had been held in the said city since the days of old, from their old site to an empty, desolate wilderness called Verabishte, three hours away from the said city. For the past two years, because our market and court are held in the aforementioned place, and especially because they are thus so far removed from our city, our old men and women have much trouble and toil in doing their shopping. Our şeriat court cases which occur in summer and winter, moreover, come to nothing because of this [difficulty in reaching Verabishte], and problems and conflicts remain continuously on the boil. These people petition and implore that, having pity upon their condition, their court and market be returned to the place where they had been held since the conquest of these territories, and that the people registered as responsible for the surety have that cancelled and lifted from them [. . .]

22 November 1764

[This petition was subsequently granted.]

8.3 Economic change: Muhammad ᶜAli's development schemes in Egypt and Syria, 1834 and 1837
Robert G. Landen

Preface

Muhammad ᶜAli's (Mehmed Ali) need to pay for his expensive military modernization program prompted him to introduce a comprehensive development program which brought sweeping change to the economies of Egypt and Syria. His reordering of agriculture smashed the Mamluk land tenure system, asserted Cairo's control over the rural economy, increased the cultivated area through the construction of irrigation works in Egypt and by re-establishing abandoned villages in Syria, and encouraged market crops such as cotton, sugar cane, and tobacco. More spectacular, although of less fundamental importance, were the paşa's attempts to build a new industrial-commercial system. Factories, many of whose machines were powered by animal-driven treadmills, were built both in the cities and the countryside. The new factories were state-owned, and by 1837 were supervised by a central Ministry of Industry. Most of them were abandoned, however, in the austerity program initiated in 1841. Commercially, there was an immense quickening of activity as Egypt became closely enmeshed with the European-dominated modern international economy. Besides controlling production, the government undertook the sale and distribution of goods through the state agencies; as a result, members of the old craft guilds, masters and workers alike, as well as laborers hired by the new factories, all became state employees. Since foreign experts and businessmen played a large role in all these projects, foreign participation in Egypt's economic life became a feature of the period and of later years as well.

In the first of these documents, the British House of Lords is presented with a report on Syrian agriculture. Bowering, author of the report, discusses soil conditions, plants cultivated, and livestock. His discussion of mulberry, olive, and grape cultivation illustrates the state of agricultural production in these traditional crops of greater Syria, and his report suggests that local capital and foreign capital alike were investing in ways to increase the production of these products. In addition, he discusses innovative crops such as tobacco, which since the 1500s had been an arena of struggle over imports and local production. Tobacco, along with coffee, was considered a stimulant and was therefore put under regulation by muftis from Arabia to Istanbul as rulers attempted to control both the consumption of these substances, and the social spaces (coffee-houses) where men could gather outside the surveillance of the state. These attempts to regulate tobacco as a social product in particular were doomed to failure, as there exist reports of Janissaries being executed for smoking tobacco—and smoking a pipe up until the very moment of their execution. The Ottomans in particular were fairly successful, however, in weaning their economies off imported tobacco through subsidies for tobacco farming, and the creation of state-run factories for pipe tobacco, cigars, and later cigarettes. State monopolies on the production of tobacco products were a key element of the Ottoman economy in particular up to the end of the empire in the early twentieth century, and as such were identified by local reformers and sultans as proof that Middle Easterners could, in fact, create their own modern, profitable economies of production and manufacture.

The second document is a British report of Muhammad ᶜAli's style of industrializing his agricultural economy. While his attempts to industrialize production of such agricultural end-products as refined sugar and milled cotton were largely unsuccessful, his investment in cotton as a cash crop paid huge dividends during the American Civil War (1860–5), when Britain's textile-manufacturing towns, such as Manchester, turned to Egypt to replace the cotton they had previously imported from the southern United States. As with mulberries, olives, and grapes, agricultural reformers used new, often Western, innovations in fertilization, irrigation, and crop rotation in order to increase areas of cultivation, levels of production, and the quality of agricultural products to compete with other providers of cotton. Consequently, Egypt was well established by the end of the Civil War as a major source of fine long-staple cotton, and has remained so to this day. This great economic success story had a horrible cost, however, as Egyptian peasants were forced to abandon their subsistence crops in order to produce cotton for their landlords. From the introduction of cotton as a major cash crop in Egypt, rates of famine, infant and maternal mortality, and deaths from water-borne diseases wiped out hundreds of thousands of Egyptian peasants for decades. In all industrializing sectors of the economy, including the military, Muhammad ᶜAli relied on slaves collected in the Sudan, but this population also fell prey to diseases of the city and the Nile. Controlling these calamitous rates of casualty from industrialization was one of the major goals of public health programs instituted by Muhammad ᶜAli's successors and funded, ironically, by revenues from cotton. This second document, then, provides a clear account of the human costs of rapid industrialization in the nineteenth century in Egypt, with relevance to other sites of rapid industrialization in Europe, the Americas, and Asia.

Texts

1. The awakening of rural Syria[31]

The agriculture produce of Syria is far less than might be expected from the extensive tracts of fertile lands and the favourable character of the climate. In the districts where hands are found to cultivate the fields, production is large and the return for capital is considerable; but the want of population for the purposes of cultivation is most deplorable. Regions of the highest fertility remain fallow, and the traveller passes over continuous leagues of the richest soil which is wholly unproductive to man. Nay, towns surrounded by lands capable of the most successful cultivation are often compelled to import corn for the daily consumption; as is the case at Antioch, in whose immediate neighbourhood the fine lands on the borders of the Orontes might furnish food for hundreds of thousands of inhabitants. But men crowd into towns for protection and security, and leave the rural districts without labourers to sow or to reap the harvest.

Agriculture knowledge is generally in a backward state; the old Roman plough, drawn by bullocks, is almost universally employed. In Mount Lebanon, however, where the scantiness of appropriate soil requires a succession of terraces for cultivation, spade husbandry is much used, the space being too narrow for the plough [. . .]

To these more important articles of export may be added wheat, barley, maize, millet, lentils, sesame seed, and other produce, consumed principally by the inhabitants. The production of which the increased cultivation is most obvious is the mulberry tree, for the use of the silkworm, which may be attributed to the demand for silk in every part of manufacturing Europe: but a considerable increase has also taken place in the cultivation of the vine, and plantations have also been made for the extension of the growth of the olive-tree, principally in the districts of Tripoli and Latakia, the localities adapted to their developments.

At Suediah, in the vale of Antioch, Latakia, Tripoli, and many other places, the cultivation of tobacco is one of the first importance, and is on the increase; and there is scarcely any place in Syria where it is not now grown, but the qualities are very various.

Mr Werry[32] thinks there is no agricultural produce whose cultivation has decreased, but that, on the contrary, grain and pulse of every kind, as well as produce for exportation, are produced to a much larger extent than formerly from one end of Syria to the other. Great exertions have been made on the part of the government to effect this object by obliging all the chief officers and the most wealthy inhabitants to take upon themselves the restoring of ruined villages, and

[31] John Bowering, 'Report on the Commercial Statistics of Syria', House of Lords, *Sessional Papers*, (1840), vol. 35, pp. 9–10.   [32] British consul in Syria.

the cultivation of the lands belonging to these villages; but it is very doubtful whether in the mode of cultivation there is any improvement.

The following is the extension given to the agriculture in the Aleppo district from 1836 to 1838.

Villages and lands belonging to the town of Aleppo:

329	Villages	Old
238	Parcels of land	
74	Villages or Hamlets	New
445	Parcels of land	
1,086	Belonging to Aleppo District	Baylan [Beilan]
410	Villages and land	Antioch
206	Villages and land	Aintab
36	Villages and land	Baylan [Beilan]
397	Old Villages	
149	Lands	Killis
27	New Villages	
2,311	In all	

And similar extension has taken place in the Damascus district.

Last year (1837) Ibrahim Pasha forced an increased cultivation throughout Syria and the inhabitants of the different towns were obliged to take upon themselves the agricultural charge of every spot of land susceptible to improvement. He himself set the example, and embarked a large sum in such enterprises. The officers of the army, down to the majors, were forced also to adventure in similar undertakings. The result was, however, extremely unfortunate, from the want of the usual periodical rains, which caused the failing of the crops generally in Syria, and in most cases a total loss of capital ensued. Mr Werry says, a considerable extension of the plantation of the mulberry and olive-tree, and vines, took place at Tripoli, Latakia, and to the south, and in fact in every place susceptible to their culture. It was the intention of his highness Ibrahim Pasha, and the government of Egypt by the increased cultivation, principally of wheat and barley, to render Syria independent of supplies from without, and, if possible, to obtain a superabundance to become an article of export. In the time of abundant crops, Syria generally produced, chiefly in the south, sufficient for its own consumption; and the north, when in want, usually received supplies from the country surrounding Urfa, across the Euphrates. The productive plans of the Adana district also supplied Syria, and were the measures undertaken by the government persevered in, there is no reason to doubt that they would in every respect become highly beneficial to the population of Syria generally, and render independent of import from any other quarter.

The chief observation to be made on these measures is, that there is no want of land generally in Syria, nor is there a want of capital for such an object, but there is want of agricultural population and of livestock.[. . .]

2. Muhammad ʿAli's attempt to make Egypt a manufacturing country[33]

Not content with imparting to his people a knowledge of the sciences, and the arts of war, Muhammad ʿAli, in 1819, was led by the advice of Europeans to attempt the introduction of the manufacturing system. In this undertaking he was deluded by fallacious calculations. Being persuaded that, with the aid of certain French and Swiss adventurers, it was possible to render Cairo a second Manchester, he commenced operations with his usual rapidity. French, Italian, Maltese, and Savoyard manufacturers and artisans were employed. Kromfish, a district of miserable houses and narrow streets, in the centre of the metropolis, infamous for murders and every other horrid crime, was cleared of its inhabitants, and the whole den of thieves and cut-throats converted, with very trifling alterations, into factories. No expense was spared in procuring every description of machinery from Europe. Magazines were formed; mills, worked by bullocks, constructed; and the machinery was erected by the principal French and Italian mechanics. This establishment was directed by M. Morel of Chamberi; and another large factory, erected at Boolak, was placed under the superintendence of M. Jumel, a Frenchman. The number of natives employed in this new species of industry amounted to eight hundred.

At Kromfish, an attempt was made to produce velvets equal to those of Genoa, and muslins not inferior to those of England; but, after a short trial, the destruction of the machinery, which could not be repaired, and the extremely inferior quality of the articles manufactured, induced the Pasha—perhaps before the experiment had been fairly tried—wholly to abandon this portion of the scheme. Kromfish was not, however, entirely forsaken. Muhammad ʿAli was still desirous of rendering Egypt a manufacturing country; a failure in one experiment not being sufficient to deter him from attempting others. The cultivation of the cotton-plant already promised to become a fertile source of revenue. He now, therefore, determined to manufacture from the raw material, and Kromfish became a cotton-mill.

On the first introduction of European manufactories into Egypt, the Turks in office, and even the people in general, openly evinced their disapprobation in their mutual discourse; and the former were often bold enough to represent to the Pasha, in open Divan, the impolicy of his conduct. But courtiers in all countries are too much the slaves of habit, too timid in their apprehensions, and

[33] James A. St John, *Egypt and Muhammad ʿAli*, vol. 2 (London, 1834), 408–414, 417, 423–5.

too ignorant of whatever concerns the public good, to be competent judges in an untried line of internal policy. The Pasha, therefore, despised their representations, which arose out of no superior degree of foresight, but from a puerile aversion to every thing new; and his will necessarily prevailed. Encouraged by the first samples produced at Kromfish, he now caused cotton-mills to be erected at Mehalet-el-Kebir, at Mansourah, and in the southern parts of the metropolis. At first, no persons were employed in the factories but black slaves from Darfour and Kordofan, who displayed great intelligence, and quickly acquired a competent knowledge of the business; but so great a change of life, co-operating with the peculiar unhealthiness of the occupation, gradually thinned their ranks, so that the Pasha was shortly compelled to have recourse to the Fellahs.[34]

It must be observed that, with the exception of a few machines adapted to each manipulation, brought out from Europe as models, no cotton-spinning apparatus has been imported into the country. The store-houses were furnished with tools; lathes, screw-tapping lathes, instruments for fluting rollers, and cutting the teeth of wheels, with other preparatory instruments—all purchased in England and France at an enormous cost; and upon these models preparatory instruments were soon multiplied by the carpenters, smiths, filers, turners, &c. formed under the tuition of the French and Italian artisans; who, under the superintendence of M. Jumel—a professional spinner and mechanic—constructed all the spinning machinery which now fills the numerous cotton-factories throughout Egypt.

The Pasha regards his manufactories in so important a light, that, to promote emulation, and confer a superior degree of respectability on the professor of the useful arts, he honours their directors with a seat in the Mashwarrah (or council), and further distinguishes them by diamond decorations, which they wear on the breast. All the operative Nazirs,[35] one of whom is placed over every mill, have likewise their badges of honour. The officers engaged in the factories deem their employment peculiarly honourable; but their conduct is too frequently directly the reverse; for though in the receipt of handsome salaries, they sordidly avail themselves of the mal-organisation of the establishments to commit dishonesty, and plunder their master and their inferiors. Being entrusted with the regulation of the expenses, and the paying of the workmen, they accept bribes to favour an indifferent artisan at the expense of the government, and commit innumerable other frauds difficult of detection. Thus it is that commissioners from the treasury are perpetually engaged in examining accounts and detecting imposition.

[34] *Fallab*: peasant; British sources often referred to this group of workers with the Egyptian singular and the British plural, as 'fellahs'. This suggests that 'fellah' was a common and familiar term to British officials and merchants concerned with overseas trade.

[35] Directors; again, an Arabic singular noun with a British plural ending.

The fellahs employed in the various manipulations have an extreme dislike to the business; being pressed into the mills, they labour only because they are compelled. Though they generally arrive at the factories in good health, the insalubrious nature of the employment, imprisonment, their scanty wages, the insufficiency of their food, and the odious vices which, by the example of their superiors, they quickly learn to commit, in a short time render them diseased and despicable. They seldom see their wives and children, nor are they allowed the requisite time for meals, ablutions, or religious duties. Inattention or misman-agement is followed by immediate chastisement; the directing Nazirs being regularly accompanied by their executioners, who flog the delinquents with the Koorbash.[36] From two hundred to five hundred blows are not unusual; so that a cotton-spinner in Egypt is no less brutally punished than a West India negro; while, in the Pasha's navy, fifty blows are considered a sufficient punishment for ordinary offences. Such being their treatment, it is not at all surprising that the operatives eagerly avail themselves of the first opportunity which presents itself of making their escape; or, where this is impracticable, of revenging their wrongs in a more serious manner. Of the twenty-three or twenty-four cotton-mills existing in Egypt, there is not one which has not, at various periods, been accid-entally or designedly set on fire. The factory at Siout, which employed about six hundred hands, was purposely burned to the ground; and, towards the close of December, 1832, the power-loom weaving mill of Khand-el-Merood was like-wise designedly destroyed by fire. In the latter establishment the loss was estimated at 35,000 lire. On the day preceding this accident, a fellah, who had been dragged against his inclination into the rope-walk, stabbed himself in three places, and, after a short struggle, expired.

In the provincial mills the raw material is beaten, carded, and spun by men and boys; and the yarn, when taken off the reefs, is put loosely into large bags, and transported to Cairo on camels. But, in some of the factories, a small portion is retained and woven into cloth, part of which being sent to the capital, the remain-der is appropriated to the payment of the operatives. For this purpose they make use of hand-looms, built after French models. At present not one of the mills keeps its full complement of machinery at work, and there are several where not one half is employed; in some cases because the machines are actually worn out; in others from the scarcity of hands. Through the ignorance and carelessness of the directors and their operatives, about fifty per cent of the raw material is wasted.[. . .]

The traveller, on his way to the upper country, is astonished at the vastness of the cotton-mills, which, though differing in dimensions, are all built on the same

[36] A kind of whip, often with multiple strands of leather, sometimes with nails at the end of each strand, attached to the whip-handle.

plan. They are constructed with rubble and mortar, and covered externally with stucco. For the small number of machines they contain, they are much more spacious than necessary. The apartments, which are flagged with stone, are extremely lofty, and the doors and windows proportionally large. All the bullock-mills, along the front of the buildings; are enclosed in large towers, adorned with bow windows, balconies, and balustrades. Spacious flights of stone steps ascend to the second story, and the entrance is generally shaded by a light wooden trellis-work. All these buildings are erected in the finest situations. At Minieh, for example, the mill is situated on the edge of the Nile, and surrounded by a grove of orange and date trees, which give it a picturesque appearance. The expense of building one of the smaller mills amounts to about 7,000 £ sterling; [. . .]

I subjoin a list of the factories of different kinds now existing in Egypt:—

1. Sugar and rum manufactory at Er Raramoun.
2. Powder manufactory at Rhouda.
3. Saltpetre refinery at Rhouda.
4. Chemical works, at Masr el Atikeh (Old Cairo).
5. Tannery, Old Cairo.
6. Found brass guns and carriages in the citadel.
7. Copper-mills.

Citadel
8. Pyrotechnic school: fire works, carcasses, stink-pots, signal rockets, &c.

Cairo
9. Cotton-mills.
10. Weaving, silk and cotton.
11. Rope walks, for Alexandria.
12. Musket manufactory: here they repair monthly 1600 old muskets, and manufacture 400 new ones, under the direction of ʿAli Aga, a French renegade, with the rank of Colonel.
13. Cloth manufactory.
14. Calico printing works.
15. Bleaching fields.
16. Iron foundry: to appearance the finest in the world. By Galloway.
17. Power-loom weaving factory. By Galloway.
18. Dyeing works.

Rosetta
19. Rice-mills. By Galloway.
20. Tannery.

21. Corn mills: there now exist about forty; but it is contemplated to increase the number to two hundred.

22. Glass-house.

23. At Malta-Fabrick, four hundred forges, employed for the fleet and army.

24. At Gallioop, one hundred and fifty forges set up, but not worked.

25. Paper mill; recently established near Cairo.

26. Manufactory of Tarbooshes, at Fouah. Directed by Tunisians.

8.4 Financial imperialism and its relationship to development; the Ottoman Public Debt Administration, 1881–1925

Robert G. Landen

Preface

The inability of Middle Eastern governments to pay off loans utilized to finance large-scale modernization schemes prompted the establishment in the late nineteenth century of various types of international debt administrations in many countries including Tunisia, Egypt, Iran, and the Ottoman Empire. The Ottoman Public Debt Administration, founded in 1881, was one of the most influential.

In 1875 the Ottoman state was eventually forced to default on the substantial foreign loans contracted at the beginning of the Crimean War. The ensuing war with Russia in 1877–8 exacerbated the situation, with the result that the empire's fiscal standing was one of virtual bankruptcy. Following the cessation of hostilities in 1878, negotiations were initiated to extract the empire and its creditors from their financial plight, and to allow for the continuation of the relationship between the empire and European lenders. The resulting solution was the creation of the Ottoman Public Debt Administration, an organization devoted to furthering the interests of the largely European holders of the Ottoman debt.

The Ottoman government turned over the collection of certain taxes and monopoly revenues to the Public Debt Administration to service the defaulted loans. The work of the Administration had a permanent influence upon the modernization of the Ottoman Empire and its successor, the Republic of Turkey. Financial collection and disbursement is at the heart of many governmental operations; thus a foreign-dominated body was given a large voice in determining Ottoman policies, political as well as economic. The Administration's bureaucracy employed thousands of locals, trained them in modern financial and tax procedures, and consequently bequeathed a well-trained core of financial officials to Turkey and other Ottoman successor states when it terminated operations in 1925. Much of the modern sector of the Ottoman economy in 1914 was the creation of the Administration as European financiers were willing to invest in railroads, public utility companies, and even banks, knowing their loans were guaranteed. The Ottoman government itself voluntarily turned over several sources of revenue for Administration collection, so impressed were they with its efficiency in amassing money.

The first document is the 1881 Ottoman decree establishing the PDA and setting out its mode of operation. The second document, dated 1906, offers excerpts from that year's annual report.

Texts

Decree of 28 Muharram, 1299 (20 December 1881)[37]

The Imperial Ottoman Government, in pursuance of the declarations made by their representative at the Congress of Berlin at the session of the 11th July, 1878, and in accordance with the engagement which they entered into by their note of the 3rd October, 1880, have, in a subsequent note of the 23rd October of the same year, invited the holders of bonds of the Ottoman Public Debt to choose a certain number of delegates to proceed as soon as possible to Constantinople for the purpose of coming to a direct agreement with the Imperial Government as to an equitable and practical settlement of the Ottoman Public Debt as well as to the means of resuming the service of the interest and sinking fund on that debt.[. . .]

Article 8

For the service of the Debt determined by article 3, the Government cede by these present, absolutely and irrevocably, from the 1st (13th) January, 1882, and until the complete extinction of the said debt:

The revenues of the monopolies and indirect taxes which form the subject of the convention of the 10th (22nd) November, 1879, which abrogated from the 1st (13th) January, 1882, in virtue of the convention annexed to the present decree, viz.:

Of the monopolies of tobacco and salt produced or consumed in the vilayets of the empire enumerated in the list annexed to the convention of the 10th (22nd) November, 1879, and appended to this decree, annex 2, not including cigars, snuffs, chewing tobacco, and imported *tombeki*, and with the exception of the tithe and the customs duties on tobacco.

Of the stamp duty (*varakai-sahiha*); of the *mirie* and *rouhsatie* duties on spirits in the vilayets of the empire enumerated in the said list, except the customs duties levied on spirits; of the duty on fish in Constantinople and its suburbs, according to the details which figure in the list relating thereto; and of the silk tithe of the suburbs of Constantinople, as also the Adrianople [Edirne], Brusa, and Samsun, according to the detail stated in the list relating thereto.

The silk tithes:

Of Tokat, a dependency of the Samsun administration.

Of Kavala, Yenidjeh, Eskidje, Dede Agatch, dependencies of the Adrianople administration.

Of Sarouhan, a dependency of the Sarouhan administration.

Of Yenikeui of Chile, a dependency of the Constantinople administration.

[37] Excerpts from Ottoman Decree of 28 Muharram 1299 (20 Dec. 1881), translated in 'Imperial Ottoman Debt', Turkey No. 1 (1911), *Sessional Papers, House of Commons* (1911), vol. 103, pp. 20, 23–6, 28–31.

Of Kartal, Guebze, and Daridja, dependencies of the Ismidt administration.

As also the duty on fish:

Of Banados, a dependency of the Rodosto administration.

Of Gallipoli, dependency of the Gallipoli administration.

Of Yalova, a dependency of the Kara Mussal administration.

Of Seyki, Mudania, Guemlek, Kurchunlu, Armudlu, Kapu Dagh, Marmora, Pasha-Liman, Erdek, Panderma, and Lake of Manias, dependencies of the Bursa administration.

The surplus of the customs receipts resulting from a modification in the tariffs in the event of a revision of the commercial treaties.

The surplus of revenue which will result from the general application of the tax on professions as compared with the actual receipts from the *temettu* tax. The means by which the revenues mentioned in paragraphs 3 and 4 will be secured to the holders of the debt shall form the subject of special provisions.

The tribute of the principality of Bulgaria. So long as this tribute shall not have been fixed by the representatives of the signatory Powers of the Treaty of Berlin, the Government shall replace it from the 1st (13th) January, 1882, by an annual sum of T100,000 pounds to be levied on the tobacco tithe.

Once the said tribute is fixed, should the Sublime Porte think fit to assign in whole or in part to some other purpose, the amount thus disposed of shall be replaced by an equivalent sum to be levied on the tobacco tithe, and, in case this should not be sufficient, on some other revenue equally secure.

The surplus revenues of the island of Cyprus.

Should the surplus revenue of the island of Cyprus not be at the disposal of the Imperial Government it will be replaced from the 1st (13th) January, 1882, by an annual sum of T130,000 pounds.

The Council of Administration (article 15) shall have the right to apply the surplus of the tobacco tithe, after deduction of the T100,000 pounds which are to replace the tribute of the principality of Bulgaria, to the payment of the aforesaid T130,000 pounds which are to replace the surplus revenues of the island of Cyprus; for the amount remaining uncovered on this sum, the Ministry of Finance shall furnish to the council half-yearly drafts on the General Customs Administration.

The revenue from Eastern Rumelia, now fixed at T240,000 pounds, plus the arrears from the 1st (13th) March, 1880, subsequent increases of which this revenue is susceptible by the terms of article 5 of the organic statute, and the sum of T5,000 pounds, representing the net annual proceeds of the customs of the said province. The Council of Administration (article 15) shall receive the aforesaid sums through the medium of the Imperial Ottoman Bank, in the safes of which they shall be deposited.

In the event of delay in the payments at the due dates, the Imperial Government shall use all diligence to see that the said province resumes the fulfillment of its engagements.

The proceeds from the duty on the *tombeki* up to a sum of T50,000 pounds.

In order to ensure the receipt of this sum by the Council of Administration, the Ministry of Finance shall issue to the council half-yearly drafts on the General Customs Administration.

All the sums accruing to the Imperial Government as the contributive portions of Servia, Montenegro, Bulgaria, and Greece to the debt mentioned in article 3 according to the provisions of the Treaty of Berlin and article 10 of the Convention of Constantinople of the 24th May, 1881.

Article 9

The revenues specified in paragraphs 1, 2, and 8, as also the tobacco tithe mentioned in paragraphs 5 and 6 of the preceding article, shall be administered in accordance with existing laws and regulations and the revenues mentioned in paragraphs 3 and 4 (surplus of customs and tax on professions) in accordance with the provisions to be enacted for that purpose.

Notwithstanding, the Council of Administration shall have the right to decide upon all modifications and improvements which may be introduced in the existing system of monopolies or contributions mentioned in Nos. 1 and 2 or the tobacco tithe mentioned in Nos. 5 and 6 of the preceding article, in case the said tithe should be applied to the service of the debt in pursuance of the provisions of the same article relating thereto, without going beyond the limits of the existing laws and regulations and without imposing fresh charges on the Ottoman subject [. . .]

Article 10

The net proceeds of the revenues indicated in article 8 shall be devoted wholly, on the 1st (13th) September and the 1st (13th) March each year, from the 1st (13th) January, 1882, to the payment of interest and sinking fund of the Debt [. . .]

Article 11

There shall be assigned every year to the service of the interest four-fifths of the net proceeds of the revenues ceded to the bondholders, not including the contributive portions of Servia, Montenegro, Bulgaria, and Greece, and after deduction of the sums representing interest on the redeemed bonds [. . .]

Article 12

There shall be assigned every year for the sinking fund one-fifth of the net proceeds of the revenues ceded to the bondholders, not including the contributive portions of Servia, Montenegro, Bulgaria, and Greece, but increased by the amount representing interest upon the redeemed bonds, as stated in the preceding article.[. . .]

Article 15

A Council of Administration is established to represent the bondholders, and to act in their interests.

This council has its head office at Constantinople.

The said council shall be composed as hereinafter stated:

One member representing the English bondholders, who also represents the Dutch bondholders, and who is to be appointed by the Council of Foreign Bondholders of London, or in default of it by the Governor of the Bank of England, or in default of him by a resolution adopted at a public meeting of English and Dutch bondholders in London;

One member representing the French bondholders;

One member representing the German bondholders;

One member representing the Austro-Hungarian bondholders; who are to be appointed by the syndicates of the financial houses of Paris, Berlin, and Vienna, which have adhered to the communication of the Imperial Ottoman Government of the 23rd October, 1880, and, if necessary, their choice shall be approved by a general meeting of the French, German, and Austro-Hungarian bondholders in each of the capitals designated above.

One member representing the Italian bondholders, who is to be appointed by the Roman Chamber of Commerce, constituted in the syndicate of the chambers of commerce of the kingdom, and, if necessary, its choice shall be approved by a general meeting of the Italian bondholders in Rome.

One member representing the Ottoman bondholders, who is to be appointed by a general meeting of the latter, assembled at Constantinople at the invitation of the prefect of the city.

One member representing the holders of the bonds provided for by the annexed convention, who will be appointed by the Imperial Ottoman Bank, or in default of it by a resolution adopted at a public meeting of the said bondholders in Constantinople [. . .]

Every employee in the service of the Imperial Ottoman Government, whether a foreigner or an Ottoman subject, who shall be appointed a member of the council shall be found to resign his public functions for the whole duration of his office [. . .]

The members of the council shall be appointed for five years, and they shall sit until the installation of the new council.

They may be re-elected on the expiration of their mandate [. . .]

The members of the council shall each have a vote. Resolutions shall be taken by a majority of votes. In case of a tie, the president shall have a casting vote [. . .]

Article 16

The Council of Administration shall have the direct administration, collection, and encashment on behalf of the bondholders and by means of agents holding its authority of the revenues and other resources enumerated in article 8, sections 1, 2, 5, 6, 7, and 9, including the tobacco tithe in the cases provided for by sections 5 and 6 of the said article, excepting, however, as regards the said tithe the obligation of rendering an account thereof to the Government, and paying annually to the Exchequer the surplus over and above the T100,000 pounds which shall take the place of the Bulgarian tribute, and eventually of the T130,000 pounds which shall take the place of the surplus revenue of the island of Cyprus.

It shall likewise have the encashment of the T50,000 pounds ceded on the proceeds of the *tombeki* duties (paragraph 8 of article 8) and of the revenues mentioned in paragraphs 3 and 4 of the said article.

The amount of the six Indirect Contributions shall be collected in cash in conformity with the regulation in force as regards the fiscal agencies of the State ('*Meskukiat Nizam-namessi*') promulgated on the 1st March, 1296.

It shall realise the value of the ceded revenues and other resources, and shall apply the whole amount thereof, after deduction of the costs of administration and collection, to the service of the interest and sinking fund of the bonds provided for by the annexed convention and of the debt fixed by article 3 in conformity with the distribution adopted.

The council shall have the right to farm or lease to third parties any of the ceded revenues; but in this case it shall remain directly responsible to the Imperial Government.

The council shall appoint a director-general of the administration who shall have, under the authority of the council, the management of affairs. He shall represent the council as regards third parties for the execution of any decisions, and in legal proceedings if required, subject to obtaining the necessary authorisation for appearing before the courts or other jurisdictions either as plaintiff or defendant in the name of the administration of the ceded revenues.

The council shall likewise appoint and dismiss the other employees of the administration of the ceded revenues.

The said employees shall be considered as State officials in the exercise of their duties. The Government shall take into favourable consideration every recommendation of the council as regards their rank, advancement, and promotion in the Ottoman hierarchy.

As regards duties, contributions, and taxes, the administration of the ceded revenues and its employees shall be treated on the same footing as the administrations of the State and its employees.

As regards employees of the State who shall enter the service of the Council of Administration, their position shall be fixed by a special regulation. The provisions of this regulation shall apply equally to the employees of the State who are already in the service of the administration of the Indirect Contributions. It is understood that this regulation shall not prejudice the right of the council to appoint and dismiss any official of this administration—a right which is already exercised, in fact, by the present administration.

The Government shall afford the council in the exercise of its administration all general assistance compatible with the existing public institutions, and, with a view to a repression of contraband trade, they undertake to apply against it the penalties enacted by law.

In case of delay in the payments of the revenue from Eastern Roumelia, the council shall have the right to apply to the Sublime Porte and to demand the necessary measures for recovery of the arrears.

The Government shall afford to the Administration of the Council the military protection indispensable for the security of its head office and its local branches.

The Government shall continue to the council the gratuitous use of the premises which they have already placed at the disposal of the actual administration of the six Indirect Contributions.

The removable stamps and stamped papers necessary for the council's transactions shall be supplied by the Government under the supervision and at the expense of the latter.

Independently of the State employees entrusted with the policing and supervision of the service to be undertaken by the State, the council may appoint auxiliary employees responsible to none but itself, as well as secret inspectors whose duty shall be to prevent frauds punishable in conformity with the laws.

The secret inspectors of the administration shall receive, like those of the Government, the usual portion of the fines and double duties to be paid by delinquents.

The council shall make regulations concerning the resolution and dispatch of business.

It shall sign the bonds to be issued in conformity with the annexed convention to discharge the debts of the signatories of the said convention indicated in article 10.

Article 17

The Council of Administration shall be found to draw up and present to the Ministry of Finance two months before the commencement of each budgetary year a budget indicating the estimates of the council as to receipts and expenditure, especially as to the sums which shall be applied during the course of the said year to the service of the bonds provided for in the annexed convention and for the service of the Debt established by article 3.

This budget must conform to the existing regulations, and shall be approved by the Imperial Government within two months.

It shall be inserted in the general budget of the Empire [. . .]

2. Annual Report, Ottoman Public Debt Administration 1905–1906, excerpts[38]

[. . .] In the London market there is no clear perception of the position and attributions of the Ottoman Public Debt Administration, and it does not seem to be understood that the Public Debt Administration is an independent Administration directed by a European Board [. . .]

[. . .] [a]s regards Turkish Fours [bonds] in particular, it should always be borne in mind that since the promulgation of the Decree of Mouharrem in 1881 [creating the Ottoman Public Debt Administration], both H.I.M. the Sultan and his successive Ministers have loyally observed the stipulation of the Act.

We have every reason to be grateful for the cordial support accorded to our Board by those in authority. We possess their entire confidence, and with a continuation of the loyal cooperation which we have enjoyed hitherto, there is every reason to hope that the interests entrusted to our charge will not suffer in the future. The interests of the Debt Administration and those of the Turkish Government are now identical. Since the Decree of 1903 the Treasury has a direct interest in our surplus, and will the more readily, I am convinced, give us, as in the past, all the support and assistance which is so necessary to the proper administration of the various important Revenues pledged to its creditors.

I maintain that these Revenues are still elastic. Time will show if my estimate is correct.

In the meantime the Council [of the Debt Administration] will neglect no opportunity of developing them, bearing in mind the interests of the Government and the people at the same time as the interests of those who have chosen us as their representatives.

Lord Fitzmaurice has been good enough to state in a recent debate that 'the Ottoman Debt Commission had been a singularly honest and successful service. [. . .] That Commission was not a body which took a certain amount of money and handed it over to certain Bondholders. No doubt that was its first origin and what called it into existence but gradually, owing to the great skill of the financiers who had control of its operations, it had been entrusted with the collection as well as the administration of various other Revenues, and the taxes

---

[38] Excerpts from Adam Block, *Special Report on the Public Debt followed by the Translation of the Annual Report of the Council of Administration for the Twenty Fourth Financial Period* (Istanbul: Ottoman Public Debt Administration, 1906), 9–11, 21–5, 27, 34–5, 89, 90, 100.

which it collected with the consent of the Ottoman Government had gradually gone on increasing.' [. . .]

I am in a position to affirm that the view is shared by many of the highest officials in this country. The financial credit of Turkey depends on our existence [. . .]

The receipts from the Revenues ceded to the Bondholders by the Decree of Mouharrem now exceeds T3,000,000 pounds, but this sum does not by any means represent the total of the sum which we collect on behalf of the Government in every part of the Empire for the service of the loans created since 1881, or for the payment of railway guarantees, etc.

[. . .] the fact that we are charged with these new services is worthy of notice, even to those who have no direct interest in the matter, inasmuch as it is a striking proof that the Government has complete confidence in the Administration, and that financial establishments and railway company promoters look to us alone for an effective guarantee of their undertakings in Turkey. [. . .]

In all, therefore, we collect a sum of T5,516,187 pounds. Considering that the Budget of the Empire is estimated at about T23,000,000 pounds—this is a high estimate—the Debt Administration collects roughly 24 percent thereof [. . .] Every year fresh Revenues are ceded to us. [. . .]

It must not be supposed that the increase in the Revenue is due only to fresh taxation. New taxes have been imposed, it is true, some sound and some, I regret to state, hardly in accordance with the ordinary rules of political economy. But the increase is due chiefly to improved methods of collection, and secondly, in certain districts, to the economic progress taking place in the country [. . .]

When Europe calls upon Turkey to reform, I am afraid it is sometimes forgotten that with restricted financial resources it is not always so easy to reorganize the administration on modern Western lines. A very distinguished diplomatist has expressed to me his astonishment that the Government manages to get along at all with the small means it possesses. At the same time, I am the first to admit that the financial measures adopted by the Government are not always profitable to the Fisc in the long run. The burden of the taxpayer is not so excessive as is generally supposed, but there are vexations and burdensome taxes which might with advantage be withdrawn; they produce little revenue, and could the Government find means to forgo them, I believe an immediate increase of the productive and purchasing power of the people would result, and the State Revenues would in the end suffer no diminution.

The Council of Administration of the Debt has never adopted the *role* of mere bailiffs of the Bondholders clamouring for their pound of flesh. Over and over again we have come to the assistance of the Government, and time out of number we have given an impetus to industries in the country. We have never hesitated to make suggestions for the adoption of sounder methods of financial administration in general calculated to develop the resources and wealth of the country, but I regret to state, not always with success.

I have said that the economic conditions of the country are improving. The chief factor in the improvement is the construction of railways. When I first came to this country, 30 years ago next year, there were only 1,230 kilometers of railways in existence.

Today there are 5,744 kilometers constructed and in the course of construction (I omit the Eregli–Bagdad Persian Gulf line, 1,800 kilometers, and the Hedjaz railway to Medina, 1,800 kilometers, and the prolongation of the Smyrna–Aidin railway to Egirdir, 60 kilometers, in all 3,660 kilometers) [. . .]

As usual where railways have been built they have brought with them increased civilization, tranquility, better administration, followed at once by increased production and prosperity [. . .]

Another proof of the growing prosperity of the country is that during the last few years many public works of permanent utility have been undertaken by foreign companies (chiefly port facilities, water works, electric light, and street railway facilities) [. . .]

Were further proof of increasing wealth required, it would be found in the establishment of new banking establishments in the capital and in the Provinces [. . .]

The total staff of the Administration in 1905–1906 was as follows:

Constantinople	1,831
Provinces	3,802

The cost in 1904–1905 (including employees engaged temporarily) was T264,749 pounds, as against T259,064 in 1905–1906:

The majority of our agents are Muslims, and there is no better employee to be found, provided the pay is good and the control severe.

We have in our employ	4,992 Muslims
	509 Christians
	132 Europeans
TOTAL	5,633

In the year 1905–1906 I took measures to increase the pay of our small officials, and the Council took what I considered to be a wise measure in deciding that no Provincial Agent should receive less than 400 piastres a month.

It is astonishing how with such insignificant salaries men can be found to serve us in responsible positions with absolute integrity, provided always that any irregularity is visited with immediate severity, and that there is a certainty of regular pay and employment with a pension to look forward to. It speaks well for the character of the people [. . .]

Since October, 1889, the Administration of the Debt has on various occasions advanced money to the Government for urgent current needs to the amount of T1,191,933 pounds. All these advances have been duly reimbursed.

8.5 Development concessions, the D'Arcy Concession for Iranian oil, 29 May 1901[39]
Robert G. Landen

Preface

Between the 1850s and World War I the grant of concessions was a device
often used by Middle Eastern governments who could command only
limited financial and technical resources but who were anxious to encourage large-scale development projects in their country. In return for small
initial payments and possibly a modest annual rent or share of anticipated
profits, European business combines undertook to construct and operate
development projects for Middle Eastern rulers. Originally, these projects
concentrated on transportation and communications schemes such as the
Suez Canal (opened 1869) or the Indo-European telegraph (completed
1865), but later included public utilities such as streetcar, gas, and electric-
ity companies, land-development corporations, and ultimately mineral
extraction combines. The D'Arcy Concession is the prototype of the
Middle Eastern oil exportation agreements, and by 1932 virtually the
entire Iran–Iraq–Persian Gulf region was reserved for exploitation by
Western oil combines. After World War II, North Africa's petroleum
reserves, too, were regulated by concession agreements. As the following
selection illustrates, the compensation originally received by the locals was
small (although the business risks were considerable too).

  In Iranian history, trade concessions were of two general types: those
that sought to create new industries, and those that sought to extract more
revenue from, or modernize, existing industries. Unlike the De Reuter
Concession of 1872, which had to be cancelled because it gave away
development rights for every conceivable new industry to a single British
subject, or the Tobacco Concession of 1890, cancelled due to the protest of
Iranian tobacco merchants and their clerical allies, the D'Arcy Concession
was narrow enough—focusing on a single industry that did not yet exist in
Iran—to avoid protests from domestic and regional interests (especially
those of Russia). Oil was not found until 1908, at which time the Anglo-
Persian Oil Company (APOC) was formed. A pipeline was created from
the oil-fields to the Persian Gulf in 1911; a refinery established in Abadan
in 1913; and in 1914 the British government gained a controlling interest
in APOC (51–49). The D'Arcy Concession was cancelled in 1932, and
renegotiated to include an area 25 per cent of the original agreement

[39] 'William Knox D'Arcy Oil Concession in Persia, 29 May 1901', in J. C. Hurewitz, *Diplomacy in the Near and Middle East: A Documentary Record, 1535–1914*, vol. 1 (Princeton: D. Van Nostrand, 1956), 249–51.

(but extending the agreement by another thirty years). The company was renamed the Anglo-Iranian Oil Company in 1935. The concession came to an end in 1951, when Iran nationalized its oil industry under the leadership of Prime Minister Muhammad Mosaddeq. Once the British and American governments had deposed the government of Mosaddeq in 1953, the D'Arcy Concession was replaced by a consortium of oil companies that included AIOC (renamed the British Petroleum Company, or BP) and shared oil profits 50–50 with the Iranian government, which established its own National Iranian Oil Company (NIOC) in 1955.

It is important to remember that in 1900 oil was mostly produced in the United States and Russia (Baku having been conquered by Russia from the Iranian Qajar Empire in the nineteenth century). It was mainly used as an illuminant, and its importance as a fuel and in plastics and synthetic textiles had not yet been realized. The industrialized countries produced all the oil they needed, and some were net exporters of oil. Oil did not provide Iran with positive balance of trade until 1922.[40] The D'Arcy Concession of 1901 was the beginning of the oil industry in the Middle East and established the framework for other oil agreements in the region until the middle of the twentieth Century.

Text

Between the Government of His Imperial Majesty the Shah of Persia, of the one part, and William Knox d'Arcy,[41] of independent means, residing in London at No. 42, Grosvenor Square (hereinafter called 'the Concessionaire'), of the other part;

The following has by these presents been agreed on and arranged—viz.:

Art. 1. The Government of His Imperial Majesty the Shah grants to the concessionaire by these presents a special and exclusive privilege to search for, obtain, exploit, develop, render suitable for trade, carry away and sell natural gas, petroleum, asphalt and ozokerite[42] throughout the whole extent of the Persian Empire for a term of sixty years as from the date of these presents.

---

[40] Julian Bharier, *Economic Development in Iran, 1900–1970* (Oxford: Oxford University Press, 1971), 114.

[41] William Knox D'Arcy (1849–1917) was already a rich man in 1901, having made money in an Australian gold mine in Mount Morgan. In 1900 he was approached by Henry Drummand Wolff, a former British ambassador to Tehran, and a former Iranian director of customs (replaced by Belgian concessionaires), to finance the concession, which they pitched to the Iranian government. Drummond Wolff had been ambassador during the days of the De Reuter concession. D'Arcy nearly lost his fortune before oil was finally struck, and remained on the board of the APOC until his death.

[42] This brownish-yellow waxy material was also known as native paraffin, mineral tallow, or mineral wax. It was used to make candles and to insulate electrically conductive materials (e.g. copper wiring).

Art. 2. This privilege shall comprise the exclusive right of laying the pipelines necessary from the deposits where there may be found one or several of the said products up to the Persian Gulf, as also the necessary distributing branches. It shall also comprise the right of constructing and maintaining all and any wells, reservoirs, stations and pump services, accumulation services and distribution services, factories and other works and arrangements that may be deemed necessary.

Art. 3. The Imperial Persian Government grants gratuitously to the concessionaire all uncultivated lands belonging to the State which the concessionaire's engineers may deem necessary for the construction of the whole or any part of the above-mentioned works. As for cultivated lands belonging to the State, the concessionaire must purchase them at the fair and current price of the province.

The Government also grants to the concessionaire the right of acquiring all and any other lands or buildings necessary for the said purpose, with the consent of the proprietors, on such conditions as may be arranged between him and them without their being allowed to make demands of a nature to surcharge the prices ordinarily current for land situated in their respective localities.

Holy places with all their dependencies within a radius of 200 Persian archines[43] are formally excluded.

Art. 4. As three petroleum mines situated at Shuster, Qasr-e Shirin, in the Province of Kermanshahan, and Daleki, near Bushehr, are at present let to private persons and produce an annual revenue of two thousand *tumans* for the benefit of the Government,[44] it has been agreed that the three aforesaid mines shall be comprised in the Deed of Concession in conformity with Article 1, on condition that, over and above the 16 per cent mentioned in Article 10, the concessionaire shall pay every year the fixed sum of 2,000 (two thousand) *tumans* to the Imperial Government.

Art. 5. The course of the pipe-lines shall be fixed by the concessionaire and his engineers.

Art. 6. Notwithstanding what is above set forth, the privilege granted by these presents shall not extend to the provinces of Azerbaijan, Gilan, Mazanderan, Asadabad and Khorasan, but on the express condition that the Persian Imperial Government shall not grant to any other person the right of constructing a pipeline to the southern rivers or to the South Coast of Persia.

Art. 7. All lands granted by these presents to the concessionaire or that may be acquired by him in the manner provided for in Articles 3 and 4 of these presents, as also all products exported, shall be free of all imposts and taxes during the term

[43] An *archine* (also *arshine, arsheen*) is a unit of measure corresponding to the ell or cubit, approximately 18–22 inches long.

[44] A *tuman* is a unit of 10,000—in this case of *dinars*. In modern Iranian currency, 10 *rials* is the equivalent of one *tuman*.

of the present concession. All material and apparatuses necessary for the exploitation, working and development of the deposits, and for the construction and development of the pipe-lines, shall enter Persia free of all taxes and Custom-House duties.

Art. 8. The concessionaire shall immediately send out to Persia and at his own cost one or several experts with a view to their exploring the region in which there exist, as he believes, the said products, and, in the event of the report of the expert being in the opinion of the concessionaire of a satisfactory nature, the latter shall immediately send to Persia and at his own cost all the technical staff necessary, with the working plant and machinery required for boring and sinking wells and ascertaining the value of the property.

Art. 9. The Imperial Persian Government authorizes the concessionaire to found one or several companies for the working of the concession.

The names, 'statutes' and capital of the said companies shall be fixed by the concessionaire, and the directors shall be chosen by him on the express condition that, on the formation of each company, the concessionaire shall give official notice of such formation to the Imperial Government, through the medium of the Imperial Commissioner, and shall forward the 'statutes,' with information as to the places at which such company is to operate. Such company or companies shall enjoy all the rights and privileges granted to the concessionaire, but they must assume all his engagements and responsibilities.

Art. 10. It shall be stipulated in the contract between the concessionaire, of the one part, and the company, of the other part, that the latter is, within the term of one month as from the date of the formation of the first exploitation company, to pay the Imperial Persian Government the sum of 20,000 pounds sterling in cash,[45] and an additional sum of 20,000 pounds sterling in paid-up shares of the first company founded by virtue of the foregoing article. It shall also pay the said Government annually a sum equal to 16 per cent of the annual net profits of any company or companies that may be formed in accordance with the said article.

Art. 11. The said Government shall be free to appoint an Imperial Commissioner, who shall be consulted by the concessionaire and the directors of the companies to be formed. He shall supply all and any useful information at his disposal, and he shall inform them of the best course to be adopted in the interest of the undertaking. He shall establish, by agreement with the concessionaire, such supervision as he may deem expedient to safeguard the interests of the Imperial Government.

The aforesaid powers of the Imperial Commissioner shall be set forth in the 'statutes' of the companies to be created.

[45] In 1901 £1 sterling was equal to 5.2 *tumans*; 1.1 *tumans* was approximately equal to US$1 in 1901.

The concessionaire shall pay the Commissioner thus appointed an annual sum of 1,000 pounds sterling for his services as from the date of the formation of the first company.

Art. 12. The workmen employed in the service of the company shall be subject to His Imperial Majesty the Shah, except the technical staff, such as the managers, engineers, borers and foremen.

Art. 13. At any place in which it may be proved that the inhabitants of the country now obtain petroleum for their own use, the company must supply them gratuitously with the quantity of petroleum that they themselves got previously. Such quantity shall be fixed according to their own declarations, subject to the supervision of the local authority.

Art. 14. The Imperial Government binds itself to take all and any necessary measures to secure the safety and the carrying out of the object of this concession of the plant and of the apparatuses, of which mention is made, for the purposes of the undertaking of the company, and to protect the representatives, agents and servants of the company. The Imperial Government having thus fulfilled its engagements, the concessionaire and the companies created by him shall not have power, under any pretext whatever, to claim damages from the Persian Government.

Art. 15. On the expiration of the term of the present concession, all materials, buildings and apparatuses then used by the company for the exploitation of its industry shall become the property of the said Government, and the company shall have no right to any indemnity in this connection.

Art. 16. If within the term of two years as from the present date the concessionaire shall not have established the first of the said companies authorized by Article 9 of the present agreement, the present concession shall become null and void.

Art. 17. In the event of there arising between the parties to the present concession any dispute or difference in respect of its interpretation or the rights or responsibilities of one or the other of the parties therefrom resulting, such dispute or difference shall be submitted to two arbitrators at Teheran, one of whom shall be named by each of the parties, and to an umpire who shall be appointed by the arbitrators before they proceed to arbitrate. The decision of the arbitrators or, in the event of the latter disagreeing, that of the umpire shall be final.

Art. 18. This Act of Concession, made in duplicate, is written in the French language and translated in Persian with the same meaning.

But, in the event of there being any dispute in relation to such meaning, the French text shall alone prevail.

8.6 Memento of a life, by Haj Mohammad Husayn Amin al-Zarb II, 1928

Shireen Mahdavi

Preface

The translated memoirs printed below give an account of the life of Haj Mohammad Hasan Amin al-Zarb through the eyes and memory of his son Haj Hosayn Aqa, Amin al-Zarb II (1289/1872–1351/1932). Haj Hosayn Aqa wrote this memoir towards the end of his life in 1347/1928 whilst on a visit to Paris. They are unfinished and end when Haj Hosayn Aqa was approximately 14 years old. As it was written from memory the dates are only approximate. The original manuscript is in the Mahdavi Archives in Tehran.[46]

The central figure of the memoirs, Haj Mohammad Hasan Amin al-Zarb (1250/1834–1316/1898), was a self-made man who was the first major Iranian entrepreneur. His life spanned the reign of three Qajar shahs. He was born in the reign of Mohammad Shah (1834–48), arrived in Tehran in the reign of Naser al-Din Shah (1848–96), and reached the zenith of his eminence during the reign of that shah. He died in the reign of Mozaffar al-Din Shah (1896–1906).

The Qajar society in which Amin al-Zarb was born was a pluralistic, socially stratified society. It was also a society that was experiencing the impact of the West. The economic conditions of the country, of which Amin al-Zarb took advantage, were also partly shaped through this impact, which had a direct effect on the social and economic life of the country, ranging from the composition of foreign trade to the balance of payments and the pattern of consumption. Amin al-Zarb made good use of the changing pattern of consumption and catered to the new demand for British textiles by importing a variety to fulfill differing tastes and budgets. Simultaneously he fulfilled the European demand for Persian carpets by becoming a major exporter.

By 1863 he had begun the most extensive commercial enterprise in Iran, and went on to become the richest and most influential merchant in the country. He had agents in all the main towns of Persia and Europe, with correspondents in Asia and America. He provided important luxury items for the royal family and the aristocracy, and carried out all foreigners'

[46] For details of the holdings of this archive, see Asghar Mahdavi, 'The Significance of Private Archives for the Study of the Economic and Social History of Iran in the Late Qajar Period', *Iranian Studies*, 16 (1983), 243–78; and Haj Husayn Aqa Amin al-Zarb, 'Yadegar-e Zendegani', in Iraj Afshar (ed.), *Savad va Bayaz*, 2 vols. (Tehran: Ketab Forushi-ye Dehkhuda, 1970), vol. 2, pp. 187–232. For the English translation of the unfinished biography, see Shireen Mahdavi, 'Memento of a Life', *Iran*, 30 (1992), 107–21.

transactions within the country, especially those of the diplomatic community. Simultaneously he invested capital in industry, importing glass, china, silk-reeling, and other factories from Europe. Moreover, he was engaged in agricultural and mining projects, having in addition constructed a railway line on the Caspian Sea. He was also appointed master of the Mint, hence the title Amin-al Zarb, and for all intents and purposes was personal banker to the shah.[47] The connection of Amin al-Zarb with the shah, the government, and the court was not only in the guise of banker and merchant but also that of financial adviser. Thus he was well placed both to protest against unfair practices affecting the merchant classes and to defend their interest when necessary. He expressed his opinions on internal economic development, foreign interference, and the importance of the merchant class both verbally and in letters to the shah and the prime minister. In critical letters, which led to the formation of the Consultative Assembly of Iranian Merchants, he attacked provincial officials for using their position to extract money from the merchants. Amin al-Zarb was very much concerned with developing the resources of the country, and considered this possible only if modern methods of banking were used. In 1878, ten years before the formation of the Imperial Bank of Iran, he wrote a letter to this effect to the shah, stating that industrial development in Iran was not possible without a national bank and proposing the formation of one. He died a famous and popular man due to his services to the community. However, the document below gives only a short account of the public man. The importance of the memoirs is that they show the private man within his family and household.

Text

In the name of God, the Merciful and the Compassionate.

The date of my birth, according to the records that my father kept at the back of a manuscript of *Zad al-maʿad*, is on the fifth of Muharram 1289/1872 of the *Hijra*.[48] The place of birth is the city of Tehran during the reign of Naser al-Din Shah Qajar (r. 1848–96). The name that I was given is Mohammad Hosayn, according to the above record.

The name of my late father was Haj Mohammad Hasan Tajer-e Esfahani, the son of Aqa Mohammad Hosayn, the son of Haj Mehdi, the son of Aqa Mohammad Rahim, may their dust be fragrant.

---

[47] For more on Amin al-Zarb see Shireen Mahdavi, 'Social Mobility in Qajar Iran: Haj Muhammad Hasan Amin al-Zarb', *Middle Eastern Studies*, 26 (1990), 582–95. Also, *For God, Mammon and Country: A Nineteenth Century Persian Merchant* (Boulder, Col.: Westview Press, 1999).

[48] *Zad al-maʿad* 'Provisions for the Hereafter', by Molla Mohammad Baqer Majlesi (1627–99); see E.G. Browne, *A Literary History of Persia*, vol. 4 (Cambridge: Cambridge University Press, 1930), 417.

The name of my late mother was Mah Begom Khanom, the daughter of the late Aqa Mohammad Ja^cfar Sarraf-e Esfahani.

The marriage of my late father to my [late] mother took place in the city of Tehran. They contracted a legal marriage according to the laws of the holy *shari*ʿ*a*, witnessed by religious scholars (*colama*).

I do not know where my great grandfather Aqa Mohammad Rahim died and I did not ask my father about it. But the late Haj Mehdi passed away in the city of Esfahan [Isfahan]; and the late Aqa Mohammad Hosayn, my grandfather, died in Kerman.

The mother of the late Haj Mohammad Hasan was Bibi Mah Khanum, who, it is said, was the daughter of one Aqa Baba from KhoY, who was a member of the dignitaries of that town (one of the cities of Azarbaijan), and I think that there is a mosque at present in Khoy named after Aqa Baba Kho'i. I do not know what transpired that the family came to Esfahan where he arranged the permanent marriage of Bibi Mah Khanom to my grandfather Aqa Mohammad Hosayn. I do not know of anyone who possesses correct information concerning them. I forgot to obtain the correct information from my late father about this subject.

I do not know the profession of my great ancestor Haj Mohammad Rahim, but the late Haj Mehdi and the late Aqa Mohammad Hosayn, his son, were both traders (*kaseb*) and merchants (*tajer*).

The late Haj Mohammad Hasan, my father, knew his grandfather Haj Mehdi and has described him to me. He was a humane, highly moral, very religious and distinguished man who was constantly engaged in reading the holy Qur'an. He [Haj Mohammad Hasan] said, when we came out of the house in the mornings he would buy all necessary provisions and send them home; then we went to his *hojreh* [business office] where he either carried out business transactions or read the Qur'an. Near noon we would go to the mosque and participate in public prayers and then go home for lunch. But often it happened that he managed to transact some business before lunchtime and then he would say, 'God has given sufficient for our expenses, why should we remain here any more?' He would then get up immediately and we would go to the mosque. He would then occupy himself in reading the Qur'an until prayer time, after which we would go home.

I do not remember the date of the passing away of the late Haj Mehdi and the late Aqa Mohammad Hosayn. My father told me, but I have forgotten. Likewise, I do not remember whether Aqa Mohammad Hosayn went to Kerman during the lifetime of his father Haj Mehdi or after his death.

From what I have gathered, my grandfather and great-grandfather did not live long enough to oversee the education of my father and his brothers. The late Bibi Mah Khanom, who was their mother, sent them to the ordinary *maktab* [primary school or Qur'an school] of that period, where they were educated in the Persian language. There was in Esfahan a famous calligrapher of the Qur'an known as Aqa Abu al-Qasem, who accepted pupils and, incidentally, made them copy Qur'ans.

Among them [the pupils] were my late father and his brother Haj Abu-Al-Qasem both of whom copied Qur'ans. Aqa Abu al-Qasem sold the Qur'ans copied by them for twelve *rials* per volume.

The late Aqa Mohammad Hosayn, my grandfather, had four male children by his wife Bibi Mah Khanom. The eldest left this world at an early age. His name was Abu al-Vahhab. The other three were as follows: Haj Mohammad Hasan Amin al-Zarb, Haj Abu al-Qasem Malek al-Tojjar of Khorasan, and Haj Mohammad Rahim Aqa.

I do not know for what reason the late Aqa Mohammad Hosayn, my grandfather, traveled to Kerman. The way my father related the story, he left Esfahan with sufficient capital, but in Kerman his transactions were not successful. Due to the fact that there were no couriers at that time, and people corresponded with each other through travelers, which took a long time, they [the family] had no news of Aqa Mohammad Hosayn for a long period. Finally, news came that Aqa Mohammad Hosayn was ill in Kerman, in dire straits, in need, and wished to see his son. The late Bibi Mah Khanom, through the sale of personal clothing, provided a small sum of money for expenses for the journey and sent the late Haj Mohammad Hasan with a muleteer to Kerman.

My late father related that he was on the road for several days, suffered much hardship as the sum of money was finished, and arrived in Kerman himself in straitened circumstances. [On arrival] he went looking for his father, and it transpired that he had passed away sometime before. He [Aqa Mohammad Hosayn] had acquired a Kermani *sigheh*[49] whom he [Haj Mohammad Hasan] met. Upon meeting her she said, 'A good thing you came, as you owe me some *mehriyeh* and the expense of your father's illness which you must pay.' Then and there, they got into a quarrel and hostilities ensued. Finally, well-wishers and peacemakers obtained a promissory note from my father in the name of that Kermani woman so that he would send the money at a specified date.

My father realized that he was stranded in the city of Kerman, a stranger with no money. He contacted two or three of the *tojjar* [merchants or traders] from Esfahan and managed to borrow a small amount of money from them and returned to [Esfahan].

In Esfahan, he met Haj Mohammad Kazem Sarraf (the father of Aqa Mohammad Ja'far Kazemov, who is working in my office at the moment). This person was an extremely humane and generous man. He comforted my father, and he lent my father the sum of money that he had borrowed from the Esfahani *tojjar* in Kerman, plus the sum of the promissory note that he had given against the claims of the *sigheh* of the late Aqa Mohammad Hosayn. The late Haj Mohammad Kazem

---

[49] *Sigheh* refers to the Twelver-Shi'i practice of temporary marriage (also known as *mut'a*). For more on this complex social phenomenon see Shahla Haeri, *Law and Desire: Temporary Marriage in Shi'i Iran* (Syracuse NY: Syracuse University Press, 1989).

obtained a promissory note from my father to pay whenever he could (May his soul rest in peace!). At the same time, he said [to my father]: 'Because you are young and an orphan, come and sit in my *hojreh* daily, and, according to my instructions, keep the day book; and from time to time I will allow you to withdraw a little money from the income of the *hojreh* so that you can make a transaction in your own name.'

At this time, the late Haj Abu al-Qasem Malik al-Tojjar and the late Haj Rahim were both in Esfahan. They each passed their days in the *hojreh* of one of the *tojjar* without any salary or wages, content to have lunch only in return for their services to the *hojreh*.

The late Bibi Mah Khanom was one of those chaste and honorable women to whom other honourable women paid respect. She acted with great decorum, sanctity, and generosity. Meanwhile, at home she made cords, braids, and buttons from cotton, silk, and wool and all things necessary for a passementerie shop and fashionable at that time, which she sent for sale. Sometimes she either sewed or knotted some other material known as *sakmaduzi* (I do not know what that is; when my late father used this word, I learned it from him), which she sent to the bazaar for sale.[50] Thus, she obtained the daily expenditure for meals and summer and winter clothing for the boys.

Some time passed in this way, and the late Haj Mohammad Kazem aided my late father Haj Mohammad Hasan financially. In that very *hojreh*, he [Haj Mohammad Kazem] would buy some property with his own money but in the name of my father and would sell it after a few days. By chance, fortune smiled during his work in the *hojreh* and from the profits of the favorable transactions of Haj Mohammad Kazem and also from the small sum of money received from those investments, he was thus able to pay his full debt to the late Haj Mohammad Kazem, including the money lent to him earlier for the Kerman debts and the financial aid made to him. About one hundred *tumans* extra remained; he received this money, said farewell to Haj Mohammad Kazem, and left his *hojreh*.

My late father, Haj Mohammad Hasan related that from this sum he provided clothes for himself, Haj Abu al-Qasem, and Haj Mohammad Rahim, gave some money to his mother for their expenditure, and left for Tehran, leaving them in Esfahan.

'When I entered Tehran, aside from a few items of clothing and an 'aba,[51] my worldly possessions consisted of a box of scales and weights (*mesqal*), made in Esfahan that I had bought for eleven *qerans* and one hundred *rials* in cash. I had nothing else besides the Grace of God and Trust in God.' (One hundred *rials* is the exact wording of my late father Haj Mohammad Hasan. May his dust be

---

[50] *Sakmaduzi* is a type of embroidery involving drawn work. For details and examples, see Iran Ala Firous, 'Needlework', in Jay Gluck and Sumi Hiramoto (eds.), *A Survey of Persian Handicraft* (Tehran: Bank Melli Iran, 1977), 228–9.   [51] A coarse cloth robe, open in front.

fragrant!) The meaning of the word *rials* is the *qeran* in circulation in Iran in which, for example, one hundred *rials* equals ten *tumans* current then and now.

He related: 'With this meager sum I acquired a shop in the bazaar and started transactions. I became the party to transactions with a number of the *tojjar*, *sarraf* [money-changer, banker], and the notables of the city and entered into social intercourse with them. I did not refrain from the buying and selling of any kind of article, and I was very careful to be faithful to my promise to people and to keep my word and to guarantee vouchers and promissory notes. In the course of eight months, after deducting the expenditures of the *hojreh* and other necessary expenditures, I sent a certain sum of money to my mother for past expenditures and the fare to Tehran for herself and my brothers (the late Haj Abu al-Qasem and Haj Mohammad Rahim). Added to that, I sent four hundred *mesqals* of gold priced at that time at one thousand two hundred *tumans* to Haj Mohammad Kazem Sarraf (whose name appears earlier) for safekeeping to remain with him. After the dispatch of the four hundred *mesqals* of gold, no other capital remained for me but I was able to conduct transactions on the basis of that credit.'

For a few months, he formed a partnership with Aqa Mohammad Jaʿfar Sarraf, who is the father of my late mother, but it was dissolved. Meanwhile, the late Bibi Mah Khanom, accompanied by the brothers, arrived in Tehran.

'In the quarter of ʿAbbas Abad near the bazaar we rented a house and lived there. The brothers were unoccupied during the day in the *hojreh*, until after a few months I provided a drapery and cloth shop for them. I bought some handkerchiefs and other material and gave it to them to sell and render accounts.'

Meanwhile, his late mother sought the hand of Mah Begom Khanom, the daughter of Aqa Mohammad Jaʿfar Sarraf, in marriage for my father. A marriage contract was drawn between them and the marriage took place. His [Haj Mohammad Hasan's] children by Mah Begom Khanom were as follows: ʿAli, who died before my birth; Mehdi who died before my birth; Khadijeh Soltan Khanom, wife of the late Haj ʿAli Naqi Kashi who died from a heart attack in 1333/1914, and she herself in 1342/1923; myself, Mohammad Hosayn; and Maʿsumeh Khanom, who died at the age of four, which I think was in the year 1304/1886.

Apparently, and according to the assertion of my late father himself and witnesses, the state of my father's fortune and luck was enormous. Whatever transaction he undertook, he made a profit. Of course, his intelligence, cleverness, wisdom, and perseverance also helped.

One of the proofs of his good fortune is a dream that Bibi Mah Khanom, the mother of the deceased had, and that I heard her relate. She said, 'When I was pregnant with Aqa Mohammad Hasan, I dreamt that a big star fell from the sky in our house and went into the sleeve of my dress. In the morning I went to Aqa Abu al-Qasem, the famous interpreter of dreams. He said, "Are you pregnant?" I said, "Yes." He said, "This child is a boy and he will possess such good fortune

and luck that he will become famous and renowned throughout the country." '
There were many incidents similar to this dream.

My late father said, 'After a few months, I audited the account of the *hojreh*
which I had given to the brothers, and discovered that they had incurred some
loss and had some unclaimed credit. Due to the fact that I had bought some
merchandise with a time limit attached from Azerbaijani *tojjars*, which I had given
them [the brothers], I was forced to pay for them myself and to forfeit the unpaid
credits. I closed that *hojreh* for a few days, but because they [the brothers] were
unoccupied, I opened it again and gave them some merchandise for sale to render
daily accounts. Some time passed in this fashion and they came home every night.
Finally, Haj Abu al-Qasem became engaged and married the daughter of Haj
Mohammad Aqa Rasul, a silk merchant. His wife was also brought into our house
to be with the late Bibi Mah Khanom.'

According to his own assertions, he [my father] made great profits from
commerce. He learnt the important know-how of commerce from one Monsieur
'Panayotti', who was at that time the only European merchant in Tehran, and
he [Haj Mohammad Hasan] related that his dealings were with him. 'One day
he took me outside the city gates; there was a great amount of cargo there. He
examined each item carefully and marked them with a big wooden seal in ink. I
asked, "What are these?" He said, "They are sheep wool." I said, "What are you
doing?" He said, "I buy them and send them to Europe. If you can buy some I will
send them in trust for you and sell them."

'From that time I became determined to engage in that trade, but my capital,
after the loss of the brothers' *hojreh* and the expenditure of my own wedding and
that of Haj Abu al-Qasem, was not worth mentioning.

'Consequently, perforce, I wrote to Haj Mohammad Kazem Sarraf to buy
sheep wool for me, according to the attached sample, with the four hundred
mesqals of gold, and send it to Tehran. I myself had about one thousand *tumans*'
worth of merchandise and bits and pieces, which I sold and turned into cash. And
because I had a reputation for honesty and good credit, I was able to borrow eight
thousand *tumans* from certain people.

'Finally, in the course of six months, with money from Esfahan and the
borrowed money, I bought ten thousand *tumans*' worth of wool and gave it to
Monsieur Panayotti and said to him, "This wool is worth ten thousand *tumans*. I
do not have any more money, and eight thousand *tumans*' worth of them belongs
to other people; you have a lot of money, please take this wool and send [it] for sale
in trust for me to Europe, and take your commission. [However,] this is on the
condition that you lend me ten thousand *tumans* in cash now, so that I can pay my
debts and have a little money in hand for commerce." Monsieur Panayotti
accepted [my conditions] cheerfully, giving me a ten-thousand *tumans* draft to
one of the bazaar *sarrafs*.

'When I wanted to leave the room, he called me and said, "Do not imagine that I gave you money on the credit of these wools; it is because during this time I have tested you and seen you to be honest and persevering. Consequently, I trust you, and henceforth the finances of my commercial office are in your charge, and you must deal with the drafts and bills of exchange." Immediately, he gave me forty thousand *tumans*' worth of *sarraf's* promissory notes.

'I went, cashed it and brought it in to the *hojreh* and gradually paid his drafts from it. At the same time, he taught me the method of buying merchandise from any place and dispatching it to any place. Every day, like a teacher, he taught me commercial methods. He also taught me the method of sending drafts to the provinces. These involved sixty-one-day and ninety-one-day drafts from Tehran to the provinces and from the provinces to Tehran, and the compensation due in lieu of these arrangements.

'I learnt his instructions with excitement, enthusiasm, and resolution. Every day he questioned me and was astounded to see how quickly I had learned; he was also happy that he was in contact with such a smart person, and he had complete confidence in the manner in which I managed his capital and financial affairs. He consulted with me on the subject of the purchase of merchandise and most other affairs.

'In the course of one year, things progressed so well that funds for the treasury and customs and the bills of exchange of merchants in the provinces were all drafted by me. When the agents of Monsieur Panayotti in the provinces needed cash for the purchase of merchandise, they would obtain it from the government, customs, or merchants, and according to the instructions of Monsieur Panayotti, they would give a draft in my name. Due to this I became very well known in Tehran to the Shah, ministers, and merchants, and others.

'Upon the instructions of Monsieur Panayotti, I was busy in Tehran purchasing certain merchandise, and I paid all the drafts a few days before they were due. An extraordinary credit was established with the government and among people both in Tehran and the provinces. As we had arranged with Monsieur Panayotti, once a week the accounts were audited and settled. One day I went to settle the accounts. After the settlement, I owed him ten thousand and seventy *tumans*. He took the book from me and wrote something in it in the European language. I thought that he had approved the authenticity of the accounts. I took the book, and when I wanted to get up, he said: "Did you understand what I have written?" I said, "No." He said, "Against the ten thousand and seventy *tumans* which you owe me I have now received ten thousand fifteen *tumans*, the profits of the sale of your wool in Europe. Therefore, you only owe me fifty-five *tumans*." '

Trade and commerce continued in Tehran and the provinces until the year 1288/1871, when there was a great famine both in Tehran and the provinces, so that it is considered to be a year of great deprivation. In keeping with his nature, my late father decided to render a service to the people. He sent all his capital, which according to his own statement consisted of ninety thousand *tumans*, to Haj Tarkhan and Baku, and as there was also wheat in Mazandaran, he sent his brother Haj Mohammad Rahim to purchase wheat there and to transport the flour from Haj Tarkhan to Tehran when it arrived in Mazandaran.[52]

In that year of extraordinary famine, this service rendered by my late father to all the people was greatly appreciated and was a source of great solace for the people. Probably a great number of people were saved from hunger and the claws of death. Even I (Mohammad Hosayn), living at that time in Tehran, repeatedly heard from aged, elderly people such as the late Aqa Sayyed Hasan Dallal, known as Siyah, the late Haj Mirza Mohammad Khalil, the late Aqa Shaykh Musa Mojtahed, the son of the late Haj Molla Mohammad Ja'far Chala Maydani, and a number of other people, who used to say that in the famine of 1288/1871, Haj Mohammad Hasan saved the lives of many people and rendered a great service to the country and to the people.

In any case, in that year, according to my late father's statements, the whole of his capital had been spent for charitable purposes, and he was left without any capital. He said: 'When I recalled my brother from Mazandaran and he came to Tehran, I discovered that, aside from two three-thousand *tumans* claims from the baker and the corn chandler, I was also under public criticism from friend and foe alike as to why I had landed myself in such a predicament. And those merchants who were in competition with me went round saying that something had gone wrong with my business and caused me to lose my credit.

'But by the grace of God and good fortune I did not owe one *dinar* to anyone, and I conducted my life with austerity and economy, so that there were no differences in outward appearances. As before, early every morning I went to my *hojreh* and slowly and prudently transacted small business in cash.

'A few months passed in this manner. The merchants of the provinces and the people of Tehran saw that those rumours were without foundation, that I did not owe anything nor was indebted to anyone and was carrying on with my own work. Then they realized that those accusations were made by my competitors. Once again they started sending commercial goods and money from the provinces in trust to me, and I would sell it for them honestly and take a small commission.

'I also looked after the brothers. Haj Mohammad Rahim had returned from Mazandaran, and it transpired that he had married while there. I wrote [to Mazandaran] and had his wife sent to Tehran also. I brought her to my own house. Both brothers with their wives lived with my mother and my own wife in the same house. We led a genteel life with great economy.

---

[52] Haj Tarkhan and Baku: two towns in Russian Azerbaijan.

'Meanwhile, there arose the necessity for me to travel by courier to Azerbaijan to settle certain accounts with merchants with whom I had been dealing. I went there and some important local merchants started transactions with me. They would transfer major merchandise to my name. Haj ʿAbd al-Hamid Tajer Esfahani, whom I knew from before, was in Tabriz. We went into partnership with each other with the objective of buying and importing goods from Istanbul to Iran and similarly buying and exporting goods from Iran to Istanbul and Europe.

'Consequently I sent Haj Abu al-Qasem to Istanbul and Haj Mohammad Rahim to Europe. For a number of years, I was engaged in commerce and became famous throughout Iran. At this point, I felt that the *hajj* [the pilgrimage to Mecca] was incumbent upon me. I made the pilgrimage to holy Mecca. I recalled Haj Abu al-Qasem from Istanbul and Haj Mohammad Rahim from Europe. I settled the accounts of the partnership with Haj ʿAbd al-Hamid Tajer Esfahani. Some cash and pieces of property in Kerman were his share from the partnership which I gave him, and we separated.'

Haj Abu al-Qasem had gone to Mashhad. Haj Mohammad Rahim had also been sent back to Europe. At this time, the extent of commerce was enormous. Important contacts were made amongst ministers and notables, including the Shah. The well-known Moʿayyer al-Mamalek, who was treasurer, was my father's client.[53]

Mirza Hosayn Khan, the prime minister, commander-in-chief in the Naseri reign, and the builder [of the future] *majles-e shura-ye melli*, was among my father's clients. The majority of the leaders, influential people, and treasurers dealt with our *hojreh*. At that time, there was no merchant who had direct agents in Europe other than my father. There was no bank whatsoever in Iran. The other merchants sent a few goods to Russia and Istanbul, but my father sent very important merchandise directly to France, Germany, and England. Whenever the government needed arms, drafts, or other goods from Europe, it was done through him. The foreign ambassadors brought money from Europe only through him.

Good luck and fortune, combined with the grace of God, were of great help, especially in the export of merchandise abroad from which great profit was made.

I remember well my father saying: 'I sought guidance from God concerning whether I should buy opium for export to Hong Kong and the answer was positive, so I started buying.[54]

---

[53] Moʿayyir al-Mamalek was treasurer and head of the Royal Household. He was also treasurer of the Privy Purse and master of the Mint, and was given the title of Nizam l-Dawla and passed his title to his son. See Mehdi Bamdad, *Tarikh-e Rejal-e Iran: Qorun-i 12–13–14*, 1 (Tehran: Kitabforushi-ye Zavvar, 1968), 495–500; Dust ʿAli Khan Moʿayyir al-Mamalek, *Rejal ʿAsr-e Naseri* (Tehran: Nashr-e Tarikh-e Iran, 1983), 33–42.

[54] Estekhareh: traditionally, before making a major decision, Persians consult a book, usually the Qur'an, or bidding beads, at random to decide the procedure to be adopted.

'Simultaneously with my attempt at purchasing opium, the price of opium fell drastically in Hong Kong and all the people in Esfahan, Borujerd, Kermanshahan, and Shiraz who bought opium annually refrained from doing so that year. All the merchants criticized me for this purchase. Finally, I bought all that I could myself and borrowed money from people at high interest rates and sent it to the provinces for the purchase of opium. All in all, I made one thousand two hundred cases of opium in Persian ports ready for shipment to Hong Kong.

'One day, Aqa ᶜAbd al-Baqi and Aqa Mohammad Amin Arbab Tehrani, who were illustrious merchants, came to my *hojreh* and said: "We have heard that you are buying opium; as we are not planning to use ours, please buy the hundred and forty cases which we have." I had no money, but because they were prominent merchants, I wished to fulfil their desire. So out of politeness I told them that I would buy, but, whatever the price, would give a promissory note for a year hence. They accepted, and we agreed on one hundred *tumans* per case to be delivered at Bushehr. They sent a telegram to Bushehr for my agent to take charge of the cases. The total of my opium holdings came to one thousand three hundred and forty cases.

'Two days after this event, Mirza Hosayn Khan, the prime minister, summoned me and said: "Aqa ᶜAbd al-Baqi and Aqa Mohammad Amin have come to me saying that your business is in trouble, that you will suffer great loss from trading in opium and they have sold your one year's promissory note to me deducting three *qerans* per tuman from it. I have accepted your promissory note. Now if you are willing, you can put your promissory note against my account at the price at which I purchased it, or let it remain and be paid on the agreed date." ' My late father said: 'I saw in this the hand of God moving. On the one hand, my debt had diminished by four thousand two hundred *tumans*; on the other hand, the household of the prime minister owed me about ten thousand *tumans*, and in this fashion our accounts would be settled. I said, "I have no objection. Please put this promissory note, as Your Excellency has bought it, against what is owing to me from the household." '

'The Prime Minister said, "Then where is my profit?" I said, "I will make a present of two hundred *tumans* to you." He accepted, gave me back my promissory note, and our account was settled.

'The opium was transported from Bushehr. As luck would have it, the price of opium increased daily until it reached three hundred and fifty *tumans* per case. I instructed them to sell. After the sale, taking into account all the necessary expenditure and the interest on the borrowed money paid to the lenders, I made a profit of roughly three hundred thousand *tumans*. "If God so desires, even the enemy can bring good fortune."

'A few days after receiving the news of the sale of opium, one day His Majesty Naser al-Din Shah summoned me and face-to-face asked me: "Did you have opium abroad?" I said, "Yes." He said, "How much profit did you make? Tell the truth, be assured, I swear by the life of the Shah that I will be happy and will not create any problems for you." Courageously and with self-confidence, I said, "I am not frightened and have full trust in the justice of the Shah, truthfully I made a profit of three hundred thousand *tumans*." Naser al-Din Shah was very pleased and appreciative. [He said], "I am delighted that during my reign merchants have the freedom and confidence to buy merchandise, that they have learned the ropes of commerce with Europe and that in one transaction they make a profit of three hundred thousand *tumans*." '

At this point, the Shah gave the letter of Malkom Khan[d.1908], the Armenian who was Iranian ambassador abroad, to my father, in which Malkom had given a report of the transaction to the Foreign Ministry and to the Shah, and pointing out that after such an important transaction, Haj Mohammad Hasan should give a sum of money as present to the Shah. The Shah said, 'Malkom has written in this manner, but it was presumptuous of him to suggest such a thing; instead of you giving me a present, I will give you a *khaĺat* [long white cashmere garment with gold lace border] so that you will be encouraged to expand your commercial activities.'[55]

I related this story as an example of the good fortune and grace of God with which he [my father] was blessed. There were many such examples of commercial transactions undertaken by my late father. It was as if whatever he touched turned into gold, which became a common saying about him by all and sundry.

Commercial activities continued in full force. In the year 1296/1878 my father met and became great friends with Aqa Ebrahim Amin al-Soltan, who had formed the government Mint that was in Tehran. He had given the administration of the Mint to my father, which involved assessing the correct standard of silver, its purchase and sale, and the settlement of clients' accounts. My father had appointed his paternal cousin Haj Mohammad Amin al-Tojjar as assayer of the Mint. In the year 1302/1884 or before that, Aqa Baqer Sa'ad al-Saltaneh

---

[55] A *khaĺat* is a robe of honor. See N.A. Stillman, *Encyclopaedia of Islam*, 1st edn., under 'Khila'. It is difficult to believe this story in its entirety, as Naser al-Din Shah was well known for accepting presents. Sir Mortimer Durand, British minister to Persia (1894–1900), says: 'The Shah's methods of collecting money from private individuals are numerous and at times amusing. Before we left Tehran last May I used to meet him driving about on a round of visits. Every notable whom he honoured in this way had to produce a "pishkish" of from 50 pounds to 200 pounds. If His Majesty makes a good shot at a moufflon, as he often does, those about him at once subscribe a purse of gold pieces as a token [of] their admiration. He is fond of playing chess in the afternoon for two or three gold pieces a game. His opponent always loses, and His Majesty pockets the gold. It is said that not long ago he was caught in a snowstorm when out shooting. He found shelter in a hut on the hillside and before leaving it he asked what "pishkish" the owner meant to offer for the honour done to him. Eventually the man produced six Russian imperials (something under 5 pounds) which the Shah carried off.' See 'Memorandum by Sir Mortimer Durand on the Situation in Persia', Confidential FO 60/581 (1894), UK Public Records Office, London, p. 2.

influenced the late Aqa Ebrahim Amin al-Soltan against Amin al-Tojjar, known as Haj Mo'yyer, resulting in his dismissal from the Mint.[56] My late father abrogated all responsibility, and Aqa Baqer entered into the activities of the Mint but did not do well.

Meanwhile, Aqa Ebrahim became ill and Naser al-Din Shah's trip to Mashhad came up.[57] Aqa Ebrahim Amin al-Soltan asked my father as a favor to look after the Mint in his absence. My father perforce accepted, and Aqa Ebrahim died on the road to Khorasan. Mirza ⁰Ali Asghar Amin al-Soltan Atabak-e A⁰zam became minister and the successor to his father. On his return from the trip, he [Atabak-e A⁰zam] gave the administration of the Mint once again to my father. Although in theory my father was under the jurisdiction of the government treasury, in practice he had full responsibility. All the time, he audited the accounts secretly and carefully. For a few years, they gave two thousand *tumans* per annum remuneration to my father. And from the year 1309/1891 or 1310/1892, they gave him five thousand *tumans*. All the profits, without any loss, waste, deficit, or defect were given to Aqa Ibrahim Amin al-Soltan during his days, and in turn to Mirza ⁰Ali Asghar Khan during his time. Most of the time, in fact, during the whole period, the collector of this income was one Tabrizi Karbalali Mohammad, who lived in their *andarun* [i.e. that of Amin al-Soltan] and was the confidant of their secrets. Once every three or six months he [Karbalali] took the accounts there [i.e. to Amin al-Soltan] and one Mirza Sayyed ⁰Abd Allah Khan who was the *mostawfi* [accountant] of the treasury, audited the accounts.[58] All the accounts and papers were taken and torn. During wintertime, they were burnt in the space heater; during the summer, they were frequently thrown into the water.

But I remember well from the year 1306 or 1307/1888 or 1889, after the return of Naser al-Din Shah from his last trip to Europe, the late Esma⁰il Khan Amin al-Molk, the brother of Atabak-e A⁰zam, became aware of the truth of the matter and started participating and being present at the time of the exchange of accounts. But I do not know what agreement he had reached with his brother. A contract had been signed between my late father and the late Aqa Ebrahim Amin al-Soltan concerning the running of the Mint. After that, the late Atabak had written in its margin that two thousand *tumans'* remuneration had been increased

---

[56] Aqa Baqer Sa⁰ad al-Saltaneh, maternal cousin of Mirza ⁰Ali Asghar Khan Amin al-Soltan, Atabak-e A⁰zam. He held many government positions through the influence of his cousin and was finally assassinated in Zanjan. See Bamdad, *Tarikh-e Rejal*, 1, 181–4.

[57] Naser al-Din Shah went to Mashhad in 1883.

[58] Sayyed ⁰Abd Allah Mostawfi. It has not been possible to establish which member of the Mustawfi family he was or what post he held. He is not mentioned at all in ⁰Abd Allah Mustawfi's *Sharh-e Zendengani-e Man*. There is a brief passing mention by E'timad al-Saltana in *Ruznameh-e Khaterat*, 141, which proves that such a person existed, but again no mention in Bamdad's *Tarikh-e Rejal*.

to four thousand *tumans*, and my late father had written his own acceptance in the same margin and signed it. This contract was put for safekeeping with Aqa Mohammad Javaheri, known as Khallalzadeh,[59] who lived in the ʿAbbas Abad district of Tehran and was a friend of the parties and known to the Shah and his ministers. After a few years, when the late Aqa Mohammad Hallalzadeh was ill (perhaps four or five days before his death), my father and I went to visit him at a time when the Mint had been taken out of the hands of Amin al-Soltan Atabak. [During this visit] he (Aqa Mohammad) said, 'As I do not have access to the prime minister, Amin al-Soltan and I know that you have settled your accounts together, and the prime minister himself has said that you have no further accounts with each other concerning the Mint, and he has received all that is owing him; in front of you and in the presence of God I burn this written document so that it does not fall into other hands and the secrets of the prime minister and his father Aqa Ebrahim are not divulged.' They brought a lamp and he burnt that paper.

The details and reports of that I will put on paper in the pages to come. Now I will write all that I remember of my own life, with the assistance of God, may He give strength.

As I wrote on the first page, I was born on the eve of Moharram 1289/1872. For a few days, I was breast-fed by my late mother, and after that, the daughter of Haj Akbar, who was our neighbour in our town house and of a genteel family, became my wet nurse and breast-fed me until I was weaned.[60]

The daughter of Haj Akbar is still living at the time of writing, Sunday 39 Rabiʿ al-Sani 1347/1928, and lives in the house of my daughter Khanom-e Khanomha, the daughter-in-law of Haji Mo'in al-Tojjar Bushehri. She is the companion of my daughter and looks after the children as though they were her own. She is very chaste and kind.

From the time I was being nursed I lived in the bedroom of the late Bibi Mah Khanom, the mother of my father. I was always in her bedroom. She loved me very much and I was used to being with her. Although she had other grandchildren, she loved me the most and held me in the highest esteem.

Although it may appear extraordinary to whomever reads this, I remember everything from my childhood. Because I am writing in candor, I have to confess that I remember my infancy when I was being nursed and in the cradle. There was a servant who was very good called Naneh ʿAli. I remember her face and figure and name, although when I was two and a half years old, she died. When I started talking, I asked after her from my late mother and the late Bibi Mah Khanom and they were astounded that I should remember her.

---

[59] In the original text this name appears first as 'Khallalzadeh' and later as 'Hallalzadeh'.

[60] Children were breast-fed until the age of 2 and not weaned before then, although in some cases breast-feeding went on for much longer.

Similarly, I have many memories of my childhood that would appear strange if I related them.

The plan of the building in which we all lived is as follows. It is the same building that is in existence today in the district of Chala Maydan. But the previous plan was different from the present one. The previous plan was as follows. There were only two compounds: one was *andaruni* and one was *biruni*. The *andaruni* compound, the living quarters of my late father and mother, faced [south]. In the middle there was an *'ursi*, that is, a big room on each side of which there were two small rooms.[61] There was a veranda in front of the small rooms with steps going into the yard. Under that *'ursi* and small rooms was a basement that was used as a storage for food and household goods.

The building facing west consisted of a five-door room in the middle and two small prayer rooms on each side. There was a *sanduqkhaneh* in the corner, behind which was a narrow corridor opening into the *kucheh* of Najarbashi.[62] (The same door still opens into the *kucheh* of Najarbashi.) In this building were the living quarters of the late Bibi. In reality, the middle room was the communal drawing room. The daughters-in-law, the sons, and the children went there to see Bibi and I slept there as well. The prayer room on the left, south of the five-door room, was a servant's bedroom.

The building on the east side consisted of a five-door room and two small rooms, which were the living quarters of the wife of the late Haj Abu al-Qasem, my uncle. The rooms on the south side similarly were three and were the living quarters of Gol Baji, the wife of the late Haj Mohammad Rahim, my uncle.[63]

My late father had also married Soghra Khanom, the daughter of Aqa Mohammad Hasan Zarrabi, who lived in her own house. Some nights, my father went to their house. By her, he had two sons and acquired a house behind our house for her to live in. But unfortunately both children died, which affected my father deeply.

In the year 1297 or 1298/1879 or 1880, my father recalled the late Haj Mohammad Rahim, my uncle, from Europe to Tehran. He was in Tehran for a

---

[61] The original text confuses the fact that an *ursi* is a sash-window rather than a room. The word originates from *Rusi*, meaning 'Russian'. Great craftsmanship went into the making of an *ursi* window: elaborate, lacelike geometrical patterns were created and the spaces in between filled with colored glass. As a status symbol and point of prestige, the design of each *ursi* had to be original.

[62] *Sanduqkhaneh*: a room assigned to the storage of clothes and valuable materials, usually in chests, hence the name *sanduq*, a chest in Persian.

[63] On Qajar domestic architecture see A.A. Bakhtiar and R. Hillenbrand, 'Domestic Architecture in Nineteenth-Century Iran: The Manzel-e Sartip Siddighi near Isfahan', in Edmund Bosworth and Carole Hillenbrand (eds.), *Qajar Iran: Political, Social and Cultural Change 1800–1925* (Edinburgh: Edinburgh University Press, 1983), and Jakob Eduard Polak, *Persien, das Land und Seine Bewohner*, 2 vols. (Leipzig, 1865), translated into Persian by Kaykavus Jahandari as *Safarnameh-e Polak: Iran va Iranian* (Tehran: Entesharat-e Khawrazmi, 1982), 45–60.

number of months. His only child was Sakineh Soltan Khanom, whom they gave in marriage to Haj Mirza Aqa, the son of Haj ᶜAbbas Sarraf. Haj Mohammad Rahim was in Tehran both for the engagement and the wedding. After the wedding of his daughter, he left for Europe via the Holy Cities [Baghdad, Karbala, and Najaf]. He also took the late Bibi with him to the Holy Cities but sent her back to Tehran after she had worshipped at the shrines, continuing to Europe himself.

I remember well both the day of the arrival of the late Haj Mohammad Rahim in Tehran and that of his departure for Europe. The late Haj Mohammad Rahim was an extremely kind and humane man. He was an extraordinarily orthodox Muslim. A few days after his return from Europe, he started fasting to make up for the days of fasting during Ramazan that he missed while in Europe. At nights, as dawn was breaking he would wake up to eat before starting his fast. I would also join him in his room coming from Bibi's room. I would stay with him until the morning, when he would say his prayers and go back to sleep. He loved me very much and showed me much kindness. He taught me the French alphabet at that young age, although I had not yet even gone to the *maktab*.

On the day he set off for the Holy Cities, the separation from the late Bibi affected me deeply. After their departure, I was ill for a number of days. Every day they promised me that Bibi would return tomorrow, the day after tomorrow, until she finally returned.

Meanwhile, they sent me to the girls' *maktab* in the neighboring house in the *kucheh* of Najarbashi. The name of the female teacher was Molla Baji. I, my sister, and the daughter of my maternal uncle Haj 'Ali, the brother of the late Bibi, went to that *maktab*. For a year we studied there, but after a year, they sent me to the boys' *maktab* that was near the *biruni* compound. (That *maktab*, at present, has turned into the building known as *talar*, in which we live.) The name of the teacher was Shaykh Esmaᶜil Shahrudi. He had a few other pupils, too. After a while, my late father bought a small house in the *kucheh* [alley] of Hammam-e Marjan, which was near the mosque of Haj Shaykh Abu al-Fath, and made that into a *maktab* where we went daily.

After a few months, Aqa Shaykh Esmaᶜil went to Shahrud. My late father asked me to go to the *hojreh* daily for the time being. There was one Aqa Mohammad Ismaᶜil who was the scribe of the *hojreh*, and it was arranged that I should study with him until another teacher should be found. Every day I went to the *hojreh* and studied Persian with him, until in the year 1299/1881, the late Aqa Mulla Shahmirzadi, the former teacher of Haj Mirza Abu al-Qasem, the bookkeeper of the *hojreh*, was recommended by him to my father and brought to the *hojreh* from Simnan. My late father commanded that he should come to the house in the mornings and give me instruction until the evening. He came the next day and started instruction in the presence of my late father. Aqa Reza, the present Ra'is al-Tojjar of Mashhad and my paternal cousin, started doing lessons with me in the same *maktab* situated in the *biruni* compound facing the *qebleh*.[64]

In passing, it should be mentioned that Aqa Reza Ra'is al-Tojjar was born in Mashhad. But at that time, he, his mother, the later Hajiyyeh Khanum, the daughter of Haj Mohammad Hasan Aqa Rasul and the wife of my late uncle, Haj Abu al-Qasem, and the three daughters of my uncle, were ordered by my father to come to Tehran.

The daughters were as follows: the eldest daughter, Khanum, who was the wife of Aqa ʿAbd al-Hosayn Sarraf, who died recently in Mashhad, was the mother of Akbar Aqa; the second daughter, Tuba Khanum, who is my own wife; the third daughter Qamar Khanum, who died after returning from Mashhad.

They had all come to Tehran on the bidding of my father, thinking that my uncle would also come, but after a two-year stay in Tehran, my father sent them again to Mashhad, accompanied by my own mother, and they stayed there and my mother returned.

For two years I was occupied in this manner with my studies. Aside from the late Molla Aqa, who had recently come to be known as Haji Akhund, there was also a Shaykh Reza, a blind man who was a reciter of the Qur'an and who was perfectly versed in the recitation of the seven versions of the Qur'an and also knew the Qur'an by heart, whom they had employed to be present in the house one hour before dawn every day.[65] He recited one section of the Qur'an and left after breakfast. After that, Persian lessons and Arabic started: the grammar of Mir, the *Amsaleh*, the *ʿAvamel* of Molla Jurjan, the *Samadiyyeh*, the *Hashiyeh* [commentary] of Molla ʿAbd Allah. After that we studied Soyuti and Jami, and later we studied the *Motavval* and *Moghni*. We completed all this in five or six years. During this period, I learnt by heart the grammar of Mir, the *Samadiyyeh*, the text of the *Mutavval*, in addition to the *Alfiyyeh*, consisting of one thousand lines of poetry.[66] One Haj Mirza, known as Gol Bulab, was in charge of cursive

---

[64] The direction to which Muslims turn in praying.

[65] *Qira'a* in the original. The term applies to the recitation of the Qur'an. After the death of the Prophet, disagreements arose on exactly how to read the revealed text. Finally, in the first half of the tenth century Ibn Mojahed (d. 324AH/936CE), the influential imam of the 'readers' in Baghdad, brought the disagreement to an end. He recognized seven 'readers' as authorities on the traditional reading of the ʿUthmani text and forbade all others, to the extent of flogging those who did not comply. The seven recognized 'readers' lived in the eighth century and included ʿAsim of Kufa (d. 128/745) and Nafi of Medina (d. 169/785). See R. Paret, *Encyclopaedia of Islam*, 2nd edn., under 'Kira'a'.

[66] The grammar of Mir by Mir Sayyed ʿAli Sharif Jurjani Astarabad (740/1339–816/1413). The *Amsaleh*: a well-known textbook for beginners on language. The *Samadiyyeh* or *Hidayeh*: a treatise on syntax. The *Hashiyeh* of Molla ʿAbd Allah is probably a commentary on logic and theology by Molla ʿAbd Allah Yazdi on a work by Saʿd al-Din Taftazan (722/1322–792/1389). Jalal al-Din Soyuti (849/1445–911/1505), a famous fifteenth-century scholar of the Mamluk period in Egypt. ʿAbd al-Rahman Jami (817/1414–898/1492), considered the last classical Persian Sufi poet. The *Motavval*

writing and was there from morning to night. And one Mirza ᶜAmu, the calli-grapher (the one who has written most of the manuscripts in the mosques and in the Naseri Sipahsalar Mosque), came every afternoon for calligraphic instruc-tion. I was engaged in studying every day but Friday. I never went out of the house, except for one day a year when my late father had given permission for me and my teachers, accompanied by two or three servants, to go to one of the parks in the town. At that time, Lalehzar and . . . were among the famous government parks where we went and had lunch and tea and returned in the evening.[67] For two years this was the regimen in the home. After two years, my late father ordered that I should no longer stay at home and that all these people should come to the upper story of the *hojreh*, which was situated in Karavansaray-e Amir, and that I should also go there in the mornings at the time of the morning *a'zan* [the call to prayer] and stay there until half an hour before sunset, when I should return home.

Until that time, Haj Akhund lived in the mosque of the *madraseh* of Amin al-Dawleh Kashi, which was in the vicinity of the *qebleh hammam*, but from this point he started living in the upper floor of Saray-e Amir. Every morning at the time of morning prayer, I would go to the upper story of the *hojreh*, either on horseback or by mule, accompanied by two trusted servants, one of whom lived near our house and the other one farther away. But some nights, Haj Akhund would still go to the *hojreh* of the *madraseh* of Amin al-Dawleh to see the theologians there. On those nights, we would arrange to meet near the ironmongers' bazaar. I would dismount and we would walk together to the *hojreh*. On the way, he would listen to the books and the *Alfiyyeh* that he had asked me to learn by heart the previous night. All the passers-by and pedes-trians were astounded and full of admiration when they saw how hard I was studying.

The late Haj Akhund was very particular and full of care for my education. During that period, his wife and children were in Shahmirzad while he was

---

by Taftazani, on rhetoric. The *Moghni*, a standard work on Arabic grammar and syntax by Jamal al-Din Ibn Hisham (708/1308–762/1360). The *Alfiyyeh* by Ibn Malik (601/1204–673/1274), on Arabic syntax.

[67] At present, Laleh is a narrow shopping street that was very fashionable up to the early 1950s. Previously, however, it was a big park, the boundaries of which were on the south bounded by Ekbatan Avenue, on the north by Mokhbir al-Dawlah Square, on the east by Saᶜdi Avenue, and on the west by the western side of the present Lalehzar Avenue. It was a royal residence. Mirza Abu al-Qasem Qaᶜem-Maqam Farahani (1193/1779–1251/1835), prime minister to Mohammad Shah Qajar, lived there before his execution. In 1886 Naser al-Din Shah turned the premises into the Ministry of Justice and finally sold it for 900,000 *rials*. See Bamdad, *Tarikh-e Rejal*, vol. 1, p. 63 and vol. 2, p. 439. Apparently Tholozan, the French court doctor, begged the shah not to sell it as it was beneficial for the air and atmosphere of Tehran, but the shah would not listen. See Mehdi Qouli, Hidaya *Khaterat va Khatarat* (Tehran: Ketab Forushi-yi Zavvar, 1965), 5. The ellipses are lacunae in the original text.

overseeing my education in Tehran. It was only in the last two years of my studies that he brought his son ʿAbd al Hosayn from Shahmirzad to study with us.

I wrote the cursive script and the lithographic script very well. I have handwritten many books, including the commentary on the morning prayer, the *Divan* of Moshtaq ʿAli Shah, [the prayer to] the twelve Imams by Mohyi al-Din ʿArabi, and *Kalileh va Dimneh* and others.[68] I have handwritten in lithographic script the collection of prayers attributed to the Commander of the Faithful [i.e. ʿAli], which was bound and covered in velvet. This volume is at present found in my own library and is actually considered well written.

Daily before sunrise, my late father would come to our place of study for inspection and was full of encouragement. He emphasized greatly the recitation and interpretation of the Qur'an, and because of this, Haj Akhund had been forced to study a number of interpretations by both Shiʿi and Sunni ʿolama. Daily, he would give us lessons in the interpretation of the Qur'an, explaining in detail the meaning and the origins of the various verses.

My late father ordered that I should be virtuous and pious and God-loving and that I should read the Qur'an and the prayers (to the Imams), and I obeyed from the bottom of my heart. Upon his instructions, I learnt by heart the Morning Prayer, the Prayer of Kamil, the *Ya Sin* chapter (in the Qur'an), the chapter [which begins with] *idha waqaʿat al-waqiʿa*, the chapter of *inna fathana laka fathan mubina*, the chapter of *Jumuʿa*, the chapter of *Munafiqun*, the chapter of *Hashr*, the chapter of *Hal a*ta, the chapter of *amma yatasa'alun*, and for each one of them he gave me a special prize and some money.[69] He was so concerned that I should be virtuous and pious that it is not possible to express it by putting it on paper. Because I considered obedience to the commands of my father obligatory and naturally believed in Islam, I did not ever refrain from piety and abstinence. From the age of twelve, I got up at dawn for morning prayers and said my prayers in the evenings. Every day, whenever I had time I would read the Qur'an and prayer book. I was very particular that I should meet devout, ascetic, God-fearing people and seek their advice and counsel. From infancy, I had great reliance and trust in God Almighty and whenever something appeared desirable and pleasing, I would ask God for it. I was extremely careful not to commit any acts against the Islamic

[68] Moshtaq ʿAli Shah (Mirza Mohammad Kermani), a Sufi master of the tariqa of Shah Neʿmat Allah Vali Kermani; he was executed in 1304/1886. Mohyi al-Din Ibn ʿArabi (561/1165–638/1240), known as al-Shaykh al-Akbar, was one of the great Sufis of Islam and one of the most prolific of Sufi writers. *Kalileh va Dimneh* is the famous book of stories narrated by animals, first translated from Sanskrit into Pahlavi, then into Arabic by the famous Ibn Muqaffaʿ, then into Persian by Nasrollah Monshi.

[69] Well-known Shiʿi prayers, the texts for which are included in Shaykh ʿAbbas Qumi, *Mafateh al-jinan*, the standard Shiʿi prayer-book. As listed in the text, these are, in order: chapters Ya-sin (36), al-Fath (48), al-Waqiʿa (56), al-Jummʿa (62), al-Munafiqin (63), al-Hashr (59), al-Insan (76), and al-Nabaʿ (78) of the Qur'an.

law and refrained from looking at those [women] not religiously permitted (*na-mahram*).[70] It was astounding the manner in which Islamic virtue had enveloped the whole of my being, and always I concealed my religiosity, asceticism, and piety from everyone.

I remember well one day in the month of Ramazan, I went to the Friday mosque for prayers in the company of Haj Akhund and others. There was one Aqa Abu Talebi from Khurasan who was famous [as] a preacher and reciter of *rawzehs* in Tehran.[71] After prayers, he usually preached. One day he spoke of the importance of the Great Name of God, saying that whoever knows it, his prayers will be granted, but that the Great Name is hidden from everyone and no one knows it. At the end, he gave an account of the glory, worth, and merit of the prayers of twelve Imams, the Prophet, and Fatima Zahra, prayer and Peace be upon them, his prayers will be answered.[72]

There and then, I said to myself that I must be very lucky to have come here and heard the preacher on these two subjects. The merit and value of the Great Name is self-evident, and the method of obtaining it has also became apparent. From the next day, I started saying daily before sunrise: 'That in Allah's grace, he grants it to whom He pleases. And Allah is the Lord of Mighty Grace', for forty-one days.[73]

It is obvious that the Grace of God that has favored me every minute and hour of every day, night, month, and year is due to those sincere prayers, for which I have always been grateful and continue to be so.

In the year 1303/1885, Naser al-Din Shah went on his trip to Mashhad and took with him Aqa Ebrahim Amin al-Soltan.[74] On the way, Aqa Ebrahim passed away and his title was given to his son Mirza ᶜAli Asghar Khan. He almost became minister of Court, in charge of everything, and held the reins of government. In Mashhad, he stayed at the house of my uncle Malek al-Tojjar. After his return to Tehran, he was extremely kind to my father. One Friday he came to lunch at out house. When he wanted to leave in the evening, they had only one carriage as we did not have one. We had a mule and a donkey. Esmaᶜil Khan Amin al-Molk, the brother of Amin al-Soltan, rode that mule, and Mohammad Qasem Khan Saheb Jamᶜ, the other brother, rode the donkey. [At that time, means of transport in the capital city was that difficult.] Two days after, my father became extremely ill,

---

[70] The term *na-mahram* is a technical term in Islamic law that refers to men in front of whom women cannot appear unveiled. Conversely, *mahram* refers to male members of the family in front of whom female members of the family can appear unveiled.

[71] *Rawzeh*: description of the tragedies of Karbala.

[72] A well-known prayer to the twelve Imams ascribed to the Isma'li philosopher of astronomer Naser al-Din Tusi (d. 672/1273).

[73] Qur'an 62: 4. Translation from Mawlana Muhammad ᶜAli, *The Holy Qur'an: Arabic Text, Translation, and Commentary* (Lahore: Ahmadiyya, 1951).

[74] Naser al-Din Shah's trip to Mashhad was actually in 1883.

suffering from a chest ailment that left him bed-ridden for a number of months. All the Persian doctors and one European doctor, Tholozan by name, sent by Amin al-Soltan and the Shah, came to visit daily.[75] My father sent a telegram to Mashhad to my uncle Haj Abu al Qasem, asking him to come to Tehran. Amin al-Soltan himself came a number of times to see how my father was doing. The doctors prescribed sweet lemons. Amin al-Soltan ordered people to go to private orangeries and buy sweet lemons at five *qerans* each. This price was considered most unusual and extraordinary by everyone and became a public byword.

Gradually my father became better and sent me in the company of Haj Mohammad Amin al-Tojjar to Ayvan-e Kayf to meet my uncle. This was the first time I left Tehran. We stayed two or three days in Ayvan-e Kayf until my uncle arrived, and then we accompanied him to Tehran. He stayed in Tehran for a few months. He was very fond of me. In the evenings, we used to come home together mounted. He, Bibi, and my father spent the nights in the five-door room on the east side of the *andarun* building. Some nights, my father would go to his own room and then it was my turn to be with my uncle. We would stay up all night, he talking of the past and I listening. My poor uncle had a stone in his bladder that troubled him very much. Physically, he was weak and ailing. After a few months he left for Mashhad, accompanied by Bibi. The first night of their departure they spent in Hazrat ʿAbd al-ʿAzim, Peace be upon Him, and left in the middle of the night.[76]

---

[75] Joseph Desiré Tholozan. Naser al-Din Shah had a number of physicians, both Persian and foreign. The foreign ones were: the Frenchman Ernest Cloquet, who died in 1855; he was succeeded by the Austrian Jakob Eduard Polak, who was already in Tehran teaching at the Dar al-Funun. Tholozan was French and was employed in Paris in 1856 by Farrokh Khan Kashi Amin al-Molk. It appears that both he and Polak were court doctors simultaneously, until Polak left in 1860 and Tholozan became the only foreign doctor. On Naser al-Din Shah's third trip to Europe Tholozan introduced the shah to Dr Feuvrier, who was appointed court doctor and remained until 1889. According to Eʿemad al-Saltaneh, *Ruznameh-e Khaterat*, 655, at the time of presenting Dr Feuvrier to the shah Tholozan stated that he wished to remain in France. However, subsequently he returned to Persia, and after Feuvrier's departure was once again the only foreign court doctor. Tholozan remained in Persia until 1896 and the accession of Mozaffar al-Din Shah Qajar, having been in that country for forty years. Unlike his predecessor, Polak, and his successor, Feuvrier, who wrote accounts of their stay in Persia, Tholozan wrote no such account, but produced many medical treatises. He appears to have been much involved in every aspect of Persian life. His two daughters were married to men who were working in Iran: one to Lemaire, the musical director of Dar al-Fonoun, and the other to Henry Lionel Churchill, who was from 1880 to 1886 with the Indo-European Telegraph Company in Tehran and in 1886 joined the British Legation as second secretary and remained in Persia until 1894. Apparently Tholozan was involved in the various concession negotiations that were taking place at that time, and he left Persia with a vast fortune. See Bamdad, *Tarikh-e Rejal*, vol. 4, p. 319.

[76] Hazrat-i ʿAbd al-ʿAzim was a descendant of Hasan b.ʿAli b. Abu Talib, the second Shiʿi imam, reputed to be a trustworthy narrator of Shiʿi Hadith. His shrine in Ray, south of Tehran, known as ShahzadehiʿAbd al-ʿAzim, is a place of Shiʿ pilgrimage.

After their departure, my father also left for town. It may have been the month of Ramazan. The only people left there were myself, Sakina Soltan, the daughter of my uncle Haj Mohammad Rahim, and Aqa Farajollah, and we returned to town in the morning (riding the donkey).

At about this time, the news of the death of Haj Mirza Sarraf, the son of Haj ᶜAbbas Sarraf, on his way to Mecca reached us. After the period of ᶜeddeh[77] was finished, Sakina Soltan was married to Aqa Farajollah, the maternal cousin of my father.

Separation from my uncle and Bibi affected me deeply; after a few days I became very ill but, thank God, recovered after a while.

In that same year, my father tore down the old *andarun* and bought the house of Mashhadi Emamqoli, the hatmaker, whose wife was my teacher. He also bought two or three small houses around there and built the *andarun*, the old side of which is three stories with a courtyard, and a bathhouse, and other extensions. Behind the courtyard known as the *talar* courtyard, he bought a small house and brought Soghra Khanum, his wife, the daughter of Aqa Mohammad Hasan Zarrabi, there. The Almighty gave my father two sons by her, but they did not have a long life and unfortunately died the same year.

My father helped the poor, theological scholars [*tollab*], and the needy enormously during the feasts of Ghadir and Fetr and during winters.[78] In the months of Moharram, during the ten days of Ashura, there was always an elaborate *rawzeh-kh*ʷ*ani* in the house, and they prepared an immense amount of food.[79] Daily, two to three *kharvars* of rice were cooked and two to three thousand men and women were fed.

His [my father's] inner belief was that help should be extended to God's creatures. The resources of God should be shared with people. He always advised me not to refrain from doing people favours and helping as much as possible, saying: 'God will repay you.' I remember well that he gave me an example [of this]. He said, 'I have estimated the cost of medicine for my family, should they fall ill, and about fifteen *tumans* is the profit that this druggist (Haji ᶜAttar, the father of Gholamhosayn) who lives near us would make. At the beginning of the year, I gave him the fifteen *tumans* and in return during the year you do not find any sick people in the house.' The point is that he held such praiseworthy beliefs.

[77] A technical term in Islamic law (ᶜ*idda* in Arabic) that refers to the period during which a divorced or widowed woman may not be married to another man.

[78] *Ghadir*: a festival celebrated by the Shiᶜis on the occasion of ᶜAli's alleged appointment as successor to the Prophet Muhammad. It is so called because the event took place near a pool in Arabia called Ghadir Khumm. *Fitr*: the festival at the end of Ramazan [Ramadan], on the first day of Shawwal on which the breaking of the fast is celebrated.

[79] Shiᶜi Muslims mourn the tenth of Muharram, the anniversary of the battle of Karbala (61/680), on which Hosayn Ibn Abu Talib fell fighting against the Umayyad forces. *Rawzeh-Kh*ʷ*ani* is a performance of a passion play on the martyrdom of Husayn.

In winter he used to buy an enormous amount of charcoal dust, about three or four hundred *kharvars*, one thousand fur vests, and a lot of shirts and trousers and distributed them among the poor. He would tell the ᶜolama that he would give them drafts to give to the poor.

During all this time I was busy studying, until one day when I came home from school I saw that an Arab *shaykh* was sitting in the *biruni*.[80] My father said, 'This Aqa is our guest and will stay with us. As I am invited to the house of Aqa Mohammad Mirza, the preacher, tonight, you stay here and entertain our guest until I return at the end of the evening.' He left. I went into the room and greeted [the guest]; he returned my greetings and said, 'Are you the son of Haji?' I said, 'Yes.' He said, 'Well done, may God preserve you. Do you study?' I said, 'Yes.' He said, 'What do you read?' I said, 'The *Motavval* and the *Moghni*.' He said, 'Where do you read?' I replied, 'I read *Zanburiyyeh*.' He quoted a sentence and asked me what its meaning was. I replied, and he said, 'That is correct. Well done!' Then he asked, 'Do you read and write Arabic?' I said, 'No.' This word had such an effect on him that the color of his face changed through anger. Angrily he said, 'How strange, how strange. You read *Motavval* and *Moghni* but you do not speak Arabic. From tomorrow you must start speaking Arabic.' After three or four hours, my father returned from his dinner. Aqa related the story to my father and said, 'I command that from tomorrow your son should write and speak Arabic. His Arabic compositions begin with his writing the incident of my arrival and our meeting. And he should translate this command of mine from Persian into Arabic. Also, Haj Mohammad Hasan, I am telling you that if in ten nights' time he manages to write a page without any mistakes you must reward your son with one hundred *ashrafis*.'[81]

My father, May God elevate him, was very keen on my progress, and considered this command a wonderful idea and encouraged me. From the day after that night, in the company of Haj Akhund, the teacher, and Shaykh Reza, a blind man who knew the Qur'an by heart and knew Arabic, we started speaking and writing in Arabic. Every night, Aqa Sayyed Jamal al-Din would write a page in Persian; the next day I would translate it into Arabic and at night he would look at it. Ten days passed in this manner. I prepared a faultless page in Arabic and showed it to him. He admired it very much but said, 'This is not sufficient, you have to write a page of Arabic in my presence.' I accepted. He chose a page of Persian and there

---

[80] This 'Arab *Shaykh*' turns out to be the Pan-Islamist Sayyed Jamal al-Din Asadabadi 'al-Afghani' (d. 1897).

[81] An Iranian gold coin. The origin of the word is not clear. Ashraf may have been the name of the shah who in ancient times minted the coin by that name, or the Afghan Ashraf, the conqueror of Esfahan in 1722, may have invented it; or alternatively, it may have been minted for the first time in the town of Ashraf. See ᶜAli Akbar, Dehkhoda, *Loghatnameh* (Tehran: Chapkhane-ye Dehkhoda Majles, 1946), under '*Ashrafi*'.

and then I turned it into faultless Arabic and gave it to him. He said, 'Wait for a while for Haji to come give you the hundred *ashrafis*.' After half an hour, my father came, and he related the incident. He [my father] also said, 'He must translate a page into Arabic in my presence. If it is correct, then I will give it [i.e., the *ashrafis*].' I obeyed and executed it immediately. He gave me a hundred *ashrafis*. This was the first reward of learning that came my way.

The late [Jamal al-Din] was in our house for some time and dictated lengthy articles every evening in Persian, which I turned into Arabic. All those articles consisted of counsels, opinions, and philosophy. Most of them are in my own handwriting and are presently in our library.

Aqa Sayyed Jamal al-Din was a man of learning and philosophy. My father held great religious beliefs in regard to him. But I was not of the same opinion, and although he was considered one of the great scholars of his time, I personally consider him an opportunist. He was impetuous, courageous, learned, and philosophical. But chance and luck were not with him. Wherever he set foot, he instigated revolts but was never able to obtain desirable results.

Finally, after a period of my father's hospitality, they took him to see Naser al-Din Shah. The Shah became very upset after discussions with him and commanded my father that Sayyed should be exiled. At this time my father wanted to go to Mazandaran to inspect the iron mines there and to establish a factory for smelting iron. So he said to the Shah, 'As he is a guest, please grant permission for me to take him courteously to Mazandaran and from there to Russia, where I will tell him the account.' The Shah accepted, and it was executed accordingly.

8.7 The population as a national economic resource: an Iranian press article, 1937

Cyrus Schayegh

Preface

The article printed below was written during the reign of Reza Shah Pahlavi (r. 1925–41), who combined accelerated social and cultural reforms—in the fields of education, secularization, jurisprudence, and women's rights, amongst others—with patrimonial one-man rule to create a system of autocratic modernization, essentially continued by his son Mohammed Reza Shah (r. 1941–79). As a result of this program, the 1930s was to witness the initiation of a first serious wave of state-led industrialization in Iran, in the wake of the global economic crisis post-1929.

It is interesting to note that the author of the article was one Dr Fereydun Keshavarz, who played an important role in the communist Tudeh Party after the forced abdication of Reza Shah in 1941 at the hands of an Anglo-Soviet invasion and occupation force (later joined by American troops).[82] Reza Shah's regime had been virulently anti-communist, banning 'collectivist ideologies' in 1931, and imprisoning fifty-three communist sympathizers after a celebrated show-trial in 1937.

Although the Iranian modernizing elite had begun to be concerned about issues of health since the mid-nineteenth century, it was only after the Constitutional Revolution of 1905–6 that the poor hygiene and 'unscientific' habits of the lower classes came under scrutiny. State officials, drawing upon the intellectual climate of the time and spurred by a desire for economic modernization coupled with an anxiety over increasing urbanization, focused on the notion that scientific state management of public health creates healthy people who 'have more desire to work—and as a result, the country thrives and progresses'.[83] Increasingly, this idea drove aspects of state economic policy. The construction of the Trans-Iranian railway (1927–38) linked health to a state-run economic project

[82] Dr Keshavarz was born in 1907 and finished his education in medicine in Paris, returning to Iran as a specialist in children's medicine in the early 1930s. According to an article published in the early 1940s by the Tudeh party entitled *Mardom baraye rawshanfekran* ('The People Support the Intellectuals'), he was also the first Iranian to establish a children's hospital in Iran in the 1930s. See Keshavarz/ShahrokhVaziri, *Man mottaham mikonam. Mosahebeh-e Shahrokh Vaziri ba Fereydun Keshavarz* ('Witness: An interview by S. Vaziri with F. Keshavarz') (Tehran: Tus, 1977), 8, 48.

[83] For additional examples, see *Mobarezeh ba kam-shodan-e jamʿiat* ('Fighting population decrease'), *Ettelaʿat*, 18 (Mehr 1315/10 Oct. 1936), and *Ahamiyyat-e behdasht* ('The importance of hygiene'), *Ettelaʿat*, 10/5 (Azar 1316/1 Dec. 1937).

for the first time, with the provision of field hospitals for workers.[84] Following previous legislation in 1922 and 1928 on child labor and working conditions in the carpet industry, Iran's parliament passed a new law on 10 August 1936 that determined the health measures with which factories had to comply—the implementation of which proved to be highly problematic for decades to come.

There was a pervasive gender bias in the association of good health with (biological) reproduction in the case of women and with (economic) production in the case of men. The fundamental 'function' of health was to 'prepare boys for work and the army, and girls for the duties of the home'.[85] It was stressed, however, that men had to be healthy not only in order to work, but also to be 'able to reproduce'. Simultaneously, some argued that women should be able to work outside their home—as long as they did not neglect their maternal and housekeeping duties—and that work at home should be considered a contribution to the national economy.

Significantly, the publication of this article coincided with the Women's Awakening Project of 1936–41, which entailed the forced unveiling of all Iranian women in exchange for increased opportunities in education and employment. Indeed, the immediate context for Keshavarz's article was a series of essays published in Iran's main daily, *Ettela'at*, on the subject of the connections between women's education, public health, child-rearing, and national economic progress.

Text

'The Need to Increase Iran's Population', by Fereydun Keshavarz

(*Ettela'at* ('Information'), 3230, 22 August 1937)[86]

[I]n our country, where raw materials, a variety of mines and much land exist, workers and farmers, and finally, a large population, are needed to utilize and exploit all these natural resources. This follows from the simple calculation that, if fifty people can build fifty meters of road in one day, five hundred meters will be prepared in one day if five hundred people exist to build the road. And, thus, more wealth is created. In the same proportion, exchange and circulation of capital and goods will also be accelerated. [. . .] In general, the way to increase a country's population is to increase the number of births and to decrease the number of deaths. Less populous European states adopt a number of methods to augment

---

[84] Translator's note: It had been pre-dated by another large industrial project in Iran, however, namely the Anglo-Persian Oil Company's activities in south-western Iran, which gave work to thousands of Iranians on a regular basis from the late 1910s. Run entirely by the British, nonetheless it influenced the views of the Iranian modernizing class and the state.

[85] *Tarbiyyat-e badani* ('Physical education'), *Ta'lim va Tarbiyyat* ('Teaching and Education'), 4/5 (1313/1934/5), 257.

[86] Fereydun Keshavarz, *Lozum-e taksir-e jam'iat dar Iran*, *Ettela'at*, 3230/31 (Mordad, 1316), 1.

their birth rates: (1) superior positions and privileges in government services are provided to persons who are married and have many children; (2) discounts on goods and taxes, the costs of educating children and such like are provided; (3) awards are given to families with many children. In Iran, this is not as urgent, because, fortunately, there are many marriages in our country. Due to the special impact of national morals and religious creeds, Iranian families have many children. We Muslims fortunately obey the command 'Marry and Reproduce! I am a father to them and you are mothers, even for miscarried fetuses.'[87] [. . .] Iranian families have on average at least five children, while in France, for example, a family has on average two to three children, roughly half the Iranian average. Therefore, the best and most necessary policy and means to increase the Iranian population is the decrease of the number of cases of death. [. . .] Another means of reducing the death rate is to prevent and increase penalties for abortions. The situation is such that it requires special attention [. . .] Fortunately, owing to the special attention to public hygiene and the establishment and increase of free hospitals and public clinics, the death rate (of persons) has been lower recently, in contrast to previous years. Nevertheless, the governmental physicians and public health can still save a large number (of people) from the claws of death and prevent the exhaustion and wasting of the country's human capital.

Something which has received too little attention in education programs for women and in the hospitals, but that seems a most important and vital element of health nonetheless, is concern for the causes of children's deaths in Iran. Due to the ignorance of Iranian mothers of (even) basic literature of child rearing, and due to the absence of sufficient means for the treatment of ill infants, more than fifty percent of all children born to Iranian families die before the age of seven. Through instruction, and by acquainting people with the literature on child rearing, as well as by providing families with free medical treatment, at least ninety percent of children under seven could live to reach adolescence, rather than [the current figure of] fifty percent. In this context, the public welfare institutions and patriotic women's organizations must carry out serious and efficient actions by which the management of the country's health shall be

[87] Editor's note: Although this passage is written in Arabic that is religiously evocative in tone it is not from the Qur'an and should probably be understood as an allusion to a Hadith, a report on the sayings and actions of the Prophet Muhammad, collections of which provide an additional scriptural source for Islamic law. If this does derive from a Hadith (which is by no means certain), the 'I' in this case would be the Prophet Muhammad referring to himself metaphorically as a father figure. The original document contained errors which obscure the intended meaning of the passage, resulting in a somewhat speculative translation. There are other instances, most notably in the nineteenth-century expatriate Persian newspaper *Qanun* ('The Law') in which similarly evocative Arabic is employed for rhetorical effect, even though what is expressed derives neither from the Qur'an nor the body of Hadith.

invigorated. Switzerland offers the best example of how a country might effect an increase in its population by the means discussed above. By strengthening the administration of public health, the number of infant deaths decreased from 25,268 per year to 5,000 per year (or one fifth of its original rate). As a result, the population has doubled in 48 years. [*France is taken as another example.*]

As long as the ignorance of many Iranian mothers continues, and there are no provisions for medicine and treatment targeted towards sick children, one must be concerned that the country's population will not change.

8.8 Diplomatic and court perspectives on the 'White Revolution' in Iran, 1958–1971
Ali M. Ansari

Preface

The White Revolution in Iran was launched with great fanfare in January 1963, following the successful administration of a popular referendum in which a suspicious 99 per cent of the population turned out to vote in favour of the reforms. The reforms, as they were originally conceived, were composed of six distinct policies. The most important, land reform, had initially been inaugurated in 1961 by Prime Minister Amini and his zealous minister of agriculture, Hasan Arsanjani, under the rubric of an ambiguously defined 'white revolution'. Subsequently appropriated by the shah, *the* White Revolution that was launched in 1963 was supplemented by another eleven points. Land reform was a popular policy among Middle Eastern rulers of various political hues during the 1950s and 1960s. In many cases, it enjoyed the support of the United States government as well as development theorists, who regarded land reform as the central means by which decaying 'feudal' governments could be arrested and replaced by modern social and economic relations which would provide a buttress against the encroachments of Soviet communism. As such, the policy was often encouraged with the Cold War in mind, and with little attention to the specificities of the case. At the same time, as is quite clear from the following documents, local rulers, including the shah, approached the implementation of land reform in political terms, sacrificing real socio-economic gains in favour of political priorities.

The following selection of documents has been drawn from British Foreign Office and Persian sources, and seeks to show not only the official representation but also the private analyses, by both Iranian and foreign observers, of the realities of reform. Whether taken from the perspective of the British diplomats in Iran who drafted reports to the Foreign Office, or the pronouncements of Mohammad Reza Shah Pahlavi, all the documents excerpted here demonstrate the political imperative behind the reform and the need to launch a 'bloodless' white revolution to anticipate and indeed prevent the further development of revolutionary tendencies from below. Document 1a reveals the genesis of the concept of the White Revolution, and together with Documents 2a and 2b, indicates the shah's initial reluctance to be involved in such a policy. Documents 2a and 2b also reveal the extent to which French political thought and historical experience served as a prism for some British diplomats and Iranian policy-makers through which to understand the politics of land reform in Iran. Documents 3a, 3b,

3c, and 3d all consider the initial impact of land reform and the response of both landowners and the peasantry. Document 4a draws attention to the growing tendency to define the White Revolution (subsequently named 'the White Revolution of the Shahanshah', and, 'the Shah–People revolution') as a distinct ideological programme. The last section contains a selection of speeches by the shah in which both the historical and utopian qualities of the programme of the White Revolution are indicated. Attention is drawn in Document 5a to the shah's allusion to the revolution as both 'legal' and 'sacred' (*moqadas*), along with his assertion (Document 5d) that the white revolution had eliminated 'serfdom' (*ra'eyat*) both practically and linguistically.

Texts

I. From British diplomatic sources

1. The Roots of the 'White Revolution'

(a. FO 371 133006 EP 1015/34, dated 15 August 1958)

[. . .] Asadullah Alam[88] went on to explain that what he had in mind was in fact a 'white revolution', which he hoped to bring about under the auspices of the shah. He was working upon His Majesty's mind to this end. He confessed he had made little progress so far but he was confident that the shah, for whose intelligence and good will he had the highest regard, would allow himself to be persuaded that he must take the lead of a popular and national crusade.

Asadullah explained that to his mind the problem of the survival of the regime was a matter not so much of economics as of psychology and public relations. Colonel Nasser had contrived to inspire the Egyptian people with new zeal by persuading them that his government was their own. Dr Musaddiq[89] [*sic*] had elicited the same enthusiasm by the same means. Asadullah had studied this phenomenon and concluded that the key to success was popularity based upon a measure of nationalistic fervour, which in turn must be founded in some patriotic aspiration, such as the recovery of Bahrain or a struggle against Arab expansion.

Asadullah added that the masses must also be shown that in the development programme of the Plan Organisation there was something for the peasant and the man in the street. The most popular man of the day was M. Moman, Mayor of Tehran, who was cleaning the streets and planting gardens which every man could see for himself and enjoy. The mayor's predecessor, M. Montasser, had

[88] Asadollah A'lam was a major landowner from Khorasan in eastern Iran; appointed head of the *Mardom* (People's) Party, he was later to become prime minister, and minister of court.

[89] Mohammad Mosaddeq, leader of the National Front, and prime minister who secured the nationalization of the Anglo-Iranian Oil Company. Overthrown in a CIA-orchestrated coup in 1953.

built an hygienic slaughter house, a much more important and fundamental improvement, but who cares about slaughter houses? [. . .]

[. . .] [Seeing in Iran] a progressive monarchy under a young ruler more popular than Colonel Nasser, Asadullah hoped to prevail upon the shah to be rid of the present 'establishment', the existing ruling classes must give place to new and younger men. The old gang were not of course to be hurt; this was a white not a red revolution; but the shah must sack them all. Asadullah proposed that the shah should dissolve the Majlis [parliament], dismiss the government and liquidate the ruling classes on the grounds that they were obstructing the necessary reforms and inhibiting the realisation of national aspirations which were the object of Imperial policy.

The *Mardom* Party was to be the instrument of this new order. Asadullah confessed, however, that the Party's progress was not rapid. He found the younger intellectuals, whose support he courted, reluctant to join; they were suspicious and sceptical. To encourage them he was trying to persuade the shah that the government should be encouraged to fight his Party, to persecute and be oppressive. He suggested that there might even be an election which his party should lose; the loss would be attributed to the riches of the old order and the honest poverty of the peoples' own *Mardom* Party. Slowly, nevertheless, young nationalists were beginning to approach him. A young man had recently called upon him calling himself a 'pan-Iranian nationalist', and told him that he stood for 'nationalism without shah'. The shah was an enemy of the people [. . .] Alam tried to persuade him otherwise. 'Not only was he, Asadullah, a king's man, willing to listen to the young man but the king himself would hear him with sympathy, for His Majesty was the champion of the people.'

Asadullah confessed that he was experiencing difficulty with the shah himself in promoting these ideas, and with Dr Eqbal.[90] The shah was wary, apprehending that Asadullah was a bit too impulsive and enthusiastic. He was afraid also that popular and nationalistic policies, however well controlled, might endanger stability [. . .]

2. The politics of the 'White Revolution'

(a. FO 371 133019 EP 1055/1, dated 13 May 1958)

[. . .] I had the strong impression, which one already gets from other evidence, that the shah is moving towards the position of a liberal autocrat relying largely on bourgeois support, not unlike Louis Philippe.[91] His antipathy to the great landed aristocracy is increasingly plain and he is manifestly bidding for popularity lower down. I think we can expect him progressively to cut out the

[90] Prime minister of Iran at the time.

[91] King of France, 1830–48, known as the 'Bourgeois or citizen King', having come to power in the Revolution of 1830 that overthrew Bourbon absolutism (for a second time) and witnessed the institutionalization of bourgeois dominance in French politics.

members of the 'thousand families' from public life and bring in more 'new men' of the Iqbal type [. . .]

(b. FO 371 140790 EP 1015/78, 4 November 1959)

The *Mardom* Party purports to be a party of the left.[92] Mr Alam [. . .] is an exponent of the idea of the 'White Revolution', believing that the only way to preserve the uneasy stability, under the Pahlavi monarchy, of society in Iran is to capture the radical movement by meeting half way the aspirations of the discontented *sans culotte*,[93] or at least of the urban middle class agitators who claim to represent the workers and the peasantry. He recognizes that Dr Musaddiq [Mosadeq] had acquired, at least at one time, the devotion of the masses to a degree unequalled by any Iranian government before or since, and he would like to emulate the success of that old demagogue, in the interest of course, of the shah and the existing order. To this end he has invited left wing elements into the Party [. . .] The game of the 'White Revolution' never appealed to His Majesty very strongly, and he is believed to have made up his mind that the *Mardom* party is not to be allowed to win the elections.

3. Perspectives on land reform

(a. FO 371 140856 EP 1461/2, dated 15 January 1959)

[. . .] The practical aim of land reform in Iran, quite apart from any considerations of social justice, must be to turn an indigent peasantry into an independent and self-reliant yeomanry, and if possible to increase production. The Government's American advisers (the United States Operations Mission) appear to be working on the assumption that anyone who owns his own land becomes *ipso facto* hard working, thrifty and enterprising in the Middle Western tradition; and they have succeeded in communicating something of their conviction to the shah. Unhappily in Iran there is, or has been until recently at any rate, some substance in the more cynical landlord's contention that, if peasants had more money, they simply smoked more opium. [. . .]

[. . .] the Iranian government are unlikely to resist the trend of the times and the example of other countries in the region. The shah himself, acutely anxious

---

[92] These political parties, in contrast with other parties and groups such as the communist *Tudeh* ('Party of the Masses', formed in 1942) or liberal constitutionalist National Front (in essence, a collection of parties that rallied around Prime Minister Mohammad Mosaddeq in the early 1950s), were formed by monarchical decree. The *Mellium* ('Nationalist') Party, founded in 1957, was headed by Prime Minister Iqbal [Eqbal] and served as the 'conservative' government party. The *Mardom* ('People's') Party was established under the stewardship of court favorite Asadollah A'lam in 1957 as the official 'opposition' party and as a popular vehicle to promote the idea of a 'white revolution'. The New Iran (*Iran-e Novin*) Party replaced the *Mellium* in 1964, and in 1975 all parties were outlawed, excepting the shah's new *Rastakhiz* ('Resurgence') Party.

[93] This was a term applied to the foot-soldiers of the French Revolution of 1789, referring to their disdain for aristocratic britches in preference for working-class 'revolutionary' attire.

to deserve the loyalty of his people as the champion of a progressive new order, claims the distribution of land to peasant proprietors as the most important of his benefactions [. . .] Like his father before him, moreover, he has probably in mind that by diminishing the holdings of the great landlords he can reduce their political powers, which are of course substantial and could be used against him. Experience has, however, taught him that there are difficulties and he will not therefore push on very fast; but there is no doubt, as he does not hesitate to repeat, that he has every intention of trying to bring about a comprehensive redistribution of agricultural lands in Iran. And whatever the dangers of trying to readjust the basis of the economy of an agricultural society, it cannot be denied that the abject poverty of the majority of the Iranian peasantry, living sometimes in conditions of bestial squalor which become the more repugnant as the possibilities of material progress become more apparent, demands a remedy.

[. . .] In political terms, the sale of Crown lands is generally acknowledged to be a contribution to social justice and a beginning of reform on the right lines. In spite of strenuous propaganda, however, it cannot be said that the shah himself derives much credit. The powerful landlords [. . .] are critical and apprehensive. The shah's opponents argue also that in fact His Majesty is giving nothing away but is selling property which is not his to sell or was illegally acquired by his tyrannical father, surrendered to the State upon his abdication in 1941 and taken back by the young shah in 1948. They claim, moreover, however improbably, that although the purchase price is to be paid by the peasants over 25 years, the shah enjoys the money now [. . .] Critical observers argue also in general terms that the notion of the self-reliant Iranian yeomanry proudly working their own farms is an American pipe-dream, for the Iranian peasant's object in life is not hard work, bigger production and independence but to work as little as he can and if possible to get rich quick [. . .]

[. . .] it is commonly argued in the light of recent developments abroad [. . .] that unless the big landowners shed some of their properties with good grace they will be found hanging before long from their own trees [. . .] There has indeed been so much talk of land reform that there is some risk that impracticable measures may be enacted for reasons of political expediency or that in the meantime private landowners uncertain of the future of their interests, will restrict the development of their lands [. . .]

(b. FO 248 1585 1461 (British Diplomat Kellas in conversation with Malek Mansur, dated 14 July 1961)

In one case, after a quite bogus exposition of the activities of a rural cooperative society by the Minister of Agriculture, His Majesty had asked a peasant upon whom he was conferring title deeds whether he had found the cooperative useful; and the peasant replied 'What cooperative?' In another case, His Majesty had asked a peasant, to whom he was about to give title deeds covering an allotment of 12 hectares, what was his annual income. The peasant replied, '30,000 [*tumans*]'. His Majesty asked that his question should be translated into Turkish and it was repeated in that language. The peasant protested that he understood Persian very well, explained that he farmed in fact a hundred hectares and that his income was indeed 30,000 [*tumans*]. Whilst a third peasant was receiving his title deeds from the Imperial hand, it was known to all present that his house was being burned by Fazlullah Beg, Khan of the Shahsavan,[94] who is the landlord in those parts [. . .]

Indeed, according to Prince Malek Mansur, the peasants were reluctant to receive their deeds, knowing that having accepted them they could no more depend upon the indispensable assistance of Fazlullah Beg in hard times, and were earning his unlimited malevolence. Mr Malek Mansur observed that the error of land reform and of so many other government projects was that they represent an ill-conceived endeavour to help the people in spite of themselves. But it was socially and economically hopeless to try and work in spite of the people, instead of with the people. In any case, in his view, the Ministry of Agriculture were totally unequal to their task; if the doors of the Ministry were closed today, it would be two years before any farmer was aware of it.

(c. FO 371 149804 EP 1461/6, dated 8 March 1960)

[. . .] Almost all critics of the bill are curiously united in blaming the 'Americans' for imposing it. Some argue that it has been thrust upon the shah and the Government by the Americans, regardless of special conditions in Iran of which they have no experience, out of a misconceived notion that the existing system of land tenure is 'feudal' or reactionary. Others are persuaded that the shah is promoting the bill in an inept endeavour to ingratiate himself to ill-informed American public opinion as a 'progressive' monarch. Some even believe that the Americans are dictating legislation in this sense in order to break the political power of the landowners, traditionally the friends of the British in Iran, regardless of the natural order of Iranian society [. . .]

(d. FO 248 1580 (British Diplomat Kellas in conversation with Dr Ram[95]), dated 30 May 1960)

Dr Ram claimed that the truth of course was that the Bill was a political measure. It was intended to show the world that Iran was not a feudal society, such as was supposed to be a liability in the struggle against communism. It might indeed enjoy some success in this respect. But the proper way to resist communism was economic, and the land reform law was not economic [. . .]

---

[94] A Turkish-speaking tribe in northern Iran.
[95] Dr Ram was a Pahlavi technocrat who would later manage the 'Bank Omran'.

II. From Iranian Sources

4. A revolutionary ideology

a. M. Honarmand, *Pahlavism—Maktab-e Naw* (Pahlavism—the new ideology) (Ordibehesht 1345/April/May 1966, Tehran, p. 50)

It is with considerable pride that one can say that in a world in which most of the countries are under the control of various ideologies which encompass five trends—feudalism, imperialism, liberalism, democracy, and socialism—the *Shahanshah*[96] has discovered a new doctrine which is ethically superior to socialism, has more freedom and rights than democracy, is more practical than liberalism [. . .]there can be little doubt that this new political doctrine among the philosophical and political doctrines existing in the world, must be recognised in political cultures, as 'Pahlavism'.

5. The imperial perspective

a. Excerpt from the message of the Shahanshah on the occasion of the national referendum on the Six Points, dated 6 Bahman 1341/January 1963

(Enghelab-e Sefid-e Shahanshah (The White Revolution of the Shahanshah), Tehran, undated)

[. . .] My dear nation, from today we have turned a page in the history of Iran together. The preceding history, written by the self-sacrificing, patriotic, and pure people of this land during long centuries and epochs, likewise was full of proud, brilliant pages. But perhaps in this prolonged period there was never such an event which profoundly and fundamentally changed Iranian social foundations, and this old society in this way, based on social justice and on the road of progress and happiness with heads held high, will emerge in a new form.

We, in this part of the world, by God's Will and with your support, will build such a country that in all aspects will be the equal of the most advanced countries in the world. We will build a country of liberty for free men and free women, where the genius of Iranians will be able, in a fruitful and pure environment, distant from the corruption of power, with their eternal creativity which is the secret of the durability of this land and nation, to manifest itself in better quality and quantity than in other times, because henceforth the chains that bound have been broken and 75 per cent of the population of this country that prior to this were constrained are now involved through the blessing of freedom.

[. . .] This social and political transformation which has taken place in Iran today, in reality is a great revolution which is both legal and sacred. It is legal because your king, who has the right to enact laws, sought your ratification, and you, meaning the Iranian nation, from whose desires and will, according to the

---

[96] *Shahanshah*, literally 'king of kings', occasionally translated as 'emperor'; ancient title of the Persian kings, adopted again by the Pahlavis.

Constitution, arises the power of the state, have ratified this legal and national revolution and with your decisive and groundbreaking vote have endorsed it, and in this way a very great transformation has begun without anyone so much as getting a bloody nose [. . .] From another respect, this revolution is a sacred revolution because both the foundations and the spirit of the high teachings of Islam, in other words justice and equity, along with the most progressive principles and hopes of contemporary civilised society, can be observed in the suggestions and legislation which form the basis of this transformation [. . .]

b. Excerpt from the Shahanshah's proclamation on the occasion of the anniversary of the 6 Bahman; dated 6 Bahman 1347/January 1969

(*Bar guzideh-i az neveshteh-ha va sokhanan-e shahanshah aryamehr* [Selections from the writings and speeches of the Shahanshah Aryamehr], Tehran, undated)

In this new epoch (*ʿasr-e jadid*) in the history of Iran, the 6 Bahman 1341 stands as the highest manifestation of the personality and spiritual (*ma ʿnavi*) genius of our nation, since in several thousand years of history this country has never expressed its national will so explicitly and decisively in the path of fundamental truth, which has been planned with Iranian intellect and Iranian actions and purely with the safeguarding of the happiness of the Iranian nation in mind. With this revolution, the page of Iranian history has turned, and a new age has begun which undoubtedly will transform Iranian society into one of the most advanced and fortunate societies in the world. But the attainment of this goal will only be achievable when the spirit of the 6 Bahman governs all aspects of this new society.

c. Excerpt from the Shahanshah's proclamation on the occasion of the Persian New Year (NowRuz); dated 1 Farvardin 1349/21 March 1970

(Ibid.)

States which have taken steps towards structural transformation, have required one and often two generations to make sacrifices and have asked them to eat less, and to wear less so that whatever they produce can be put to work to strengthen the foundations of the economy and defence of the country. But we, through God's Will, in place of such privations have secured 10 per cent growth per annum for you, and this is truly a miracle that just as the most profound social revolution is taking place in our country, and the strongest political, economic and military infrastructure is being founded in this state, general life has been subject to such progress and economic growth and average income has risen to such an extent. Of course, there was no need for us to expect the Iranian nation to accept sacrifices and privations, but I am sure that if such sacrifices were necessary, without doubt, the nation of Iran like any other living nation, would have been ready.

d. Excerpt from the Shahanshah's speech to deputies of the Mardom Party, dated 28 Ordibehesht 1350/May 1971

(Ibid.)

The society which we see today, meaning the society of the free men and free women of Iran, was not possible in the last ten years. The formation of the 'corps' of the revolution, drawn from the young boys and girls of the country who as a result of faith and conviction are busy serving [their country] in the farthest points of the country, would not have been possible. The forces of reaction, or to use my own old phrase, the alliance of the red and the black would oppose any type of advance, because for every step we took in this direction, they would automatically and involuntarily take a step backwards. At the end of this summer one person (I won't say *ra' iyat* because this word was eliminated on the very first day of the Iranian revolution), but maybe even a single tenant farmer will not remain, in other words whatever person in whichever field in which he works will be his own lord and master. I see no need to explain the condition of the workers, nor of the other ranks of the country, along with the social classes. Each one of you, from wherever you come, quickly compare your situation today at its weakest point with what it was like in Bahman 1341?

Selected bibliography

ANSARI, A. M., 'The Myth of the White Revolution: Mohammad Reza Shah, "Modernisation" and the Consolidation of Power', *Middle Eastern Studies*, 37/3 (July 2001), 1–24.

——*Modern Iran Since 1921: The Pahlavis and After* (London: Longman, 2003).

BANANI, A., *The Modernization of Iran, 1921–1941* (Stanford: Stanford University Press, 1961).

BARBIR, KARL, 'Getting and Spending in Eighteenth-Century Damascus', in Abdeljelil Temimi (ed.), *La Vie sociale dans les provinces arabes à l'époque ottomane*, 3 (Zaghouan: Tunisia, 1988), 63–76.

BEININ, JOEL, *Workers and Peasants in the Modern Middle East* (New York: Cambridge University Press, 2001).

BURKE, EDMUND, III, (ed.), *Struggle and Survival in the Modern Middle East* (Berkeley: University of California Press, 1993).

—— *Ottoman Rule in Damascus, 1708–1758* (Princeton: Princeton University Press, 1980).

CLAY, CHRISTOPHER, *Gold for the Sultan: Western Bankers and Ottoman Finance 1856–1881: A Contribution to Ottoman and to International Financial History* (London: I. B. Tauris, 2000).

DANKOFF, ROBERT and ROBERT ELSIE, *Evliya Çelebi in Albania and Adjacent Regions: Kosovo, Montenegro, Ohrid* (Boston: Brill, 2000).

FAGHIH, M. A., 'Behdari', in E. Yarshater (ed.), *Encyclopaedia Iranica*, 4 (London and New York: Routledge & Kegan Paul, 1990).

FAHMY, KHALED, *All the Pasha's Men: Mehmed Ali, His Army, and the Making of Modern Egypt* (Cambridge: Cambridge University Press, 1997).

FINDLEY, CARTER V., *Bureaucratic Reform in the Ottoman Empire: The Sublime Porte, 1789–1922* (Princeton: Princeton University Press, 1980).

GHARAIBEH, FAWZI A., *The Economics of the West Bank and Gaza Strip* (Boulder, Col. and London: Westview Press, 1987).

GIBB, H. A. R. and HAROLD BOWEN, *Islamic Society and the West*, 2 vols. (London: Oxford University Press, 1957).

GOLDBERG, ELLIS, *The Social History of Labor in the Middle East* (Boulder, Col.: Westview Press, 1996).

HOOGLUND, E., *Land and Revolution in Iran, 1960–1980* (Austin: University of Texas Press, 1982).

HOURANI, ALBERT, 'The Fertile Crescent in the XVIIIth Century', in *A Vision of History* (Beirut: Khayats, 1961), 35–70.

—— 'Aspects of Islamic Culture', in Thomas Naff and Roger Owen (eds.), *Studies in Eighteenth Century Islamic History* (Carbondale: Southern Illinois University Press, 1977).

ISSAWI, CHARLES (ed.), *The Economic History of Iran, 1800–1914* (Chicago: University of Chicago Press, 1971).

—— *An Economic History of the Middle East and North Africa* (New York: Columbia University Press, 1982).

—— (ed.), *The Fertile Crescent, 1800–1914: A Documentary Economic History* (Oxford: Clarendon Press, 1988).

KEENAN, BRIGID, *Damascus: Hidden Treasures of the Old City* (London: Thames & Hudson, 2000).

KIEL, MACHIEL, *Ottoman Architecture in Albania, 1385–1912* (Istanbul: IRCICA, 1990).

LAMBTON, A. K. S., *The Persian Land Reform 1962–66* (Oxford: Clarendon Press, 1969).

—— *Landlord and Peasant in Persia* (London: I. B. Tauris, 1991).

LANDES, DAVID, *Bankers and Pashas: International Finance and Economic Imperialism in Egypt* (Cambridge, Mass.: Harvard University Press, 1958).

LOCKMAN, ZACHARY (ed.), *Workers and Working Classes in the Middle East: Struggles, Histories, Historiographies* (Albany: State University of New York Press, 1994).

MARCUS, ABRAHAM, *The Middle East on the Eve of Modernity: Aleppo in the Eighteenth Century* (New York: Columbia University Press, 1989).

MITCHELL, TIMOTHY, *Colonising Egypt* (Cambridge: Cambridge University Press, 1998).

NAJMABADI, A., 'Crafting an Educated Housewife', in L. Abu-Lughod (ed.), *Remaking Women: Feminism and Modernity in the Middle East* (Princeton: Princeton University Press, 1998).

OWEN, ROGER, *The Middle East and the World Economy, 1800–1914* (London: Methuen, 1981).

PAIDAR, P., *Women and the Political Process in Twentieth Century Iran* (Cambridge: Cambridge University Press, 1995).

PETERS, F. E., *The Hajj: The Muslim Pilgrimage to Mecca and the Holy Places* (Princeton: Princeton University Press, 1994).

RAFEQ, ABDUL-KARIM, *The Province of Damascus: 1723–1783* (Beirut: Kehayats, 1966).

—— 'Changes in the Relationship Between the Ottoman Central Administration and the Syrian Provinces from the Sixteenth to the Eighteenth Centuries', in Thomas Naff and Roger Owen (eds.), *Studies in Eighteenth Century Islamic History* (Carbondale: Southern Illionis University Press, 1977).

—— 'Craft Organization, Work Ethics, and the Strains of Change in Ottoman Syria', *Journal of the American Oriental Society*, 3/3 (July–Sept. 1991), 502–7.

RAYMOND, ANDRE, *The Great Arab Cities in the 16th–18th Centuries: An Introduction* (New York: New York University Press, 1984).

SCHAYEGH, CYRUS, 'Sport, Health, and the Formation of the Iranian Modern Middle Class, 1920s–1930s', *Iranian Studies*, 35/4 (2002), 341–69.

SCHILCHER, LINDA, *Families in Politics: Damascene Factions and Estates of the 18th and 19th Centuries* (Weisbaden: F. Steiner, 1985).

TAMARI, STEVE, 'Biography, Autobiography, and Identity in Early Modern Damascus', in Mary Ann Fay (ed.), *Auto/Biography and the Construction of Identity and Community in the Middle East* (New York: Palgrave, 2001).

TUCKER, JUDITH E., *Women in Nineteenth-Century Egypt* (Cambridge: Cambridge University Press, 1985).

Glossary

Note: Most terms are defined in document annotation. This is a list of terms that appear often in our text, but also in the literature on Middle East studies generally. An attempt has been made to indicate how the same word may appear in different linguistic contexts; a dash indicates that word does not appear commonly in a particular linguistic context.

Key

Arabic, Persian, Turkish: definition

—, *akhund*,—: cleric

aʿlim, aʿlem,—: 'learned person', cleric

ayatullah, ayatollah,—: 'sign of God', honorific title of a ranking Twelver Shiʿi cleric

fatwa, fatva, fetva: legal opinion

fiqh, feqh,—: the entire corpus of Islamic legal jurisprudence

hadith, hadis, hedis: 'report' on the life and sayings of the Prophet Muhammad, used as a scriptural source for Islamic law; for Shiʿi, reports on the Imams are also used

hijra, hejrat, hicret,—: 'emigration' refering to the Prophet Muhammad's emigration from Mecca to Medina in 622 GE. It marks the first year of the Muslim lunar calender (AH) and Iran's solar calender.

hujjat al-islam, hojjat al-eslam,—: 'proof of Islam', honorific title of a low-ranking Twelver Shiʿi cleric

ilitzam,—, *iltizam*: Ottoman tax farm

imam, emam, imam: 'leader' in a generic sense, but the leader of a prayer or a mosque in its most basic religious meaning. For Shiʿi, imam implies something much more—the rightful leader of the entire Islamic community, enjoying the power to interpret Islamic law authoritatively (though not able to receive new Koranic revelation as the Prophet Muhammad did)

iqtaʿ, eqtaʿ, ikta: state property, the use of which was given to military or administrative official in lieu of or in addition to a salary

janissary: see *yeni çeri*

qadi, qazi, Kadi: judge

—, —, *kapı kul*: 'servant of the [royal] threshold', elite slave troops of the Ottoman Empire, of which the janissary corps was a part

madrasah, madraseh, medrese: religious school; in Persian also the generic term for school

majlis, majles, meclis: gathering, parliament

marjaʿ al-taqlid, marjaʿ-e taqlid,—: 'source of imitation', in Twelver Shiʿi Islam, a ranking cleric who provides sole guidance for the ordinary believer until the return of the Twelfth (Hidden) Imam

mufti, mofti, müfti: cleric who renders a legal opinion

mulla, molla,—: cleric

multazim,—, *mültazim*: tax farmer

—, *padešah, padisah*: see *shah*

—, —, *paşa*: senior Ottoman official

—, *pir,*—: 'old man', the head of a mystical order

—, *sadr-e aᶜzam, sadr-i azem*: Qajar Persian title for 'prime minister', and Ottoman title for head of bureaucracy, often translated as 'grand vizier'

—, *shah,*—: king in Persian

—, *shahanshah,*—: king of kings, emperor in Persian

shariᶜa, shariᶜa, şeriat: Islamic law

shaykh al-islam,—, *şeyhüleslam*: chief mufti in the Ottoman Empire

—,—, *sipahi*: Ottoman cavalry mustered from the Muslim population and rewarded with the use of state lands for their service

—, *soyurghal,*—: Safavid and Qajar Iranian system of *iqtaᶜ*

sufi, sufi, sufi: an Islamic mystic

sultan, soltan, sultan: 'the one who rules', king

—,—, *timar*: Ottoman system of *iqtaᶜ* for *sipahi* troops and ranking officials

—, *tuyul,*—: Safavid and Qajar Iranian system of *iqtaᶜ*

ᶜ*ulama,* ᶜ*olama, ulema*: the learned scholars of Islam

wakil, vakil, vekil: representative, member of parliament

wilaya, velayat, vilayet: province

wilayat al-faqih, velayat-e faqih,—: 'deputyship of the jurist', Twelver Shiᶜi concept that a well-respected cleric should rule until the return of the Twelfth (Hidden) Imam; it is the organizing principle of the Islamic Republic of Iran

—,—, *yeni çeri*: elite unit of the Ottoman Empire, conscripted from European Christian provinces in the Empire

Index

Note: References in *italics* refer to illustrations and tables. The Arabic and Hebrew articles (al-, el- and ha-) are ignored in filing.